Craft and Micro Distilleries in the U.S. and Canada

The definitive guide to small batch, artisanal spirits

4th Edition

David J. Reimer Sr.

Craft and Micro Distilleries in the U.S. and Canada, Fourth Edition
The definitive guide to small batch, artisanal spirits

Copyright © 2014, by David J. Reimer, Sr.

Cover Design by: Jerry F. Cavill Jr.

Website: www.microdistillerybooks.com
Email: david@microdistillerybooks.com, sales@microdistillerybooks.com
Facebook: Micro Distilleries, Micro-Distilleries in the U.S. and Canada
Twitter: @djreimersr, @microdbooks

Printed in the United States of America
April 2014

B/W Print Edition ISBN: 978-0-9852599-4-5

Color Print Edition ISBN: 978-0-9852599-5-2

Published by:
Crave Press

www.cravepress.com

Acknowledgements

I would like to thank everyone at the distilleries that took the time to talk with me and had the patience to answer all my questions. It was their expertise, enthusiasm, and cooperation that helped to steer me in the right direction to make this fourth edition possible.

I would be remiss if I didn't thank Christina Steffy, Jerry F. Cavill Jr., and Enchanted Acres Photography by Roxanne Richardson for helping to bring all of this together again.

Front Cover
Row 1 — Thistle Finch Rye Whiskey – Thistle Finch Distilling, PA
Wild Buck Whiskey – NJoy Spirits LLC, FL
High West Double Rye Whiskey – High West Distillery, UT
Koval Single Barrel Rye Whiskey – Koval Distillery, IL
Blaum Bros. Gin – Blaum Bros. Distilling Co., IL
Schramm Gin – Pemberton Distillery Inc., BC
Copperworks Distilling Company Gin – Copperworks Distilling Co., WA
Delaware Distilling Company Premium Gin – Delaware Distilling Co., DE
Far North Spirits Alander Spiced Rum – Far North Spirits, MN

Row 2 — Queen Charlotte's Carolina Rum – Muddy River Distillery, NC
Montanya Oro Rum – Montanya Distillers LLC, CO
Busted Barrel Dark Rum – Jersey Artisan Distilling, NJ
JP Trodden Small Batch Bourbon – J.P. Trodden Small Batch Bourbon, WA
Wiggly Bridge Bourbon Whisky – Wiggly Bridge Distillery, ME
A & G Reserve Michigan Brandy – St. Julian Winery, MI
Spring44 Straight Bourbon – Spring44 Distilling, CO
Lyon Distilling Company Rum – Lyon Distilling Company, MD
Kaua`i Coconut Rum – Kōloa Rum Company, HI

Row 3 — Rhine Hall Apple Brandy – Rhine Hall, IL
Humboldt Distillery Organic Vodka – Humboldt Distillery, CA
Twenty 2 Vodka – Northern Maine Distilling Company, ME
High Wire Distilling Co. Vodka – High Wire Distilling, SC
Ozark Moonshine – Ozark Distillery LLC, MO

Row 4 — Few Bourbon – Few Spirits LLC, IL
Beanball Bourbon – Cooperstown Distillery, NY
Railroad Rye Whiskey – Hidden Marsh Distillery, NY
American Single Malt Whiskey – Westland Distillery, WA
Iris™ - Elixir Inc., OR
Corbin CA Estate Grown Sweet Potato Vodka – Sweet Potato Spirits, CA
Boyd & Blair Potato Vodka – Pennsylvania Pure Distilleries LLC, PA
Dorothy Parker American Gin – New York Distilling Company, NY
Big Gin – Captive Spirits, WA

Back Cover — Endeavour Gin – The Liberty Distillery, BC
Eau de Vie de Pomme – Clear Creek Distillery, OR

Preface

A micro distillery, often referred to as an "artisan", "boutique" or "craft distillery", is a small distillery producing premium spirits in small batches. While this term is most commonly used in the United States, micro distilleries exist all over the world; however this book concentrates on the distilleries in the U.S. and Canada.

For a trade that dates back to the 1600s in America, it has taken a long time to recover from Prohibition. For the first time since the days of Al Capone, small distilleries are being reestablished. It was during Prohibition in the United States that most small distilleries were forced out of business, leaving only the mega-distilleries to resume operation when Prohibition was repealed. However, within the last decade, the number of micro distilleries in the United States and Canada has rocketed from a couple dozen to more than a couple hundred. This number represents not only stand-alone distilleries, but also includes many micro-breweries and small wineries that established distilleries within their brewing or winemaking operations. The west coast of the U.S. has experienced the highest number of micro distillery openings as these are states with more relaxed legislation.

Today's micro distillery trend is a long way from where it was before Prohibition. After the repeal of the eighteenth amendment, what remained of the country's liquor industry was consolidated into a few large companies. While these mammoths substantially profited from Prohibition, they also greatly lowered consumer expectations. At the time, America's large but then underground drinking population wasn't fussy, and many drinkers believed they were getting the real deal from bootleggers or speakeasy bartenders who often rebottled homemade gin or whiskey and sold it as top-shelf liquor.

Despite the recent economic recession in the U.S., people with a passion for hand crafted sprits are opening micro distilleries. And, contrary to myths about the foolishness of starting a business in an economic downturn, many are holding their own financially and finding audiences for their award winning, hand-crafted superior spirits.

While micro distilleries represent less than 5% of the overall spirits market, micro distillers appeal to individuals who appreciate quality over mass production.

Alabama

    High Ridge Spirits -- Still Crossroads   1

Alaska

    Alaska Distillery -- Wasilla   2
    Bare Distillery -- Anchorage   3
    High Mark Distillery -- Sterling   4
    Port Chilkoot Distillery -- Haines   5
    Ursa Major Distilling -- Fairbanks   6

Arizona

    Arizona High Spirits Distillery -- Flagstaff   7
    Desert Diamond Distillery -- Kingman   8

Arkansas

    Arkansas Moonshine Inc. -- Newport   9
    Rock Town Distillery Inc. -- Little Rock   10

California

    1512 Spirits -- Rohnert Park   11
    Amador Distillery -- Jackson   12
    Ascendant Spirits -- Buellton   13
    Autry Cellars -- San Luis Obispo   14
    Ballast Point Spirits -- San Diego   15
    BNS Brewing & Distilling Company -- Santee   16
    Bowen's Spirits Inc. -- Bakersfield   17
    Cal-Czech Distillery -- Angels Camp   18
    Charbay Distillers -- St. Helena   19
    Cutler's Artisan Spirits -- Santa Barbara   20
    Distillery No. 209 -- San Francisco   21
    Essential Spirits Alambic Distilleries -- Mountain View   22
    Falcon Spirits LLC -- Richmond   23
    Fog's End Distillery -- Gonzales   24
    Germain-Robin -- Redwood Valley   25
    GreenBar Collective -- Los Angeles   26
    Greenway Distillers -- Ukiah   27
    Hanson Spirits LLC -- Sonoma   28
    HelloCello -- Sonoma   29
    High Roller Spirits -- Atwater   30
    Humboldt Distillery -- Fortuna   31
    Kill Devil Spirit Company -- San Diego   32
    Lost Spirits Distillery -- Salinas   33
    Malahat Spirits -- San Diego   34
    Manzanita Distilling Company -- Santee   35

California

Mosswood Distillers Inc. -- San Francisco	36
Napa Valley Distillery -- Benica	37
Napa Valley Distillery -- Napa	38
Old Harbor Distilling Company -- San Diego	39
Old World Spirits LLC -- Belmont	40
RE:FIND Distillery -- Paso Robles	41
Saint James Spirits -- Irwindale	42
Spirit Works Distillery -- Sebastopol	43
St. George Spirits -- Alameda	44
Stark Spirits -- Pasadena	45
Stillwater Spirits -- Petaluma	46
Sweet Potato Spirits -- Atwater	47
Tamar Distillery Inc. -- Redwood Valley	48
Tahoe Moonshine Distillery Inc. -- South Lake Tahoe	49
Treasure Island Distillery -- San Francisco	50
Valley Spirits LLC -- Modesto	51
Ventura Limoncello Company -- Ventura	52

Colorado

Altitude Spirits -- Boulder	53
Black Canyon Distillery -- Longmont	54
Boathouse Distillery -- Salida	55
Boulder Distillery -- Boulder	56
Breckenridge Distillery -- Breckenridge	57
Colorado Gold Distillery -- Cedaredge	58
Dancing Pines Distillery -- Loveland	59
Deerhammer Distilling Company -- Buena Vista	60
Distillery 291 -- Colorado Springs	61
Downslope Distilling -- Centennial	62
Feisty Spirits -- Fort Collins	63
Golden Moon Distillery -- Golden	64
Honey House Distillery -- Durango	65
K J Wood Distillers LLC -- Berthoud	66
Leopold Bros. -- Denver	67
Mancos Valley Distillery -- Mancos	68
Mile High Spirits LLC -- Denver	69
Montanya Distillers LLC -- Crested Butte	70
Mystic Mountain Distillery LLC -- Larkspur	71
Peach Street Distillers -- Palisade	72
Peak Spirits® Farm Distillery -- Hotchkiss	73
Rocky Mountain Distilling Co. -- Colorado Springs	74
Roundhouse Spirits -- Boulder	75
Spirit Hound Distillers -- Lyons	76

Colorado

Spring44 Distilling -- Loveland	77
State 38 Distilling -- Golden	78
Still Cellars -- Longmont	79
Stranahan's Colorado Whiskey Distillery -- Denver	80
Syntax Spirits LLC -- Greeley	81
Tesouro Distillery -- Longmont	82
Trail Town Still -- Ridgway	83
Two Guns Distillery -- Leadville	84
Wood's High Mountain Distillery -- Salida	85
Woody Creek Distillers -- Basalt	86

Connecticut

Elm City Distillery LLC -- Wallingford	87
Onyx Spirits Company LLC -- East Hartford	88
Westford Hill Distillers -- Ashford	89

Delaware

Delaware Distilling Company -- Rehoboth Beach	90
Dogfish Head Craft Brewery -- Rehoboth Beach	91
Painted Stave Distillery -- Smyrna	92

District of Columbia

New Columbia Distillers -- Washington DC	93

Florida

Alchemist Distilleries Inc. -- Miami	94
Cape Spirits Inc. -- Cape Coral	95
Drum Circle Distilling -- Sarasota	96
Empire Winery & Distillery -- New Port Richey	97
Fat Dog Spirits LLC -- Tampa	98
Fish Hawk Spirits LLC -- Ocala	99
Florida Farm Distillers -- Umatilla	100
NJoy Spirits LLC -- Weeki Wachee	101
Peaden Brothers Distillery -- Crestview	102
Rollins Distillery -- Gulf Breeze	103
Spirits of the USA LLC -- Jacksonville	104
The Florida Distillery -- Tampa	105

Georgia

Dawsonville Moonshine Distillery -- Dawsonville	106
Georgia Distilling Company -- Milledgeville	107
Ivy Mountain Distillery LLC -- Mt. Airy	108
Moonrise Distillery Inc. -- Clayton	109

Georgia

	Richland Distilling Company -- Richland	110
	Thirteenth Colony Distilleries -- Americus	111

Hawaii

	Haleakala Distillers -- Kula	112
	Hawaii Sea Spirits LLC -- Kula	113
	Island Distillers Inc. -- Honolulu	114
	Kōloa Rum Company -- Kalaheo	115

Idaho

	44° North Vodka -- Rigby	116
	Bardenay Inc. -- Boise	117
	Grand Teton Distillery -- Driggs	118
	Koenig Distillery -- Caldwell	119

Illinois

	Blaum Bros. Distilling Co. -- Gelena	120
	CH Distillery -- Chicago	121
	Chicago Distilling Company -- Chicago	122
	Few Spirits LLC -- Evanston	123
	Hum Spirits Company -- Chicago	124
	J.K. Williams Distilling LLC -- East Peoria	125
	Koval Distillery -- Chicago	126
	Letherbee Distillers -- Chicago	127
	Mastermind Vodka -- Pontoon Beach	128
	Mid-Oak Distillery -- Midlothian	129
	North Shore Distillery -- Lake Bluff	130
	Premiere Distillery LLC -- Gurnee	131
	Quincy Street Distillery -- Riverside	132
	Rhine Hall -- Chicago	133
	Rumshine Distilling LLC -- Tilton	134
	Tailwinds Distilling Company -- Plainfield	135

Indiana

	Heartland Distillers -- Indianapolis	136
	Huber's Starlight Distillery -- Starlight	137
	The Indiana Whiskey Company -- South Bend	138
	Virtuoso Distillers LLC -- Mishawaka	139

Iowa

	Broadbent Distillery -- Norwalk	140
	Cedar Ridge Distillery -- Swisher	141
	Iowa Distilling Company -- Cumming	142

Iowa

Mississippi River Distilling Co. -- LeClaire	143
Paradise Distilling Company LLC -- Dubuque	144
Templeton Rye Distillery -- Templeton	145
Werner Distilling LLC -- Holstein	146

Kansas

D and J Distilling -- Winfield	147
Dark Horse Distillery -- Lenexa	148
Dodge City Distillery -- Olathe	149
Good Spirits Distilling -- Olathe	150
Wheat State Distilling -- Wichita	151

Kentucky

Barrel House Distilling Co. -- Lexington	152
Corsair Artisan Distillery -- Bowling Green	153
E.H. Taylor, Jr. Old Fashioned Copper Distillery	154
Kentucky Artisan Distillery -- Crestwood	155
Limstone Branch Distillery -- Lebanon	156
MB Roland Distillery -- Pembroke	157
Old Pogue Distillery -- Maysville	158
Silver Trail Distillery -- Hardin	159
Whiskey Thief Distilling Company -- Graefenburg	160
Wilderness Trace Distillery -- Danville	161
Willett Distillery -- Bardstown	162

Louisiana

Atelier Vie -- New Orleans	163
Cajun Spirits Distillery -- New Orleans	164
Celebration Distillation -- New Orleans	165
Donner-Peltier Distillers -- Thibodaux	166
Lifted Spirits LLC -- New Orleans	167
Louisiana Spirits LLC -- Lacassine	168
Rank Wildcat Spirits LLC -- Lafayette	169
VooDoo Distillery -- New Orleans	170

Maine

Artisan Distillery LLC -- Oxford	171
Maine Distilleries LLC -- Freeport	172
New England Distilling -- Portland	173
Northern Maine Distilling Company -- Brewer	174
Spirits of Maine Distillery -- Gouldsboro	175
Sweetgrass Farm Winery & Distillery -- Union	176
Tree Spirits -- Oakland	177

Maine

Wiggly Bridge Distillery -- York Beach	178

Maryland

Blackwater Distilling Inc. -- Stevensville	179
Fiore Winery & Distillery -- Plyesville	180
Lyon Distilling Company -- Saint Michaels	181

Massachusetts

Berkshire Mountain Distillers Inc. -- Gr. Barrington	182
Bully Boy Distillers -- Boston	183
Cape Cod Distilling Company LLC -- Hyannis	184
Damnation Alley Distillery -- Belmont	185
Dirty Water Distillery -- Plymouth	186
GrandTen Distilling -- Boston	187
Nashoba Valley Distillery Ltd. -- Bolton	188
Privateer Rum -- Ipswich	189
Ryan & Wood Inc. -- Gloucester	190
Triple Eight Distillery -- Nantucket	191
Turkey Shore Distilleries -- Ipswich	192

Michigan

Artesian Distillers -- Grand Rapids	193
Big Cedar Distilling Inc. -- Sturgis	194
Chateau Chantal -- Traverse City	195
Coppercraft Distillery LLC -- Holland	196
Corey Lake Orchards -- Three Rivers	197
Entente Spirits LLC -- Baroda	198
Grand Traverse Distillery -- Traverse City	199
Journeyman Distillery -- Three Oaks	200
New Holland Artisan Spirits -- Holland	201
Northern Latitudes Distillery -- Lake Leelanau	202
Northern United Brewing Co. & Dist. -- Traverse City	203
St. Julian Winery -- Paw Paw	204
Two James Spirits -- Detroit	205
Ugly Dog Distillery LLC -- Chelsea	206
Uncle Don's Apple Pie Craft Distillery -- Cadillac	207
Valentine Distilling Company -- Ferndale	208

Minnesota

Du Nord Craft Spirits -- Minneapolis	209
Far North Spirits -- Hallock	210
Loon Liquors -- Northfield	211
Noreseman Distillery -- Minneapolis	212

Minnesota

Panther Distillery -- Osakis	213
Sherwoods Winery & Distillery LLC -- Duluth	214

Mississippi

Cathead Distillery LLC -- Gluckstadt	215

Missouri

Copper Run Distillery -- Walnut Shade	216
Crown Valley Distilling Co. -- Ste. Genevieve	217
Mad Buffalo Distillery -- Union	218
Mid-Best Distillery Inc. -- Gravois Mills	219
Missouri Spirits -- Springfield	220
Of The Earth Farm Distillery -- Rayville	221
Ozark Distillery LLC -- Osage Beach	222
Pinckney Bend Distillery -- New Haven	223
S.D. Strong Distilling -- Parkville	224
Square One Brewery and Distillery -- St. Louis	225
St. Louis Distillery -- St. Charles	226
StilL 630 -- St. Louis	227
Wood Hat Spirits LLC -- New Florence	228

Montana

Glacier Distilling Company -- Coram	229
Headframe Spirits -- Butte	230
Montgomery Distillery -- Missoula	231
RoughStock Distillery -- Bozeman	232
Steel Toe Distillery -- Potomac	233
Swanson's Mountain View Apple Orchard and Dist.	234
The Montana Distillery-1889 -- Missoula	235
Trailhead Spirits -- Billings	236
Triple Divide Spirits -- Helena	237
Vilya Spirits LLC -- Kalispell	238
Whistling Andy Distillery -- Bigfork	239
Willie's Distillery -- Ennis	240

Nebraska

Copper's Chase Distillery LLC -- West Point	241
Cut Spike Distillery -- La Vista	242

Nevada

Churchill Vineyards and Distillery -- Fallon	243
Las Vegas Distillery -- Henderson	244

New Hampshire
    Flag Hill Winery & Distillery -- Lee   245
    Sea Hagg Distillery -- North Hampton   246

New Jersey
    Big Still Liquors LLC -- Clifton   247
    Cooper River Distillers -- Camden   248
    Jersey Artisan Distilling -- Fairfield   249

New Mexico
    Don Quixote Distillery & Winery -- Los Alamos 250
    Rancho de Los Luceros Destilaria -- Alcalde   251
    Santa Fe Spirits -- Santa Fe   252

New York
    Adirondack Distilling Company -- Utica   253
    Albany Distilling Company -- Albany   254
    Beak & Skiff Distillery -- LaFayette   255
    Black Button Distilling -- Rochester   256
    Black Dirt Distillery -- Pine Island   257
    Breuckelen Distilling Company Inc. -- Brooklyn 258
    Buffalo Distilling Co. -- Bennington   259
    Cacao Prieto LLC -- Brooklyn   260
    Catskill Distilling Company Ltd. -- Bethel   261
    Celk Distilling -- Williamson   262
    Clayton Distillery -- Clayton   263
    Cooperstown Distillery -- Cooperstown   264
    Coppersea Distillery -- West Park   265
    Delaware Phoenix Distillery -- Walton   266
    Demarest Hill Winery -- Warwick   267
    Finger Lakes Distilling -- Burdett   268
    Five & 20 Spirits -- Westfield   269
    Greenhook Ginsmiths -- Brooklyn   270
    Harvest Spirits LLC -- Valatie   271
    Hidden Marsh Distillery -- Senaca Falls   272
    Hillrock Estate Distillery -- Ancram   273
    Industry City Distillery Inc. -- Brooklyn   274
    Jack From Brooklyn Inc. -- Brooklyn   275
    Kings County Distillery -- Brooklyn   276
    KyMar Farm Distillery -- Charlotteville   277
    Lake George Distilling Company -- Fort Ann   278
    Lake Placid Spirits LLC -- Lake Placid   279
    Lockhouse Distillery -- Buffalo   280
    Long Island Spirits -- Baiting Hollow   281

New York

Luckey Spirits -- Greenwich	282
Magnanini Farm Winery Inc. -- Wallkill	283
Myer Farm Distillers -- Ovid	284
Nahmias et Fils -- Yonkers	285
New York Distilling Company -- Brooklyn	286
Port Morris Distillery -- Bronx	287
Prohibition Distillery LLC -- Roscoe	288
Proof of Concept LLC -- Brooklyn	289
Saratoga Distilleries Inc. -- Galway	290
Shinn Estate Vineyards and Farmhouse -- Mattituck	291
Six Mile Creek Winery & Distillery -- Ithaca	292
StilltheOne Distillery LLC -- Port Chester	293
Stoutridge Distillery -- Marlboro	294
The Noble Experiment NYC -- Brooklyn	295
Tirado Distillery -- Bronx	296
Tuthilltown Spirits Distillery -- Gardiner	297
Van Brunt Stillhouse -- Brooklyn	298
Warwick Valley Distillery -- Warwick	299

North Carolina

Adam Dalton Distillery -- Asheville	300
Asheville Distilling Company -- Asheville	301
Blue Ridge Distilling Company -- Bostic	302
Broadslab Distillery LLC -- Benson	303
Call Family Distillers -- Wilkesboro	304
Carolina Distillery LLC	305
Covington Spirits LLC -- Snow Hill	306
Devil's Distillery -- Pittsboro	307
Howling Moon Distillery -- Asheville	308
Mayberry Spirits -- Mount Airy	309
Muddy River Distillery -- Belmont	310
Piedmont Distillers -- Madison	311
Southern Artisan Spirits -- Kings Mountain	312
The Brothers Vilgalys Spirits Company -- Durham	313
Top of the Hill Distillery -- Chapel Hill	314
Windsor Run Cellars -- Hamptonville	315

North Dakota

Maple River Distillery -- North Casselton	316
Moon River Distillery Inc. -- Park River	317

Ohio

25th Street Spirits -- Cleveland	318
Belle of Dayton -- Dayton	319
Black Swamp Distillery -- Fremont	320
Buckeye Distillery Inc. -- Tipp City	321
Cleveland Whiskey LLC -- Cleveland	322
Crystal Spirits LLC -- Dayton	323
Ernest Scarano Distillery -- Fremont	324
Fifth Element Spirits -- Shade	325
Flat Rock Spirits -- Fairborn	326
Indian Creek Distillery -- New Carlisle	327
Middle West Spirits LLC -- Columbus	328
Mill St. Distillery LLC -- Utica	329
Portside Distillery -- Cleveland	330
Red Eagle Spirits -- Geneva	331
Renaissance Artisan Distillers -- Akron	332
S and G Artisan Dist. LLC -- Yellow Springs	333
Seven Brothers Distilling Co. -- Painesville	334
Tom's Foolery -- Chagrin Falls	335
Watershed Distillery -- Columbus	336
Woodstone Creek -- Cincinnati	337

Oklahoma

Prairie Wolf Spirits -- Guthrie	338

Oregon

4 Spirits Distillery -- Adair Village	339
Bendistillery -- Bend	340
Big Bottom Distilling -- Hillsboro	341
Black Rock Distillery LLC -- Spray	342
Brandy Peak Distillery -- Brookings	343
Bull Run Distilling Company -- Portland	344
Cascade Peak Spirits Distillery -- Ashland	345
Clear Creek Distillery -- Portland	346
Dogwood Distilling -- Forest Grove	347
Eastside Distilling -- Portland	348
Elixir Inc. -- Eugene	349
Glaser Estate Winery and Dist. -- Roseburg	350
Hard Times Distillery LLC -- Monroe	351
HillCrest Winery and Distillery -- Roseburg	352
House Spirits Distillery -- Portland	353
Immortal Spirits & Distilling Co. -- Medford	354
Indio Spirits -- Portland	355
LiL'BiT Distillery Inc. -- Woodburn	356

Oregon

McMenamins Cornelius Pass Roadhouse -- Hillsboro	357
McMenamins Edgefield Distillery -- Troutdale	358
New Deal Distillery -- Portland	359
Oregon Ryegrass Spirits -- Corvallis	360
Oregon Spirit Distillers -- Bend	361
Ransom Spirits -- Sheridan	362
Rogue Spirits -- Newport	363
Rolling River Spirits -- Portland	364
Sinister Distilling Company -- Albany	365
Stein Distillery -- Joseph	366
Stillwagon Distillery -- Coos Bay	367
Stone Barn Brandyworks -- Portland	368
Stringer's Orchard Winery and Dist. -- New Pine Creek	369
Sub Rosa Spirits -- Dundee	370
Superfly Distilling Company -- Brookings	371
Vinn Distillery -- Wilsonville	372
Vivacity Spirits -- Corvallis	373
Ye Ol' Grog Distillery -- Saint Helens	374

Pennsylvania

Allegheny Distilling LLC -- Pittsburgh	375
Blackbird Distillery -- Brookville	376
Hewn Spirits LLC -- Pipersville	377
Manatawny Still Works -- Pottstown	378
Mountain Laurel Spirits LLC -- Bristol	379
Mountain View Distillery -- Stroudsburg	380
Naoj and Mot Inc. -- Philadelphia	381
Old Republic Distillery -- Seven Valleys	382
Pennsylvania Pure Distilleries LLC -- Glenshaw	383
Philadelphia Distilling -- Philadelphia	384
Pittsburgh Distillery Co. -- Pittsburgh	385
Stay Tuned Distillery LLC -- Munhall	386
Thistle Finch Distilling -- Lancaster	387

Rhode Island

Newport Distilling Company -- Newport	388
Sons of Liberty Spirits Co. -- South Kingstown	389

South Carolina

Dark Corner Distillery -- Greenville	390
Firefly Distillery -- Wadmalaw Island	391
High Wire Distilling -- Charleston	392
Lucky Duck Distillery -- Yemassee	393

South Carolina

Palmetto Moonshine -- Anderson	394
Six & Twenty Distillery -- Piedmont	395
Striped Pig Distillery -- Charleston	396
Tiger Juice Distillery -- Hartsville	397

South Dakota

Black Hills Dakota Distillery -- Rapid City	398
Dakota Spirits Distillery LLC -- Pierre	399

Tennessee

Chattanooga Whiskey Co. -- Chattanooga	400
Collier and McKeel -- Nashville	401
Corsair Artisan Distillery -- Nashville	402
East Tennessee Distillery -- Piney Flats	403
Nelson's Green Brier Distillery -- Nashville	404
Ole Smoky Distillery LLC -- Gatlinburg	405
Popcorn Sutton's Distillery -- Nashville	406
Prichard's Distillery Inc. -- Kelso	407
Short Mountain Distillery -- Woodbury	408
SPEAKeasy Spirits -- Nashville	409
Tenn South Distillery -- Lynnville	410

Texas

Azar Distillery -- San Antonio	411
Balcones Distillery -- Waco	412
Banner Distilling Co. -- Manor	413
Big Thicket Distilling Company -- Conroe	414
Bone Spirits -- Smithville	415
D.E.W. Distillation LLC -- Wimberley	416
Firestone & Robertson Dist. Co. -- Fort Worth	417
Garrison Brothers Distillery -- Hye	418
Hideous LC -- Lockhart	419
JEM Beverage Company -- Carrollton	420
Quentin D. Witherspoon Dist. LLC -- Lewisville	421
Railean Distillers -- San Leon	422
Ranger Creek Brewing & Dist. -- San Antonio	423
Rebecca Creek Distillery LLC -- San Antonio	424
San Luis Spirits -- Dripping Springs	425
SAVVY Distillers LP -- Austin	426
South Congress Distillery -- Manor	427
Spink Distillery -- San Antonio	428
Spirit of Texas LLC -- Pflugerville	429
Texacello LLC -- Austin	430

Texas

The Original Texas Legend Distillery -- Orange	431
Tito's Handmade Vodka -- Austin	432
Treaty Oak Distilling Co. -- Austin	433
Whitmeyer's Distilling Co. LLC -- Houston	434
Yellow Rose Distilling LLC -- Houston	435

Utah

High West Distillery -- Park City	436
Ogden's Own Distillery -- Ogden	437

Vermont

Boyden Valley Winery & Spirits -- Cambridge	438
Caledonia Spirits Inc. -- Hardwick	439
Dunc's Mill -- St. Johnsbury	440
Elm Brook Farm -- East Fairfield	441
Flag Hill Farm -- Vershire	442
Green Mountain Distillers -- Stowe	443
Mad River Distillers -- Warren	444
Saxtons River Distillery LLC -- Brattleboro	445
Shelburne Orchards Distillery -- Shelburne	446
Smugglers' Notch Distillery -- Jeffersonville	447
Vermont Distillers -- West Marlboro	448
Vermont Spirits Distilling Co. -- Quechee	449
WhistlePig Farm -- Shoreham	450

Virginia

A. Smith Bowman Distillery -- Fredericksburg	451
Appalachian Mountain Spirits LLC -- Marion	452
Belmont Farms Distillery -- Culpeper	453
Catoctin Creek Distilling Co. LLC -- Purcellville	454
Chesapeake Bay Distillery LLC -- Virginia Beach	455
Copper Fox Distillery -- Sperryville	456
Parched Group LLC -- Richmond	457
Reservoir Distillery -- Richmond	458
Three Brothers' Whiskey Distillery -- Disputanta	459
Virginia Distillery Company -- Lovingston	460
Woods Mill Distillery -- Faber	461

Washington

2 Loons Distillery -- Loon Lake	462
2bar® Spirits -- Seattle	463
3 Howls Distillery -- Seattle	464
Bainbridge Organic Dist. -- Bainbridge Island	465

Washington

Batch 206 Distillery -- Seattle	466
BelleWood Distilling -- Lynden	467
Black Heron Spirits Dist. -- West Richland	468
Black Rock Spirits LLC -- Seattle	469
Black Sam Distillery Co. -- Montesano	470
Blue Flame Spirits -- Prosser	471
Blue Spirits Distilling -- Chelan	472
Bluewater Distilling -- Everett	473
broVo Spirits -- Seattle	474
Captive Spirits -- Seattle	475
Carbon Glacier Distillery -- Wilkeson	476
Chuchanut Bay Distillery -- Bellingham	477
Copperworks Distilling Company -- Seattle	478
Dark Moon Artisan Distillery -- Snohomish	479
Deception Distilling LLC -- Anacortes	480
Double V Distillery -- Battle Ground	481
Dry County Distillery LLC -- Marysville	482
Dry Fly Distilling -- Spokane	483
Evanson Handcrafted Dist. LLC -- Spokane	484
Ezra Cox Distillery -- Centralia	485
Four Lakes -- Chelan	486
Freemont Mischief -- Seattle	487
Glacier Basin Distillery -- Yakima	488
Glass Distillery -- Seattle	489
Gnostalgic Spirits Distillery -- Seattle	490
Golden Distillery -- Bow	491
Heritage Distilling Co. Inc. -- Gig Harbor	492
It's 5 Artisan Distillery -- Cashmere	493
J.P. Trodden Small Batch Bourbon	494
Kayak Spirits Distillery LLC -- Freeland	495
Letterpress Distilling -- Seattle	496
Mac Donald Distillery -- Snohomish	497
Meriwether Distilling Co. -- Seattle	498
Mount Baker Distillery -- Bellingham	499
Mt. Index Brewery & Distillery -- Index	500
Nightside Distillery -- Edgewood	501
Old Ballard Liquor Co. -- Seattle	502
OOLA Distillery -- Seattle	503
Pacific Distillery LLC -- Woodinville	504
Parliament Distillery -- Sumner	505
Port Steilacoom Distillery -- Steilacoom	506
Project V Distillery and Sausage Co. -- Woodinville	507
Rain City Spirits -- Seattle	508

Washington

RiverSands Distillery -- Kennewick	509
San Juan Island Distillery -- Friday Harbor	510
Sandstone Distillery LLC -- Tenino	511
Seattle Distilling Company -- Vashon	512
Sidetrack Distillery -- Kent	513
Skip Rock Distillers -- Snohomish	514
Sodo Spirits Distillery -- Seattle	515
Soft Tail Spirits -- Woodinville	516
Sound Spirits -- Seattle	517
Sun Liquor Distillery -- Seattle	518
Tatoosh Craft Distillery -- Seattle	519
The Ellensburg Distillery -- Ellensburg	520
The Hardware Distillery Co. -- Hoodsport	521
Valley Shine Distillery -- Mount Vernon	522
Walla Walla Distilling Company -- Walla Walla	523
Westland Distillery -- Seattle	524
Whidby Island Distillery -- Langley	525
Wishkah River Distillery -- Aberdeen	526
Woodinville Whiskey Co. -- Woodinville	527

West Virginia

Bloomery Plantation Distillery -- Charles Town	528
Forks of Cheat Distillery -- Morgantown	529
Pinchgut Hollow Distillery -- Fairmont	530
Smooth Ambler Spirits Company -- Maxwelton	531
WV Distilling Co. LLC -- Morgantown	532

Wisconsin

45th Parallel Distillery -- New Richmond	533
AEppelTreow Winery & Distillery -- Burlington	534
Death's Door Spirits -- Middleton	535
Door County Distillery -- Carlsville	536
Great Lakes Distillery LLC -- Milwaukee	537
Hendricks Family Distillery LLC -- Omro	538
Lo Artisan Distillery LLC -- Sturgeon Bay	539
Minhas Micro Distillery -- Monroe	540
Old Sugar Distillery -- Madison	541
The North Woods Distillery LLC -- Coleman	542
White Wolf Distillery -- Shell Lake	543
Yahara Bay Distillers -- Madison	544

Wyoming

Kolts Fine Spirits -- Sheridan	545
Single Track Spirits -- Cody	546
Wyoming Whiskey Distillery -- Kirby	547

Canada

British Columbia

Central City Brewers and Distillers -- Surrey	548
Deep Cove Brewers and Distillers -- North Vancouver	549
Island Spirits Distillery -- Hornby Island	550
Long Table Distillery Ltd. -- Vancouver	551
Maple Leaf Spirits Inc. -- Penticton	552
Merridale Ciderworks Corp. -- Cobble Hill	553
Odd Society Spirits -- Vancouver	554
Okanagan Spirits -- Kelowna	555
Pemberton Distillery Inc. -- Pemberton	556
Shelter Point Distillery -- Campbell River	557
Sons of Vancouver Dist. Ltd. – N. Vancouver	558
The Dubh Glas Distillery -- Oliver	559
The Liberty Distillery -- Vancouver	560
Urban Distilleries -- Kelowna	561
Victoria Spirits -- Victoria	562
Yaletown Distilling Company -- Vancouver	563

New Brunswick

Winegarden Estate Ltd. -- Baie Verte	564

Nova Scotia

Glenora Distillery -- Cape Breton	565
Ironworks Distillery -- Lunenburg	566
Jost Vineyards Ltd. -- Malagash	567

Ontario

66 Gilead Distillery -- Bloomfield	568
Forty Creek Distillery -- Grimsby	569
Mary Jane's -- Niagara Falls	570
Still Waters Distillery -- Concord	571
The Ottawa Distillery Co. -- Ottawa	572
Waverley Spirits -- Perth	573

Prince Edward Island

Myriad View Artisan Distillery Inc. -- Rollo Bay	574
Prince Edward Distillery -- Hermanville	575

Quebec

Cidrerie Michel Jodoin -- Rougemont	576
The Subversives Distillers -- Longueuil	577

Saskatchewan

Last Mountain Distillery Ltd. -- Lumsden	578
LB Distillers -- Saskatoon	579

Yukon

Klondike River Distillery -- Dawson City	580
Yukon Spirits -- Whitehorse	581

Distilling Associations and Guilds	583
Resources and Information	586
Spirit Events and Festivals	590
Miscellaneous	594
Seminars and Certification for Craft Distilling	595
Index by Spirit Type	597

High Ridge Spirits

Bullock County Road 7
Stills Crossroads, AL 36081
334-474-3942

Owners / Operators
Robert Hall, Owner
Jamie Ray, Master Distiller

Email: info@highridgespirits.com
Website: www.highridgespirits.com
Facebook: High Ridge Spirits, LLC
Twitter: @alabamashine
Instagram: @highridgespirits

Type: Micro Distillery. Opened in 2013.

Hours of operation: Not provided

Tours: Available by appointment

Types of spirits produced: Moonshine

Names of spirits:
- Stills Crossroads Shine
- Flavored Shine

Best known for / most popular:
Stills Crossroads Shine

Average bottle price: Not provided

Distribution: AL

Interesting facts:
- First legal distillery in Alabama since Prohibition.
- High Ridge Spirits operates in a former horse barn in rural Bullock County.

Alaska Distillery

1540 North Shoreline Drive
Wasilla, AK 99654
907-382-6250

Owners / Operators:
Toby Foster, Founder / CEO

Email: toby@alaskadistillery.com
Website: www.alaskadistillery.com
Facebook: Alaska Distillery
Twitter: @AK_Distillery

Type: Micro Distillery. Opened in 2007.

Hours of operation:
Monday through Friday, 8 a.m. to 5 p.m.

Tours: Available

Types of spirits produced:
Gin, vodka, whiskey, moonshine

Names of spirits:
- Permafrost Alaska Vodka
- Smoked Salmon Vodka
- Alaska Outlaw Whiskey
- Purgatory Hemp Seed Vodka
- Birch Syrup Vodka
- Fireweed Vodka
- Honey Vodka
- Bristol Bay Glacier Gin
- Rhubarb Vodka
- Chocolate Moouse Vodka
- Alaska Apple Pie Moonshine
- Blueberry Vodka
- High Bush Cranberry Vodka
- Mountain Blackberry Vodka
- Raspberry Vodka
- FrostBite Alaska Vodka
- Lavender Vodka

Best known for / most popular: Alaska Distillery Smoked Salmon Vodka

Average bottle price: $24.99 to $37.99

Distribution: AK, AZ, CA, CO, GA, IL, IN, KY, MT, TN, TX, WA; Canada AB, BC

Interesting facts:
- Alaska Distillery is Alaska's first distillery.
- Award winning portfolio of Alaska themed spirits.

Bare Distillery

6310 A Street
Anchorage, AK 99518
907-561-2100

Owners / Operators:
Kyle T. Ryan, President / Founder
Jeremy Loyer, VP / Founder

Email: vodka@truulipeak.com
Website: www.truulipeak.com
Facebook: Truuli Peak Vodka
Twitter: @TruuliPeakVodka
Blog: Truuli Peak Vodka Blog
YouTube: Hot Mixology, Truuli Peak Vodka

Type: Micro Distillery. Opened in 2011.

Hours of operation: Daily, 9 a.m. to 5 p.m.

Tours: Available by appointment

Types of spirits produced: Vodka

Names of spirits:
- Truuli Peak Vodka

Best known for / most popular: Truuli Peak Vodka

Average bottle price: $39.99

Distribution: AK

Interesting facts:
- Truuli Peak Vodka is named after the highest elevation in the Kenai Mountain range, situated just outside of Anchorage. Rising at 6,612 feet above sea level, Truuli Peak is a majestic summit within the pristine Alaskan environment. The word Truuli is the ancient Alaska native term for the Kenai Mountain Range.
- Truuli Peak Vodka is made from local barley, honey and Eklutna glacier water.

High Mark Distillery

37200 Thomas Street
Sterling, AK 99672
907-260-3399

Owners / Operators:
Felicia Keith-Jones, Owner / Distiller
Ray Keith, Distiller

Email: highmarkdistillery@hotmail.com
Website: www.highmarkdistillery.com
Facebook: HighMark Distillery

Type: Micro Distillery. Opened in December 2012.

Hours of operation:
Monday through Saturday, noon to 8 p.m.
Sunday, Closed

Tours: Available

Types of spirits produced:
Vodka, moonshine, apple jack

Names of spirits:
- High Mark Vodka
- Blind Cat Moonshine
- Nickel Back Apple Jack

Best known for / most popular:
Nickel Back Apple Jack

Average bottle price: $29.00 to $36.00

Distribution: AK

Interesting facts:
- Known to be the youngest female owner/distiller in the U.S.
- High Mark Distillery is named for Felicia's late husband's favorite extreme sport, High Mark Snowmachining (extreme snow mobiling).

Port Chilkoot Distillery

34 Blacksmith Street
Haines, AK 99827
907-766-3434

Owners / Operators:
Heather Shade, Owner / Head Distiller
Sean Copeland, Owner / Production & Warehouse Manager

Email: portchilkootdistillery@gmail.com
Website: www.portchilkootdistillery.com
Facebook: Port Chilkoot Distillery
Twitter: @PortChilkott

Type: Micro Distillery. Opened in October 2013.

Hours of operation:
Monday through Friday, 9 a.m. to 5 p.m.

Tours: Available by appointment

Types of spirits produced:
Vodka, moonshine, gin, whiskey, bourbon

Names of spirits:
- Icy Strait Vodka
- 12 Volts Moonshine
- 50 Fathoms Gin

Best known for / most popular: 12 Volts Moonshine

Average bottle price: $32.00 to $36.00

Distribution: AK

Interesting facts: "Creating fine spirits is a natural extension of the Alaskan way of life. Putting up hand-crafted food and goods in large volumes comes naturally to Alaskans. Even during the Klondike Gold Rush days and beyond, bootleggers were producing and selling moonshine in Southeast Alaska. We are merely two of many who are committed to harvesting from the land, creating our own quality goods, and following our dreams in a place that can be wild and unpredictable. We wouldn't trade it for anything." – Heather Shade

Ursa Major Distilling

3738 Mariposa Lane
Fairbanks, AK 99709
907-455-6811

Owners / Operators:
Rob Borland, Owner
Tara Borland, Co-owner

Email: sales@ursamajordistilling.com
Website: www.ursamajordistilling.com
Facebook: Ursa Major Distilling
Twitter: @UrsaMajorDistil

Type: Craft Distillery. Opened in January 2013.

Hours of operation: Continuous

Tours: Not available

Types of spirits produced: Vodka, gin

Names of spirits:
- Long Winter Vodka
- Summer Harvest Gin

Best known for / most popular: Long Winter Vodka

Average bottle price: $38.00

Distribution: Local distribution

Interesting facts:
- Everything is made from scratch with local ingredients.
- Ursa Major Distilling is America's farthest north distillery.

Arizona High Spirits Distillery

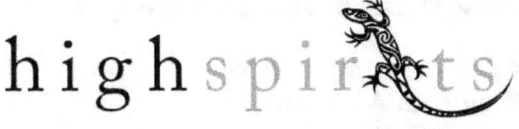

4366 E. Huntington Drive, Bldg. 2
Flagstaff, AZ 86004
928-853-1021

Owners / Operators:
Dana Kanzler, Managing Partner / Head Distiller

Email: dskanzler@yahoo.com
Website: www.arizonahighspirits.com
Facebook: Mogollon Brewing Company
Twitter: @AZHighSpirits
YouTube: Arizona High Spirits

Type: Micro Distillery. Opened in 2006.

Hours of operation: Monday through Friday, 7 a.m. to 5 p.m.

Tours: Available by appointment

Types of spirits produced: Vodka, gin, rum, whisky

Names of spirits:
- Prickly Pear Vodka
- Chili Vodka
- American Vodka
- Desert Dry Gin
- Pieces of Eight Spiced Rum
- Prickly Pear Liqueur
- Single Malt Mesquite Smoked Whisky

Best known for / most popular: Prickly Pear Vodka

Average bottle price: $20.00 to $30.00

Distribution: AZ, CA, NV, TX

Interesting facts: Arizona High Spirits is located at an elevation of 7,000 feet.

Desert Diamond Distillery

4875 N. Olympic Drive
Kingman, AZ 86401
928-757-7611

Owners / Operators:
The Patt Family

Email: Contact through website
Website: www.desertdiamonddistillery.com
Facebook: Desert Diamond Distillery
Twitter: @D3Spirits

Type: Micro Distillery. Opened in 2009.

Hours of operation:
Monday through Thursday, 10 a.m. to 5 p.m.
Friday and Saturday, 10 a.m. to 6 p.m.
Sunday by appointment only

Tours: Tours are ongoing Monday through Saturday, Sunday by appointment only.

Types of spirits produced: Vodka, rum

Names of spirits:
- Desert Diamond Distillery Gold Miner Vodka
- Desert Diamond Distillery Gold Miner Rum
- Desert Diamond Distillery Gold Miner Agave Rum
- Desert Diamond Distillery Gold Miner Dark Rum
- Desert Diamond Distillery Gold Miner Barrel Reserve Rum

Best known for / most popular: Agave Rum

Average bottle price: Not provided

Distribution: AZ, CA, NV

Interesting facts: The Desert Diamond Dark Rum and Barrel Reserve Rum are both platinum and gold medal award winning rums in significant contests.

Arkansas Moonshine Inc.

421 Beech Street
Newport, AR 72112
870-373-0888

Owners / Operators:
Hayden Wyatt, Owner / Distiller

Email: info@arkansasmoonshine.com
Website: www.arkansasmoonshine.com

Type: Craft Distillery. Opened in March 2010.

Hours of operation: Dictated by demand

Tours: Not available

Types of spirits produced: Moonshine

Names of spirits:
- Blue Flame Moonshine

Best known for / most popular: Blue Flame Moonshine

Average bottle price: $19.00

Distribution: AR

Interesting facts: Not provided

Rock Town Distillery Inc.

1216 East 6th Street
Little Rock, AR 72202
501-907-5244

Owners / Operators:
Phil Brandon, Owner

Email: phil@rocktowndistillery.com
Website: www.arkansaslightning.com
Facebook: Rock Town Distillery
Twitter: @rocktowndistill
Instagram: @rocktowndistill

Type: Micro Distillery. Opened in 2010.

Hours of operation:
Sunday through Friday, 1 p.m. to 5 p.m.; Saturday, 1 p.m. to 6 p.m.

Tours: Monday through Friday, 2 p.m. to 4 p.m.;
Saturday, 1:30 p.m., 3 p.m., 4:30 p.m.; Sunday, 1:30 p.m. and 3 p.m.

Types of spirits produced:
Vodka, gin, rum, bourbon, rye and wheat whiskey, moonshine, flavored moonshines

Names of spirits:
- Brandon's Vodka
- Brandon's Gin
- Brandon's Gin Barrel Reserve
- Rock Town Vodka
- Rock Town Barrel Aged Rum
- Rock Town Arkansas Bourbon Whiskey
- Rock Town Arkansas Rye Whiskey
- Rock Town Hickory Smoked Whiskey
- Arkansas Lightning
- Apple Pie Arkansas Lightning
- Lightning Hot Cinnamon Arkansas Lightning
- Peach Arkansas Lightning
- Blackberry Cobbler Arkansas Lightning
- Grape Arkansas Lightning

Best known for / most popular: Apple Pie Arkansas Lightning

Average bottle price: $29.99

Distribution: AR, FL, GA, IL, MO, MS, OK, OR, TN, TX; UK

Interesting facts:
Rock Town Distillery is Arkansas' first legal distillery since Prohibition.

1512 Spirits

Rohnert Park, CA 94928

Owners / Operators:
Salvatore P. Cimino, Owner / Master Distiller

Email: info@1512spirits.com
Website: www.1512spirits.com
Facebook: 1512 Spirits
Twitter: @1512Spirits

Type: Nano Distillery. Opened in 2011.

Hours of operation: Not provided

Tours: Not provided

Types of spirits produced: Whiskey, grappa, poitin

Names of spirits:
- 1512 Barbershop Rye Whiskey
- 1512 Spirits Aged 100% Rye Whiskey
- 1512 Spirits 2nd Chance Wheat Whiskey
- 1512 Spirits Signature Poitin
- 1512 Spirits Grappa
- 1512 Spirits Bourbon #1

Best known for / most popular:
1512 Spirits Aged 100% Rye Whiskey

Average bottle price: $115.00

Distribution: CA, NY; UK

Interesting facts: Smallest commercial distillery in CA.

Amador Distillery

260 Scottsville Boulevard
Jackson, CA 95642
209-304-1740

Owners / Operators:
Adam Stratton, Owner / Operator

Email: adam@amadordistillery.com
Website: www.amadordistillery.com
Facebook: Amador Distillery
Twitter: @AmadorDistiller

Type: Craft Distillery. Opened March 14, 2013.

Hours of operation:
Wednesday through Friday, 10 a.m. to 4 p.m.
Tastings are offered on Fridays, 4 p.m. to 7 p.m.

Tours: Available by appointment

Types of spirits produced:
Bourbon, rye whiskey, single malt whiskey, vodka, gin, light rum, brandy

Names of spirits:
- Amador Distillery Gin
- Amador Distillery Rum
- Amador Distillery Vodka
- Amador Distillery Bourbon
- Amador Distillery Whiskey

Best known for / most popular: Amador Distillery Gin

Average bottle price: $20.00 to $30.00

Distribution:
Through Southern Wine and Spirits

Interesting facts:
The distillery is all electric in anticipation of installing solar panels on the roof. The goal is to be "net-zero" power consumer within a couple of years.

Ascendant Spirits

37 Industrial Way, Ste. 102
Buellton, CA 93427
805-691-1000

Owners / Operators:
Steve Gertman, President / Master Distiller
Paul Gertman, Chief Financial Officer
Sarah Manski, Operations Manager
Kyle Herman, VP of Sales

Email: info@ascendantspirits.com
Website: www.ascendantspirits.com
Facebook: Ascendant Spirits Distillery & Tasting Room
Twitter: @ASDistillery
Yelp: Ascendant Spirits Distillery & Tasting Room

Type: Craft Distillery. Opened in March 2013.

Hours of operation:
Friday, 4 p.m. to 8 p.m.
Saturday and Sunday, 1 p.m. to 7 p.m.

Tours: Available during tasting room hours

Types of spirits produced:
Bourbon, vodka, caviar lime vodka, strawberry vodka, moonshine

Names of spirits:
- Breaker Bourbon
- American Star Vodka
- American Star Caviar Lime Vodka
- American Star Strawberry Vodka
- Silver Lightning Moonshine
- Pink Lightning Moonshine
- Sempre Fi Moonshine

Best known for / most popular: Breaker Bourbon

Average bottle price: $40.00 to $50.00

Distribution: TBA

Interesting facts:
First distillery in Santa Barbara County since Prohibition.

Autry Cellars

5450-B Edna Road (Hwy 227)
San Luis Obispo, CA 93401
805-546-8669

Owners / Operators:
Stephen P. Autry, Owner / Wine Maker / Distiller

Email: wine@autrycellars.com
Website: www.autrycellars.com
Facebook: Autry Cellars Artisan Wines

Type: Micro Distillery. Opened in January 2012.

Hours of operation: Daily 11 a.m. to 5 p.m.

Tours: Available daily, 11 a.m. to 5 p.m.

Types of spirits produced: Brandy

Names of spirits:
- Autry Cellars Grappa
- Autry Cellars American Oaked
- Autry Cellars Hungarian Oaked
- Autry Cellars Apple Brandy

Best known for / most popular: Not provided

Average bottle price: $35.00 to $60.00

Distribution: Direct sales

Interesting facts: Not provided

Ballast Point Spirits

10051 Old Grove Road, Ste. B1
San Diego, CA 92131
858-695-2739

Owners / Operators:
Jack White and Yuseff Cherney, Owners

Email: yuseff@ballastpoint.com
Website: www.ballastpoint.com
Facebook: Ballast Point Brewing & Spirits
Twitter: @BPbrewing

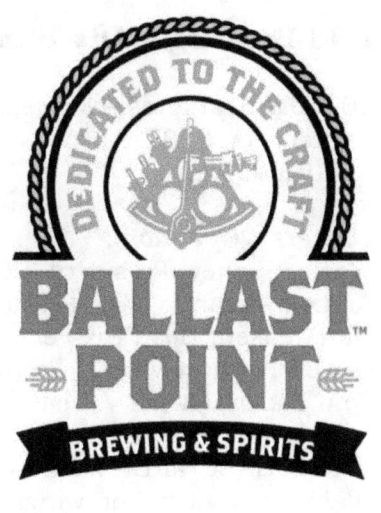

Type: Brewery / Micro Distillery
Brewery established in 1996; distillery established in 2008.

Hours of operation:
Monday through Saturday, 11 a.m. to 9 p.m.
Sunday, 11 a.m. to 7 p.m.

Tours: Available daily* at 1 p.m., 3 p.m., 5 p.m., 7 p.m.
*No 7 p.m. tour on Sunday

Types of spirits produced: Bourbon, gin, rum, vodka, whiskey

Names of spirits:
- Old Grove Gin
- Three Sheets Barrel Aged Rum
- Three Sheets White Rum
- Devil's Share Whiskey
- Devils' Share Bourbon
- Devil's Share Moonshine
- Fugu Vodka

Average bottle price:
$24.00 to $65.00

Distribution:
CA, GA, IL, NJ, NV, NY, WA

Interesting facts:
First licensed distillery in San Diego since Prohibition.

BNS Brewing & Distilling Company

10960 Wheatlands Avenue, Ste. 101
Santee, CA 92071
619-956-0952

Owners / Operators:
Wesley Richey, President / Owner / Brewer
Andrew Arrabito, Vice President / Owner / Distiller
Dan Jensen, Head Brewer / Owner
Gene Chaffin, Owner / Production Manager
Tom Paden, Owner / Distribution Manager

Email: BNSCraftBrew@gmail.com
Website: www.bnsbrewinganddistilling.com
Facebook: BNS Brewing & Distilling Co.
Instagram: BNSBrewinganddistilling

Type: Craft Distillery. Opened in June 2013.

Hours of operation: Daily, noon to 10 p.m.

Tours: Not available

Types of spirits produced:
Vodka, gin, blended malt whiskey, single malt whiskey, bourbon, rum

Names of spirits:
- TBA

Best known for / most popular: TBA

Average bottle price: TBA

Distribution: TBA

Interesting facts: Not provided

Bowen's Spirits Inc.

Bakersfield, CA 93308
661-343-2041

Owners / Operators:
Wade Bowen, Owner / CEO
JoJo Bowen, VP Sales
Dave Plivelich, VP Marketing

Email: Wade@BowenSpirits.com
JoJo@BowenSpirits.com
Dave@BowenSpirits.com
Website: www.bowenspirits.com
www.bowenswhiskey.com
Facebook: Bowen's Whiskey

Type: Micro Distillery. Opened in 2012.

Hours of operation: Not provided

Tours: Not provided

Types of spirits produced: Whiskey

Names of spirits:
- Bowen's Whiskey

Best known for / most popular: Bowen's Whiskey

Average bottle price: $38.99

Distribution:
CA, DC, FL, IL, MD, VA, WY; Canada MB

Interesting facts:
- Bowen's unique smoky flavor comes from reclaimed, forest fire ravaged Red Oak from the local central California mountains.

Awards and Recognitions:
Bowen's Whiskey
- 94 Points, The Tasting Panel. "Smoky + sweet + soft + smooth = sensational. This newcomer is original and memorable - a buttery caramel-driven campfire in a bottle."

Cal-Czech Distillery

1209 Highway 49
Angels Camp, CA 95222
209-736-2990

Owners / Operators:
Rocky Cozzo, Owner / Distiller

Email: rocky@vodkamorava.com
Website: www.vodkamorava.com
Facebook: Cal-Czech Distillery
Twitter: @VodkaMorava

Type: Micro Distillery. Opened in 2012.

Hours of operation: Monday through Friday, 9 a.m. to 5 p.m.

Tours: Available by appointment

Types of spirits produced: Vodka

Names of spirits:
- Vodka Morava

Best known for / most popular: Vodka Morava

Average bottle price: $30.00 to $40.00

Distribution: Available through distributors

Interesting facts: Techniques are inspired by Czech and Ukrainian distillers.

Charbay Distillers

4001 Spring Mountain Road
St. Helena, CA 94574
707-963-9327

Owners / Operators:
Miles and Susan Karakasevic, Owners
Miles Karakasevic, Grand Master Distiller
Susan Karakasevic, General Manager
Marko Karakasevic, Master Distiller

Email: info@charbay.com
Website: www.charbay.com
Facebook: Charbay Distillery & Winery
Twitter: @Charbay
Blog: www.charbay.com

Type: Micro Distillery. Opened in 1983.

Hours of operation: Closed to the public.

Tours: Not available

Types of spirits produced: Whiskey, vodka, rum, grappa, brandy, liqueurs, tequila (made in Mexico by Miles/Marko)

Names of spirits:
- Charbay Whiskey, Release III
- Charbay R5 Whiskey
- Charbay 'S' Whiskey
- Charbay Tahitian Vanilla Bean Rum
- Charbay Brandy No. 89
- Charbay Vodka (clear)
- Charbay Fresh Fruit Vodkas (Blood Orange, Ruby Red Grapefruit, Meyer Lemon, Pomegranate & Green Tea)
- Charbay Black Walnut Liqueur
- Charbay Tequila Blanco

Best known for / most popular: Charbay Vodka and Whiskey

Average bottle price: $38.00 to $350.00

Distribution:
Nationwide in high end shops, restaurants, and clubs

Interesting facts:
- Charbay is family owned and operated by 12th and 13th generation distillers and winemakers.
- Considered founding pioneers in the American micro distillery movement with many firsts in their 30 year history.

Cutler's Artisan Spirits

137 Anacapa Street, Ste. D
Santa Barbara, CA 93101
805-680-4009

Owners / Operators:
Ian Cutler, Owner / Head Distiller

Email: info@cutlersartisan.com
Website: www.cutlersartisan.com
Facebook: Cutler's Artisan Spirits

Type: Micro Distillery. Opened in 2013.

Hours of operation: Monday through Thursday, 1 p.m. to 5 p.m.
Saturday and Sunday, 10 a.m. to 5 p.m.

Tours: Available by appointment

Types of spirits produced: Whiskey, vodka, gin, liqueurs

Names of spirits:
- TBA

Best known for / most popular: TBA

Average bottle price: TBA

Distribution: TBA

Interesting facts: Not provided

Distillery No. 209

Pier 50 Shed B, Mailbox 9
San Francisco, CA 94158
415-369-0209

Owners / Operators:
Leslie Rudd, Founder
Samantha Rudd, Owner
Arne Hillesland, Ginerator
Joe Fairchild, COO

Email: Joe Fairchild, joe.fairchild@distillery209.com
Arne Hillesland, arne@distillery209.com
Website: www.distillery209.com, www.209gin.com
Facebook: Distillery No. 209
Twitter: @distillery209

Type: Micro Distillery. Opened in 2005.

Hours of operation: Not open to the public

Tours: Not available

Types of spirits produced: Gin, vodka

Names of spirits:
- No. 209 Gin
- No. 209 Kosher-for-Passover Gin
- No. 209 Kosher-for-Passover Vodka
- No. 209 Cabernet Sauvignon Barrel Reserve Gin
- No. 209 Sauvignon Blanc Barrel Reserve Gin

Best known for / most popular:
Basil Gimlet and Last Word

Average bottle price: $29.99 to $54.99

Distribution: 34 states and internationally

Interesting facts: Distillery No. 209 was the 209th registered distillery permitted in the United States. No. 209 Kosher-for-Passover Gin is the first and only known Passover certified gin in the world.

Essential Spirits Alambic Distilleries

144 A&B, South Whisman Road
Mountain View, CA 94041
650-962-0546

Owners / Operators:
Dave Classick Sr., Owner / Master Distiller
Andrea Mirenda, Owner / President
Dave Classick Jr., Distiller / ITO
Audrey Classick, Brand Ambassador

Email: service@essentialspirits.com
Website: www.essentialspirits.com
Facebook: Sgt. Classick Hawaiian Rum
Twitter: @SgtClassick

Type: Micro Distillery. Opened in 1998.

Hours of operation:
January to November – Monday through Friday, 10 a.m. to 7 p.m.
December – Closed

Tours: Available

Types of spirits produced: Rum, gin, grappa, pear eau-de-vie, vodka

Names of spirits:
House Brands
- Sergeant Classick Hawaiian Rum (Silver and Gold)
- Classick Grappa di Cabernet - Stags Leap
- Classick Pure Pear Eau-de-Vie

Contract Brands
- DH Krahn Gin
- Hana Gin
- Ice Fox Vodka
- Island Rum (Silver and Gold)
- Hula Girl RTD Cocktails
- U4RIK Grape based Vodka
- Del Dotto Estates - Howell Mountain Grappa de Cabernet
- Vino Robles Grappa de Petite Syrah

Best known for / most popular:
Sgt. Classick Rumadillo (rum and tonic with fresh lime)

Average bottle price: $20.00 to $38.00

Distribution: CA, FL, NY, WA

Falcon Spirits LLC

3701 Collins Avenue, 1 B & C
Richmond, CA 94806
510-234-3252

Owners / Operators:
Farid Dormishian, Owner / Operator

Email: faridd@falconspirits.com
Website: www.falconspirits.com
Facebook: Falcon Spirits
Twitter: @FalconSpirits

Type: Micro Distillery. Opened in 2011.

Hours of operation: Not provided

Tours: Available by appointment

Types of spirits produced: Gin

Names of spirits:
- Botanica Spiritvs

Best known for / most popular: Botanica Spiritvs

Average bottle price: $40.00

Distribution: CA, CT, OR, NY, UT, WA

Interesting facts: "Botanica Spiritvs Gin is produced in less than 300 bottles per batch. It is a vapor infused gin where the alcohol vapor extracts the flavors from the botanicals during distillation. The base alcohol is non-GMO grain spirit that has been 6 times distilled and then carbon filtered to remove all impurities. Some of the botanicals are distilled in season and not available year round. Each batch is the product of 2-3 separate distillations that are then blended and allowed to age for a period of three weeks before being brought to bottling strength of 45% ABV. The high proof gin is brought to bottling strength using cucumber water that is prepared by macerating fresh fragrant Persian cucumbers and then adding water from the Sierra Mountains and freezing the mixture to burst the cells open thus releasing the cucumber flavor. The frozen mixture is thawed, vacuum filtered, and then used to bring the gin to bottling strength. This mixture is allowed to rest at least a day and then polished by bringing the gin to 4 degrees Celsius and then passing them through six stage diatomaceous earth filters; bottled and hand labeled with a stamp signifying the batch number." - Farid Dormishian

Fog's End Distillery

425 Alta Street, Bldg. #25
Gonzales, CA 93926

Owners / Operators:
Craig Pakish, Founder

Email: fogsenddistillery.craig@gmail.com
Website: www.fogsenddistillery.com

Type: Micro Distillery. Opened in 2008.

Hours of operation: Not provided

Tours: By appointment, call 831-809-5941

Types of spirits produced: Whiskey, moonshine, rye

Names of spirits:
- White Dog
- Monterey Rye
- California Moonshine
- Primo Aqua Ardiente

Best known for / most popular: Monterey Rye

Average bottle price: $30.00

Distribution: CA

Awards and Recognitions:
Monterey Rye
- Gold Medal, October 2013, TheFiftyBest.com

Germain-Robin

1110 Bel Arbres Road
Redwood Valley, CA 95470
707-468-7899

craft distillers®
pure, beautifully made spirits

Owners / Operators:
Ansley Coale, President
Joe Corley, Distiller

Email: alambic@pacific.net
Website: www.craftdistillers.com
Facebook: Craft Distillers

Type: Micro Distillery. Opened in 1982.

Hours of operation: Monday through Friday, 9 a.m. to 5 p.m.

Tours: Not available

Types of spirits produced:
Absinthe, apple brandy, brandy, grappa, liqueurs

Names of spirits:
- Germain-Robin Brandy
- Germain-Robin Apple Brandy
- Germain-Robin Grappa
- Germain-Robin Créme de Poète Liqueur
- Germain-Robin Absinthe Superieure

Best known for / most popular: Grape Brandy

Average bottle price: $48.00 to $350.00

Distribution: Distillery and retail locations nationwide

Interesting facts: Hubert Germain-Robin was the first known distiller to use wines from world-class varietal grapes.

GreenBar Collective

2459 E. 8th Street
Los Angeles, CA 90021
213-375-3668

Owners / Operators:
Melkon Khosrovian, Owner
Litty Mathew, Owner

Email: info@greenbar.biz
Website: www.greenbar.biz
Facebook: Greenbar
Twitter: @GreenBarDrinks
Instagram: @GreenbarDistillery

Type: Micro Distillery. Opened in 2004.

Hours of operation: Not provided

Tours: Not provided

Types of spirits produced:
Vodka, gin, tequila, rum, whiskey, liqueur

Names of spirits:
- TRU Vodka
- TRU Gin
- IXÁ Tequila
- CRUSOE Rum
- FRUITLAB Liqueur
- GRAND POPPY Bitter Liqueur

Best known for / most popular:
TRU organic vodka & IXÁ organic tequila

Average bottle price: Not provided

Distribution: Not provided

Interesting facts:
- All organic spirits
- Tasting Room to open Summer 2014
- We plant one tree for every bottle sold.

Greenway Distillers Inc.

5000 Low Gap Road
Ukiah, CA 95482
707-485-2941

Owners / Operators:
Crispin Cain, President / Distiller / Spirits Master
Tamar Kaye, Vice President

Email: acwd.1@netzero.net , crispin@greenwaydistillers.com
Website: www.greenwaydistillers.com
Facebook: Greenway Distillers, Inc.

Type: Micro Distillery. Incorporated in 2010.

Hours of operation: Monday through Friday, 6 a.m. to 5 p.m.

Tours: Available by appointment

Types of spirits produced: Absinthe, liqueur

Names of spirits:
- Crispin's Rose Liqueur ($50)
- Germain-Robin Absinthe ($85)

Best known for / most popular: Crispin's Rose Liqueur

Average bottle price: $50.00 to $85.00

Distribution: See www.caddellwilliams.com

Awards and Recognitions:
Germain-Robin Absinthe
- Five Star Review, F. Paul Pacult's Spirit Journal
Crispin's Rose Liqueur
- Five Star Review, F. Paul Pacult's Spirit Journal
- Best of the Best Issue of the Robb Report, 2008.

Hanson Spirits LLC

21750 Eighth Street East
Sonoma, CA 95476
415-407-5150

Owners / Operators:
Chris Hanson, Owner / Operator
Brandon Hanson, Owner / Operator
Scott Hanson, Owner / Operator

Email: info@hansonspirits.com
        chris@hansonspirits.com
Website: www.hansonspirits.com
Facebook: Hanson of Sonoma Vodka

Type: Craft Distillery. Opened in January 2013.

Hours of operation:
Monday through Friday, 9 a.m. to closing

Tours: Not available

Types of spirits produced: Organic Vodka

Names of spirits:
- Hanson of Sonoma Organic Vodka - Original
- Hanson of Sonoma Organic Vodka - Cucumber
- Hanson of Sonoma Organic Vodka - Espresso
- Hanson of Sonoma Organic Vodka - Mandarin
- Hanson of Sonoma Organic Vodka - Ginger
- Hanson of Sonoma Organic Vodka - Boysenberry

Best known for / most popular: Original Vodka

Average bottle price: $34.95

Distribution: CA, 6 other states (not provided)

Interesting facts:
- Family owned and operated
- Certified organic craft distillery
- Certified Gluten Free and certified Non-GMO

Awards and Recognitions:
- Original Vodka, 2013 Sip Awards Platinum Award
- Original Vodka, 2013 Sip Awards Best of Vodka Class
- Espresso Vodka, 2013 Sip Awards Platinum Award
- Two Gold Medals, The 2013 Vodka Masters in London

HelloCello
Prohibition Spirits

21877 8th Street East #4
Sonoma, CA 95476
707-721-6390

Owners / Operators:
Fred Groth, Founder / Distiller / Ambassador
Amy Groth, Founder / Distiller / Ambassador

Email: info@hellosonoma.com
Website: www.hellosonoma.com, www.prohibition-spirits.com
Facebook: HelloCello-Limoncello di Sonoma
Twitter: HelloSonoma

Type: Micro Distillery. Opened in 2009.

Hours of operation: Available by appointment

Tours: Available by appointment

Types of spirits produced: Vodka, rum, whiskey, liqueur

Names of spirits:
- Solano Vodka
- Sugar Daddy Light Rum
- Sugar Daddy Amber Rum
- Sugar Daddy Dark Rum
- Hooker's House Bourbon
- Hooker's House Rye
- Hooker's House General's Reserve
- Hooker's House Corn Whiskey
- Limoncello di Sonoma
- OrangeCello di Sonoma
- FigCello di Sonoma
- Nocino
- Chauvet Brandy

Best known for / most popular:
Hookers House Bourbon and Limoncello di Sonoma

Average bottle price: $32.00

Distribution: Not provided

Interesting facts: Not provided

High Roller Spirits

3133 Hull Road
Atwater, CA 95301
209-385-2966

Owners / Operators:
David Souza, Founder / Master Distiller
Sharon Ambrosia, Operations Manager

Email: david@highrollerspirits.com
Website: www.highrollerspirits.com
Facebook: High Roller Premium Vodka
Twitter: @HighRollerVodka

Type: Micro Distillery. Opened in 2011.

Hours of operation: Not provided

Tours: Not provided

Types of spirits produced: Vodka

Names of spirits:
- High Roller Premium Vodka

Best known for / most popular: High Roller Premium Vodka

Average bottle price: Not provided

Distribution: CA, NE, TN

Interesting facts:
Gluten free vodka made from sweet potatoes

Humboldt Distillery

735 10th Street
Fortuna, CA 95540
707-725-1700

Owners / Operators:
Abe Stevens, Owner / Distiller

Email: info@humboldtdistillery.com
Website: www.humboldtdistillery.com
Facebook: Humboldt Distillery

Type: Micro Distillery. Established in 2012.

Hours of operation:
Monday through Friday, 10 a.m. to 6 p.m.

Tours: Tastings and tours conducted by appointment, or during public hours posted on website.

Types of spirits produced:
Vodka, spiced rum, seasonal fruit brandies

Names of spirits:
- Humboldt Distillery Organic Vodka
- Humboldt Distillery Organic Spiced Rum
- Humboldt Distillery Pear Brandy
- Humboldt Distillery Apple Brandy

Best known for / most popular: Not provided

Average bottle price: $15.99 to $19.99

Distribution: Northern CA

Interesting facts: Spirits are certified organic

Kill Devil Spirit Company

2766 Via Orange Way, Ste. O
San Diego, CA 91978

Owners / Operators:
Ray Digilio, Owner
Luke Oskam, Head Brewer / Distiller

Email: Ray@killdevilspiritco.com
Website: www.killdevilspiritco.com
Facebook: Kill Devil Spirit Co.
Twitter: @killdevilspirit

Type: Boutique Distillery. Opened in 2011.

Hours of operation: Not provided

Tours: Available by appointment through the website

Types of spirits produced: Vodka, whiskey

Names of spirits:
- Rx Vodka
- Ugly California Moonshine

Best known for / most popular: Ugly California Moonshine

Average bottle price: Not provided

Distribution: Countywide

Interesting facts: California's smallest distillery

Lost Spirits Distillery

Monterey County, CA 93907

Owners / Operators:
Bryan Davis, Co-owner
Joanne David, Co-owner

Email: info@lostspirits.net
Website: www.lostspirits.net
Facebook: Lost Spirits Distillery
Twitter: @LostSpirits1

Type: Micro Distillery. First release in 2012.

Hours of operation: Available by appointment

Tours: Available by reservation. See website.

Types of spirits produced: Whiskey

Names of spirits:
- Leviathan American Peated Single Malt Whiskey
- Paradiso Peated American Single Malt Whiskey

Best known for / most popular:
Leviathan Peated American Single Malt Whiskey

Average bottle price: $55.00

Distribution: CA, DC, IL, NY, TN; Germany, Sweden, Denmark, UK

Interesting facts:
- Lost Spirits is best known for producing some of the world's most heavily peated whiskeys. What sets the distillery apart from other peated malt houses is the use of exotic and rare peat sources such as peat harvested from Canadian forests, California islands, and tropical climates.
- The distillery is also home to one of the only operational log and copper pot stills left in the United States. Log and copper pot stills are made of oak tanks fitted with a copper neck.
- The entire distillery, including the equipment, was built by hand by the founders.

Malahat Spirits

8706 Production Avenue
San Diego, CA 92121
858-999-2326

Owners / Operators:
Ken Lee, Partner
Antonio Grillo, Partner
Thomas Bleakley, Partner

Email: rumrunner@malahatspirits.com
Website: www.malahatspirits.com
Facebook: Malahat Spirits
Twitter: @MalahatSpirits

Type: Micro Distillery. Opened in 2012.

Hours of operation: TBA

Tours: TBA

Types of spirits produced: Rum, whiskey

Names of spirits:
- Malahat Spirits Rum
- Malahat Spirits Spiced Rum

Best known for / most popular: Malahat Spirits Rum

Average bottle price: TBA

Distribution: Local distribution

Interesting facts: The Malahat was the "Queen of Rum Row." Her call to glory came during Prohibition. Loaded with the finest spirits available, she would set sail down the U.S. West Coast to 'Mexico'.

When she reached Southern California, the Malahat would rendezvous with smaller boats, "Rum Runners," and deliver her precious cargo. The Malahat was the source for rum, whiskey and other spirits available in Southern California.

Malahat Spirits will continue that tradition by handcrafting and distilling the best spirits.

Manzanita Distilling Company

10149 Prospect Avenue
Santee, CA 92071
619-749-3653

Owners / Operators:
Jeff Trevaskis, Owner / Founder
Jacob Pittman, Head Distiller / Co-Founder

Email: jeff@twistedmanzantia.com
Website: www.twistedmanzanitaspirits.com
Facebook: Twisted Manzanita Spirits
Twitter: @ManzanitaSpirits
Instagram: ManzanitaSpirits

Type: Craft Distillery. Opened in November 2013.

Hours of operation: Friday 4 p.m. to 8 p.m.; Saturday 4 p.m. to 8 p.m.

Tours: Available

Types of spirits produced: Moonshine, vodka

Names of spirits:
- Manzanita Moonshine
- Manzanita Oaked Moonshine
- Orange Vodka

Best known for / most popular: Manzanita Moonshine

Average bottle price: $30.00 to $70.00

Distribution: CA

Awards and Recognitions:
Manzanita SoCal Moonshine
- Silver Medal, 2013 San Diego International Spirits Festival

Manzanita Orange Vodka
- Bronze Medal, 2013 San Diego International Spirits Festival

Mosswood Distillers Inc.

751 13th Street, Bldg. 264 #3
Treasure Island
San Francisco, CA 94130
415-439-0585

Owners / Operators:
Therese Agnew, Co-owner / Operator
Jake Chevedden, Co-owner / Operator

Email: info@drinkmosswood.com
Website: www.drinkmosswood.com
Facebook: Mosswood Distillers
Twitter: @drinkmosswood
Instagram: @drinkmosswood

Type: Rectifer. Opened in August 2013.

Hours of operation: Not provided

Tours: Available by appointment

Types of spirits produced: Whiskey

Names of spirits:
- Mosswood American Whiskey Apple Brandy Barreled Bourbon
- Mosswood American Whiskey Espresso Barreled Bourbon
- Mosswood American Whiskey California Ale Barreled Bourbon

Best known for / most popular:
Mosswood American Whiskey, Apple Brandy Barreled Bourbon
Mosswood American Whiskey, Espresso Barreled Bourbon

Average bottle price: $40.00

Distribution: San Francisco Bay Area

Interesting facts: Not provided

Napa Valley Distillery

4812 E. Second Street
Benicia, CA 94510
510-334-8923

Owners / Operators:
Robert Contreras, Owner

Email: robert@napavalleydistillery.com
Website: www.napavalleydistillery.com
Facebook: Napa Valley Distillery
Twitter: @NapaValleyDist
Pinterest: Napa Valley Distillery

Type: Craft Distillery. Opened in April 2014.

Hours of operation: Varies

Tours: Available by appointment

Types of spirits produced:
Vodka, gin, rum, whiskey

Names of spirits:
- TBA

Best known for / most popular: TBA

Average bottle price: TBA

Distribution: TBA

Interesting facts: Not provided

Napa Valley Distillery

225 Walnut Street
Napa, CA 94558
707-265-NAPA

Tasting Room and Bar Shop
(at the Oxbow Public Market)

610 First Street
Napa, CA 94559
707-22-OXBOW

Owners / Operators:
Arthur and Lusine Hartunian

Email: sales@napadistillery.com
Website: www.napadistillery.com
Facebook: Napa Valley Distillery
Twitter: @NapaVodka

Type: Micro Distillery. Opened in 2009.

Hours of operation: Daily, 10 a.m. to 8 p.m.

Tours: Not available

Barrel-Aged Cocktails

Types of spirits produced: Brandy, vodka, whiskey, liqueur

Names of spirits:
- Napa Vodka Vintage Reserve
- Barrel-Aged Cocktails
  Old Hollywood, Negroni, Mint Julep, East India, Manhattan
- Old Hollywood Gin
- Napa Valley Meyer Lemon Liqueur

Best known for: Japanese James Bond
Served at Iron Chef Morimoto's restaurant in Napa, CA

Average bottle price: $30.00

Distribution:
CA, DC, FL, IL, LA, MD, NV, TN, WI; Canada AB, QC

Interesting facts:
- This is the world's first known "vintage vodka," handcrafted entirely from premium Napa Valley Sauvignon Blanc from a single vintage and a single Napa Valley Estate.
- Is the original Napa Valley Distillery and the first in the city of Napa since Prohibition.

Old Harbor Distilling Company

270 17th Street
San Diego, CA 92101
619-630-7048

Owners / Operators:
Michael Skubic, Founder / Distiller

Email: info@oldharbordistilling.com
Website: www.oldharbordistilling.com
Facebook: Old Harbor Distilling
Twitter: @Old_Harbor
Instagram: @OldHarborDistilling

Type: Craft Distillery. Opened in March 2014.

Hours of operation: Friday and Saturday

Tours: Friday and Saturday by appointment

Types of spirits produced: Gin, rum, coffee liqueur, rye, bourbon, single malt, applejack, amaro

Names of spirits:
- San Miguel: Southwestern Gin
- 1542: California Native Botanical Gin
- Barrelman: Navy Strength Rum
- Ampersand: Cold Brew Coffee Liqueur
- The Judge: Rye Whiskey
- The Kid: Single Malt Whisky

Best known for / most popular: TBA

Average bottle price: $25.00 to $55.00

Distribution: CA

Interesting facts: Located in East Village San Diego, just a few blocks away from the historic Gaslamp District.

Services offered other than production:
Tastings, tours and merchandise

Old World Spirits LLC

121 Industrial Road, #3-4
Belmont, CA 94002
650-622-9222

Owners / Operators:
Davorin Kuchan, President

Email: info@oldworldspirits.com
Website: www.oldworldspirits.com
Facebook: Old World Spirits, LLC
Twitter: @oldworldspirits
YouTube: Old World Spirits Product Feature
Yelp: Old World Spirits
foursquare: OldWorldSpirits

Type: Micro Distillery. Opened in 2008.

Hours of operation: Monday through Saturday, 9 a.m. to 5 p.m.

Tours: Available on the last Friday of the month and by appointment

Types of spirits produced: Whiskey, gin, absinthe, liqueurs, brandies, bitters

Names of spirits:
- Kuchan Eaux De Vie
  - Poire Williams
  - Indian Blood Peach
  - O'Henry Oak Aged Peach
- Kuchan Nocino Black Walnut Liqueur
- La Sorciere Absinthe Verte and Bleue
- Blade California Small Batch Gin
- Rusty Blade Barrel Aged Gin
- Kuchan Alambic Brandy
- Goldrun Rye Whiskey

Best known for / most popular: Blade Gin, Rusty Blade, La Sorciere Absinthe, Kuchan Nocino and Goldrun 100% Rye Whiskey

Average bottle price: $30.00 to $75.00

Distribution: CA, CO, ID, NV, OR, WA

Interesting facts: First known U.S. distillery to release "blanche" clear style absinthe and Rusty Blade Barrel Aged Gin.

RE:FIND Distillery

2725 Adelaida Road
Paso Robles, CA 93446
805-239-9456

Owners / Operators:
Alex Villicana, Owner / Distiller
Monica Villicana, Owner

Email: alex@refinddistillery.com, monica@refinddistillery.com
Website: www.refinddistillery.com
Facebook: Re:Find Distillery
Twitter: @re_find

Type: Micro Distillery. Opened in 2011.

Hours of operation: Monday through Friday, 8 a.m. to 5 p.m.

Tours: Daily, 11 a.m. to 5 p.m.

Types of spirits produced: Vodka, gin, brandy, whiskey

Names of spirits:
- RE:FIND Vodka
- RE:FIND Gin
- RE:FIND Neutral Brandy
- RE:FIND Botanical Brandy
- RE:FIND Limoncello
- RE:FIND Cucumber Vodka
- RE:FIND Rye Whiskey

Best known for / most popular: RE:FIND Gin

Average bottle price: $35.00 to $38.00

Distribution: CA

Saint James Spirits

5220 Fourth Street, Unit 17
Irwindale, CA 91701
626-856-6930

Owners / Operators:
James Busuttil, Owner

Email: sjspirits@earthlink.net
Website: www.saintjamesspirits.com

Type: Micro Distillery. Opened in 1995.

Hours of operation: Not provided

Tours: Not provided

Types of spirits produced: Brandy, rum, agave, grappa, whisky

Names of spirits:
- Mojo Vodka
- California Gold Agave
- Saint James Spirits Grappa
- Royale Hawaiian Pineapple Rum
- Saint James Spirits Pineapple Brandy
- Saint James Spirits Kirsch (Eau de Vie)
- Peregrine Rock – California Pure Malt Whisky

Best known for / most popular: Not provided

Average bottle price: Not provided

Distribution: CA

Interesting facts: Not provided

Spirit Works Distillery

6790 McKinley Street #100
Sebastopol, CA 95472
707-634-4793

Owners / Operators:
Ashby Marshall, Owner / Distiller
Timo Marshall, Owner / Distiller

Email: hello@spiritworksdistillery.com
Website: www.spiritworksdistillery.com
Facebook: Spirit Works Distillery

Type: Micro Distillery. Opened in 2013.

Hours of operation: Thursday through Sunday, 11 a.m. to 4 p.m.

Tours: Available Friday through Sunday at 4 p.m. (reserve online)

Types of spirits produced: Gin, sloe gin, vodka, whiskey

Names of spirits:
- Spirit Works Gin
- Spirit Works Sloe Gin
- Spirit Works Wheat Whiskey
- Spirit Works Rye Whiskey
- Spirit Works Vodka

Best known for / most popular: Spirit Works Sloe Gin

Average bottle price: Not provided

Distribution: Southern Wine & Spirits Artisanal Group

Interesting facts:
Spirit Works Sloe Gin is currently one of the only U.S. made traditional sloe gins, meaning they use whole sloe berries in their recipe that has been passed down through the Marshall family for generations.

St. George Spirits

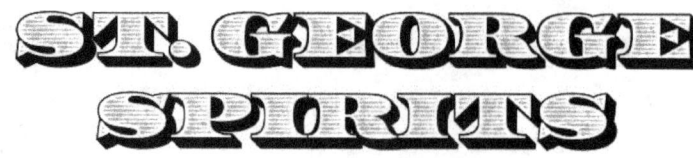

2601 Monarch Street
Alameda, CA 94501
510-769-1601

Owners / Operators:
Lance Winters, Owner / Master Distiller

Email: info@stgeorgespirits.com
tastingroom@stgeorgespirits.com
Website: www.stgeorgespirits.com
Facebook: St. George Spirits
Twitter: @StGeorgeSpirits
Flickr: St. George Spirits
YouTube: St. George Spirits
Yelp: St. George Spirits Alameda

Type: Micro Distillery. Opened in 1982.

Hours of operation: Tasting room and on-site store - Wednesday through Saturday, noon to 7 p.m.; Sunday noon to 5 p.m.

Tours: Available Wednesday through Sunday. Check website for times.

Types of spirits produced: Fruit brandies, fruit liqueurs, single malt whiskey, absinthe, agricole rum, gin, bourbon

Names of spirits:
- St. George Brandy
- St. George Liqueur
- St. George Single Malt Whiskey
- St. George Absinthe Verte
- St. George California Agricole Rum
- St. George Botanivore Gin
- St. George Terroir Gin
- St. George Dry Rye Gin
- Breaking & Entering Bourbon

Best known for / most popular:
St. George Absinthe Verte

Average bottle price: $20.00 to $80.00

Distribution: Nationwide, on-site store

Interesting facts: St. George Spirits is housed in a 65,000 square foot airplane hangar on the former Alameda Naval Air Station.

Stark Spirits

1260 Lincoln Avenue, Ste. 1100
Pasadena, CA 91103
626-798-1377

Owners / Operators:
Gregory Stark and Karen Robinson-Stark

Email: info@starkspirits.com
Website: www.starkspirits.com

Type: Micro Distillery. Opened in December 2013.

Hours of operation: Monday through Friday, 9 a.m. to 6 p.m.

Tours: Not available

Types of spirits produced:
Rum, rye whiskey, single malt whiskey, aquavit, fruit schnapps, brandy

Names of spirits:
- California Silver Rum
- California Gold Rum
- Rye Whiskey
- Single Malt Whiskey

Best known for / most popular: TBA

Average bottle price: $25.00 to $50.00

Distribution: CA

Stillwater Spirits

611 2nd Street
Petaluma, CA   94952
707-778-6041

Owners / Operators:
John Moylan, Co-owner
Donald Payne, Co-owner
Paddy Giffen Co-owner
Brendan Moylan, General Manager
Tim Welch, Distiller

Email: stillwaterspirits@gmail.com
Website: www.stillwaterspirits.com
Facebook: Stillwater Spirits & Moylan's Distilling

Type: Micro Distillery. Opened in 2004.

Hours of operation:
Monday through Friday, 10 a.m. to 6 p.m.

Tours: Not available

Types of spirits produced:
Vodka, gin, rum, whisky, brandy

Names of spirits:
- Stillwater Spirits Gin
- Stillwater Spirits Vodka 80°
- Stillwater Spirits Vodka 100°
- Stillwater Spirits Asian Pear Brandy
- Stillwater Spirits Cabernet Sauvignon Grappa
- Moylan's Distilling Bourbon Cask Strength
- Moylan's Distilling Rye Whisky
- Moylan's Distilling Beer Schnapps
- Moylan's Distilling American Single Malt Whisky
- Moylan's Distilling American Single Malt Cask Strength
- Moylan's Distilling Cherry Wood Malt Cask Strength

Best known for / most popular: Stillwater Spirits Gin

Average bottle price: $30.00 to $60.00

Distribution: San Francisco, CA area

Interesting facts: Not provided

Sweet Potato Spirits

3241 Hull Road
Atwater, CA 95301
209-358-2966

Owners / Operators:
David J. Souza, Owner / Founder / Master Distiller
Sharon Ambrosia, Office / Operations Manager
Erik Teague, Brand Manager / Assistant Distiller

Email: info@sweetpotatospirits.com
Website: www.sweetpotatospirits.com
Facebook: Sweet Potato Spirits, Corbin Sweet Potato Vodka
Twitter: @spspirits

Type: Craft Distillery. Opened in October 2010

Hours of operation:
Monday through Friday, 8 a.m. to 5 p.m.

Tours: Available by appointment only

Types of spirits produced:
Vodka, gin, rye whiskey, sweet potato liqueur, brandy

Names of spirits:
- Corbin California Estate Grown Sweet Potato Vodka
- Corbin Western Dry Gin
- Corbin Cash Merced Rye Whiskey

Best known for / most popular: Sweet Potato Vodka

Average bottle price: $30.00 to $50.00

Distribution: CA, GA

Interesting facts: Sweet Potato Spirits is proudly one of the few distilleries in the U.S. that creates their products from what they grow on their farm. With nearly a century of farming history, they create 100% handcrafted farm to bottle products.

Awards and Recognitions:
Double Gold, San Francisco World Spirits Competition; Double Gold, Wine and Spirits Wholesalers of America

Services offered other than production:
Contract distilling

47

Tamar Distillery Inc.
American Craft Whiskey Distillery

1110 Bel Arbres Road
Redwood Valley, CA 95470
707-485-2941

Owners / Operators:
Crispin Cain, President / Distiller / Spirits Master
Tamar Kaye, Vice President

Email: acwd.1@netzero.net , crispin@greenwaydistillers.com
Website: www.craftdistillers.com
Facebook: Greenway Distillers, Inc.

Type: Micro Distillery. Opened in 2010.

Hours of operation:
Monday through Friday, 6 a.m. to 5 p.m.

Tours: Available by appointment

Types of spirits produced:
Whiskey, gin, vodka, aged cocktails

Names of spirits:
Low Gap Whiskies
 Malted Bavarian Wheat, Malted Rye, Bourbon, Blended
Russell Henry Gins
 London Dry, Ginger, Lime
Fluid Dynamics Barrel Aged Cocktails
 The 1850 Cocktail, The Saratoga, The Rye, Manhattan
Vodkas
 Straight, Citron, Lime, Tangerine

Best known for / most popular: Low Gap Whiskey

Average bottle price: $20.00 to $75.00

Distribution: See www.caddellwilliams.com

Awards and recognitions:
Low Gap Clear Rye Whiskey
- Five Star Review, Paul Pacult's *Spirit Journal*
Low Gap 2-Year Old Malted Bavarian Wheat Whiskey
- Gold Medal, San Francisco International Spirits Competition
Russell Henry London Dry Gin
- Five Star Review, Paul Pacult's *Spirit Journal*
- Number 11 on Paul Pacult's *Spirit Journal* list of the "130 Best Spirits Available in the World Market Today". The only American spirit in the top 10%.

Tahoe Moonshine Distillery Inc.

1611 Shop Street #4B
South Lake Tahoe, CA 96150
530-416-0313

Owners / Operators:
Jeffrey VanHee, Owner / Master Distiller

Email: jeffrey@tahoemoonshine.com
Website: www.tahoemoonshine.com
Facebook: Tahoe Moonshine Distillery

Type: Micro Distillery. Opened in 2010.

Hours of operation: Not provided

Tours: Available

Types of spirits produced:
Whiskey, gin, rum, vodka, liqueur

Names of spirits:
- Stormin' Whiskey
- Jagged Peaks Gin
- California Dreamin' Rum
- Jug Dealer Rum
- Snowflake Vodka
- Hot Stinkin' Garlic Vodka
- Peanut Butter Vodka

Best known for / most popular: Stormin' Whiskey

Average bottle price: $29.00

Distribution: CA, NV

Interesting facts: All spirits are hand-crafted, distilled, and bottled in Lake Tahoe with all-natural and organic ingredients. No artificial flavoring, preservatives, or any unnatural additives of any kind are ever used.

Treasure Island Distillery

990 13th Street
San Francisco, CA 94130
415-935-7989

Owners / Operators:
Owned and operated by the William Smith family

Email: william@sfvodka.com
Website: www.sfvodka.com
Facebook: SFVodka
Twitter: @SFVodka

Type: Micro Distillery. Opened in 2009.

Hours of operation:
Monday through Saturday, 9 a.m. to 6 p.m.

Tours: Not open to the public

Types of spirits produced:
Vodkas made from corn, grapes, and cane

Names of spirits:
- China Beach San Francisco Vodka
- Ocean Beach San Francisco Vodka
- Baker Beach San Francisco Vodka

Best known for / most popular:
China Beach San Francisco Vodka

Average bottle price: $35.00

Distribution: San Francisco Bay area

Interesting facts: Treasure Island Distillery operates out of the old Navy brig on Treasure Island in San Francisco. The space consists of the solitary confinement cells, intake and processing areas, the guard's room, the infirmary, and one of the two exercise yards.

Valley Spirits LLC

553 Mariposa Road, Ste. #1
Modesto, CA 95354
209-484-0311

Owners / Operators:
Lee Palleschi, Proprietor

Email: masterdistiller@drinkvalleyspirits.com
Website: www.drinkvalleyspirits.com
Facebook: Cold House Vodka
Twitter: @ColdHouseVodka

Type: Micro Distillery. Opened in 2010.

Hours of operation: 8 a.m. to 5 p.m.

Tours: Available

Types of spirits produced: Vodka, moonshine, whiskey

Names of spirits:
- Cold House Vodka
- Moonshine Bandits Outlaw Moonshine
- Prohibition Spirits

Best known for / most popular: Cold House Vodka

Average bottle price: $24.00

Distribution: CA, NV

Interesting facts: Not provided

Ventura Limoncello Company

2646 Palma Drive, Ste. 160
Ventura, CA 93003
805-658-0881

Owners / Operators:
James Carling, President
Manuela Zaretti-Carling, Vice President

Email: General info, info@venturalimoncello.com
James Carling, james@venturalimoncello.com
Website: www.venturalimoncello.com
Facebook: Ventura Limoncello
Twitter: @VLimoncello
YouTube: Ventura Limoncello Channel
LinkedIn: James Carling

Type: Micro Distillery. Opened in 2008.

Hours of operation: Monday through Friday, 9 a.m. to 5 p.m.

Tours: By appointment only

Types of spirits produced: Liqueur

Names of spirits:
- Ventura Limoncello Originale
- Ventura Limoncello Crema
- Ventura Orangecello Blood Orange

Best known for / most popular:
Ventura Limoncello Originale

Average bottle price: $16.00 to $28.00

Distribution: AK, AZ, CA, CT, HI, IL, MO, NJ, NV, NY, OR

Interesting facts:
- All citrus used is grown in Ventura County, CA.

Awards and Recognitions:
Ventura Limoncello Originale
- Gold Medal 2013, Spirit of the Americas
- Gold Medal 2011, 2008 SF World Spirits Competition
- Gold Medal 2011, MicroLiquor Awards

Ventura Orangecello Blood Orange
- Double Gold Medal - Best in Class
- 2011 San Francisco World Spirits Competition

Ventura Limoncello Crema
- Gold Medal, 2010 LA SIP Awards

Altitude Spirits

Boulder, CO 80306
303-245-8773

Owners / Operators:
Mitch Baris, Co-founder
Matthew Baris, Co-founder

Email: info@altitudespirits.com
Website: www.vodka14.com, www.altitudespirits.com
Facebook: Vodka 14
Twitter: @Vodka14, @AltitudeSpirits

Type: Micro Distillery. Opened in 2005.

Hours of operation: Not provided

Tours: Not provided

Types of spirits produced: Vodka

Names of spirits:
- Vodka 14

Best known for / most popular: Not provided

Average bottle price: Not provided

Distribution: Not provided

Interesting facts: Organic vodka

Black Canyon Distillery

13710 Deere Court #B
Longmont, CO 80504
720-204-1909

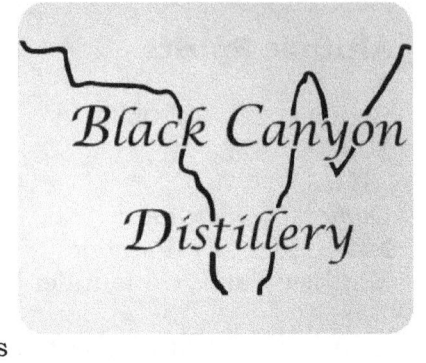

Owners / Operators:
Fred Lesnick, Co-owner / Master Distiller
Susan Lesnick, Co-owner / V.P. and Secretary
Chris Broadfoot, Co-owner / Director of Promotions
Jeannetta Broadfoot, Co-owner / Account Manager

Email: susan@blackcanyondistillery.com
Website: www.blackcanyondistillery.com
Facebook: Black Canyon Distillery

Type: Micro Distillery. Opened in 2011.

Hours of operation:
Wednesday through Friday, 9 a.m. to 5 p.m.
Saturday, 8 a.m. to 4 p.m. (call first)

Tours: Available by appointment

Types of spirits produced: Whiskey

Names of spirits:
- Black Canyon Sour Mash Corn Whiskey
- Black Canyon Rita

Best known for / most popular: Black Canyon Sour Mash Corn Whiskey

Average bottle price: $25.00 to $28.00

Distribution: CO

Interesting facts:
- Co-owner Fred Lesnick fabricated two stills and all eight of mash tuns.
- Member of Colorado Proud
- Buys local grain and is a grain to glass distillery.

Boathouse Distillery

6573 Ridge Road
Salida, CO 81201
719-239-0390

Owners / Operators:
Jerry Mallett, President

Email: jmallett123@yahoo.com
Website: www.boathousedistillery.com

Type: Micro Distillery. Opening in 2013.

Hours of operation: 8 a.m. to 4 p.m.

Tours: Not available

Types of spirits produced: Single malt whiskey, bourbon, various vodkas

Names of spirits:
- Colorado Bourbon
- Colorado Moonshine

Best known for / most popular: Colorado Bourbon, Colorado Moonshine

Average bottle price: $22.00 to $35.00

Distribution: CO

Boulder Distillery
Clear Spirit Company Inc.

2500 47th Street, Unit 10
Boulder, CO 80301
303-442-1244

Owners / Operators:
Steve Viezbicke, Owner

Email: info@303vodka.com
Website: www.303vodka.com
Facebook: 303 Vodka – Boulder Distillery – Clear Spirit
Twitter: @303Vodka

Type: Micro Distillery. Opened in 2009.

Hours of operation:
Sunday through Tuesday, Closed
Wednesday through Saturday, 2 p.m. to 10 p.m.

Tours: Available

Types of spirits produced: Vodka, whiskey

Names of spirits:
- Viezbicke 303 Vodka
- Viezbicke 303 Whiskey

Best known for / most popular: Viezbicke 303 Vodka

Average bottle price: Not provided

Distribution: CO

Interesting facts: Boulder's first distillery since Prohibition.

Breckenridge Distillery

1925 Airport Road
Breckenridge, CO 80424
970-547-9759

Owners / Operators:
Bryan Nolt, President
Jordan Via, Master Distiller
Maya Berthoud, National Sales Manager
Litch Polich, Colorado Brand Ambassador

Email: Bryan Nolt, bryan@breckenridgedistillery.com
Jordan Via, jordan@breckenridgedistillery.com
Maya Berthoud, mya@breckenridgedistillery.com
Litch Polich, litch@breckenridgedistillery.com
Website: www.breckenridgedistillery.com
Facebook: Breckenridge Distillery
Twitter: @breckdistillery

Type: Micro Distillery. Opened in 2010.

Hours of operation:
Tasting Room, 11 a.m. to 9 p.m. (closed Tuesday)
Distillery, 11 a.m. to 6 p.m. (closed Monday)

Tours: Available

Types of spirits produced:
Vodka, bourbon, whiskey, rum, bitters

Names of spirits:
- Breckenridge Bourbon
- Breckenridge Vodka
- Breckenridge Bitters
- Breckenridge Spiced Rum
- Turin-Style Bitters

Best known for / most popular: Breckenridge Bourbon

Average bottle price: $30.00 to $40.00

Distribution: AL, AR, CA, CO, CT, DC, FL, GA, IA, IL, IN, KS, KY, LA, MA, MI, MN, MO, MS, NC, ND, NE, NJ, NM, NV, NY, OK, OR, PA, SC, SD, TX, VA, WA, WI, WY

Interesting facts: One of the world's highest distilleries in elevation.

Colorado Gold Distillery

1290 S. Grand Mesa Drive
Cedaredge, CO 81413
970-856-2600

Owners / Operators:
Peter Caciola, Owner

Email: coop2@sopris.net
Website: www.coloradogolddistillers.com
Facebook: Colorado Gold Spirits

Type: Micro Distillery. Opened in 2007.

Hours of operation: Tuesday through Saturday, 10 a.m. to 4 p.m.

Tours: Available

Types of spirits produced:
Agave spirits, whiskey, gin, vodka, bourbon whiskey, brandy

Names of spirits:
- Colorado Gold Premium Gin
- Colorado Gold Premium Vodka
- Colorado Gold's Own Agave Spirits
- Colorado's Own Corn Whiskey
- Colorado Gold Straight Bourbon Whiskey
- Colorado Gold Brandy

Best known for / most popular:
Colorado's Own Corn Whiskey

Average bottle price: $19.55 to $55.00

Distribution: AZ, CA, CO, LA, NM, OR, TX, WY

Interesting facts: Not provided

Dancing Pines Distillery

1527 Taurus Court, #110
Loveland, CO 80537
970-635-3426

Owners / Operators:
Christopher McNay, Co-owner
Kristian Naslund, Co-owner
Kimberly Naslund, Co-owner

Email: info@dpdistillery.com
Website: www.dancingpinesdistillery.com
Facebook: Dancing Pines Distillery
Twitter: @DPDistillery

Type: Micro Distillery. Opened in 2010.

Hours of operation: Open to the public Saturdays, 1 p.m. to 7 p.m.

Tours: Saturdays at 2 p.m., 4 p.m., and 6 p.m. by reservation

Types of spirits produced: Rum, whiskey, gin, liqueurs

Names of spirits:
- Dancing Pines Bourbon
- Dancing Pines Black Walnut Bourbon
- Dancing Pines Gin
- Dancing Pines Rum
- Dancing Pines Cask Rum
- Dancing Pines Spice Rum
- Dancing Pines Brulee Liqueur
- Dancing Pines Chai Liqueur
- Dancing Pines Cherry Tart Liqueur
- Dancing Pines Espresso Liqueur

Best known for / most popular:
Dancing Pines Bourbon

Average bottle price: $30.00 to $50.00

Distribution: AZ, CA, CO, CT, DC, DE, FL, GA, ID, IL, LA, MA, MD, NJ, NV, NY, SC, VA, WA, WV, WY

Interesting facts: Not provided

Deerhammer Distilling Company

321 East Main Street
Buena Vista, CO 81211
719-395-9464

Owners / Operators:
Lenny Eckstein, Owner / Manager
Amy Eckstein, Owner / Barmaid

Email: info@deerhammer.com
Website: www.deerhammer.com
Facebook: Deerhammer Distilling Company
Twitter: @Deerhammer

Type: Micro Distillery. Opened in 2010.

Hours of operation:
Winter Hours
Thursday through Saturday, 4 p.m. to 10 p.m.

Summer Hours
Wednesday through Sunday, 2 p.m. to 10 p.m.

Tours: Available

Types of spirits produced: Whiskey, brandy, gin

Names of spirits:
- Whitewater Whiskey
- Down Time Single Malt Whiskey
- Buena Vista Brandy
- Bullwheel Gin

Best known for / most popular:
Whitewater Whiskey

Average bottle price: $38.00

Distribution: CO

Interesting facts: Deerhammer is located at 8,000 feet above sea level in the Arkansas River Valley and is surrounded by the highest concentration of 14,000 foot peaks in the country.

Distillery 291

1647 S. Tejon Street
Colorado Springs, CO 80905
719-323-8010

Owners / Operators:
Michael Myers, Owner

Email: info@distillery291.com
Website: www.distillery291.com
Facebook: Distillery 291
Twitter: @distillery291

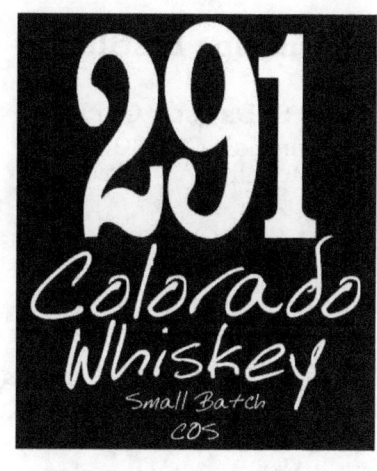

Type: Craft Distillery. Opened in 2011.

Hours of operation: Not provided

Tours: Not provided

Types of spirits produced: Whiskey

Names of spirits:
- 291 Colorado Whiskey Aspen Stave Finished (aged)
- 291 Fresh Colorado Whiskey (corn, unaged)
- 291 Colorado Rye Whiskey White Dog
- 291 American Whiskey

Best known for / most popular: Not provided

Average bottle price: Not provided

Distribution: Self distribution

Interesting facts:
- From grain to barrel to bottle in 339 square feet.
- First craft distillery in Colorado Springs, CO.

Downslope Distilling

6770 S. Dawson Circle
Centennial, CO 80122
303-693-4300

Owners / Operators:
Andrew Causey, Owner
Mitch Abate, Head Distiller

Email: General info, spirits@downslopedistilling.com
Media / Business, andy@downslopedistilling.com
Technical / Product, mitch@downslopedistilling.com
Website: www.downslopedistilling.com
Facebook: Downslope Distilling
Twitter: @DownslopeDist

Type: Micro Distillery. Opened in 2009.

Hours of operation: Daily

Tours: Available Friday through Sunday, noon to 4 p.m.

Types of spirits produced: Vodka, rum, whiskey

Names of spirits:
- Downslope Cane Vodka
- Downslope Grain Vodka
- Downslope Pepper Vodka
- Downslope White Rum
- Downslope Gold Rum
- Downslope Spiced Rum
- Downslope Vanilla Rum
- Downslope Wine Barrel Aged Rum
- Downslope Double-Diamond Whiskey
- Downslope Malt Whiskey

Best known for / most popular:
Vodka from Maui cane, Vanilla Rum, Wine Barrel Aged Rum, Pepper Vodka, Double Diamond Whiskey

Average bottle price: $25.00 to $32.00

Distribution: CA, CO, IL, LA, MA, NM, OR

Interesting facts: The barrels used at Downslope originate from wineries. When they are retired from aging spirits, they house beer at local breweries.

Feisty Spirits

1708 E. Lincoln Avenue, #1
Fort Collins, CO 80524
970-444-2FUN

Owners / Operators:
David Monahan, Co-founder
Jamison Gulden, Co-founder

Email: info@FeistySpirits.com
Website: www.FeistySpirits.com
Facebook: Feisty Spirits
Twitter: @FeistySpirits

Type: Micro Distillery. Opened in 2012.

Hours of operation: Check website

Tours: Check website

Types of spirits produced: Whiskey

Names of spirits:
- Feisty Spirits Blue Corn Bourbon
- Feisty Spirits Rye
- Feisty Spirits Elementals
  A line of single grain whiskeys

Best known for / most popular: Bourbon Whiskey

Average bottle price: $40.00

Distribution: CO

Interesting facts:
Made with organic grains and natural ingredients.

Golden Moon Distillery
Maison De La Vie Ltd.

412 Violet Street
Golden, CO 80401
303-993-7174

Owners / Operators:
Stephen Gould, Co-proprietor / Distiller
Karen Knight, Co-proprietor

Email: s.gould@gouldgobal.com
Website: www.goldenmoondistillery.com
Facebook: Golden Moon Distillery
Twitter: @goldenmoondistillery

Type: Micro Distillery. Opened in 2008.

Hours of operation: Monday through Friday, 9 a.m. to 5 p.m.

Tours: Available

Types of spirits produced: Gin, absinthe, grappa, apple jack, crème de violette, dry curacao, amer dit picon

Names of spirits:
- Golden Moon Gin
- Redux Absinthe
- Redux Absinthe No.2
- Golden Moon Colorado Grappa
- Golden Moon Colorado Apple Jack
- Golden Moon Crème de Violette
- Golden Moon Dry Curacao
- Golden Moon Amer dit Picon

Best known for / most popular: Golden Moon Gin

Average bottle price: $27.00 to $86.00

Distribution: U.S.

  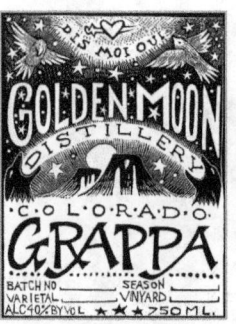 

Honey House Distillery

33633 Highway 550, Ste. A
Durango, CO 81301
970-247-1474

Owners / Operators:
Adam Bergal, Co-owner
Kevin Culhane, Co-owner
Sheree Culhane, Co-owner
Danny Culhane, Co-owner

Email: kevin@honeyhousedistillery.com
Website: www.honeyhousedistillery.com
Facebook: Honey House Distillery

Type: Micro Distillery. Opened in 2013.

Hours of operation:
Memorial Day to Labor Day, 8 a.m. to 6 p.m.
Labor Day to Memorial Day, 9 a.m. to 5 p.m.

Tours: Available

Types of spirits produced:
Rocky Mountain Honey infused Bourbon Whiskey

Names of spirits:
- Colorado Honey
- Wildflower Gin

Best known for / most popular: Colorado Honey

Average bottle price: $33.00

Distribution: CO

Interesting facts:
Colorado Honey is made from fine bourbon whiskey infused with 100% pure Rocky Mountain Honey from Honeyville, a third generation family beekeeping business. Unlike most major brands of honey whiskey, Colorado Honey is made with pure honey, not honey liqueur.

K J Wood Distillers LLC

403 5th Street, Unit C
Berthoud, CO 80513
303-517-7697

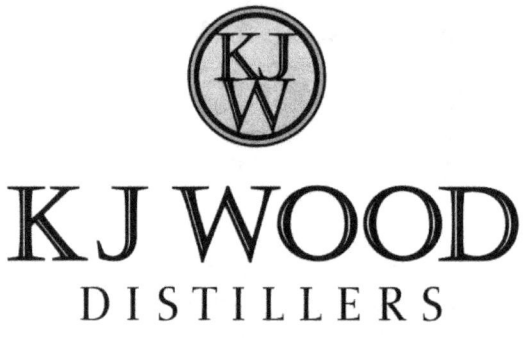

Owners / Operators:
K John Wood, Owner / Distiller
Kenneth Wood, Owner
Matt Throop, Fermentation Specialist

Email: KJWdistillers@gmail.com
Website: www.kjwooddistillers.com
Facebook: K J Wood Distillers, LLC

Type: Craft Distillery. Opened in July 2013.

Hours of operation:
Monday through Saturday

Tasting room hours:
Thursday through Saturday, 3 p.m. to 8 p.m.

Tours: Not available

Types of spirits produced:
Gin, bourbon, single malt whiskey

Names of spirits:
- Jinn Gin
- Dead Drift Whiskey
- Dalgleish Single Malt (2018)

Best known for / most popular: Not provided

Average bottle price: $38.00 to $54.99

Distribution: On-site retail, CO

Interesting facts: Not provided

Leopold Bros.

4950 Nome Street
Denver, CO 80239

Owners / Operators:
Todd Leopold, Co-owner
Scott Leopold, Co-owner

Email: sales@leopoldbros.com
Website: www.leopoldbros.com
Facebook: Leopold Bros.
Twitter: @LeopoldBros

Type: Micro Distillery. Opened in 1999.

Hours of operation: Not provided

Tours: Not provided

Types of spirits produced:
Vodka, gin, whiskey, liqueur, absinthe

Names of spirits:
- Silver Tree American Small Batch Vodka
- Leopold Bros. American Small Batch Gin
- Leopold Bros. American Small Batch Whiskey
- Leopold Bros. New York Apple Whiskey
- Leopold Bros. Rocky Mountain Blackberry Whiskey
- Leopold Bros. Rocky Mountain Peach Whiskey
- Leopold Bros. Georgia Peach Whiskey
- Leopold Bros. Rocky Mountain Blackberry Liqueur
- Leopold Bros. Michigan Tart Cherry Liqueur
- Leopold Bros. New England Cranberry Liqueur
- Leopold Bros. American Orange Liqueur
- Leopold Bros. Frenchpress Style American Coffee Liqueur
- Leopold Bros. Three Pins Alpine Herbal Liqueur
- Leopold Bros. Absinthe Verte

Best known for / most popular: Not provided

Average bottle price: Not provided

Distribution: AZ, CA, CO, DC, GA, ID, IL, NV, VA, WY

Interesting facts: Not provided

Mancos Valley Distillery

116 N. Main Street
Mancos, CO 81328
970-946-0229

Owners / Operators:
Ian James, Owner / Distiller

Email: events@mancosvalleydistillery.com
Website: www.mancosvalleydistillery.com
Facebook: Mancos Valley Distillery, LLC
Twitter: @MVDistillery

Type: Micro Distillery. Opened in 2010.

Hours of operation: Friday 5 p.m. to 10 p.m.; Saturday 5 p.m. to 10 p.m.

Tours: Available

Types of spirits produced: Rum, liqueur

Names of spirits:
- Ian's Alley Rum
- Ian's Alley Spiced Rum
- Colorado Coffee Liqueur

Best known for / most popular: Ian's Alley Rum

Average bottle price: Not provided

Distribution: CO

Interesting facts: Not provided

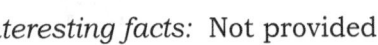

Mile High Spirits LLC

2920 Larimer Street
Denver, CO 80205
303-601-3499

Owners / Operators:
Joe Vonfeldt, Co-owner
Chase Campbell, Co-owner
Wyn Ferrell, Co-owner

Email: info@milehighspiritsllc.com
Website: www.milehighspiritsllc.com
Facebook: Mile High Spirits
Twitter: @MileHighSpirits

Type: Micro Distillery. Opened in 2012.

Hours of operation:
Monday through Friday, 4 p.m. to midnight
Saturday and Sunday, 11 a.m. to 1 p.m.
Sunday, 11 a.m. to 8 p.m.

Tours: Not available

Types of spirits produced:
Vodka, whiskey, gin, rum

Names of spirits:
- Fireside Bourbon
- Elevate Vodka
- Peg Leg Rum
- Denver Dry Gin
- Distroya Liqueur

Best known for / most popular:
Fireside Bourbon and Elevate Vodka

Average bottle price: $19.00 to $30.00

Distribution: On-site retail

Interesting facts:
- Mile High Spirits is one of only a few distilleries in the world to use an all glass still for its distillation.

Awards and Recognitions:
- Micro Liquor Awards 2012, Fireside, Gold in Flavor, Silver in Packaging.
- Micro Liquor Awards 2012, Elevate, Silver in flavor and Silver in packaging.
- Denver International Spirits Competition 2013, Silver Medal Fireside
- Denver International Spirits Competition 2013, Gold Medal Elevate

Montanya Distillers LLC

Distillery and Tasting Room:
212 Elk Avenue
Crested Butte, CO 81224

Silverton Tasting Room:
1309 Greene Street
Silverton, CO 81433

970-799-3206 or 800-975-6154

Owners / Operators:
Karen Hoskin, President / Co-owner
Brice Hoskin, Vice President / Co-owner

Email: info@montanyadistillers.com
Website: www.montanyadistillers.com
Facebook: Montanya Distillers
Twitter: @montanyarum
LinkedIn: Montanya Distillers
Yelp: Montanya Distillers
Trip Advisor: Montanya Distillers
Instagram: montanyarum
Pinterest: Montanya Rum

Type: Micro Distillery. Opened in 2008.

Hours of operation: Daily, 11 a.m. to 9 p.m.

Tours: Available

Types of spirits produced: Light and dark rum

Names of spirits:
- Montanya Oro Rum
- Montanya Platino Rum

Average bottle price:
$24.99 to $32.99

Distribution: Available in 38 states

Interesting facts:
Montanya Distillers is one the few U.S. distilleries owned and operated by a woman, with a female distiller and a female general manager.

Mystic Mountain Distillery LLC

11505 Spring Valley Road
Larkspur, CO 80118
303-663-9375

Owners / Operators:
Fred Linneman, General Manager

Email: info@mysticmtnspirits.com
Website: www.mysticmtnspirits.com
Facebook: Mystic Mountain Distillery

Type: Micro Distillery. Opened in 2005.

Hours of operation: 9 a.m. to 2 p.m.

Tours: Not available

Types of spirits produced: Gin, moonshine, rum, tequila, vodka, whiskey

Names of spirits:
- Colorado Blue Vodka
- BOHICA Vodka
- Colorado Crystal Vodka
- Rocky Mountain Moonshine
- Colorado Fog Gin
- Blackjack Aces High Whiskey

Average bottle price: $20.00 to $25.00

Distribution: Not provided

Interesting facts: Not provided

Peach Street Distillers

144 South Kluge Avenue, Bldg. #2
Palisade, CO 81526
970-464-1128

Owners / Operators:
Rory Donovan, Owner

Email: info@peachstreetdistillers.com
Website: www.peachstreetdistillers.com
Facebook: Peach Street Distillers
Twitter: @PSDistillers

Type: Micro Distillery. Opened in 2005.

Hours of operation:
Monday through Thursday, noon to 10 p.m.
Friday and Saturday, noon to midnight
Sunday, 10 a.m. to 10 p.m.

Tours: Available May through September, Fridays 3 p.m.

Types of spirits produced: Bourbon, vodka, gin, brandy, grappa, agave spirit

Names of spirits:
- Colorado Straight Bourbon
- Goat Artisan Vodka
- Jackelope Gin
- Jackelope and Jenny Gin
- Jack & Jenny Peach Brandy
- Jack & Jenny Pear Brandy
- Aged Peach Brandy
- Aged Pear Brandy
- Grappa of Gewurztraminer
- Grappa of Viognier
- Grappa Muscat
- Dagave Gold
- Dagave Extra
- Dagave Silver

Best known for / most popular:
Colorado Straight Bourbon

Average bottle price: $30.00 to $60.00

Distribution: CA, CO, IL, LA, NJ, NY, TX

Interesting facts: 2012 American Distillers Institute Distillery of the Year

Peak Spirits® Farm Distillery

26567 North Road
Hotchkiss, CO 81419
970-361-4249

Owners / Operators:
Lance Hanson, Owner / Distiller

Email: lance@peakspirits.com
Website: www.peakspirits.com
Facebook: Peak Spirits
Twitter: @peakspirits

Type: Micro Distillery. Opened in 2005.

Hours of operation: Vary

Tours: Available by appointment

Types of spirits produced:
Gin, vodka, eaux de vie

Names of spirits:
- CapRock® Organic Gin
- CapRock® Organic Vodka
- CapRock® Organic Eaux de Vie
- CapRock® Biodynamic® Estate Grappa

Best known for / most popular: Gin

Average bottle price: $35.00

Distribution: CA, CO, DC, IL, MA, MD, RI, SC, VA

Interesting facts:
All products are 100% USDA-certified organic or Demeter-certified biodynamic.

Rocky Mountain Distilling Co.

6660 Delmonico Drive, Ste. D-223
Colorado Springs, CO 80919
970-306-6222

Owners / Operators:
Todd Ficken, Owner

Email: info@rockymountaindistilling.com
Website: www.rockymountindistilling.com
Foursquare: Rocky Mountain Distilling Co.

Type: Micro Distillery. Opening in 2013.

Hours of operation: Monday through Friday, 10 a.m. to 6 p.m.

Tours: Available by appointment

Types of spirits produced: Vodka

Names of spirits:
- VR Vodka

Best known for / most popular: VR Vodka

Average bottle price: Not provided

Distribution: Not provided

Interesting facts: Not provided

Roundhouse Spirits

5311 Western Avenue, Ste. 180
Boulder, CO 80301
303-819-5598

Owners / Operators:
Charles (Ted) Palmer, Co-owner
Michael Belochi, Co-owner / Director of Sales

Email: info@roundhousespirits.com
Website: www.roundhousespirits.com
Facebook: Roundhouse Spirits
Twitter: @RndhouseSpirits

Type: Micro Distillery. Opened in 2008.

Hours of operation: Vary

Tours: Available

Types of spirits produced: Gins, agave spirit, liqueurs

Names of spirits:
- Roundhouse Gin
- Imperial Barrel Aged Gin
- Corretto Coffee Liqueur
- Pumpkin King Cordial
- Tatanka Agave Spirit

Best known for / most popular:
Roundhouse Gin as a sipping gin on the rocks

Average bottle price: $25.00 to $55.00

Distribution: CO, DC, IL, NJ, NY; Italy

Interesting facts:
Roundhouse Spirits is the 6th licensed distillery in CO.

Spirit Hound Distillers

4196 Ute Highway
Lyons, CO 80540

Owners / Operators:
Matthew Rooney, Co-founder / President
Craig Engelhorn, Co-founder / Head Distiller
Neil Sullivan, Co-founder / VP Operations
Wayne Anderson, Co-founder / Business Development
Rick England, Distillery partner

Email: info@spirithounds.com
Website: www.spirithounddistillers.com
Facebook: Spirit Hound Distillers

Type: Micro Distillery. Opened in 2012.

Hours of operation: Vary

Tours: Available

Types of spirits produced:
Whisky, vodka, gin, liqueur, rum

Names of spirits:
- Spirit Hound Gin
- Mountain Bum Rum
- Richardo's Coffee Liqueur
- White Dog Moonshine

Best known for: Whisky

Distribution: CO through BDC

Interesting facts:
- First craft distillery in Lyons CO.
- In September 2013, Lyons experienced a 1000 year flood. The town and the distillery were devastated. The first barrel of rum, 'flood rum' was saved and bottled with some of the proceeds from sales to go to the local fire department.

Spring44 Distilling

505 West 66th Street
Loveland, CO 80538
970-445-0744

SPRING44

THE PROOF IS IN THE WATER

Owners / Operators:
Jeff Lindauer, Co-founder / CEO
Russ Wall, Co-founder / CMO
Jeff McPhie, Co-founder / COO
Robin Marisco, CFO
Rob Masters, Head Distiller
Ryan Jackson, Production Manager

Email: info@spring44.com
Website: www.spring44.com
Facebook: Spring44
Twitter: @Spring44spirits
YouTube: Spring44Distilling's Channel

Type: Craft Distillery. Opened in 2012.

Hours of operation:
Friday, 4 p.m. to 7 p.m.; Saturday, 2 p.m. to 7 p.m.

Tours: Available

Types of spirits produced: Vodka, gin, old tom gin, straight bourbon, single barrel bourbon

Names of spirits:
- Spring44 Gin (ABV 44%)
- Spring44 Vodka (ABV 40%)
- Spring44 Honey Vodka (ABV 40%)
- Rob's Mountain Gin (44%)
- Spring44 Old Tom Gin (ABV 44%)
- Spring44 Straight Bourbon (ABV 45%)
- Spring44 Single Barrel Bourbon (ABV 50%)

Best known for / most popular: Spring44 Gin

Average bottle price: $25.00 to $55.00

Distribution: AZ, CA, CO, CT, FL, IL, MA, NJ, NY, RI

Interesting facts:
Spring44 Spirits are made with Rocky Mountain artesian mineral spring water from a private source at 9,000 foot elevation located in the Buckhorn Canyon, CO.

State 38 Distilling

400 Corporate Circle, Ste. B
Golden, CO 80401
720-242-7219

Owners / Operators:
Sean Smiley, Owner / Head Distiller

Email: sean@state-38.com
Website: www.state-38.com
Facebook: State 38 Distilling
Twitter: @state38
Pinterest: State 38 Distilling

Type: Craft Distillery.
Opened in November 2013.

Hours of operation:
Vary. Check social media for schedule

Tours: Available. Times vary.

Types of spirits produced:
Vodka, gin, blanco, reposado, anejo, liquor

Names of spirits:
- State 38 Agave Blanco
- State 38 Agave Reposado
- State 38 Agave Anejo
- State 38 Agave Vodka
- State 38 Agave Gin
- State 38 Agave Liquor

Best known for / most popular:
All of the above

Average bottle price: $35.00 to $55.00

Distribution: On-site retail, Golden and Denver CO area

Still Cellars
a distillery and arthouse

1115 Colorado Avenue, Ste. C
Longmont, CO 80501
720-204-6064

Owners / Operators:
Jason R. Houston, Founder / Owner / Operator / Zymologist
Sadye Rose W., Founder / Owner / Operator / Arthouse Maven

Email: spirits@stillcellars.com
Website: www.stillcellars.com

Type: Micro Distillery. Opened in 2012.

Hours of operation:
Friday, 3 p.m. to 8 p.m.; Saturday 2 p.m. to 7 p.m.
Recommended to call in advance to confirm

Tours: Available by appointment

Types of spirits produced:
Single malt whiskey, vodka, apple spirits

Names of spirits:
- Still Cellars Vodka
- Still Cellars Whiskey Barley
- Still Cellars Apple Cinnamon
- Still Cellars Apple Ginger
- Still Cellars Apple Straightup

Best known for / most popular:
Apple spirits made from Colorado apples and infused with spices

Average bottle price: $38.00 to $44.00

Distribution: CO

Interesting facts:
- Certified organic
- Tasting room is an arthouse featuring local artists

Stranahan's Colorado Whiskey Distillery

200 S. Kalamath Street
Denver, CO 80223
303-296-7440

Owners / Operators:
Proximo Distillers, LLC
Pete Macca, General Manager
Rob Dietrich, Head Distiller
Kristin Forsch, Brand Ambassador
Marlene Steiner, Brand Manager

Email: info@stranahans.com
Website: www.stranahans.com
Facebook: Stranahans Colorado Whiskey
Twitter: @Stranahans

Type: Craft Distillery. Opened in 2004.

Distillery hours: Daily

Gift Shop hours: Daily, noon to 5 p.m.

Tours: Available Wednesday through Monday
Register at website

Types of spirits produced: Whiskey

Names of spirits:
- Stranahan's Colorado Whiskey
- Snowflake

Best known for / most popular: Snowflake

Average bottle price: $60.00 to $99.00

Distribution: CO

Interesting facts:
- Stranahan's is the first legal distillery in CO.
- Bottles are filled and packaged by hand by distillery staff and volunteers.

Syntax Spirits LLC

625 3rd Street, Unit C
Greeley, CO 80631
970-352-5466 (hours and location)

Owners / Operators:
Heather Bean, Owner
Jeff Copeland, Owner

Email: info@syntaxspirits.com
Website: www.syntaxspirits.com
Facebook: Syntax Spirits Distillery
Twitter: @SyntaxSpirits

Type: Micro Distillery. Opened in 2010.

Hours of operation:
Wednesday and Thursday, 4 p.m. to 9 p.m.
Friday, 4 p.m. to 11 p.m.
Saturday, noon to 11 p.m.; Sunday, noon to 6 p.m.

Tours:
Wednesday through Saturday, 5 p.m. and 7 p.m.;
Sunday, 3 p.m.

Types of spirits produced:
Vodka, rum, whisky, bourbon, infused spirits, liqueurs

Names of spirits:
- Class V™ Vodka
- Powder™ White Rum
- White Cat™ Whiskey
- Big Cat™ Whisky
- Perky Pepper™ Pepper Flavored Vodka

Best known for / most popular:
Class V™ Vodka, Powder™ White Rum

Average bottle price: $25.00 to $35.00

Distribution: CO, WY

Interesting facts:
- One of Colorado's few 100% grain-to-glass distilleries where all alcohol is made in-house from local grain and American molasses.
- One of the few woman owned-and-operated distilleries in the U.S.
- Unique label art is by acclaimed pinball artist Greg Freres.

Photo by: Jafe Parsons

Tesouro Distillery

105 South Sunset Street, Ste. A
Longmont, CO 80501
303-746-2819

Tesouro
Premium Handcrafted Small-Batch Rum from the Colorado Rocky Mountains

Owners / Operators:
Greg Dubbe', Owner

Email: info@tesourodistillery.com
Website: www.tesourodistillery.com

Type: Micro Distillery. Opened in 2011.

Hours of operation: Vary

Tours: Vary

Types of spirits produced: Rum

Names of spirits:
- Tesouro Rum

Best known for / most popular: Tesouro Rum

Average bottle price: $30.00 to $35.00

Distribution: CO

Interesting facts: Not provided

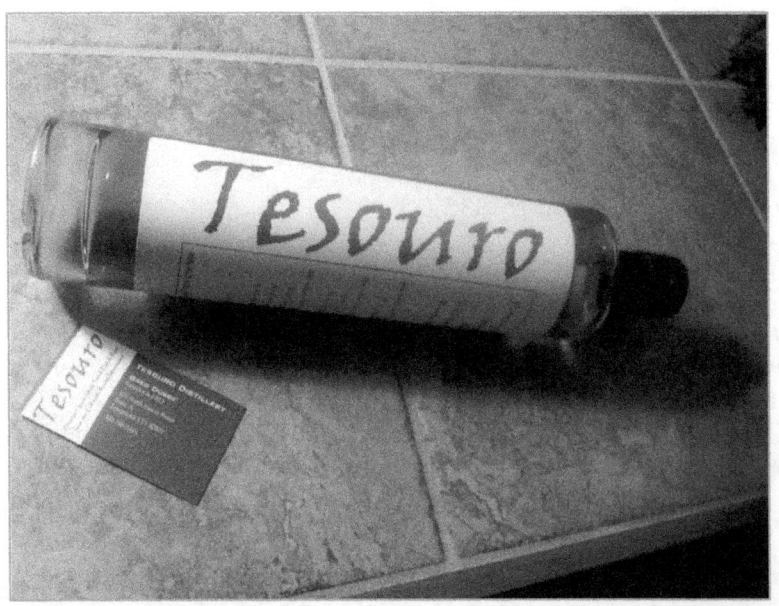

Trail Town Still

240 Palomino Trail, Unit A
Ridgway, CO 81432
970-626-3060

Owners / Operators:
Joe Alaimo, General Manager / Distiller
Lynda Gegauff, Sommelier

Email: still@trailtownstill.com
Website: www.trailtownstill.com
Facebook: Trail Town Still
Twitter: @trailtownstill
YouTube: trailtownstill

Type: Micro Distillery. Opened in 2011.

Hours of operation:
Monday through Saturday, 4 p.m. to 11 p.m.

Tours: Available

Types of spirits produced: Gin, vodka, light whiskey, agave liquor, rum

Names of spirits:
- Trail Town Still Colorado Gin
- Trail Town Still Colorado Vodka
- Trail Town Still Coyote Light Whiskey
- Trail Town Still Colorado Agave Liquor Desert Water

Average bottle price: $38.00 to $54.00

Distribution: Not provided

Two Guns Distillery

401 Harrison Avenue
Leadville, CO 80461

Owners / Operators:
B.A. Dallas, Owner / Operator / Distiller
Dave Dawson, Owner
Jeff Thomas, Owner
Sarah Dallas, General Manager

Email: Not provided
Website: www.twogunsdistillery.com
Facebook: Two Guns Distillery

Type: Micro Distillery. Opened in May 2013.

Production hours: Daily

Public hours:
Monday through Thursday, 5 p.m. to 10 p.m.
Friday and Saturday, noon to 11 p.m.
Sunday, noon to 6 p.m.

Tours: Available. The entire operation is located right behind the bar.

Types of spirits produced: Whiskey, moonshine

Names of spirits:
- Two Guns Wild West Whiskey
- Single Six Rocky Mountain Moonshine
- Cowboy Coffee
  (coffee infused moonshine)
- Dirty Gin (Summer 2014)

Best known for / most popular: Not provided

Average bottle price: $30.00 to $45.00

Distribution: CO, On-site retail

Interesting facts:
- Two Guns is a micro distillery mashing, fermenting, distilling, and aging all of their own spirits.
- "Our Whiskey is based upon a historical 1880's Leadville recipe of frontier whiskey. This is what you would have bellied up to the bar and had next to Doc Holiday, Oscar Wilde, Horace Tabor, and many other Wild West legends that came or lived in Leadville Boom days." B.A. Dallas

Wood's High Mountain Distillery

144 W. 1st Street
Salida, CO 81201
719-207-4315

Owners / Operators:
P.T. Wood, Owner
Lee Wood, Owner

Email: info@woodsdistillery.com
Website: www.woodsdistillery.com
Facebook: Wood's High Mountain Distillery
Twitter: @WoodsDistillery

Type: Micro Distillery. Opened in 2012.

Hours of operation:
Tasting room open daily, 4 p.m. to 8 p.m.

Tours: Available

Types of spirits produced: Gin, whiskey

Names of spirits:
- Treeline Gin
- Tenderfoot Whiskey

Best known for / most popular: Treeline Gin

Average bottle price: Not provided

Distribution: CO

Interesting facts:
- The still at WHMD was built in Germany around 1880.
- Wood's High Mountain Distillery is making "Treeline Barrel Rested" Gin. They refill their empty whiskey barrels and age their standard "treeline" gin in them for 2-6 months.

Woody Creek Distillers

60 Sunset Drive
Basalt, CO 81621
970-279-5110

Owners / Operators:
Mary Scanlan, CEO
Mark Kleckner, CFO / COO
Pat Scanlan, Founder / Partner
Keith Hemeon, Vice President of Sales
David Matthews, Distillery Manager

Email: mark@woodycreekdistillers.com
Website: www.woodycreekdistillers.com
Facebook: WoodyCreekDistillers
Twitter: @WoodyCreekDisti
YouTube: WoodyCreekDistillers
Vimeo: Woody Creek Distillers
Flickr: WoodyCreekDistillers

Type: Craft Distillery. Opened in 2012.

Hours of operation:
Tuesday through Saturday, 2 p.m. to 8 p.m.
Sunday, noon to 6 p.m.

Tasting room: Woody Creek spirits, signature cocktails, snack boards
Retail shop: Spirits, clothing, gifts

Tours: Available by appointment

Types of spirits produced:
Potato vodka, bourbon, whiskey, apple brandy, pear eau de vie, gin

Names of spirits:
- Woody Creek Colorado 100% Potato Vodka
- Woody Creek Colorado Reserve Vodka (from 100% Stobrawa Potatoes)
- Woody Creek Colorado Apple Brandy
- Woody Creek Colorado Pear Brandy (Eau De Vie)
- Woody Creek Colorado 4 Grain Whiskey
- Woody Creek Colorado Rye Whiskey
- Woody Creek Colorado White Whiskey (from 100% Olathe Sweet Corn)

Best known for / most popular:
Woody Creek Colorado 100% Potato Vodka

Average bottle price: $30.00

Distribution: CO, FL, GA, KS, NY, TN

Interesting facts:
Woody Creek Distillers is a farm-to-bottle distillery. They control every aspect of the production, starting with growing all their own potatoes. All other grains and fruits used are sourced exclusively in Colorado.

Elm City Distillery LLC

53 Capital Drive
Wallingford, CT 06492
203-285-8830

Owners / Operators:
Eric Kotowski, Owner

Email: info@elmcitydistillery.com
Website: www.elmcitydistillery.com
Facebook: Elm City Distillery
Twitter: @ECDistillery

Type: Micro Distillery. Opened in 2010.

Hours of operation:
Monday through Friday, 9 a.m. to 5 p.m.

Tours: Available by appointment

Types of spirits produced: Vodka, whiskey

Names of spirits:
- Velocipede Vodka
- Nine Square Rye

Best known for / most popular: Not provided

Average bottle price: $24.00

Distribution: CT

Interesting facts: Not provided

Onyx Spirits Company LLC

64D Oakland Avenue
East Hartford, CT 06108
860-550-1939

Owners / Operators:
Adam von Gootkin, Co-founder
Peter Kowalczyk, Co-founder

Email: contact@onyxspirits.com
Website: www.onyxspirits.com
Facebook: Onyx Spirits Company
Twitter: @OnyxSpirits
YouTube: OnyxSpirits's Channel

Type: Micro Distillery. Opened in 2011.

Hours of operation:
Monday through Friday, 9 a.m. to 6 p.m.

Tours: Not available

Types of spirits produced:
New England style ultra-premium American moonshine

Names of spirits:
- Onyx Moonshine
  (in .750ml, .375ml, and 1.75ml)
- Releasing soon:
  High proof Onyx Moonshine
  Barrel Aged Onyx Moonshine

Best known for: Onyx Moonshine

Average bottle price: $22.00 to $28.00

Distribution: CT, MA, RI
Purchase online: drinkbetter.com/onyx

Interesting facts:
Onyx Moonshine is the first legal moonshine to be produced in New England since Prohibition.

ONYX SPIRITS Co
PRODUCERS OF FINE LIQUOR
MANCHESTER, CONNECTICUT

Westford Hill Distillers

196 Chatey Road
Ashford, CT 06278
860-429-0464

Owners / Operators:
Louis Chatey, Co-owner
Margaret Chatey, Co-owner

Email: info@westfordhill.com
Website: www.westfordhill.com
Facebook: Westford Hills Distillers

Type: Micro Distillery. Opened in 1997.

Hours of operation: Not provided

Tours: Not available

Types of spirits produced: Brandy, vodka

Names of spirits:
- Aged Apple Brandy
- Framboise Eau de vie
- Pear William Eau de vie
- Kirsch Eau de vie
- Fraise Eau de vie
- Poire Prisonniere
- Rime Organic Vodka

Best known for / most popular: Aged Apple Brandy

Average bottle price: $20.00

Distribution: CA, CT, MA, RI

Interesting facts: Not provided

Delaware Distilling Company

18693 Coastal Highway
Rehoboth Beach, DE 19971
302-645-8273

Owners / Operators:
Zachary King, Owner
Steve Funk, Owner
Jonathon Bedi, Head Distiller

Email: info@delawaredistilling.com
Website: www.delawaredistilling.com
Facebook: Delaware Distilling Company
Twitter: @DeDistill
Yelp: Delaware Distilling Company

Type: Craft Distillery. Opened in May 2013.

Restaurant hours:
Friday through Sunday, noon to 1 a.m.
Monday through Thursday, 4 p.m. to 1 a.m.

Tours: Available by appointment only

Types of spirits produced:
Vodka, whiskey, gin, spiced rum

Names of spirits:
- Delaware Distilling Company Premium Gin
- Delaware Distilling Company Premium Vodka
- Delaware Distilling Company Spiced Rum
- Delaware Distilling Company White Rum
- Delaware Distilling Company White Whiskey
- Delaware Distilling Company Bourbon
- Delaware Distilling Company Potato Vodka

Best known for / most popular: Spiced Rum

Average bottle price: $18.00 to $32.00

Distribution: On-site retail, DC, DE, MD

Interesting facts: Not provided

Services offered other than production:
Full service restaurant/bar with made from scratch distillery inspired cuisine, and live entertainment. Also offers an infusion bar with over 20 fresh infusions of their liquors. Tastings available in 4 and 6 shot tastings, and have specialty cocktails for all of them.

Dogfish Head Craft Brewery

320 Rehoboth Avenue
Rehoboth Beach, DE 19971
302-226-BREW (2739)

Owners / Operators:
Sam Calagione, Founder / President
Alison Schrader, Off-Centered Distiller
Graham Hamblett, Lead Distiller

Email: info@dogfish.com
Website: www.dogfish.com
Facebook: Dogfish Head Beer
Twitter: @dogfishbeer
YouTube: Dogfish Head
Google Plus: Dogfish Head Craft Brewery

Type: Micro Distillery. Opened in 2002.

Hours of operation:
Sunday through Thursday, noon to 11 p.m.
Friday and Saturday, noon to 1 a.m.

Tours: Not available

Types of spirits produced: Rum, vodka, gin

Names of spirits:
- Brown Honey Rum
- White Light Rum
- Wit Spiced Rum
- Blue Hen Vodka
- Peanut Butter Vodka
- Chocolate Vodka

Best known for / most popular: Brown Honey Rum, Peanut Butter Vodka

Average bottle price: $25.00

Distribution: DE

Interesting facts: Not provided

Painted Stave Distilling

106 W. Commerce Street
Smyrna, DE 19977
302-653-6834

Owners / Operators:
Mike Rasmussen, Co-owner
Ron Gomes Jr., Co-owner

Email: hello@paintedstave.com
Website: www.paindedstave.com
Facebook: Painted Stave Distilling

Type: Craft Distillery. Opened in Fall 2013.

Tasting room hours: Friday 3 p.m. to 8 p.m.; Saturday 11 a.m. to 6 p.m.; Sunday noon to 5 p.m.

Tours: Offered at the top of the hour ($10, includes a cocktail and tasting)

Types of spirits produced:
Vodka, gin, whiskey, brandy, grappa

Names of spirits:
- Silver Screen Vodka
- Candy Manor Gin
- Old Cooch's Corn Whiskey

Best known for / most popular:
Candy Manor Gin

Average bottle price: $30.00

Distribution: TBA

Interesting facts:
- First standalone distillery in Delaware.
- Housed in a renovated 1940's movie theater.

New Columbia Distillers

1832 Fenwick Street NE
Washington, DC 20002
202-733-1710

Owners / Operators:
John Uselton, Owner / Distiller
Michael Lowe, Owner / Distiller
Saul Mutchnick, VP of Sales

Email: cheers@greenhatgin.com
Website: www.greenhatgin.com
Facebook: New Columbia Distillers
Twitter: @dcdistillers

Type: Micro Distillery. Opened in 2012.

Hours of operation: Monday through Friday, 8 a.m. to 5:30 p.m.

Tours: Available Saturday, 1 p.m. to 4 p.m.

Types of spirits produced: Gin, rye whiskey

Names of spirits:
- Green Hat Gin
- Green Hat Seasonal Gin

Best known for / most popular: Green Hat Gin

Average bottle price: $32.00 to $36.00

Distribution: DC, MD, VA

Interesting facts:
First DC distillery since before Prohibition

Alchemist Distilleries Inc.

6468-6470 NW 77th Court
Miami, FL 33166
718-360-3123

Owners / Operators:
D.J. Noel, President

Email: djno@alchemistdistillery.com
Website: www.alchemistdistillery.com
Facebook: Alchemist Distilleries

Type: Micro Distillery. Opened in 2013.

Hours of operation: Vary

Tours: Available by appointment

Types of spirits produced: Whiskey, vodka, rum

Names of spirits:
- Alchemist Distillery Whiskey
- Alchemist Distillery Vodka
- Alchemist Distillery Rum

Best known for / most popular: Alchemist Distillery Whiskey

Average bottle price: $24.99 to $32.99

Distribution: FL

Interesting facts:
In addition to their core spirits, Alchemist Distilleries creates spirits using farm fresh produce. They buy seasonal, local produce from Florida farmers and craft unique spirits using these fresh ingredients. Like the produce, theses unique spirits are available only on a seasonal basis.

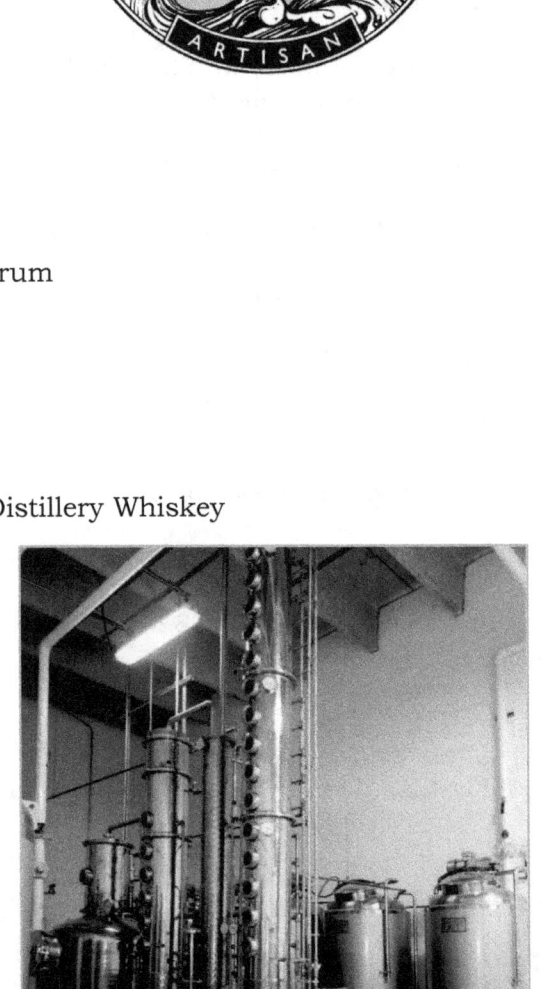

Cape Spirits Inc.

131 SW 3rd Place
Cape Coral, FL 33991

Owners / Operators:
JoAnn Elardo, President

Email: info@wickeddolphin.com
Website: www.wickeddolphin.com
Facebook: Wicked Dolphin
Twitter: @GettingWicked

Type: Micro Distillery. Opened in 2012.

Hours of operation:
Monday through Friday, 9 a.m. to 5 p.m.

Tours:
Available Thursday and Saturday, 11 a.m. to 2 p.m.

Types of spirits produced: Rum

Names of spirits:
- Wicked Dolphin Rum
- Wicked Dolphin Spiced Rum

Best known for / most popular: The Wicked Dolphin Punch

Average bottle price: $24.99

Distribution: Republic National Distributing Co.

Interesting facts:
- The first distillery in Lee County, FL.
- One of the first distilleries in FL to sell spirits since Prohibition.
- "Our Spiced Rum is distinctly Florida. Made with Florida oranges, local honey and spices it has creamy vanilla undertones with notes of Florida oranges, sweet honey and a spicy citrus finish we also add some aged rum to give it a mature smooth taste – If you like Spiced Rum and Coke try our Wicked Coke!" – JoAnn Elardo

Drum Circle Distilling

2212 Industrial Boulevard
Sarasota, FL 34234
941-358-1900

Owners / Operators:
Troy Roberts, Founder / CEO / Distiller
Tom Clarke, Partner / COO
Ryan Adams, Partner

Email: info@drumcircledistilling.com
Website: www.drumcircledistilling.com
Facebook: Siesta Key Rum
Twitter: @SiestaKeyRum

Type: Micro Distillery. Opened in 2007.

Hours of operation: Not provided

Tours: Available by appointment

Types of spirits produced: Rum

Names of spirits:
- Siesta Key Spiced Rum
- Siesta Key Silver Rum
- Siesta Key Gold Rum

Best known for / most popular: Not provided

Average bottle price: Not provided

Distribution: AZ, CA, CT, DE, GA, MD, NJ, NV, TX, WA

Interesting facts: Not provided

Empire Winery & Distillery

11807 Little Road
New Port Richey, FL 34654
727-819-2821

Owners / Operators:
Henry Kasprow, Owner

Email: empirewinery@msn.com
Website: www.empirewineryanddistillery.com
Facebook: V6 Vodka

Type: Winery / Micro Distillery. Opened in 2002.

Hours of operation: Not provided

Tours: Not provided

Types of spirits produced: Vodka, grappa, mead, liqueur

Names of spirits:
- T & W V6 Rye Vodka
- T & W Grappa Di Muscatto
- T & W Royal Mead Honey Wine
- T & W Lemonela Liqueur
- T &W Limonela Liqueur
- T & W Orangela Liqueur

Best known for / most popular: Not provided

Average bottle price: Not provided

Distribution: Not provided

Interesting facts: Not provided

Fat Dog Spirits LLC

3212 North 40th Street
Tampa, FL 33605
813-503-5995

Owners / Operators:
Nick Carbone, Proprietor

Email: fatdogspirits@earthlink.net
Website: www.fatdogspirits.com
Facebook: Fat Dog Spirits

Type: Micro Distillery. Opened in 2004

Hours of operation: Vary

Tours: Available upon request.

Types of spirits produced: Absinthe verte, gin, vodka

Names of spirits:
- Nicholas Gin
- Touch Vodka-Original
- Touch Red Grapefruit Flavored Vodka
- Touch Key Lime Flavored Vodka
- Touch Valencia Orange Flavored Vodka
- Artemisia Superior Absinthe Verte

Best known for / most popular: Nicholas Gin

Average bottle price: $32.00 to $34.00

Distribution: FL, IL

Interesting facts: Fat Dog Distillery is the second U.S. distillery to be approved to make Artemisia Absinthe in over 100 years.

Fish Hawk Spirits LLC

16162 SW 44th Street
Ocala, FL 34481

Owners / Operators:
R. Matthew Bagdanovich, Managing Member
James M. Brady, Managing Member
A. Christian Howard, Managing Member

Email: fishhawk@fishhawkspirits.net
Website: www.fishhawkspirits.net
Facebook: Fish Hawk Spirits
Twitter: @FHspirits

Type: Micro Distillery. Opened in 2012.

Hours of operation: Not provided

Tours: Not provided

Types of spirits produced: Absinthe

Names of spirits:
- Absinthia Rubra
- Marion Black 106

Best known for / most popular: Not provided

Average bottle price: Not provided

Distribution: FL

Interesting facts: Not provided

Florida Farm Distillers

Umatilla, FL 32784
352-455-7232

Owners / Operators:
Dick & Marti Waters, Owners / Distillers

Email: whiskey@palmridgereserve.com
Website: www.palmridgereserve.com
Facebook: Palm Ridge Reserve
Twitter: @handmadewhiskey

Type: Micro Distillery. Opened in 2008.

Hours of operation: Vary

Tours: Available

Types of spirits produced: Whiskey

Names of spirits:
- Palm Ridge Reserve

Best known for / most popular: Palm Ridge Reserve

Average bottle price: $50.00 to $60.00

Distribution: FL, MO, Nashville TN area

Interesting facts: Not provided

Handmade Micro Batch
Florida Whiskey

NJoy Spirits LLC

7237 Wild Buck Road
Weeki Wachee, FL 34613
352-592-9622

Owners / Operators:
Natalie Joy Goff, Co-owner
Kevin S. Goff, Co-owner

Email: njoyspirits@att.net

Type: Micro Distillery. Opened in 2013.

Hours of operation: TBA

Tours: TBA

Types of spirits produced: Whiskey

Names of spirits:
- Wild Buck Whiskey

Best known for / most popular:
Wild Buck Whiskey

Average bottle price: $49.99

Distribution: Not provided

Interesting facts: Not provided

Peaden Brothers Distillery

382 Main Street
Crestview, FL 32536
251-583-5660

Owners / Operators:
Trey Peaden, Co-owner
Tyler Peaden, Co-owner
Robert Ellis, Co-owner / International Sales

Email: info@peadenbrothersdistillery.com
Website: www.peadenbrothersdistillery.com
Facebook: Peaden Brothers Distillery
Twitter: @peadenbrothers

Type: Micro Distillery. Opened February 2014.

Hours of operation: TBA

Tours: Available after opening. Watch website.

Types of spirits produced:
Flavored whiskeys, aged rums

Names of spirits:
- TBA

Best known for / most popular:
TBA

Average bottle price: TBA

Distribution: U.S., Canada

Interesting facts:
The Peaden Brothers are third generation distillers of southern whiskey.

Rollins Distillery

5680 Gulf Breeze Parkway., D-10
Gulf Breeze, FL 32563
850-503-1275

Owners / Operators:
Paul Rollins, Co-Owner / President / Master Distiller
Lamia Rollins, Co-Owner / Administrative Director
Patrick Rollins, Marketing Director

Email: info@rollinsdistillery.com
Website: www.rollinsdistillery.com, www.espritdekrewe.com
Facebook: Rollins Distillery
Twitter: @CraftyRams

Type: Craft Distillery. Opened in 2012.

Hours of operation: Daily, 8 a.m. to 5 p.m.

Tours: Available

Types of spirits produced: Rum, vodka

Names of spirits:
- Esprit de Krewe™ Crystal Rum
- Esprit de Krewe™ Spiced Rum
- Esprit de Krewe™ Vodka

Best known for / most popular: Not provided

Average bottle price: Not provided

Distribution: Not provided

Interesting facts: First distillery in the Florida Panhandle.

Spirits of the USA LLC

Jacksonville, FL 35522
866-795-5463

Owners / Operators:
Michael Gerard, Founder / CEO

Email: info@spiritsoftheusa.com
Website: www.spiritsoftheusa.com
Facebook: Spirits of the USA
Twitter: @SPIRITSUSA

Type: Craft Distillery. Opened in 2008.

Hours of operation: Not provided

Tours: Not provided

Types of spirits produced: Vodka, gin, rum

Names of spirits:
- Coyote Vodka
- Coyote Ice Peppermint Flavored Vodka
- Coyote Jalapeño Flavored Vodka
- Coyote Mango Flavored Vodka
- Black Window Gin
- Rattlesnake Tequila
- Rattlesnake Jalapeño Tequila
- Deadman's Mango Flavored Rum
- Deadman's Dark & Spice Rum
- Runner Energy Drink

Best known for / most popular: Not provided

Average bottle price: Not provided

Distribution: FL

Interesting facts: Not provided

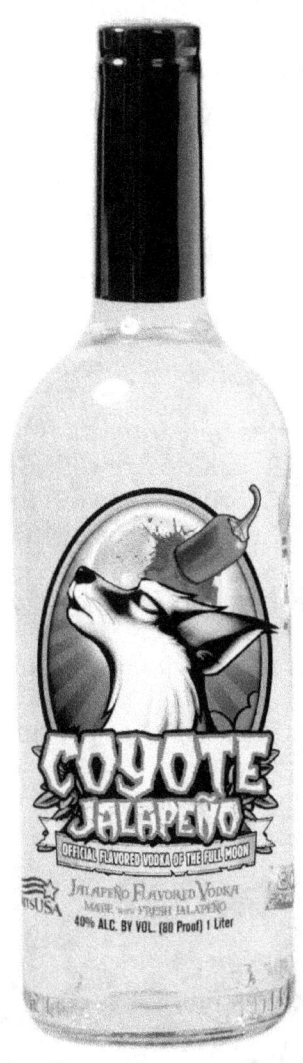

The Florida Distillery

501 S. Falkenburg Road, Ste. C-6
Tampa, FL 33619
813-347-6565

Owners / Operators:
Lee Nelson, Co-owner
Pat O'Brian, Co-owner
Nefreteri Jacobsen, Operations Assistant

Email: info@floridadistillery.net
Website: www.cane-vodka.com
Facebook: The Florida Cane Distillery
Twitter: @FLVODKA
Instagram: CaneVodka
Pinterest: Cane Vodka

Type: Micro Distillery. Opened in 2012.

Hours of operation: Daily

Tours: Not available

Types of spirits produced: Vodka

Names of spirits:
- Cane Vodka
- Cane Vodka Gator Grape
- Cane Vodka Orlando Orange
- Cane Vodka Buccaneer Blueberry
- Cane Vodka Plant City Strawberry

Best known for / most popular: Cane Vodka

Average bottle price: $30.00

Distribution: FL

Interesting facts: Not provided

Dawsonville Moonshine Distillery
Free Spirits Distillery

415 Highway 53 East
Dawsonville, GA 30534
770-401-1211

Owners / Operators:
Cheryl Wood, Owner

Email: moonshiners@dawsonvillemoonshinedistillery.com
Website: www.dawsonvillemoonshinedistillery.com
Facebook: Dawsonville Moonshine Distillery
Twitter: @Moonshiners_

Type: Micro Distillery. Opened in 2012.

Hours of operation:
Monday through Saturday, 10 a.m. to 4 p.m.
Sunday, noon to 4 p.m.

Tours: Available

Types of spirits produced: Whiskey

Names of spirits:
- Dawsonville Moonshine Georgia Corn Whiskey

Best known for / most popular:
Dawsonville Moonshine Georgia Corn Whiskey

Average bottle price: $25.00

Distribution: GA

Interesting facts: The distillery is under the same roof as the Georgia Racing Hall of Fame and City Hall.

Georgia Distilling Company

121 Blandy Way
Milledgeville, GA 31061
478-453-1086

Owners / Operators:
Shawn Hall, Co-owner
Bill Mauldin, Co-owner

Email: info@georgiadistillingcompany.com
Website: www.georgiadistilling.com
Facebook: Georgia Distilling Company, Inc.
Twitter: @GeorgiaDistiCo, @GrandaddyMimms

Type: Micro Distillery. Opened in 2009.

Hours of operation: Not provided

Tours: Not available

Types of spirits produced: Moonshine, vodka, whiskey

Names of spirits:
- Georgia Vodka
- Bear Creek Sippin' Shine
- Grandaddy Mimm's Whiskey
- Tootsie's Apple Pie Whiskey
- Doc Holliday Rye Whiskey
- Copperhead Georgia Sour Mash

Best known for / most popular: Grandaddy Mimm's

Average bottle price: $20.00

Distribution: Not provided

Interesting facts: Not provided

Ivy Mountain Distillery LLC

1896 Dick's Hill Parkway
Mt. Airy, GA 30563

Owners / Operators:
Carlene Holder, Owner
Carlos Lovell, Master Distiller

Email: carlene@ivymountaindistillery.com
Website: www.ivymountaindistillery.com
Facebook: Ivy Mountain Distillery

Type: Micro Distillery. Opened in 2011.

Hours of operation: Not provided

Tours: Available first Tuesday, third Friday of each month, 9 a.m. and 3 p.m.

Types of spirits produced: Whiskey, brandy

Names of spirits:
- Ivy Mountain Georgia Sour Mash Whiskey™
- Ivy Mountain Georgia Sour Mash Spirits™
- Ivy Mountain Apple Brandy™
- Ivy Mountain Georgia Peach Brandy™

Best known for / most popular: Not provided

Average bottle price: $24.00

Distribution: Not provided
Eagle Rock Distributors and Atlanta Beverage (GA)
Southern Wine & Spirits (SC, FL)

Interesting facts:
- The master distiller is 85 years young.
- The recipe belongs to his father and was used to make illegal whiskey generations ago.

Moonrise Distillery Inc.

31 Webb Road
P.O. Box 829
Clayton, GA 30525
404-697-8800

Owners / Operators:
Jim Harris, Owner / Distiller

Email: jimharris@windstream.net
Website: www.moonrisedistillery.com

Type: Craft Distillery. Opened in August 2013.

Hours of operation:
Monday through Friday, 9 a.m. to 5 p.m.
Saturday and Sunday reserved for special occasions

Tours: Available

Types of spirits produced:
Whiskey, moonshine, brandy

Names of spirits:
- Corn Squeezins (Moonshine)
- James Henry Barrel Aged Whiskey
- Moonrise Distillery Apple Brandy
- Moonrise Distillery Peach Brandy
- Moonrise Distillery Blackberry Brandy

Best known for / most popular: Not provided

Average bottle price: $20.00 to $40.00

Distribution: GA

Interesting facts: Not provided

Richland Distilling Company

333 Broad Street
Richland, GA 31825
229-887-3537 / 941-545-4311

Owners / Operators:
Erik Vonk, Founder / Proprietor
Karin Vonk, Marketing and Public Relations

Email: cheers@richlandrum.com
Website: www.richlandrum.com
Facebook: Richland Distilling Company

Type: Artisan Rum Distillery. Opened in 2011.

Hours of operation:
Monday through Friday, 9 a.m. to 5 p.m.

Tours: Available weekends and by appointment

Types of spirits produced: Ultra-premium rum

Names of spirits:
- Richland Rum

Best known for: Unique, authentic sipping rum, best enjoyed neat or on the rocks

Average bottle price: $55.00

Distribution: FL, GA, TN; Duty free stores at major airports and on cruise ships

Interesting facts:
- Field-to-glass premium rum made with home grown sugar cane.
- The Richland Distilling Company is one of only a few distilleries in the entire United States solely dedicated to hand-crafting Rum from pure cane syrup. Annual production is approximately 6,000 cases.

Thirteenth Colony Distilleries

305 N. Dudley Street
Americus, GA 31709
229-924-3310

Owners / Operators:
Alton Darby, Chairman / CEO
Kent Cost, President
Gilbert S. Klemann MD, VP of Product Development
Lindsey Cotton, Marketing / Office Manager
Graham Arthur, Production and Facility Manager / Distiller
Elizabeth Warnock, Distillery Representative
Anna Payne, Office Administrator

Email: info@13colony.net
Website: www.13colony.net
Facebook: Southern Vodka
Twitter: @13thColony

Type: Micro Distillery. Opened in 2009.

Hours of operation: Not provided

Tours: Not provided

Types of spirits produced: Gin, vodka, whiskey

Names of spirits:
- Plantation Vodka
- Southern Gin
- Southern Vodka
- Southern Corn Whiskey

Best known for / most popular: Plantation Vodka

Average bottle price: Not provided

Distribution: AL, GA, LA, MS, NJ, WV, WY

Interesting facts: Not provided

Haleakala Distillers

Kula, HI 96790

Owners / Operators:
Jim Sargent, Master Distiller
Leslie Sargent, Managing Director

Website: www.haleakaladistillers.com

Type: Micro Distillery. Opened in 2003.

Hours of operation: Vary

Tours: Not available

Types of spirits produced: Rum, liqueur

Names of spirits:
- Maui Dark Rum ®
- Maui Gold Rum ®
- Maui Platinum Rum ®
- Maui Reserve Gold Rum ®
- Maui Pineapple Flavored Rum ®
- Maui Okolehao ® (made from Ti root)
- Braddah Kimo's Extreme 155 Proof Rum ®

Best known for / most popular: Maui Dark Rum ®

Average bottle price: $20.00 in Hawaii

Distribution: AK, HI, WA. Visit www.mauirum.biz for details.

Interesting facts: Haleakala Distillers is Hawaii's oldest distillery, one of the most awarded and the only known Hawaiian distillery that ferments only local ingredients to make their rum.

Hawaii Sea Spirits LLC

4051 Omaopio Road
Kula, HI 96790
866-77-OCEAN

Owners / Operators:
Shay Smith, President / CEO
Kyle Smith, Production Director
Don Freytag, Chief Marketing Officer / Sales Director
Sye Vasquez, Board Member / Advisor
Craig Duvall, Board Member / Advisor

Email: Sales, sales@oceanvodka.com
Shay Smith, shay@oceanvodka.com
Kyle Smith, kyle@oceanvodka.com
Don Freytag, don@oceanvodka.com
Website: www.oceanvodka.com
Facebook: Ocean Vodka
Twitter: @OceanVodka
Instagram: @oceanvodkamaui
#: #oceanvodkamaui

Type: Craft Distillery. Opened in 2006.

Hours of operation: Daily, 9:30 a.m. to 5 p.m.

Tours: Available, check website for reservation information

Types of spirits produced: Vodka

Names of spirits:
- Ocean Vodka

Best known for / most popular:
Ocean Vodka

Average bottle price: $32.00

Distribution: U.S.; Japan, Canada

Interesting facts:
- 100% gluten free
- Uses only 100% USDA Certified Organic sugar cane
- The only known vodka in the world made from organic sugar cane
- The only known spirit in the world made with deep ocean mineral water, sourced 3,000 feet below the Kona coast of the island of Hawaii.
- 100% solar powered
- Craft distillery and organic farm are located 1,000 feet above the ocean on the slopes of Mt. Haleakala in Kula, Maui.
- Give back to oceanic causes every year.

Island Distillers Inc.

220 Puuhale Road, #B3
Honolulu, HI 96819
808-492-4632

Owners / Operators:
Dave Flintstone, Owner

Email: dave@islanddistillers.com
Website: www.islanddistillers.com
Facebook: Hawaiian Vodka
YouTube: Hawaiianvodka's Channel

Type: Micro Distillery. Opened in 2009.

Hours of operation: Open daily, hours vary

Tours: Not available

Types of spirits produced: Vodka, moonshine

Names of spirits:
- Hawaiian Vodka
- Hawaiian Coconut Vodka
- Hawaiian Moonshine

Best known for / most popular: Hawaiian Moonshine

Average bottle price: $25.00 to $33.00

Distribution: Hawaii

Interesting facts:
Island Distillers is Honolulu's only licensed distillery.

Kōloa Rum Company

2-2741 Kaumualii Highway, Ste. C
Kalaheo, HI 96741
808-332-9333

Owners / Operators:
Bob Gunter, President / CEO
Alicia Iverson, CFO
Jeanne Toulon, Director of Business & Public Relations
Edie Hafdahl, Western Regional Brand Manager
Rex Riddle, Hawaii State Sales Manager

Email: info@koloarum
Website: www.koloarum.com
Facebook: Koloa Rum Company
Twitter: @KoloaRumCompany
Pinterest: Koloa Rum Company

Type: Micro Distillery. Opened in 2009.

Hours of operation: Vary. Visit website for tasting room and store hours

Tours: Not available

Types of spirits produced: Rum and related spirits products

Names of spirits:
- Kaua`i White
- Kaua`i Gold
- Kaua`i Dark Rum
- Kaua`i Spice Rum
- Kaua`i Coconut Rum
- Kōloa Mai Tai Cocktail
- Kōloa Rum Punch Cocktail

Best known for / most popular:
Kaua`i Dark Rum

Average bottle price:
$29.95 to $32.95

Distribution: AZ, CA, DC, FL, GA, HI, IA*, ID*, IL, MD, MN, MT*, NC*, NV, OR*, PA*, UT*, VT*, WA, WY*, Western Canada, China, Australia (* special order)

Interesting facts: The history of Hawaii's first sugar plantation lives within each bottle of Kōloa Rum. The rum is carefully handcrafted in single batches from Kaua`i grown raw crystal sugar from the west side of the island and from pure mountain rainwater that is captured and slowly filtered through layers of volcanic strata before finally reaching vast underground aquifers from Mt. Wai`ale`ale and the nearby mountain peaks and rainforests. It is distilled in a 1,210 gallon vintage copper-pot still that was manufactured in New England shortly after World War II.

44° North Vodka

134 N. 3300 E.
Rigby, ID 83442
206-649-3598

Owners / Operators:
Ken Wyatt, Co-Founder
Ron Zier, Co-Founder

Email: ken@44northvodka.com
Website: www.44northvodka.com
Facebook: 44° North Vodka
Twitter: @44NorthVodka

Type: Micro Distillery. Opened in 2004.

Hours of operation: Not provided

Tours: Not provided

Types of spirits produced: Vodka

Names of spirits:
- 44° North Magic Valley Vodka
- 44° North Rainier Cherry Vodka
- 44° North Mountain Huckleberry Vodka

Best known for / most popular: Not provided

Average bottle price: Not provided

Distribution: Nationwide

Interesting facts: Not provided

Bardenay Inc.

610 Grove Street
Boise, ID 83702
208-426-0538

Bardenay Eagle
155 E. Riverside Drive
Eagle, ID 83616

Bardenay Coeur d'Alene
1710 W. Riverstone Drive
Coeur d'Alene, ID 83814

Owners / Operators:
Kevin Settles, Owner

Email: info@bardenay.com
Website: www.bardenay.com
Facebook: Bardenay
Twitter: @Bardenay
UrbanSpoon: Bardenay
Yelp: Bardenay Restaurant & Distillery
Trip Advisor: Bardenay Restaurant & Distillery

Type: Micro Distillery. Opened in 1999.

Hours of operation: Vary

Tours: Available

Types of spirits produced: Gin, rum, vodka

Names of spirits:
- Bardenay Vodka
- Bardenay London Dry Gin
- Bardenay Small Batch Rum
- Ginger Spiced Rum
- Lemon Vodka

Best known for / most popular:
Bardenay Vodka

Average bottle price: $12.00 to $22.00

Distribution: ID

Interesting facts: Bardenay Distillery is the nation's first restaurant distillery.

Grand Teton Distillery

1755 North Highway 33
Driggs, ID 83422
208-354-7263

Owners / Operators:
Lea Beckett, President
William Beckett, VP
John Boczar, VP / Master Distiller

Email: info@tetonvodka.com
Website: www.tetonvodka.com
Facebook: Grand Teton Vodka
Twitter: @TetonVodka
LinkedIn: Grand Teton Vodka

Type: Micro Distillery. Opened in 2012.

Hours of operation:
Monday through Friday, 9 a.m. to 5 p.m.

Tours: Available by appointment

Types of spirits produced: Vodka, moonshine

Names of spirits:
- Grand Teton Vodka
- Teton Moonshine
- Spiced Apple Pie Moonshine
- Vishnovka, Russian style cherry vodka

Best known for / most popular: Grand Teton Vodka

Average bottle price: $18.95 to $21.95

Distribution:
AR, CA, CT, GA, ID, MT, OR, SC, WA, WY

Awards and Recognitions:
- Gold Medal, 94 points from Beverage Testing Institute in Chicago in 2013.
- Gold Medal, 94 Points from Beverage Testing Institute in Chicago in 2012.
- Double Gold Medal at the 2013 San Francisco Spirits Competition.
- Ranked #1 on Proof66.com for vodka distilled from potatoes.

Koenig Distillery

20928 Grape Lane
Caldwell, ID 83607
208-455-8386

Owners / Operators:
Andrew Koenig, Owner / Master Distiller
Jill Koenig, Owner / Vice-President

Email: info@koenigdistilleryandwinery.com
Website: www.koenigdistilleryandwinery.com
Facebook: Koenig Distillery and Winery
Twitter: @DrinkKoenig

Type: Micro Distillery and custom bottling operation. Opened in 1999.

Tasting room hours:
Friday through Sunday, noon to 5 p.m.

Tours: Private tours are available.

Types of spirits produced:
Bourbon, vodka, grappa, brandy

Names of spirits:
- Seven Devils Straight Bourbon Whiskey
- Koenig Potato Vodka
- Koenig Huckleberry Flavored Vodka
- Koenig Pear Brandy
- Koenig Apricot Brandy
- Koenig Cherry Brandy
- Koenig Plum Brandy
- Koenig Grappa

Best known for / most popular:
Koenig Huckleberry Vodka

Average bottle price: $19.95

Distribution: CA, ID, MT, OR, PA, WA

Interesting facts:
It takes more than 15 pounds of fresh fruit to make each bottle of brandy.

Blaum Bros. Distilling Co.

9380 W. U.S. Highway 20
Galena, IL 61036
815-777-1000

Owners / Operators:
Matthew Blaum Co-founder / Distiller
Michael Blaum Co-founder / Distiller

Email: info@BlaumBrosDistilling.com
Website: www.BlaumBros.com
Facebook: Blaum Bros. Distilling Co. of Galena

Type: Craft Distillery. Opened in 2013.

Hours of operation: Monday through Sunday

Tours: Available daily

Types of spirits produced: Vodka, gin, bourbon, moonshine, rye whiskey, malt whiskey

Names of spirits:
- Blaum Bros. Vodka
- Blaum Bros. Gin
- Lead Mine Moonshine
- Galena Bourbon Whiskey
- Fever River Rye Whiskey
- Blaum Bros. Malt Whiskey

Best known for / most popular: Vodka and Gin

Average bottle price: $30.00

Distribution: On-site tasting room, IA, IL, MO, WI

Interesting facts:
The Blaum Bros. Distillery is located in the former Mormon Church of Galena.

CH Distillery

564 West Randolph Street
Chicago, IL 60661
312-707-8780

Owners / Operators:
Tremaine Atkinson, Managing Director
Mark Lucas, Managing Director / Sales
Kevin McDonald, Assist. Distillery Manager

Email: info@chdistillery.com
Website: www.chdistillery.com
Facebook: CH Distillery & Cocktail Bar
Twitter: @CHDistillery
Pinterest: CHDistillery & Cocktail Bar
Vine: CHDistillery

Type: Micro Distillery. Opened in August 2013.

Distillery operation: Monday through Saturday

Cocktail bar hours:
Tuesday through Thursday, 5 p.m. to 11 p.m.
Friday and Saturday, 5 p.m. to midnight

Tours: Available Saturday, 5:30 p.m.;
every other Tuesday, 5:30 p.m.

Types of spirits distilled: Vodka, gin, rum, whiskey

Types of spirits produced: Limoncello, bourbon

Names of spirits:
- CH Vodka
- CH Key Gin
- CH London Dry Gin
- CH Bourbon
- Giuliana's Crema di Limoncello
- CH Rum (cocktail bar only)
- CH Whiskey (cocktail bar only)

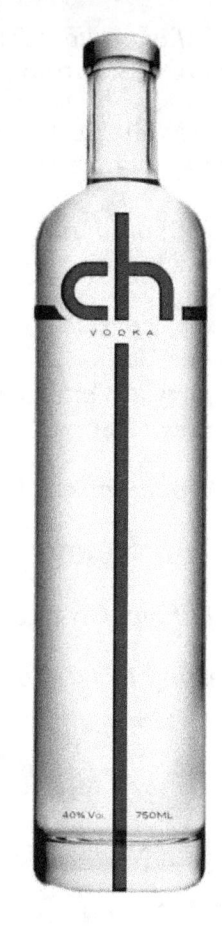

Average bottle price: $34.99

Distribution: On-site retail, IL

Interesting facts:
All CH Distillery products are made from scratch using only Illinois sourced grains.

Chicago Distilling Company

2359 N. Milwaukee Avenue
Chicago, IL 60647
872-206-2774

Owners / Operators:
Jay DiPrizio, Co-founder
Vic DiPrizio, Co-founder
Noelle DiPrizio, Co-founder

Email: drink@chicagodistilling.com
Website: www.chicagodistilling.com
Facebook: Chicago Distilling Company
Twitter: @chidistilling
Yelp: Chicago Distilling Company

Type: Craft Distillery. Opened in January 2014.

Hours of operation: Thursday, 5 p.m. to 11 p.m.;
Friday and Saturday, 5 p.m. to 1 a.m.; Sunday, 3 p.m. to 11 p.m.

Tours: Available Thursday and Saturday at 6:30 p.m.; Sunday at 3:30 p.m. Book in advance on website. Private tours available by request.

Types of spirits produced:
Vodka, whiskey, gin, specialty spirits

Names of spirits:
- Ceres Vodka
- Shorty's White Whiskey
- Finn's Gin

Best known for / most popular: Craft cocktails

Average bottle price: $22.00 to $45.00

Distribution: On-site retail

Interesting facts: Not provided

Few Spirits LLC

918 Chicago Avenue
Evanston, IL 60202
847-920-8628

Owners / Operators:
Paul Hletko, Founder

Email: info@fewspirits.com
Website: www.fewspirits.com
Facebook: Few Spirits
Twitter: @fewspirits
Blog: fewspirits.tumblr.com
Yelp: Few Spirits
LinkedIn: Few Spirits

Type: Micro Distillery. Opened in 2011.

Hours of operation:
Tours every Saturday, 2 p.m. and 3 p.m.

Tours: Available

Types of spirits produced: Gin, whiskey

Names of spirits:
- Few American Gin
- Few White Whiskey
- Few Bourbon
- Few Rye

Average bottle price: $35.00 to $80.00

Distribution: IL

Interesting facts:
- Few Spirits is the first legal alcohol ever produced in Evanston, IL.
- Few Rye was named Whiskey Advocate's Craft Whiskey of the Year in 2013.

Hum Spirits Company

676 N. LaSalle Drive, Unit 329
Chicago, IL 60654
312-735-1838

Owners / Operators:
Jennifer Piccione, Chief Executive Officer
Adam Seger, Chief Innovative Officer
Bryce Williford, Chief Financial Officer
Erin Ramsay, Social Media Coordinator / Executive Assistant

Email: info@humspirits.com
Website: www.humspirits.com
Facebook: The Hum Spirits Company
Twitter: @humspirits
YouTube: Hum Channel
Foursquare: Adam S.

Type: Contract distilled at Pennsylvania Pure Distilleries. Opened in 2009.

Hours of operation: 9 a.m. to 6 p.m.

Tours: Available

Types of spirits produced: Liqueur

Names of spirits:
- Hum Botanical Spirit

Best known for / most popular:
Hum Botanical Spirit

Average bottle price: $36.00

Distribution: AZ, CA, DC, DE, FL, GA, ID, IL, LA, MD, MN, MT, NJ, NV, NY, TN, TX, WA, VA

Interesting facts: Bottles used for samples and R&D are re-purposed into hummingbird feeders.

J.K. Williams Distilling LLC

526 High Point Lane
East Peoria, IL 61611
309-839-0591

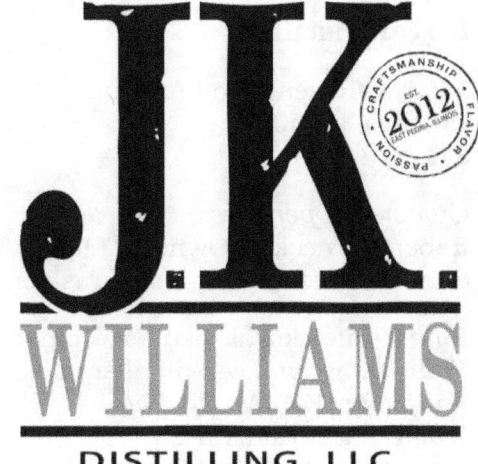

Owners / Operators:
Jon Williams, Owner / President
Jesse Williams, Owner / Master Distiller
Kassi Williams, Owner
Kristin Williams, Owner

Email: info@jkwilliamsdistilling.com
Website: www.jkwilliamsdistilling.com
Facebook: J.K. Williams Distilling
YouTube: J.K. Williams Distilling
Blog: www.blogspot.com/jkwilliamsdistilling

Type: Craft Distillery. Opened in October 2013.

Hours of operation: Saturday, 10 a.m. to 4 p.m.; Sunday, noon to 4 p.m.

Tours: Available with tastings

Types of spirits produced:
Whiskey, bourbon

Names of spirits:
- J.K.'s Original Corn Whiskey
- J.K.'s Peach Whiskey
- Smitty's Apple Pie Whiskey
- J.K.'s Lemon Whiskey
- Young Buck Bourbon
- J.K.'s Straight Bourbon

Best known for / most popular:
"Craftsmanship, Passion, and Flavor"

Average bottle price: $24.00 to $50.00

Distribution: IL

Interesting facts: "As the descendants of bootleg whiskey-making master J.K. Williams, we feel a certain responsibility to bring craft whiskey-and bourbon-making back to the Peoria area. Just like J.K. in his day, the current Williams generation is in the midst of raising families in Central Illinois while creating our own craft whiskey legacy. We're taking J.K.'s vision into the future while retaining the heritage of incredible small-batch whiskey that is tied to the Williams name." – Kristin Williams

Koval Distillery

5121 N. Ravenswood Avenue
Chicago, IL 60640
312-878-7988

Owners / Operators:
Robert Birnecker, Owner / Master Distiller
Sonat Birnecker, Owner / President

Email: info@koval-distillery.com
Website: www.koval-distillery.com
Facebook: KOVAL Distillery
Twitter: @kovaldistillery
Instagram: kovaldistillery

Type: Micro Distillery. Opened in 2008.

Hours of operation: Not provided

Tours: Available. Sign up online.

Types of spirits produced:
Brandy, beer spirit, whiskey, liqueurs

Names of spirits: KOVAL Brand

Aged Whiskey:
- Rye
- Millet
- Oat
- Bourbon
- Four Grain
- Limited Edition Charred Barrel Wheat
- Limited Edition Charred Barrel Spelt
- Limited Edition Toasted Barrel Rye
- Limited Edition Toasted Barrel Wheat
- Limited Edition Toasted Barrel Oat
- Limited Edition Toasted Barrel Millet
- Limited Edition Toasted Barrel Spelt

Brandy:
- Pear Brandy (Williams)
- Apple Brandy

White Whiskey:
- White Rye
- Limited Edition White Wheat
- Limited Edition White Oat
- Limited Edition White Spelt
- Limited Edition White Millet

Beer spirit:
- Bierbrand

Liqueurs:
- Jasmine
- Coffee
- Rose Hip
- Ginger
- Orange Blossom
- Chrysanthemum & Honey
- Caraway
- Walnut

Average bottle price: $25.00 to $45.00

Distribution:
CA, CT, DC, DE, FL, GA, IL, IN, KY, LA, MA, MD, MI, MN, MO, MS, NE, NJ, NM, NY, OR, PA, RI, TN, WI; Ontario, Germany, Austria, Japan, Australia

Interesting facts: Koval Distillery is the first boutique distillery located in Chicago since Prohibition.

LETHERBEE DISTILLERS
CHICAGO ILLINOIS

Letherbee Distillers

1815 W. Berteau Avenue
Chicago, IL 60647

Owners / Operators:
Brenton Engel, Owner / Distiller

Email: brenton@letherbee.com
Website: www.letherbee.com
Facebook: Letherbee Distillers
Twitter: @letherbee

Type: Micro Distillery. Opened in 2012.

Hours of operation: Vary

Tours: Not available

Types of spirits produced:
Gin, absinthe, malört, herbal liquors and liqueurs, specialty seasonal spirits

Names of spirits:
- Letherbee Gin
- Absinthe Brun (Barrel-Aged)
- Malört Liqueur
- Autumnal Gin
- Vernal Gin

Best known for:
Letherbee Gin

Average bottle price:
Affordable

Distribution:
IL, NY, MA, MN

Photo by Clayton Hauck

Mastermind Vodka

4262 State Route 162
Pontoon Beach, IL 62040
618-512-1039

Owners / Operators:
Carl Levering, President
Chris Egan, Brand Executive
Julie Martin, Controller
Travis McDonald, Asst. Distiller / Tour Coordinator

Email: info@mastermindvodka.com
Website: www.mastermindvodka.com
Facebook: Mastermind Vodka
Twitter: @MastermindVodka

Type: Micro Distillery. Opened in 2011.

Hours of operation:
Tuesday through Saturday, 10 a.m. to 9 p.m.

Tours: Available

Types of spirits produced: Vodka, moonshine

Names of spirits:
- Mastermind Vodka
- LPR Moonshine

Best known for / most popular: Mastermind Vodka

Average bottle price: $27.00 to $35.00

Distribution: IL, MO

Mid-Oak Distillery

4704 W. 147th Street
Midlothian, IL 60445
708-925-9318

Owners / Operators:
Matthew Altman, President / Master Distillery
Dominic D'Ambrosio, Vice President of Marketing

Email: admin@cdvodka.com
Website: www.cdvodka.com
Facebook: Mid-Oak Distillery
   Mid-Oak Distillery Featuring CD Vodka

Type: Micro Distillery. Opened in 2012.

Hours of operation:
Tasting room - Wednesday through Saturday, 5 p.m. to 10 p.m.
       Sunday, noon to 5 p.m.
Distillery operations - Monday and Tuesday

Tours: Available by appointment

Types of spirits produced: Vodka

Names of spirits:
- CD Vodka

Best known for / most popular:
CD Vodka

Average bottle price: $25.00

Distribution: IL, WI

Interesting facts: What's in a name?
The CD on the bottle's label symbolizes the reign of Russia's Catherine the Great in the late 1700s. Catherine allowed only the noble class of Russia to distill vodka in their homes; however, they were not allowed to sell it. With no commercial interest in producing vodka, the focus was on the spirit's quality and so only the most stringent methods of production were followed. Because of this, it is said that the finest vodka in the history of the world was made during Catalina Dynastii or, loosely translated, Catherine's Dynasty.

North Shore Distillery

28913 Herky Drive, Unit 308
Lake Bluff, IL 60044
847-574-2499

Owners / Operators:
Derek Kassebaum, Co-owner
Sonja Kassebaum, Co-owner

Email: tours@northshoredistillery.com
Website: www.northshoredistillery.com
Facebook: North Shore Distillery
Twitter: @NSDistillery

Type: Micro Distillery. Opened in 2004.

Hours of operation: Monday through Friday, 10 a.m. to 6 p.m.

Tours: Available

Types of spirits produced: Vodka, absinthe, gin

Names of spirits:
- Distiller's Gin No. 6
- Distiller's Gin No. 11
- Sirène Absinthe Verte
- North Shore Vodka
- Aquavit Private Reserve
- Sol Chamomile Citrus Vodka

Best known for / most popular: Not provided

Average bottle price: Not provided

Distribution: CA, IA, IL, IN, KY, MN, MO, MT, PA, WI

Interesting facts: Not provided

Premiere Distillery LLC

Gurnee, IL 60031
847-662-4444

Owners / Operators:
Inna Feldman-Gerber, President
Gregory Feldman, Master Distiller

Email: info@premieredistillery.com
Website: www.premieredistillery.com
Facebook: Premiere Distillery
Twitter: @premieredistill
Pinterest: Inna Feldman-Gerber

Type: Micro Distillery. Opened in 2012.

Hours of operation: Vary

Tours: Not available

Types of spirits produced: Vodka

Names of spirits:
- Real Russian Vodka

Best known for / most popular: Real Russian Vodka

Average bottle price: $19.99

Distribution: CA, IL, IN, MI, MO, NY, TN, WI

Interesting facts:
- Third generation master distiller is from Russia
- Only known American vodka handcrafted by real Russians
- Heirloom family recipe that dates back to 1905
- Distilled 6 times from winter wheat
- Filtered 10 times through a proprietary filtration system designed by the master distiller
- Woman-owned distillery

Awards and Recognitions:
- 92 Point, The Tasting Panel Magazine
- 92 Points, Wine Enthusiast
- 2013 Gold Medal, Craft Spirits Awards
- 2013 Gold Medal, Beverly Hills International Spirits Awards
- 2013 & 2012 Silver Medal, San Francisco World Spirits Competition

Quincy Street Distillery

39 E. Quincy Street
Riverside, IL 60546
708-870-5987

Owners / Operators:
Derrick C. Mancini, Owner

Email: manager@quincystreetdistillery.com
Website: www.quincystreetdistillery.com
Facebook: Quincy Street Distillery
Twitter: @QSDistillery

Type: Micro Distillery. Opened in 2012.

Speakeasy cocktail bar and retail shop hours:
Friday, 4 p.m. to 9 p.m.
Saturday, 2 p.m. to 9 p.m.

Tours: $10, Friday to Sunday, reservations required made via website scheduler.

Types of spirits produced:
Gin, whiskey, absinthe, aquavit, honey spirit, liqueur

Names of spirits:
- Water Tower White Lightning™ Un-aged Illinois Corn Whiskey
- Bourbon Spring™ Young Rested Illinois Bourbon Whiskey
- North American Steamship Rye™ Single Malt Rye Whiskey
- Old No. 176™ Railroad Gin
- Old No. 176™ Barrel Reserve Gin
- Prairie Sunshine™ Wildflower Honey Spirit
- Prairie Moonshine™ Corn & Honey Spirit

Best known for: Artisanal spirits crafted with creative historical interpretations

Average bottle price: $22.00 to $56.00

Distribution: IL

Interesting facts:
- The Riverside landmark water tower burned down "like a giant candle" on New Year's Eve one hundred years ago.
- Engine No. 176 was the first to be custom built for the Chicago, Burlington, & Quincy Railroad, and gives its name to our interpretation of Prohibition-era "railroad" gin.
- Bourbon Spring is a historical site near the distillery where in 1834 the Cook County militia was formed with the election of Colonel Beaubien; this is celebrated with bourbon barrels in the spring.

Rhine Hall

2010 W. Fulton Street, Ste. #F-104F
Chicago, IL 60612
312-243-4313

Owners / Operators:
Jenny Solberg, Co-owner
Charlie Solberg, Co-owner / Master Distiller

Email: jenny@rhinehall.com
Website: www.rhinehall.com
Facebook: Rhine Hall
Twitter: @rhinehall

Type: Craft Distillery. Opened in November 2013.

Hours of operation:
Thursdays 5 p.m. to 9 p.m.
Saturdays 2 p.m. to 7 p.m.

Tours: Saturdays, 3 p.m. and 4 p.m.
Reservations recommended via sales@rhinehall.com

Types of spirits produced: Fruit brandy and grappa

Names of spirits:
- Rhine Hall Apple Brandy
- Rhine Hall Oaked Apple Brandy
- Rhine Hall Grappa
- Rhine Hall Oaked Grappa

Best known for / most popular: Fruit brandy

Average bottle price: $29.00 to $60.00

Distribution: On-site tasting room, IL

Services offered other than production: Tours, tastings, private events

Interesting facts: Rhine Hall is a family owned-operated handcraft distillery.

Rumshine Distilling LLC

8 S. Hodge Street
Tilton, IL 61833
217-446-6960

Owners / Operators:
Ernie L. Trinkle II, Owner
L. Tyler Langston Jr., Owner

Website: www.rumshinedistilling.com
Facebook: Rumshine Distilling
Twitter: @_Rumshine

Type: Craft Distillery. Opened in August 2013.

Hours of operation:
Tuesday through Friday, 5 p.m. to 8:30 p.m.
Saturday, noon to 6 p.m.

Tours: Available

Types of spirits produced: Specialty spirits, rum, whiskey

Names of spirits:
- Apple Strudel
- That Purple Stuff
- 8
- Brass
- A Buck and a Quarter

Best known for / most popular: Apple Strudel

Average bottle price: $10.00 to $38.00

Distribution: On-site retail, local distribution

Tailwinds Distilling Company

14912 S. Eastern Avenue, Unit 103
Plainfield, IL 60544
815-290-0786

Owners / Operators:
Toby Beall, Founder / Head Distiller
Brad Beall, Manager
Jillian Beall, Founder
Jamey Beall, Operator/ Manager/ Distiller

Email: info@tailwindsdistilling.com
Website: www.tailwindsdistilling.com
Facebook: Tailwinds Distilling
Twitter: @Tailwinds_Rum

Type: Micro Distillery. Opened in 2012.

Hours of operation:
Friday and Saturday, noon to 8 p.m.; Sunday, noon to 5 p.m.

Tours: Available on Saturdays, 1 p.m. and 3 p.m.

Types of spirits produced: Rum, 100% blue agave spirit

Names of spirits:
- Taildragger White Rum
- Taildragger Amber Rum
- Midnight Caye Silver 100% Blue Agave Spirit
- Midnight Caye Rested 100% Blue Agave Spirit

Best known for / most popular: Taildragger Rum

Average bottle price: $27.00 to $40.00

Distribution: IL

Interesting facts: "Tailwinds" is a sendoff given to pilots...life is just easier with the wind at your back.

Heartland Distillers

9402 Uptown Drive, Ste. 1000
Indianapolis, IN 46256
800-417-0150

Owners / Operators:
Stuart Hobson, Owner / Distiller

Email: stuart@heartlanddistillers.com
Websites: www.heartlanddistillers.com, www.springmillbourbon.com
www.indianavodka.com, www.indianainfusions.com
www.sorgrhum.com
Facebook: Heartland Distillers, Indiana Vodka, Indiana Infusions
Spring Mill Bourbon, Sorgrhum
Twitter: @Indiana_Vodka, @springmillbourb

Type: Micro Distillery. Opened in 2009.

Hours of operation: Closed to the public

Tours: Available by appointment

Types of spirits produced:
Gin, vodka, whiskey, sweet sorghum spirits, bourbon

Names of spirits:
- Heartland Distiller's Reserve Vodka
- Heartland Distiller's Reserve Bourbon
- Indiana Vodka
- Indiana Infusions
- Prohibition Gin
- Spring Mill Straight Bourbon Whiskey
  (90 proof and Cask Strength)
- Sorgrhum White – America's First Sweet Sorghum Spirit
- Sorgrhum Barrel Aged

Best known for: Indiana Vodka

Average bottle price: $17.00 to $25.00

Distribution: Glazers Wholesale, Southern Wine & Spirits

Interesting facts:
- Heartland Distillers is Indiana's first new legal distillery since Prohibition.
- Sorgrhum is produced from Amish harvested and pressed sorghum cane. The sorghum cane is pressed on a horse drawn press and then cooked into a syrup over open wood flames before fermentation and distillation.
- Spring Mill Bourbon is twice barreled in new charred oak and then bottled in ceramic stone bottles.

Huber's Starlight Distillery

19816 Huber Road
Starlight, IN 47106
812-923-9463

Owners / Operators:
Ted Huber, Co-owner
Greg Huber, Co-owner

Email: contactus@huberwinery.com
Website: www.starlightdistillery.com
Facebook: Huber's Orchard & Winery

Type: Winery / Micro Distillery.
Winery opened in 1978. Distillery opened in 2000.

Hours of operation: Daily, noon to 6 p.m.

Tours: Available upon request

Types of spirits produced:
Brandy, grappa, ports, fruit infusions

Names of spirits:
- Starlight Distillery Grappa
- Starlight Distillery Brandy
- Starlight Distillery Apple Brandy
- Starlight Distillery Applejack Brandy
- Starlight Distillery Private Reserve Brandy

Best known for / most popular: Apple Brandy & Applejack

Average bottle price: $20.99 to $59.99

Distribution: IL, IN, KY, MO, OH

Interesting facts:
- Huber's Starlight Distillery primarily uses fruits and grapes grown on their 600 acre estate that was founded in 1843 by their ancestors from Baden-Baden Germany.
- Huber's Starlight Distillery will be expanding their product line in June of 2014 to include vodka, gin, whiskey, and bourbon.

Photo collage by Brianne DeRolph

The Indiana Whiskey Company

1216 W. Sample Street
South Bend, IN 46619
574-855-3453

Owners / Operators:
Charles Florance, President / Distiller
Rich Hall, Brewer
Braden Weldy, Operations Officer

Email: distillery@inwhiskey.com
Website: www.inwhiskey.com
Facebook: The Indiana Whiskey Company
Twitter: @inwhiskey
Google+: inwhiskey

Type: Craft Distillery.
Opened in September 2011.

Hours of operation:
Monday through Friday, 9 a.m. to 5 p.m.

Tours: Available by appointment

Types of spirits produced: Whiskey

Names of spirits:
- The Silver Sweet Corn Whiskey
- The Indiana Straight Leg Infantry Whiskey

Best known for / most popular: Not provided

Average bottle price: $25.00

Distribution: IN

Interesting facts: Not provided

Services offered other than production: Tastings, on-site retail

Virtuoso Distillers LLC

4211 Grape Road
Mishawaka, IN 46545
574-876-4450

Owners / Operators:
Steve Ross, Owner

Email: steve@18vodka.com
Website: www.18vodka.com
Facebook: 18 Vodka
Twitter: @18Vodka

Type: Micro Distillery. Opened in 2008.

Hours of operation: Daily, 10 a.m. to 5 p.m.

Tours: Available by appointment

Types of spirits produced: Vodka, whiskey, lemoncello

Names of spirits:
- 18 Vodka

Best known for: Vodka

Average bottle price: $23.00 to $28.00

Distribution: DC, IL, IN

Interesting facts: 18 Vodka is made from 100% rye.

Broadbent Distillery

6175 50th Avenue
Norwalk, IA 50211
515-981-0011

Owners / Operators:
E. John Broadbent, President

Email: ejab2@aol.com
Website: www.twojaysiowa.com
Facebook: Broadbent Distillery

Type: Micro Distillery. Opened in 2012.

Hours of operation: Vary

Tours: Available by appointment

Types of spirits produced: Whiskey, grappa

Names of spirits:
- Two Jays Corn Whiskey
- Two Jays Corn Whiskey Country Style
- Grappa

Best known for / most popular:
Two Jays Iowa Corn Whiskey Country Style

Average bottle price: $16.00 to $35.00

Distribution: IA

Interesting facts: Broadbent Distillery is Iowa's fourth licensed micro distillery since Prohibition and is the smallest legal distillery in Iowa.

Cedar Ridge Distillery

1441 Marak Road
Swisher, IA 52338
319-857-4300

Owners / Operators:
Jeff Quint, Owner

Email: info@crwine.com
Websites: www.crwine.com, www.clearheartspirits.com, www.crdistillery.com
Facebook: Cedar Ridge Winery & Distillery
Twitter: @CedarRidge4
Yelp: Cedar Ridge Vineyards, Winery and Distillery
YouTube: Cedar Ridge
Instagram: cedarridgevineyards

Type: Winery / Micro Distillery. Opened in 2005.

Hours of operation: Wednesday through Friday from 11 a.m. to 9 p.m.
Saturday and Sunday from 11 a.m. to 5 p.m.

Tours: Available upon request

Types of spirits produced:
Brandy, bourbon whiskey, gin, grappa, liqueur, rum, vodka

Names of spirits:
- ClearHeart Vodka
- ClearHeart Gin
- ClearHeart Light Rum
- Cedar Ridge Dark Rum
- Cedar Ridge Single Malt Whiskey
- Cedar Ridge Iowa Bourbon Whiskey
- Cedar Ridge Apple Brandy
- Cedar Ridge Grape Brandy
- Cedar Ridge Lemoncella (lemon liqueur)
- Cedar Ridge Lamponcella (raspberry liqueur)
- Cedar Ridge Grappa

Best known for / most popular: ClearHeart Vodka

Average bottle price: Not provided

Distribution: IA, IL, MO, NE

Interesting facts: Cedar Ridge Distillery is Iowa's first micro distillery.

Iowa Distilling Company

4349 Cumming Avenue
Cumming, IA 50061
515-981-4216

Owners / Operators:
Todd E. Dunkel, President / Distiller
Phil Bubb, General Counsel / Distiller

Email: info@iowadistilling.com
Website: www.iowadistilling.com
Facebook: Iowa Distilling
Twitter: @IowaDistilling

Type: Craft Distillery. Opened in March 2012.

Hours of operation: Monday through Saturday

Tours & Tastings: Daily, Monday through Friday. Private events are happening each week.

Types of spirits produced: Rum, whiskey

Names of spirits:
- Steel Drum Rum
- Prairie Fire Cinnamon Whiskey
- Iowa Shine Corn Whiskey

Best known for / most popular:
Prairie Fire Cinnamon Whiskey and Steel Drum Rum

Average bottle price: $25.00

Distribution: IA, IL

Interesting facts: Not provided

Services offered other than production:
- Tours, tasting, on-site retail
- Custom distilling and bottling

Mississippi River Distilling Company

303 North Cody Road
LeClaire, IA 52753
563-484-4342

Owners / Operators:
Ryan and Garrett Burchett, Owners

Email: info@mrdistilling.com
Website: www.mrdistilling.com
Facebook: Mississippi River Distilling Company
Twitter: @mrivrdistilling
YouTube: Mississippi River Distilling
Pinterest: Mississippi River Distilling Company

Type: Micro Distillery. Opened in 2010.

Hours of operation:
Monday through Saturday, 10 a.m. to 5 p.m.
Sunday noon to 5 p.m.

Tours: Available

Types of spirits produced: Bourbon whiskey, gin, vodka

Names of spirits:
- River Pilot Vodka
- River Rose Gin
- River Baron Artisan Spirit
- Cody Road Bourbon Whiskey
- Cody Road Rye Whiskey

Best known for / most popular:
River Pilot Vodka

Average bottle price: $25.00 to $30.00

Distribution:
AL, AR, CA, DC, FL, GA, IA, IL, IN, KY, MD, MN, MO, MS, ND, NE, NJ, NY, SC, SD, TN, TX, WI

Interesting facts:
100% of the grain is sourced from within 25 miles of the distillery.

Paradise Distilling Company LLC

245 Railroad Avenue
Dubuque, IA 52003
563-587-8142

Owners / Operators:
Joseph P Berger, Owner

Email: ParadiseDistilling@gmail.com
Website: www.paradisedistilling.com
Facebook: Paradise Distilling Company LLC

Type: Micro Distillery. Opened in March 2014.

Hours of operation:
Friday, 2 p.m. to 8 p.m.
Saturday, 1 p.m. to 7 p.m.
Sunday, 1 p.m. to 5 p.m.

Tours: Available

Types of spirits produced: Rum

Names of spirits:
- Island Bay Rum - a 90 Proof Clear Rum
- Caribbean Mist Rum - a 80 Proof Spiced Rum
- White Sand Rum - a 80 Proof Heavy Oaked rum

Best known for / most popular: Rum

Average bottle price: $28.00 to $38.00

Distribution: Tasting room

Templeton Rye Distillery

209 East 3rd Street
Templeton, IA 51463
712-669-8793

Owners / Operators:
Kevin Boersma, Distillery Manager

Email: info@templetonrye.com
Website: www.templetonrye.com
Facebook: Templeton Rye
Twitter: @TempletonRye
YouTube: Templeton Rye Whiskey

Type: Micro Distillery. Opened in 2005.

Hours of operation: 8 a.m. to 5 p.m.

Tours: Available

Types of spirits produced: Whiskey

Names of spirits:
- Templeton Rye Whiskey

Best known for / most popular: Templeton Rye

Average bottle price: $39.00

Distribution: CA, IA, IL, NY

Interesting facts: Templeton Rye was Al Capone's whiskey of choice.

Werner Distilling LLC

101 N. Hamburg Street
Holstein, IA 51025
712-368-2806

Owners / Operators:
Gregory and Karen Brunelle, Managers

Email: sales@wernerdistilling.com
Facebook: Werner Distilling

Type: Micro Distillery. Opened in 2012.

Hours of operation: Vary

Tours: Available by appointment

Types of spirits produced: Rum

Names of spirits:
- Holstein Rum
- Holstein Coconut Flavored Rum
- Holstein Single Barrel Sippin' Rum

Best known for / most popular:
Holstein Rum

Average bottle price: $20.00 to $25.00

Distribution: IA

Interesting facts: Pictured on the label are Karen's grandfather and great-grandfather working the field on the family farm in 1931.

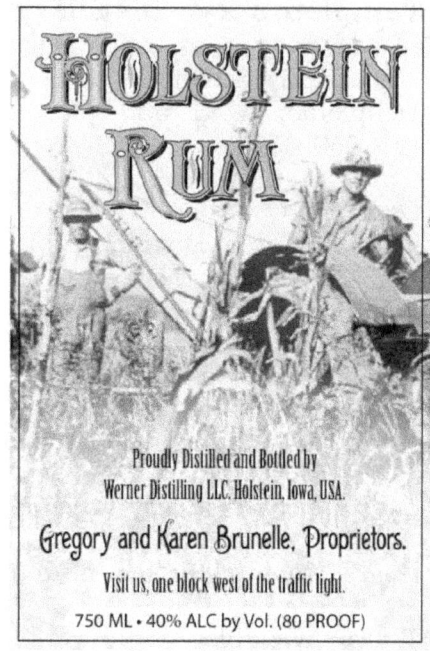

D and J Distilling

3 Leed Road
Winfield, KS 67156

Owners / Operators:
Derek Redenius, Owner / Operator
Cory Brock, Founder / Investor
Jimmy Spillman, Investor
John Eck, Investor

Email: dandjredenius@gmail.com
Website: www.honorvodka.com

Type: Rectifier. Opening in 2014.

Hours of operation: TBA

Tours: TBA

Types of spirits produced: Vodka

Names of spirits:
- Honor Vodka

Best known for / most popular:
Honor Vodka

Average bottle price: $13.00 to $16.00

Distribution: KS

Interesting facts:
Uses NGS to render to 80 proof vodka.

Dark Horse Distillery

11740 West 86th Terrace
Lenexa, KS 66214
913-492-3275

Owners / Operators:
Kris Hennessy, CEO
Damian Garcia, Director of Sales and Marketing
Patrick Garcia, Master Distiller / COO
Eric Garcia, General Manager
Mary Garcia, Director of Special Events

Email: info@dhdistillery.com
Website: www.dhdistillery.com
Facebook: Dark Horse Distillery
Twitter: @DHDistillery
Pinterest: Dark Horse Distillery

Type: Micro Distillery. Opened in 2010.

Hours of operation:
Monday through Friday, 8 a.m. to 5 p.m.

Tours: Available for both public and private

Types of spirits produced: Whiskey, vodka

Names of spirits:
- Long Shot White Whiskey
- Dark Horse Distillery Reunion Rye Whiskey
- Dark Horse Distillery Reserve Bourbon Whiskey
- Rider Vodka

Best known for / most popular:
Dark Horse Reserve Bourbon
Dark Horse Reunion Rye

Average bottle price: $18.00 to $42.00

Distribution: CT, KS, MO, NJ, NY

Interesting facts:
- Dark Horse is family owned and operated.
- Dark Horse sources their grains locally and mills them on site.
- Dark Horse uses the traditional sour mash process in their whiskey production.
- Dark Horse uses an American made, copper column pot still know as Chester Copperpot by the distillers.
- Their spirits have won numerous awards (13 in all) including Double Gold from The Fifty Best for their Dark Horse Reunion Rye and a Gold, 91 point rating from BTI for their Dark Horse Reserve Bourbon.

Dodge City Distillery

11935 S. Blackbob Road
Olathe, KS 66062
620-253-7306

Owners / Operators:
Hayes Kelman, Owner / Operator / Distiller
Brian Marshall, Owner
Roger Kelman, Owner
Rick Marshall, Owner
Chris Holovach, Owner
James Cox, Manager

Email: info@dodgecitydistillery.com
Website: www.dodgedistillery.com
Facebook: Dodge City Distillery
Twitter: @DodgeDistillery

Type: Micro Distillery. Opened in July 2011.

Hours of operation: Daily, 11 a.m. to midnight

Types of spirits produced: Bourbon, vodka

Names of spirits:
- Miss Kitty's Velvet Vodka
- Double Barrel Bourbon

Best known for / most popular: Vodka, bourbon

Average bottle price: $16.00 to $25.00

Distribution: KS

Interesting facts:
Currently, spirits are contract bottled with Good Spirits Distilling. The owners xxpect to relocate and produce independently in 2014.

Services offered other than production:
On-site restaurant

Good Spirits Distilling

2019 E. Spruce Circle, #A
Olathe, KS 66062
913-397-8815

Owners / Operators:
Todd Bukaty, President
Ron Bailey, Vice President

Email: tbukaty@goodspiritsdistilling.com
Website: www.goodspiritsdistilling.com
Facebook: Clear10 Vodka
Twitter: @CLEAR10Vodka

Type: Micro Distillery. Opened in 2008.

Hours of operation: Daily, 9 a.m. to 5 p.m.

Tours: Not available

Types of spirits produced: Vodka, triple sec, flavored vodka, private label

Names of spirits:
- Czar
- CLEAR10 Vodka
- Twister Vodka
- Aeroplano Vodka
- Tailgater's Vodka
- Miss Kitty's Velvet Vodka
- Dizzythree Expresso Vodka
- Dodge City Distillery Bourbon Whiskey

Best known for / most popular: Asian Mahito

Average bottle price: $20.00

Distribution: AR, KS, MO, OK

Interesting facts: CLEAR10 Vodka is gluten free.

Wheat State Distilling

1635 E. 37th Street North, Ste. 6
Wichita, KS 67219
785-341-5755

Owners / Operators:
David Bahre, Owner / Master Distiller
Kim Bahre, Owner

Email: info@wheatstatedistilling.com
Website: www.wheatstatedistilling.com
Facebook: Wheat State Distilling

Type: Craft Distillery. Opened in December 2013.

Hours of operation: Saturday

Tours: Available Saturday by appointment

Types of spirits produced: Whiskey, vodka, gin, bourbon, rum

Names of spirits:
- Wheat State Distilling Gin
- Wheat State Distilling Rum
- Wheat State Distilling Spiced Rum
- Wheat State Distilling Barrel Rested Gin
- Wheat State Distilling Bella Bahre's Bourbon
- Wheat State Distilling Wheat Whiskey
- Wheat State Distilling Wheat Vodka

Best known for / most popular:
Wheat State Distilling Wheat Whiskey
Wheat State Distilling Wheat Vodka

Average bottle price: $25.00 to $65.00

Distribution:
On-site retail, KS

Interesting facts:
- Wichita's first legal distillery.
- Wheat State Distilling is a field to bottle facility.
- Wheat State Distilling operates a custom built still and an automated 2000L still with two 18 foot vodka columns with twin deflegmators.
- Offer quarterly distilling and whiskey workshops.

Barrel House Distilling Co.

1200 Manchester Street
Lexington, KY 40504
859-259-0159

Owners / Operators:
Jeff Wiseman, Owner
Peter Wright, Owner
Frank Marino, Owner

Email: barrelhousedistillery@yahoo.com
Website: www.barrelhousedistillery.com, www.purebluevodka.com
Facebook: Barrel House Distilling Company
Twitter: @DevilJohnShine

Type: Micro Distillery. Opened in 2008.

Hours of operation: Vary

Tours: Available

Types of spirits produced: Moonshine, rum, vodka, whiskey

Names of spirits:
- Pure Blue Vodka
- Devil John Moonshine
- Kentucky Honey (rum)

Best known for / most popular:
The Winchester and the KY Martini

Average bottle price: $20.00 to $25.00

Distribution: DC, IL, KY, MD, TN

Interesting facts:
Barrel House Distilling is spearheading stream and watershed cleanup in Kentucky as a service to its community.

Corsair Artisan Distillery

400 E. Main Street, #110
Bowling Green, KY 42101
270-904-2021

1200 Clinton Street, #110
Nashville, TN 37203
615-200-0320

Owners / Operators:
Darek Bell and Andrew Webber, Owners

Email: info@corsairartisan.com
Website: www.corsairartisan.com
Facebook: Corsair Artisan Distillery
Twitter: @corsairartisan
YouTube: Corsair Artisan

Type: Micro Distillery. Opened TN in 2010. Open KY in 2008.

Hours of operation:

Nashville, TN	Bowling Green, KY
Mon. through Sat., 9 a.m. to 8 p.m.	Mon. through Sat., 8 a.m. to 6 p.m.

Tours: Available
Nashville, TN; Tuesday through Saturday from 3 p.m. to 8 p.m.
Bowling Green, KY; Friday and Saturday from 10 a.m. to 6 p.m.

Types of spirits produced: Gin, rum, absinthe, vodka, whiskeys

Names of spirits:
- Corsair Gin
- Corsair Spiced Rum
- Corsair Red Absinthe
- Corsair Vanilla Vodka
- Corsair Barrel Aged Gin
- Corsair Wry Moon Un-aged Rye Whiskey
- Corsair Triple Smoke Single Malt Whiskey
- Corsair Pumpkin Spice Moonshine
- Corsair Quinoa Whiskey
- Corsair Ryemageddon Whiskey
- Corsair Genever
- Corsair Rasputin Hopped Whiskey

Best known for / most popular: Corsair Triple Smoke Whiskey

Average bottle price: $25.00 to $55.00

Distribution: AK, CA, CO, CT, DC, DE, FL, GA, IL, KY, MD, MI, MO, NC, NJ, NV, NY, OR, TN, TX, WA, WV

Awards and Recognitions:
- 2013 Craft Whiskey of the Year, Whisky Advocate
- 2013 Craft Distillery of the Year, Whisky Magazine
- 2013 Innovator of the Year, Whisky Magazine

E.H. Taylor, Jr. Old Fashioned Copper Distillery
Microstill is located at Buffalo Trace Distillery

113 Great Buffalo Trace
Frankfort, KY 40601
502-223-7641

Owners / Operators:
Buffalo Trace Distillery

Email: info@buffalotrace.com
Website: www.buffalotracedistillery.com
Facebook: Buffalo Trace Distillery
Twitter: @BuffaloTrace
YouTube: Buffalo Trace Distillery

Type: Micro Distillery. Opened in 2009.

Hours of operation:
Monday through Saturday, 9 a.m. to 5:30 p.m.
Sunday (April to October), noon to 5:30 p.m.

Gift shop hours:
Monday through Saturday, 9 a.m. to 5:30 p.m.
Sunday (April to October), noon to 5:30 p.m.

Tours: Five complimentary tours available. See website for details.

Types of spirits produced: Bourbon Whiskey

Names of spirits:
- E.H. Taylor, Jr. Straight Kentucky Bourbon Whiskey

Best known for: E.H. Taylor, Jr. Straight Kentucky Bourbon Whiskey

Average bottle price: Not provided

Distribution: Not provided

Interesting facts: Today, Buffalo Trace Distillery carries on Col. E. H. Taylor Jr's spirit of innovation through its E.H. Taylor Jr. Old Fashioned Copper Distillery, a microstill located on the grounds of Buffalo Trace Distillery. This microstill allows the distillery to conduct experiments on a smaller scale and has received many awards for its creations. The Experimental Collection, as the product line is called, has been responsible for such ground breaking experiments as unique mash bills, various types of wood, and barrel toasts. Currently there are more than 1500 experimental barrels of whiskey aging in the warehouses of Buffalo Trace Distillery.

Kentucky Artisan Distillery

6230 Old Lagrange Road
Crestwood, KY 40014
502-241-3070

Owners / Operators:
Stephen Thompson, Managing Director / Co-owner
Michael Loring, President / Co-owner
Chris Miller, Machinery Operations / Co-owner
Jeremy Dever, Assistant Managing Director
Connor Shaughnessy, Distiller / Lab Operations
Daniel Morgan, Distiller / Mechanical Operations

Email: Not provided
Website: www.whiskeyrow.com
Facebook: The Kentucky Artisan Distillery

Type: Craft Distillery. Opened in 2013.

Hours of operation: TBA

Tours: TBA

Types of spirits produced:
Gin, rum, whiskey, vodka, GNS, infusions

Names of spirits:
- TBA

Best known for / most popular: TBA

Average bottle price: TBA

Distribution: TBA

Interesting facts: Not provided

Services offered other than production:
Contract distilling, bottling, *processing and blending.*

Limestone Branch Distillery

1280 Veterans Memorial Highway
Lebanon, KY 40033
270-699-9004

Owners / Operators:
Steve Beam, Owner
Paul Beam, Owner

Email: steve@limestonebranch.com
Website: www.limestonebranch.com
Facebook: Limestone Branch Distillery
Twitter: @limestonebranch

Type: Micro Distillery. Opened in 2011.

Hours of operation:
Monday through Saturday, 10 a.m. to 5 p.m.; Sunday 1 p.m. to 5 p.m.

Tours: Available

Types of spirits produced: Moonshine

Names of spirits:
- TJ Pottinger Sugar Shine
- TJ Pottinger Kentucky Whiskey
- Revenge

Best known for / most popular:
TJ Pottinger Sugar Shine

Average bottle price: $17.50 to $30.00

Distribution: IN, KY

Interesting facts: Not provided

MB Roland Distillery

137 Barkers Mill Road
Pembroke, KY 42266
270-640-7744

Owners / Operators:
Paul Tomaszewski, Owner
Merry Beth (Roland) Tomaszewski, Owner

Email: info@mbrdistillery.com
Website: www.mbrdistillery.com
Facebook: MB Roland Distillery
Twitter: @MBRDistillery

Type: Micro Distillery. Opened in 2009.

Hours of operation: Tuesday through Saturday, 10 a.m. to 6 p.m.

Tours: Available on the hour, every hour

Types of spirits produced:
Bourbon/whiskey, shine, flavored shines

Names of spirits:
- MBR Kentucky Bourbon Whiskey
- MBR Kentucky Black Patch Whiskey
- MBR Kentucky White Dog
- MBR Kentucky Black Dog
- MBR True Kentucky Shine
- MBR Kentucky Apple Pie
- MBR Kentucky Blueberry Shine
- MBR Kentucky Pink Lemonade
- MBR Kentucky Strawberry Shine
- MBR St. Elmo's Fire
- MBR Kentucky Mint Julep
- MBR Kentucky Blackberry Shine
- MBR Kentucky Dark Cherry Shine

Best known for / most popular:
Kentucky Bourbon Whiskey and Kentucky Black Dog

Average bottle price: $17.00 to $32.00

Distribution: DC, DE, GA, IL, IN, KY, MD, MI, MO, TN

Interesting facts: MB Roland Distillery was built on a former Amish dairy farm.

Old Pogue Distillery

716 W. 2nd Street
Maysville, KY 41056
317-697-5039

Owners / Operators:
Peter H. Pogue, President
Paul K. Pogue, Principal / Head Distiller
John P. Pogue, Sr., Principal / Supervisor Emeritus
John P. Pogue, Jr., Principal / Vice President of Sales and Marketing
Henry E. Pogue V, Principal / Vice President Facilities Management
Robert W. Pogue, Principal / Vice President of Corporate Compliance
John A. Pogue, Partner / Distiller

Email: info@oldpogue.com
Website: www.oldpogue.com
Facebook: Old Pogue Bourbon
Twitter: @OldPogueBourbon

Type: Micro Distillery. Opened in 2011.

Hours of operation: Monday through Friday, 10 a.m. to 4:30 p.m.

Tours: Available by appointment

Types of spirits produced: Bourbon whiskey, rye whiskey

Names of spirits:
- Old Pogue "Master's Select" Kentucky Straight Bourbon
- Limestone Landing Single Malt Rye Un-aged Whiskey
- Old Maysville Club Rye Whiskey
- Five Fathers Pure Rye Whisky

Best known for/ most popular: Old Pogue

Average bottle price: $40.00 to $45.00

Distribution: U.S.; Canada

Interesting facts: The original H.E. Pogue Distillery operated from 1876-1951 with 3 generations of Pogues serving as owners and distillers. The 5th, 6th, and now 7th generation of Pogues, original descendants of H.E. Pogue, have located their micro distillery on the same property as the original distillery. The new distillery was started as a way to carry on the family tradition using all the original recipes from their forefathers.

Silver Trail Distillery

5402 Aurora Highway
Hardin, KY 42048
270-354-6209

Owners / Operators:
Spencer Balentine, Owner

Email: silvertraildistillery@gmail.com
Website: www.lblmoonshine.com
Facebook: Silver Trail Distillery

Type: Micro Distillery. Opened in 2011.

Hours of operation: Not provided

Tours: Not provided

Types of spirits produced: Moonshine

Names of spirits:
- LBL Most Wanted Moonshine

Best known for / most popular:
LBL Most Wanted Moonshine

Average bottle price: Not provided

Distribution: KY

Interesting facts: Not provided

Whiskey Thief Distilling Company

283 Crab Orchard Road
Graefenburg, KY 40601
970-447-8007

Owners / Operators:
Ross Caldwell, Co-owner / Distiller
Heather Caldwell, Co-owner

Email: ross@whiskeythief.us

Type: Micro Distillery. Opened in 2013.

Hours of operation: Daily, 9 a.m. to 5 p.m.

Tours: Available by appointment

Types of spirits produced:
White dog, flavored white dog

Names of spirits:
- Foggy Dog Whiskey
- White Dog Whiskey

Best known for / most popular: Not provided

Average bottle price: $19.00 to $29.00

Distribution: KY, OH

Interesting facts:
- The "Still House" is built in the style of a Kentucky Tobacco barn.
- Bourbon recipe is used for all White Dog spirits.
- Plan to release an uncut, unfiltered aged spirit in six or seven years.

Wilderness Trace Distillery

445 Roy Arnold Avenue
Danville, KY 40422
859-402-8707

Owners / Operators:
Shane Baker, Master Distiller
Pat Heist, Master Distiller
Mike Heist, Distillery / Operator
Jerod Smith, Tours
Melissa Baker, Accounts / Gift Shop

Email: inquiries@wildernesstraceky.com
Website: www.wildernestracedistillery.com
Facebook: Wilderness Trace Distillery
Twitter: @WTDistillery
Instagram: WildernessTraceDistillery
YouTube: Wilderness Trace Distillery

Type: Micro Distillery. Opened in November 2013.

Hours of operation:
Monday through Friday, 10 a.m. to 4 p.m.;
Saturday, 10 a.m. to 4 p.m.

Tours: Available Wednesday through Saturday, on the hour from 10 a.m. to 3 p.m.

Types of spirits produced:
Bourbon, whiskey, rum, vodka

Names of spirits:
- Blüe Heron Premium Vodka
- Settlers Select Rye Whiskey
- Harvest Rum Bourbon Barrel Aged
- Kentucky Straight Bourbon

Best known for / most popular:
Harvest Rum Bourbon Barrel Aged

Average bottle price: $20.00 to $45.00

Distribution: On-site retail, expanding in 2014.

Interesting facts:
- Member of the Kentucky Bourbon Trail Craft Tour.
- All grain is locally sourced from a family farm.
- All products are unfiltered.

Willett Distillery

1869 Loretto Road
Bardstown, KY 40004
502-348-0899

Owners / Operators:
Mr. Even Kulsveen, Executive Director

Email: visitorcenter@willettdistillery.com
Website: www.willettdistillery.com
Facebook: Willett Distillery
Twitter: @WillettWhiskey

Type: Micro Distillery. Opened in 1936.

Hours of operation:
Gift shop - Monday through Friday, 9 a.m. to 4:30 p.m.
   Saturday, 10 a.m. to 3:30 p.m.
   Sunday, noon to 3:30 p.m. (April - December)

Tours: Available April through December

Types of spirits produced: Bourbon, rye whiskey

Names of spirits:
- Willett Pot Still Reserve Bourbon
- Willett Family Estate Bottled Bourbon
- Willett Family Estate Bottled Rye
- Rowan's Creek
- Noah's Mill
- Johnny Drum Private Stock

Best known for / most popular:
Willett Pot Still Reserve Bourbon

Average bottle price: $15.00 to $300.00

Distribution: AZ, CA, CO, CT, DC, DE, FL, GA, HI, IL, IN, KY, LA MA, MD, MI*, MN, MO, MT*, NC*, NJ, NV, NY, OR, PA, SC, TN, TX, VA*, WA, WI, WY*

(* denotes a state where they do not have a distributor, but still deliver product via special orders.)

Atelier Vie

1001 S. Broad Street
New Orleans, LA 70125
504-813-4700

Owners / Operators:
Jedd Haas, President
Brennan Steele, Ambassador
Skylar Rosenbloom, Chief Bean Hunter
Amelia Walch, The Gold Standard

Email: jedd@ateliervie.com
Website: www.ateliervie.com
Facebook: Atelier Vie, LLC
Twitter: @AtelierVie
YouTube: Atelier Vie

Type: Micro Distillery. Opened in 2012.

Hours of operation:
Bottle Sales Hours are now every weekend. Hours vary throughout the year, but generally are 10 a.m. to 2 p.m. See the Visit page of their website for details and directions (don't trust GPS!).

Tours: Tours aren't officially offered due to the small size of the facility. Once you're inside, you've seen the whole distillery.

Types of spirits produced: Vodka, abinsthe, whiskey, gin

Names of spirits:
- Toulouse Red, Absinthe Rouge
- Toulouse Green, Absinthe Verte
- Riz, Louisiana Rice Whiskey
- Buck 25 Vodka
- Euphrosine Gin #9

Best known for / most popular: Toulouse Red, Toulouse Green, Riz

Average bottle price: $20.00 to $60.00

Distribution: AR, DC, IL, LA

Interesting facts:
- Toulouse Green, a new traditional-style absinthe verte, is made with locally grown wormwood. Seeds were distributed to area farmers with the first harvests over the summer of 2013. This commitment to use local ingredients took a year to yield results.
- Riz, a Louisiana Rice Whiskey, is distilled from 100% Louisiana rice obtained from an area rice mill. Riz is officially recognized as whiskey by the TTB and is a distinctive product of Louisiana.
- Euphrosine Gin #9, is a contemporary-style American gin and won a Gold Medal at the 2013 American Craft Distillers Association spirits competition.

Cajun Spirits Distillery

2532 Poydras Street
New Orleans, LA 70119
504-875-3592

Owners / Operators:
Gus Haik, Owner / Operator / Distiller

Email: gus@cajunspirits.com
Website: www.cajunspirits.com
Facebook: TBA
Twitter: @cajunspirits

Type: Micro Distillery. Opened in January 2014.

Hours of operation: TBA

Tours: Available by reservation. Please call.

Types of spirits produced: Rum, vodka, gin

Names of spirits:
- Tresillo Rum
- Crescent Vodka
- 3rd Ward Gin

Best known for / most popular: Not provided

Average bottle price: Not provided

Distribution: On-site retail, Southeast LA

Interesting facts:
- In an industrial corner of the 3rd Ward, you'll find the Cajun Spirits Distillery, where they take the raw materials provided by Louisiana's agricultural bounty and produce top-quality spirits.
- All of their spirits start with 100% Louisiana sugarcane specifically chosen for each spirit. They then ferment the select sugarcane juice using a proprietary yeast strain, which helps yield their distinct flavors.

Celebration Distillation

2815 Frenchmen Street
New Orleans, LA 70122
504-945-9400

Owners / Operators:
James Michalopoulos, Founder / Owner
Jim Colwell, General Manager
Erick Lewko, Sales Manager
Jason Coleman, Marketing Manager

Email: info@oldneworleansrum.com
Website: www.oldneworleansrum.com
Facebook: Old New Orleans Rum
Myspace: Old New Orleans Rum
Twitter: @NewOrleansRum

Type: Micro Distillery. Opened in 1995.

Hours of operation:
Monday through Friday, 9 a.m. to 5 p.m.
Saturday, 1:30 p.m. to 5 p.m.

Tours: Available

Types of spirits produced: Rum

Names of spirits:
- Old New Orleans Crystal Rum
- Old New Orleans Amber Rum
- Old New Orleans Cajun Spice Rum
- Old New Orleans 10 Year Rum
- Gingeroo – an Old New Orleans Rum Bottled Cocktail

Best known for / most popular: Old New Orleans Cajun Spice Rum

Average bottle price: $17.00 to $21.00

Distribution: CA, FL, IL, LA, MI, MO, MS, NC, NE, NY, VA, WI

Interesting facts:
- Celebration Distillation is the oldest continuously licensed and operating rum distillery in the continental United States.
- Cajun Spice Rum has been the highest rated flavored rum four years in a row from 2007 to 2010 by the Beverage Testing Institute.
- In 2012 Celebration Distillation partnered with a local sugar cane mill to install a pump and pipeline to extract B-cut molasses from the milling process. Using the B-cut molasses has produced a more flavorful and fully integrated rum.

Donner-Peltier Distillers

1635 St. Patrick Highway
Thibodaux, LA 70301
985-446-0002

Owners / Operators:
Tom Donner, Co-owner
Elizabeth Donner, Co-owner
Henry M. Peltier, Co-owner
Jennifer N. Peltier, Co-owner
Taryn Clement, Distillery Manager

Email: info@dpdspirits.com
Website: www.dpdspirits.com
Facebook: Donner-Peltier Distillers
Twitter: @DonnerPeltier

Type: Micro Distillery. Opened in 2012.

Hours of operation:
Monday through Saturday, noon to 6 p.m.

Tours: Available. Monday through Saturday at 4 p.m.

Types of spirits produced: Vodka, rum, gin, whiskey

Names of spirits:
- Oryza Vodka
- Oryza Gin
- Rougaroux Sugarshine Rum
- Rougaroux Full Moon Dark Rum
- Rougaroux 13 Pennies Praline Rum
- LA 1 Whiskey

Best known for / most popular:
Not provided

Average bottle price: Not provided

Distribution: KY, LA, MT

Awards and Recognitions:
Rougaroux Sugarshine won Double Gold, 2013 San Francisco Spirits Competition.

Lifted Spirits LLC
Yvelise Limoncello

3169 Law Street
New Orleans, LA 70117
504-298-9451

Owners / Operators:
Mark C. Stevens, Owner
Thomas Rush, Manager
Michael Szczachor, Chief Engineer

Email: info@yveliselimoncello.com
Website: www.yveliselimoncello.com
Facebook: Yvelise Limoncello
Twitter: @YveLimoncello
Pinterest: Yvelise Limoncello
Instagram: Yvelise Limoncello

Type: Micro Distillery. Opening in 2015.

Hours of operation: TBA

Tours: Available

Types of spirits produced: Liqueurs

Names of spirits:
- Yvelise Limoncello

Best known for / most popular: Not provided

Average bottle price: $19.00 to $24.00

Distribution: LA

Copyright 2014, Yvelise Limoncello. All Rights Reserved.
Yvelise™ is a registered trademark of Lifted Spirits, LLC

Louisiana Spirits LLC

20909 S. I-10 Frontage Road
Lacassine, LA 70650

Owners / Operators:
Tim Litel, Co-founder
Skip Cortese, Co-founder
Trey Litel, Co-founder

Email: info@laspirits.net
Website: www.laspirits.net, www.bayourum.com
Facebook: Louisiana Spirits, Bayou Rum
Twitter: @BayouRum

Type: Micro Distillery. Opened in June 2013.

Hours of operation: Call for reservations

Tours: Available Tuesday through Sunday

Types of spirits produced: Rum

Names of spirits:
- Silver Bayou Rum
- Spiced Bayou Rum

Best known for / most popular: Bayou Rum

Average bottle price: TBA

Distribution: Republic National Distributing Co.

Interesting facts: Bayou Rum is handmade using 100% natural Louisiana cane sugar and molasses in a traditional pot still.

Rank Wildcat Spirits LLC

619 Bonin Road
Lafayette, LA 70508
337-257-3385

Owners / Operators:
David C. Meaux, Founder / Co-owner / Distiller
Cole G. LeBlanc, Founder / Co-owner / Distiller
David J. Buchholz, Co-owner
Kevin R. Guarino, Co-owner
John B. Sledge III, Co-owner

Email: davidcmeaux@rankwildcat.com
colegleblanc@rankwildcat.com
Website: www.rankwildcat.com
Facebook: Rank Wildcat Spirits, LLC
YouTube: Rank Wildcat Spirits, LLC

Type: Micro Distillery. Opened in 2011.

Hours of operation: Non-traditional

Tours: Upon request

Types of spirits produced: Rum

Names of spirits:
- Sweet Crude Rum

Best known for / most popular: Sweet Crude Rum

Average bottle price: $19.00 to $22.00

Distribution: LA

Interesting facts:
- Rank Wildcat Spirits, LLC is Acadiana's first micro-distillery and is the second licensed rum distillery to open in Louisiana. Additionally, Rank Wildcat Spirits is solely owned and operated by two Acadiana locals. They built everything from the ground up including their one-of-a-kind stainless steel and copper still they named Lulu.
- Having no high-dollar investors, government aid or industrial professionals to grease the wheels, Rank Wildcat is truly a "grass roots" Acadiana project.

VooDoo Distillery
Soc Au Lait Distillerie

301 N. Claiborne Avenue
New Orleans, LA 70112
866-827-2124

Owners / Operators:
Ian Nygren, Owner / Operator

Email: info@neworleansvodkas.com
Website: www.seersuckervodka.com
Facebook: Seersucker Vodka, Voo Doo Distillery

Type: Micro Distillery. Founded in 2009, opened in March 2014.

Hours of operation: Closed to the public

Tours: Not available

Types of spirits produced: Vodka

Names of spirits:
- Seersucker Vodka

Best known for / most popular: Not provided

Average bottle price: $25.00

Distribution: LA

Interesting facts: One of the first micro distilleries in New Orleans.

Artisan Distillery LLC

1487 Main Street
Oxford, ME 04270
207-744-9323

Owners / Operators:
Stuart Littlefield, Owner / Distiller

Email: stuart@adistillery.com
Website: www.adistillery.com

Type: Craft Distillery. Opened in June 2010.

Hours of operation:
Monday through Friday, 10 a.m. to 4 p.m.

Tours: Available by appointment

Types of spirits produced:
Whiskey, rum, vodka, fruit brandies, liquors

Names of spirits:
- Columbian Dark Roast Brandy
- Hazelnut Coffee Brandy
- French Vanilla Coffee Brandy

Best known for / most popular: Not provided

Average bottle price: $12.00 to $24.99

Distribution: ME

Interesting facts: Artisan Distillery LLC operates one of the only vacuum distilling systems in the country. They are able to distill at very low temperatures which protects delicate flavor notes.

Maine Distilleries LLC

437 U.S. Route 1
Freeport, ME 04032
207-865-4828

Owners / Operators:
Chris Dowe, Owner / CEO
Lee Thibodeau, Owner
Don Thibodeau, Owner
Bob Harkins, Owner

Email: info@coldrivervodka.com
Website: www.mainedistilleries.com
Facebook: Maine Distilleries
Twitter: @MaineSpirits

Type: Micro Distillery. Opened in 2005.

Hours of operation: Daily, 6 a.m. to 11 p.m.

Tours: Available

Types of spirits produced: Vodka, gin

Names of spirits:
- Cold River Classic Vodka
- Cold River Blueberry Vodka
- Cold River Gin

Best known for / most popular: Cold River Classic Vodka

Average bottle price: $27.99 to $38.99

Distribution: CO, CT, DC, DE, GA, ID, IN, MA, MD, ME, MT, NC, NJ, OR, PA, RI, TN, WY; Great Britain, Ireland and the western provinces of Canada.

Interesting facts:
- Spirits are gluten free
- Spirits are certified Kosher

New England Distilling

26 Evergreen Drive, Unit B
Portland, ME 04103
207-878-9759

Owners / Operators:
Ned Wight, Owner / Distiller
Tim Fisher, Owner / Distiller

Email: info@newenglanddistilling.com
Website: www.newenglanddistilling.com
Facebook: New England Distilling
Twitter: @NEDistilling

Type: Micro Distillery. Opened in 2012.

Hours of operation: Mon. through Fri., noon to 5 p.m.; Sat., 10 a.m. to 3 p.m.

Tours: Available Mon. through Fri., noon to 4 p.m.; Sat. 10 a.m. to 3 p.m.

Types of spirits produced: Gin, whiskey, rum

Names of spirits:
- Ingenium Gin
- Eight Bells Rum
- Gunpowder Rye Whiskey

Best known for / most popular: Ingenium Gin

Average bottle price: Not provided

Distribution: CT, MA, ME, NY

Interesting facts:
Handcrafted on 150 years and six generations of family tradition.

Northern Maine Distilling Company

55 Baker Boulevard, Ste. 22
Brewer, ME 04412
207-974-3055

Owners / Operators:
Scott Galbiati, Co-owner
Jessica Jewell, Co-owner

Email: scott@twenty2vodka.com
Website: www.twenty2vodka.com
Facebook: Twenty2
Twitter: @Twenty2Vodka
Pinterest: Scott @ Twenty2 Vodka
Tumblr: Twenty2vodka
Flickr: Twenty2Vodka

Type: Micro Distillery. Opened in 2009.

Hours of operation: Not provided

Tours: Not provided

Types of spirits produced: Vodka

Names of spirits:
- Twenty 2 Vodka
- Twenty 2 Create*
  *(150 proof neutral spirit designed for infusing)

Best known for / most popular:
Twenty 2 Vodka

Average bottle price: $26.99

Distribution: DC, MD, ME, NH, NJ

Interesting facts: Not provided

Spirits of Maine Distillery

175 Chicken Mill Road
Gouldsboro, ME 04607
207-546-2408

Owners / Operators:
Robert and Kathe Bartlett, Owners

Email: info@bartlettwinery.com
Website: www.bartlettwinery.com
Facebook: Bartlett Maine Estate Winery

Type: Winery / Micro Distillery. Opened in 2007.

Hours of operation:
Open June to mid-October - Monday through Saturday, 10 a.m. to 5 p.m.
Closed Sundays and holidays
Open by appointment after season

Tours: Not available

Types of spirits produced: Brandy, eau de vie, rum, geist

Names of spirits:
- Fine Apple Brandy
- Pear Eau de Vie
- Peach Eau de Vie
- Honey Eau de Vie
- Raspberry Geist
- Light Rum and Dark Rum

Best known for / most popular:
Pear Eau de Vie

Average bottle price: $30.00 to $40.00

Distribution: ME

Interesting facts:
- Bartlett Maine Estate Winery became Maine's first licensed winery in 1982.
- Spirits of Maine Distillery became Maine's second distillery in 2007.

Sweetgrass Farm Winery & Distillery

Farm Winery & Distillery
347 Carroll Road
Union, ME 04862
207-785-3024

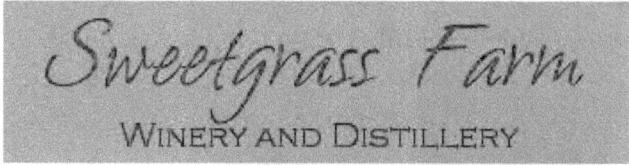

Sweetgrass Farm Winery & Distillery Gin Room
324 Fore Street
Portland, ME 04101
207-761-8446

Owners / Operators:
Keith and Constance Bodine, Owners

Email: info@sweetgrasswinery.com
Website: www.sweetgrasswinery.com
          www.backrivergin.com
Facebook: Back River Gin
          Sweetgrass Farm Winery & Distillery
Twitter: @BackRiverGin

Type: Winery / Micro Distillery. Opened in 2005.

Hours of operation:
Union, ME - Daily, 11 a.m. to 5 p.m. (Mid-May to December 31)
Portland, ME – Year round

Tours: Available

Types of spirits produced:
Gin, rum, apple brandy, whiskey, liqueurs, wines, vanilla extract, bitters, fortified wines

Names of spirits:
- Back River Gin
- Three Crow Rum
- Cranberry Gin
- Maple Smash Liqueur
- Vermouth

Best known for / most popular:
Back River Gin

Average bottle price: $12.00 to $34.00

Distribution: ME

Tree Spirits

152 Fairfield Street
Oakland, ME 04963
207-861-2723

Owners / Operators:
Bruce Olson, Co-owner
Karen Heck, Co-owner

Email: bruce@treespiritsofmaine.com
Website: www.treespiritsofmaine.com
Facebook: Tree Spirits

Type: Micro Distillery. Opened in 2010.

Hours of operation: Vary
Check social media for current schedule.

Tours: Available

Types of spirits produced: Applejack, brandy, absinthe

Names of spirits:
- Tree Spirits Applejack
- Tree Spirits Knotted Maple
- Tree Spirits Pear Brandy
- Tree Spirits Absinthe (March 2014)

Best known for / most popular:
Maple spirit distilled from maple wine and absinthe

Average bottle price: $35.00

Distribution: ME

Interesting facts:
- All spirits except absinthe, have won double gold, silver and bronze medals, in international competitions.
- All spirits are produced from Tree Spirits' wine made from locally sourced apples, pears and maple syrup.

hand crafted wine and distilled spirits

Wiggly Bridge Distillery

19 Railroad Avenue
York Beach, ME 03909
207-363-9322

Owners / Operators:
David Woods and David Woods II
Managing Members

Email: info@wigglybridgedistillery.com
Website: www.wigglybridgedistillery.com
Facebook: Wiggly Bridge Distillery
Twitter: @wigglybridgedistillery

Type: Craft Distillery. Opened in July 2013.

Hours of operation: Daily, 10 a.m. to 4 p.m.

Tours: Available by appointment

Types of spirits produced:
Bourbon, rum, whiskey, vodka

Names of spirits:
- Wiggly Bridge Bourbon
- Wiggly Bridge Rum
- Wiggly Bridge Whiskey
- Wiggly Bridge Vodka

Best known for / most popular: Not provided

Average bottle price: Not provided

Distribution: On-site retail

Interesting facts:
The Wiggly Bridge is the world's smallest pedestrian suspension bridge.

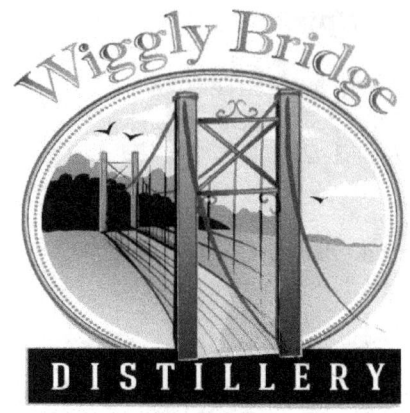

Blackwater Distilling Inc.

184 Log Canoe Circle
Stevensville, MD 21666
443-249-3123

Owners / Operators:
Christopher Cook, CEO
Jon Cook, COO
Mark Troxler, VP of Business Development
Jon Blair, Production Manager

Email: info@blackwaterdistilling.com
Website: www.blackwaterdistilling.com, www.sloopbetty.com
Facebook: Sloop Betty, Blackwater Distilling
Twitter: @sloopbetty
YouTube: Sloop Betty TV
LinkedIn: Sloop Betty Vodka

Type: Micro Distillery. Opened in 2010.

Hours of operation: Not provided

Tours: Not available

Types of spirits produced: Vodka

Names of spirits:
- Sloop Betty

Best known for / most popular: Sloop Betty

Average bottle price: $29.99

Distribution: DC, DE, MD

Interesting facts:
Blackwater Distilling is the first licensed distillery in MD in nearly 40 years.

Fiore Winery & Distillery

3026 Whiteford Road
Pylesville, MD 21132
410-879-4007, 410-452-0132

Owners / Operators:
Mike Fiore, Owner
Rose Fiore, Owner
Eric Fiore, Owner

Email: mike.fiore@fiorewinery.com
Website: www.fiorewinery.com
Facebook: Fiore Winery
Twitter: @FioreWinery

Type: Winery / Micro Distillery. Opened in 2009.

Hours of operation:
Monday through Saturday, 10 a.m. to 5 p.m.; Sunday, noon to 5 p.m.

Tours: Available

Types of spirits produced: Brandy, grappa, limoncello

Names of spirits:
- Fiore Grappa
- Fiore Limoncello

Best known for / most popular:
Wine and grappa

Average bottle price: $15.00 to $25.00

Distribution: MD

Interesting facts: Not provided

Lyon Distilling Company

605 S. Talbot Street, #6
Saint Michaels, MD 21663
443-333-9181

Owners / Operators:
Ben Lyon, Owner / Distiller
Jaime Windon, Owner

Email: liquor@lyondistilling.com
Website: www.lyondistilling.com
Facebook: Lyon Distilling Company

Type: Craft Distillery. Opened in December 2013.

Hours of operation: Tastings, tours, sales; Daily noon to 6 p.m.

Tours: Private tours available by appointment

Types of spirits produced:
Rum, whiskey, moonshine

Names of spirits:
- Lyon Distilling Company Rum
- Maryland Free State Rye Whiskey

Best known for / most popular: Rum

Average bottle price: $33.00 to $99.00

Distribution: On-site retail, MD

Interesting facts:
"We are Maryland's first craft distillery." - Ben Lyon

Berkshire Mountain Distillers Inc.

Great Barrington, MA 01230
413-229-0219

Owners / Operators:
Chris Weld, Owner

Email: cweld@berkshiremountaindistillers.com
Website: www.berkshiremountaindistillers.com
Facebook: Berkshire Mountain Distillers
Twitter: @BerkshireMtDist

Type: Micro Distillery. Opened in 2007.

Hours of operation: Open for tours Summer 2014

Tours: See above

Types of spirits produced:
Vodka, gin, bourbon, corn whiskey, rum, bitters

Names of spirits:
- Greylock Gin
- Ethereal Gin
- Barrel Aged Ethereal Gin
- Ragged Mountain Rum
- Ice Glen Vodka
- Berkshire Bourbon
- New England Corn Whiskey
- Cocktail Kingdom Bitters

Best known for / most popular: Greylock Gin

Average bottle price: $25.99 to $45.99

Distribution: Available in more than 20 states

Interesting facts:
Berkshire Mountain Distillers is the Berkshire's first legal distillery since prohibition and located in a renovated 1950 hay barn that sits in the midst of an apple orchard.

Bully Boy Distillers

35 Cedric Street
Boston, MA 02119
617-442-6000

Owners / Operators:
Will Willis, Co-owner
Dave Willis, Co-owner

Email: info@bullyboydistillers.com
Website: www.bullyboydistillers.com
Facebook: Bully Boy Distillers
Twitter: @bullyboybooze
Blog: bullyboydistillers.blogspot.com

Type: Micro Distillery. Opened in 2010.

Hours of operation: Open for tours

Tours: Available by appointment

Types of spirits produced: Vodka, whiskey, rum

Names of spirits:
- Bully Boy Vodka
- Bully Boy Boston Rum
- Bully Boy Bully Boy White Rum
- Bully Boy White Whiskey
- Bully Boy American Straight Whiskey

Best known for / most popular: Bully Boy Boston Rum

Average bottle price: Not provided

Distribution: MA, NH, RI

Interesting facts:
The distillery is named after Bully Boy, a favorite farm workhorse.

Cape Cod Distilling Company LLC

92 Barnstable Road
Hyannis, MA 02601
508-428-2882

Owners / Operators:
Rick Wrightson, Managing Director
Skip Wrightson, Distiller
Rachel Wrightson, Store Manager

Email: rick@capecodwhisky.com
Website: www.capecodwhisky.com
Facebook: Cape Cod Whisky
Twitter: @CapeCodWhisky

Type: Craft Distillery.
Currently under construction.

Hours of operation:
Monday through Saturday

Tours: Not currently available

Types of spirits produced:
Moonshine, single malt whisky

Names of spirits:
- Massachusetts Moonshine
- Old Barnstable American Single Malt Whisky

Best known for / most popular: Old Barnstable American Single Malt Whisky

Average bottle price: TBA

Distribution: TBA

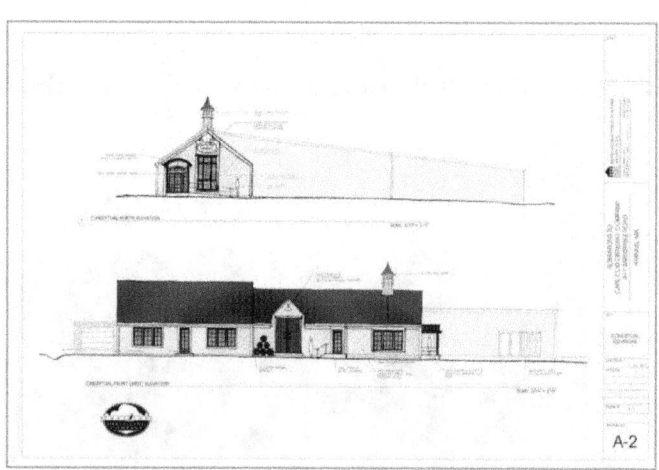

Damnation Alley Distillery

7 Brighton Street
Belmont, MA 02478
617-932-1360

Owners / Operators:
Alison DeWolfe, Ministry of Propaganda
Jeremy Gotsch, Ministry of Dreams
Jessica Gotsch, Ministry of Ecology
Alex Thurston, Ministry of Yeast Ranching
Emma Thurston, Ministry of Indecision

Email: info@damnationalleydistillery.com
Website: www.damnationalleydistillery.com
Facebook: Damnation Alley Distillery
Twitter: @damndistillery
Instagram: @damndistillery

Type: Micro Distillery. Opened in April 2013.

Hours of operation:
Wednesday and Thursday, 4 p.m. to 8 p.m.
Friday, 4 p.m. to 9 p.m.
Saturday, noon to 8 p.m.
Sunday, noon to 5 p.m.

Tours: Not available

Types of spirits produced: Whiskey, vodka, bourbon

Names of spirits:
- Nick the Sipper
  (a gently filtered vodka)
- The Re-Mixer (Vodka)
- One Night in Bangkok Flavored Vodka
  (sweet Thai chili pepper vodka)
- Massachusetts Whiskey
  (aged and white)

Best known for / most popular: Nick the Sipper

Average bottle price: $35.00 to $100.00

Distribution: On-site retail

Interesting facts:
"We're unique in that we don't use a single ingredient from out of state, including all of our grain, which is actually quite difficult to do." - Emma Thurston

Dirty Water Distillery

10 Water Street
Plymouth, MA 02360
508-927-3260

Owners / Operators:
Steve Neidhardt, Owner / Distiller / Miscreant
Petras "Pepi" Avizonis, Owner / Distiller / Miscreant

Email: info@dirtywaterdistillery.com
Website: www.dirtywaterdistillery.com
Facebook: Dirty Water Distillery
Twitter: @LoveDirtyWater

Type: Craft Distillery. Opened in April 2013.

Hours of operation: Daily, 10 a.m. to 6 p.m.

Tours: Available

Types of spirits produced: Rum, liqueur, gin, vodka

Names of spirits:
- What Knot White Rum
- Velnias Spiced Honey Liqueur
- Bog Monster Gin
- Dirty Water Cranberry Vodka
- Dirty Water Clementine Vodka

Best known for / most popular: The Knotty Toddy

Average bottle price: $19.99 to $27.99

Distribution: On-site retail, MA

Interesting facts:
All label artwork is done by local tattoo artist Tony Ciavarro, owner of Stinky Monkey Tattoos in Kingston, MA.

GrandTen Distilling

383 Dorchester Avenue
Boston, MA 02127
617-269-0497

Owners / Operators:
Spencer McMinn, Co-founder
Matthew Nuernberger, Co-founder

Email: info@grandten.com
Website: www.grandten.com
Facebook: GrandTen Distilling
Twitter: @GrandTen

Type: Micro Distillery. Opened in 2012.

Hours of operation: Not provided

Tours: Saturday, noon to 4 p.m., or by appointment

Types of spirits produced: Rum, vodka, gin, liqueur

Names of spirits:
- Wire Works American Gin
- Wire Works Special Reserve Gin
- Fire Puncher Vodka
- Fire Puncher Black Vodka
 (Barrel aged pepper vodka, infused with Taza Chocolate)
- South Boston Irish Whiskey
- Angelica - Botanical Liqueur
- Amandine - Barrel Aged Almond Liqueur
- Craneberry - Massachusetts Cranberry Liqueur

Best known for / most popular:
Wire Works American Gin

Average bottle price: $25.00 to $35.00

Distribution: CT, MA, PA, WA

Interesting facts:
Distillery is housed in an old Boston iron foundry.

Nashoba Valley Spirits Ltd.

100 Wattaquadoc Hill Road
Bolton, MA 01740
978-779-5521

Email: email@nashobawinery.com
Website: www.nashobawinery.com
Facebook: Nashoba Valley Winery
Twitter: @NashobaWinery

Type: Winery / Farm Distillery. Opened in 2003.

Hours of operation: Monday through Friday, 10 a.m. to 5 p.m.

Tours: Available on weekends

Types of spirits produced: Vodka, brandies, eau de vie, cordials

Names of spirits:
- Foggy Bog Brandy
- Nashoba Vodka
- Cherry Eau de vie
- Vidal Grappa
- Raspberry Eau de vie
- Elephant Heart Plum-infused Brandy
- Silk Peach Brandy
- Apple Brandy
- Elderberry Brandy
- Baerenfang Fruit and Honey Blended Brandy
- Northern Comfort Brandy
- Johnny Hop Appl and Hop flower-infused Brandy
- Nashoba Single-malt Whiskey

Best known for / most popular: Foggy Bog Brandy

Average bottle price: $21.00 to $26.00

Distribution: Not provided

Interesting facts: Not provided

Privateer Rum

28 Mitchell Road
Ipswich, MA 01938
978-356-0477

Owners / Operators:
Andrew Cabot, Owner

Email: info@privateerrum.com
Website: www.privateerrum.com
Facebook: Privateer Rum
Twitter: @PrivateerRum

Type: Micro Distillery. Opened in 2011.

Hours of operation: Not provided

Tours: Not provided

Types of spirits produced: Rum

Names of spirits:
- Privateer Silver Reserve Rum
- Privateer True American Rum

Best known for / most popular: Not provided

Average bottle price: Not provided

Distribution: MA

Interesting facts: Not provided

Ryan & Wood Inc.

15 Great Republic Drive
Gloucester, MA 01930
978-281-2282

Owners / Operators:
Bob Ryan and Dave Wood, Owners
Kathy Ryan and Maryann Wood, Owners

Email: Bob Ryan: bob@ryanandwood.com
Kathy Ryan: kathy@ryanandwood.com
Website: www.ryanandwood.com
Facebook: Ryan & Wood Inc., Distilleries
Twitter: @ryanandwood

Type: Micro Distillery. Opened in 2006.

Hours of operation: Daily, 8 a.m. to 5 p.m.

Tours: Available

Types of spirits produced: Gin, rum, vodka, whiskey

Names of spirits:
- Beauport Vodka
- Folly Cove Rum
- Knockabout Gin
- Ryan & Wood Straight Rye Whiskey
- Ryan & Wood Straight Wheat Whiskey

Best known for: Knockabout Gin

Average bottle price: $28.00

Distribution: MA

Interesting facts: Not provided

Triple Eight Distillery

5 Bartlett Farm Road
Nantucket, MA 02554
508-325-5929

Owners / Operators:
Jay Harman, Owner
Dean Long, Owner
Randy Hudson, Owner

Email: jay@ciscobrewers.com
Website: www.ciscobrewers.com/distillery
Facebook: Cisco Brewers Nantucket
Twitter: @ciscobrewers

Type: Micro Distillery. Opened in 2000.

Hours of operation: Daily, 10 a.m. to 7 p.m.

Tours: Available by appointment

Types of spirits produced:
Gin, rum, notch single malt whisky, vodka

Names of spirits:
- Triple Eight Vodka
- Hurricane Rum
- Gale Force Gin
- Notch Single Malt Whisky

Best known for / most popular: Triple Eight Vodka

Average bottle price: Not provided

Distribution: CO, MA

Interesting facts:
One of the first micro distilleries in Massachusetts.

Turkey Shore Distilleries

23 Hayward Street, #8
Ipswich, MA 01938
978-356-0048

Owners / Operators:
Mat Perry, Co-founder
Evan Parker, Co-founder

Email: info@turkeyshoredistilleries.com
Website: www.turkeyshoredistilleries.com
Facebook: Turkey Shore Distilleries
Twitter: @OldIpswichRum

Type: Craft Distillery. Opened in 2010.

Hours of operation: Monday through Friday, 9 a.m. to 5 p.m.

Tours: Available

Types of spirits produced: Rum

Names of spirits:
- Old Ipswich "White Cap" Rum
- Old Ipswich "Tavern Style" Rum
- Old Ipswich "Greenhead" Spiced Rum
- Old Ipswich "Golden Marsh" Spiced Rum

Best known for / most popular: Not provided

Average bottle price: Not provided

Distribution: MA

Interesting facts: Not provided

Artesian Distillers

955 Ken O Sha Industrial Park Drive SE
Grand Rapids, MI 49508
616-252-1700

Owners / Operators:
Amir Haririan, CEO
Leslie Haririan, Co-founder

Email: amir@artesiandistillers.com
Website: www.artesiandistillers.com
Facebook: Artesian Distillers
Twitter: @Adistillers

Type: Micro Distillery. Opened in 2009.

Hours of operation: Daily, 10 a.m. to 3 p.m.

Tours: Available

Types of spirits produced:
Rum, vodka, gin, bourbon whiskey

Names of spirits:
- 1492 Cristobal Rum
- Shipwreck Spiced Pirate Rhum
- RMD Vodka
- RMD Gin
- RMD Rum
- Glen Scotch Whisky
- Prohibition Edition Bourbon

Best known for / most popular: Not provided

Average bottle price: Not provided

Distribution: MI

Interesting facts: Not provided

Big Cedar Distilling Inc.

29130 Maystead Road
Sturgis, MI 49061
269-998-3610

Owners / Operators:
Dong Stanke, Co-owner
Tina Stanke, Co-owner

Email: doug@incentivevodka.com
Website: www.incentivevodka.com
Facebook: Incentive Vodka
Twitter: @BigCedarDistill

Type: Micro Distillery. Opened in 2009.

Hours of operation: Not provided

Tours: Not provided

Types of spirits produced: Vodka

Names of spirits:
- Incentive Vodka

Best known for / most popular: Incentive Vodka

Average bottle price: Not provided

Distribution: MI

Interesting facts: Incentive Vodka is gluten free.

Chateau Chantal

15900 Rue de Vin
Traverse City, MI 49686
231-223-4110

Owners / Operators:
Robert Begin, Founder
James Krupka, CEO
Mark Johnson, Winemaker
Brian Hosmer, Winemaker

Email: wine@chateauchantal.com
mjohnson@chateauchantal.com
Website: www.chateauchantal.com
Facebook: Chateau Chantal Winery
Twitter: @chateauchantal
Blog: chateauchantal.wordpress.com

Type: Winery / Micro Distillery. Opened in 2001.

Hours of operation:
June through August: Monday through Saturday, 11 a.m. to 9 p.m.
September through October: Monday through Saturday, 11 a.m. to 7 p.m.
November through mid-June: Monday through Saturday, 11 a.m. to 5 p.m.
Sundays year round: 11 a.m. to 5 p.m.
Closed: Thanksgiving, Christmas, New Year's, Easter

Tours: Tours available June through August

Types of spirits produced: Brandy, eau de vie

Names of spirits:
- Chateau Chantal Cherry Eau de Vie
- Chateau Chantal Pear Eau de Vie
- Chateau Chantal Plum Eau de Vie
- Chateau Chantal Brandy – "Cinq à Sept"
- Chateau Chantal Cerise
- Chateau Chantal Cerise Noir
- Chateau Chantal Entice

Best known for / most popular: Chateau Chantal Cerise

Average bottle price: $24.99 to $34.00

Distribution: IL, MI

Coppercraft Distillery LLC

184 120th Avenue
Holland, MI 49424

Owners / Operators:
Walter Catton, Owner / Operator
Mark Fellwock, Owner / Operator
Adam Irrer, Owner / Operator

Email: info@coppercraftdistillery.com
Website: www.coopercraftdistillery.com
Facebook: Coppercraft Distillery
Twitter: @CCDistillery
Instagram: CCDistillery

Type: Craft Distillery.
Opened in September 2012.

Hours of operation:
Check website for current hours

Tours:
Check website for current hours

Types of spirits produced: Bourbon, whiskey, gin, barrel aged gin, rum, brandy, vodka, citrus vodka

Names of spirits:
- Coopercraft Bourbon
- Coopercraft Whiskey
- Coopercraft Gin
- Coopercraft Barrel Aged Gin
- Coopercraft Rum
- Coppercraft Applejack
- Coppercraft Vodka
- Coppercraft Citrus Vodka

Best known for / most popular: Gin and Rum

Average bottle price: $30.00 to $60.00

Distribution: CO, IL (Chicago), MI

Services offered other than production:
Tours, tastings, retail

Corey Lake Orchards

12147 Corey Lake Road
Three Rivers, MI 49093
269-244-5690

Owners / Operators:
Dayton Hubbard, Owner

Email: oreylakeorchards@gmail.com
Website: www.coreylakeorchards.com
Facebook: Corey Lake Orchards

Type: Micro Distillery. Opened in 1999.

Hours of operation: Open May through October, 8 a.m. to 6 p.m.

Tours: Available Saturday afternoons and by appointment

Types of spirits produced: Brandy

Names of spirits:
- Hubbard's Apple Brandy
- Hubbard's Cherry Brandy
- Hubbard's Grape Brandy
- Hubbard's Peach Brandy
- Hubbard's Pear Brandy

Best known for / most popular:
Hubbard's Apple Brandy

Average bottle price: $10.00 to $30.00

Distribution: Corey Lake Orchards

Interesting facts: All Hubbard's brandies are made from fruit grown on its farm.

Entente Spirits LLC

10983 Hills Road
Baroda, MI 79101
269-422-1617

Owners / Operators:
Moersch Family, Owners

Email: info@roundbarnwinery.com
Website: www.roundbarndistillery.com
Facebook: The Round Barn Winery
Twitter: @RoundBarnWinery
YouTube: Round Barn Winery

Type: Winery / Micro Distillery / Brewery
Distillery opened in 1999.

Hours of operation: Open year-round

Tours: Not available

Types of spirits produced:
Bourbon, rum, vodka, brandies

Names of spirits:
- DiVine Bourbon
- DiVine Rum
- DiVine Vodka
- Other products are labeled under Free Run Cellars

Best known for / most popular: DiVine Vodka

Average bottle price: $15.00 to $30.00

Distribution: IL, IN, MI

Interesting facts:
- Entente Sprits tasting rooms are located in turn of the century barns, including an Amish-built round barn.
- DiVine Vodka is made from grapes.

Grand Traverse Distillery

781 Industrial Circle, Ste. 5
Traverse City, MI 49696
231-947-8635

Owners / Operators:
Kent Rabish, Owner / Distiller
Landis Rabish, Production Manager / Lead Distiller
Perry Harmon, Retail Manager / Spirits Ambassador

Email: kent@grandtraversedistillery.com
info@grandtraversedistillery.com
Website: www.grandtraversedistillery.com
Facebook: Grand Traverse Distillery

Type: Micro Distillery. Opened in 2007.

Retail Sales / Tastings / Cocktails:
Monday through Saturday, 11 a.m. to 5:30 p.m.;
Sunday, noon to 4 p.m.

Tasting Rooms:
Frankenmuth, MI; Leland, MI; Traverse City, MI

Tours:
Available Thursday through Saturday 11:30 a.m. to 4:30 p.m.

Types of spirits produced: Vodka, whiskey, gin, rum (2014)

Names of spirits:
- True North Vodka
- True North Wheat Vodka
- True North Cherry Flavored Vodka
- True North Chocolate Flavored Vodka
- Ole George 100% Straight Rye Whiskey
- Straight Bourbon Whiskey
- Cherry Whiskey
- 100% Corn Whiskey (un-aged)
- Double Barreled Ole George 100% Straight Rye Whiskey
- Peninsula Gin

Best known for / most popular: True North Vodka, Ole George

Average bottle price: $31.00 to $62.00

Distribution: IL, MI – Looking for more U.S. distribution.
Contact Perry Harmon, perry@grandtraversedistillery.com

Interesting facts:
Grand Traverse Distillery is northern Michigan's oldest "grain to bottle" and craft certified micro distillery.

Journeyman Distillery

109 Generations Drive
Three Oaks, MI 49128
269-820-2050

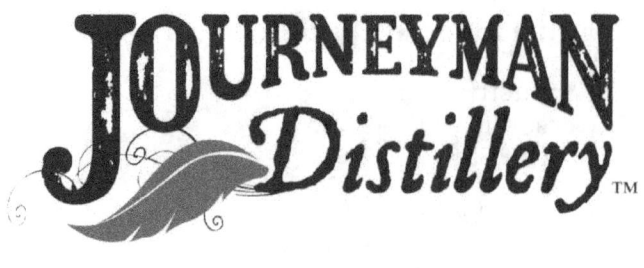

Owners / Operators:
Bill Welter, Founder
Nick Gurniewicz, Partner

Email: info@journeymandistillery.com
Website: www.journeymandistillery.com
Facebook: Journeyman Distillery
Twitter: @JourneymanDist
YouTube: JourneymanDistillery's Channel

Type: Micro Distillery. Opened in 2011.

Hours of operation: Vary by season

Tours: Available, register on website

Types of spirits produced:
White whiskey, wheat whiskey, rye whiskey, vodka, gin, bourbon, rum

Names of spirits:
- W.R. Whiskey (White Whiskey)
- Ravenswood Rye (Rye Whiskey)
- Buggy Whip Wheat (Wheat Whiskey)
- Red Arrow Vodka
- Road's End Rum
- Bilberry Black Heart's Gin
- Featherbone Bourbon
- Three Oaks Single Malt
- Bilberry Black Heart's Gin Barrel Aged
- New Zealand Single Malt (Around the World Series)
- Humdinger Jalapeno Spirit
- Road's End Rum Barrel Aged (Navy Strength)
- Silver Cross Whiskey
- Snaggle Tooth Coffee Liqueur

Best known for / most popular: Ravenswood Rye

Average bottle price: $19.99 to $49.99

Distribution: CA, IN, IL, MA, MI, MO, NJ, TN, WI, On-site retail

Interesting facts: Certified Organic by Midwest Organic Services Association, and USDA. Also Kosher Certified by Kosher Organics.

New Holland Artisan Spirits

66 East 8th Street
Holland, MI 49423
616-355-6422

Owners / Operators:
Not provided

Email: info@newhollandbrew.com
Website: www.newhollandbrew.com
Facebook: New Holland Artisan Spirits
Twitter: @NHAS_Spirits

Type: Micro Distillery. Opened in 2005.

Hours of operation: Not provided

Tours: Available

Types of spirits produced: Bourbon, gin, whiskey, brandy

Names of spirits:
- Knickerbocker Gin
- Beer Barrel Bourbon
- Walleye Rye Whiskey
- Malthouse Whiskey
- Hatter Royale Hopquila
- Dutchess Vodka
- Dutchess Citrus Vodka
- Double Down Barley Whiskey
- Bill's Michigan Wheat Whiskey
- Zeppelin Bend Straight Whiskey
- Freshwater Superior Single Barrel Rum
- Freshwater Michigan Amber Rum
- Freshwater Huron White Rum

Best known for / most popular: Dutchess Vodka

Average bottle price: Not provided

Distribution: Not provided

Interesting facts: Not provided

Northern Latitudes Distillery

112 E. Philip Street, Ste. B
Lake Leelanau, MI 49653
231-256-2700

Owners / Operators:
Mark Moseler, Co-owner
Mandy Moseler, Co-owner

Email: info@nldistillery.com
Website: www.nldistillery.com
Facebook: Northern Latitudes Distillery
Twitter: @NLatitudes

Type: Micro Distillery. Opened in 2012.

Hours of operation:
Monday through Thursday, 11 a.m. to 6 p.m.
Friday and Saturday, 11 a.m. to 8 p.m.
Sunday, noon to 5 p.m.

Tours: Available by appointment

Types of spirits produced: Gin, vodka, liqueur

Names of spirits:
- Jack Pine Gin
- Ice Dunes Vodka
- Deer Camp Vodka
- Limoncello di Leelanau Lemon Liqueur
- Manitou Passage Rum - White Rum
- Whaleback Spiced Rum
- Apollo Horseradish Vodka
- Northern Roots Ginger Liqueur
- Mackinac Island Fudge Chocolate Liqueur

Best known for / most popular: Jack Pine Gin

Average bottle price: Not provided

Distribution: Not provided

Interesting facts: First full service distillery in Leelanau County MI.

Northern United Brewing Company & Distilling

13512 Peninsula Drive
Traverse City, MI 49686
231-223-8700

Owners / Operators:
Mike Hall, Head Distiller
Michael Wooster, Manager
Josh Lentz, Supervisor
Kaleb Longworth, Assistant Distiller
Sam Maxbauer, Assistant Distiller
Charles Psenka, Sr., Chief Liaison

Email: jpbrewery.traverse@nubco.net
Website: www.civilizedspirits.com
Facebook: Civilized Spirits
Twitter: @DrinkCivilized

Type: Micro Distillery. Opened in 2010.

Hours of operation: As demand dictates

Tours: Available by appointment

Types of spirits produced:
Vodka, rum, gin, cherry spirit, agave, whiskey, apple spirit

Names of spirits:
- Civilized Vodka
- Civilized Sakura
- Civilized Whiskey
- Civilized White Dog
- Civilized Single Malt Whiskey
- Civilized Rum
- Civilized Gin

Best known for / most popular: Civilized Vodka

Average bottle price: $30.00 to $40.00

Distribution: MI

Interesting facts: "Civilized Spirits — a family of liquors created for the woodland gentleman of yore; the sort of man who cut wood for a living and wrestled grizzlies for fun, but still found time to wax his mustache and comb some pomade through his hair. Although the grizzlies may be gone, the dedication and appreciation of artisanal spirits lives on in every Civilized Spirit we hand-bottle." – Mike Hall

St. Julian Winery

716 S. Kalamazoo Street
Paw Paw, MI 49079
800-732-6002

Owners / Operators:
David Braganini, President
Larry Gilbert, Resident Distiller
Eric Kempisty, Chief Engineer / Distiller

Email: wines@stjulian.com
Website: www.stjulian.com
Facebook: St. Julian Winery
Twitter: @stjulianwinery
Pinterest: St. Julian Winery

Type: Winery / Micro Distillery.
Opened in 2000.

Hours of operation:
Monday through Saturday, 9 a.m. to 6 p.m.
Sunday, 11 a.m. to 6 p.m.
(Seasonal Winter Hours)

Tours: Available

Types of spirits produced: Brandy, vodka

Names of spirits:
- A & G Brandy
- Michigan Dew Vodka
- Grey Heron Vodka

Best known for / most popular: Grey Heron Vodka

Average bottle price: $34.99

Distribution:
MI tasting locations in Paw Paw, Union Pier, Frankenmuth, and Dundee.

Interesting facts:
- Family owned and operated, St. Julian produces all of its wines and spirits from 100% Michigan grown fruit.
- A & G Brandy is aged in Michigan oak.

Two James Spirits

2445 Michigan Avenue
Detroit, MI 48216

Owners / Operators:
David Landrum, President
Peter Bailey, Vice President

Email: David Landrum, david@twojames.com
Peter Bailey, peter@twojames.com
Website: www.twojames.com
Facebook: Two James Spirits
Twitter: @TwoJamesSpirits

Type: Micro Distillery. Opened in March 2012.

Hours of operation:
Tuesday through Thursday, 2 p.m. to 8 p.m.
Friday and Saturday, 2 p.m. to 10 p.m.; Sunday, noon to 4 p.m.

Tours: Available by appointment

Types of spirits produced: Vodka, gin, bourbon, whiskey

Names of spirits:
- Two James Gin
- Two James Vodka
- Two James Bourbon
- Two James Rye Whiskey
- Two James "Reserve" Single Malt Whiskey

Average bottle price: $30.00 to $50.00

Distribution: Detroit, MI metro area.

Interesting facts: Two James is located in Corktown, Detroit's oldest neighborhood, and is the first licensed distillery in Detroit since Prohibition.

Ugly Dog Distillery LLC

14496 North Territorial Road
Chelsea, MI 48118
734-444-0433

Owners / Operators:
Jon Dyer, Owner / Master Distiller
Dewey Winkle, Director of Operations

Email: jon@uglydogdistillery.com
Website: www.uglydogvodka.com
Facebook: Ugly Dog Distillery
Twitter: @UglyDogBooze, @UglyDogVodka

Type: Micro Distillery. Opened in 2010.

Hours of operation: Monday through Saturday, 10 a.m. to 6 p.m.

Tours: Available by appointment

Types of spirits produced:
Vodka, rum, gin

Names of spirits:
- Ugly Dog Gin
- Ugly Dog Rum
- Ugly Dog Vodka
- Ugly Dog Bacon Vodka
- Ugly Dog Raspberry Vodka
- Ugly Dog Black Cherry Vodka
- Ugly Dog Whipped Cream Vodka

Best known for / most popular: Ugly Dog Vodka

Average bottle price: $16.98 to $19.97

Distribution: MI

Interesting facts:
- The vodka is distilled from 100% Michigan grown wheat.
- The rum is made from Florida grown sugar cane.

Awards and Recognitions:
- Ugly Dog Vodka, Gold Medal, 2012 Micro Liquor Spirits Award
- Ugly Dog Bacon Vodka, Bronze Medal, 2012 WA Cup Spirits Competition
- Ugly Dog Raspberry Vodka, Gold Medal, 2013 The Fifty Best Competition
- Ugly Dog Bacon Vodka, Silver Medal, 2013 The Fifty Best Competition

Uncle Don's Apple Pie Craft Distillery

805 N. Mitchell Street
Cadillac, MI 49601
231-779-6939

Owners / Operators:
Don "Uncle Don" Gondzar, Owner

Email: dgondzar@uncledonsapplepie.com
Website: www.uncledonsapplepie.com
Facebook: Uncle Don's Apple Pie, LLC
LinkedIn: Uncle Don's Apple Pie

Type: Craft Distillery. Opened in 2012.

Hours of operation:
Tuesday through Thursday, noon to 5 p.m.
Friday and Saturday, noon to 6 p.m.

Tours: Available

Types of spirits produced: Vodka, spirits

Names of spirits:
- Big Gun Vodka
- Uncle Don's Shining Spirits
- Uncle Don's Country Cocktails
  Old Fashion Apple, Fuzzy Peach, Black Cherry, Blueberry, Raspberry

Best known for / most popular: Not provided

Average bottle price: Not provided

Distribution: Not provided

Interesting facts: First craft distillery in Cadillac, MI.

Valentine Distilling Company

161 Vester Street
Ferndale, MI 48220
248-629-9951

Owners / Operators:
Rifino Valentine, President / Founder

Email: info@valentinedistilling.com
Website: www.valentinedistilling.com
Facebook: Valentine Vodka
Twitter: @valentinevodka

Type: Micro Distillery. Opened in 2007.

Hours of operation: Wednesday and Thursday, 4:30 p.m. to 11 p.m.
Friday and Saturday, 4:30 p.m. to 1 a.m.; Sunday noon to 6 p.m.

Tours: Available by appointment

Types of spirits produced:
Vodka, gin, barrel aged gin, whiskey

Names of spirits:
- Valentine Vodka
- Valentine White Blossom Elderflower Flavored Vodka
- Valentine Liberator Gin
- Valentine Woodward Limited Whiskey
- Valentine Liberator Old Tom Gin

Best known for / most popular: Vodka

Average bottle price: $30.00

Distribution: CT, DC, DE, IL, MD, MI, NY, TN

Interesting facts: Valentine Distilling Co. is located in a refurbished building that once housed a Packard Body Shop and was built 1927.

Remarks: "I have always believed in the quality of handmade, premium products. Whether it is jam made with fresh fruit on a small family farm or a pint from my favorite microbrewery, I've always appreciated the care and quality of ingredients that a small, local producer uses in their products. It is also a good feeling knowing that I'm not only getting a better product, but that my hard earned money is going to a true artisan rather than a faceless corporation in a far away country. So when I found myself craving a premium martini, with imported vodka being my only option, I made it my mission to create one of the world's best vodka, right here in the USA!"
       - Rifino Valentine, President and Founder, Valentine Distilling Co.

Du Nord Craft Spirits

2610 E. 32nd Street
Minneapolis, MN 55406
612-382-7236

Owners / Operators:
Shanelle Montana, Owner / Operator
Chris Montana, Owner / Operator

Email: info@dunordcraftspirits.com
Website: www.dunordcraftspirits.com
Facebook: Du Nord Craft Spirits
Twitter: @DuNordCS

Type: Micro Distillery. Opened in July 2012.

Hours of operation: Monday through Saturday

Tours: Available. Call or check website for more information.

Types of spirits produced: Vodka, gin

Names of spirits:
- L'etoile Vodka
- Fitzgerald Gin

Best known for / most popular: TBA

Average bottle price: $25.00 to $35.00

Distribution: Twin cities, St. Cloud area

Interesting facts:
"Du Nord Craft Spirits is a small batch distillery producing artisan gin, vodka, apple whiskey, and bourbon. We are a 'grain to glass' craft distillery meaning we mill, mash, and distill our own product; every step of the process will happen in our Minneapolis location. All of our ingredients are sourced as locally as possible. We hope that you come visit us and see how your spirits are produced. The best things come from the north." - Shanelle Montana

Far North Spirits

2045 220th Avenue
Hallock, MN 56728
612-720-3738

Owners / Operators:
Michael Swanson, Owner / Distiller
Cheri Reese, Owner / Director of Marketing
Ian Lowther, Director of Sales
Dave Pickerell, Consultant / Master Distiller

Email: cheri@farnorthspirits.com
Website: www.farnorthspirits.com
Facebook: Far North Spirits
Twitter: @FarNorthSpirits
Pinterest: Far North Spirits
Instagram: FarNorthSpirits

Type: Micro Distillery. Opened in October 2013.

Hours of operation: Daily

Tours: Available Saturday, 1 p.m. to 4 p.m.

Types of spirits produced:
American Style gin, spiced rum, rye whiskey

Names of spirits:
- Solveig (Gin)
- Ålander (Rum)
- Roknar (Rye Whiskey)

Best known for / most popular: Solveig Gin

Average bottle price: $30.00 to $48.00

Distribution: MN, ND

Interesting facts:
- Far North Spirits is a field-to-glass craft distillery located on a working family farm.
- Far North Spirits is licensed as "MN Grown" by the Minnesota Department of Agriculture.
- Far North Spirits may very well be the northernmost distillery in the contiguous U.S.

Loon Liquors

1325 Armstrong Road, Ste. 165
Northfield, MN 55057
952-905-8709

Owners / Operators:
Simeon Rossi, Chief Artisan
Mark Schiller, Chief Business Officer

Email: thankyou@loonliquors.com
Website: www.loonliquors.com
Facebook: Loon Liquors
Twitter: @loonliquors
YouTube: Loon Liquors
Instagram: Loonliquors

Type: Micro Distillery. Opened in January 2014.

Hours of operation: Evenings

Tours: Available by appointment

Types of spirits produced: Whiskey, gin

Names of spirits:
- Loonshine
- MetropoliGin

Best known for / most popular: TBD

Average bottle price: $35.00 to $40.00

Distribution: MN

Interesting facts: Certified organic

Norseman Distillery

1101 Stinson Boulevard
Minneapolis, MN 55413
612-643-1933

Owners / Operators:
Scott Ervin, Owner / Master Distiller

Email: scott@norsemandistillery.com
Website: www.norsemandistillery.com
Facebook: Norseman Distillery

Type: Micro Distillery. Opened in January 2013.

Hours of operation: Daily, 9 a.m. to 8 p.m.

Tours: Available Saturdays on the hour

Types of spirits produced:
Gin, rum, vodka, whiskey, bourbon

Names of spirits:
- Norseman Vodka
- Heirloom Gin

Best known for / most popular: Not provided

Average bottle price: $25.00

Distribution: On-site retail. MN

Interesting facts:
"As legend has it, when Northwoods lumberjacks had felled their lot of trees, they would come charging south into the quiet hamlets of a young Minnesota. Surly by nature and wielding heavy axes, these vulgar beasts of men ransacked house after house in search of food to replenish their stores. The gentle townsfolk endured this tyranny for generations, until one day they decided they'd had enough. Using the finest grains from their own fields, they began distilling specially formulated alcohols capable of inspiring great merriment in those who drank them. The spirits were distributed to each home, where they were prominently displayed in bottles that bore the name of content's owner – 'NORSEMAN.' When the woodsmen returned, angry and violent as ever, they immediately snatched the bottles and drank greedily from them. Just as the villagers intended, within minutes the marauders became jovial and full of cheer, and the threat to peace and property was ended. Taking our name from this little-known bit of regional heritage, Norseman Distillery was founded with similar principals of using the very best local ingredients to produce small batches of exceptionally fine spirits." - Scott Ervin

Awards and Recognitions:
Norseman Vodka, 2013 Tasters Choice MN Award

Panther Distillery

300 East Pike Street
Osakis, MN 56360
320-859-2256

Owners / Operators:
Adrian Panther, Owner
Brett Grinager, Master Distillery

Email: pantherdistillery@gmail.com
Website: www.pantherdistillery.com
Facebook: Panther Distillery

Type: Micro Distillery. Opened in 2011.

Hours of operation:
Monday through Saturday, 10 a.m. to 4 p.m.

Tours: Available

Types of spirits produced: Whiskey, bourbon

Names of spirits:
- White Water Whiskey
- Spiked Apple Spirits

Best known for / most popular: White Water Whiskey

Average bottle price: $19.99

Distribution: MN, ND

Interesting facts: First legal whiskey distillery in MN.

Sherwoods Winery & Distillery LLC

Duluth, MN 55803
218-340-8511

Owners / Operators:
Davin Sherwood, Owner / Operator
Kristen Sherwood, Owner / Operator

Email: kristen@sherwoodspirits.com
Website: www.sherwoodspirits.com
Facebook: Sherwoods Winery

Type: Farm Winery / Distillery.
Opened in December 2012.

Hours of operation:
Monday through Friday, 9 a.m. to 3:30 p.m.

Tours: Not available

Types of spirits produced: Vodka

Names of spirits:
- 3BEES Vodka

Best known for / most popular: 3BEES Vodka

Average bottle price: $48.00

Distribution: MN

Interesting facts:
- The first registered distillery in our immediate area.
- Uses only fresh ingredients, including raw northern Minnesota honey.
- It takes 3 pounds of honey to produce one of our bottles of 3BEES Vodka.
- Each batch of vodka is currently made from a 40 gallon wash and is distilled in small quart sized cuts.

Cathead Distillery LLC
Bottle Tree Beverage Company

Gluckstadt, MS 39110
601-667-3038

Owners / Operators:
Austin Evans, Owner
Richard Patrick, Owner

Email: info@catheadvodka.com
Website: www.catheadvodka.com
Facebook: Cathead Vodka
Twitter: @CATHEADVodka

Type: Micro Distillery. Opened in 2010.

Hours of operation: Monday through Friday, 9 a.m. to 5 p.m.

Tours: Available

Types of spirits produced:
Vodka, gin, moonshine, whiskey, liqueur

Names of spirits:
- Cathead Vodka
- Cathead Honeysuckle Vodka
- Gold Coast White Whiskey
- Gold Coast Bourbon
- Bristow Gin
- Hoodoo Chicory Liqueur

Best known for / most popular: Lazy Cat

Average bottle price: $19.99

Distribution:
AL, AR, CO, FL, GA, IN, LA, MS, SC, TN, VA

Interesting facts:
The first legal commercial distillery in MS.

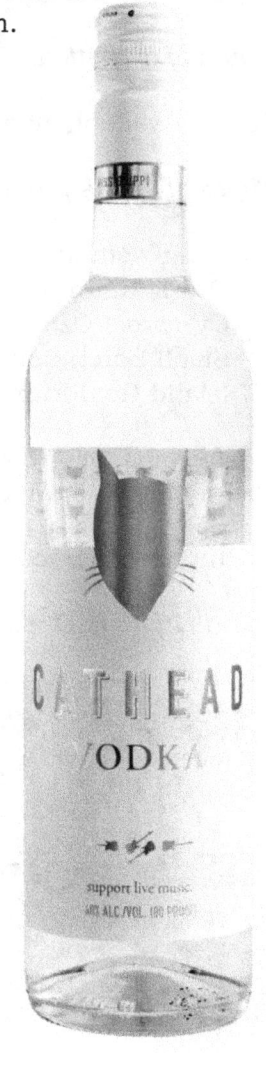

Copper Run Distillery

1901 Day Road
Walnut Shade, MO 65771
417-587-3456

Owners / Operators:
Jim Blansit, Owner / Master Distiller

Email: info@copperrundistillery.com
Website: www.copperrundistillery.com
Facebook: Copper Run Distillery
Foursquare: Copper Run Distillery
Yelp: Copper Run Distillery
Instagram: copperrundistillery

Type: Micro Distillery. Opened in 2008.

Hours of operation: Daily, 11 a.m. to 7 p.m.

Tours: Available noon, 2 p.m., 4 p.m., 6 p.m.

Types of spirits produced: Whiskey, spirit whiskey, rum

Names of spirits:
- Ozark Mountain Moonshine
- Overproof Ozark Mountain Moonshine
- Small Batch Spirit Whiskey
- Island Gold Rum

Best known for / most popular:
Ozark Mountain Moonshine

Average bottle price: $31.00

Distribution: MO, ship to most states

Crown Valley Distilling Company

13326 State Route F
Ste. Genevieve, MO 63670
573-756-9700

Owners / Operators:
Joe and Loretta Scott, Owners
Bryan Siddle, Director of Operations

Email: Bryan Siddle: bsiddle@crownvalleywinery.com
          Scott Eckl, Distiller: seckl@crownvalleywinery.com
Website: www.crownvalleybrewery.com, www.missourimoonshine.com
Facebook: Crown Valley Brewing and Distilling, Crown Valley Vodka
Twitter: @CrownValleyBrew
Blog: blog.crownvalleybrewery.com

Type: Brewery / Micro Distillery. Opened in 2009.

Hours of operation: Vary by season

Tours: Available

Types of spirits produced:
Whiskey, vodkas, absinthe, flavored spirits

Names of spirits:
- Missouri Moonshine
- Downhome Sweetwater

Best known for / most popular:
Missouri Moonshine

Average bottle price: $25.00 to $45.00

Distribution: On-site, AL, DE, FL, IL, KS, KY, LA, MD, MO, MS, NC, OK, TN

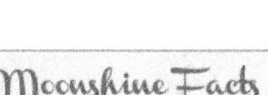

- Moonshine has several different nicknames, such as white lightnin', corn liquor, corn squeezins', etc.

- "Bootleggers," are what they called the people that transport and sold moonshine. They got their name from colonial times when they would hide the bottles in their tall riding boots.

- After the Revolutionary War, the government needed money to pay for that war and started taxing liquors and spirits. Against those liquor taxes and the President, George Washington, called on the militia to quell the uprising and take the leaders into custody. This is known as, The Whiskey Rebellion.

Mad Buffalo Distillery

Shawnee Bend Farms
7616 Shawneetown Spur
Union, MO 63084
636-395-7418

Owners / Operators:
Chris Burnette, President
William Uphouse, VP of Operations
Elise Burnette, VP of Marketing
Josh Johnson, VP of Sales
Jason Wink, VP of Production

Email: info@madbuffalodistillery.com
Website: www.madbuffalodistillery.com
Facebook: Mad Buffalo Distillery
Twitter: @madbuffalobrew
Pinterest: Mad Buffalo Distillery

Type: Micro Distillery. Opened in January 2013.

Hours of operation: By appointment only

Tours: Available by appointment only

Types of spirits produced: Vodka, bourbon, corn whiskey

Names of spirits:
- Thunderbeast Storm Moonshine Corn Whiskey
- Thunderbeast Stampede Vodka
- Thunderbeast Baby Buffalo Bourbon
- Thunderbeast Baby Buffalo Bourbon Single Barrel

Best known for / most popular:
Thunderbeast Storm Moonshine

Average bottle price: $24.99 to $35.99

Distribution: DC, DE, MD, MO, NV, TN

Interesting facts:
- Family owned and operated farm distillery.
- All products are made from ingredients grown, ground, malted, mashed, distilled, bottled and labeled on site in a true ground to glass process.

Mid-Best Distillery Inc.

423 Valley Road
Gravois Mills, MO 65037
816-838-3139

Owners / Operators:
Brian Dixon, Operator
Mike Anderson, Distillery

Email: mike@mid-bestdistillery.com
brian@mid-bestdistillery.com
sales@mid-bestdistillery.com
Website: www.mid-bestdistillery.com
Facebook: Mid-Best Distillery

Type: Micro Distillery. Opened in June 2013.

Hours of operation:
Wednesday through Saturday, 10 a.m. to 6 p.m.
April through December

Tours: Available

Types of spirits produced: Whiskey, rum

Names of spirits:
- Not provided

Best known for / most popular: Not provided

Average bottle price: $25.00

Distribution: MO

Interesting facts:
Family owned and operated.

Missouri Spirits

507 W. Walnut
Springfield, MO 65806
417-501-4674

Owners / Operators:
Scott Shotts, Manager

Email: info@missourispirits.com
Website: www.missourispirits.com
Facebook: Missouri Spirits
Twitter: @missourispirits

Type: Currently contract distilled. Opening distillery soon (2014)

Hours of operation: TBD

Tours: TBD

Types of spirits produced:
Bourbon, single malt whiskey, gin, vodka, rum

Names of spirits:
- Missouri Spirits Bourbon
- Missouri Spirits Single Malt Whiskey
- Missouri Spirits Gin
- Missouri Spirits Vodka
- Missouri Spirits Rum

Best known for / most popular: TBD

Average bottle price: $22.00

Distribution: On-site retail, MO

Of The Earth Farm Distillery LLC

38391 West 176th Street
Rayville, MO 64084

Owners / Operators:
JD Pierce, Owner / Distiller
Sarah Burnett Pierce, Owner / Accounts Manager
Jim C. Pierce, Assistant Distiller
Patricia Sappington Pierce, Marketing Support Staff

Email: info@oftheearthfarm.com
Website: www.oftheearthfarm.com
Facebook: Of The Earth Farm Distillery

Type: Craft Distillery. Opened in October 2012.

Hours of operation: By appointment only

Tours: Available by appointment

Types of spirits produced: Brandy, grappa, whisky

Names of spirits:
- Apple Brandy
- Apple Eau de Vie
- Grappa
- Ray County Rye

Best known for / most popular: Not provided

Average bottle price: $24.00 to $30.00

Distribution: Kansas City, MO area

Interesting facts:
- The first distillery in Ray County Missouri since Prohibition.
- The distillery was started by JD as a value-added project for the seven acre apple, pear and peach orchard owned by Jim C. and Patricia Pierce.
- The apple brandy and eau de vie is made from apples grown in the orchard.
- The Ray County Rye is made with a combination of rye grown in Ray County and Canadian rye.
- Spent mashes are returned to the earth after passing through pasture raised Berkshire hogs on the farm.

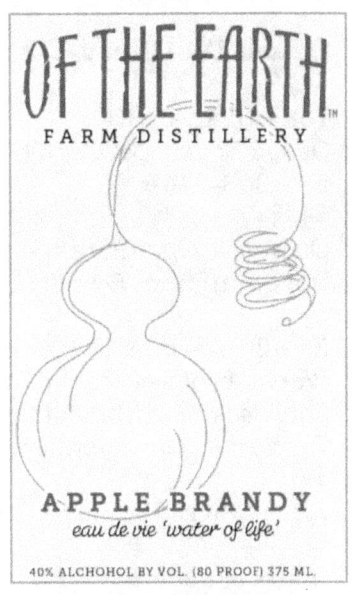

Ozark Distillery LLC

1684 Highway KK
Osage Beach, MO 65065
573-348-2449

Owners / Operators:
Dave Huffman, Owner / Head Distiller

Email: ozarkdistillery@gmail.com
Website: www.ozarkdistillery.com
Facebook: Ozark Distillery
Twitter: @ozarkdistillery

Type: Micro Distillery. Opened in March 2013.

Hours of operation: Daily, 9 a.m. to 5 p.m.

Tours: Available by appointment

Types of spirits produced:
Corn whiskey, bourbon whiskey, vodka

Names of spirits:
- Ozark Moonshine
- Ozark Apple Pie Moonshine
- Vanilla Bean Moonshine
- Pink Lemonade Moonshine
- Blackberry Moonshine
- Butterscotch Moonshine
- Ozark Premium Vodka
- Ozark Bourbon Whiskey

Best known for / most popular:
Ozark Moonshine Corn Whiskey

Average bottle price: $24.95

Distribution: MO

Interesting facts:
Family owned and operated distillery.

Pinckney Bend Distillery

Pinckney Bend Distillery
1101B Miller Street
P.O. Box 15
New Haven, MO 63068
573-237-5559

Owners / Operators:
Jerome Meyer, President / CEO
Thomas Anderson, V.P. Production / Product Development
Ralph Haynes, V.P. Sales and Marketing
Curtis Reis, National Sales Manager

Email: ralph@pinckneybend.com
Website: www.pinckneybend.com
Facebook: Pinckney Bend Distillery
Twitter: @PinckneyBend

Type: Micro Distillery. Opened in 2011.

Hours of operation:
Saturday and Sunday, noon to 6 p.m., or by appointment

Tours: Available during above hours

Types of spirits produced: Gin, vodka, corn whiskey, rested whiskey

Names of spirits:
- Pinckney Bend American Gin
- Pinckney Bend Three-Grain Vodka
- Pinckney Bend Corn Whiskey
- Pinckney Bend Rested American Whiskey

Best known for / most popular:
Pinckney Bend American Gin

Average bottle price:
$27.00 to $40.00

Distribution:
AR, IL (Southern IL and Chicago metro), KS, MO, NE, OK, SD; Singapore

Interesting facts: Pinckney Bend was a navigational hazard that was well known to generations of Missouri River boatmen. From 1818 until 1824 it was also the last town on the journey westward.

S. D. Strong Distilling

8500 NW River Park Road, #136A
Parkville, MO 64152
816-686-8269

Owners / Operators:
Steve Strong, President

Email: info@sdstrongdistilling.com
Website: www.sdstrongdistilling.com
Facebook: S.D. Strong Distilling
Twitter: @StillStrongMO
Instagram: sdstrongdistiller

Type: Micro Distillery. Opened in 2012.

Hours of operation: Not open to the public

Tours: Available by appointment

Types of spirits produced: Vodka, gin (coming soon), whiskey (coming soon)

Names of spirits:
- S.D. Strong Vodka

Best known for / most popular: S.D. Strong Vodka

Average bottle price: $19.99

Distribution: MO

Interesting facts:
The nation's first and only known micro distillery located in a cave.

Square One Brewery and Distillery

1727 Park Avenue
St. Louis, MO 63104
314-231-2537

Owners / Operators:
Steve Neukomm, Owner

Email: steve@squareonebrewery.com
Website: www.squareonebrewery.com
  www.spiritsofstlouisdistillery.com
Facebook: Square One Brewery & Distillery
Twitter: @SquareOneBrews

Type: Brewery / Micro Distillery. Opened in 2008.

Hours of operation:
Monday through Saturday, 11 a.m. to 1:30 a.m., Sunday 10 a.m. to midnight

Tours: Available by appointment

Types of spirits produced: Agave blue, gin, liqueurs, rum, whiskey, vodka

Names of spirits:
Under the brand name "Spirits of St. Louis"
- JJ Neukomm American Malt Whiskey
- Vermont Night Whiskey Liqueur
- Midwest Spring Wheat Vodka
- Island Time Amber Rum
- Regatta Bay Gin
- Agave Blue

Average bottle price: $25.00 to $48.00

Distribution: MO

Interesting facts:
Square One is the first legal distillery in St. Louis since Prohibition.

St. Louis Distillery

755 Friedens Road, Ste. B
St. Charles, MO 63303
636-925-1577

Owners / Operators:
Bill Schroer, Owner / Distiller
Greg Deters, Owner / Distiller
Steve Herberholt, Owner / Distiller

Email: info@stldistillery.com
Website: www.cardinalsinvodka.com
Facebook: Cardinal Sin Vodka
Twitter: @CardinalSinVod

Type: Micro Distillery. Opened in 2012.

Hours of operation: Vary

Tours: Available by appointment

Types of spirits produced: Vodka

Names of spirits:
- Cardinal Sin Vodka

Best known for / most popular:
Cardinal Sin Vodka

Average bottle price: $27.99 to $29.99

Distribution: IL, MO

Interesting facts: Not provided

Steve   Bill   Greg

StilL 630

1000 S. 4th Street
St. Louis, MO 63104
314-513-2275

Owners / Operators:
David Weglarz, Owner / Distiller
Jim Schultz, Owner
Dyke Minix, Owner
Ben Pippenger, Owner

Email: distillery@still630.com
Website: www.still630.com
Facebook: StilL 630 Distillery
Twitter: @StilL630

Type: Micro Distillery. Opened in 2012.

Hours of operation: Monday through Sunday, 1 p.m. to 6:30 p.m.

Tours: Friday through Sunday at 1 p.m., 3 p.m., 5 p.m.

Types of spirits produced: Rum, whiskey, bourbon

Names of spirits:
- Sir Whisquila
- Bell Bourbon
- Barrel Master
- Expedition Rum
- American Whiskey
- Rally Point Rye Whiskey
- Big Jake White Dog Whiskey
- S.S. Sorghum Whiskey

Best known for / most popular:
Rally Point Rye Whiskey, Sir Whisquila, and S.S. Sorghum Whiskey

Average bottle price: $28.00 to $35.00

Distribution: MO
Interesting facts:
Located just south of Busch Stadium in downtown St. Louis.
The "630" in the name derives from the height and width of the Gateway Arch, which itself is a monument to the indomitable spirit of the frontiersmen and women.

Wood Hat Spirits LLC

489 Booneslick Road
New Florence, MO 63363
573-835-1000

Owners / Operators:
Gary Hinegardner, Owner / Distiller

Email: gary@woodhatspirits.com
Website: www.woodhatspirits.com
Facebook: Wood Hat Spirits

Type: Micro Distillery. Opened in December 2013.

Hours of operation:
Monday through Saturday, 10 a.m. to 5 p.m.
Sunday, 1 p.m. to 5 p.m.

Tours: Available

Types of spirits produced:
Whiskey, bourbon, cordials

Names of spirits:
- Berry Berry Cordial
- Bourbon Rubenesque
- Montgomery County Bourbon
- Blue Corn Whiskey
- Aged Blue Corn Whiskey

Best known for / most popular: Not provided

Average bottle price: $20.00 to $38.00

Distribution: Self distribution

Interesting facts: Field to glass distillery.

Glacier Distilling Company

10237 Highway 2 E.
Coram, MT 59913
406-387-9887

Owners / Operators:
Nicolas Lee, Distiller
Lauren Oscilowski, Assistant Distiller

Email: info@glacierdistilling.com
Website: www.glacierdistilling.com
Facebook: Glacier Distilling Company
Twitter: @GlacierWhiskey

Type: Micro Distillery. Opened in 2011.

Hours of operation: Vary by season

Tours: Available

Types of spirits produced:
Whiskey, brandy, liqueur

Names of spirits:
- Glacier Dew Rye Spirit
- North Fork Whiskey
- Bad Rock Rye
- Wheatfish Whiskey

Best known for / most popular: Glacier Dew

Average bottle price: $28.00 to $64.00

Distribution: MT

Interesting facts: The recipe for Glacier Dew was inspired by legendary moonshiner Josephine Doody who produced some renowned shine in Glacier Park back in the early 1900s.

Headframe Spirits

21 S. Montana
Butte, MT 59701
406-299-2886

Owners / Operators:
John McKee, Co-owner
Courtney McKee, Co-owner

Email: cheers@headframespirits.com
Website: www.headframespirits.com
Facebook: Headframe Spirits
Twitter: @HeadframeSpirit

Type: Micro Distillery. Opened Leap Day, 2012.

Hours of operation:
Monday through Saturday, 10 a.m. to 8 p.m.
Sunday, noon to 5 p.m.

Tours: Available

Types of spirits produced: Gin, vodka, whiskey, liqueur

Names of spirits:
- Anselmo Gin
- High Ore Vodka
- Destroying Angel Whiskey
- Neversweat Bourbon Whiskey
- Orphan Girl Bourbon Cream Liqueur

Best known for / most popular:
Orphan Girl Bourbon Cream Liqueur

Average bottle price: $25.00

Distribution: IL, MT, WA

Montgomery Distillery

129 West Front Street
Missoula, MT 59802
406-926-1725

Owners / Operators:
Ryan Montgomery, Stillworks Director
Jenny Montgomery, Tasting Room Director
Tom and Chris Montgomery, Sales Managers
Chad Larrabee, Head Distiller

Email: info@montgomerydistillery.com
Website: www.montgomerydistillery.com
Facebook: Montgomery Distillery
Twitter: @montstill

Type: Micro Distillery. Opened in 2012.

Hours of operation:
Monday through Saturday, noon to 8 p.m.
Sunday, 1 p.m. to 6 p.m.

Tours: Available Wednesday through Saturday at 8 p.m. or by appointment

Types of spirits produced: Gin, vodka, aquavit, bierschnapps and other limited edition spirits. Single malt and rye whiskies will begin release in 2016.

Names of spirits:
- Whyte Laydie Gin
- Quicksilver Vodka
- Skadi Aquavit

Best known for / most popular: Whyte Laydie Gin

Average bottle price: Not provided

Distribution: MA, MD, MT

Inteesting facts: Ryan Montgomery studied with Frank McHardy of Springbank Distillery in Campbeltown, Scotland. Montgomery and distillers Chad Larrabee and Christopher Conley interpret old world spirits from around the globe using Montana grain. Their tasting room offers award-winning craft cocktails featuring fresh, local ingredients and an abundance of house-made syrups, shrubs, bitters and liqueurs.

RoughStock Distillery

81211 Gallatin Road, Ste. A
Bozeman, MT 59718

Owners / Operators:
Bryan Schulz, Co-owner
Kari Schulz, Co-owner

Website: www.montanawhiskey.com
Facebook: RoughStock Montana Whiskey

Type: Micro Distillery. Opened in 2008.

Hours of operation:
Monday through Friday, 11 a.m. to 6 p.m.
Saturday, 11 a.m. to 3 p.m.; Sunday, Closed

Tours: Available

Types of spirits produced: Whiskey

Names of spirits:
- RoughStock Montana Pure Malt Whiskey
- RoughStock Montana Black Label Whiskey
- RoughStock Montana Spring Wheat Whiskey
- RoughStock Montana Straight Rye Whiskey
- RoughStock Montana Sweet Corn Whiskey

Interesting facts: RoughStock Distillery is Montana's first legal distillery since Prohibition and the first to make whiskey in Montana in more than 100 years.

Steel Toe Distillery

23545 Highway 200 East
Potomac, MT 59823
406-244-4567

Owners / Operators:
Carl and Christina Bock, Owners

Email: cbock@steeltoedistillery.com
Website: www.steeltoedistillery.com

Type: Micro Distillery. Opened in October 2013.

Hours of operation:
Tuesday through Sunday, noon to 7 p.m.

Tours: Available

Types of spirits produced: Whiskey, gin

Names of spirits:
- Uncle Carls Prohibition Style Whiskey
- Show Pony Gin

Best known for / most popular:
Uncle Carl's Prohibition Style Whiskey

Average bottle price: $30.00

Distribution: On-site retail, MT

Interesting facts:
Steel Toe Distillery is family owned and operated.

Swanson's Mountain View Apple Orchard and Distillery

1752 Mountain View Orchards Road
Corvallis, MT 59828
406-961-3434

Owners / Operators:
Swanson family

Email: mountain.view.orchards@gmail.com
Website: https://sites.google.com/site/mountainvieworchards
Facebook: Swanson's Mountain View Distillery

Type: Micro Distillery. Opened in 2011.

Hours of operation: Daily, 9 a.m. to 5 p.m.

Tours: Available

Types of spirits produced: Honey spirit, brandy, cider

Names of spirits:
- Legendary Gold Honey Spirit
- Bitterroot Heritage Apple Brandy
- Harvest Legacy Dessert Cider

Best known for / most popular:
Legendary Gold Honey Spirit

Average bottle price: $8.00 to $30.00

Distribution: Not provided

Interesting facts: Not provided

234

The Montana Distillery-1889
Flathead Distillers

Missoula, MT

Owners / Operators:
Mark Hlebichuk, Co-owner
Sharie McDonald-Hlebichuk, Co-owner

Email: info@flatheadvodka.com
Website: www.themontanadistillery.com
Facebook: Flathead Vodka

Type: Micro Distillery. Opened in 2010.

Hours of operation: TBA

Tours: TBA

Types of spirits produced: Vodka

Names of spirits:
- Flathead Vodka
- Flathead Cherry Vodka
- Flathead Coffee Vodka

Best known for / most popular:
Flathead Vodka

Average bottle price: $25.00

Distribution: Not provided

Interesting facts:
84 proof vodka is made from sugar beets which are gluten free

Trailhead Spirits
Bootleg Distillery Inc.

2314 Montana Avenue
Billings, MT 59101
406-969-1627

Owners / Operators:
Casey McGowan, President
Steffanie McGowan, Vice President

Email: casey@trailheadspirits.com, steffanie@trailheadspirits.com
Website: www.trailheadspirits.com
Facebook: Trailhead Spirits

Type: Micro Distillery. Opened in 2013.

Hours of operation:
Monday through Sunday, noon to 8 p.m.
Cocktail service from 4 p.m. to 8 p.m.

Tours: Available

Types of spirits produced: Vodka, gin

Names of spirits:
- Great North Vodka
- Healy's Gin
- Healy's Reserve - Cask Rested Gin

Best known for / most popular: Great North Vodka

Average bottle price: $27.00

Distribution: MT

Interesting facts:
The wheat used is sourced from from the McGowan family farms in Highwood, MT.

Triple Divide Spirits

790 Front Street
Helena, MT 59601
406-459-0815

Owners / Operators:
Karen Powell, Owner
J.P. Crowley, Distiller
Jennifer Quick, Operations Manager

Email: drinks@tripledividespirits.com
Website: www.tripledividespirits.com
Facebook: Triple Divide Spirits
Twitter: @HelenaDistiller
Yelp: Triple Divide Spirits

Type: Micro Distillery. Opened in November 2013.

Winter hours:
Wednesday through Saturday 4 p.m. to 8 p.m.

Summer hours:
Tuesday through Saturday 2 p.m. to 8 p.m.

Tours: Not available

Types of spirits produced: Vodka, flavored vodkas, gin

Names of spirits:
- Triple Divide Spirits Vodka

Average bottle price: $27.00

Distribution: MT

Interesting facts:
Triple Divide Spirits is a woman-owned, family-operated business.

Vilya Spirits LLC
Formerly Ridge Distillery LLC

19 Artemisia Way
Kalispell, MT 59901
406-756-5964

Owners / Operators:
Joe and Julie Legate, Owner / Operators

Email: info@vilyaspirits.com
Website: www.vilyaspirits.com
Facebook: Vilya Spirits

Type: Micro Distillery. Opened in 2008.

Hours of operation: Not open to the public

Tours: Available by appointment

Types of spirits produced: Gin, absinthe

Names of spirits:
- Silvertip American Dry Gin
- Extrait d'Absinthe Verte
- Extrait d'Absinthe Blanche

Best known for / most popular: Absinthe

Average bottle price: $30.00 to $68.00

Distribution: AZ, CA, CT, DC, DE, FL, GA, IL, MA, MD, MT, NJ, NV, NY, RI, SC, TN, WA, WV

Interesting facts: The distillery is powered by hydroelectric energy.

Whistling Andy Distillery

8541 Mt. Highway 35
Bigfork, MT 59911
406-837-2620

Owners / Operators:
Brian Anderson, Owner / Distiller
Mike Marchetti, Owner
Dana Marchetti, Bookeeping
Chandra Hodges, Operations
Lisa Cloutier, Outside Sales and Marketing

Email: brian@whistlingandy.com, marketing@whistlingandy.com
Website: www.whistlingandy.com
Facebook: Whistling Andy
Twitter: @WhistlingAndy

Type: Micro Distillery. Opened in 2010.

Hours of operation: Monday through Sunday, noon to 8 p.m.

Tours: Available by appointment

Types of spirits produced: Rum, gin, whiskey, vodka, kirsch

Names of spirits:
- Whistling Andy Gin
- Whistling Andy Vodka
- Whistling Andy Silver Rum
- Whistling Andy Moonshine
- Whistling Andy Hopshnop
- Whistling Andy Harvest Select
- Whistling Andy Hibiscus-Coconut Rum

Best known for / most popular: Hibiscus Crush

Average bottle price: $24.00 to $48.00

Distribution: AZ, CA, IL, MO, MT, NV, OR; Canada

Interesting facts:
A veteran-owned distillery, hires returning veterans.

Willie's Distillery

312 E. Main Street
Ennis, MT 59729
406-682-4117

Owners / Operators:
Willie Blazer, Co-owner
Robin Blazer, Co-owner

Email: info@williesdistillery.com
Website: www.williesdistillery.com
Facebook: Willie's Distillery, Inc
Twitter: @mtmoonshine

Type: Micro Distillery. Opened in 2012.

Hours of operation: Daily with varied hours. Normally 10 a.m. to 8 p.m. (seasonal)

Tours: Available

Types of spirits produced:
Moonshine, whiskey, vodka, gin, liqueurs, brandy

Names of spirits:
- Bighorn Whiskey
- Snowcrest Vodka
- Montana Moonshine
- Montana Honey Moonshine
- Montana Wild Chokecherry Liqueur

Best known for / most popular:
Montana Moonshine

Average bottle price: $20.00 to $40.00

Distribution: MT

Interesting facts:
- Located in a small cowboy town of 840 people and around 11,000,000 trout.
- Just 200 yards from Blue Ribbon Fly-Fishing on the Madison River.

Cooper's Chase Distillery LLC

584 18th Road
West Point, NE 68788
402-380-0233

Owners / Operators:
Doug Throener, Owner

Email: info@cooperschase.com
Website: www.cooperschase.com
Facebook: Cooper's Chase Distillery

Type: Micro Distillery. Opened in 2009.

Hours of operation: Not provided

Tours: Not provided

Types of spirits produced: Vodka

Names of spirits:
- Chase Nebraska Vodka

Best known for / most popular: Chase Nebraska Vodka

Average bottle price: Not provided

Distribution: Not provided

Interesting facts: Not provided

Cut Spike Distillery

11941 Centennial Road
La Vista, NE 68128
402-763-8868

Owners / Operators:
Jason Payne, President / Founder
Mike Cunningham, Master Distiller

Email: info@cutspike.com
Website: www.cutspikedistillery.com
Facebook: Cut Spike Distillery
Twitter: @CutSpike
Pinterest: Lucky Bucket Brew and Cut Spike Distillery
Instagram: @Cutspike

Type: Craft Distillery. Opened in February 2008.

Hours of operation:
Wednesday through Friday, 4 p.m. to 10 p.m.
Saturday, 11 a.m. to 5 p.m.

Tours: Available Wednesday through Friday at 5:30 p.m.
Saturday, noon, 1 p.m. and 2 p.m.

Types of spirits produced:
Barrel aged rum, premium vodka, single malt whiskey

Names of spirits:
- Cut Spike Single Malt Whiskey
- Cut Spike Premium Vodka
- Cut Spike Barrel-Aged Rum

Best known for / most popular:
Not provided

Average bottle price: $23.99 to $54.99

Distribution: NE

Interesting facts:
Cut Spike is a nod to Omaha's railroad history aligning with the philosophy of doing the work by hand.

Services offered other than production: Tasting room, store

242

Churchill Vineyards and Distillery

1045 Dodge Lane
Fallon, NV 89406
775-423-4000

Owners / Operators:
Colby Frey, Owner / Winemaker / Distiller
Ashley Frey, Owner / Marketing

Email: info@churchillvineyards.com
   Ashley Frey: Ashley@churchillvineyards.com
   Colby Frey: Colby@churchillvineyards.com
Website: www.churchillvineyards.com
Facebook: Churchill Vineyards
Twitter: @churchillwines

Type: Winery / Micro Distillery. Opened in 2010.

Hours of operation: Open by appointment

Tours: Available by appointment

Types of spirits produced:
Whiskey, vodka, brandy, grappa

Names of spirits:
- Nevada Vodka
- Nevada Brandy
- Nevada Single Malt Whiskey

Best known for / most popular:
Churchill Vineyards Grappa and Coke

Average bottle price: $20.00 to $50.00

Distribution: NV

Interesting facts: Spirits grown, produced, and bottled on-site by fifth generation Nevada farmer, Colby Frey.

Las Vegas Distillery

7330 Eastgate Road, Ste. 100
Henderson, NV 89011
702-629-7534

Owners / Operators:
Katalin and George Rácz, Owners

Email: info@lasvegasdistillery.com
Website: www.lasvegasdistillery.com
Facebook: Las Vegas Distillery
Twitter: @VegasDistillery

Type: Micro Distillery. Opened in 2011.

Hours of operation: Not provided

Tours: Available

Types of spirits produced: Vodka, rumskey

Names of spirits:
- Nevada Vodka
- Seven Grain Vodka
- White Rumskey

Best known for / most popular: Nevada Vodka

Average bottle price: Not provided

Distribution: NV

Interesting facts:
Las Vegas Distillery is one of the first legal distilleries in the history of Nevada.

Flag Hill Winery & Distillery

297 North River Road
Lee, NH 03861
603-659-2949

Owners / Operators:
Frank W. Reinhold, Jr, Owner

Email: wine-info@flaghill.com
Website: www.flaghill.com
Facebook: Flag Hill Winery & Distillery
Twitter: @flaghillwinery

Type: Winery / Micro Distillery. Opened in 2004.

Hours of operation:
Wednesday through Sunday, 11 a.m. to 5 p.m.

Tours:
Available weekends from June to September

Types of spirits produced:
Absinthe, brandy, grappa, gin, liqueurs, vodka, rum

Names of spirits:
- General John Stark Vodka
- Josiah Bartlett Barrel Aged Apple Brandy
- Karner Blue Gin
- Moonshine
- Graham's Grappa
- Sugar Maple Liqueur
- Blueberry Liqueur
- Raspberry Liqueur
- Cranberry Liqueur
- Flag Hill White Rum

Best known for / most popular: Karner Blue Gin

Average bottle price: $15.00 to $26.00

Distribution: MA, NH, NY, PA

Interesting facts:
In 2004, Flag Hill became the first distillery in NH.

Sea Hagg Distillery

135 Lafayette Road, Unit 9
North Hampton, NH 03862
603-379-2274

Owners / Operators:
Heather Hughes, Managing Member

Email: info@seahaggdistillery.com
Website: www.seahaggdistillery.com
Facebook: The Sea Hagg Distillery LLC

Type: Micro Distillery. Opened in 2012.

Hours of operation: Vary

Tours: Available

Types of spirits produced: Rum, eau de vie

Names of spirits:
- Sea Hagg Rum (Amber)
- Sea Hagg Silver Rum
- Sea Hagg Peach Rum
- Sea Hagg Blueberry Rum
- Sea Hagg Eau de Vie Pear
- Sea Hagg Eau de Vie Apple

Best known for / most popular: Sea Hagg Rum

Average bottle price: $28.00 to $30.00

Distribution: NH

Interesting facts: Not provided

Big Still Liquors LLC

23 Sebago Street
Clifton, NJ 07013
304-690-2012

Owners / Operators:
Ron Haberman, President / Founder

Email: ron@300joules.com
Website: www.300joules.com
Facebook: 300 Joules Liqueur
Twitter: @Drink300

Type: Mixing / Bottling. Opened in 2011.

Hours of operation:
Monday through Friday, 9 a.m. to 4 p.m.

Tours: Not available

Types of spirits produced: Liqueur

Names of spirits:
- 300 Joules Lemon Infusion
- 300 Joules Ginger Infusion

Best known for / most popular: TBA

Average bottle price: $21.95

Distribution: TBA

Interesting facts:
Joules is a nod to the former profession of the founder, a cardiology specialist.

Cooper River Distillers

34 N. 4th Street
Camden, NJ 08102
856-295-1273

Owners / Operators:
James Yoakum, Founder / Chief Distiller

Email: info@CooperRiverDistillers.com
Website: www.cooperriverdistillers.com
Facebook: Cooper River Distillers
Twitter: @NJDistiller

Type: Craft Distillery. Opened 2014.

Hours of operation: Vary

Tours: Not available

Types of spirits produced: Rum, whiskey, brandy

Names of spirits:
- Petty's Island Rum
- Petty's Island Rum Rye Oak Reserve (aged rum)
- Silver Fox Rye (unaged rye spirits)

Best known for / most popular: TBA

Average bottle price: $24.99 to $29.99

Distribution: NJ (Camden County area)

Interesting facts:
One of the first new distilleries in New Jersey since Prohibition.

Jersey Artisan Distilling

32B Pier Lane West
Fairfield, NJ 07004
973-521-7623

Owners / Operators:
Brant Braue, President / Master Distiller
Krista Haley, CFO / COO
Fred Braue Sr., Shareholder
Fred Braue Jr., Shareholder

Email: info@jerseyartisandistilling.com
Website: www.jerseyartisandistilling.com
Facebook: Jersey Artisan Distilling
Twitter: @JerseyRum
YouTube: JerseyDistilling

Type: Craft Distillery. Opened in January 2013.

Hours of operation: Daily from 9 a.m. to 7 p.m.

Tours: Not available

Types of spirits produced: Rum

Names of spirits:
- Busted Barrel Dark Rum
- Busted Barrel Silver Rum

Best known for / most popular: Busted Barrel Rum

Average bottle price: $25.00 to $35.00

Distribution: NJ

Interesting facts: One of the first legal distilleries in NJ since Prohibition.

Don Quixote Distillery & Winery

236 Rio Bravo
Los Alamos, NM 87544
505-695-0864

Owners / Operators:
Ron and Olha Dolin, Owners

Email: ron@dqdistillery.com
Website: www.dqdistillery.com
Facebook: Don Quixote Winery and Distillery

Type: Winery / Micro Distillery. Opened in 2003.

Hours of operation: Tuesday through Sunday, noon to 6 p.m.

Tours: Available

Types of spirits produced:
Eau de vie, vodka, bourbon, gin, whiskey, brandy, grappa

Names of spirits:
- Don Quixote Angelica
- Don Quixote Blue Corn Vodka
- Don Quixote Blue Corn Bourbon
- Don Quixote Gin
- Don Quixote Pisco
- Don Quixote Qalvados – Apple Brandy
- Don Quixote Grappa
- Don Quixote Malvasia Bianca Grappa
- Don Quixote Mon Cherie Cherry Eau de Vie
- Spirit of Santa Fe Gin
- Spirit of Santa Fe Brandy
- Spirit of Santa Fe Vodka

Best known for / most popular: Blue Corn Vodka, Pisco, Angelica, Gin

Average bottle price: $25.00 to $50.00

Distribution: NM

Interesting facts:
Don Quixote Distillery is New Mexico's first distillery specializing in premium spirits made from New Mexico agricultural products.

Rancho de Los Luceros Destilaría

183 County Road 41
Alcalde, NM 87511
505-404-6101

Owners / Operators:
John Bernasconi, President / Owner
George Shurman, Owner
Karen Lubliner, Owner
Caitlin Richards, Operation Manager
Steven Jarrett, Distiller
John Cox, Sales Manager

Website: www.KGBspirits.com

Type: Micro Distillery. Opened in 2012.

Hours of operation: Vary

Tours: Not available

Types of spirits produced:
Gin, vodka, liqueur, absinthe, bourbon, rye

Names of spirits:
- Los Luceros Hacienda Gin
- Vodka Viracocha
- Brimstone Absinthe
- Naranjo Orange Liqueur
- John David Albert's Taos Lightning
  Single barrel straight Rye Whiskey, 5 year
- Ceran St. Vrain's Taos Lightning
  Single barrel straight Rye Whiskey, 15 year
- Thomas Tate Tobin's Taos Lightning
  Single barrel straight Bourbon
- Simeon Turley's Taos Lightning
  Single barrel straight Bourbon, 6 year

Best known for / most popular: Taos Lightning Rye

Average bottle price: $35.00 to $90.00

Distribution: NM

Interesting facts: Rancho de Los Luceros Destilaría is located on the property of the historic ranch of the same name in Alcalde, NM, in the straw bale building that was once home to the Los Luceros Winery – the second straw bale-built winery in the U.S.

Santa Fe Spirits

7505 Mallard Way, Unit I
Santa Fe, NM 87507
505-467-8892

Downtown Tasting Room
308 Read Street
Santa Fe, NM 87501
505-780-5906

Owners / Operators:
Colin Keegan, Owner
John Couchot, Master Distiller

Email: info@santafespirits.com
Website: www.santafespirits.com
Facebook: Santa Fe Spirits
Twitter: @SantaFeSpirits

Type: Micro Distillery. Opened in 2011.

Distillery Hours of operation:
Wednesday through Saturday, 3 p.m. to 7 p.m.

Downtown Tasting Room Hours:
Monday through Saturday, 3 p.m. to 9 p.m.

Tours: Available

Types of spirits produced:
Single malt whiskey, brandy, gin, vodka, un-aged whiskey

Names of spirits:
- Colkegan Single Malt
- Santa Fe Apple Brandy
- Wheelers Gin
- Expedition Vodka
- Silver Coyote Un-aged Whiskey

Best known for / most popular:
Barrel Aged Manhattan
(single malt aged Manhattan drink, aged for a month in new oak)

Average bottle price: $29.99 to $55.00

Distribution: CO, NM, OK, OR, TX

Interesting facts:
All products have a distinctive Southwest flair, from botanicals to aging processes.

Adirondack Distilling Company

601 Varick Street
Utica, NY 13502
315-316-0387

Owners / Operators:
Steve Cox, Principal
Bruce Elsell, Principal
Jordan Karp, Principal

Email: info@adirondackdistilling.com
Website: www.adirondackdistilling.com
Facebook: Adirondack Distilling Company
Twitter: @ADKDistillingCo
YouTube: Adirondack Distilling
Pinterest: AdirondackDistilling

Type: Micro Distillery. Opened in 2012.

Hours of operation: Friday, 5 p.m. to 8 p.m.
Saturday, 1 p.m. to 4 p.m.

Tours: Available

Types of spirits produced: Vodka, gin, whiskey, bourbon

Names of spirits:
- Adirondack ADK Vodka
- Adirondack ADK Gin
- 1,000 Stills White Whiskey
- 601 Bourbon

Best known for / most popular: Adirondack ADK Vodka

Average bottle price: $32.95

Distribution: CA, CT, NY

Interesting facts:
Adirondack ADK Vodka is made from 100% New York Corn - thus it is gluten free - and is filtered through Herkimer Diamonds.

Albany Distilling Company

78 Montgomery Street
Albany, NY 12207
518-621-7191

Owners / Operators:
John Curtin, Co-owner
Matthew Jager, Co-owner

Email: info@albanydistilling.com
Website: www.albanydistilling.com
Facebook: The Albany Distilling Company, Inc.
Twitter: @AlbDistCo

Type: Micro Distillery. Opened in 2012.

Hours of operation: Vary

Tours: Available Tuesdays, 4 p.m. to 8 p.m. Saturdays, noon to 8 p.m. or by appointment.

Types of spirits produced: Whiskey, rum

Names of spirits:
- Coal Yard New Make Whiskey
- Ironweed Whiskey
- Quackenbush Still House Rum

Best known for / most popular: Ironweed

Average bottle price: $35.00 to $50.00

Distribution: Albany, NY area

Interesting facts:
The distillery occupies a renovated, century old building.

Beak & Skiff Distillery

4472 Cherry Valley Turnpike
LaFayette, NY 13084
316-677-5105

Owners / Operators:
Steve Morse, Co-owner
Candy Morse, Co-owner
David Pittard, Co-owner
Tim Beak, Co-owner
Jackie Beak, Co-owner
Ed Brennan, Co-owner
Steve Brennan, Co-owner

Email: beakandskiff@gmail.com
Website: www.1911spirits.com
Facebook: 1911 Spirits
Twitter: @1911spirits

Type: Micro Distillery. Opened in 2009.

Hours of operation: Daily, 10 a.m. to 5 p.m. (May 15th to December 31st)

Tours: Available

Types of spirits produced: Vodka, gin, hard cider

Names of spirits:
- 1911 Vodka
- 1911 Gin
- 1911 Hard Cider
- 1911 Wine

Best known for / most popular: 1911 Vodka

Average bottle price: $9.99 to $34.99

Distribution: NY

Interesting facts: Not provided

Black Button Distilling

85 Railroad Street
Rochester, NY 14609
585-730-4512

Owners / Operators:
Jason Barrett, President / Head Distiller
Richard Barrett, Operations Manager

Email: cheers@blackbuttondistilling.com
Website: www.blackbuttondistilling.com
Facebook: Black Button Distilling
Twitter: @BlackButton85
Yelp: Black Button Distilling

Type: Craft Distillery. Opened in June 2012.

Hours of operation:
Tuesday through Friday, noon to 6 p.m.;
Saturday, 9 a.m. to 4 p.m.; Sunday, noon to 4 p.m.

Tours: Available every hour, on the hour

Types of spirits produced: Vodka, whiskey, gin

Names of spirits:
- Black Button Citrus Forward Gin
- Black Button Moonshine
- Black Button Wheat Vodka
- Black Button Lilac Gin (seasonal)
- Black Button Professional Proof Vodka
- Black Button Four Grain Bourbon
- Black Button Unaged Rye

Best known for / most popular:
Black Button Moonshine

Average bottle price: $34.00 to $48.00

Distribution: Upstate NY, on-site retail.

Interesting facts: "Since 1922 my family has provided some of the finest men's suit buttons available. For four generations these buttons have closed suits worn by presidents, popes, kings, and businessmen the world over. From a young age I went to work in my grandfather's factory but it was clear I was meant for a different path. I broke tradition and decided to make whiskey, but the lessons I learned in his factory as a kid still guide me to this day; work hard, work with your hands, make your product the best on the market, and you can't cheat time. My distillery pays homage to my grandfather and the world he knew - where real men worked hard and drank real pot distilled whiskey." - Jason Barrett

Black Dirt Distillery

385 Glenwood Road
Pine Island, NY 10969
845-258-6020

Owners / Operators:
Jeremy Kidde, Co-owner
Jason Grizzanti, Co-owner

Email: info@blackdirtdistillery.com
Website: www.blackdirtdistillery.com
Facebook: Black Dirt Distillery
Twitter: @BDDistillery

Type: Craft Distillery. Opened in 2012.

Hours of operation: Not provided

Tours: Not available

Types of spirits produced: Apple Jack, bourbon

Names of spirits:
- Black Dirt Bourbon

Best known for / most popular: Black Dirt Bourbon

Average bottle price: $44.00

Distribution: NJ, NY

Interesting facts: Not provided

Breuckelen Distilling Company Inc.

77 19th Street
Brooklyn, NY 11232
347-725-4985

Owners / Operators:
Brad Estabrooke, Founder

Email: info@brkdistilling.com
Website: www.brkdistilling.com
Facebook: Breuckelen Distilling
Twitter: @BrkDistilling

Type: Micro Distillery. Opened in 2010.

Hours of operation: By appointment or check website

Tours: Available

Types of spirits produced: Gin, whiskey

Names of spirits:
- Glorious Gin
- 77 Whiskey

Best known for / most popular: 77 Whiskey

Average bottle price: $40.00

Distribution: U.S.; Europe, Australia

Interesting facts: Not provided

Buffalo Distilling Co.

611 Woodley Road
Bennington, NY 14004

Owners / Operators:
Andrew Wegrzyn, President / Distiller
Frank J Weber III, Vice President / Distiller
Eric Kempisty, Chief Engineer/ Distiller

Email: info@bflodistilling.com
Website: www.Buffalodistillingcompany.com
Facebook: Buffalo Distilling Co.
Twitter: @BuffaloDistill

Type: New York State Farm Distillery. Opened in January 2012.

Hours of operation: Monday, Wednesday, Saturday

Tours: Available by appointment

Types of spirits produced:
Brandy, bourbon, whiskey

Names of spirits:
- One Foot Cock Apple Brandy
- One Foot Cock Bourbon
- One Foot Cock Whiskey

Best known for / most popular: Not provided

Average bottle price: $30.00 to $35.00

Distribution: Western NY

Interesting facts: Buffalo Distilling Co. originally opened in 1895, closed during Prohibition, was born again 100 years later.

259

Cacao Prieto LLC

218 Conover Street
Brooklyn, NY 11231
347-225-0130

Owners / Operators:
Daniel Preston
Michele Clark
Michael Dirksen
Matthew Jones, Head Distiller

Email: info@widowjane.com
Website: www.widowjane.com, www.cacaoprieto.com
Facebook: Cacao Prieto or Widow Jane Distillery
Twitter: @CacaoPrieto
YouTube: CacaoPrieto
Vimeo: CacaoPrieto
Instagram: cacao_prieto or widow_jane

Type: Micro Distillery. Opened in 2008.

Hours of operation: Daily

Tours: Available by appointment

Types of spirits produced: Whiskey, rum, vodka, rye, gin, rum liqueur, bourbon whiskey, white dog

Names of spirits:
- Widow Jane Rye
- Widow Jane Bourbon Whiskey
- Widow Jane Wapsie Valley Bourbon Whiskey
- Bloody Butcher High Rye Bourbon Whiskey
- Bloody Butcher Bourbon Whiskey
- Mamajuana
- Chamomile Rum
- Cacao Prieto White Rum
- Cacao Prieto Don Rafael Cacao Rum
- Cacao Prieto Don Daniel Cacao Rum Liqueur
- Cacao Prieto Don Esteban Cacao Rum Liqueur
- Brooklyn Roasting Company Coffee Liqueur

Best known for / most popular: Widow Jane Bourbon Whiskey

Average bottle price: $29.00 to $53.00

Distribution: NY

Interesting facts: Not provided

Catskill Distilling Company Ltd.

2037 Route 17B
Bethel, NY 12720
845-583-3141

Owners / Operators:
Monte Sachs, President
Stacy Cohen, Vice President

Email: msachs@hvc.rr.com
Website: www.catskilldistillingco.com
Facebook: Catskill Distilling Company, Dancing Cat Distillery and Saloon
Twitter: @catskillDistill

Type: Micro Distillery. Opened in 2011.

Hours of operation: Friday through Sunday, 2 p.m. to 8 p.m.

Tours: Available

Types of spirits produced: Vodka

Names of spirits:
- Peace Vodka

Best known for / most popular: Peace Vodka

Average bottle price: $34.99

Distribution: Not provided

Interesting facts: Not provided

Celk Distilling
Apple Country Spirits

3274 Eddy Road
Williamson, NY 14589
315-589-8733

Owners / Operators:
David DeFisher, Founder

Email: info@applecountryspirits.com
Website: www.applecountryspirits.com
Facebook: Tree Vodka

Type: Micro Distillery. Opened in 2012.

Hours of operation: Monday through Friday, by appointment
Saturday, 11 a.m. to 5 p.m.; Sunday, noon to 5 p.m.

Tours: Available

Types of spirits produced: Vodka

Names of spirits:
- Tree Vodka

Best known for / most popular: Tree Vodka

Average bottle price: Not provided

Distribution: NY

Interesting facts: Tree Vodka is gluten free.

Clayton Distillery

40164 NYS Route 12
Clayton, NY 13624
315-285-5004

Owners / Operators:
Michael Aubertine, Majority Owner / Operator
Michael Ingerson, Investor
Roger Howard, Investor

Email: info@claytondistillery.com
Website: www.claytondistillery.com
Facebook: Clayton Distillery
Twitter: @claytondistillery

Type: Craft Distillery. Opened in April 2013.

Hours of operation:
June 15 to September 5
    Monday through Wednesday, 10 a.m. to 5 p.m.
    Thursday through Saturday, 10 a.m. to 8 p.m.
    Sunday, noon to 5 p.m.
September 6 to June 14
    Closed Monday and Tuesday
    Wednesday and Thursday, noon to 5 p.m.
    Friday and Saturday, 10 a.m. to 6 p.m.
    Sunday, noon to 5 p.m.

Tours: Available daily.
$10 per person (includes a complimentary shot glass)

Types of spirits produced: Vodka, gin, whisky, liqueur

Names of spirits:
- Bourbon
- Flagship Vodka
- Shoal Finder Gin
- Apple Pie Moonshine
- Cherry Moonshine
- Lemonade Moonshine
- Raspberry Liqueur
- Maple Strawberry Liqueur
- Limoncello Lemon Liqueur
- Two Dog Moonshine Un-aged corn whisky
- Rhubarbe Fraise
- Strawberry rhubarb liqueur

Best known for / most popular: Flagship Vodka

Average bottle price: $30.99

Distribution: Northern and Central NY State counties

Interesting facts: "I grew up on a small fifth generation dairy farm about fifteen miles from the distillery. In 2006, my parents sold the cows and now we grow our own corn and wheat on the family farm." – Michael Aubertine

Cooperstown Distillery

11 Railroad Avenue
Village of Cooperstown, NY 13326
607-282-4246

Owners / Operators:
Gene Marra, Owner / Distiller
Montell Marra, Owner / Marketing
Rory Gallagher, Distiller / Compliance

Email: cooperstowndistillery@gmail.com
montellmarra@yahoo.com
Website: www.cooperstowndistillery.com
Facebook: Cooperstown Distillery
Cooperstown Distillery Like Page
Twitter: CooperstownDi
Pinterest: Cooperstown Distillery

Type: Craft Distillery. Opened in 2013.

Hours of operation: Daily, 11 a.m. to 6 p.m.

Tours: Available

Types of spirits produced: Bourbon, gin, vodka

Names of spirits:
The Glimmerglass Collection
- Fenimore Gin
- Glimmerglass Vodka

The Baseball Line-up
- Abner Doubleday Double-play Vodka
- Beanball Bourbon

Best known for / most popular:
Beanball Bourbon, Fenimore Gin

Average bottle price: $35.00 to $45.00

Distribution: NY

Interesting facts: This husband and wife team has decades of combined experience in food, wine, viticulture, agriculture and design. They were teaching and promoting "lifestyle" before it was a buzzword. The spirit at Cooperstown Distillery is one of generosity where there is always food, drink, and advice being given away.

Coppersea Distilling

1592 Broadway (Rte. 9W)
West Park, NY 12493
845-444-1044

Owners / Operators:
Angus MacDonald, Master Distiller
Christopher Williams, Distillery Manager
Michael Kinstlick, CEO

Email: michael@coppersea.com
christopher@coppersea.com
angus@coppersea.com
Website: www.coppersea.com
Facebook: Coppersea Distilling

Type: NY Farm Distillery. Opened in 2012.

Hours of operation:
Monday through Friday, 9 a.m. to 5 p.m.

Tours: Available by appointment

Types of spirits produced: Eaux de Vie, whiskey

Names of spirits:
- Coppersea New York Raw Rye
- Coppersea New York Peach Eau de Vie
- Coppersea New York Plum Eau de Vie
- Coppersea New York Pear Eau de Vie
- Coppersea New York Cherry Eau de Vie

Best known for / most popular:
Coppersea New York Raw Rye

Average bottle price: $50.00 to $60.00

Distribution: CA, NY

Interesting facts:
Coppersea Distilling is currently the only known American craft distillery adhering to traditional practices to the extent of growing and malting their own grains, fermenting in wooden, open-top tanks, gravity-feeding mash, and using direct-fired, simple alembic stills.

Delaware Phoenix Distillery

144 Delaware Street
Walton, NY 13856
610-865-5056

Owners / Operators:
Cherl Lins, Owner / Distiller

Email: cheryllins@frontiernet.net
Website: www.delawarephoenix.com
Facebook: Delaware Phoenix Distillery Absinthes

Type: Micro Distillery. Opened in 2011.

Hours of operation: Not provided

Tours: Not provided

Types of spirits produced: Whiskey, absinthe

Names of spirits:
- Delaware Phoenix Walton Waters Absinthe
- Delaware Phoenix Meadow of Love Absinthe
- Delaware Phoenix Corn Whiskey
- Delaware Phoenix Rye Whiskey
- Delaware Phoenix Rye Dog

Best known for / most popular: Not provided

Average bottle price: Not provided

Distribution: Not provided

Interesting facts: Not provided

Demarest Hill Winery

81 Pine Island Turnpike
Warwick, NY 10990
845-986-4723

Owners / Operators:
Francesco Ciummo, Owner

Email: info@demaresthillwinery.com
Website: www.demaresthillwinery.com
Facebook: Demarest Hill Winery

Type: Winery / Micro Distillery. Opened in 2010.

Hours of operation: Daily, 11 a.m. to 6 p.m.

Tours: Available

Types of spirits produced: Grappa, brandy, liqueur, limoncella, orancella

Names of spirits:
- Demarest Hill Winery Grappa
- Demarest Hill Winery Special Reserve Brandy
- Demarest Hill Winery Tropical Liqueur
- Demarest Hill Winery Amarena Aperitivo
- Demarest Hill Winery Limoncella
- Demarest Hill Winery Orancella

Best known for / most popular: Not provided

Average bottle price: Not provided

Distribution: Not provided

Interesting facts: Not provided

Finger Lakes Distilling

4676 NYS Route 414
Burdett, NY 14818
607-546-5510

Owners / Operators:
Brian McKenzie, President / Owner
Thomas McKenzie, Distiller

Email: brian@fingerlakesdistilling.com
Website: www.fingerlakesdistilling.com
Facebook: Finger Lakes Distilling

Type: Craft Distillery. Opened in 2008.

Hours of operation: Daily, 11 a.m. to 5 p.m.

Tours: Saturdays, May through November

Types of spirits produced: Vodka, gin, whiskey, liqueurs, grappa, brandy

Names of spirits:
- Vintner's Vodka
- Vintner's Wild Berry Vodka
- Seneca Drums Gin
- McKenzie Distiller's Reserve Gin
- McKenzie Pure Potstill Whiskey
- McKenzie Bourbon Whiskey
- McKenzie Rye Whiskey
- Glen Thunder Corn Whiskey
- Pear Brandy
- Riesling Grappa
- Gewurztraminer Grappa
- White Pike Whiskey
- Maplejack Liqueur
- Cassis Liqueur
- Raspberry Liqueur
- Cherry Liqueur
- Grape Brandy

Best known for / most popular: McKenzie Whiskeys

Average bottle price: $19.00 to $48.00

Distribution: CT, DC, IL, MA, MD, NJ, NY, PA

Interesting facts: The first standalone distillery in the Finger Lakes region.

Five & 20 Spirits
Mazza Chautauqua Cellars

8398 West Main Road (Route 20)
Westfield, NY 14787
716-793-9463

Owners / Operators:
Mazza Family

Email: info@fiveand20.com
Website: www.fiveand20.com
Facebook: Five & 20
Twitter: @fiveand20

Type: Winery / Micro Distillery.
Opened in 2006; expanded in 2013

Hours of operation:
July – August
    Monday through Saturday, 10 a.m. to 8 p.m.
    Sunday, 11 a.m. to 6 p.m.
September – June
    Monday through Saturday, 10 a.m. to 6 p.m.
    Sunday, 11 a.m. to 5 p.m.

Tours: Available when distiller is present

Types of spirits produced: Eau de vie, grappa, grain based spirits (whiskey, bourbon), specialty spirits, liqueur

Names of spirits:
- Pear in the Bottle Pear Eau de Vie
- Apple Eau de Vie
- Plum Eau de Vie
- Cherry Eau de Vie
- Pear Eau de Vie
- Grappa of Steuben
- Rye Whiskey
- Corn Whiskey
- Bourbon (coming soon)
- White Rye Whiskey (coming soon)
- Bierschnapps (coming soon)
- Limoncello (coming soon)

Best known for / most popular: Rye Whiskey (aged)

Average bottle price: $24.95 to $79.95

Distribution: Not provided

Interesting facts:
- The area's first grain-to-glass distillery.
- Soon to be one of only a handful of places in the U.S. to house wine, spirits and beer under one roof.

Greenhook Ginsmiths

208 Dupont Street
Brooklyn, NY 11222
646-339-3719

Owners / Operators:
Steven DeAngelo, Ginsmith

Email: steven@greenhookgin.com
Website: www.greenhookgin.com
Facebook: Greenhook Ginsmiths
Twitter: @GreenhookGin

Type: Micro Distillery. Open in 2012.

Hours of operation: Not open to the public

Tours: Not available

Types of spirits produced: Gin, liqueur

Names of spirits:
- Greenhook Ginsmiths American Dry Gin
- Greenhook Ginsmiths Beach Plum Gin Liqueur

Best known for / most popular: Greenhook Ginsmiths American Dry Gin

Average bottle price: Not provided

Distribution: Not provided

Interesting facts: Not provided

Harvest Spirits LLC

3074 US Route 9
Valatie, NY 12184
518-261-1625

Owners / Operators:
Derek Grout, Owner

Email: info@harvestspirits.com
Website: www.harvestspirits.com
Facebook: Harvest Spirits Farm Distillery
Twitter: @HarvestSpirits

Type: Micro Distillery. Opened in 2008.

Hours of operation: Saturday and Sunday, noon to 5 p.m.

Tours: Available

Types of spirits produced: Vodka, brandy, grappa and applejack. In development: Himbeer Geist, frozen applejack, bacon-washed applejack, fruit-in-bottle and various fruit and herbal infused spirits

Names of spirits:
- Core Vodka
- Cornelius Applejack
- Apple Eau de Vie
- Pear Eau de Vie
- Grappa
- Rare Pear Brandy

Best known for / most popular: Applejack, vodka

Average bottle price: $25.00 to $40.00

Distribution: NY

Interesting facts: Not provided

Hidden Marsh Distillery

2981 Auburn Road (U.S. Route 20)
Seneca Falls, NY 13148
315-568-8190

Owners / Operators:
George, Ginny, Bill & Ed Martin, Owners

Email: info@beevodka.com
Website: www.beevodka.com
Facebook: Montezuma Winery & Hidden Marsh Distillery
Twitter: @MontezumaWinery

Type: Winery / Micro Distillery. Opened in 2008.

Hours of operation: Daily, 9 a.m. to 6 p.m.

Tours: Not available

Types of spirits produced:
Vodka, brandy, whiskey, liqueurs

Names of spirits:
- Judd's Wreckin' Ball Corn Whiskey
- Duck Blind Shine Wheat Whiskey
- Tangle Foot Corn Whiskey
- Lone Loggers Bourbon Whiskey
- Railroad Rye Whiskey
- Orchard Vodka (distilled from apples)
- BEE Hot Vodka
  (infused with Jalapeno and Habanera peppers)
- Elderberry Liqueur

Best known for / most popular:
BEE Vodka

Average bottle price:
$24.99 to $48.99

Distribution: NY

Hillrock Estate Distillery

408 Pooles Hill Road
Ancram, NY 12502
518-329-1023

Owners / Operators:
Jeffrey Baker, Owner
Dave Pickerell, Master Distiller
Tim Welly, Head of Operations / Distiller
Danielle Eddy, Director of PR Marketing & Sales

Email: info@hillrockdistillery.com
Website: www.hillrockdistillery.com
Facebook: Hillrock Estate Distillery

Type: Micro Distillery. Opened in 2011.

Hours of operation: Available by appointment

Tours: Available by appointment

Types of spirits produced: Whiskey

Names of spirits:
- Hillrock Soera Aged Bourbon Whiskey
- Estate Single Malt
- Estate Rye

Best known for / most popular:
Hillrock Soera Aged Bourbon Whiskey

Average bottle price: Not provided

Distribution: NY

Interesting facts: Field-to-glass operation with on-site floor malthouse.

Industry City Distillery Inc.

33 35th Street, Unit 6
Brooklyn, NY 11232
917-727-5309

Owners / Operators:
Dave Kyrejko, Co-founder / Chief Engineer
Zachary Bruner, Co-founder/ Fabricator & Machinist / CEO
Peter Simon, Co-founder / Director of Sales and Operations

Email: tours@drinkicd.com
Website: www.drinkicd.com
Facebook: Industry City Distillery
Twitter: @drinkicd
Instagram: @drinkicd
Flickr: The City Foundry

Type: Micro Distillery. Opened in 2011.

Hours of operation:
Monday through Friday, 9:30 a.m. to 6 p.m.
Saturday and Sunday, 10 a.m. to 5 p.m.

Tours: Available upon request

Types of spirits produced: Vodka

Names of spirits:
- Industry Standard Vodka
- Technical Reserve Neutral Spirit

Best known for / most popular:
Industry Standard Vodka

Average bottle price: $36.00

Distribution: NYC area

Interesting facts:
ICD uses a custom-built immobilized cell bioreactor system for continuous fermentation. This, along with their steam stripping still and their batch fractional column still, was designed and built in-house by the team.

Jack From Brooklyn Inc.

177 Dwight Street
Brooklyn, NY 11231

Owners / Operators:
Alan Camlet, Co-founder
Timothy Kealey, Co-founder

Email: info@jackfrombrooklyn.com
Website: www.jackfrombrooklyn.com
Facebook: The Liquortarian
Twitter: @TheLiquortarian

Type: Micro Distillery. Opened in 2011.

Hours of operation: Not provided

Tours: Not provided

Types of spirits produced: Liqueur

Names of spirits:
- Sorel

Best known for / most popular: Sorel

Average bottle price: Not provided

Distribution: Not provided

Interesting facts: Sorel is a hibiscus-based liqueur.

Kings County Distillery

Brooklyn Navy Yard, Bldg. 121
Brooklyn, NY 11205

Owners / Operators:
Colin Spoelman, Co-founder / Master Distiller
David Haskell, Co-founder
Nicole Austin, Master Blender
Matthew Million, Distillery Manager

Email: info@kingscountydistillery.com
Website: www.kingscountydistillery.com
Facebook: Kings County Distillery
Twitter: @KingsCoWhiskey

Type: Micro Distillery. Opened in 2010.

Hours of operation: Daily, 9 a.m. to midnight

Tours: Available on Saturdays from 2:30 p.m. to 5:30 p.m.

Types of spirits produced: Whiskey, bourbon

Names of spirits:
- Kings County Moonshine
- Kings County Bourbon
- Kings County Chocolate Whiskey

Best known for / most popular: Kings County Moonshine, neat

Average bottle price: $20.00 to $40.00

Distribution: NJ, NY

Interesting facts:
Kings County Distillery operates out of the century old Paymaster Building in the Brooklyn Navy Yard.

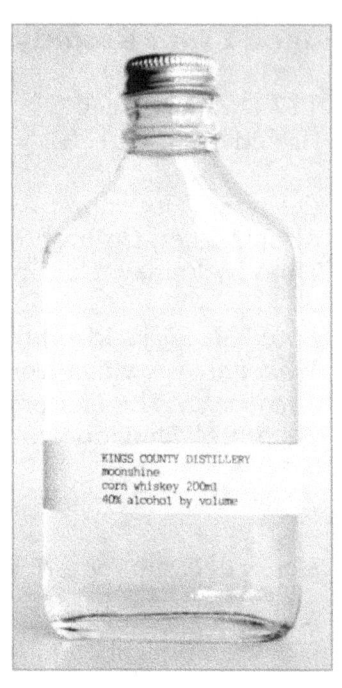

KyMar Farm Distillery

P.O. Box 72
Charlotteville, NY 12036
518-290-0051

Owners / Operators:
Kenneth Wortz, Founder / Managing Member / Distiller
Lori Wortz, Managing Member / Operations
Bill Martz, Member / Operations

Email: info@ky-mar.com
Website: www.ky-mar.com
Facebook: KyMar Farm Distillery

Type: Micro Distillery. Opened in 2011.

Hours of operation: Weekends by appointment only

Tours: Available Summer 2014

Types of spirits produced: Eau de Vie, shine, liqueur

Names of spirits:
- Schoharie Mapple Jack
- Schoharie Shine
- Schoharie Eau de Vie de Pomme

Best known for / most popular:
Schoharie Mapple Jack

Average bottle price: $30.00 to $35.00

Distribution: CT, MA, NY

Interesting facts:
- Schoharie Mapple Jack is the perfect liqueur served neat, on the rocks or in cocktails.
- Schoharie Shine is made from sweet sorghum in lieu of traditional grains and cane sugar.

Photo by Lea Sophie

Lake George Distilling Company

11262 State Route 149
Fort Ann, NY 12827
518-639-1025

Owners / Operators:
Robin McDougall, CEO / CFO
John McDougall, Distiller

Email: info@lakegeorgedistillingcompany.com
Website: www.lakegeorgedistillingcompany.com
Facebook: Lake George Distilling Company
Twitter: @LG_DISCO

Type: New York State Farm Distillery. Opened in September 2013.

Hours of operation:
Wednesday through Friday, 5 p.m. to 8 p.m.
Saturday, noon to 7 p.m.; Sunday, noon to 5 p.m.

Tours: Available as schedule allows

Types of spirits produced:
Bourbon, rye whiskey, corn whiskey (moonshine), smoked corn whiskey

Names of spirits:
- Bullhead Bourbon
- Red Rock Rye
- 32 Mile Moonshine
- Indian Kettles Smoke
- Apple Pie Moonshine
- Lake George Lemonade

Best known for / most popular:
Purple Moon

Average bottle price: $20.00 to $30.00

Distribution: On-site retail, NY

Services offered other than production:
Tours, tastings, merchandise

Lake Placid Spirits LLC

Lake Placid, NY 12946

Owners / Operators:
Ann Stillman O'Leary, Owner
Twig McGlynn, Manager

Email: info@lakeplacidspirits.com
Website: www.lakeplacidspirits.com
Facebook: P3 Placid Vodka, Lake Placid Spirits, LLC
YouTube: Lake Placid Spirits--Cool Runnings

Type: Craft Distillery. Opened in 2007.

Hours of operation: Daily

Tours: Not available

Types of spirits produced: Vodka, gin

Names of spirits:
- 46 Peaks Potato Vodka
- P3 Placid Vodka
- Alpenglow Cranberry Maple Vodka
- Blue Line Gin

Best known for / most popular:
46 Peaks Potato Vodka

Average bottle price: $28.00 to $32.00

Distribution: NY

Interesting facts:
- The word Adirondack means "barkeater" or "tree eater" and the indigenous people used the white pine bark and needles to obtain vitamin C.
- Blue Line refers to the boundary of the Adirondack Park of New York State, the largest park in the lower 48 states.
- A certified Women Owned Business of NY State (W.B.E.)
- Blue Line Gin uses a local Adirondack botanical, northern white pine. The new spring growth is harvested in a sustainable manner in the Lake Placid Olympic Region and is combined with other classic gin botanicals.

Awards and Recognitions:
Blue Line Gin
- Silver Medal, 2013 New York State Wine & Grape Foundation Watkins Glen

Lockhouse Distillery

255 Great Arrow Avenue, Ste. 31
Buffalo, NY 14207
716-983-4025

Owners / Operators:
Niko Georgiadis, Partner / President
Chad Vosseller, Partner / Vice President of Operations
Jon Mirro, Partner / Vice President of Marketing
Thomas Jablonski, Business Manager

Email: info@lockhousedistillery.com
Website: www.lockhousedistillery.com
Facebook: Lockhouse Distillery
Twitter: @LockhouseDist

Type: Micro Distillery. Open in 2013.

Hours of operation: Not provided

Tours: Not available

Types of spirits produced: Vodka

Names of spirits:
- Lockhouse Vodka

Best known for / most popular: Lockhouse Vodka

Average bottle price: $30.00 to $50.00

Distribution: Not provided

Interesting facts: Buffalo's first operating distillery since Prohibition.

Long Island Spirits

2182 Sound Avenue
Baiting Hollow, NY 11933
631-630-9322

Owners / Operators:
Richard Stabile, Owner / Founder / Master Distiller

Email: info@lispirits.com
Website: www.lispirits.com
Facebook: LiV® Vodka
Twitter: @LiVGUY

Type: Micro Distillery. Opened in 2007.

Tasting room hours: Monday through Thursday, 10 a.m. to 5 p.m. Friday and Saturday, 10 a.m. to 6 p.m.; Sunday, 11 a.m. to 6 p.m.

Tours: Not available

Types of spirits produced:
Potato Vodka, liqueurs, single malt whisky, bourbon, rye

Names of spirits:
- LiV Vodka
  Original LiV, Ristretto Espresso Flavored Vodka
- Sorbetta Liqueurs
  Lemon, Lime, Orange, Strawberry, Raspberry
- Pine Barrens Single Malt Whisky
- Rough Rider Rye
- Rough Rider Straight Bourbon Whisky

Best known for / most popular: LiV Vodka

Average bottle price: $27.00

Distribution: CO, CT, DC, GA, IL, MA, NJ, NY, PA, RI

Interesting facts:
- Long Island Spirits is the first craft distillery on Long Island since the 1800s.
- LiV Vodka is crafted from 100% locally and sustainable marcy russet Long Island Potatoes, creating a gluten-free product.
- The Sorbetta Liqueurs are the first ever known potato based liqueurs to be available in the U.S. They are crafted using all natural macerated fruits, including Long Island strawberries and raspberries.

Luckey Spirits

112 Mountain Road
Greenwich, NY 12834
518-369-4329

Owners / Operators:
Frederick Luckey, Owner / Operator
Florence Luckey, Owner / Operator

Email: frederick@luckeyspirits.com
Website: www.luckeyspirits.com

Type:
New York State Class-D Farm Distillery. Opened in October 2013.

Hours of operation: Open to the public by appointment

Tours: Available by appointment

Types of spirits produced: Vodka, brandy

Names of spirits:
- TBA

Best known for / most popular: TBA

Average bottle price: TBA

Distribution: Self distribution

Interesting facts:
- Inspired by Bavarian relatives' tradition of small scale distillation of fruit brandies, the Luckey's see their distillery as a way to get in touch with nature's cycles and to help revive rural traditions of farm distilling.
- A traditional European style 80 gallon wood-fired Kothe 3-plate still, custom made in Eislingen, Germany, is the work horse of the distillery supplemented by a 50 gallon Trident Welding packed column still made in Port Chester, Maine. Cooling water for the stills, as well as water for blending spirits, is gravity fed from Willard Mountain springs. Spent fruit mash and waste fruit are provided to local pig farmers.
- All alcohol is produced through on-site fermentation of their fruit and honey, supplemented by produce from local farms.

Services offered other than production: Tasting room

Magnanini Farm Winery Inc.

172 Strawridge Road
Wallkill, NY 12589
845-895-2767

Owners / Operators:
Richard Magnanini, Owner
Robert Magnanini, Operator / Manager
David Magnanini, Operator
Rachel Magnanini, Owner / Operator

Email: info@magnanini.com
Website: www.magwine.com

Type: Winery / Micro Distillery. Opened in 2008.

Hours of operation: Saturday and Sunday

Tours: Available by appointment

Types of spirits produced: Grappa, liqueur

Names of spirits:
- Grappa Del Nonno
- Grappa & Miele
- Grappa & Limone
- Grappa & Walnut
- Pear Liqueur

Best known for / most popular: Grappa Del Nonno

Average bottle price: $24.00 to $34.00

Distribution: On-site retail

Interesting facts:
- Magnanini Farm Winery Grappa del Nonno is one of the only grappas in the world that is made in small batches from Dechaunac grape marc.
- Grappa Del Nonno won a Bronze Medal at the 7th Annual Judging of Artisan American Spirits.
- Grappa Del Nonno won a Double Gold Medal at the 2013 Hudson Valley Wine and Spirits Competition.

Myer Farm Distillers

7350 State Route 89
Ovid, NY 14521
607-532-4800

Owners / Operators:
Joseph Myer, President / Master Distiller
John Myer, Vice President

Email: joe@myerfarmdistillers.com
Website: www.myerfarmdistillers.com
Facebook: Myer Farm Distillers
Twitter: @MFDistillers

Type: Micro Distillery. Opened in 2012.

Tasting room hours: Open seven days
Spring through Fall - 10:30 a.m. to 5:30 p.m.
Winter - 11 a.m. to 5 p.m.

Tours: Available by appointment

Types of spirits produced:
Vodka, flavored vodkas, gin, aged whiskeys, clear whiskeys

Names of spirits:
- Myer Farm Gin
- Myer Farm Vodka
- Myer Farm Blueberry Orange Vodka
- Myer Farm Ginger Vodka
- Myer Farm White Dog Wheat Spirit
- Myer Farm White Dog Corn Whiskey
- John Myer Wheat Whiskey
- John Myer Four Grain Whiskey
- John Myer Bourbon Whiskey
- John Myer Rye Whiskey

Best known for / most popular: Myer Farm Gin, Myer Farm Ginger Vodka, John Myer Four Grain Whiskey, and John Myer Bourbon Whiskey

Average bottle price: $18.00 to $45.00

Distribution: NY

Interesting facts:
- Founded and operated by fifth generation farmers on land that has been in the family since 1868.
- Products use International Services Certified Organic Grain produced by John Myer.
- Won the American Distilling Institute's 7th Annual Judging of Artisan American Spirits Best of Category in two categories (contemporary gin and clear whiskey) their first year in production.

Nahmias et Fils

201 Saw Mill River Road, Bldg. C
Yonkers, NY 10701
914-294-0055

Owners / Operators:
Dorit Nahmias, President
David Nahmias, Master Distiller

Email: Dorit Nahmias: dorit@baronnahmias.com
David Nahmias: david@baronnahmias.com
Website: www.nahmiasetfils.com
Facebook: Nahmias et Fils distillery
Twitter: @nahmiasetfils

Type: Micro Distillery. Opened in 2012.

Hours of operation:
Monday through Friday, 8 a.m. to 6 p.m.

Tours: Available by appointment

Types of spirits produced:
Mahia, un-aged rye whiskey, aged rye whiskey

Names of spirits:
- Mahia
- Legs Diamond Whiskey

Best known for / most popular: Mahia

Average bottle price: $34.99 to $44.99

Distribution: CA, CT, MA, NJ, NY, PA, RI

Interesting facts: Not provided

Awards and Recognitions:
Mahia
- Silver Medal, 2012 New York International Spirits Competition
- 93 Points, Tasting Panel Magazine

Legs Diamond Rye Whiskey
- Bronze Medal, Beverage Testing Institute
- 92 Points, Tasting Panel Magazine

New York Distilling Company

79 Richardson Street
Brooklyn, NY 11211
718-412-0874

Owners / Operators:
Tom Potter, Co-founder / President
Allen Katz, Co-founder / Vice-president
Bill Potter, Co-founder / Production Manager

Email: info@nydistilling.com
Website: www.nydistilling.com
Facebook: New York Distilling Company
Twitter: @nydistilling

Type: Micro Distillery. Opened in 2011.

Hours of operation:
Monday, 6 p.m. to midnight; Tuesday through Friday, 6 p.m. to 2 a.m.
Saturday, 3 p.m. to 2 a.m.; Sunday, 3 p.m. to midnight

Tours: Saturday and Sunday, 3 p.m. to 5 p.m.
Free and no reservation required.

Types of spirits produced: American rye whiskey, gin

Names of spirits:
- Perry's Tot - Navy Strength Gin
- Dorothy Parker - American Gin
- Chief Gowanus - New-Netherland Gin
- Mister Katz's Rock & Rye

Best known for / most popular:
Dorothy Parker – American Gin

Average bottle price: $31.00

Distribution: Regional distribution

Interesting facts:
- Chief Gowanus - New-Netherland Gin is based on an early 19th century recipe for Resemblance of Holland Gin that was made in the U.S. to mimic Genever
- New York Distilling Company was the backdrop for a scene in Season 4 Episode 11 of *White Collar*.

Port Morris Distillery

780 E. 133rd Street
Port Morris
Bronx, NY 10454
718-585-3192

Owners / Operators:
Rafael Barbosa, Co-owner
William Valentin, Co-owner

Email: rbarbosa@portmorrisdistillery.com
wvalentin@portmorrisdistillery.com
Website: www.portmorrisdistillery.com
Facebook: Port Morris Distillery

Type: Micro Distillery. Opened in 2012.

Hours of operation:
Monday through Friday, 9 a.m. to 6 p.m.
Saturday, 9 a.m. to 8 p.m.

Tours: Available by appointment

Types of spirits produced: Rum

Names of spirits:
- Pitorro Añejo
- Pitorro Shine

Best known for / most popular: Pitorro Shine

Average bottle price: $35.00

Distribution: NY

Interesting facts:
- The legacy of pitorro also known as "moonshine rum" began in the lush mountains of Guayama, Puerto Rico.
- Port Morris Distillery became one of the first moonshine distillers to age pitorro in wood cast barrels. The 80 proof añejo is cured by resting the Pitorro in American-made used and new barrels for about two years.
- Port Morris Distillery's pitorro uses a prolonged fermentation process of 14 to 21 days, which gives the pitorro a glassy look similar to perlas (pearls)—meaning the pitorro is of the highest quality.

Prohibition Distillery LLC

10 Union Street
Roscoe, NY 12776
917-685-8989

Owners / Operators:
Brian Facquet, Co-founder
John Walsh, Co-founder

Email: brian@prohibitiondistillery.com
Website: www.prohibitiondistillery.com
Facebook: Bootlegger 21 New York Vodka
Twitter: @Bootlegger21

Type: Micro Distillery. Opening in 2013.

Hours of operation: Daily

Tours: Available

Types of spirits produced: Vodka

Names of spirits:
- Bootlegger 21 Vodka

Best known for / most popular: Bootlegger 21 Vodka

Average bottle price: $25.00 to $29.00

Distribution: AZ, CA, CT, GA, MA, MD, NJ, NY, RI, TN

Interesting facts:
- The distillery is located in an old, restored, firehouse.
- Starting to make bourbon, rye, moonshine and gin.

Proof of Concept LLC
Barrow's Intense Ginger Liqueur

67 35th Street, Ste. C405
Brooklyn, NY 11232
917-597-1084

Owners / Operators:
Josh Morton, Owner

Email: taste@barrowsintense.com
Website: www.barrowsintense.com
Facebook: Barrow's Intense Ginger Liqueur
Twitter: @barrowsintense
Instagram: @barrowsintense

Type: Small Batch Rectifier. Opened in November 2012.

Hours of operation: Not open to the public

Tours: Available by appointment

Types of spirits produced: Liqueur

Names of spirits:
- Barrow's Intense Ginger Liqueur

Best known for / most popular:
Barrow's Intense Ginger Liqueur

Average bottle price: $30.00 to $35.00

Distribution: CT, MA, NH, NJ, NY, PA

Interesting facts:
A quarter pound of fresh ginger goes into every bottle.

Awards and Recognitions:
- SIPS 2013 - "Best of Class" Platinum Award

Saratoga Distilleries Inc.

2474 Old Mill Road
Galway, NY 12074
518-879-1793

Owners / Operators:
Richard F. DeVall, President / Head Distiller
David F. DeVall, Vice President / Plant Manager

Email: richdevall@saratogadistilleries.com
Website: www.saragogadistilleries.com
Facebook: Saratoga Distilleries, Inc.

Type: Micro Distillery. Opened in 2011.

Hours of operation: Vary

Tours: Available by appointment

Types of spirits produced: Bourbon

Names of spirits:
- Saratoga Single Barrel Bourbon

Best known for / most popular:
Saratoga Single Barrel Bourbon

Average bottle price: Not provided

Distribution: NY

Interesting facts: Not provided

Shinn Estate Vineyards and Farmhouse

2000 Oregon Road
Mattituck, NY 11952
631-804-0367

Owners / Operators:
David Page, Owner / Distiller

Email: info@shinnestatevineyards.com
Website: www.shinnestatevineyards.com
Facebook: Shinn Estate Vineyards
Twitter: @shinnvineyard

Type: Winery / Micro Distillery. Opened in 2010.

Hours of operation:
Monday through Thursday, 10:30 a.m. to 5 p.m.
Friday and Saturday, 10:30 a.m. to 8 p.m.; Sunday, 10:30 a.m. to 5 p.m.

Tours: Available

Types of spirits produced: Brandy, grappa

Names of spirits:
- Shinn Estate Vineyards Eau de Vie
- Shinn Estate Vineyards Shine

Best known for / most popular: Shinn Estate Vineyards Shine

Average bottle price: $25.00 to $48.00

Distribution: NY

Interesting facts: Not provided

Six Mile Creek Winery & Distillery

1551 Slaterville Road
Ithaca, NY 14850
607-272-9463

Owners / Operators:
Nancy and Roger Battistella, Owners
Paul King, Production Supervisor
Peter Masse, General Manager
Will Adams, Tasting Room Manager
Melissa Croes, Asst. Tasting Room Manager

Email: info@sixmilecreek.com
Website: www.sixmilecreek.com
Facebook: Six Mile Creek
Twitter: @SixMileCreek
Yelp: Six Mile Creek Vineyard

Type: Winery / Micro Distillery. Opened in 1987.

Hours of operation:
Monday through Thursday, 11 a.m. to 6 p.m.
Friday and Saturday, 10 a.m. to 6 p.m.; Sunday, 11 a.m. to 5 p.m.

Tours: Available

Types of spirits produced: Vodka, gin, limoncella, grappa

Names of spirits:
- Six Mile Creek Vodka
- Six Mile Creek Gin
- Six Mile Creek Grappa
- Six Mile Creek Limoncella

Best known for / most popular: Six Mile Creek Vodka

Average bottle price: Not provided

Distribution: Not provided

Interesting facts: Not provided

StilltheOne Distillery LLC

1 Martin Place
Port Chester, NY 10573
914-217-0347

Owners / Operators:
Ed and Laura Tiedge, Owners

Email: ed@stilltheonedistillery.com
Website: www.combvodka.com
Facebook: COMB Vodka, StilltheOne Distillery
Twitter: @Comb_CTO

Type: Micro Distillery. Opened in 2007.

Hours of operation: Daily, 7 a.m. to 5 p.m.

Tours: Available by appointment

Types of spirits produced: Vodka, whiskey, gin, brandy

Names of spirits:
- COMB Vodka
- COMB 9 Gin
- COMB Blossom Brandy
- Westchester Whiskey

Best known for / most popular: COMB Vodka

Average bottle price: $34.00

Distribution: CA, CT, IL, ND, NY

Interesting facts: This is the first legal distillery in Westchester since Prohibition.

COMB VODKA • COMB 9 GIN

Stoutridge Distillery

10 Ann Kaley Lane
Marlboro, NY 12542
845-236-7620

Owners / Operators:
Stephen Osborn, Owner / Operator
Kimberly Wagner, Owner / Operator

Email: steve@stoutridge.com
Website: www.stoutridge.com

Type: Winery / Micro Distillery. Opened in 2009.

Hours of operation: Friday through Sunday, 11 a.m. to 6 p.m. year-round

Tours: Available.

Types of spirits produced:
Brandy, grappa, vodka, gin, corn, rye whiskey

Names of spirits:
- Northern Threat Yankee Bourbon
- Wagner's White Lightning
- Stoutridge Vodka
- Stoutridge Gin

Best known for / most popular: Stoutridge Gin

Average bottle price: Not provided

Distribution: On-site retail

Interesting facts: The distillery is built on the site of a Prohibition era distillery.

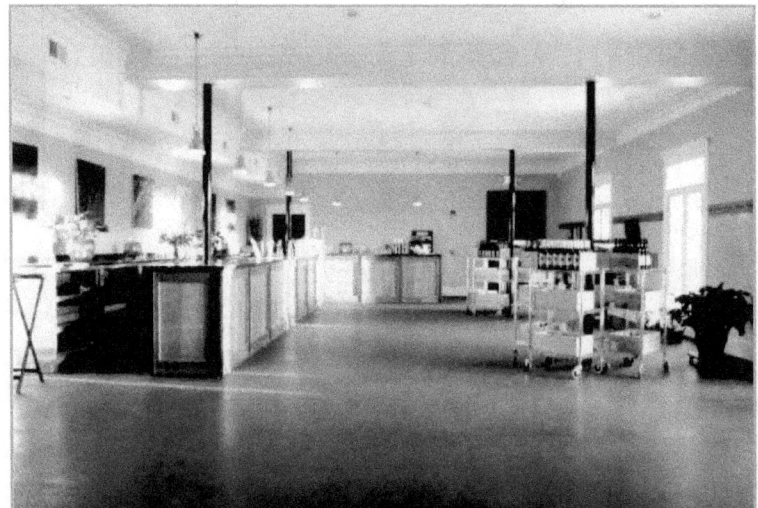

The Noble Experiment NYC

23A Meadow Street
Brooklyn, NY 11206
718-381-3693

Owners / Operators:
Bridget C. Firtle, Founder / Head Distiller

Email: info@tnenyc.com
Website: www.tnenyc.com
Facebook: The Noble Experiment NYC
Twitter: @tneNYC
Instagram: tnenyc

Type: Micro Distillery. Opened in 2012.

Hours of operation: Monday through Saturday, 10 a.m. to 6 p.m.

Tours: Available Saturday at 4 p.m.

Types of spirits produced: Rum

Names of spirits:
- Owney's NYC Rum

Best known for / most popular: Owney's NYC Rum

Average bottle price: $34.00 to $36.00

Distribution: NY

Interesting facts: The distillery is housed in a turn of the century warehouse.

Tirado Distillery

888 E. 163rd Street
Bronx, NY 10459

Owners / Operators:
Dr. Renee Hernandez Tirado, Owner

Email: madhern@yahoo.com
Website: www.tiradowhiskey.com
Facebook: Tirado Whiskey

Type: Micro Distillery. Opened in 2011.

Hours of operation: Monday through Friday, 9 a.m. to 5 p.m.

Tours: Available

Types of spirits produced: Whiskey, rum, liqueur

Names of spirits:
- Tirado Gold
- Tirado NY Corn Whiskey
- Tirado El Caribe Whiskey
- Tirado Maple Delight
- Tirado El Pitito Rum

Best known for / most popular: Not provided

Average bottle price: Not provided

Distribution: NY

Interesting facts:
First legal distillery in the Bronx since Prohibition.

Tuthilltown Spirits Distillery

14 Grist Mill Lane
Gardiner, NY 12525
Tuthilltown office: 845-255-1527
Retail store / Tour reservations: 845-633-8734

Owners / Operators:
Ralph Erenzo, Founder / Distiller
Brian Lee, Founder / Distiller
Gable Erenzo, Distiller / Ambassador / Manager
Joel Elder, Chief R & D Distiller
Cathy Erenzo, Executive Manager
Michael Chichetti, Whiskey Production Manager
Brendan O'Rourke, Operations Manager

Email: ambassador@tuthilltown.com
Website: www.tuthilltown.com
Facebook: Tuthilltown Spirits, Hudson Whiskey
Twitter: @Tuthilltown, @HudsonWhiskey

Type: Micro Distillery. Opened in 2005.

Hours of operation:
Thursday through Monday, 11 a.m. to 6 p.m.
Sunday, noon to 6 p.m.

Tours: Available

Types of spirits produced:
Bourbon, gin, rum, whiskey, vodka, seasonal liqueurs, eau de vie

Names of spirits:
Hudson Whiskeys
- Single Malt
- Baby Bourbon
- Four Grain Bourbon
- Manhattan Rye
- New York Corn Whiskey
- Indigenous Vodka: Empire State Wheat and Fresh Pressed Apple
- Half Moon Orchard Gin
- Tuthilltown Barrel Aged Cassis
- Basement Bitters
- Roggen's Rum

Best known for: Hudson Baby Bourbon

Average bottle price / most popular: $28.00 to $45.00

Distribution: International

Interesting facts:
- Tuthilltown Spirits is New York's first whiskey distillery since Prohibition.
- Hudson Baby Bourbon was the first bourbon whiskey to be distilled in NY.

Van Brunt Stillhouse

6 Bay Street
Brooklyn, NY 11231
718-852-6405

Owners / Operators:
Daric Schlesselman, Owner / Distiller

Email: info@VanBruntStillhouse.com
Website: www.vanbruntstillhouse.com
Facebook: Van Brunt Stillhouse
Twitter: @VBStillhouse

Type: Micro Distillery. Opened in 2012.

Hours of operation: Saturday and Sunday, 1 p.m. to 5 p.m.

Tours: Saturday and Sunday at 2 p.m. and 4 p.m.

Types of spirits produced: Rum, whiskey, grappa

Names of spirits:
- Due North Rum
- Red Hook Grappa
- Van Brunt Stillhouse Whiskey

Best known for / most popular: Due North Rum

Average bottle price: $25.00 to $50.00

Distribution: NYC metro area

Interesting facts: Not provided

Warwick Valley Distillery

114 Little York Road
Warwick, NY 10990
845-258-6020

Owners / Operators:
Jason Grizzanti, Owner
Jeremy Kidde, Owner
Joseph Grizzanti, Owner

Email: wvwinery@warwick.net
Website: www.wvwinery.com
Facebook: Warwick Valley Winery and Distillery

Type: Winery / Micro Distillery. Opened in 2002.

Hours of operation: Daily, 11 a.m. to 6 p.m.

Tours: Available by appointment only

Types of spirits produced: Bourbon, gin, brandy, liqueurs

Names of spirits:
- American Fruits™ Apple Brandy
- American Fruits™ Pear Brandy
- American Fruits™ Black Currant Cordial
- American Fruits™ Bartlett Pear Liqueur
- American Fruits™ Sour Cherry Cordial
- American Fruits™ Burbon Barrel Aged Apple Liqueur
- Warwick Rustic American Gin

Best known for / most popular: Warwick Rustic American Gin

Average bottle price: Not provided

Distribution: U.S.

Interesting facts:
In 2002, Warwick Valley Winery & Distillery became the first licensed distillery in the Hudson Valley since Prohibition.

Adam Dalton Distillery

251 Biltmore Avenue
Asheville, NC 28801
336-413-1657

Owners / Operators:
Adam Dalton, Owner / Manager / Distiller
Joan Dalton, Owner / Manager / CFO

Email: adamdaltondistillery@gmail.com
Website: www.addistillery.com
Facebook: Adam Dalton Distillery
Twitter: @ADDistillery

Type: Micro Distillery. Opened in 2011.

Hours of operation:
Monday through Friday, 5 p.m. until close
Saturday and Sunday, 3 p.m. until close

Tours: Available by appointment

Types of spirits produced: Rum, blue agave, vodka, moonshine, whiskey

Names of spirits:
- White Widow

Best known for / most popular: White Widow

Average bottle price: $19.99

Distribution: NC

Interesting facts: First legal distillery in Asheville, NC since Prohibition.

Asheville Distilling Company

12 Old Charlotte Highway
Asheville, NC 28803
828-575-2000

Owners / Operators:
Troy Ball, Owner / Founder
Charlie Ball, Master Distiller

Email: info@troyandsons.com
Website: www.troyandsons.com
Facebook: Troy and Sons
Twitter: @troyandsons
Youtube: Asheville Distilling

Type: Micro Distillery. Opened in 2010.

Hours of operation:
Monday through Saturday

Tours:
Available Friday and Saturday at 5 p.m. and 6 p.m.

Types of spirits produced:
Whiskey, premium moonshine

Names of spirits:
- Blonde Whiskey
- Troy & Sons Oak Reserve Whiskey
- Troy & Sons Platinum Heirloom Moonshine Whiskey

Best known for / most popular:
Troy & Sons Platinum Moonshine

Average bottle price: $29.95 to $49.95

Distribution: CA, CT, GA, NC, SC, TN, TX

Interesting facts:
Troy is the first woman to start a whiskey distillery in modern times.

Blue Ridge Distilling Company

228 Redbud Lane
Bostic, NC 28018
828-245-2041

Owners / Operators:
Tim Ferris, Owner

Email: info@blueridgedistilling.com
Website: www.blueridgedistilling.com
Facebook: Blue Ridge Distilling Co., Inc.
Twitter: @DefiantWhisky
Instagram: Defiantwhisky

Type: Micro Distillery. Opened in 2010.

Hours of operation: Daily

Tours: Available by appointment

Types of spirits produced: Whisky

Names of spirits:
- Defiant Whisky, An American Single Malt

Best known for / most popular:
Defiant American Single Malt Whisky

Average bottle price: $39.99

Distribution:
CT, DC, DE, GA, MD, NC, NJ, NY, RI, TN, VA; online at forwhiskeylovers.com.

Personal message:
Blue Ridge Distilling Company is "Defiantly Redefining Whisky" - Tim Ferris

Broadslab Distillery LLC

4870 NC Highway 50 South
Benson, NC 27504
919-291-0691

Owners / Operators:
Jeremy Norris, Owner / Distiller

Email: broadslabdistillery@gmail.com
Website: www.broadslabdistillery.com
Facebook: Broadslab Distillery
Twitter: @BroadslabStill

Type: Micro Distillery. Opened in 2011.

Hours of operation: Not open to the public

Tours: Available by appointment

Types of spirits produced: Moonshine, rum

Names of spirits:
- Broadslab Legacy Shine
- Broadslab Legacy Reserve
- Carolina Coast Rum

Best known for / most popular: Broadslab Legacy Shine

Average bottle price: $22.95 to $25.95

Distribution: GA, NC, SC

Interesting facts: Broadslab Distillery is located in "Broadslab" which is the infamous moonshine capital of Johnston County, NC.

Call Family Distillers

1611 Industrial Drive
Wilkesboro, NC 28697
336-262-4128

Owners / Operators:
Brian Call, Founder / Master Distiller
Brad Call, Founder / Chief Operations Officer

Email: callfamilydistillers@gmail.com
Website: www.callfamilydistillers.com
Facebook: Call Family Distillers LLC
Twitter: @Call_Distillers
Instagram: CallFamilyDisitillers

Type: Craft Distillery. Opening in Fall 2014.

Hours of operation: Monday through Saturday, 8 a.m. to 5 p.m.

Tours: Available

Types of spirits produced: Moonshine

Names of spirits:
- TBD

Best known for / most popular: TBD

Average bottle price: $22.00

Distribution: NC, SC, VA

Interesting facts:
The Call family traces its heritage back to Dan Call, the man who taught Jasper Newton to make whiskey that later became Jack Daniels. Brian Call, the master distiller was taught by his father Willie Clay Call, who is best known for his legendary moonshining in the past.

Carolina Distillery LLC

1001 West Avenue NW
Lenoir, NC 28645

Owners / Operators:
Keith Nordan, Owner
Chris Hollified, Owner
Tim Sisk (Hippy), Master Distiller
Lisa Jett, Marketing/Sales Director

Email: carolinadistillery@gmail.com
Website: www.carolinadistillery.com
Facebook: Carolina Distillery, Carriage House Apple Brandy

Type: Craft Distillery. Opened in November 2008.

Hours of operation:
Monday through Friday, 9 a.m. to 4 p.m.

Tours: Available by appointment

Types of spirits produced: Brandy

Names of spirits:
- Carriage House Apple Brandy
- Carriage House Strawberry Infusion
- Carriage House White
- Good Old Mountain Shine Apple Pie

Best known for / most popular:
Carriage House Apple Brandy

Average bottle price: $19.95 to $23.95

Distribution: NC

Covington Spirits LLC

310 Kingold Boulevard
Snow Hill, NC 28580
252-747-9267

Owners / Operators:
James Eason, Co-owner
John Kimber, Co-owner
Bobby Ham, Co-owner
Jimmy Burch, Co-owner

Email: info@covingtonvodka.com
Website: www.covingtonvodka.com
Facebook: Covington Vodka
YouTube: Covington Vodka

Type: Craft Distillery. Opened in January 2013.

Hours of operation:
Monday through Friday, 8 a.m. to 5 p.m.

Tours: Not available

Types of spirits produced: Vodka

Names of spirits:
- Covington Gourmet Vodka

Best known for / most popular:
Slogan - "The Best Yam Vodka On Earth"

Average bottle price: $29.95

Distribution: NC

Interesting facts:
- Distilled in North Carolina from sweet potatoes.
- 100% gluten-free

Awards and Recognitions:
- Gold Medal, 2013 San Francisco International Spirits Competition

Devil's Distillery

193 Lorax Lane
Pittsboro, NC 27312
919-245-5434

Owners / Operators:
Chris Jude, Head Distiller / Chief Operations Officer
Andy Zeman, Managing Partner / Vintner
Lyle Estill, Managing Partner

Email: chris@devilsdistillery.com
Website: www.fairgamebeverage.com
Facebook: Devil's Distillery

Type: Micro Distillery. Opened in January 2014.

Tasting room hours: Thursday and Friday, noon to 5 p.m.

Tours: Available with advance notice

Types of spirits produced: Brandy, sorghum rum, port and sherry style wines, cordials, amaro wine, bitters

Names of spirits:
- TBA

Best known for / most popular: TBD

Average bottle price: $15.00 to $30.00

Distribution: On site

Interesting facts: Not provided

Howling Moon Distillery

Asheville, NC 28814

Owners / Operators:
Cody Bradford, Owner / CEO
Chivous Downey, President
Austin Bradford, Bottling and Packaging / Operations Manager

Email: info@howlingmoonshine.com
Website: www.howlingmoonshine.com
Facebook: Howling Moon Distillery

Type: Micro Distillery. Opened in 2010.

Hours of operation: Not open to the public

Tours: Not available

Types of spirits produced: Moonshine

Names of spirits:
- Mountain Moonshine
- Apple Pie Moonshine
- Strawberry Moonshine

Best known for / most popular: Apple Pie Moonshine

Average bottle price: $24.95

Distribution: NC

Interesting facts:
- Cody is a fifth generation moonshiner.
- Some of his equipment belonged to his great-great-grandfather.
- The moonshine recipe is 150 years old.

Mayberry Spirits

461 N. South Street
Mount Airy, NC 27030
336-719-6860

Owners / Operators:
Steve Cox, Owner
Vann McCoy, Owner

Email: hiccup@mayberryspirits.com
Website: www.mayberryspirits.com

Heritage Appalachian Moonshine

Type: Craft Distillery. Opened in Spring 2014.

Hours of operation: Daily, 6 a.m. to 6 p.m.

Tours: Thursday through Monday, 10 a.m. to 5 p.m.

Types of spirits produced: Moonshine, brandy, whiskey

Names of spirits:
- Really Fine Drink – Heritage Appalachian Moonshine
- Dutch Apple Pie

Best known for / most popular: TBA

Average bottle price: $20.00 to $30.00

Distribution: NC

Interesting facts: Not provided

Muddy River Distillery

1500 River Drive, Ste. 100
Belmont, NC 28012
336-516-4190

Owners / Operators:
Robbie Delaney, Owner

Email: muddyriverdistillery@gmail.com
Website: www.muddyriverdistillery.com
Facebook: Muddy River Distillery LLC
Twitter: @1stCarolinaRum
Instagram: muddyriverdistillery

Type: Micro Distillery. Opened in 2012.

Tours: Available by appointment

Types of spirits produced: Rum

Names of spirits:
- Carolina Rum
- Queen Charlotte's Reserve (barrel aged rum)

Best known for / most popular: Carolina Rum

Distribution: NC, SC

Interesting facts:
- First legal rum distillery in NC
- American made equipment designed and built by the distiller.

Awards and Recognitions:
- Spirituous Liquor, 2012 Big Sip Cup Best in Show
- 2013 Big Sip Cup Best Spirits and the Overall competition
- 2013 Best of Charlotte - Best Locally Made Spirits

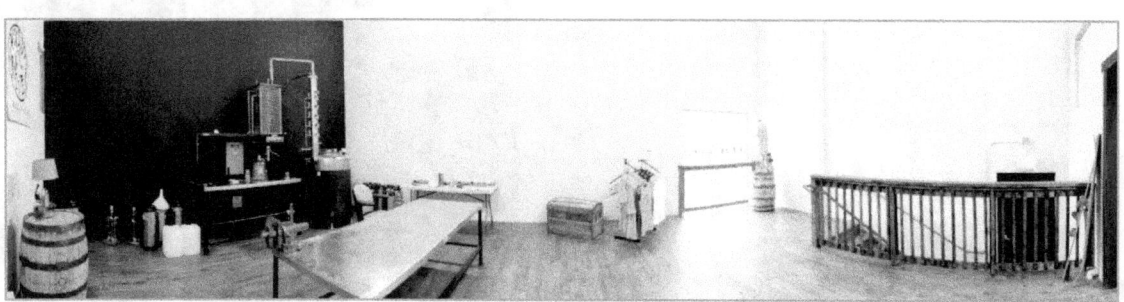

Piedmont Distillers

3690 U.S. Highway 220
Madison, NC 27025
336-445-0055

Owners / Operators:
Joe Michalek, Founder
Junior Johnson, Co-owner

Email: info@piedmontdistillers.com
Website: www.piedmontdistillers.com
Facebook: Junior Johnson's Midnight Moon
 Catdaddy Carolina Moonshine
Twitter: @JJMidnightMoon, @CatdaddyShine

Type: Micro Distillery. Opened in 2005.

Hours of operation: Not available

Tours: Not available

Types of spirits produced: Moonshine

Names of spirits:
- Junior Johnson's Midnight Moon
- Catdaddy Spiced Moonshine

Best known for / most popular:
Junior Johnson's Midnight Moon
Catdaddy Spiced Moonshine

Average bottle price: $20.00 to $30.00

Distribution: Available in all 50 states

Interesting facts:
Midnight Moon is one of the only legal moonshines made with real fruit.

Southern Artisan Spirits

Kings Mountain, NC 28086
704-297-0191

Owners / Operators:
Charlie Mauney, Co-owner
Alex Mauney, Co-owner

Email: info@southernartisanspirits.com
Website: www.southernartisanspirits.com
Facebook: Southern Artisan Spirits
Twitter: @CardinalGin

Type: Micro Distillery. Opened in 2010.

Hours of operation: Not provided

Tours: Not provided

Types of spirits produced: Gin

Names of spirits:
- Cardinal Gin

Best known for / most popular: Not provided

Average bottle price: Not provided

Distribution: DC, GA, MD, NC, NJ, SC, VA

Interesting facts: Not provided

The Brothers Vilgalys Spirits Company

803 D Ramseur Street
Durham, NC 27701

Owners / Operators:
Rimas Vilgalys, Founder / CEO

Email: vilgalys@gmail.com
Website: www.brothersvilgalys.com
Facebook: Brothers Vilgalys Spirits
Twitter: @BrosVilgalys

Type: Micro Distillery. Opened in 2012.

Hours of operation: Vary

Tours: Not available

Types of spirits produced: Spiced Honey Liqueur (presently from GNS)

Names of spirits:
- Krupnikas

Best known for / most popular: Krupnikas

Average bottle price: $29.95

Distribution: NC

Interesting facts:
Krupnikas is a spiced honey liqueur traditional in Lithuanian and Polish communities.

Top of the Hill Distillery

505 W. Franklin Street, Ste. C
Chapel Hill, NC 27516
919-699-8703

Owners / Operators:
Scott Maitland, Proprietor
Esteban McMahan, Spirit Guide
George Dusek, Head Distiller
Keith Crissman, Distiller

Email: info@topodistillery.com
Website: www.topodistillery.com
Facebook: TOPO Distillery
Twitter: @TOPOdistillery

Type: Micro Distillery. Opened in 2012.

Hours of operation:
Monday through Friday, 8 a.m. to 5 p.m.

Tours: Available. Schedule via website.

Types of spirits produced:
Vodka, gin, whiskey

Names of spirits:
- TOPO Vodka
- TOPO Carolina Whiskey
- TOPO Piedmont Gin
- TOPO Age Your Own Whiskey Kits

Best known for / most popular:
TOPO Vodka

Average bottle price: $21.95 to $28.95

Distribution: NC

Interesting facts: TOPO is one of the only exclusively local and certified USDA organic distillery in the U.S.

Windsor Run Cellars

6531 Windsor Road
Hamptonville, NC 27020
336-468-8400

Owners / Operators:
Chuck Johnson, Co-owner
Jamey Johnson, Co-owner

Email: info@windsorrun.com
Website: www.windsorrun.com
Facebook: Windsor Run Cellars

Type: Micro Distillery. Opened in 2012.

Hours of operation: Wednesday through Saturday, 10 a.m. to 5 p.m.
Sunday, 1 p.m. to 5 p.m.

Tours: Available

Types of spirits produced: TBA

Names of spirits:
- TBA

Best known for / most popular: TBA

Average bottle price: TBA

Distribution: TBA

Interesting facts: Not provided

Maple River Distillery

4 Langer Avenue
North Casselton, ND 58012
701-347-5900

Owners / Operators:
Greg Kempel, Co-owner
Susan Kempel, Co-owner

Email: greg@mapleriverwinery.com
Website: www.mapleriverdistillery.com
Facebook: Maple River Distillery
Twitter: @MapleRiverWine
YouTube: Maple River Winery

Type: Winery / Micro Distillery. Opened in 2009.

Hours of operation: Monday through Saturday, 9 a.m. to 5 p.m.

Tours: Not available

Types of spirits produced: Vodkas, cordials, brandies

Names of spirits:
- Maple River Distillery Flavored Vodka
  Rhubarb, Chokecherry, Apple, Apricot, Grape, Pear, Wild Plum
- Maple River Distillery Cordial
  Chokecherry, Apple, Pear, Red Currant, Aronia Black Currant, Wild Plum
- Maple River Distillery Brandy
  Rhubarb, Chokecherry, Apricot, Apple, Grape, Pear, Wild Plum, Aronia

Best known for / most popular:
Chokecherry Brandy

Average bottle price: $9.99 to $29.99

Distribution: ND

Interesting facts:
- Only known Chokecherry Brandy in the world.
- All brandy is produced with fruit grown within an approximate 150 mile radius of the distillery.

Moon River Distillery Inc.

6966 Highway 18
Park River, ND 58270
281-513-8778

Owners / Operators:
Scott Thompson, President
John Thompson, Vice President / Operations Manager

Type: Craft Distillery. Opened in January 2014.

Hours of operation: Varies

Tours: Not available

Types of spirits produced: Vodka

Names of spirits:
- TBA

Best known for / most popular: TBA

Average bottle price: TBA

Distribution: TBA

Interesting facts: Not provided

25th Street Spirits

1947 West 25th Street
Cleveland, OH 44113
216-621-4000

Owners / Operators:
Sam McNulty, Partner
Mark Priemer, Partner
Mike Foran, Partner
Andy Tveekrem, Partner

Email: marketgardenbrewery@gmail.com
Website: www.25thstreetspirits.com
Facebook: 25th Street Spirits
Twitter: @25thSpirits

Type: Micro Distillery. Opened in 2012.

Hours of operation: Monday through Friday, 8 a.m. to 8 p.m.

Tours: Available by appointment

Types of spirits produced: Whiskey, gin

Names of spirits:
- McNulty Whiskey
- Starling Gin

Best known for / most popular: McNulty Whiskey

Average bottle price: Not provided

Distribution: Not provided

Interesting facts: Not provided

Belle of Dayton

122 Van Buren Street
Dayton, OH 45402
937-776-4634 / 937-558-6578

Owners / Operators:
Murphy LaSelle, Owner / Distiller
Mike LaSelle, Owner / Distiller

Email: murphy@belleofdayton.com
mike@belleofdayton.com
Website: www.belleofdayton.com
Facebook: Belle of Dayton

Type: Micro Distillery. Opened in February 2014.

Distillery store hours:
Thursday through Saturday 5 p.m. to 9 p.m.

Tours:
Available with free tastings, Thursday through Saturday by appointment for $7.00 per person. Call or check their website for availability.

Types of spirits produced:
Vodka, rum, bourbon, moonshine, single malt whiskey

Names of spirits:
- Belle Vodka
- Belle 1775 Colonial Reserve Rum
- Belle Bourbon Barrel Rum
- Belle Bourbon
- Belle Single Malt

Best known for / most popular:
Belle Bourbon Barrel Rum and "Age Your Own" Moonshine Kits

Average bottle price: $24.99 to $59.99

Distribution: On-site retail, OH

Interesting facts: The distillery store resembles a pre-Prohibition style bar with a full tasting room and Belle of Dayton branded products. The room is available for private tours, business events, and parties.

The LaSelle brothers, Murphy and Mike

Black Swamp Distillery

4148 State Route 53
Fremont, OH 43420
419-344-4347

Owners / Operators:
Darrin Critchet, Owner / Distiller

Email: bsdistillery@yahoo.com
Facebook: Black Swamp Distillery

Type: Craft Distillery. Opened in 2013.

Hours of operation: Vary

Tours: Available

Types of spirits produced: Moonshine

Names of spirits:
- Apple Betty
- Pattys Peach
- Shellys Strawberry
- Blackberry Bev
- Mango Marge

Best known for / most popular: Not provided

Average bottle price: $22.00

Distribution: On-site retail

Interesting facts: Not provided

Buckeye Distillery Inc.

130 W. Plum Street
Tipp City, OH 45371
937-877-1901

Owners / Operators:
Aaron Lee, Owner

Email: info@buckeyedistillery.com
Website: www.buckeyedistillery.com
Facebook: Buckeye Distillery

Type: Micro Distillery. Opened in 2009.

Hours of operation: Monday through Friday, 9 a.m. to 5 p.m.

Tours: Not available

Types of spirits produced: Liqueurs

Names of spirits:
- Buckeye Distillery Cherry Liqueur
- Buckeye Distillery Blackberry Liqueur
- Buckeye Distillery Raspberry Liqueur

Best known for / most popular: Buckeye Distillery Cherry Liqueur

Average bottle price: $16.95 to $19.00

Distribution: IL, MI, OH, TN

Interesting facts: Not provided

Cleveland Whiskey LLC

1768 E. 25th Street
Cleveland, OH 44114
216-881-8481

Owners / Operators:
Tom Lix, CEO

Email: tlix@clevelandwhiskey.com
Website: www.clevelandwhiskey.com
LinkedIn: www.linkedin.com/in/tomlix
Facebook: Cleveland Whiskey
Twitter: @CleveWhiskey
Pinterest: Cleveland Whiskey

Type: Micro Distillery. Opened in 2009.

Hours of operation: Daily

Tours: Available by appointment

Types of spirits produced: Bourbon whiskey

Names of spirits:
- Black Reserve Bourbon Whiskey

Best known for / most popular: Black Reserve

Average bottle price: $34.95

Distribution: Limited

Interesting facts:
The bourbon is Pressure-Aged™.

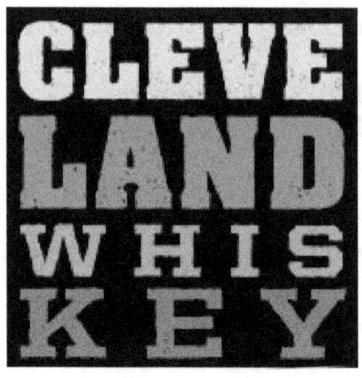

Crystal Spirits LLC

Dayton, OH

Owners / Operators:
Jim Finke, CEO
Tom Rambasek, President
Chris Finke, Co-founder

Email: info@crystalspiritsllc.com
Website: www.buckeyevodka.com
Facebook: Buckeye Vodka
Twitter: @BuckeyeVodka

Type: Micro Distillery. Opened in 2011.

Hours of operation: Not provided

Tours: Not provided

Types of spirits produced: Vodka

Names of spirits:
- Buckeye Vodka

Best known for / most popular: Buckeye Vodka

Average bottle price: $20.00

Distribution: Available through The Party Source

Interesting facts: Not provided

Ernest Scarano Distillery

4487 Hayes Avenue
Fremont, OH 43420
419-205-8734

Owners / Operators:
Ernest Scarano, Owner

Email: ernie@esdistillery.com
Website: www.esdistillery.com
Facebook: Ernest Scarano Distillery

Type: Micro Distillery. Opened in 2010.

Hours of operation:
Monday through Thursday, 9 a.m. to 4 p.m.; Saturday, 8 a.m. to noon

Tours: Available by appointment. One week notice required.

Types of spirits produced: Whiskey

Names of spirits:
- Old Homicide
- Whiskey Dick
- Widmer Winter Rye

Best known for / most popular: Old Homicide

Average bottle price: $45.00 to $95.00

Distribution: Not provided

Interesting facts: Not provided

Fifth Element Spirits

41625 Bearwallow Ridge Road
Shade, OH 45776
740-696-1159

Owners / Operators:
Kelly Sauber, Owner / Distiller
Deanna Schwartz, Project Coordinator

Email: kelly@fifthelementspirits.com
Website: www.fifthelementspirits.com
Facebook: Fifth Element Spirits
Twitter: @fifthspirits

Type: Micro Distillery. Opened in 2011.

Hours of operation: Available by appointment

Tours: Available by appointment

Types of spirits produced: Vodka, gin

Names of spirits:
- Fifth Element Spirits Spicebush Gin
- Fifth Element Spirits Vodka from grapes
- Fifth Element Spirits Vodka from grains
- Fifth Element Spirits Coffee Liqueur
- Seasonal Spirits:
  - Elderberry Brandy
  - Sorghum Rum
  - Whiskey Is In The Wood
  - Chardonnay Grappa
  - Apple Brandy

Best known for / most popular: Fifth Element Spirits Gin

Average bottle price: $35.00

Distribution: OH

Interesting facts:
100% distilled on premises; locally sourced, organic and non-GMO ingredients.

Flat Rock Spirits

5380 Intrastate Drive
Fairborn, OH 45324
937-879-4447

Owners / Operators:
James Bagford, Co-founder
Brad Measel, Co-founder
Shawn Measel, Co-founder

Email: james@flatrockspirits.com
Website: www.flatrockspirits.com
Facebook: Flat Rock Spirits
Twitter: @FlatRockSpirits

Type: Micro Distillery. Opened in 2010.

Hours of operation: Not provided

Tours: Not provided

Types of spirits produced: Bourbon

Names of spirits:
- Stillwrights Bourbon

Best known for / most popular: TBA

Average bottle price: TBA

Distribution: OH

Interesting facts: Bourbon is currently aging.

Indian Creek Distillery

7095 Staley Road
New Carlisle, OH 45344
937-846-1443

Owners / Operators:
Joe and Melissa Duer, Owners

Email: jmduer76@gmail.com
Website: www.staleymillfarmanddistillery.com
Facebook: Indian Creek Distillery

Type: Early American Stillhouse. Opened in December 2012.

Hours of operation:
Thursday, 10 a.m. to 5 p.m.
Friday, 10 a.m. to 7 p.m.
Saturday, 10 a.m. to 5 p.m.

Tours:
Available Saturday at noon, 2 p.m., 4 p.m.

Types of spirits produced: Rye whiskey

Names of spirits:
- Staley Rye Whiskey
- Elias Staley Un aged Rye Whiskey

Best known for / most popular:
Double Copper Distilled Rye Whiskey

Average bottle price: $50.00 to $65.00

Distribution: On-site, OH, The Party Source KY

Interesting facts:
"Created and crafted in the hearts and hands of the 6th generation, this rare and unique early American distillery brings the flavor of our storied American Rye Whiskey out of the 1800's and dares to create a hand-made authentic spirit, distinct and relevant for today." – Indian Creek Distillery

Middle West Spirits LLC

1230 Courtland Avenue
Columbus, OH 43201
614-299-2460

Owners / Operators:
Brady Konya, General Manager / Owner
Ryan Lang, Head Distiller / Owner
Eric Boettcher, Production Manager
Josh Daily. Director of Sales
Cris Dehlavi, Brand Mixologist

Email: info@middlewestspirits.com
Website: www.middlewestspirits.com
Facebook: Middle West Spirits
Twitter: @MiddleWestSpts
LinkedIn: Middle West Spirits, LLC

Type: Craft Distillery. Opened in 2010.

Hours of operation:
Office Hours: Monday through Friday, 9 a.m. to 6 p.m.
Gift Shop: Monday through Friday, noon to 6 p.m.
Gift Shop Holiday Hours: Monday through Saturday, 10 a.m. to 7 p.m.

Tours: Available Friday and the first Saturday of each month starting at 6 p.m. There is a $15 fee per person.

Types of spirits produced:
Vodka, infused seasonal vodkas, whiskey, bourbon

Names of spirits:
- OYO Vodka
- OYO Honey Vanilla Bean Vodka
- OYO Stone Fruit Vodka
- OYO Whiskey (100% Wheat)
- OYO Bourbon, Michelone Reserve (4-Grain)
- OYO Rye Whiskey (100% Dark Pumpernickel)

Best known for / most popular: OYO Whiskey

Average bottle price: $30.00 to $45.00

Distribution: DC, FL, GA, KY, LA, MD, NJ, NY, OH, PA

Interesting facts:
Middle West Spirits is the first modern craft distillery to operate in Columbus, OH, the birthplace of Prohibition.

Mill St. Distillery LLC

10 Mill Street
Utica, OH 43080
740-892-9333

Owners / Operators:
Paul Taiganides, CEO / Founder
Carlos Ogden, COO / Founder
Jeff Thompson, CSO / Founder
Hernando Posada, CFO
Mark Bubnick, CTO

Email: carlos@millstdistillery.com
Website: www.millstdistillery.com
Facebook: Mill St. Distillery
Twitter: @MSDdistillery

Type: Micro Distillery. Opened in 2013.

Hours of operation:
Monday through Thursday, 11 a.m. to 5 p.m.
Friday and Saturday, 11 a.m. to 6 p.m.

Tours: Available. Sign up at website.

Types of spirits produced: Moonshine, aged grappa

Names of spirits:
- Mill St. Moonshine
- Mill St. Grappa
- Mill Street Bourbon / Aged Whiskey

Best known for / most popular:
All products especially Mill St. Moonshine

Average bottle price: $28.50 to $90.00

Distribution: On-site retail, OH liquor stores

Interesting facts:
Mill Street Distillery uses high quality locally sourced grain and fruit and combines it with their collective global experience, using traditional recipes from New and Old World, to produce hand crafted spirits.

Portside Distillery

983 Front Street
Cleveland, OH 44113
216-568-6633

Owners / Operators:
Dan Malz, Co-owner
Keith Sutton, Co-owner
John Marek, Co-owner
Matt Zappernick, Co-owner

Email: dan@portsidedistillery.com
Website: www.portsidedistillery.com
Facebook: Portside Distillery
Twitter: @_Portside_

Type: Micro Distillery. Opened in 2011.

Hours of operation:
Monday through Friday, 5 p.m. to 8 p.m.
Saturday, noon to 4 p.m.

Tours: Not provided

Types of spirits produced: Rum

Names of spirits:
- Portside Distillery Silver Rum

Best known for / most popular:
Portside Distillery Silver Rum

Average bottle price: Not provided

Distribution: Not provided

Interesting facts: Portside Distillery is the first craft distillery in Cleveland, OH, since Prohibition.

Red Eagle Spirits

6202 South River Road
Geneva, OH 44041
440-466-6604

Owners / Operators:
Gene and Heather Sigel, Owners

Email: info@redeaglespirits.com
Website: www.redeaglespirits.com
Facebook: Red Eagle Distillery

Type: Micro Distillery. Opened in 2012.

Hours of operation:
Saturday, 1 p.m. to 9 p.m.
Sunday, 1 p.m. to 6 p.m.

Tours: Available

Types of spirits produced: Bourbon

Names of spirits:
- TBA

Best known for / most popular: TBA

Average bottle price: $23.00

Distribution: OH

Interesting facts: Bourbon is currently aging.

Renaissance Artisan Distillers

915 Home Avenue
Akron, OH 44310
800-695-9870

Owners / Operators:
John and Jim Pastor, Owners
Ron Petrosky, Head Distiller

Email: info@renartisan.com
Website: www.renartisan.com
Facebook: Renaissance Artisan Distillers

Type: Artisan Distillery. Opened in November 2013.

Hours of operation: Monday through Thursday, 10 a.m. to 5 p.m.

Tasting room: Monday through Friday, 10 a.m. to 7 p.m.
Saturday, 10 a.m. to 5 p.m.

Tours: Available upon request

Types of spirits produced: Rum, gin, grappa, whiskey, brandy

Names of spirits:
- TBA

Best known for / most popular: TBA

Average bottle price: $20.00 to $40.00

Distribution: On-site retail

S and G Artisan Distillery LLC

305 N. Walnut Street, Ste. J
Yellow Springs, OH 45387
937-623-6814

Owners / Operators:
Meg Solomon-Gujer, Business Manager
Steven Gujer, Production Manager
Hajo Scheuner, Sales and Marketing Manager
Kerry Scheuner, Sales and Marketing Manager

Email: sandgartisandistillery@woh.rr.com
Website: www.sandgartisandistillery.com
Facebook: The Spirits of Yellow Springs

Type: Micro Distillery. Opened in October 2012.

Tasting room hours:
Thursday and Friday, 4 p.m. to 7 p.m.
Saturday, noon to 7 p.m.

Tours: Not available

Types of spirits produced: Rum

Names of spirits:
- The Spirits of Yellow Springs® Apple Pie Moonshine
- The Spirits of Yellow Springs® Apple Pie Moonshine Distiller's Reserve

Best known for / most popular:
The Spirits of Yellow Springs® Apple Pie Moonshine

Average bottle price: $20.00 to $24.00

Distribution: OH, On-site retail

Interesting facts: Coming soon is a product called Sneaky Monk, a nocino walnut bitter liqueur.

Seven Brothers Distilling Company

7755 Brakeman Road
Painesville, OH 44077
440-897-9311

Owners / Operators:
Kevin Suttman, President

Email: promo@seven-brothers.com
Website: www.seven-brothers.com
Facebook: Seven Brothers Distilling Co

Type: Micro Distillery. Opened in 2010.

Hours of operation: Vary

Tours: Available by appointment

Types of spirits produced: Vodka, white rum, aged rum, spice rum, aged whiskey, flavored vodkas, flavored rums, flavored whiskey

Names of spirits:
- Seven Brothers Vodka
- Seven Brothers Silver Rum
- Seven Brothers 100-Proof Spiced Rum

Best known for / most popular: Seven Brothers Vodka

Average bottle price: $24.50 to $32.00

Distribution: OH

Interesting facts:
- Seven Brothers Distilling Company is one of the smallest and most unique distilleries in America.
- Seven Brothers Distilling Company has pioneered a unique "low-temperature" distillation technique. This process significantly lowers the distillation temperature, creating unique flavor profiles. They plan to use this technology to create many more unique and flavorful products.

Tom's Foolery
Tomsfoolery LLC

Chagrin Falls, OH 44023

Owners / Operators:
Tom Herbruck, President / Head Distiller
Lianne Herbruck, Plant Manager
Erik Rothschiller, Brewer / Distiller

Email: tom@tomsfoolery.com
lianne@tomsfoolery.com
Website: www.tomsfoolery.com
www.applejackohio.com
Facebook: Tom's Foolery—A Spirited Venture

Type: Micro Distillery. Opened in 2008.

Hours of operation: Daily, hours vary

Tours: Not available

Types of spirits produced: Applejack, bourbon, rye

Names of spirits:
- Tom's Foolery Applejack

Best known for / most popular: Tom's Foolery Applejack

Average bottle price: $42.00

Distribution: OH

Interesting facts: Their first bourbon and rye will be released in late 2014.

Watershed Distillery

1145-D Chesapeake Avenue
Columbus, OH 43212
614-357-1936

Owners / Operators:
Greg Lehman, Co-owner
Dave Rigo, Co-owner

Email: info@watersheddistillery.com
Website: www.watersheddistillery.com
Facebook: Watershed Distillery
Twitter: @Watershed_Ohio

Type: Micro Distillery. Opened in 2010.

Hours of operation: Monday through Friday, 9 a.m. to 6 p.m.

Tours: Available. See website

Types of spirits produced: Vodka, gin, bourbon

Names of spirits:
- Watershed Distillery Bourbon
- Watershed Distillery Bourbon Barrel Gin
- Watershed Distillery Four Peel Gin
- Watershed Distillery Vodka

Best known for / most popular: Four Peel Gin

Average bottle price: $25.00 to $40.00

Distribution: IL, KY, OH

Interesting facts:
- The first bourbon distilled in Columbus since Prohibition.
- Watershed's use of spent grains reduces the cost of farming and provides for a more sustainable Ohio.

Woodstone Creek

4712 Vine Street
Cincinnati, OH 45217

Owners / Operators:
Donald Outterson, Owner / Distiller

Email: woodstonecreek@yahoo.com
Website: www.woodstonecreek.com
Facebook: Woodstone Creek

Type: Micro Distillery. Opened in 1999.

Hours of operation: Saturday, 1 p.m. to 5 p.m.

Tours: Not available

Types of spirits produced: Bourbon, single malt (peated and unpeated), white dogs, varietal whisky (barley, rye, wheat, corn), vodka, rum, gin, grape brandy, honey brandy, bierschnaps

Names of spirits:
- Woodstone Creek 5 Grain Straight Bourbon Whisky
- Woodstone Creek Vodka
- Woodstone Creek Single Barrel Peated Single Malt Whisky

Best known for / most popular:
Woodstone Creek 5-Grain Straight Bourbon Whiskey

Average bottle price: $20.00 to $185.00

Distribution: CO, IL, IN, KY, OH

Interesting facts:
- Woodstone Creek is Ohio's first licensed micro distillery.
- Donald originated the micro distillery license in Ohio in 1998. Additionally, he worked to change the liquor law in 2008 when he introduced legislation to allow self-sales for micros in the state. Legislation to allow spirits tastings was finally passed in 2012.

Prairie Wolf Spirits

124 East Oklahoma Avenue
Guthrie, OK 73044
405-590-7619

Owners / Operators:
David Merritt, President
Hunter Merritt, Manager
Blake Merritt, Head Distiller

Email: info@prairiewolfspirits.com
Website: www.prairiewolfspirits.com
Facebook: Prairie Wolf Spirits
Twitter: @PWSpirits

Type: Micro Distillery. Opened in 2013.

Hours of operation: Not open to the public

Tours: Not available

Types of spirits produced: Vodka, liqueur

Names of spirits:
- Prairie Wolf Vodka
- DARK (Coffee Liqueur)

Best known for / most popular:
Prairie Wolf Vodka

Average bottle price: $20.00

Distribution: OK

Interesting facts:
- Prairie Wolf Spirits is fully wind powered.
- The first licensed active distillery in Oklahoma.

4 Spirits Distillery

6040 NE Marcus Harris Avenue
Adair Village, OR 97330
541-760-0696

Owners / Operators:
Dawson Officer, Owner / Distiller
Sarah Wayt, Marketing and Sales Director

Email: dawson@4spiritsdistillery.com, sarah@4spiritsdistillery.com
Website: www.4spiritsdistillery.com
Facebook: 4 Spirits Distillery

Type: Micro Distillery. Opened in 2011.

Hours of operation: Vary

Tours: Available

Types of spirits produced:
Vodka, whiskey, rum

Names of spirits:
- WebFoot Vodka
- SlapTail Vodka
- 4 Spirits Vodka
- 4 Spirits Whiskey

Best known for / most popular: All

Average bottle price: $11.95 to $26.50

Distribution: ID, OR, WA, WY

Interesting facts: 4 Spirits Distillery pays homage to all U.S. war veterans and active service members so that we should never forget their service and sacrifice to our country. Specifically and on a very personal level of the owner, the distillery is dedicated to four combat soldiers who he served with in the Oregon National Guard 2 Battalion, 162 Infantry Brigade. They are Lt. Erik McCrae, Sgt. Justin Linden, Sgt. Justin Eyerly and Sgt. David Roustum. These four men lost their lives in 2004 serving in Baghdad, Iraq. They were combat soldiers and fought side by side in Delta Co. 2-162 Infantry.

Bendistillery

19330 Pinehurst Road
Bend, OR 97701
541-318-0200

Owners / Operators:
Jim Bendis, Founder / Chairman
Alan Dietrich, Chief Executive Officer
Jennah Padilla, Vice President / Operations
James Padilla, National Sales Manager
Francoise Labbe, Private Label Director

Email: info@bendistillery.com
Website: www.bendistillery.com
Facebook: Crater Lake Spirits
Twitter: @bendistillery

Type: Micro Distillery. Opened in 1995.

Hours of operation:
Monday through Saturday, 11 a.m. to 5 p.m.
Sunday, 11 a.m. to 4 p.m.

Tours: Available

Types of spirits produced:
Gin, vodka, flavored vodka, rye whiskey

Names of spirits:
- Crater Lake Gin
- Crater Lake Vodka
- Crater Lake Reserve Vodka
- Crater Lake Hazelnut Espresso Vodka
- Crater Lake Pepper Vodka
- Crater Lake Sweet Ginger Vodka
- Crater Lake Rye Whiskey

Best known for / most popular: Crater Lake Gin

Average bottle price: $22.95 to $29.95

Distribution: AZ, CA, DC, GA, HI, ID, IL, MA, MD, MN, MT, NM, OR, PA, RI, TN, TX, WA, WI, WY

Interesting facts: Will be launching an Estate line of spirits that are crafted from products grown entirely at the distillery. The first in the series will be a gin.

Big Bottom Distilling

21420 NW Nicholas Court, Ste. D-9
Hillsboro, OR 97124
503-608-7816

Owners / Operators:
Ted Pappas, Founder / Owner

Email: info@bigbottomwhiskey.com
Website: www.bigbottomwhiskey.com
    www.calhounbros.com
Facebook: Big Bottom Whiskey
    Calhoun Bros. Adventure Spirits
Twitter: @bbwhiskey

Type: Small Batch Distillery / Independent Bottler. Opened in 2010.

Tasting room hours:
Saturdays, noon to 4 p.m. or by appointment

Tours: Available by appointment

Types of spirits produced:
Straight bourbon whiskey, blended whiskey, aged rum

Names of spirits:
- Big Bottom Whiskey American Straight Bourbon Whiskey
- Big Bottom Whiskey Straight Bourbon Whiskey (finished in Port casks)
- Big Bottom Whiskey Straight Bourbon Whiskey (finished in Zinfandel casks)
- Big Bottom Whiskey, Straight Bourbon Whiskey 111 Proof
- Big Bottom Whiskey, Straight Bourbon Whiskey (finished in Cabernet Sauvignon casks)
- Calhoun Bros. Straight Bourbon Whiskey
- Calhoun Bros. Aged Rum 4 Years

Best known for / most popular: Pear's Big Bottom

Average bottle price: $21.95 to $44.95

Distribution: CA, GA, IL, NV, OR, SC, WA

Black Rock Distillery LLC

32405 Highway 19-207
Spray, OR 97874
541-420-4748

Owners / Operators:
Galen B. Fischer, Co-owner
Isaiah Fischer, Co-owner
Andrew Richardson, Co-owner

Email: 9rocksvodka@gmail.com
Website: www.blackrockdistillery.com, www.ninerocksvodka.com
    www.9rocksvodka.com
Facebook: 9 Rocks Vodka
Twitter: @9rocksvodka

Type: Micro Distillery. Opened in 2010.

Hours of operation: Not available

Tours: Available by appointment

Types of spirits produced: Vodka

Names of spirits:
- 9 Rocks Vodka

Best known for / most popular:
9 Rocks Vodka

Average bottle price: $22.95

Distribution: OR

Interesting facts:
- 9 Rocks Vodka is gluten free.
- Made in Spray, OR, a small rural outpost located on the unabated John Day River 2.5 hrs NE of Bend, OR.

Brandy Peak Distillery

18526 Tetley Road
Brookings, OR 97415
541-469-0194

Owners / Operators:
David and Georgia Nowlin, Owners

Email: distiller@brandypeak.com
Website: www.brandypeak.com
Facebook: Brandy Peak Distillery

Type: Micro Distillery. Opened in 1994.

Hours of operation:
Open March through the first weekend of January
Tuesday through Saturday, 1 p.m. to 5 p.m.

Tours: Available

Types of spirits produced:
Brandy, grappa, liqueur

Names of spirits:
- Brandy Peak Natural Pear Brandy
- Brandy Peak Aged Pear Brandy
- Brandy Peak Aged Pinot Noir Brandy
- Brandy Peak Spirit of Muscat Brandy
- Brandy Peak Aged Muscat Brandy
- Brandy Peak Grappa
- Brandy Peak Aged Grape Brandy
- Brandy Peak Blackberry Liqueur

Best known for / most popular:
Brandy Peak Aged Pear Brandy

Average bottle price: $20.00 to $42.00

Distribution: CA, OR

Interesting facts
- Spirits are distilled in wood-fired pot stills that are unique in the industry.
- It takes fourteen pounds of pears to make a 375ml bottle of the pear brandy.
- No artificial additives, colorings or flavorings are used.
- Brandy Peak is named after the highest mountain in Curry County.

Bull Run Distilling Company

2259 NW Quimby Street
Portland, OR 97210
503-224-3483

Owners / Operators:
Lee Medoff, Co-founder / Head Distiller
Patrick Bernards, Co-founder / Chief Enthusiast
John Rudi, President

Email: spirits@bullrundistillery.com
Website: www.bullrundistillery.com
Facebook: Bull Run Distilling Company
Twitter: @BullRunSpirits
YouTube: BullRunDistillingCo.

Type: Micro Distillery. Opened in 2011.

Distillery Office Hours: Monday through Friday, 9 a.m. to 5 p.m.

Tasting Room & Retail Store Hours:
Wednesday through Sunday, noon to 6 p.m.

Tours: Available by chance or by reservation.

Types of spirits produced: Aquavit, gin, rum, single malt whiskey, vodka, and a limited release line of unique, small-batch spirits.

Names of spirits:
- Bull Run Pacific Rum
- Medoyeff Vodka
- Bull Run Gin
- Oregon Single Malt Whiskey (Spring 2016)
- Temperance Trader Straight Bourbon Whiskey
- Temperance Trader Barrel Strength Bourbon
- Temperance Small Batch

Best known for / most popular: Temperance Trader Bourbon

Average bottle price: $24.95 to $42.95

Distribution: CA, IL, IN, MA, NY, OR, WA

Interesting facts:
- Bull Run Distilling Company is named for its famed water source, the Bull Run Watershed, considered to be one of the purest, raw water sources in all of North America.
- Bull Run's twin 800-gallon pot stills are among the largest of all craft distillers in the west, and were designed and built locally in Portland, OR.
- Bull Run Distillery was named "One of the Coolest Distilleries in America" by Travel + Leisure Magazine in 2013.

Cascade Peak Spirits Distillery
Home of Organic Nation

280 E. Hersey Street
Ashland, OR 97520
541-482-3160

Owners / Operators:
Diane Paulson, Co-founder / Owner
David Eliasen, Co-founder / Owner / Distiller

Email: spirits@organicnationspirits.com
Website: www.organicnationspirits.com
Facebook: Organic Nation Spirits
Twitter: @OGNationSpirits
LinkedIn: Diane Paulson
YouTube: Certified Organic Spirits

Type: Micro Distillery. Opened in 2007.

Hours of operation: Open year-round on a short schedule and by appointment

Tours: Available by appointment only

Types of spirits produced:
Certified organic vodka, gin, rye whiskey

Names of spirits:
- Organic Nation Vodka
- Organic Nation Gin
- Oldfield Rye Whiskey

Best known for / most popular:
Organic Nation Gin and Vodka, and a Bees Knees cocktail

Average bottle price: $30.00 to $55.00

Distribution: CA, OR

Interesting facts:
Cascade Peak Spirits is the first certified organic artisan distiller in the Pacific Northwest creating uniquely crafted organic spirits.

Awards and Recognitions:
Gold Medals for Oldfield Rye and Organic Nation Gin, 2014 Good Food Awards

Clear Creek Distillery

2389 NW Wilson
Portland, OR 97210
503-248-9470

Owners / Operators:
Steve McCarthy, Owner

Email: steve@clearcreekdistillery.com
Website: www.clearcreekdistillery.com
Facebook: Clear Creek Distillery

Type: Micro Distillery. Opened in 1985.

Hours of operation: Vary by season
Tasting Room and Store hours: Monday through Saturday, 9 a.m. to 5 p.m.

Tours: Not available

Types of spirits produced: Whiskey, brandy, grappa, liqueur

Names of spirits:
- Williams Pear Brandy
- Pear in the Bottle
- Eau de Vie de Pomme
- Apple Brandy
- Apple in the Bottle
- Kirschwasser (Cherry Brandy)
- Blue Plum Brandy (Slivovitz)
- Framboise (Raspberry)
- Eau de Vie of Douglas Fir
- Grappa Moscato
- Marc de Gewürztraminer
- Grappa of Oregon Pinot Noir
- McCarthy's Oregon Single Malt Whiskey
- Grappa of Pinot Grigio
- Cavatappi Nebbiolo Grappa
- Cavatappi Sangiovese Grappa
- Oregon Pot Distilled Brandy
- Cranberry Liqueur
- Marion Blackberry Liqueur
- Loganberry Liqueur
- Cassis Liqueur
- Cherry Liqueur
- Raspberry Liqueur
- Pear Liqueur
- Mirabelle Plum

Best known for / most popular: Pear Brandy

Average bottle price: $18.00 to $80.00

Distribution: 35 states

Interesting facts: Not provided

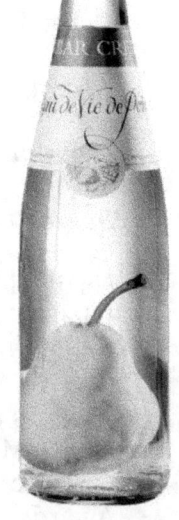

Dogwood Distilling

1835 19th Avenue
Forest Grove, OR 97116
503-359-7705

Owners / Operators:
Matt Hottenroth, Owner

Email: info@dogwooddistilling.com
Website: www.dogwooddistilling.com
Facebook: Dogwood Distilling
Twitter: @UnionGin

Type: Craft Distillery. Opened in 2010.

Hours of operation: Not provided

Tours: Not provided

Types of spirits produced: Gin, vodka

Names of spirits:
- Union Gin
- DL Franklin Vodka

Best known for / most popular: DL Franklin Vodka

Average bottle price: $15.95 to $21.95

Distribution: OR

Interesting facts: Not provided

Eastside Distilling
Formerly Deco Distilling

1512 SE 7th Avenue
Portland, OR 97214
503-926-7060

Owners / Operators:
Lenny Gotter, Owner
Bill Adams, Owner

Email: info@eastsidedistilling.com
         events@eastsidedistilling.com
Website: www.eastsidedistilling.com
Facebook: Eastside Distilling
Twitter: @eastsidedistill
Yelp: Eastside Distilling
YouTube: Eastside Distilling Channel

Type: Micro Distillery. Opened in 2008.

Tasting room hours:
Monday through Thursday, noon to 5 p.m.
Friday, noon to 7:30 p.m.
Saturday, 11 a.m. to 6 p.m.
Sunday, noon to 5 p.m.

Tours: Available with Groupon, Living Social, Mercperk, and Fox12 Daily Deals

Types of spirits produced:
Rum, bourbon, vodka, seasonal liqueurs

Names of spirits:
- Below Deck Silver Rum
- Below Deck Coffee Rum
- Below Deck Ginger Rum
- Burnside Bourbon
- Double Barrel Burnside Bourbon
- Portland Potato Vodka
- Cherry Bomb Whiskey
- Peppermint Bark Liqueur
- Egg Nog Advocaat Liqueur
- Holiday Spiced Liqueur

Best known for / most popular: Burnside Bourbon

Average bottle price: $15.95 to $43.95

Distribution: OR, WA

Interesting facts: Not provided

Elixir Inc.

1050 Bethel Drive
Eugene, OR 97405
541-345-2257

Owners / Operators:
Andrea Loreto, President / CEO

Email: contact@elixir-us.com
Website: www.calisaya.net, www.irisliqueur.com
Twitter: @CalisayaLiqueur, @IrisLiqueur

Type: Micro Distillery. Opened in 2011.

Hours of operation:
Monday through Friday, 9 a.m. to 5 p.m.

Tours: Available by appointment

Types of spirits produced: Liqueurs

Names of spirits:
- Calisaya®
- Iris™

Best known for / most popular: Calisaya®

Average bottle price: $47.00

Distribution: CA, DC, MA, NY, OR

Interesting facts:
- Elixir® craft distillery, founded by Italian brothers Andrea and Mario Loreto in Eugene, Oregon, is dedicated to revivifying traditional spirits in the Italian tradition using the finest all-natural ingredients. All of Elixir's spirits are composed of pure McKenzie River water and grain neutral spirit.
- Elixir® is producing two botanical liqueurs Calisaya® and Iris™. Iris™ is a floral liqueur derived from pure iris root and Calisaya® is an amaro based on cinchona bark.

Glaser Estate Winery and Distillery

213 Independence Lane
Roseburg, OR 97471
541-580-4867

Owners / Operators:
David and Sandra Glaser, Owners
Leon Glaser, Master Distiller

Email: info@glaserestatewinery.com
Website: www.glaserestatewinery.com
Facebook: Glaser Estate Winery

Type: Winery / Micro Distillery. Opened in 2011.

Hours of operation: Friday through Sunday, 11 a.m. to 5 p.m.

Tours: Not available

Types of spirits produced: Rum, vodka, whisky, liqueur, limoncello

Names of spirits:
- TBA

Best known for / most popular: Not provided

Average bottle price: Not provided

Distribution: Not provided

Interesting facts: Not provided

Hard Times Distillery LLC

175 S. 5th
Monroe, OR 97456
541-207-8354

Owners / Operators:
Dudley Clark, Owner / Distiller

Email: info@hardtimesdistillery.com
            dudley@hardtimesdistillery.com
Website: www.hardtimesdistillery.com
Facebook: Hard Times Distillery LLC
Twitter: @hardtimesdstlry
YouTube: Hardtimesdistillery's Channel

Type: Micro Distillery. Opened in 2009.

Hours of operation:
Saturday and Sunday, noon to 5 p.m.

Tours: Available

Types of spirits produced: Vodka, whiskey

Names of spirits:
- Apple Shine
- Green Geisha
- Sweet Baby Moonshine
- Hard Times Blue Collar Vodka

Best known for / most popular:
Green Geisha Wasabi Bloody Mary

Average bottle price: $13.95 to $27.00

Distribution: OR

Interesting facts: Not provided

HillCrest Winery and Distillery

240 Vineyard Lane
Roseburg, OR 97471
541-673-3709

Owners / Operators:
Dyson and Susan DeMara, Owners

Email: info@hillcrestvineyard.com
Website: www.hillcrestvineyard.com
Facebook: HillCrest Winery and Distillery
Yelp: Hillcrest Winery & Distillery
Tripadvisor: HillCrest Winery and Distillery

Type: Winery / Micro Distillery. Opened in 2003.

Hours of operation: Not provided

Tours: Not provided

Types of spirits produced: Eaux de Vie, vodka

Names of spirits:
- Not provided

Best known for / most popular: Not provided

Average bottle price: Not provided

Distribution: Not provided

Interesting facts: Oregon's oldest estate winery.

House Spirits Distillery

2025 SE 7th Avenue
Portland, OR 97214
503-235-3174

Owners / Operators:
Christian Krogstad, Co-owner
Thomas Mooney, Co-owner

Email: info@housespirits.com
Website: www.housespirits.com, www.avaiationgin.com
www.westwardwhiskey.com
Facebook: Westward Whiskey, Aviation American Gin, House Spirits Distillery
Twitter: @AviationGin
Pinterest: House Spirits

Type: Micro Distillery. Opened in 2004.

Hours of operation:
Wednesday through Saturday, noon to 6 p.m.
Sunday, noon to 5 p.m.

Tours: Available on Saturday

Types of spirits produced:
Gin, whiskey, liqueur, rum, white dog, aquavit

Names of spirits:
- Aviation American Gin
- House Spirits Rum
- House Spirits White Dog
- House Spirits Coffee Liqueur
- Krogstad Festlig Aquavit
- Krogstad Gamel Aquavit
- Westward Oregon Straight Malt Whiskey
- Volstead Vodka

Best known for / most popular:
Aviation American Gin

Average bottle price: $29.95

Distribution: U.S. and 15 countries

Interesting facts: Aviation American Gin is Wine Enthusiast Magazine's highest rated gin ever.

Immortal Spirits & Distilling Company

3582 S. Pacific Highway, Unit D.
Medford, OR 97504
541-646-8144

Owners / Operators:
Jesse Gallagher, Co-owner / Operator
Enrico Carini, Co-owner / Operator

Email: info@immortalspirits.com
Website: www.immortalspirits.com
Facebook: Immortal Spirits and Distilling Company
Twitter: @immortalspirits

Type: Craft Distillery. Opened in 2010.

Hours of operation: Not provided

Tours: Available by appointment

Types of spirits produced:
Whiskey, rum, brandy, absinthe

Names of spirits:
- Oregon Single Malt Whiskey
- Early Whiskey
- Eua de Vie Poire
- Knarr Absinthe Verte
- State of Jefferson Rum

Best known for / most popular:
Knarr- Absinthe Verte

Average bottle price: $44.00

Distribution: OR

Interesting facts: The stills were made in-house by the owners: a 1,200 gallon pot still for beer stripping and an 88 gallon pot still for spirit runs. They recently completed their 60 barrel mash tun. Currently they are producing Oregon Single Malt Whiskey, distilled from locally grown Rogue Valley, Oregon barley. 2014 marks 2 years of ageing on Oregon Oak barrels for their first batches. Straight Oregon Whiskey will be released soon.

Indio Spirits

7272 SW Durham Road #100
Portland, OR 97224
503-620-0313

Owners / Operators:
John Ufford, Chairman / CEO
Bob Turner, President
Mark Ryan White, Distiller

Email: mark@indiospirits.com
Website: www.indiospirits.com
Facebook: Indio Spirits Distillery & Tasting Room
Twitter: @IndioSpirits

Type: Contract distilled spirits. Opened in 2004.

Hours of operation: Daily

Tours:
Available Friday through Sunday, 2 p.m. to 7 p.m.

Types of spirits produced: Vodka, gin, whisky, rum

Names of spirits:
- Indio Vodka
- Cricket Club Gin
- Red Island Rum
- Snake River Stampede
- James Oliver Rye

Best known for / most popular: James Oliver Rye

Average bottle price: $20.00 to $27.00

Distribution: National

Interesting facts: Not provided

Awards and Recognitions:
- James Oliver Rye, 90 Points, Beverage Testing Institute
- Indio Vodka, Silver Medal, San Francisco International Spirits Competition
- Snake River Stampede, Silver Medal, Great American Distillers Festival

LiL'BiT Distillery Inc.

1501 NE Industrial Avenue
Woodburn, OR 97071
503-701-5780

Owners / Operators:
Mihai Talvan, CEO
Ioan Talvan, Master Distiller

Email: info@lilbitinc.com
Website: www.milibit.com

Type: Micro Distillery. Opened in 2012.

Hours of operation: Daily, 9 a.m. to 5 p.m.

Tours: Not available

Types of spirits produced: Brandy

Names of spirits:
- MiLi BiT Țuică

Best known for / most popular: MiLi BiT Țuică

Average bottle price: $25.00 to $30.00

Distribution: Not provided

Interesting facts:
Romanians know MiLi BiT Țuică as tuică ('tsuj.kə), Germans call it schnapps (not to be confused with the liquored drink), Serbs know it as slivovitz, Hungarians will call this palinka, and the French call it eau de vie. The U.S. government classifies it as brandy.

McMenamins Cornelius Pass Roadhouse Distillery

4045 N.W. Cornelius Pass Road
Hillsboro, OR 97124
503-640-6174

Owners / Operators:
Clark McCool, Distillery Manager
Bart Hance, Head Distiller
Arthur Price, Distiller

Email: cpr@mcmenamins.com
Website: www.mcmenamins.com
Facebook: McMenamins Cornelius Pass Roadhouse

Type: Micro Distillery. Opened in 2011.

Hours of operation: Daily, 9 a.m. to 5 p.m.

Tours: Available

Types of spirits produced: Whiskey, brandy, gin

Names of spirits:
- White Owl Whiskey
- Morning Dew
- Gables Gin
- 3 Year Old Whiskey (Sept. 2014)
- Hazelnut Liqueur (Nov. 2014)

Best known for / most popular: Gables Gin

Average bottle price: $17.50 to $39.50

Distribution: OR, WA

Interesting facts:
Set in an old granary barn constructed by the pioneer Imbrie family in the mid-1850s, the Cornelius Pass Roadhouse Distillery boasts a century-year-old, 160-gallon Alambic Charentais pot still.

McMenamins Edgefield Distillery

2126 SW Halsey Street
Troutdale, OR 97060
503-669-8610

Owners / Operators:
Clark McCool, Manager
James Whelan, Head Distiller
Jarod Davis, Distiller

Email: distillery@mcmenamins.com
Website: www.mcmenamins.com
Facebook: McMenamins Edgefield Distillery
YouTube: McMenaminsVIDEO's channel
Pinterest: McMenamins
Flickr: McMenamins Photos' photostream

Type: Micro Distillery. Opened in 1998.

Hours of operation: Daily, 9 a.m. to 5 p.m.

Tours: Available

Types of spirits produced:
Whiskey, brandy, gin, liqueur, rum

Names of spirits:
- Hogshead Whiskey
- White Dog Whiskey
- Monkey Puzzle Whiskey
- Devils Bit Whiskey
- Alambic 13 Brandy
- Edgefield Potstill Brandy
- Pear Brandy
- Longshot Brandy
- Penny's Gin
- Professors Gin
- Coffee Liqueur
- Herbal Liqueur
- Edgefield Rum

Best known for / most popular: Hogshead Whiskey

Average bottle price: $12.75 to 37.50

Distribution: OR, WA

Interesting facts: Edgefield also has a brewery and a winery.

New Deal Distillery

900 SE Salmon Street
Portland, OR 97214
503-234-2513

Owners / Operators:
Tom Burkleaux, Owner
Matthew VanWinkle, Owner

Email: info@newdealdistillery.com, tom@newdealdistillery.com
Website: www.NewDealDistillery.com
Facebook: New Deal Distillery
Twitter: @NewDealPDX

Type: Micro Distillery. Opened in 2004.

Hours of operation:
Wednesday through Sunday, noon to 5 p.m.

Tours: Available

Types of spirits produced: Vodka, infused vodka, rum, liqueurs, gin, whiskey

Names of spirits:
- New Deal Vodka
- Portland 88 Vodka
- Hot Monkey Pepper-Flavored Vodka
- Mud Puddle Bitter Chocolate Vodka
- Coffee Liqueur
- Ginger Liqueur
- Gin No. 1
- Portland Dry Gin 33
- Distiller's Workshop Rum
- Distiller's Workshop Whiskey

Photo by: Jeremy Dunham, Polara Studios, 2009

Best known for / most popular: New Deal Vodka

Average bottle price: $20.00 to $50.00

Distribution: CT, IL, OR, VT, WA; Canada, Singapore

Interesting facts:
New Deal uses water from the Bull Run Reservoir, one of North America's largest gravity-fed water supplies. This water, which comes from the melted snow pack from Mt. Hood's annual accumulation of 500-600 inches of snow each season, is considered by many to be among the most pure water in the nation.

Oregon Ryegrass Spirits

720 NE Granger Avenue, Bldg. B
Corvallis, OR 97330
541-990-0337

Owners / Operators:
Chris Beatty, Founder / Spirit Chemist

Email: chris@ryegrassspirits.com
Website: www.ryegrassspirits.com, www.spiritopia.com
Facebook: Spiritopia Liqueurs

Type: Micro Distillery. Opened in June 2013.

Hours of operation:
Monday through Friday, 9 a.m. to 5 p.m.

Tours: Available by appointment

Types of spirits produced: Liqueurs

Names of spirits:
- Spiritopia

Best known for / most popular:
Spiritopia Ginger Liqueur

Average bottle price: $30.00

Distribution: OR

Interesting facts:
The ginger used is from an organic farm in Peru.

Oregon Spirit Distillers

490 NE Butler Market Road, Ste. 110
Bend, OR 97701
541-382-0002

Owners / Operators:
Brad and Kathy Irwin, Owners / Operators

Email: info@oregonspiritdistillers.com
Website: www.oregonspiritdistillers.com
Facebook: Oregon Spirit Distillers
Twitter: @oregonspirit

Type: Micro Distillery. Opened in 2009.

Hours of operation:
Monday through Saturday, noon to 5 p.m.

Tours: Available during open hours

Types of spirits produced: Vodka, genever, bourbon, spiced rum, absinthe, cordial

Names of spirits:
- Merrylegs Genever
- Wild Card Absinthe
- Oregon Spirit Vodka
- C.W. Irwin Straight Bourbon
- Black Mariah (Marionberry Cordial)
- One-Eyed Jon Spiced Rum

Average bottle price: $30.00 to $50.00

Distribution: ID, OR, WA

Interesting facts: Not provided

RANSOM

Ransom Spirits

23101 Houser Road
Sheridan, OR 97378
503-876-5022

Owners / Operators:
Tad Seestedt, Sole Proprietor

Email: info@ransomspirits.com
Website: www.ransomspirits.com
Facebook: Ransom Spirits

Type: Winery / Micro Distillery. Opened in 1997.

Hours of operation: Not open to the public

Tours: Not available

Types of spirits produced:
Gin, whiskey, brandy, grappa, vodka

Names of spirits:
- WhipperSnapper Oregon Spirit Whiskey
- Old Tom Gin
- Small's Gin
- Gewürztraminer Grappa
- The Vodka

Best known for / most popular: Old Tom Gin

Average bottle price: $25.00 to $37.00

Distribution:
CA, CO, DC, IL, MA, MO, NJ, NV, NY, OR, TN, TX, WA, WI

Interesting facts:
The name Ransom was initially chosen to represent the investment necessary to become self-employed. It has since come to represent the amount of debt owed to banks and other loaning institutions.

Photos courtesy of Ransom Spirits. Photos by: "Eye of the Lady Photography Studio"

Rogue Spirits

Rum Distillery:
Rogue Ales Public House and Distillery
1339 Northwest Flanders Street
Portland, OR 97209
503-222-5910

Main Distillery:
Rogue House of Spirits
2122 Marine Science Drive
Newport, OR 97365
541-867-3673

Owners / Operators:
Mike Higgins, President Rogue Spirits
Jeff Alexander, Master Distiller

Email: m.higgins@rogue.com
Website: www.rogue.com
　　　　www.roguespirits.com
Facebook: Rogue Ales

Twitter: @RogueAles
YouTube: Rogue Ales HQ
Instagram: rogueales

Type: Brewery / Micro Distillery. Opened Portland in 2003, Newport in 2006.

Hours of operation:
Portland
Sun. through Thur., 11 a.m. to midnight
Fri. and Sat., 11 a.m. to 10 a.m.

Newport
Friday, 4 p.m. to 8 p.m.
Saturday, noon to 8 p.m.
Sunday, noon to 6 p.m.

Tours: Available at both facilities. Days and times vary.

Types of spirits produced: Artisan, varietal whiskey, gin, rum, vodka

Names of spirits:
- Rogue Spruce Gin
- Rogue Pink Gin
- Rogue Dead Guy Whiskey
- Rogue Oregon Single Malt Whiskey
- Rogue Chipotle Whiskey
- Rogue Hazelnut Spice Rum
- Rogue Dark Rum
- Rogue Vintage Vodka
- Rogue Oregon Single Malt Vodka
- Rogue Oregon Rye Whiskey

Best known for / most popular: Rogue Spirits are best known for creating spirits using ingredients fresh from Rogue Farms.

Average bottle price: $34.00 to $44.00

Distribution: 45 states and 5 countries

Interesting facts: The Rogue distillery in Portland was Oregon's first rum distillery.

Rolling River Spirits

1215 SE 8th Avenue, Ste. H
Portland, OR 97214
503-236-3912

Owners / Operators:
Richard Rickard, General Manager
Joan Rickard, Distiller
Tim Rickard, Master Distiller

Email: info@rollingriverspirits.com
Website: www.rollingriverspirits.com
Facebook: Rolling River Spirits
Twitter: @RollingRiverPDX

Type: Micro Distillery. Opened in March 2014.

Hours of operation: Monday through Friday, hours vary

Tasting room hours: Friday, 4:30 p.m. to 7:30 p.m.
Saturday and Sunday, noon to 5 p.m.

Tours:
Available during tasting room hours and by appointment

Types of spirits produced: Vodka, gin, whiskey

Names of spirits:
- Rolling River Spirits Vodka
- Rolling River Spirits Gin
- Rolling River Spirits Whiskey

Best known for / most popular: Rolling River Spirits Vodka

Average bottle price: $21.50 to $37.50

Distribution: On-site retail, OR

Interesting facts:
Rolling River Spirits uses custom designed and custom built stills.

Sinister Distilling Company

635 NE Water Avenue, Ste. D
Albany, OR 97321
541-639-4257

Owners / Operators:
Eric Howard, Owner / Head Distiller
Jamie Howard, Owner

Email: howie@sinisterdeluxe.com
Website: www.sinisterdistilling.com
Facebook: Sinister Distilling
Twitter: @sinisterdeluxe

Type: Craft Distillery. Opened in September 2013.

Hours of operation: Check website for hours.

Tours: Call or email for a tour.

Types of spirits produced: Whiskey, gin

Names of spirits:
- Sinner

Best known for / most popular: TBA

Average bottle price: TBA

Distribution: TBA

Interesting facts:
- Deluxe Brewing and Sinister Distilling is Albany's first brewstillery.
- Sinister Distilling Company and Deluxe Brewing Company is the dream of Albany Steamworks, LLC, otherwise known as Eric "Howie" and Jamie Howard. The couple decided long ago that a brewstillery was exactly what they needed to start. After several years of research and the help of family, friends and the community, the Howards are realizing their dream.
- Sinister Distilling Company uses a whiskey pot still from Portugal to produce their spirits.

Stein Distillery

604 N. Main Street
Joseph, OR 97846
503-642-2659

Owners / Operators:
Austin Stein, Co-owner
Heather Stein, Co-owner

Email: whiskey@steindistillery.com
Website: www.steindistillery.com

Type: Micro Distillery. Opened in 2012.

Hours of operation: Not provided

Tours: Not provided

Types of spirits produced: Whiskey

Names of spirits:
- TBA

Best known for / most popular: Not provided

Average bottle price: Not provided

Distribution: OR

Interesting facts: Not provided

Stillwagon Distillery

63848 Seven Devils Road
Coos Bay, OR 97420
253-732-8458

Owners / Operators:
Richard and Karen Stillwagon, Owners / Operators

Email: stillwagondistillery@yahoo.com
Website: www.stillwagondistillery.com
Facebook: Stillwagon Distillery

Type: Craft Distillery. Opened in September 2013.

Hours of operation:
Monday through Friday, 9 a.m. to 5 p.m.

Tours: Available by appointment

Types of spirits produced: Rum

Names of spirits:
- Devil's Own Wicked Rum
- Devil's Own Gold Rum

Best known for / most popular: TBA

Average bottle price: TBA

Distribution: OR

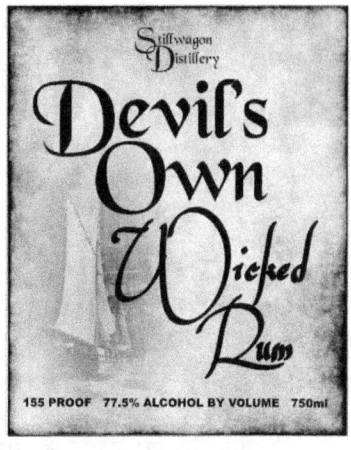

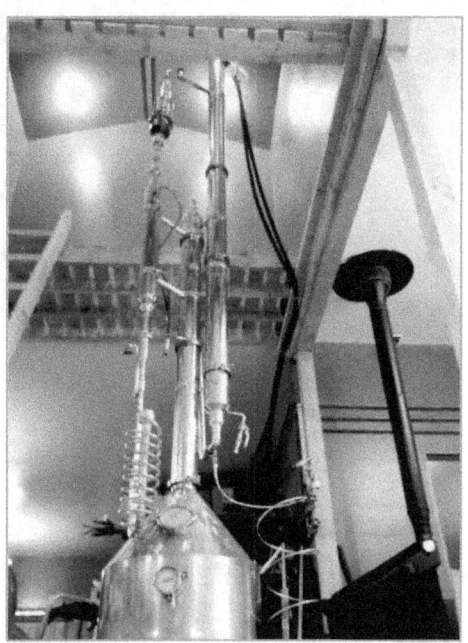

Stone Barn Brandyworks

3315 SE 19th, Ste. B
Portland, OR 97202
503-775-6747

Owners / Operators:
Sebastian and Erika Degens, Founders

Email: degens@stonebarnbrandyworks.com
Website: www.stonebarnbrandyworks.com
Facebook: Stone Barn Brandyworks

Type: Micro Distillery. Opened in 2009.

Hours of operation:
Saturday and Sunday, noon to 6 p.m.
Monday, noon to 7 p.m.

Tours: Available during above hours

Types of spirits produced:
Brandy, liqueur, grappa, whiskey

Names of spirits:
- Oregon Apple Brandy (oaked)
- Bartlett Pear Brandy
- Comice Pear Brandy
- Pacific Northwest Cherry Brandy
- Pacific Northwest Plum Brandy
- Biggs Junction Apricot Liqueur
- Golden Quince Liqueur
- Cranberry Liqueur
- Oregon Blush Rhubarb Liqueur
- Strawberry Liqueur
- Red Wing Roast Coffee Liqueur
- Nocino Green Walnut Liqueur
- Easy Eight Unoaked Oat Whiskey
- Hard Eight Rye Whiskey
- Hoppin' Eights Whiskey
- Pinot Noir Grappa
- Eastside Ouzo

Best known for / most popular: Fruit liqueurs, brandies; rye and oat whiskey

Average bottle price: $25.00 to $32.00

Distribution: OR

Interesting facts: Stone Barn's whiskeys are made from Bob's Red Mill Flour.

Stringer's Orchard Winery and Distillery

New Pine Creek, OR 97635
530-946-4112

Owners / Operators:
Joanne and John Stringer, Owners

Email: winemaker@stringersorchard.com
Website: www.stringersorchard.com

Type: Winery / Micro Distillery. Opened in 2005.

Hours of operation:
Closed January through March
April to December, Monday through Saturday, 10 a.m. to 5 p.m.

Tours: Available

Types of spirits produced: Brandy, liqueur

Names of spirits:
- Wild Plum Wine
- Plum Brandy (Slivovitz)
- Pacific Plum Liqueur
- Pacific Plum Gin
- Plum Jam and Syrup

Best known for / most popular: Pacific Plum Liqueur

Average bottle price: $19.95 to $28.00

Distribution: Sold locally

Interesting facts:
Only known distillery making alcohol from wild Pacific plum.

Sub Rosa Spirits

876 SW Alder Drive
Dundee, OR 97115
503-476-2808

Owners / Operators:
Michael Sherwood, Owner

Email: sub-rosa@comcast.net
Website: www.subrosaspirits.com
Facebook: Sub Rosa Spirits

Type: Craft Distillery. Opened in 2007.

Hours of operation: Not provided

Tours: Not provided

Types of spirits produced: Vodka

Names of spirits:
- Sub Rosa Tarragon Vodka
- Sub Rosa Saffron Vodka

Best known for / most popular:
Sub Rosa Tarragon Vodka and Sub Rosa Saffron Vodka

Average bottle price: $29.95

Distribution: CA, DC, IL, OR, WA

Interesting facts:
Sub Rosa Saffron Vodka is the first commercial savory spiced vodka that captures the flavors of India and Asia.

The words "sub rosa" come from the Latin "under the rose," from the association of the rose with confidentiality. Use of a rose at secret meetings was a symbol of the sworn confidence of the participants. The ceilings of ancient banquet rooms were often decorated with roses to remind guests that what was spoken within was private.

Lovers of Sub Rosa distillates carry on the tradition of elixirs consumed in private, a shared secret with a select few. Anyone who is familiar with secret societies such as the Illuminati, Freemasons, Priory of Scion, or Knights Templar will be familiar with the concept of "sub rosa." By sampling Sub Rosa elixirs, you become part of the cadre. Membership is open to a select few who quest after the true spirit.

Superfly Distilling Company

16399 Lower Harbor Road, Ste. B
Brookings, OR 97415
530-520-8005

Owners / Operators:
Ryan Webster, Owner

Email: ryanwebster@msn.com
Website: www.superflybooze.com
Facebook: Superfly Distilling Company

Type: Micro Distillery. Opened in 2008.

Hours of operation: Not provided

Tours: Available occasionally

Types of spirits produced: Vodka, rum, whiskey

Names of spirits:
- Superfly Vodka

Best known for / most popular: Superfly Vodka

Average bottle price: $20.00

Distribution: Not provided

Interesting facts: Not provided

Vinn Distillery

7990 SW Boeckman Road
Wilsonville, OR 97070
503-957-9210

Owners / Operators:
Michelle Ly, Co-owner
Quyen Ly, Co-owner
Vicki Ly, Co-owner
Lien Ly, Co-owner

Email: Michelle Ly, michelle@vinndistillery.com
Quyen Ly, quyen@vinndistillery.com
Vicki Ly, vicki@vinndistillery.com
Lien Ly, lien@vinndistillery.com
Website: www.vinndistillery.com
Facebook: Vinn Distillery
Twitter: @vinndistillery

Type: Micro Distillery. Opened in 2009.

Tasting room location / hours:
833 SE Main Street Ste. 125, Portland, OR 97214
Saturday and Sunday, noon to 5 p.m.

Tours: Not available

Types of spirits produced: Rice vodka, baijiu, rice wine

Names of spirits:
- Vinn Mijiu (pronounced "Mee-Je-oh") Ice
- Vinn Mijiu (pronounced "Mee-Je-oh") Fire
- Vinn Baijiu (pronounced "By-Je-oh")
- Vinn Vodka
- Vinn Whiskey

Best known for / most popular: Vinn Baijiu

Average bottle price: $18.95 to $35.95

Distribution: OR

Interesting facts:
- The recipe used to make all three of Vinn Distillery spirits is over 7 generations old.
- Baijiu - considered the national drink of China - is a Chinese distilled alcoholic beverage. The name baijiu literally means "white liquor."
- Vinn Distillery products are gluten free.
- First known rice vodka produced and bottled in the U.S.
- Vinn Whiskey was the first and one of the only rice based barrel-aged whiskey produced and bottled in the U.S.

Vivacity Spirits

720 NE Granger Avenue #C
Corvallis, OR 97330
541-286-4285

Owners / Operators:
Caitlin Prueitt, Owner / Distiller
Chris Neumann, Owner / Distiller

Email: vivacityspirits@gmail.com
Website: www.vivacityspirits.com
Facebook: Vivacity Spirits
Twitter: @VivacitySpirits

Type: Micro Distillery. Opened in 2011.

Hours of operation: Tasting room open first and third Saturday of the month

Tours: Available by appointment

Types of spirits produced:
Vodka, gin, rum, liqueur

Names of spirits:
- Vivacity Fine Vodka
- Vivacity Bankers' Gin
- Vivacity Native Gin
- Turkish Coffee Liqueur

Best known for / most popular:
Turkish Coffee Liqueur

Average bottle price: $23.95 to $28.95

Distribution: OR

Interesting facts:
The base for the vodka and gin are made with American grown organic corn.

Ye Ol' Grog Distillery

35855 Industrial Way, Unit C
Saint Helens, OR 97051
503-366-4001

Owners / Operators:
Lloyd Williams, Owner
Ken McFarland, Owner
Greg Scott, Owner
Marcus Alden, Owner

Email: info@yeolgrogdistillery.com
Website: www.yeolgrogdistillery.com, www.grogme.com
Facebook: Ye Ol Grog Distillery, Grog Wench Libations
Twitter: @GrogMe

Type: Micro Distillery. Opened in 2009.

Hours of operation:
Monday through Friday, 1 p.m. to 5 p.m.
Saturday and Sunday, 1 p.m. to 4 p.m.

Tours: Available by appointment

Types of spirits produced:
Specialty distilled spirits, vodka

Names of spirits:
- Dog Watch Vodka
- Dutch Harbor Breeze Grog
- Good Morning Glory Grog
- St Helens Vodka

Best known for / most popular:
Dutch Harbor Breeze Grog

Average bottle price: Mid-range

Distribution: AK, CA, CO, DC, DE, FL, GA, HI, IL, MD, MO, OR, PA, WA and online at www.cellar.com

Interesting facts:
"Our philosophy is to distill vodka to a smoothness, texture, and purity that doesn't require carbon filtration. After all, if you had to filter your water at home 10 times, you probably wouldn't drink it." – Ken McFarland

You'll notice that most of Ye Ol' Grog products have an "FPC" brand; that is their corporate take on political correctness. PC is for politically correct, the "F," well, you can figure that out for yourself.

Allegheny Distilling LLC

3212A Smallman Street
Pittsburgh, PA 15201
412-709-6480

Owners / Operators:
Tim Russell, Founder / Distiller
Moss Clark, Partner / Distiller

Email: tim@maggiesfarmrum.com
Website: www.maggiesfarmrum.com
Facebook: Maggie's Farm Rum
Twitter: @MaggiesFarmRum

Type: Craft Distillery. Opened in November 2013.

Hours of operation:
Wednesday and Thursday, 11 a.m. to 7 p.m.
Friday and Saturday, 11 a.m. 10 p.m.
(Cocktail sales Friday and Saturday evenings)

Tours: Available by request

Types of spirits produced: Rum, liqueur, brandy

Names of spirits:
- Maggie's Farm Rum
- Queen's Share Overproof

Best known for / most popular: Maggie's Farm Rum

Average bottle price: $28.00

Distribution: PA

Interesting facts:
Maggie's Farm is the first Pennsylvania made craft rum available for commercial sale since Prohibition.

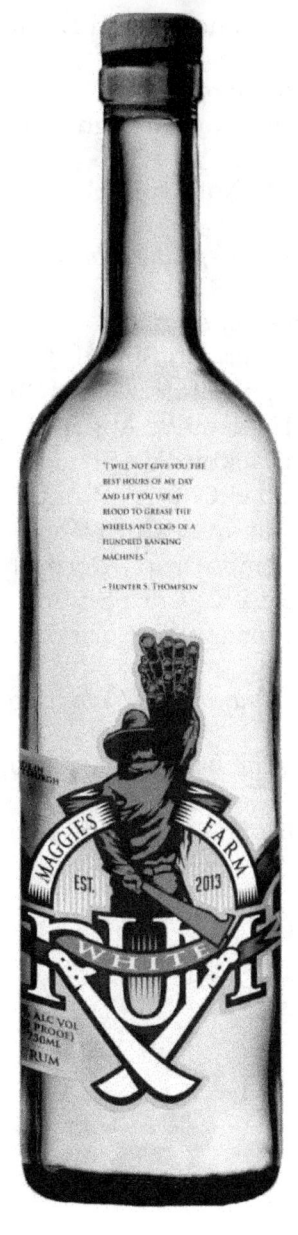

Blackbird Distillery

93 Blackout Alley
Brookville, PA 15825
814-849-0915

Owners / Operators:
David W. Black Jr., Co-owner
Jennifer M. Black, Co-owner

Email: blackbirdmoonshine@gmail.com
Website: www.blackbirddistillery.com

Type: Small Batch Distillery. Opened in March 2014

Hours of operation:
Wednesday through Sunday, 11 a.m. to 7 p.m.

Tours: Not available

Types of spirits produced: Moonshine

Names of spirits:
- American Shine - Charred Oak
- AppleBlack - Corn Shine
- Homemade ApplePie - Corn Shine
- Blackbird's - Straight Shine
- BlackCherry - Corn Shine
- Banana - Corn Shine
- LemonDrop - Corn Shine
- Peach - Corn Shine
- Pineapple - Corn Shine

Best known for / most popular: TBD

Average bottle price: $30.00 to $50.00

Distribution: On-site retail

Hewn Spirits LLC

31B Appletree Lane
Pipersville, PA 18947

Owners / Operators:
Sean Tracy, Managing Member

Email: info@hewnspirits.com
Website: www.hewnspirits.com
Facebook: Hewn Spirits

Type: Micro Distillery. Opened in September 2013.

Hours of operation: TBD

Tours: Available

Types of spirits produced:
Rum, whiskey, gin, vodka

Names of spirits:
- Shipmate Rum
- Red Barn Rye
- New Moon White Whiskey

Best known for / most popular:
Not provided

Average bottle price:
$25.00 to $38.00

Distribution: PA, NJ

Interesting facts: Not provided

Manatawny Still Works

320 Circle of Progress Drive, Ste. 104
Pottstown, PA 19464
484-624-8271

Owners / Operators:
Randy McKinley, VP Sales & Marketing
Max Pfeffer, Head Distiller

Email: info@manatawnystillworks.com
randym@manatawnystillworks.com
Website: www.ManatawnyStillWorks.com
Facebook: Manatawny Still Works
Twitter: @manatawnysw
Instagram: ManatawnyStillWorks

Type: Craft Distillery. Opened in February 2014.

Hours of operation:
Monday through Friday, 9 a.m. to 6 p.m.
Saturday, noon to 6 p.m.

Tours: Available

Types of spirits produced: Vodka, rum, whiskey

Names of spirits:
- Rutter Rum - Light Rum
- Manatawny Hearts of Darkness Rum - Dark/Aged Rum
- J. Potts Whiskey - White Whiskey
- Manatawny Batch Whiskey - One-Year Old Aged
- Manatawny Pennsylvania Whiskey - Two-Year Old Aged

Best known for / most popular: Not provided

Average bottle price: $18.99 to $45.00

Distribution: DE, MD, NJ, NY, PA, VA, WV

Mountain Laurel Spirits LLC

925 Canal Street
Bristol, PA 19007
215-781-8300

Owners / Operators:
Herman C. Mihalich, Co-owner
John S. Cooper, Co-owner

Email: info@dadshatrye.com
Website: www.dadshatrye.com
Facebook: Dad's Hat Rye
Twitter: @dadshatrye

Type: Craft Distillery. Opened in 2011.

Hours of operation: Not provided

Tours:
Available Saturday afternoons by appointment

Types of spirits produced: Rye whiskey, white rye

Names of spirits:
- Dad's Hat™ Pennsylvania Rye Whiskey
- Dad's Hat™ Pennsylvania White Rye
- Dad's Hat™ Pennsylvania Rye Whiskey Finished in Vermouth Barrels
- Dad's Hat™ Pennsylvania Rye Whiskey Finished in Sweet Wine Barrels

Best known for / most popular:
Dad's Hat™ Pennsylvania Rye Whiskey

Average bottle price: $30.00 to $40.00

Distribution:
CA, DC, ID, KY, MA, NH, NJ, NY, OR, PA, RI

Interesting facts: Not provided

Mountain View Distillery
Mountain View Vineyard Inc.

5866 Neola Road
Stroudsburg, PA 18360
570-619-0053

Owners / Operators:
Randall A. Rice, Owner / Distiller

Email: info@maountainviewvineyard.com
Website: www.mountainviewvineyard.com
Facebook: Mountain View Vineyard and Winery
Tripadvisor: Mountain View Vineyard and Distillery

Type: Craft Distillery. Opened in September 2013.

Hours of operation:
November to April: Friday through Sunday, noon to 6 p.m.
May to October: Monday through Saturday, 11 a.m. to 6 p.m.
                       Sunday, noon to 4 p.m.

Tours: Available Saturday and Sunday at 3 p.m.

Types of spirits produced:
Vodka, brandy, moonshine

Names of spirits:
- Apple Pie Shine (40 & 80 Proof)
- Original Shine
- Randy's Brandy
- Red Raspberry Vodka
- Pear Vodka
- Peach Vodka – Coming soon
- Blueberry Vodka – Coming soon

Best known for / most popular:
Apple Pie Shine

Average bottle price: $20.00 to $24.00

Distribution: On-site retail

Interesting facts:
One of only a couple winery/distillery combinations in PA.

Naoj and Mot Inc.

2519 Moore Street
Philadelphia, PA 19145
215-271-1161

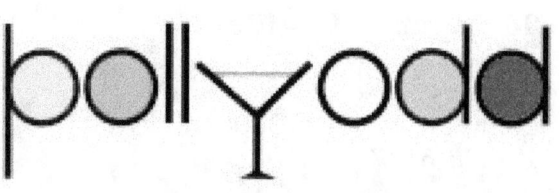

Owners / Operators:
Joan Verratti, CEO / President
Tom Cavaliere, Plant Manager

Email: joan@naojandmotinc.com
Website: www.pollyodd.com
Facebook: Pollyodd

Type: Micro Distillery. Opened in 2012.

Hours of operation:
Monday through Friday, 8 a.m. to noon

Tours: Not available

Types of spirits produced: Liqueurs

Names of spirits:
- Pollyodd Lemoncello
- Pollyodd Limecello
- Pollyodd Orangecello
- Pollyodd Chocolatecello
- Pollyodd Mangocello
- Pollyodd Lemoncreamcello
- Pollyodd Orangecreamcello
- Pollyodd Bananacreamcello
- Pollyodd Chocolatecreamcello
- Pollyodd Strawberrycreamcello

Best known for / most popular: Pollyodd Lemoncello

Average bottle price: $23.00 to $26.00

Distribution: PA

Interesting facts:
One of only a few woman owned and operated distilleries in the U.S.

Old Republic Distillery

47 Cherry Street
Seven Valleys, PA 17360
717-428-6177

Owners / Operators:
Bill Mathias, Owner / Distiller
Denise Mathias, Owner

Email: cheers@drinkORD.com
Website: www.DrinkORD.com
Facebook: Old Republic Distillery
Twitter: @DistilleryORD
Yelp: Old Republic Distillery

Type: Micro Distillery. Opened in March 2013.

Hours of operation:
Thursday, 4:30 p.m. to 7:30 p.m.
Friday and Saturday, noon to 6 p.m.
Seasonal hours posted on social media

Tours: Not available

Types of spirits produced:
Liqueur, vodka, moonshine

Names of spirits:
- Battlefield Vodka
- Blackberry Vodka
- Apple Pie Moonshine
- Love Potion
- Love Potion Black Cherry
- Blueberry Apple Pie Moonshine

Best known for / most popular: Love Potion

Average bottle price: $14.00 to $35.00

Distribution: On-site retail

Interesting facts:
- Old Republic Distillery is the 1st distillery in South-Central PA since Prohibition.
- Old Republic Distillery incorporates local history stories on their labels.

Pennsylvania Pure Distilleries LLC

1101 William Flinn Highway
Glenshaw, PA 15116
412-486-8666

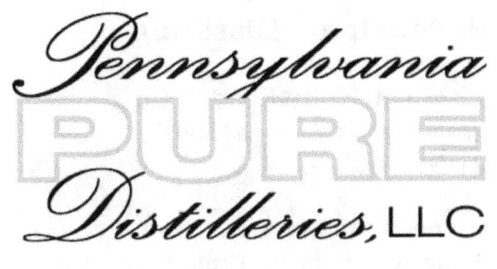

Owners / Operators:
Barry L. Young, Owner
C. Prentiss Orr, Owner

Email: info@boydandblair.com
Website: www.boydandblair.com
Facebook: Boyd and Blair Potato Vodka
Twitter: @BoydBlairVodka
LinkedIn: Pennsylvania Pure Distilleries LLC

Type: Micro Distillery. Opened in 2008.

Hours of operation:
Monday through Friday, 9:30 a.m. to 6 p.m.

Tours:
By appointment for industry professionals

Types of spirits produced: Potato vodka

Names of spirits:
- Boyd & Blair Potato Vodka (80 proof)
- Boyd & Blair Professional Proof 151 Potato Vodka

Best known for / most popular:
Boyd & Blair Potato Vodka

Average bottle price: $29.00 to $49.00

Distribution: AZ, CA, CO, CT, DC, DE, FL, GA, IA, ID, IL, IN, KY, LA, MA, MD, MI, MN, MO, NC, NH, NJ, NV, NY, OR, PA, RI, TN, TX, VA, WA, WI, WV; Canada AL, ON; Hong Kong; Singapore

Interesting facts: Pennsylvania Pure Distilleries LLC was founded as Pennsylvania's first vodka distillery.

Philadelphia Distilling

12285 McNulty Road #105
Philadelphia, PA 19154
215-671-0346

Owners / Operators:
Andrew Auwerda, President
Tim Yarnall, Vice President

Email: info@philadelphiadistilling.com
Website: www.philadelphiadistilling.com, www.bluecoatgin.com
www.penn1681vodka.com, www.vieuxcarreabsinthe.com
www.shinewhiskey.com, www.thebayvodka.com
Facebook: Bluecoat American Dry Gin, Penn 1681 Rye Vodka
Vieux Carré Absinthe Supérieure, Shine Whiskey
Philadelphia Distilling, THE BAY Seasoned Vodka
Twitter: @bluecoatgin, @vcabsinthe, @TheBayVodka
@Penn1681Vodka, @shinewhiskey

Type: Micro Distillery. Opened in 2005.

Hours of operation: Regular

Tours: Available

Products produced: Absinthe, gin, vodka, whiskey

Names of spirits:
- Bluecoat American Dry Gin
- Penn 1681 Rye Vodka
- Vieux Carré Absinthe Supérieure
- XXX Shine Whiskey (range)
- The Bay Seasoned Vodka

Best known for / most popular:
Bluecoat American Dry Gin

Average bottle price: $28.00

Distribution:
40 U.S. States; Bermuda, France, Spain, Italy, East Africa

Interesting facts:
- The first craft distillery in Pennsylvania since Prohibition.
- The first spirit released was Bluecoat American Dry Gin.
- The first East Coast distillery to distill authentic absinthe in over 100 years.

Pittsburgh Distilling Co.

2401 Smallman Street
Pittsburgh, PA 15222
412-728-0053

Owners / Operators:
Alex Grelli, Meredith Grelli,
Eric Meyer, Mark Meyer, Mary Ellen Meyer

Email: meredith@wiglewhiskey.com
Website: www.wiglewhiskey.com
Facebook: Wigle Whiskey
Twitter: @WigleWhiskey

Type: Micro Distillery. Opened in 2012.

Hours of operation:
Monday through Saturday, 10 a.m. to 6 p.m.
Sunday, 10 a.m. to 4 p.m.

Tours:
Available Saturdays and by appointment.
Register on website.

Types of spirits produced:
Whiskey, Genever-style gin, rum, bitters

Names of spirits:
- Wigle Organic White Rye Whiskey
- Wigle Organic White Wheat Whiskey
- Wigle Organic Ginever
- Organic Aged Wheat Whiskey – Small Cask Series
- Organic Aged Rye Whiskey-Small Cask Series
- Wigle Landlocked

Best known for / most popular:
Small batch, from scratch organic whiskey

Average bottle price: $25.00 to $50.00

Distribution:
On-site retail, PA, online for DC residents

Interesting facts:
Pittsburgh Distilling makes Monongahela Rye, the original form of American whiskey, and offers historical tours about the whiskey.

Stay Tuned Distillery LLC

810 Ravine Street
Munhall, PA 15120
412-461-4555, 724-309-2942

Owners / Operators:
Lee Ann Sommerfeld, General Manager
Peter Streibig, Production Manager

Email: las@staytunedstills.com
Website: www.staytunedstills.com
Facebook: Stay Tuned Distillery
Twitter: @StayTunedStills

Type: Craft Distillery. Opened in November 2013.

Tasting room hours:
Thursday and Friday, 11 a.m. to 7 p.m.
Saturday, 11 a.m. to 5 p.m.
Sunday and Monday, Closed

Tours: Available by appointment only

Types of spirits produced: Gin

Names of spirits:
- Stay Tuned Distillery PathoGin

Best known for / most popular: Mason Dawson Gimlet

Average bottle price: $36.00 to $50.00

Distribution: PA

Interesting facts: The distillery is located in the historic John Munhall Neighborhood House built in 1920.

Services offered other than production:
Tasting room and a small gallery space.

Thistle Finch Distilling

417 W. Grant Street
Lancaster, PA 17603
717-478-8472

Owners / Operators:
Andrew Martin, Owner / Distiller

Email: martin@thistlefinch.com
Website: www.thistlefinch.com
Facebook: Thistle Finch Distillery
Twitter: @ThistleFinchRye
Instagram: @thistlefinchrye

Type: Craft Distillery. Opened in December 2013.

Hours of operation:
Wednesday and Friday, 6 p.m. to 10 p.m.
Saturday, 2 p.m. to 10 p.m.

Tours: Not available

Types of spirits produced: Rye whiskey

Names of spirits:
- Small Batch White Rye Whiskey

Best known for / most popular:
Small Batch White Rye Whiskey

Average bottle price: $32.00

Distribution: PA

Interesting facts:
Lancaster County's first whiskey since Prohibition.

Newport Distilling Company

293 JT Connell Road
Newport, RI 02840
401-849-5232

Owners / Operators:
Brent Ryan, President / Head Distiller
Derek Luke, Founder / Brewmaster

Email: information@thomastewrums.com
Website: www.thomastewrums.com
Facebook: Thomas Tew Rum
Twitter: @ThomasTewRum

Type: Micro Distillery. Opened in 2006.

Hours of operation:
Open 6 days a week (Closed Tuesdays), noon to 5 p.m.

Tours: Available

Types of spirits produced: Rum

Names of spirits:
- Thomas Tew Single Barrel Rum

Best known for / most popular:
Thomas Tew Single Barrel Rum

Average bottle price: $30.00 to $35.00

Distribution:
CT, DC, DE, FL, GA, IL, MA, MD, MI, NJ, NY, RI

Interesting facts:
- Newport Distilling Company received the first license to distill in the state since the close of the John Dyer Distillery in Providence in 1872.
- Subject of the 2011 episode, "Rum Distiller" on Dirty Jobs with Mike Rowe.

AUTHENTIC POT-STILL
RUM
NEWPORT, RI USA

Sons of Liberty Spirits Co.

1425 Kingstown Road
South Kingstown, RI 02879
401-284-4006

Owners / Operators:
Mike Reppucci, Owner / Founder
Chris Guillette, The Fashionista
Danny Murphy, The Mayor
Bryan Ricard, The Gopher

Email: info@solspirits.com
Website: www.solspirits.com
Facebook: Sons of Liberty Spirits Co.
Twitter: @solspirits

Type: Micro Distillery. Opened in 2011.

Hours of operation: Vary

Tours: Wednesdays and Saturdays, noon to 4 p.m.

Types of spirits produced: American single malt whiskey, seasonal whiskey, vodka, seasonal vodka

Names of spirits:
- UPRISING American Single Malt Whiskey
- BATTLE CRY American Single Malt Whiskey
- Hop Flavored Whiskey (Spring/Summer)
- Pumpkin Spice Flavored Whiskey (Fall/Winter)
- Loyal 9 Vodka
- Loyal 9 Mint Cucumber Flavored Vodka (Spring/Summer)
- Loyal 9 Dark Chocolate Vanilla Bean Flavored Vodka (Fall/Winter)

Best known for / most popular:
UPRISING and BATTLE CRY American Single Malt Whiskey

Average bottle price: $27.00 to $42.00

Distribution: MA, RI

Interesting facts:
- Sons of Liberty's American Single Malts are all born from different beers and crafted to bring forth the unique flavors of that beer.
- UPRISING is born from a stout beer, BATTLE CRY is born from a Belgian-Style Ale.
- Sons of Liberty Seasonals is the first ever seasonal line of whiskies.
- The 2013 release of Pumpkin Spice Flavored Whiskey used over 4,000 lbs of Rhode Island grown pumpkins
- Loyal 9 Seasonal Vodkas are made with fresh and locally grown ingredients.

Dark Corner Distillery

241-B North Main Street
Greenville, SC 29601
864-631-1144

Owners / Operators:
Joe Fenten, Founder

Email: joe@darkcornerdistillery.com
Website: www.darkcornerdistillery.com
Facebook: Dark Corner Distillery
Twitter: @DCDistillery

Type: Micro Distillery. Opened in 2011.

Hours of operation:
Monday through Saturday, noon to 6 p.m.

Tours: Available by appointment

Types of spirits produced:
Whiskey, bourbon, gin, absinthe

Names of spirits:
- Moonshine
- Stumphouse Whiskey
- Apple-achian Shine
- Butterscotch Shine
- Carolina Peach Shine
- Lewis Redmond Carolina Bourbon Whiskey

Best known for / most popular:
Apple-achian Margarita

Average bottle price: $32.00

Distribution: DC, GA, MD, NC, SC

Interesting facts:
- "World's Best Moonshine" – Joe Fenton
- One of the most awarded moonshines in the world.
- One of the few distilleries that mashes and pot distills over an open flame.

Firefly Distillery

6775 Bears Bluff Road
Wadmalaw Island, SC 29487
843-557-1405

Owners / Operators:
Jim Irvin and Scott Newitt

Email: info@fireflyvodka.com
info@fireflymoonshine.com
Website: www.fireflyvodka.com, www.fireflymoonshine.com
Facebook: The Official Firefly Sweet Tea Vodka Page, Firefly Moonshine
Twitter: @FireflyVodka, @TheFireflyShine

Type: Micro Distillery. Opened in 2007.

Production hours:
Monday through Friday, 8:30 a.m. to 4:30 p.m. (closed to public)

Retail hours: Tuesday through Saturday, 11 a.m. to 5 p.m. Closed January

Tours: Video tour is available

Types of spirits produced:
Vodka, moonshine, rum, liqueur, ready-to-drink cocktails

Names of spirits:
- Firefly Sweet Tea Flavored Vodka
- Firefly Skinny Tea
- Firefly Handcrafted Vodka
- Firefly Peach and Raspberry Flavored Tea Vodkas
- Firefly Moonshines:
    - White Lightning
    - Strawberry
    - Cherry
    - Peach
    - Caramel
    - Apple Pie
    - Blackberry
- Sea Island Gold, Java and Spiced Rums
- Southern Accents Liqueurs

Best known for / most popular:
Firefly Sweet Tea Vodka

Average bottle price: Under $20.00

Distribution: Nationwide

Interesting facts:
Firefly was the first distillery to make a sweet tea flavored vodka.

High Wire Distilling

652 King Street
Charleston, SC 29403
843-755-4664

Owners / Operators:
Ann Marshall and Scott Blackwell, Owners

Email: info@highwiredistilling.com
Website: www.highwiredistilling.com
Facebook: High Wire Distilling Co.
Twitter: @HighWireCHS
Instragram: @highwirechs

Type: Craft Distillery. Opened in August 2013.

Tasting room hours:
Thursday through Saturday, 11 a.m. to 6 p.m.

Types of spirits produced:
Gin, rum, whiskey, vodka, bitters

Names of spirits:
- Hat Trick Botanical Gin
- High Wire Distilling Co. Belonger's Rum
- High Wire Distilling Co. Quarter Acre Sorghum Whiskey
- High Wire Distilling Co. Home Team Vodka

Best known for / most popular: Hat Trick Botanical Gin

Average bottle price: $27.99

Distribution: On-site retail, SC

Interesting facts:
Quarter Acre Sorghum Whiskey is made from sorghum grown on a Mennonite farm in East Tennessee. It takes a full quarter acre of sorghum to produce one batch.

Lucky Duck Distillery

17B Yemassee Highway
Yemassee, SC 29945
843-589-5440

Owners / Operators:
Fletcher Chase Flowers, Owner / Distiller

Email: luckyduckdistillery@gmail.com
Website: TBA
Facebook: Lucky Duck Distillery

Type: Micro Distillery. Opened in March 2014.

Hours of operation:
Tuesday through Saturday, 10 a.m. to 5 p.m.

Tours: Available

Types of spirits produced: Moonshine, bourbon

Names of spirits:
- Fletcher's Finest

Best known for / most popular:
Fletcher's Finest

Average bottle price: $24.50 to $35.00

Distribution: SC, On-site retail

Interesting facts:
Fletcher is one of the youngest distillers in the U.S. (age 22).

Palmetto Moonshine

200 W. Benson Street
Anderson, SC 29624
864-226-9917

Owners / Operators:
Trey Boggs, Owner / Operator
Bryan Boggs, Owner / Operator

Email: info@palmettomoonshine.com
Website: www.palmettomoonshine.com
Facebook: Palmetto Moonshine
Twitter: @palmettomoonshn
YouTube: PalmettoMoonshine

Type: Micro Distillery. Opened in January 2011.

Hours of operation:
Monday through Friday, 10 a.m. to 7 p.m.
Saturday, 9 a.m. to 7 p.m.

Tours: Available with free tasting

Types of spirits produced: Moonshine

Names of spirits:
- White Lightning, 105 proof
- Palmetto Apple Pie Moonshine, 45 proof
- Palmetto Blackberry Moonshine, 45 proof
- Palmetto Peach Moonshine, 45 proof

Best known for / most popular:
Raging Bull and Redneck Tea

Average bottle price: $24.95 to $34.90

Distribution: AR, CT, DC, DE, GA, IL, IN, KS, KY, LA, MA, MD, MI, MO, NH, NJ, NV, NY, RI, SC, TN, TX

Interesting facts:
Palmetto Moonshine is South Carolina's first legal moonshine distillery.

Six & Twenty Distillery

3109 Highway 153
Piedmont, SC 29673
864-263-8312

Owners / Operators:
David Raad, Head Distiller
Robert Redmond, Marketing and Sales

Email: info@sixandtwentydistillery.com
Website: www.sixandtwentydistillery.com
Facebook: Six & Twenty Distillery

Type: Micro Distillery. Opened in 2012.

Hours of operation:
Monday through Saturday, 9 a.m. to 6:30 p.m.

Tours: Available by appointment

Types of spirits produced: Whiskey

Names of spirits:
- Six & Twenty Whiskey "Blue"
- Carolina Virgin Wheat Whiskey

Best known for / most popular: Six & Twenty Whiskey "Blue"

Average bottle price: $49.95

Distribution: Not provided

Interesting facts:
- Blue was named after the old adage, "something old, something new, something borrowed, something blue."
- Take the five year old bourbon (something old) and the virgin wheat whiskey (something new), and re-barrel age those together (something borrowed--time in a barrel) to get perfect harmony (something "Blue").
- According to the label "At first sight, you see its youthfulness. Your nose alerts you to the sweetness of South Carolina's soft red winter wheat. The pride of the Carolinas comes out when you taste this hand-crafted spirit made from the pure Blue Ridge Mountain water. This is why we call it Virgin Wheat Whiskey."

Striped Pig Distillery

2225-A Old School Drive
Charleston, SC 29405
843-276-3201

Owners / Operators:
James Craig, Owner / Vice-President
Boris Van Dyck, Owner / Mixologist
Casey Lillie, Owner / President
John Pieper, Owner / Head Distiller
Todd Weiss, Owner / Distiller

General Email: info@stripedpigdistillery.com
Media Contact: Juliana Harless, Marketing Director
juliana@stripedpigdistillery.com
Website: www.stripedpigdistillery.com
Facebook: Striped Pig Distillery
Twitter: @DstillD
Pinterest: Striped Pig
Instagram: Striped Pig Distillery

Type: Micro Distillery. Opened in 2013.

Hours of operation: Tue. through Fri., 10 a.m. to 7 p.m.; Sat., noon to 5 p.m.

Tours and tastings: Wednesday through Friday, 3 p.m. to 7 p.m.; Saturday, noon to 5 p.m. (or during open hours of operation by signing up on their website)

Types of spirits produced: Vodka, rum, 'shine, whiskey

Names of spirits:

- Striped Vodka
- Striped Rum
- Striped 'Shine

Best known for: Hand-crafted spirits made in small batches from fresh, local ingredients; corn used for vodka and 'shine from Myer's Farm in Bowman, SC, and molasses used for rum from Savannah, GA.

Average bottle price: $19.00 to $29.00

Distribution: SC

Interesting facts: Charleston's first distillery since Prohibition.
What's in a name? The earliest temperance laws sought to eliminate the rum seller's trade by prohibiting the sale of liquor in quantities less than 15 gallons. Traditionally, during militia musters, tents would set up on the side streets selling food, games and drinks; the 15 gallon law was aimed at eliminating the drinking. A clever gentleman got a license not to sell liquor, but to exhibit a striped pig at these musters. The price of admission to his tent coincided with the usual price of a drink and, when guests entered his tent, they not only saw his pig painted with stripes but were also served glass of free rum.

Tiger Juice Distillery

1438 Cedar Creek Road
Hartsville, SC 29550
843-498-7202

Owners / Operators:
Michael Joseph Flynn

Email: tiger6@shtc.net
Website: www.tigerjuicedistillery.com
Facebook: Tiger Juice Distillery
Twitter: @TJ_Distillery

Type: Micro Distillery. Opened in 2011.

Hours of operation: Not provided

Tours: Not provided

Types of spirits produced: Whiskey

Names of spirits:
- New Age Spirit Whiskey

Best known for / most popular: New Age Spirit Whiskey

Average bottle price: Not provided

Distribution: SC

Interesting facts: Not provided

Michael Joseph Flynn

Sometimes the best ideas are in your own backyard. Whether your roots are Native American or Scotch/Irish like mine, some traditions are time-honored for great and delicious reasons. With a combination of family tradition, adventurous spirit and an innovative, patented technology, we're proud to share our New Age Spirit Whiskey. Virtually free of impurities, it's still full of nuanced flavor and an ultimately smooth taste you'll want to sip and savor.

To all of you, thanks – and enjoy our libations responsibly. And please, do your part to support the farmers who nurture the land and harvest our favorite grains. Be kind to your fellow man and animals that share this earth we've been chosen to explore. Welcome to the New Age of Spirits.

~Michael Joseph Flynn

Black Hills Dakota Distillery

2902 W. Main Street, Ste. 1
Rapid City, SD 57702
605-645-2571

Owners / Operators:
Paul Lewis, Co-manager
Michael Lewis, Co-manager

Email: plewis@BHDDistllery.com
mlewis@BHDDistllery.com
Website: www.bhddistillery.com
Facebook: Black Hills Dakota Distillery, LLC

Type: Micro Distillery. Opened in April 2010.

Hours of operation: As demand requires

Tours: Not available

Types of spirits produced: Potcheen

Names of spirits:
- Sturgis Shine

Best known for / most popular: Sturgis Shine

Average bottle price: $35.00 to $40.00

Distribution: SD

Interesting facts:
Sturgis Shine is based on a reincarnated ancient recipe for Irish pocheen. The recipe was brought from Ireland with the managing brothers' great-grandfather who came to America as a stowaway on a cattle boat. Potcheen was outlawed in Ireland in 1661 and today is produced for export only. Sturgis Shine is a 100-proof spirit made form barley, sugar, and clove honey. This spirit is triple distilled and charcoal filtered to give it a clean distinct flavor.

Dakota Spirits Distillery LLC

3601 Airport Road
Pierre, SD 57501
605-494-1009

Owners / Operators:
Jamison Rounds, Co-founder
Tom Rounds, Co-founder

Email: info@dakotaspirits.com
Website: www.dakotaspirits.com
Facebook: Dakota Spirits Distillery LLC

Type: Micro Distillery. Opened in 2010.

Hours of operation: Not provided

Tours: Not provided

Types of spirits produced: Vodka, whiskey, brandy

Names of spirits:
- Ringneck Vodka
- Blended Whiskey
- Coyote 100 Light Whiskey
- Bickering Brothers Brandy

Best known for / most popular: Not provided

Average bottle price: Not provided

Distribution: SD

Interesting facts: Dakota Spirits Distillery is South Dakota's first legal distillery.

Chattanooga Whiskey Company

Chattanooga, TN

Owners / Operators:
Joe Ledbetter, Co-founder
Tim Piersant, Co-founder

Email: info@chattanoogawhiskey.com
Website: www.chattanoogawhiskey.com
Facebook: Chattanooga Whiskey
Twitter: @ChattWhiskey
Pinterest: Chattanooga Whiskey

Type: Chattanooga Whiskey Company is currently in the planning and business development stage.

Hours of operation: Not provided

Tours: Not provided

Types of spirits produced: Whiskey

Names of spirits:
- 1816 Reserve
- 1816 Cask

Best known for / most popular: TBA

Average bottle price: TBA

Distribution: TBA

Interesting facts: TBA

Collier and McKeel

1200 Clinton Street
Nashville, TN 37212

Owners / Operators:
Mike Williams, Owner

Email: info@collierandmckeel.com
Website: www.collierandmckeel.com
Facebook: Collier and McKeel Handcrafted Tennessee Whiskey
Twitter: @TNsourmash

Type: Micro Distillery. Opened in 2011.

Hours of operation: Not provided

Tours: Not provided

Types of spirits produced: Vodka, whiskey

Names of spirits:
- Snow Creek Vodka
- Collier and McKeel White Dog
- Collier and McKeel Tennessee Whiskey
- Collier and McKeel Sour Mash Whiskey
- Collier and McKeel Fiery Gizzard Cinnamon Whiskey

Best known for / most popular: Not provided

Average bottle price: Not provided

Distribution: TN

Interesting facts: As a sign of the distillery's commitment to quality and attention to detail, the master distiller personally puts his thumbprint on every single bottle of Collier and McKeel Handcrafted Tennessee Whiskey that is produced.

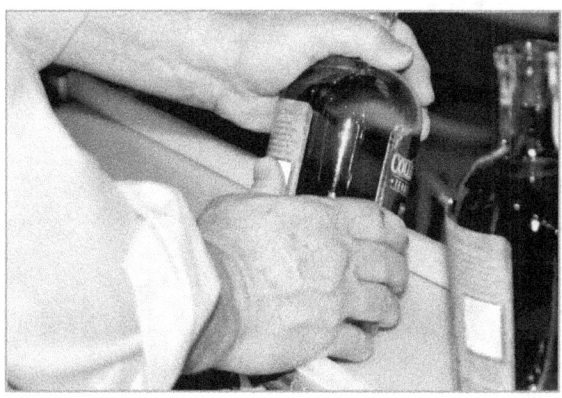

Corsair Artisan Distillery

1200 Clinton Street, #110
Nashville, TN 37203
615-200-0320

400 E. Main Street, #110
Bowling Green, KY 42101
270-904-2021

Owners / Operators:
Darek Bell and Andrew Webber, Owners

Email: info@corsairartisan.com
Website: www.corsairartisan.com
Facebook: Corsair Artisan Distillery
Twitter: @corsairartisan
YouTube: Corsair Artisan

Type: Micro Distillery. Opened TN in 2010. Open KY in 2008.

Hours of operation:

Nashville, TN
Mon. through Sat., 9 a.m. to 8 p.m.

Bowling Green, KY
Mon. through Sat., 8 a.m. to 6 p.m.

Tours: Available
Nashville, TN; Tuesday through Saturday from 3 p.m. to 8 p.m.
Bowling Green, KY; Friday and Saturday from 10 a.m. to 6 p.m.

Types of spirits produced: Gin, rum, absinthe, vodka, whiskeys

Names of spirits:
- Corsair Gin
- Corsair Spiced Rum
- Corsair Red Absinthe
- Corsair Vanilla Vodka
- Corsair Barrel Aged Gin
- Corsair Wry Moon Un-aged Rye Whiskey
- Corsair Triple Smoke Single Malt Whiskey
- Corsair Pumpkin Spice Moonshine
- Corsair Quinoa Whiskey
- Corsair Ryemageddon Whiskey
- Corsair Genever
- Corsair Rasputin Hopped Whiskey

Best known for / most popular: Corsair Triple Smoke Whiskey

Average bottle price: $25.00 to $55.00

Distribution: AK, CA, CO, CT, DC, DE, FL, GA, IL, KY, MD, MI, MO, NC, NJ, NV, NY, OR, TN, TX, WA, WV

Awards and Recognitions:
- 2013 Craft Whiskey of the Year, Whisky Advocate
- 2013 Craft Distillery of the Year, Whisky Magazine
- 2013 Innovator of the Year, Whisky Magazine

East Tennessee Distillery

220 Piney Flats Road
Piney Flats, TN 37686

Owners / Operators:
Neil "Tiny" Roberson, President / Master Distiller
Byron Reece, VP Sales & Marketing
Gary Melvin, VP Finance
Darrell Hunt, Chairman of the Board

Email: byronreece@gmail.com
Website: www.mellomoon.com
Facebook: East Tennessee Distillery

Type: Micro Distillery. Opened in 2011.

Hours of operation: 8 a.m. to 6 p.m.

Tours: Monday through Saturday, 10 a.m. to 6 p.m.; Sunday, 2 p.m. to 5 p.m.

Types of spirits produced: Moonshine

Names of spirits:
- Roberson's Tennessee Mellomoon

Best known for / most popular: Roberson's Tennessee Mellomoon 150 Proof, 100 Proof Straight, 70 proof Caramel, Peach, Strawberry, Coconut, Apple Pie, Grape, Banana, Honey Ginseng, Cinnamon Roll

Average bottle price: $25.00

Distribution: CO, FL, KY, NC, NJ, NY, SC, TN, VA, WV

Interesting facts:
- ETD was the ninth federally licensed distillery in TN since Prohibition.
- ETD was the first legal distillery in Sullivan County, TN.
- Roberson's Tennessee Mellomoon Caramel Shine, Awarded Platinum "Best of Show" at the 2014 World Beverage Competition in Geneva Switzerland.

Nelson's Green Brier Distillery

1414 Clinton Street
Nashville, TN 37203
615-207-7467

Owners / Operators:
Charlie Nelson
Andy Nelson

Email: Charlie, charlie@greenbrierdistillery.com
Andy, andy@greenbrierdistillery.com
Website: www.greenbrierdistillery.com
Facebook: Nelson's Green Brier Distillery
Twitter: @TNWhiskeyCo, @BelleMeadeBRBN
Instagram: @TNWhiskeyCo

Type: Micro Distillery. Opened in 2009.

Hours of operation: Not provided

Tours: TBD

Types of spirits produced: Whiskey

Names of spirits:
- Belle Meade™ Bourbon

Best known for / most popular:
Belle Meade Manhattan, Fortified Belle, Belle Meade Mint Julep

Average bottle price: $35.00 to $40.00

Distribution: AL, AR, CA, DC, FL, GA, IL, KY, MD, NV, SC, TN, TX, VA

Interesting facts: Nelson's Green Brier Distillery was one of the largest distilleries in the country before Prohibition; it was known as "Old No. 5." The founder, Charles Nelson, produced the original Tennessee whiskey and was one of the first to bottle and sell whiskey rather than selling it by the barrel or jug.

Ole Smoky Distillery LLC

903 Parkway
Gatlinburg, TN 37738
865-436-6995

Owners / Operators:
Justin King, Master Distiller

Email: General info: shine@osdistillery
         Justin King: justin@osdistillery.com
Website: www.olesmokymoonshine.com
Facebook: Ole Smoky Moonshine Distillery
Twitter: @OleSmoky
Instagram: @olesmokymoonshine

Type: Micro Distillery. Opened in 2010.

Hours of operation: Daily, 10 a.m. to 10 p.m.
No alcohol sold on Sunday. Tastings, noon to 7 p.m.

Tours: Self-guided tours are available. Guests can read the storyboards, see the working still, and speak with the distillers.

Types of spirits produced: Moonshine

Names of spirits:
- Ole Smoky® Original Moonshine (Corn Whiskey)
- Ole Smoky® White Lightnin'™ (Neutral Spirits)
- Ole Smoky® Moonshine Cherries™
- Ole Smoky® Apple Pie Moonshine™
- Ole Smoky® Blackberry Moonshine™
- Ole Smoky® Strawberry Moonshine™
- Old Smoky® Lemon Drop Moonshine™
- Ole Smoky® Grape Moonshine™ (seasonal)
- Ole Smoky® Hunch Punch Moonshine™ (seasonal)
- Ole Smoky® Peach Moonshine™ (seasonal)

Best known for / most popular: Moonshine

Average bottle price: $24.95 to $34.95

Distribution: 49 U.S. states; Canada

Interesting facts:
- Tennessee's first legal moonshine distillery.
- The original un-aged corn whiskey is made from a 100-year-old family recipe.

Popcorn Sutton's Distillery

Nashville, TN 37209

Owners / Operators:
Jamey Grosser, Master Distiller

Email: info@popcornsuttonswhiskey.com
Website: www.popcornsuttonswhiskey.com
Facebook: Popcorn Sutton's Tennessee White Whiskey

Type: Micro Distillery. Opened in 2011.

Hours of operation: Not provided

Tours: Not provided

Types of spirits produced: Whiskey

Names of spirits:
- Popcorn Sutton's Tennessee White Whiskey

Best known for / most popular: Popcorn Sutton's Tennessee White Whiskey

Average bottle price: Not provided

Distribution: AR, GA, KY, MO, SC, TN

Interesting facts: Not provided

Prichard's Distillery Inc.

11 Kelso Smithland Road
Kelso, TN 37348
931-433-5454

Owners / Operators:
Phil Prichard, President / Master Distiller

Email: phil@pdspirits.com
Website: www.pdspirits.com
Facebook: Prichard's Distillery
Twitter: @prichardspirits
Pinterest: Pricard's Distillery

Type: Micro Distillery. Opened in 1999.

Hours of operation: 8 a.m. to 4 p.m.

Tours: Available

Types of spirits produced: Rum, whiskey, liqueurs

Names of spirits:
Rums
- Prichard's Fine Rum
- Prichard's Cranberry Rum
- Prichard's Crystal Rum
- Prichard's Key Lime Rum
- Prichard's Private Stock Rum
- Prichard's Sweet Georgia Bell

Whiskey
- Benjamin Prichard's Double Barreled Bourbon
- Benjamin Prichard's Double Chocolate Bourbon Whiskey
- Benjamin Prichard's Lincoln County Lightning
- Benjamin Prichard's Rye Whiskey
- Benjamin Prichard's Single Malt Whiskey
- Benjamin Prichard's Tennessee Whiskey

Liqueurs
- Benjamin Prichard's Cranberry Liqueur
- Benjamin Prichard's Sweet Lucy Bourbon Liqueur
- Benjamin Prichard's Sweet Lucy Bourbon Cream Liqueur

Best known for / most popular: Sweet Lucy

Average bottle price: $19.95 to $72.00

Distribution: 44 U.S. states; 8 European countries

Interesting facts: The first legal distillery in Tennessee in almost fifty years.

Short Mountain Distillery
Golden Rule Distilling Company

119 Mountain Spirits Lane
Woodbury, TN 37190
615-216-0830

Owners / Operators:
Billy Kaufman, CEO
David Kaufman, CFO
Ben Kaufman, Marketing / Promotions Director
Josh Smotherman, Master Distiller
Ryan Smotherman, Second Distiller

Email: david@shortmountaindistillery.com
Website: www.shortmountaindistillery.com
Facebook: Short Mountain Distillery

Type: Craft Distillery. Opened in March 2012.

Hours of operation:
Thursday through Saturday, 9 a.m. to 4 p.m.

Tours: Available

Types of spirits produced: Moonshine

Names of spirits:
- Short Mountain Shine
- Short Mountain Apple Pie Shine

Best known for / most popular: Moonshine

Average bottle price: $28.00 to $38.00

Distribution: GA, IL, TN

Interesting facts:
The distillery is owned and operated by the Kaufman brothers. In 1910 their great grandfather, Jesse Shwayder, founded the iconic American brand Samsonite. Shwayder never missed an opportunity to attribute his company's success to the Golden Rule: "Do unto others as you would have them do unto you." He believed in this deep value so much that he started a tradition of handing out marbles engraved with the Golden Rule. The Kaufman brothers carry on this tradition to honor their great grandfather with a collectable coin inscribed with this philosophy on every bottle.

Awards and Recognitions:
- Gold Medal, 2012 Beverage Testing Institute
- Apple Pie Shine, 90/100, 2013 Wine Enthusiast

SPEAKeasy Spirits

900 44th Avenue North, Ste. 100
Nashville, TN 37209
615-347-9543

Owners / Operators:
Jeff Pennington, Co-owner
Jenny Pennington, Co-owner

Email: jenny@speakeasymarketing.com
Website: www.tennesseesippingcream.com
Facebook: Speakeasy Spirits
Twitter: @TNSippingCream

Type: Micro Distillery. Opened in 2012.

Hours of operation: Not provided

Tours: Available

Types of spirits produced:
Whiskey, Liqueur/Cordial

Names of spirits:
- Whisper Creek Tennessee Sipping Cream
- Pennington's Strawberry Rye Whiskey

Best known for / most popular:
Whisper Creek Tennessee Sipping Cream

Average bottle price: $19.99

Distribution: AR, CA, CO, CT, DE, FL, GA, IA, IL, IN, KS, KY, MA, MD, MI, MO, NC, NE, NH, NY, OH, OK, OR, RI, SC, TN, WI, WY; Canada, Mexico

Interesting facts: Not provided

Awards and Recognitions:
Silver Medal, 2013 Craft Spirits Awards

Services offered other than production:
Contract distilling, rectifying and bottling services

Tenn South Distillery

1800 Abernathy Road
Lynnville, TN 38401
931-527-0027

Owners / Operators:
Blair Butler, Proprietor
Clayton Cutler, Chief Distiller

Email: info@tennsouthdistillery.com
Website: www.tennsouthdistillery.com
Facebook: Tenn South
Twitter: @TennSouth

Type: Craft Distillery. Opened in January 2013.

Tasting room hours:
Tuesday through Friday, noon to 5 p.m.
Saturday, 10 a.m. to 3 p.m.

Tours:
Available Friday, noon to 5 p.m.
Saturday 10 a.m. to 3 p.m.

Types of spirits produced:
Tennessee whiskey, Tennessee moonshine, flavored moonshines gin, vodka

Names of spirits:
- Abernathy Gin
- Black Mule Vodka
- Clayton James Tennessee Whiskey (mid 2014)
- All Purpose Shine -100 proof TN moonshine
- Blackberry Shine*
- Apple Pie Shine*
- Peach Pie Shine*
  *50 proof flavored All Purpose Shine using real juice

Best known for / most popular: All Purpose Shine

Average bottle price: $20.00 to $30.00

Distribution: On-site retail, TN

Interesting facts: Not provided

Azar Distillery

8501 Cover Road
San Antonio, TX 78263
210-648-1500

Owners / Operators:
Richard N. Azar III (Trey), Founder / Master Distiller
Kimberly R. Azar, Founder

Email: trey@cincovodka.com
Website: www.cincovodka.com
Facebook: Cinco Vodka
Twitter: @CincoVodka
YouTube: Azar Distilling
Flickr: Cinco Vodka

Type: Micro Distillery. Opened in 2011.

Hours of operation:
Monday through Friday, 9 a.m. to 5 p.m.

Tours: Available by appointment

Types of spirits produced: Vodka

Names of spirits:
- Cinco ~ The Five Star Vodka

Best known for / most popular:
Cinco Martini (Cincotini)

Average bottle price: $19.99 to $36.99

Distribution: CA, GA, TX

Interesting facts:
- Handcrafted from 100% American wheat
- Copper pot distilled in small batches
- Unfiltered for superior balance and flavor
- No sugar or artificial flavorings added
- Made in San Antonio, TX

Awards and Recognitions:
Triple Gold, 2013 Los Angeles International Spirits Competition

Balcones Distillery

212 S. 17th Street
Waco, TX 76701
254-755-6003

Owners / Operators:
Chip Tate, President / Head Distiller

Email: info@balconesdistilling.com
Website: www.balconesdistilling.com
Facebook: Balcones Distillery
Twitter: @BalconesWhisky

Type: Micro Distillery. Opened in 2008.

Hours of operation:
Monday through Friday, 9 a.m. to 5 p.m.

Tours: Available by appointment only

Types of spirits produced:
Whisky, rumble (sugar, honey and fig spirit), rum

Names of spirits:
- Rumble
- Rumble Cask Reserve
- Baby Blue Whisky
- True Blue Whisky
- Brimstone Whisky
- '1' Texas Single Malt Whisky

Best known for / most popular:
Baby Blue Corn Whisky and '1' Texas Single Malt Whisky

Average bottle price: $35.00 to $65.00

Distribution: CA, CT, DC, DE, FL, IL, KY, LA, MD, MN, NJ, NM, NY, TX

Interesting facts
Balcones Distilling is the producer of the first legal Texas whiskey since Prohibition, the only 100% Blue Corn whisky, and Texas' first single malt.

Banner Distilling Co.

13201 Jacobson Road, #11
Manor, TX 78653
512-815-2326

Owners / Operators:
Logan Simpson, Co-founder / Head Distiller
Anthony Jimenez: Co-founder / Distiller

Email: info@bannerdistilling.com
Website: www.bannerdistilling.com
Facebook: Banner Distilling Co.
Twitter: @BannerDistiller
Pinterest: Banner Distilling Co.

Type: Micro Distillery. Opened in November 2013.

Hours of operation: Saturday and Sunday, 9 a.m. to 5 p.m.

Tours: Available by appointment on Saturday between 10 a.m. and 5 p.m.

Types of spirits produced: Vodka, whiskey

Names of spirits:
- Banner Natural Vodka
- Banner Texas Wheat Whiskey

Best known for / most popular: Vodka and whiskey

Average bottle price: $20.00 to $40.00

Distribution: TX

Big Thicket Distilling Company

512 Bryant Road, Ste. 1
Conroe, TX 77303
936-666-1341

Owners / Operators:
Daniel Bass, President / Head Distiller
Joseph Breda, Chief Financial Officer
Gretchen Bass, Vice President of Marketing and Public Relations
Melissa Breda, Vice President

Email: info@bigthicketdistilling.com
Website: www.bigthicketdistilling.com
Facebook: Big Thicket Distilling Company
Twitter: @BigThicketTX
Pinterest: Big Thicket Distilling Company
Yelp: Big Thicket Distilling Company
YouTube: Big Thicket Distilling

Type: Craft Distillery. Opened in January 2014.

Hours of operation:
Monday through Friday, 8 a.m. to 5 p.m.
Saturday, 10 a.m. to 6 p.m.

Tours:
Available on Saturday at 10 a.m., 2 p.m., and 4 p.m.
Group tours may be scheduled anytime with reservation

Types of spirits produced:
Vodka, rum, whiskey, gin, specialty spirits

Names of spirits:
- Dog Trot Vodka
- Dry Dock Rum

Best known for / most popular:
Dog Trot Vodka

Average bottle price: $20.00 to $50.00

Distribution: On-site retail, TX

Interesting facts:
The virgin forests of Texas's Big Thicket region were logged in the early late 1800s and in the 1900s. Beautiful white oaks were among the trees logged; these white oaks were fit to use for staves in the manufacture of wine and whiskey barrels.

Bone Spirits

802 Northeast 1st Street
Smithville, TX 78957
512-237-5000

Owners / Operators:
Jeff Peace, Founder

Email: info@bonespirits.com
Website: www.bonespirits.com
Facebook: Bone Spirits LLC
Twitter: @BoneSpiritsLLC
LinkedIn: Jeff Peace

Type: Micro Distillery. Opened in 2010.

Hours of operation: Not provided

Tours: Not provided

Types of spirits produced:
Vodka, moonshine, whiskey, gin

Names of spirits:
- Smiths Premium Vodka
- Fitch's Goat Moonshine
- Fitch's Goat 100% Corn Whiskey
- Moody June American Dry Gin

Best known for / most popular: Not provided

Average bottle price: Not provided

Distribution: FL, GA, LA, OK, TN, TX

Interesting facts: Not provided

D.E.W. Distillation LLC

1400 Jacob's Well Road
Wimberley, TX 78676
512-847-6874

Owners / Operators:
David Watson, Owner / President
Laura Watson, Vice President
Walter Smith, General Manager

Email: David Watson, david@cypresscreekreserve.com
Laura Watson, laura@cypresscreekreserve.com
Walter Smith, walterlsmithjr@yahoo.com
Website: www.cypresscreekreserve.com
Facebook: Cypress Creek Reserve Rum

Type: Micro Distillery. Opened in 2010.

Hours of operation: Tuesday through Saturday, 11:30 a.m. to 6 p.m.

Tours: Available by appointment

Types of spirits produced: Rum

Names of spirits:
- Cypress Creek Reserve Crystal Rum
- Cypress Creek Reserve Vanilla Flavored Rum

Best known for / most popular: Cypress Creek Reserve Vanilla Citrus Martini

Average bottle price: $17.00 to $25.00

Distribution: TX

Interesting facts: Owner David Watson designed and built the distillery.

Firestone & Robertson Distilling Co.

901 W. Vickery
Fort Worth, TX 76104
817-840-9140

Owners / Operators:
Leonard Firestone, Co-founder / Distiller
Troy Robertson, Co-founder / Distiller

Email: info@frdistilling.com
Website: www.frdistilling.com
Facebook: Firestone & Robertson Distilling Co.
Twitter: @FRDistilling

Type: Micro Distillery. Opened in 2012.

Hours of operation: Not provided

Tours: Available

Types of spirits produced: Bourbon, whiskey

Names of spirits:
- TX Blended Whiskey
- Straight Bourbon

Best known for / most popular: TX Blended Whiskey

Average bottle price: Not provided

Distribution: TX

Interesting facts: Not provided

Garrison Brothers Distillery

1827 Hye Albert Road
Hye, TX 78635
830-392-0246

Owners / Operators:
Dan Garrison, Proprietor

Email: dan@garrisonbros.com
Website: www.garrisonbros.com
Facebook: Garrison Brothers Distillery
Twitter: @garrisonbros

Type: Craft Distillery. Opened in 2005.

Hours of operation: Daily, 10 a.m. to 6 p.m.

Tours: Available Wednesday through Sunday, 10 a.m., noon, 2 p.m., 4 p.m.

Types of spirits produced: Straight Bourbon Whiskey

Names of spirits:
- Garrison Brothers Texas Straight Bourbon Whiskey

Best known for / most popular:
Garrison Brothers Texas Straight Bourbon Whiskey

Average bottle price: Not provided

Distribution: TX

Hideous LC

5276 Barth Road
Lockhart, TX 78644
512-443-3687

Owners / Operators:
Michael E. Klein, Owner

Email: hideousinfo@hideous.com
Website: www.hideous.com
Facebook: Hideous Liqueur
Twitter: @hideousliqueur

Type: Micro Distillery. Opened in 2012.

Hours of operation: Not open to the public

Tours: Not available

Types of spirits produced: Liqueur

Names of spirits:
- Hideous Liqueur

Best known for / most popular: Hideous Liqueur

Average bottle price: $27.00

Distribution: TX

Interesting facts:
- Hideous Liqueur is an all-natural 70 proof berry citrus liqueur that was created at a fraternity house in 1999 while Michael Klein was an undergraduate at The University of Texas at Austin.
- Hideous is one of the top selling on-premise spirits in Texas.
- The H-Bomb (Hideous and energy drink) is the most popular drink with the brand, however Hideous is great in margaritas, martinis, or as a mixer with almost any other spirit or flavor.

JEM Beverage Company

2525 Tarpley Road #104
Carrollton, TX 75006

Owners / Operators:
Evan Batt, Co-owner
John Straits, Co-owner
Mike Pfeiffer, Co-owner

Email: info@jembevco.com
Website: www.westernsonvodka.com, www.redriverwhiskey.com
www.stingrayspicedrum.com, www.southernsonvodka.com
Facebook: Western Son Vodka, Southern Son Vodka
Red River Whiskey, Stingray Spiced Rum
Twitter: @westernsonvodka, @StingrayRum, @SouthrnSonVodka

Type: Micro Distillery. Opened in 2011.

Hours of operation: Vary

Tours: Available by appointment

Types of spirits produced: Rum, whiskey, vodka

Names of spirits:
- Stingray Spiced Rum
- Southern Son Vodka
- Western Son Texas Vodka
- Red River Texas Bourbon Whiskey
- Red River Texas Young Rye Whiskey
- South House Southern Moonshine*
(* also available in Apple Pie, Cherry Lemonade, and Peach)

Best known for / most popular: Western Son Texas Vodka

Average bottle price: $17.99 to $27.99

Distribution:
AK, GA, LA, MA, MS, NV, OK, RI, TN, TX

Interesting facts: JEM donates to two charities for its brands, — the Peter Burks Unsung Hero Fund for both vodkas and the Native Texas Wildlife Conservation for the whiskey.

Quentin D. Witherspoon Distillery LLC

Lewisville, TX

Owners / Operators:
Quentin D. Witherspoon, Master Distiller / President
M. Ryan Dehart, CFO
Natasha Dehart, VP-Sales
Laurent Spamer, CMO

Email: info@witherspoondistillery.com
Website: www.witherspoondistillery.com
Facebook: Quentin D. Witherspoon Distillery
Twitter: @River_Rum
Pinterest: Quentin Witherspoon

Type: Micro Distillery. Opened in 2011.

Hours of operation:
Tuesday through Saturday, 9 a.m. to 5 p.m.

Tours:
Available Saturday at 11 a.m., 1 p.m., 3 p.m., 5 p.m.

Types of spirits produced:
Rum, bourbon, malt whiskey

Names of spirits:
- Witherspoon's River Rum
- Witherspoon's Texas Straight Bourbon Whiskey
- Cross Timbers Texas Malt Whiskey

Best known for / most popular: All

Average bottle price: $20.00 to $55.00

Distribution: TX

Interesting facts:
Quentin Witherspoon began distilling spirits in Africa over 20 years ago, using water purification equipment to convert spoiled beer and wine into liquor. For 15 years Quentin took his hobby and passion throughout the Southeastern US and the Caribbean Islands, mastering the craft of whiskey and rum making. In 2012 Quentin trademarked the Cross Timbers Texas Malt Whiskey process, which is only the second region in the US to claim exclusive rights to a whiskey process and is a mark of Texas pride in the industry. The waiting list for Cross Timbers grows daily.

Railean Distillers
Eagle Point Distillery

341 5th Street
San Leon, TX 77539
713-545-2742

Owners / Operators:
Kelly Railean, Owner / Master Distiller
Erik Bauer, EVP Sales

Email: Kelly Railean: krailean@railean.com
         Erik Bauer: ebauer@railean.com
Website: www.railean.com
Facebook: Railean Handmade Texas Rum
Twitter: @RaileanRum
Flickr: Railean Rum

Type: Micro Distillery. Opened in 2007.

Hours of operation: Open to the public for tours, bottle sales and gift shop most Fridays and Saturdays. Call or check the website for tour times and hours.

Tours: Available by appointment for individual and group during most week days, Monday through Thursday. You must be 21 years or older with valid ID to enter the Railean Distillery.

Types of spirits produced: Vodka, rum (white and aged), 100% blue agave spirit

Names of spirits:
- Railean Vodka
- Railean Texas White Rum
- Railean Reserve XO Dark Rum
- Railean Small Cask Single Barrel Dark Rum
- Railean "El Perico" 100% Blue Agave Spirit
- Railean Spiced Rum
- Railean "El Perico" Blue Agave Reposado

Best known for / most popular:
Reserve XO Dark Rum

Average bottle price: $16.99 to $29.99

Distribution: AK, AZ, CA, TX

Interesting facts:
- First and only distillery in the Houston / Galveston area
- First and only known certified American made rum in the USA
- Blue Agave Spirit is certified "Made in America"

Ranger Creek Brewing & Distilling

4834 Whirlwind Drive
San Antonio, TX 78217
210-775-2099

Owners / Operators:
Mark McDavid, Co-founder, Sales / Marketing
TJ Miller, Co-founder / Operations / Head Distiller
Dennis Rylander, Co-founder / Finance / Accounting

Email: General Info, info@drinkrangercreek.com
           Mark McDavid, mark@drinkrangercreek.com
Website: www.drinkrangercreek.com
Facebook: Ranger Creek Brewing & Distilling
Twitter: @rangercreek
YouTube: DrinkRangerCreek

Type: Brewery / Micro Distillery. Opened in 2010.

Hours of operation: Open for tours only

Tours: Saturdays, 2 p.m. to 4 p.m.
         Check the website for availability and to RSVP

Types of spirits produced: Whiskey

Names of spirits:
- Ranger Creek .36 Texas Bourbon Whiskey
- Ranger Creek Rimfire Mesquite Smoked Texas Single Malt Whiskey
- Ranger Creek. 44 Texas Rye Whiskey
- Ranger Creek La Bestia Defavorable Belgian White Whiskey

Best known for / most popular:
Ranger Creek .36 Texas Bourbon Whiskey

Average bottle price: $35.00

Distribution: TX

Interesting facts: Ranger Creek is a combined brewery/distillery located in San Antonio, TX. They make beer and whiskey in their "brewstillery" and make it by hand one batch at a time. They primarily focus on the relationship between beer and whiskey. As a combined operation, they can do things to highlight this relationship that no one else can. For example, they age their own beer in bourbon barrels and distill their beers into whiskeys. They also use much of the same equipment to make both beer and whiskey because there are a lot of similarities between the two processes.

Awards and Recognitions:
- Double Gold Medal, The Fifty Best, 2014
- Beverage Testing Institute, 90 points (Exceptional)
- Bronze Medal, American Distilling Institute 2012

Rebecca Creek Distillery LLC

26605 Bulverde Road, Ste. B
San Antonio, TX 78260
830-714-4581

Owners / Operators:
Mike Cameron, Co-founder / Owner
Steve Ison, Co-founder / Owner

Email: info@rebeccacreekdistillery.com
Website: www.rebeccacreekdistillery.com, www.texasvodka.com
www.rebeccacreekwhiskey.com
Facebook: Enchanted Rock Vodka,
Rebecca Creek Fine Texas Spirit Whiskey
Twitter: @TXvodka

Type: Micro Distillery. Opened in 2010.

Hours of operation: Monday through Friday, 8 a.m. to 5 p.m.

Tours: Available Saturdays, noon to 5 p.m.

Types of spirits produced: Vodka, whiskey

Names of spirits:
- Enchanted Rock Vodka
- Rebecca Creek Fine Texas Whiskey

Best known for / most popular:
Enchanted Rock Ultra-Premium Texas Vodka

Average bottle price: $18.00 to $35.00

Distribution: TX

Interesting facts:
Rebecca Creek Distillery was the first legal distillery in south Texas since Prohibition.

San Luis Spirits

Dripping Springs, TX 78620
512-858-1199

Owners / Operators:
Kevin Kelleher, Owner

Email: info@sanluisspirits.com
Website: www.drippingspringsvodka.com
Facebook: Dripping Springs Vodka
Twitter: @DSVodka

Type: Micro Distillery. Opened in 2007.

Hours of operation: Not provided

Tours: Not provided

Types of spirits produced: Vodka

Names of spirits:
- Dripping Springs Vodka
- Dripping Springs Orange
- Well No 1876

Best known for / most popular:
Dripping Springs Vodka

Average bottle price: $18.99

Distribution: AZ, CO, LA, MN, NE, ND, NM, NV, OK, SD, TX, WI

Interesting facts:
Award winning Dripping Springs Vodka is made in the Texas Hill Country in small 50 gallon copper pot stills with mineral rich artesian spring water.

Awards and Recognitions:
Gold Medal, Best in Class and the prestigious Vodka Purity Trophy at the International Wine and Spirits Competition. Judges call it "a great sipping vodka."

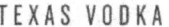

SAVVY Distillers LP

13805 Quitman Pass
Austin, TX 78728
512-476-4477

Owners / Operators:
Chad Auler, Founder / President
Clayton Christopher, CEO
John Potts, VP of Sales
Brandon Cason, VP of Marketing
John Scarborough, CFO
Gary Crowell, Special Operations
Kevin Coles, Production Manager

Email: info@savvyvodka.com
Website: www.savvyvodka.com
Facebook: SAVVY Vodka
Twitter: @SavvyMartini

Type: Micro Distillery. Opened in 2007.

Hours of operation: Monday through Friday, 8 a.m. to 5 p.m.

Tours: Not available

Types of spirits produced: Vodka

Names of spirits:
- SAVVY Vodka

Best known for / most popular: SAVVY Vodka

Average bottle price: $20.00 to $25.00

Distribution: TX

Interesting facts: Not provided

South Congress Distillery

16525 Decker Creek Drive
Manor, TX 78563
512-589-3939

Owners / Operators:
Mike Jakle, Owner
Miles Ponder, Owner

Email: mike@whitehatrum.com
Website: www.whitehatrum.com
Facebook: White Hat Rum
Twitter: @WhiteHatRum

Type: Micro Distillery. Opened in 2009.

Hours of operation: Monday through Friday, 8 a.m. to 5 p.m.

Tours: Available by request

Types of spirits produced: Rum

Names of spirits:
- White Hat Rum

Best known for / most popular:
White Hat Rum

Average bottle price: $19.99

Distribution: TX

Awards and Recognitions:
- Gold Medal, The Fifty Best White Rum Tasting 2013 NYC
- Silver Medal, Ministry of Rum Tasting Competition 2012 Chicago

Spink Distillery

12732 Cimarron Path, Ste. 102
San Antonio, TX 78249
210-896-5070

Owners / Operators:
Nick Spink, Owner / Founder / Master Distiller

Email: info@spikevodka.com
Website: www.spikevodka.com
Facebook: Spike Vodka

Type: Artisan Micro Distillery. Opened 2012.

Hours of operation:
Monday through Friday, 9 a.m. to 5 p.m.

Tours: Not available

Types of spirits produced: Vodka

Names of spirits:
- Spike Vodka

Best known for / most popular:
Spiked Lemon and Spikerita

Average bottle price: $22.00

Distribution: TX

Interesting facts:
- Spike Vodka is the first and only known vodka in the world made from prickly pear cactus. Spike Vodka is true artisan vodka – everything from harvest to bottle is done by hand and by the distillers in San Antonio.
- "Spike has a character that is smooth and original. Spike is not your normal vodka. Some say Spike has an organic character with hints of pepper and spices while others say it is almost agave-like, but all agree it is original and unique and shows that vodka can have character. After you taste Spike you will know why Spike will become the next signature of Texas." – Nick Spink

Spirit of Texas LLC

1715 Dalshank Street, Ste. A
Pflugerville, TX   78660
512-789-1600

Owners / Operators:
Shaun Siems, Co-founder
Jason Malik, Co-founder
Michael Rajski, Partner

Email: General info, info@spiritoftx.com
Shaun Siems, shaun.siems@spiritoftx.com
Jason Malik, jason.malik@spiritoftx.com
Michael Rajski, michael.rajski@spiritoftx.com
Website: www.spiritoftx.com , www.pecanstreetrum.com
Facebook: Spirit of Texas Distillery, Pecan Street Rum
Twitter: @spiritoftx1

Type: Micro Distillery. Opened in 2010.

Hours of operation:
Monday through Friday, 8 a.m. to 5 p.m.

Tours: Not available

Types of spirits produced: Rum

Names of spirits:
- Pecan Street Rum
- Spirit of Texas Rum

Best known for / most popular: Pecan Street Rum

Average bottle price: $20.00

Distribution: TX

Interesting facts:
Pecan Street Rum is the first known rum to be aged in American oak barrels with Texas pecans.

Texacello LLC

5214 Burleson Road
Austin, TX 78744
512-636-6389

Owners / Operators:
Paula Angerstein, Founder / Owner
Dee Kelleher, Managing Partner

Email: info@paulastexasspirits.com
Website: www.paulastexasspirits.com
Facebook: Paula's Texas Spirits
Twitter: @PaulasTXSpirits

Type: Small batch macerate. Opened in 2004.

Hours of operation: Vary

Tours: Not available

Types of spirits produced: Liqueur

Names of spirits:
- Paula's Texas Orange
- Paula's Texas Lemon

Best known for / most popular:
Margarita, Lemon Drop

Average bottle price: $22.00

Distribution: TX

Interesting facts:
- Paula is the organizer and charter board member of Texas Distilled Spirits Association.
- Paula's Texas Lemon is one of only a handful of limoncellos made in the USA.
- Paula's Texas Orange is one of only a few orange liqueurs made in the USA.

The Original Texas Legend Distillery

1501 Simmons
Orange, TX 77630

Owners / Operators:
Thomas Germann, CEO

Email: tger68@yahoo.com
Website: www.theoriginaltexaslegenddistillery.com
Facebook: Friends of The Original Texas Legend Distillery

Type: Micro Distillery. Opened in 2012.

Hours of operation: Vary

Tours: Not available

Types of spirits produced: Vodka, bourbon, blended whiskey

Names of spirits:
- Troubadour Vodka
- Troubadour Texas Bourbon
- Troubadour Blended Whiskey
- Troubadour Barrel Strength Bourbon, 116 proof
- TLD Vodka, Neutral Spirit Corn Vodka, 80 proof

Best known for / most popular: Troubador Vodka

Average bottle price: $18.00

Distribution: United Wine & Spirits, Houston TX

Interesting facts:
- True handcrafted batch blended vodka.
- Each and every bottle of Troubadour Vodka is hand signed by the distiller that made that vodka.

Tito's Handmade Vodka
Fifth Generation, Inc.
Mockingbird Distillery

1406 Smith Road
Austin, TX 78721
512-389-9011

Owners / Operators:
Tito Beveridge, Owner

Email: info@titosvodka.com
Website: www.titosvodka.com
Facebook: Titos Handmade Vodka
Twitter: @TitosVodka
Flicker: Titos Vodka
Pinterest: TitosVodka

Type: Micro Distillery. Opened in 1995.

Hours of operation:
Monday through Friday, 8 a.m. to 5 p.m.

Tours: Not available

Types of spirits produced: Vodka

Names of spirits:
- Tito's Handmade Vodka

Best known for / most popular: Tito's Handmade Vodka

Average bottle price: $20.00

Distribution: Throughout the U.S. and Canada

Interesting facts:
- Tito's Handmade Vodka is Texas' first and oldest legal distillery.
- Tito's Handmade Vodka is gluten free.

Treaty Oak Distilling Co.

13011 DeBarr Drive
Austin, TX 78729
512-699-5041

Owners / Operators:
Daniel R. Barnes, Owner

Email: info@treatyoakrum.com
Website: www.treatyoakdistilling.com
Facebook: Treaty Oak Distilling Co.
Twitter: @TreatyOakTX

Type: Micro Distillery. Opened in 2005.

Hours of operation: Please check website

Tours: Please check website

Types of spirits produced:
Rum, gin, vodka

Names of spirits:
- Treaty Oak Platinum Rum
- Treaty Oak Aged Rum
- Waterloo Gin
- Starlite Vodka
- Graham's Texas Tea
- Waterloo Antique Aged Gin
- Red Handed Bourbon

Average bottle price: $18.00 to $28.00

Distribution: Not provided

Interesting facts:
Treaty Oak Distillery is named after a 500-year-old oak tree in Austin, Texas, that symbolizes the strength and vitality of our products.

Awards and Recognitions:
Treaty Oak Rum
- Gold Medal, 2013 50 Best White Rum Tasting
- Silver 'Best Value', 2012 BTI International Review of Spirits
- Gold Medal in Taste, 2011 Microliquor Spirit Award

Treaty Oak Reserve Rum
- Gold Medal, 2013 Great American Distillery Festival

Starlite Vodka
- Gold Medal, 2013 Spirits of the Americas

Whitmeyer's Distilling Co. LLC

12821 Duncan Road, Bldg. 5 Ste. G
Houston, TX 77067
713-623-1637

Owners / Operators:
Travis Whitmeyer, Founder / Owner
Chris Whitmeyer, Founder / Owner
Wesley Whitmeyer, Founder / Owner
Sam Freeman, Director of Operations

Email: info@whitmeyers.com
Website: www.whitmeyers.com
Facebook: Whitmeyer's Distilling
Twitter: @HOU_Distillery

Type: Micro Distillery. Opened in 2012.

Hours of operation: Open for tours only

Tours: Available

Types of spirits produced: Vodka, bourbon whiskey, moonshine whiskey, flavored whiskey

Names of spirits:
- Space City Vodka
- Whitmeyer's Texas Moonshine Whiskey
- Whitmeyer's Texas Peach Whiskey
- Whitmeyer's Texas Single Barrel
- Cask Strength Straight Bourbon Whiskey

Best known for / most popular: Not provided

Average bottle price: $18.00 to $70.00

Distribution: TX

Interesting facts: Not provided

Yellow Rose Distilling LLC

1224 North Post Oak, Ste. 100
Houston, TX 77055
281-886-8757

Owners / Operators:
Troy Smith, Founding Partner / Master Distiller
Ryan Baird, Founding Partner
Randy Whitaker, Managing Partner

Email: info@yellowrosedistilling.com
Website: www.yellowrosedistilling.com
Facebook: Yellow Rose Distilling
Twitter: @YR_Distilling

Type: Micro Distillery. Opened in 2012.

Hours of operation: Monday through Friday, 10 a.m. to 4 p.m.

Tours: Call for hours

Types of spirits produced: Whiskey

Names of spirits:
- Outlaw Bourbon Whiskey
- Straight Rye Whiskey
- Double Barrel Bourbon Whiskey
- Blended Whiskey

Best known for / most popular: Outlaw Bourbon Whiskey

Average bottle price: $30.00 to $65.00

Distribution: TX

Interesting facts: Houston's first legal whiskey distillery.

High West Distillery

703 Park Avenue
Park City, UT 84060
435-649-8300

Owners / Operators:
David Perkins, Proprietor

Email: info@highwest.com
Website: www.highwest.com
Facebook: High West Distillery
Twitter: @HighWest
Yelp: High West Distillery & Saloon

Type: Micro Distillery. Sold first whiskey in Dec. 2007. The Saloon opened in 2009

Hours of operation: Daily, 11 a.m. to 10 p.m.

Tours: Available

Types of spirits produced:
Whiskey, vodka, barrel aged cocktails

Names of spirits:
- High West Whiskey Rendezvous® Rye
- High West Double Rye! ®
- High West Whiskey Son of Bourye®
- High West Whiskey American Prairie Reserve
- High West Whiskey Campfire®
- High West Vodka 7000' ®
- High West Vodka 7000' ® Peach
- High West Silver Whiskey® Western Oat
- High West Silver Whiskey OMG Pure Rye®
- The 36th Vote Barreled Manhattan
- The Barreled Boulevardier

Best known for / most popular: High West Double Rye! ®

Average bottle price: $30.00 to $130.00

Distribution: AK, AZ, AR, CA, CO, CT, DC, DE, FL, GA, IA, ID, IL, IN, KS, KY, LA, MA, MD, MI, MN, MO, MT, NC, NE, NJ, NM, NY, NV, OK, OR, PA, SC, TN, TX, UT, VA, WA, WI, WY; Canada, Singapore, Australia, UK/EU, China

Interesting facts:
- High West Distillery became the first legal distillery in Utah since 1870.
- High West Distillery and Saloon is the only ski-in gastro-distillery in the world.

Ogden's Own Distillery

2679 Midland Drive #4
Ogden, UT 84401
801-458-1995

Owners / Operators:
Tim Smith, Founder / Distiller
Steve Conlin, Partner / Marketing
Mike Glasmann, Partner / Executive
Stu Smith, Partner / Executive

Email: info@ogdensown.com
Website: www.ogdensown.com
Facebook: Five Wives Vodka
   Underground Herbal Spirit
Twitter: @OgdensOwn

Type: Micro Distillery. Opened in 2009.

Hours of operation: Monday through Friday, 9 a.m. to 5 p.m.

Tours: Not available

Types of spirits produced: Liqueur, vodka

Names of spirits:
- Underground Herbal Spirit
- Five Wives Vodka
- Five Wives Sinful Vodka

Best known for / most popular:
Underground Herbal Spirit and Five Wives Vodka

Average bottle price: $19.95

Distribution: AK, AL, CA, CO, ID, MI, MO, MT, NV, OR, PA, TX, UT, WA, WY

Awards and Recognitions:
"Distillery of the Year", 2012 New York International Spirits Competition

Underground Herbal Spirit
- 2013 Best of Category "Liqueurs" in Spirits of the Americas Competition
- Gold Medal, 2013 Denver International Spirits Competition

Five Wives Vodka
- Bronze Medal, 2013 New York International Spirits Competition
- Silver Medal, 2013 in Spirits of the Americas Competition
- Silver Medal, 2013 Denver International Spirits Competition
- Silver Medal, 2013 San Francisco World Spirits Competition

Boyden Valley Winery & Spirits

64 Vermont Route 104
Cambridge, VT 05444
802-644-8151

Owners / Operators:
David Boyden, Co-owner
Linda Boyden, Co-owner

Email: info@boydenvalley.com
Website: www.boydenvalley.com
Facebook: Boyden Valley Winery
Twitter: @Bwinery

Type: Micro Distillery. Opened in 2010.

Hours of operation: Daily, 10 a.m. to 5 p.m.

Tours: Available

Types of spirits produced: Liqueurs

Names of spirits:
- Vermont Ice Apple Crème
- Vermont Ice Maple Crème

Best known for / most popular: Not provided

Average bottle price: Not provided

Distribution: Not provided

Interesting facts: Not provided

Caledonia Spirits Inc.
Caledonia Winery Inc.

46 Buffalo Mountain Commons Drive
Hardwick, VT 05843
802-472-8000

Owners / Operators:
Todd Hardie, Owner

Email: info@caledoniaspirits.com
Website: www.caledoniaspirits.com
Facebook: Caledonia Spirits & Winery
Twitter: @CaledoniaSpirit

Type: Winery / Micro Distillery. Opened in 2011.

Hours of operation: Monday through Saturday, 10 a.m. to 6 p.m.

Tours: Not provided

Types of spirits produced: Vodka, cordial

Names of spirits:
- Barr Hill Vodka
- Barr Hill Honey Vodka
- Caledonia Spirits Elderberry Cordial

Best known for / most popular: Not provided

Average bottle price: Not provided

Distribution: DC, MA, MD, NJ, NY, VT

Interesting facts: Not provided

Dunc's Mill

622 Keyser Hill Road
St. Johnsbury, VT 05819
802-745-9486

Owners / Operators:
Duncan Holaday, Owner

Email: duncan@duncsmill.com
Website: www.duncsmill.com

Type: Micro Distillery. Opened in 1998.

Hours of operation: Not provided

Tours: Available by appointment

Types of spirits produced: Rum

Names of spirits:
- Dunc's Mill Maple Flavored Rum
- Dunc's Mill Elderflower Flavored Rum
- Backwoods Reserve Straight Rum

Best known for / most popular: Dunc's Mill Elderflower Flavored Rum

Average bottle price: Not provided

Distribution: Not provided

Interesting facts: The oldest continuously operating distillery in VT.

Elm Brook Farm

250 Elm Brook Road
East Fairfield, VT 05448
802-782-5999

Owners / Operators:
David Howe, Owner

Email: ebf@elmbrookfarm.com
Website: www.elmbrookfarm.com
Twitter: @ElmBrookFarm

Type: Micro Distillery. Opened in 2012.

Hours of operation:
Available by appointment

Tours: Available by appointment

Types of spirits produced:
Vodka, barrel aged specialty spirit

Names of spirits:
- Literary Dog Premium Sipping Vodka
- Rail Dog Barrel Aged Maple Spirit

Best known for / most popular: Not provided

Average bottle price: $55.99 to $93.99

Distribution:
Elm Brook Farm, Burlington VT Farmers' Market and, most VT Liquor Outlets

Interesting facts:
- Literary Dog Vodka is distilled more than 20 times.
- Elm Brook Farm does not use charcoal filtering.
- Both products are distilled on their farm using 100% pure maple.

Flag Hill Farm

135 Ewing Road
Vershire, VT 05079
802-685-7724

Owners / Operators:
Sebastian Lousada and Sabra Ewing, Owners

Email: flaghillfarm@wildblue.net
Website: www.flaghillfarm.com
Facebook: Flag Hill Farm Vermont Hard Cyder

Type: Micro Distillery. Winery in 1986. Distillery in 2002

Hours of operation: Appointment only

Tours: Appointment only

Types of spirits produced: Brandy

Names of spirits:
- Pomme de Vie - Vermont Apple Brandy
- Stair's Pear - Vermont Pear Brandy

Best known for / most popular: Apple Brandy

Average bottle price: $17.50 to $20.00

Distribution: VT

Interesting facts:
- Produced the first legal Vermont brandies since Prohibition.
- Flag Hill Farm Winery and Distillery is certified organic.

Green Mountain Distillers

192 Thomas Lane, Ste. 1
Stowe, VT 05672
802-253-0064

Owners / Operators:
Timothy Danahy, Founder / Distiller
Harold Faircloth III, Founder / Distiller

Email: info@greendistillers.com
Website: www.greendistillers.com
Facebook: Green Mountain Distillers

Type: Micro Distillery. Opened in 2002.

Hours of operation: Not provided

Tours: Not provided

Types of spirits produced: Vodka, gin

Names of spirits:
- Green Mountain Organic Gin
- Green Mountain Organic Sunshine Vodka
- Green Mountain Organic Lemon Vodka
- Green Mountain Organic Orange Vodka
- Green Mountain Organic Maple Liqueur

Best known for / most popular: Not provided

Average bottle price: Not provided

Distribution: Not provided

Interesting facts: Not provided

Mad River Distillers

156 Cold Spring Farms Road
Warren, VT 05674
802-496-6973

Owners / Operators:
John Egan Founder / Chairman
Brett Little Founder / President
Alex Hilton General Manager / Partner

Email: alex@madriverdistillers.com
Website: www.madriverdistillers.com
Facebook: Mad River Distillers

Type: Craft Distillery. Opened in July 2013.

Hours of operation: Tuesday through Saturday

Tours:
Available Friday and Saturday, noon to 5 p.m.

Types of spirits produced:
Rum, corn whiskey, rye, bourbon, apple brandy

Names of spirits:
- Mad River Rum
- Mad River Corn Whiskey
- Mad River Rye
- Mad River Bourbon
- Mad River Apple Brandy

Best known for / most popular: TBA

Average bottle price: $15.00 to $45.00

Distribution: VT, Boston, On-line

Interesting facts:
They use pure spring water from their farm to blend all of their spirits.

Saxtons River Distillery LLC

485 West River Road
Brattleboro, VT 05301
802-246-1128

Owners / Operators:
Christian Stromberg, Owner

Email: sapling@saplingliqueur.com
Website: www.saplingliqueur.com
Facebook: Sapling Vermont Maple Liqueur

Type: Micro Distillery. Opened in 2007.

Tasting room hours:
Monday through Friday, 9 a.m. to 5 p.m.
Saturday and Sunday, 10 a.m. to 5 p.m.

Tours: Not available

Types of spirits produced: Liqueur, bourbon, rye

Names of spirits:
- Sapling Vermont Maple Liqueur
- Sapling Maple Bourbon
- Sapling Maple Rye
- Perc Coffee Liqueur

Best known for / most popular: Sapling Vermont Maple Liqueur

Average bottle price: Not provided

Distribution: CA, MA, ME, MT, NH, NJ, NV, PA, VT

Interesting facts: Not provided

Shelburne Orchards Distillery

216 Orchard Road
Shelburne, VT 05482
802-985-2753

Owners / Operators:
Nick Cowles, Owner

Email: apple100@together.net
Website: www.shelburneorchards.com
Facebook: Shelburne Orchards

Type: Micro Distillery. Opened in 2009.

Hours of operation:
Monday through Saturday, 9 a.m. to 6 p.m.
Sunday, 9 a.m. to 5 p.m.

Tours: Available

Types of spirits produced: Brandy

Names of spirits:
- Dead Bird Apple Brandy

Best known for / most popular:
Dead Bird Apple Brandy

Average bottle price: Not provided

Distribution: Not provided

Interesting facts: Not provided

Smugglers' Notch Distillery

276 Main Street
Jeffersonville, VT 05464
802-309-3077

Owners / Operators:
Ron Elliott, Co-owner / Chairman
Jeremy Elliott, Co-owner / President

Email: jeremy@smugglersnotchdistillery.com
Website: www.smugglersnotchdistillery.com
Facebook: Smugglers Notch Distillery

Type: Micro Distillery. Opened in 2010.

Hours of operation: Monday through Sunday, 1 p.m. to 5 p.m.

Tours: Available by appointment

Types of spirits produced: Vodka, rum, gin, straight bourbon whiskey, whiskey

Names of spirits:
- Smugglers' Notch Vodka
- Smugglers' Notch Gin
- Smugglers' Notch Hopped Gin
- Smugglers' Notch Rum
- Smugglers' Notch Bourbon
- Smugglers' Notch Rye

Best known for / most popular: Smugglers' Notch Vodka

Average bottle price: $26.99 to $59.99

Distribution: CT, MA, NH, NY, VT

Interesting facts:
- Smugglers' Notch Distillery is a father/son partnership.
- The distillery was founded in 2006 at the foot of the famed Smugglers' Notch, site of many a clandestine bootlegger's run through the rugged Vermont mountain pass.

Awards and Recognitions:
Smugglers Notch Vodka
- 95 points, The Wine Enthusiast
- Double Gold, San Francisco World Spirits Competition

Vermont Distillers

7755 Route 9 East
West Marlboro, VT 05363
802-464-2003

Owners / Operators:
Edward C. Metcalfe, Jr., CEO
Augustus (Gus) Metcalfe, Production and Marketing
Dominic Metcalfe, Marketing and Sales

Email: info@vermontdistillers.com
Website: www.vermontdistillers.com
Facebook: Vermont Distillers

Type: Micro Distillery. Opened in 2012.

Hours of operation: Daily, 10 a.m. to 5 p.m.

Tours: Not available

Types of spirits produced: Cordials, vodka

Names of spirits:
- Metcalfe's Vermont Maple Cream Liqueur
- Metcalfe's Raspberry Liqueur
- Ciriaco's Limoncello
- Mount Snow Vodka

Best known for / most popular:
Metcalfe's Vermont Maple Cream Liqueur

Average bottle price: $24.95 to $29.95

Distribution: AZ, CT, FL, MA, MN, ND, NH, NJ, NV, NY, OR, TX, VT, WA, WI

Interesting facts: Not provided

Vermont Spirits Distilling Co.

Quechee Gorge Village
5573 Woodstock Road
Quechee, VT 05059
866-998-6352

Owners / Operators:
Steve Johnson, President / CEO
Joe Buswell, Master Distiller / Vice President
Harry Gorman, Distiller / Vice President
Mimi Buttenheim, General Manager

Email: info@vermontspirits.com
Website: www.vermontspirits.com
Facebook: Vermont Spirits Distilling Co.
Twitter: @VermontSpirits

Type: Micro Distillery. Founded in 1999. Retail Store opened in 2012

Hours of operation:
Monday through Sunday, 10 a.m. to 5 p.m.
Call for seasonal hours

Tours: Not available

Types of spirits produced: Vodka, gin, whiskey, bourbon, brandy

Names of spirits:
- Vermont Gold Vodka
- Vermont White Vodka
- Vermont Crimson Vodka
- Coppers Gin
- No. 14 Bourbon
- No. 14 Apple Brandy
- Black Snake Whiskey
- VS Limited Release Vodka

Best known for / most popular:
Vermont Gold Vodka and No. 14 Bourbon

Average bottle price: $20.00 to $50.00

Distribution: CT, DC, DE, ID, MA, MD, ME, NH, NJ, NY, OR, RI, TN, VT, WY

Interesting facts:
- Vermont White Vodka is lactose free.
- All vodkas are gluten free.
- No. 14 Bourbon is flavored with pure maple syrup.
- Black Snake Whiskey is made from 100% Vermont Corn and is un-aged.
- Coppers Gin is distilled with Vermont wild juniper.
- Vermont Crimson is distilled from apples from Vermont's Champlain Valley.

WhistlePig Farm

2139 Quiet Valley Road
Shoreham, VT 05770

Owners / Operators:
Raj Peter Bhakta, Founder / Chief Steward

Email: info@whistlepigrye.com
Website: www.whistlepigwhiskey.com
Facebook: WhistlePig Whiskey
Twitter: @WhistlePigRye

Type: Micro Distillery. Opened in 2014.

Hours of operation: Daily

Tours: Not available

Types of spirits produced: Whiskey

Names of spirits:
- WhistlePig Straight Rye Whiskey

Best known for / most popular:
WhistlePig Straight Rye Whiskey

Average bottle price: $70.00 to $250.00

Distribution: TBA

Interesting facts: Not provided

A. Smith Bowman Distillery

One Bowman Drive
At Deep Run
Fredericksburg, VA 22408
540-373-4555

Email: pioneer@asmithbowman.com
Website: www.asmithbowman.com
Facebook: A. Smith Bowman Distillery

Type: Micro Distillery. Opened in 1935, moved in 1988.

Hours of operation:
Distillery is open Monday through Saturday; 9 a.m. to 4 p.m.
Gift shop is open from 9 a.m. to 4 p.m.

Tours: Available. Complimentary. Depart every hour; 9 a.m. to 3 p.m.

Types of spirits produced:
Bourbon, limited edition whiskeys, gin, vodka, rum

Names of spirits:
- Bowman Brothers Small Batch Virginia Straight Bourbon Whiskey
- John J. Bowman Single Barrel Virginia Straight Bourbon Whiskey
- Abraham Bowman Limited Edition Whiskey
- George Bowman Colonial Era Dark Caribbean Rum
- Deep Run Virginia Vodka
- Sunset Hills Virginia Gin
- Virginia Gentleman

Best known for / most popular:
Hand crafted small batch VA bourbons

Average bottle price: Not provided

Distribution: CO, DC, FL, GA, IN, IL, KS, KY, LA, MA, MD, MI, MO, NJ, NY, OH, PA, SC, TN, TX, VA, WA

Interesting facts:
- One of the first licensed distilleries in Virginia after repeal of Prohibition.

Awards and Recognitions:
Bowman Brothers Small Batch Virginia Straight Bourbon Whiskey
- 2013 Double Gold Medal Winner

John J. Bowman Single Barrel Virginia Straight Bourbon Whiskey
- 2013 Gold Medal Winner

Appalachian Mountain Spirits LLC
Virginia Sweetwater Distillery

760 Walkers Creek Road
Marion, VA 24365
276-782-0932

Owners / Operators:
Scott Schumaker, Owner

Email: appmtnspirits@yahoo.com
Website: www.virginiasweetwaterdistillery.com
Facebook: Appalachian Mountain Spirits LLC

Type: Micro Distillery. Opened in 2013.

Hours of operation: Not provided

Tours: Not provided

Types of spirits produced: Moonshine, whiskey

Names of spirits:
- Virginia Sweetwater Moonshine
- War Horn Whiskey

Best known for / most popular:
Virginia Sweetwater Moonshine

Average bottle price: Not provided

Distribution: Not provided

Interesting facts: Not provided

Belmont Farms Distillery

13490 Cedar Run Road
Culpeper, VA 22701
540-825-3207

Owners / Operators:
Chuck and Jeanette Miller, Owners

Email: jtmiller46@aol.com
Website: www.belmontfarmdistillery.com

Type: Micro Distillery. Opened in 1987.

Hours of operation:
Tuesday through Saturday, 10 a.m. to 5 p.m.

Tours:
Available from April 1st through December 15th
Tuesday through Saturday, 10 a.m. to 5 p.m.

Types of spirits produced:
Virginia whiskey, corn whiskey

Names of spirits:
- Kopper Kettle Virginian Whiskey
- Virginia Lightning Whiskey
- Virginia Lightning Apple Pie
- Virginia Lightning Cherry

Best known for / most popular:
Virginia Lightning Whiskey

Average bottle price: $17.95 to $29.95

Distribution: VA

Interesting facts:
Belmont Farms Distillery has appeared on "How It's Made" on the Science Channel and has been featured on "The History Channel" and "The National Geographic Channel." Additionally, Author Patricia Cornwell visited the still and did her own filming.

Catoctin Creek Distilling Co. LLC

120 W. Main Street
Purcellville, VA 20132
540-751-8404

Owners / Operators:
Scott and Becky Harris, Owners

Email: info@catoctincreek.com
Website: www.catoctincreek.com
Facebook: Catoctin Creek Distilling Company
Twitter: @catoctincreek
YouTube: Catoctin Creek Distilling Company
LinkedIn: Catoctin Creek Distilling Company

Type: Micro Distillery. Opened in 2009.

Hours of operation:
Monday through Friday, 10 a.m. to 5 p.m.
Saturday, noon to 5 p.m.

Tours: Available

Types of spirits produced:
Rye whiskey, gin, fruit spirits

Names of spirits:
- Catoctin Creek Organic Roundstone Rye™
- Catoctin Creek Organic Mosby's Spirit™
- Catoctin Creek Organic Watershed Gin®
- Catoctin Creek Pearousia®
- Catoctin Creek 1757 Virginia Brandy™

Best known for / most popular: Catoctin Creek Organic Roundstone Rye™

Average bottle price: $38.90

Distribution:
CA, DC, GA, KY, MD, TN, VA, WA

Interesting facts:
- First legal distillery in Loudoun County, VA since Prohibition.
- Certified organic and kosher.

Still photo by: Rick Martin

Chesapeake Bay Distillery LLC

2669 Production Road #106
Virginia Beach, VA 23454
757-692-4083

Owners / Operators:
Chris Richeson, Managing member

Email: info@chesapeakebaydistillery.com
Website: www.chesapeakebaydistillery.com
Facebook: Spirits of the Blue Ridge Vodka
Twitter: @blueridgevodka

Type: Micro Distillery. Opened in 2006.

Hours of operation: Not open to the public

Tours: Not available

Types of spirits produced: Vodka, rum

Names of spirits:
- Spirits of the Blue Ridge Vodka
- Chick's Beach Rum

Best known for / most popular:
Spirits of the Blue Ridge Vodka

Average bottle price: $19.95 to $22.45

Distribution: VA

Interesting facts: Not provided

Copper Fox Distillery

9 River Lane
Sperryville, VA 22740
540-987-8554

COPPER FOX DISTILLERY

Owners / Operators:
Richard Wasmund, Owner / Master Distiller

Email: rwasm@aol.com
Website: www.copperfox.biz
Facebook: Copper Fox Distillery
Twitter: @cufoxdistillery
YouTube: Copper Fox Distillery

Type: Micro Distillery. Opened in 2005.

Hours of operation:
Monday through Saturday, 10 a.m. to 6 p.m.

Tours: Available

Types of spirits produced: Single malt whisky, rye whisky

Names of spirits:
- Wasmund's Single Malt Whisky
- Wasmund's Single Malt Spirit
- Copper Fox Rye Whisky
- Wasmund's Rye Spirit

Best known for / most popular:
Wasmund's Single Malt Whisky

Average bottle price: Not provided

Distribution: 24 U.S. states

Parched Group LLC

2700 Hardy Street
Richmond, VA 23220
804-231-3000

Owners / Operators:
Paul McCann, Owner

Email: info@cirrusvodka.com
Website: www.cirrusvodka.com
Facebook: Cirrus Vodka
Twitter: @CirrusVodka

Type: Micro Distillery. Opened in 2009.

Hours of operation: Not provided

Tours: Not provided

Types of spirits produced: Vodka

Names of spirits:
- Cirrus Vodka

Best known for / most popular: Cirrus Vodka

Average bottle price: Not provided

Distribution: DC, GA, IN, MD, MI, TN, VA

Interesting facts: Not provided

Reservoir Distillery

1800 A Summit Avenue
Richmond, VA 23230
804-912-2621

Owners / Operators:
David Cuttino, Co-owner / General Manager
James H. Carpenter, Co-owner / Master Distiller

Email: info@reservoirdistillery.com
Website: www.reservoirdistillery.com
Facebook: Reservoir Distillery
Twitter: @ReservoirDist

Type: Micro Distillery. Opened in 2009.

Hours of operation: Daily

Tours: Not available

Types of spirits produced: Bourbon, whiskey

Names of spirits:
- Reservoir Bourbon
- Reservoir Rye Whiskey
- Reservoir Wheat Whiskey

Best known for / most popular: Not provided

Average bottle price: $40.00 to $80.00

Distribution: DC, DE, FL, MD, VA

Three Brothers' Whiskey Distillery

9935 County Line Road
Disputanta, VA 23842
757-204-1357

Owners / Operators:
David Reavis, Owner / Distiller

Email: info@threebrotherswhiskey.com
Website: www.threebrotherswhiskey.com
Facebook: Three Brothers Whiskey
Twitter: @3BrosWhiskey
YouTube: Three Brothers Whiskey
Google +: Threebrotherswhiskey
Tumblr: threebrotherswhiskey.tumblr.com

Type: Craft Distillery.
Opened in September 2014.

Hours of operation:
Saturday and Sunday, noon to 6 p.m.

Tours: Available by appointment

Types of spirits produced:
Rye whiskey, white whiskey, gin

Names of spirits:
- George (Rye Whiskey)
- Old Point Comfort Gin
- Deputy Dave's Contraband Liquor

Best known for / most popular: TBD

Average bottle price: $25.00 to $45.00

Distribution: On-site retail, VA

Interesting facts: Not provided

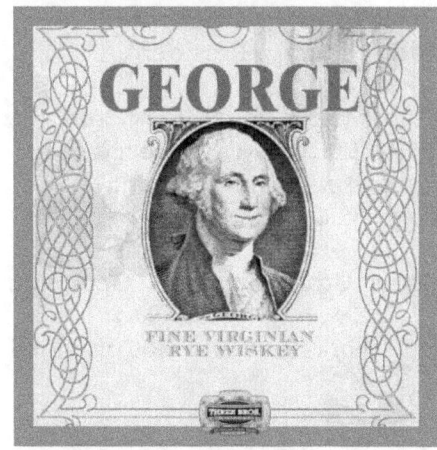

Virginia Distillery Company

299 Eades Lane
Lovingston, VA 22949
434-325-1299

Owners / Operators:
George Moore, Chairman
John McCray, President

Email: info@vadistillery.com
Website: www.vadistillery.com
Facebook: Virginia Distillery
Twitter: @VADistillery

Type: Craft Distillery. Opened in 2010.

Hours of operation: Not provided

Tours: Not provided

Types of spirits produced: Whisky

Names of spirits:
- Virginia Highland Malt Whisky

Best known for / most popular: Not provided

Average bottle price: $55.00

Distribution: DC, DE, IL, MA, MD, NYC, VA

Interesting facts: Not provided

Woods Mill Distillery

1625 River Road
Faber, VA 22938
434-361-1215

Owners / Operators:
Jim Taggart, Managing Partner / Distiller
Jeff Fletcher, Managing Partner / Distiller

Email: info@woodsmilldistillery.com
Website: www.woodsmilldistillery.com
Facebook: Woods Mill Distillery

Type: Micro Distillery.
Opened in November 2012.

Hours of operation: By appointment

Tours: Available by appointment

Types of spirits produced:
Brandy, whisky

Names of spirits:
- Harvest Apple Brandy

Best known for / most popular:
Harvest Apple Brandy

Average bottle price: $25.00

Distribution: VA

Services offered other than production: Contract distilling

2 Loons Distillery

3950 3rd Ave
Loon Lake, WA 99148
509-998-0330

Owners / Operators:
Greg Schwartz, Owner
Trish Schwartz, Owner

Email: info@2loonsdistillery.com
Website: www.2loonsdistillery.com
Facebook: 2 Loons Distillery

Type: Craft Distillery. Opened in 2014.

Hours of operation: By appointment

Tours: Available by appointment

Types of spirits produced: Vodka, moonshine, whiskey, bourbon

Names of spirits:
- TBA

Best known for / most popular: Not provided

Average bottle price: TBA

Distribution: On-site retail

2bar® Spirits

2960 4th Avenue S., #106
Seattle, WA 98134
206-801-1113

Owners / Operators:
Nathan Kaiser, Owner

Email: info@2barspirits.com
Website: www.2barspirits.com
Facebook: 2bar Spirits
Twitter: @2bar
Pinterest: 2bar Spirits
Flicker: 2bar Spirits' Photostream
Vimeo: 2bar Spirits

Type: Micro Distillery. Opened in 2012.

Hours of operation: Monday through Friday, 9 a.m. to 5 p.m.

Tours: Available Monday through Sunday, 2 p.m. to 6 p.m.

Types of spirits produced: Bourbon, moonshine, vodka

Names of spirits:
- 2bar Vodka
- 2bar Moonshine
- 2bar Bourbon

Best known for / most popular: Moonshine over Manhattan

Average bottle price: $30.00

Distribution: OR, WA

Interesting facts:
2bar Spirits is descended from five generations who ranched their land under the 2bar brand. For more than a century they have stood for quality, independence and hard work. Now those characteristics transcend to 2bar Spirits, handcrafted in Seattle, Washington.

3 Howls Distillery

426 S. Massachusetts Street
Seattle, WA 98134
206-747-8400

Owners / Operators:
Will Maschmeier, CEO / Distiller
Craig Phalen, COO / Distiller

Email: speak@3howls.com
Website: www.3howls.com
Facebook: 3 Howls Distillery
Twitter: @3Howls

Type: Craft Distillery. Opened in July 2013.

Hours of operation: Monday through Friday, 8 a.m. to 5 p.m.

Tours: Available

Types of spirits produced: Rum, whiskey, gin, flavored vodkas

Names of spirits:
- Single Malt Whiskey
- Hopped Whiskey
- Rye Whiskey
- Good Old Fashioned Gin
- Navy Strength Gin
- White Label Rum
- Gold Label Rum
- Bananas Foster Vodka
- Blood Orange Vodka
- Rosemary Vodka

Best known for / most popular: Whiskey, rum, gin and flavored vodkas

Average bottle price: $25.00

Distribution: ID, OR, WA

Interesting facts:
The name, 3 Howls, is based off of a Scottish hell hound called the Cu-Sith.

Bainbridge Organic Distillers

9727 Coppertop Loop NE, Unit 101
Bainbridge Island, WA 98110
206-842-3184

Owners / Operators:
Keith Barnes, Owner / Distiller

Email: info@bainbridgedistillers.com
Website: www.bainbridgedistillers.com
Facebook: Bainbridge Organic Distillers
Yelp: Bainbridge Organic Distillers

Type: Craft Distillery. Opened in 2009.

Hours of operation:
May to Oct.: Monday through Sunday, noon to 5 p.m.
Nov. to April: Monday through Saturday, noon to 5 p.m.

Tours: Available

Types of spirits produced: Vodka, whiskey, gin

Names of spirits:
- Bainbridge Legacy Organic Vodka
- Bainbridge Battle Point Organic Whiskey
- Bainbridge Heritage Organic Gin
- Bainbridge Rolling Bay Organic Rye
- Bainbridge 'The Whiskey Forty Saloon' Organic Whiskey

Best known for / most popular: Bainbridge Battle Point Whiskey

Average bottle price: $34.95 to $48.95

Distribution: CA, WA

Interesting facts: Not provided

Batch 206 Distillery

1417 Elliott Avenue West
Seattle, WA 98119

Owners / Operators:
Jeff and Daleen Steichen, Owners
Rusty Figgins, Master Distiller

Email: info@batch206.com
Website: www.batch206.com
Facebook: Batch 206
Twitter: @batch206

Type: Micro Distillery. Opened in March 2012.

Hours of operation:
Wednesday through Friday, 2 p.m. to 7 p.m.
Saturday and Sunday, noon to 6 p.m.

Tours: Available

Types of spirits produced: Vodka, gin, moonshine

Names of spirits:
- Batch 206 Vodka
- Batch 206 Mad Mint Vodka
- Counter Gin
- See 7 Stars Moonshine

Best known for / most popular:
Batch 206 Vodka and Counter Gin

Average bottle price: $24.95

Distribution: AZ, CA, CT, DE, FL, GA, MD, NJ, NM, NV, OR, SC, TX, WA

Interesting facts: Not provided

BelleWood Distilling

6140 Guide Meridian
Lynden, WA 98264
360-318-7720

Owners / Operators:
John & Dorie Belisle, Owners
Jessie Parker, Distiller

Email: info@bellewoodfarms.com
Website: www.bellewoodfarms.com, www.bellewooddistilling.com
Facebook: BelleWood Acres - Apples and Apple Cider
YouTube: BelleWood Acres TV Commerical
Flickr: BelleWood Acres

Type: Micro Distillery. Opened in 2012.

Hours of operation: Daily, 10 a.m. to 5 p.m.

Tours: Available

Types of spirits produced:
Eau de Vie, brandy, gin, vodka, liqueurs

Names of spirits:
- BelleWood Vodka
  (distilled from apples)
- BelleWood Apple Eau de Vie
- BelleWood Gin
- BelleWood Vodka
  (infused with fresh raspberries)
- BelleWood Aged Apple Brandy
- BelleWood Pumpkin Spice Liqueur

Best known for / most popular:
BelleWood Vodka

Average bottle price: $23.00 to $49.00

Distribution:
On-farm sales at BelleWood Acres; Haggen and Top Food, a 28-store local grocery chain; plus local restaurants and bars. A complete list can be found on our web site.

Interesting facts: They are growers as well as distillers. They raise 25,000 trees in the most Northwest corner of our nation which results in over 1.7 million pounds of fruit. Their farm provides a true farm to glass experience.

Black Heron Spirits Distillery

8011 Keene Road
West Richland, WA 99353
509-967-0781

Owners / Operators:
Mark Williams, Owner

Email: info@blackheronspirits.com
Website: www.blackheronspirits.com
Facebook: Black Heron Spirits

Type: Micro Distillery. Opened in 2010.

Hours of operation:
Friday and Saturday, noon to 5:00 pm

Tours: Available

Types of spirits produced:
Vodka, whisky, lemoncello

Names of spirits:
- Black Heron Vodka
- Desert Lightning Corn Whisky
- Lemoncello
- Black Heron Brandy
- Coyote Howl Whisky
- Finn Huckleberry Vodka
- Black Heron Bourbon
- Huckleberry Cordial
- Black Heron Moonshine

Best known for / most popular:
Desert Lightning and Lemoncello

Average bottle price: $30.00

Distribution: WA

Interesting facts: Not provided

Black Rock Spirits LLC

1952 1st Avenue South #5
Seattle, WA 98134

Owners / Operators:
Sven Liden, Co-founder / Owner
Stefan Schachtell, Co-founder / Owner
Chris Marshall, Co-founder / Owner

Email: info@blackrockspirits.com
Website: www.blackrockspirits.com, www.bakonvodka.com
www.sparkledonkey.com
Facebook: Black Rock Spirits, Bacon Vodka
Twitter: @baconvodka, @BlackRockSp
LinkedIn: Black Rock Spirits LLC

Type:
Contract distilled at Koenig Distillery, ID. Opened in 2008.

Hours of operation:
Monday through Friday, 9 a.m. to 6 p.m.

Tours: Not available

Types of spirits produced: Vodka

Names of spirits:
- Bakon Vodka

Best known for / most popular: Bakon Bloody Mary

Average bottle price: $28.00

Distribution: 46 U.S. states; 5 countries

Interesting facts:
Passed $1 million in sales of Bakon Vodka in 2012.

Black Sam Distillery Co.

430 South First Street
Montesano, WA 98563
360-580-0304

Owners / Operators:
Bob & Myrna Bellamy, Owners

Email: blacksaminc@comcast.net
Website: www.blacksamdistillery.com
Facebook: Black Sam Distillery

Type: Micro Distillery. Opened in 2012.

Hours of operation: Daily, 10 a.m. to 5 p.m.

Tours: Available by appointment

Types of spirits produced: Whiskey, vodka, gin

Names of spirits:
- Black Sam
- Down & Dirty

Best known for / most popular: Not provided

Average bottle price: Not provided

Distribution: On-site, local liquor stores

Interesting facts:
- The distillery was named after Pirate Black Sam Bellamy, a family ancestor.
- The still was hand fabricated on site from copper and stainless steel.
- The mash cooker and still are heated with a glycol hot water system instead of steam.

Blue Flame Spirits

2880 Lee Road, Ste. B
Prosser, WA 99350
509-778-4036

Owners / Operators:
Brian Morton, Co-owner
Charles Isley, Co-owner

Email: info@blueflamespirits.com
Website: www.blueflamespirits.com
Facebook: Blue Flame Spirits
Twitter: @BlueFlamespirit
Yelp: Blue Flame Spirits

Type: Craft Distillery. Opened in 2010.

Hours of operation:
Monday through Saturday, 11 a.m. to 5 p.m.

Tours: Available

Types of spirits produced:
Whiskey, vodka, gin, brandy

Names of spirits:
- Blue Flame Grappa
- Blue Flame Brandy
- Blue Flame Gin
- Blue Flame Ultra Premium Gin
- Blue Flame Vodka
- Blue Flame Peppered Vodka
- Blue Flame Ultra Premium Vodka
- Blue Flame Rye
- Blue Flame Wheat Whiskey

Best known for / most popular: All products

Average bottle price: $35.00

Distribution: CA, OR, WA

Interesting facts:
- 100% percent handcrafted farm to bottle.
- All ingredients are sourced within 45 miles of the distillery.

Awards and Recognitions:
- Grappa, Gold Medal, 2012 San Francisco World Spirits Competition
- Rye Whiskey, Silver Medal, The Washington Cup Domestic

Blue Spirits Distilling

324 Minneapolis Beach Road
Chelan, WA 98116
206-310-3945

Owners / Operators:
Jeffrey Soehren, Owner
Heidi Soehren, Owner

Email: jeff@bluespiritsdistilling.com
Website: www.bluespiritsdistilling.com
Facebook: Blue Spirits Distilling

Type: Distiller / Rectifier. Opened in 2012.

Hours of operation: Daily, noon to 5 p.m.

Tours: Available by appointment

Types of spirits produced: Vodka, gin, whiskey

Names of spirits:
- Blue Spirits Vodka
- Blue Spirits Gin
- Blue Spirits Whiskey

Best known for / most popular:
Cucumber Vodka

Average bottle price: $38.00

Distribution: WA; Ontario

Interesting facts:
- New for 2014 - Bespoke Vodka, Gin and Whisky Studio in Leavenworth, WA
- On the shores of Lake Chelan.
- The only boat up distillery in WA state.

Bluewater Distilling

1205 Craftsman Way, Ste. 116
Everett, WA 98201
206-369-0739

Owners / Operators:
John Lundin, Founder / Distiller

Email: info@bluewaterdistilling.com
Website: www.bluewaterdistilling.com
Facebook: Bluewater Distilling
Twitter: @BWDistilling
Instagram: bluewaterdistilling

Type: Micro Distillery. Opened in 2012.

Hours of operation: Tuesday through Sunday, noon to 7 p.m.

Tours: Available

Types of spirits produced: Vodka, gin, akvavit, specialty spirits

Names of spirits:
- Bluewater Organic Vodka
- Halcyon Organic Distilled Gin
- Ekström's Organic Akvavit

Best known for / most popular:
Halcyon Organic Distilled Gin
Named "Gin of the Year" - theGinIsIn.com

Average bottle price: $24.00 to 32.00

Distribution: CA, KS, MT, NJ, NY, OR, WA

Interesting facts:
- Certified organic
- American-made bottles
- Member of 1% for the Planet

broVo Spirits

Seattle, WA 98117
206-496-2613

Owners / Operators:
Erin Brophy, Co-founder / COO
Mhairi Voelsgen, Co-founder / CEO
Kat Uzzelle, Co-founder

Email: info@brovospirits.com
Website: www.brovospirits.com
Facebook: BroVo Spirits
Twitter: @broVoSpirits

Type: Micro Distillery. Opened in 2011.

Hours of operation: Not provided

Tours: Not provided

Types of spirits produced: Liqueur, amaro

Names of spirits:
- broVo+RG Rose Geranium Liqueur
- broVo+L Lavender Liqueur
- broVo+LB Lemon Balm Liqueur
- broVo+G Ginger Liqueur
- broVo+DF Douglas Fir Liqueur
- broVo Amaro No 1
- broVo Amaro No 2
- broVo Amaro No 3
- broVo Amaro No 4
- broVo Amaro No 5
- broVo Amaro No 6

Best known for / most popular:
broVo+RG Rose Geranium Liqueur

Average bottle price: Not provided

Distribution: WA; Canada, BC

Interesting facts: Not provided

Captive Spirits

1518 NW 52nd Street, Ste. A
Seattle, WA 98107
206- 852-4794

Owners / Operators:
Ben Capdevielle, Owner / Founder / Head Distiller
Todd Leabman, Owner / Founder / CFO
Holly Robinson, Owner / Head of Marketing and PR

Email: ben@captivespiritsdistilling.com
todd@captivespiritsdistilling.com
holly@captivespiritsdistilling.com
Website: www.captivespiritsdistilling.com
Facebook: Captive Spirits
Twitter: @captivespirits

Type: Micro Distillery. Opened in 2012.

Hours of operation: Vary

Tours: Available by appointment

Types of spirits produced: Gin

Names of spirits:
- Big Gin
- Bourbon Barrel Aged Big Gin

Best known for / most popular: Big Gin

Average bottle price: $30.00 to $45.00

Distribution:
AZ, IL, ND, NY, WA; British Columbia, United Kingdom

Interesting facts:
- Ben is a third generation distiller.
- Captive Spirits is the only known strictly gin distillery in Washington.
- Captive Spirits uses a custom built Vendome pot still specifically designed to make gin.

Carbon Glacier Distillery

533 Church Street
Wilkeson, WA 98396
360-989-9700

Owners / Operators:
Christopher W. Lyons, Owner
Keith Quimby, Owner

Email: admin@carbonglacierdistillery.com
Website: www.carbonglacierdistillery.com
Facebook: Carbon Glacier Distillery
Twitter: @CGDistillery
Pinterest: Carbon Glacier Distillery

Type: Micro Distillery. Opened in 2012.

Hours of operation:
Monday, Thursday, Friday, 2 p.m. to 6 p.m.
Saturday and Sunday, noon to 6 p.m.

Tours: Available upon request

Types of spirits produced: Vodka, gin, whiskey (apple brandy and absinthe coming soon)

Names of spirits:
- Stocking Stuffer Whiskey
  (Seasonal Avail. Dec. 1st)
- Pump Trolley Whiskey
  (Seasonal – Avail. 3rd weekend in July)
- B4 Premium Handcrafted Vodka
- Quimby and Jack's Distilled Dry Gin
- Moose Shine Pacific Northwest Un-aged Whiskey

Best known for / most popular:
Moose Shine Pacific Northwest Un-aged Whiskey
B4 Premium Handcrafted Vodka

Average bottle price: $25.00 to $35.00

Distribution: WA

Interesting facts: Founded by Keith Quimby (a Washington native) and Christopher Lyons (a transplant from Kentucky), Carbon Glacier Distillery is nestled in the foothills of the Cascade Mountains just a few miles from the entrance to Mount Rainier National Park on WA State Route 165 in the historic town of Wilkeson.

Chuckanut Bay Distillery

1115 Railroad Avenue
Bellingham, WA 98225
360-739-0361

Owners / Operators:
Kelly Andrews, Co-owner
Rob Andrews, Co-owner
Ethan Lynette, Co-owner
Matt Howell, Co-owner

Email: chuckanutbaydistillery@yahoo.com
Website: www.chuckanutbaydistillery.com
Facebook: Chuckanut Bay Distillery
Twitter: @ChuckanutBay

Type: Micro Distillery. Opened in 2011.

Hours of operation: Friday through Sunday, noon to 4 p.m.

Tours: Not provided

Types of spirits produced: Vodka, gin

Names of spirits:
- Chuckanut Bay Gin
- Chuckanut Bay Vodka

Best known for / most popular: Not provided

Average bottle price: Not provided

Distribution: Not provided

Interesting facts: Not provided

Copperworks Distilling Company

1250 Alaskan Way
Seattle, WA 98101
206-504-7604

Owners / Operators:
Jason Parker, Owner / Distiller
Micah Nutt, Owner / Distiller

Email: info@copperworksdistilling.com
Website: www.copperworksdistilling.com
Facebook: Copperworks Distilling & Tasting Room
Twitter: @CopperworksDist

Type: Micro Distillery. Opened in 2013.

Hours of operation: Vary by season. Visit website.

Tours: Available. Visit website for details.

Types of spirits produced:
Gin, vodka, all-malt whiskey (aging)

Names of spirits:
- Copperworks Gin
- Copperworks Vodka

Best known for / most popular: TBA

Average bottle price: $35.00

Distribution: Select locations in Seattle, WA

Interesting facts:
- Each Copperworks product is distilled in a traditional Scottish copper still best suited to that individual spirit.
- The company's copper pot and column stills were designed specifically for Copperworks' unique processes and chosen ingredients and were hand-built by the expert coppersmiths at Forsyths in the highlands of Scotland.
- With more than 10,000 pounds of copper stills representing 1,800 gallons of capacity, Copperworks can produce up to 350,000 bottles of spirits per year.
- Copperworks plans to offer additional styles of gin in 2014 and beyond and expects to release its first all-malt whiskey in 2016.

Awards and Recognition:
Copperworks Ginm Gold Medal, 2014 World Beverage Competition

Dark Moon Artisan Distillery

1830 Bickford Avenue, Ste. 108
Snohomish, WA 98290

Owners / Operators:
Kathy Alley, Owner
John Dawson, Master Distiller

Email: info@darkmoondistillery.com
Facebook: Dark Moon Artisan Distillery

Type: Micro Distillery. Opened in 2012.

Hours of operation:
Monday through Friday, 7:30 a.m. to 5 p.m.
Saturday, 11 a.m. to 5 p.m.

Tours: Available

Types of spirits produced:
Apple-based vodka, rum, mixed cider and vodka

Names of spirits:
- Singing Whale Vodka
- Turtle Island Rum-style Spirits
- Apple Knocker

Best known for / most popular: Apple Knocker
(A 40 proof mixed cider and vodka with cinnamon, vanilla and other natural flavors.)

Average bottle price: $20.00

Distribution: OR, WA

Interesting facts:
All spirits are distilled from Washington apples.

Deception Distilling LLC

996 Padilla Heights Road
Anacortes, WA 98221
360-588-1000

Owners / Operators:
Harold Christenson, Manager

Email: deceptiondistilling@hotmail.com
Website: www.deceptiondistilling.com
Facebook: Deception Distilling

Type: Craft Distillery.
Opened in January 2013.

Hours of operation:
Monday through Friday, 8 a.m. to 4:30 p.m.
Saturday, 9 a.m. to 2:30 p.m.

Tours: Available

Types of spirits produced: Vodka, moonshine, whiskey

Names of spirits:
- Deception Vodka
- Skagit Moon Moonshine

Best known for / most popular: Apple Pie Moonshine

Average bottle price: $20.00 to $30.00

Distribution: WA

Awards and Recognitions:
- Silver Medal, 2013 San Francisco World Spirits Competition

Double V Distillery

1315 SE Grace Avenue, Unit 118
Battle Ground, WA 98604
360-723-5282

Owners / Operators:
John Vissotzky, Owner / Spirit Master
Steve Vissotzky, Co-owner
Nicholas Vissotzky, Operations

Email: vvspirits@gmail.com
Website: www.doublevdistillery.com
Facebook: Double V Distillery
Twitter: @DoubleVspirits

Type: Craft Distillery. Opened in 2009.

Hours of operation:
Tuesday through Friday, 9 a.m. to 6 p.m.
Saturday, 10 a.m. to 3 p.m.

Tours: Available by appointment

Types of spirits produced: Vodka, gin, corn whiskey, apple pie, whiskey, bourbon

Names of spirits:
- Viscova (vodka)
- Griffon (gin)
- Colonel Cobb Corn Whiskey
- Colonel Cobb Apple Pie

Best known for / most popular: Viscova Craft Vodka, Griffon Gin

Average bottle price: $28.00 to $32.00

Distribution: Self

Interesting facts:
- Mashes are hand made using an open vat style fermentation process.
- Uses only organically grown corn and barley from the state of Washington.
- Their copper still was manufactured in Germany and it features a 21 plate vodka tower.
- They distill their vodka and gin three times for the best overall character.
- They age their whiskey for a minimum of 4 years in charred oak barrels made in Kentucky.

Dry County Distillery LLC

1326 6th Street
Marysville, WA 98270
425-343-8021

Owners / Operators:
Howard V.O. Johnston, Owner
Jennifer Johnston, Manager

Email: info@drycountydistillery.com
Website: www.drycountydistillery.com
Facebook: Dry County Distillery

Type: Micro Distillery. Opened in June 2012.

Hours of operation:
Monday through Friday, 11 a.m. to 6 p.m.; Sunday by appointment

Tours: Available by appointment

Types of spirits produced: Gin, vodka, whisky, liqueur

Names of spirits:
- Dry County Gin
- Dry County Copper Still Vodka
- Black Rope Anise
- Dry County Rum
- Dry County Apple Pie

Best known for / most popular: Black Rope Anise

Average bottle price: $25.50 to $45.00

Distribution: Pilchuck Distributors Inc.

Interesting facts: Not provided

Dry Fly Distilling

1003 E. Trent, Ste. 200
Spokane, WA 99202
509-489-2112

Owners / Operators:
Don Poffenroth, Owner
Kent Fleischmann, Owner
Patrick Donovan, Lead Distiller

Email: don@dryflydistilling.com, kent@dryflydistilling.com
Website: www.dryflydistilling.com
Facebook: Dry Fly Distilling
Twitter: @dryflydistiller

Type: Micro Distillery. Opened in 2007.

Hours of operation:
Monday through Friday, 8 a.m. to 5 p.m.
Saturday, 10 a.m. to 3 p.m.

Tours: Available

Types of spirits produced: Vodka, gin, whisky

Names of spirits:
- Dry Fly Washington Wheat Vodka
- Dry Fly Washington Wheat Gin
- Dry Fly Washington Straight Wheat Whiskey
- Dry Fly Washington Straight Bourbon Whiskey
- Dry Fly Washington Straight Triticale Whiskey
- Dry Fly Cask Straight Wheat Whiskey
- Dry Fly Port Barrel Finish Wheat Whiskey
- Dry Fly Barrel Reserve Gin

Best known for / most popular:
A "PMD" - Dry Fly Vodka from the freezer and a splash of cranberry juice

Average bottle price: $29.95 to $49.95

Distribution:
40 U.S. states; Canada, The Pacific Rim, Caribbean, and Europe

Interesting facts
- Dry Fly Distillery is Washington's first craft distillery producing vodka, gin, and whiskey.
- The "Dry Fly" company name stemmed from Kent and Don's mutual shared passion for fly fishing.
- One of America's most respected craft distilleries - named a 2014 Master Class Distillery.

Evanson Handcrafted Distilling LLC

1620 E. Houston Avenue, Ste. 600
Spokane, WA 99217
509-481-8847

Owners / Operators:
Joel Evanson, Co-owner / Distiller
Kelly Evanson, Co-owner / Artist

Email: evanson.handcrafted.distilling.llc@hotmail.com
Website: www.evansonhandcrafteddistilling.com
Facebook: Evanson Handcrafted Distilling LLC

Type: Craft Distillery. Opened in July 2013.

Hours of operation:
Thursday, noon to 5 p.m.
Friday noon to 6 p.m.
Saturday noon to 4 p.m., or by appointment

Tours: Available by appointment

Types of spirits produced: Vodka, gin, whiskey

Names of spirits:
- E Vodka
- E-VO-DKA Vodka
- SPOKANE FALLS-Single Malt-White Dog Whiskey

Best known for / most popular: E Vodka

Average bottle price: $20.00 to $40.00

Distribution: On-site tasting room

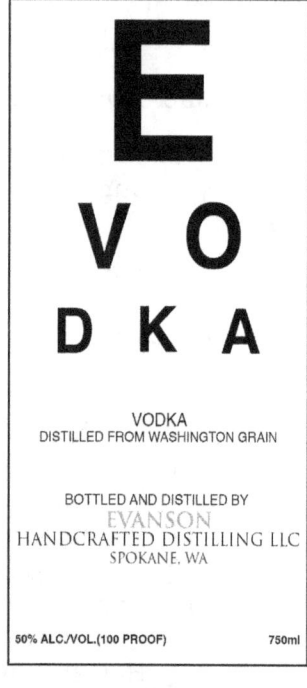

Ezra Cox Distillery

719 N. Tower Avenue
Centralia, WA 98531
360-736-1033

Owners / Operators:
Ezra Cox III, Distiller / Manager

Email: ezracoxiii@gmail.com
Website: www.ezracox.com
Facebook: Ezra Cox Distillery

Type: Micro Distillery. Opened in 2011.

Hours of operation: Advanced notice requested

Tours: Available

Types of spirits produced: Moonshine, whiskey, vodka, flavored moonshine

Names of spirits:
- Ezra Cox Moonshine
- Ezra Cox Single Malt Whiskey
- Ezra Cox Single Malt Vodka

Best known for / most popular: Ezra Cox Moonshine, Flavored Moonshine

Average bottle price: $20.00 to $30.00

Distribution: WA

Interesting facts:
Specializing in spirits made from single malt mash and a variety of real fruit flavored moonshines.

Four Lakes

223 Howard Flats Road
Chelan, WA 98816
509-542-7927

Owners / Operators:
Don Koester, Owner
Karl Koester, Manager / Winemaker / Grower

Email: info@fourlakeswinery.com
Website: www.fourlakeswinery.com
Facebook: Four Lakes Winery
Twitter: @FourLakesWinery

Type: Winery / Micro Distillery. Opened in 2004.

Hours of operation: Not provided

Tours: Not provided

Types of spirits produced: Grappa, brandy

Names of spirits:
- Not provided

Best known for / most popular: Not provided

Average bottle price: Not provided

Distribution: Not provided

Interesting facts: Not provided

Fremont Mischief

132 N. Canal Street
Seattle, WA 98103
206-632-0957

Owners / Operators:
Mike Sherlock, Founder

Email: info@fremontmischief.com
Website: www.fremontmischief.com
Facebook: Fremont Mischief
Twitter: @FremontMischief

Type: Micro Distillery. Opened in 2011

Hours of operation:
Wednesday through Friday, noon to 6 p.m.
Saturday, 11 a.m. to 6 p.m.; Sunday, noon to 5 p.m.

Tours: Available Friday through Sunday at 1 p.m., 3 p.m.

Types of spirits produced:
Whiskey, gin, vodka, rum, bitters

Names of spirits:
- John Jacob Rye Whiskey
- Worker's No 9 Vodka
- Fremont Mischief Whiskey, aged 8 years
- Fremont Mischief Gin
- Fremont Mischief Vodka
- Sherlock's "Mischief Well" Vodka
- Sintillation Low Calorie Vodka
- Mischief Mariner Rum
- Bitter Face Bitters
- Rex Velvet Sinister Spirit

Best known for / most popular:
John Jacob Rye Whiskey, Worker's No. 9 Vodka

Average bottle price: $26.00 to $33.00

Distribution: CA, OR, WA

Interesting facts:
- Mischief spirits are made from local grains.
- A portion of their proceeds benefit local charities.

Glacier Basin Distillery

2604 Draper Road
Yakima, WA 98903
509-930-0817

Owners / Operators:
Cragg Gilbert, Partner / Manager
Chris Bolm, Partner / Manager
Karl Hale, Partner / Manager
Putnam Barber, Partner / Manager
Thomas Hale, Partner / Distiller / Operator

Email: thomas@glacierbasin.com
Website: www.glacierbasin.com
Facebook: Glacier Basin Distillery

Type: Craft Distillery. Opened in May 2013.

Hours of operation:
Open by appointment and on event days

Tours: Available by appointment

Types of spirits produced: Fruit brandy

Names of spirits:
- Grappa
- Kirschwasser Cherry Brandy

Best known for / most popular:
Kirschwasser Cherry Brandy

Average bottle price: $31.00 to $38.00

Distribution: On-site retail

Interesting facts:
Fruits used are grown on their own ranch.

Glass Distillery

1712 1st Avenue S.
Seattle, WA 98134
206-686-7210

Owners / Operators:
Ian MacNeil, Founder / Distiller

Email: tastings@glassdistillery.com
Website: www.glassdistillery.com
Facebook: Glass Distillery
Twitter: @GlassDistillery

Type: Micro Distillery. Opened in 2012.

Hours of operation: Available by appointment

Tours: Available by appointment
(call or email tastings@glassdistillery.com)

Types of spirits produced: Vodka

Names of spirits:
- Glass Vodka
- Glass Honey Vodka
- Gridiron Vodka
- Glass Kona Coffee Vodka

Best known for / most popular: Glass Vodka

Average bottle price: $20.00 to $50.00

Distribution: CA, HI, MI, TX, WA; Canada BC

Interesting facts:
- Glass Vodka is distilled from grapes harvested from the Pacific Northwest and distilled using a state-of-the-art, 17.5 foot tall copper German still.
- Glass Vodka won a Bronze in the Vodka category and Best in Class Platinum for bottle/package design at the 2012 International SIP Awards.
- Gridiron Vodka was recently introduced as a premium vodka selection at Century Link Field, home of the Seattle Seahawks and Seattle Sounders.
- Glass Kona Coffee Vodka is an infusion of Keala's Hapuna Blend Kona Coffee.

Gnostalgic Spirits Distillery

1518 NW 52nd Street
Seattle, WA 98107
206-257-2306

Owners / Operators:
Gwydion Stone, Owner

Email: contact@gnostalgicspirits.com
Website: www.gnostalgicspirits.com
Facebook: Gnostalgic Spirits Distillery

Type: Micro Distillery. Opened in 2012.

Hours of operation: Not provided

Tours: Not provided

Types of spirits produced: Absinthe

Names of spirits:
- Marteau Absinthe de la Belle Époque

Best known for / most popular:
Marteau Absinthe de la Belle Époque

Average bottle price: Not provided

Distribution: Not provided

Interesting facts: Not provided

Golden Distillery

9746 Samish Island Road
Bow, WA 98232
360-542-8332

Owners / Operators:
Bob Stilnovich and Jim Caudill, Owners

Email: goldendistillery@gmail.com
Website: www.goldendistillery.com
Facebook: Golden Distillery

Type: Micro Distillery. Opened in 2010.

Hours of operation:
Thursday through Sunday, 11 a.m. to 5 p.m.

Tours: Available

Types of spirits produced: Whiskey, brandy

Names of spirits:
- Golden Samish Bay Single Malt Whiskey
- Golden Samish Bay Whiskey Reserve
- Golden White Gold Whiskey
- Golden Apple Brandy

Best known for / most popular: Golden Samish Bay Single Malt Whiskey

Average bottle price: $40.00 to $50.00

Distribution: WA

Interesting facts:
- Golden Distillery is the first distillery to open in Skagit County.
- Golden Apple Brandy is being aged in used whiskey barrels.

Awards and Recognitions:
- Samish Bay Single Malt Whiskey won Gold at the ADI convention in KY.
- Samish Bay Single Malt Whiskey received 88.5 points in the Whiskey Bible.

Heritage Distilling Company

3207 57th Street Court NW
Gig Harbor, WA 98335
253-509-0008

Owners / Operators:
Jennifer Stiefel, Co-founder / President
Justin Stiefel, Co-founder / CEO / Head Distiller

Email: info@heritagedistilling.com
Website: www.heritagedistilling.com
Facebook: Heritage Distilling Company, Inc.
Twitter: @heritagedistill
Pinterest: Heritage Distilling Company
LinkedIn: Heritage Distilling Co.
Flickr: Heritage Distilling Company's Photostream
Blog: Official HDC™ Blog: On the Rocks
Tripadvisor: Heritage Distilling Company

Type: Micro Distillery. Opened in 2012.

Hours of operation: Vary. Refer to website.

Tours: Available daily at 4 p.m. or by appointment

Types of spirits produced: Whiskey, gin, vodka

Names of spirits:
- HDC Vodka
- HDC Charr Barrel Finished Vodka
- HDC Soft Gin
- HDC Fall Classic – Apple Cider Flavored Whiskey
- Commander's Rye Whiskey
- Elk Rider Vodka
- Elk Rider Crisp Gin
- Elk Rider Whiskey

Best known for / most popular: HDC Vodka, triple distilled

Average bottle price: $29.00 to $47.00

Distribution: WA

Awards and Recognitions:
Elk Rider Vodka
- 2013 Gold Medal, 93 Points. Tastings.com, Best Buy.

Commander's Rye Whiskey
- 2013 Silver Medal, San Francisco World Spirits Competition

HDC Vodka
- 2013 Double Gold Medal – Best Vodka, FiftyBest.com International Tasting

HDC Soft Gin
- 2013 Double Gold Medal – Best Gin, FiftyBest.com International Tasting

It's 5 Artisan Distillery

207 Mission Avenue
Cashmere, WA 98801
509-679-9771

Owners / Operators:
Colin Levi, Owner

Email: 5@its5distillery.com
Website: www.its5distillery.com
Facebook: It's 5

Type: Micro Distillery. Opened in 2009.

Hours of operation: Daily, 11 a.m. to 5 p.m.

Winter Hours: 11 a.m. to 4 p.m., Wednesday by appointment, Closed Sunday

Tours: Available by appointment

Types of spirits produced:
Eau de vie, brandy, grappa, whiskey, gin, liqueurs

Names of spirits:
- Block and Tackle Moonshine
  100% Corn Whiskey Un-aged
- Corn Whiskey Moonshine
  100% Corn Whiskey Aged
- Reserve Bourbon (aged 4 years)
- Vodka
- Northwest Dry Gin
- Grappa
- Eaux de Vie: Voignier, Apple, Pear, Apricot, Cherry, Plum
- Liqueur: Raspberry, Blueberry, Elderberry, Blackberry, Pear, Apricot, Cherry

Best known for / most popular: Reserve Bourbon

Average bottle price: $30.00

Distribution: CA, IN, MN, MT, NV, OR, PA, TN, WA

Interesting facts:
Seventh craft distillery in North Central WA since Prohibition.

J.P. Trodden Small Batch Bourbon

18646 142nd Avenue NE
Woodinville, WA 98072
206-399-6291

Owners / Operators:
Mark Nesheim, Owner / Distiller
Jennifer Seversen, Owner

Email: Mark Nesheim, mark@jptroddendistilling.com
Jennifer Seversen, jennifer@jptroddendistilling.com
Website: www.jptroddendistilling.com
Facebook: JP Trodden, JP Trodden Distilling

Type: Micro Distillery. Opened in 2011.

Hours of operation:
Monday through Friday, 7 a.m. to 5 p.m.
Saturday, 1 p.m. to 5 p.m.

Tours: Available by appointment

Names of spirits: Bourbon

Names of spirits:
- JP Trodden Small Batch Bourbon

Best known for / most popular:
JP Trodden Small Batch Bourbon

Average bottle price: $59.00

Distribution: WA

Interesting facts: JP Trodden loved to share whiskey with his friends. He was a U.S. mail carrier in the Okanogan highlands during Prohibition and was known to stash a few bottles in his mail bag whenever he crossed the nearby British Columbia border. His grandson Mark named the distillery in JP's honor and carries on the tradition of sharing whiskey with friends.

"JP Trodden is a 100% true craft distillery using only Washington grown grains that are ground and cooked in our own mash recipe, fermented, distilled, barrel aged and bottled on premise to our own exacting standards. No NGS is ever used in creating our handcrafted small batch Bourbon".
– Mark Nesheim

Kayak Spirits Distillery LLC

5490 Cameron Road
Freeland, WA 98249
360-672-4920

Owners / Operators:
Eric R. Stallman, Co-owner
Kathy Stallman, Co-owner

Email: lwa@whidbey.com
Website: www.sites.google.com/site/kayakspiritsdistillery
Facebook: Kayak Spirits Distillery LLC

Type: Craft Distillery. Opening in 2013.

Hours of operation: Not provided

Tours: Not provided

Types of spirits produced: Whiskey, vodka

Names of spirits:
- TBA

Best known for / most popular: TBA

Average bottle price: TBA

Distribution: TBA

Interesting facts: TBA

Letterpress Distilling

85 S. Atlantic Street, #110
Seattle, WA 98134
206-227-4522

Owners / Operators:
Skip Tognetti, Owner / Distiller

Email: skip@letterpressdistilling.com
Website: www.letterpressdistilling.com
Facebook: Letterpress Distilling
Twitter: @lp_distilling

Type: Micro Distillery. Opened in 2012.

Hours of operation: Saturday and Sunday, noon to 6 p.m. and by appointment

Tours: Available with prior arrangement.
If time allows, tours may be given when open.

Types of spirits produced: Vodka, limoncello

Names of spirits:
- Letterpress Vodka
- Letterpress Limoncello

Best known for / most popular:
Letterpress Limoncello

Average bottle price: Not provided

Distribution: Self distributed

Mac Donald Distillery

104 Avenue C
Snohomish, WA 98290
425-275-1328

Owners / Operators:
Glen Mac Donald, Owner

Email: info@macdonalddistillery.com
Website: www.macdonalddistillery.com
Facebook: Mac Donald Distillery

Type: Micro Distillery. Opened in 2010.

Hours of operation:
Monday through Friday, 8 a.m. to 5 p.m.
Saturday, noon to 5 p.m.

Tours: Available

Types of spirits produced: Gin, vodka, whiskey

Names of spirits:
- Isis Vodka
- Isis Premium Gin
- Ty Wolfe Whiskey

Best known for / most popular: Isis Vodka

Average bottle price: Not provided

Distribution: Not provided

Interesting facts: Not provided

Meriwether Distilling Co.

5840 Airport Way S., Ste. 200
Seattle, WA 98108

Owners / Operators:
Whitney D. Meriwether, Owner / Distiller

Email: info@meriwetherdistilleries.com
Website: www.meriwetherdistilleries.com
Facebook: Meriwether Distilling Company
Twitter: @Daily_Drinker

Type: Craft Distillery. Opened in 2011.

Hours of operation: Not provided

Tours: Not provided

Types of spirits produced: Vodka

Names of spirits:
- Speakeasy Vodka

Best known for / most popular: Speakeasy Vodka

Average bottle price: Not provided

Distribution: Not provided

Interesting facts: Not provided

Mount Baker Distillery

1305 Fraser Street, Ste. D2
Bellingham, WA 98229
360-734-3301

Owners / Operators:
Troy Smith, Owner

Email: info@mountbakerdistillery.com
Website: www.mountbakerdistillery.com
Facebook: Mount Baker Distillery
Twitter: @MtBDistillery

Type: Craft Distillery. Opened in 2011.

Hours of operation:
Friday and Saturday, 11 a.m. to 6 p.m.

Tours: Available by appointment

Types of spirits produced: Vodka, moonshine

Names of spirits:
- Mount Baker Vodka
- Mount Baker Moonshine

Best known for / most popular: Mount Baker Moonshine

Average bottle price: Not provided

Distribution: WA

Interesting facts: The recipe for the moonshine comes from an old family recipe perfected by Grandpa Abe Smith. The story of Abe Smith is told on the label of MBD's Moonshine.

Mt. Index Brewery & Distillery

49315 SR 2
Index, WA 98256
360-793-6584

Owners / Operators:
Charles Tucker, Master Distiller / Manager
Anthony Gross, Richard Gross

Email: charles@barbarian-beverage.com
Facebook: Mt. Index Brewery & Distillery

Type: Craft Distillery. Opened in August 2013.

Hours of operation: Daily, 11 a.m. to 7 p.m.

Tours: Available

Types of spirits produced:
Vodka, coriander vodka, coffee liquor

Names of spirits:
- Mt. Index Vodka
- Mt. Index Coriander Flavored Vodka
- Black Cat Coffee Liquor

Best known for / most popular:
Mt. Index Coriander Flavored Vodka

Average bottle price: $20.00

Distribution: On-site retail; Red Apple in Sultan, WA

Interesting facts: Not provided

Nightside Distillery

2908 Meridian E. #116
Edgewood, WA 98371
253-377-1379

Owners / Operators:
Tom Greene, Owner / Distiller

Email: tom@nightsidedistillery.com
Website: www.nightsidedistillery.com
Facebook: Nightside Distillery

Type: Craft Distillery. Opened in December 2013.

Hours of operation: By appointment

Tours: Available by appointment

Types of spirits produced: Vodka

Names of spirits:
- TBA

Best known for / most popular: TBA

Average bottle price: $25.00 to $35.00

Distribution: On-site retail

Interesting facts: Apple based vodka

Old Ballard Liquor Co.

4421 Shilshole Avenue NW
Seattle, WA 98107
206-858-8010

Owners / Operators:
Lexi, Owner / Operator

Email: info@oldballardliquorco.com
Website: www.oldballardliquorco.com
Facebook: Old Ballard Liquor Co.
Twitter: @OldBallardLiq
Yelp: Old Ballard Liquor Co

Type: Craft Distillery. Opened in June 2013.

Hours of operation: Seasonal. Visit social media for the current hours.

Tours: Available

Types of spirits produced: Cherry bounce, vodka, aquavit, seasonal specials

Names of spirits:
- Cherry Bounce
- Riktig Aquavit
- Älskar Aquavit
- Well Vodka

Best known for / most popular:
Cherry Bounce, Riktig Aquavit

Average bottle price:
$20.00 to $40.00

Distribution: Greater Seattle area independent liquor stores, on-site retail

Interesting facts: The Old Ballard Liquor Co. is an artisan nano-distillery in the Ballard neighborhood of Seattle. Paying homage to the area's history as a Scandinavian fishing and blue collar neighborhood, their focus is on forgotten and neglected traditional old-fashioned liquors and liqueurs.

OOLA Distillery

1314 E. Union Street
Seattle, WA 98122
206-709-7909

Owners / Operators:
Kirby Kallas-Lewis, Founder / Distiller
Jeana Harrington, Managing Director

Email: info@ooladistillery.com
Website: www.ooladistillery.com
Facebook: OOLA Distillery
Twitter: @OOLADistillery

Type: Micro Distillery. Opened in 2011.

Sales room hours:
Thursday through Saturday, noon to 8 p.m.

Tours: Available Saturday, 3 p.m. by reservation

Types of spirits produced: Gin, vodka, whiskey

Names of spirits:
- OOLA Gin
- OOLA Vodka
- OOLA Citrus Vodka
- OOLA Chili Pepper Vodka
- OOLA Rosemary Vodka
- OOLA Waitsburg Bourbon Whiskey
- OOLA Waitsburg Barrel-Finished Gin

Best known for / most popular:
OOLA Gin, 5 awards including a MicroLiquor Triple Gold

Average bottle price: $20.00 to $50.00

Distribution: CA, CT, DC, DE, FL, GA, ID, IL, MD, NJ, NV, NY, OR, TN, TX, WA, WY
All products online via Binnys.com

Interesting facts:
- OOLA is also the name of Kirby's German Shepherd.
- OOLA Distillery is located in Seattle's dense, urban Capitol Hill neighborhood.

Photos by: David Clugston

Pacific Distillery LLC

18808 142nd Avenue NE, #4B
Woodinville, WA 98072
425-350-9061

Owners / Operators:
Marc Bernhard, Owner / Master Distiller

Email: mbernhard@pacificdistillery.com
Website: www.pacificdistillery.com
Facebook: Pacific Distillery
Twitter: @PacificDistill

Type: Micro Distillery. Opened in 2008.

Hours of operation: Not provided

Tours: Available

Types of spirits produced: Absinthe, gin

Names of spirits:
- Voyager Single Batch Distilled Gin
- Pacifique Absinthe Verte

Best known for / most popular: Pacifique Absinthe

Average bottle price: $30.00 to $63.00

Distribution:
CA, CT, DC, FL, GA, ID, KY, LA, OR, NJ, NY, TX, WA

Interesting facts: Pacific Distillery products are distilled in a genuine direct-fired 500 liter copper alambic-pot still using all-organic botanicals.

Parliament Distillery

13708 24th Street, Ste. 103
Sumner, WA 98390
253-447-8044

Owners / Operators:
Jarrett Tomal, Owner / Distiller

Email: ghostowlsales@gmail.com
Website: www.ghostowlwhisky.com
Facebook: Parliament Distillery
Twitter: @ghostowlwhisky

Type: Micro Distillery. Opened in 2012.

Hours of operation:
Thursday through Saturday, noon to 6:30 p.m.

Tours: Available by appointment

Types of spirits produced: Whisky, moonshine

Names of spirits:
- Ghost Owl Whisky
- Rack House Caramel Apple
- Rack House Apple Pie w/ Graham Cracker Crust
- Rack House Yucca

Best known for / most popular: Whisky

Average bottle price: $29.99 to $39.99

Distribution: AK, ID, OR, WA

Interesting facts: Not provided

Port Steilacoom Distillery

1601 Lafayette Street
Steilacoom, WA 98388
253-212-0090

Owners / Operators:
Kevin Laughlin Stewart, Co-owner
Jennifer Laughlin Stewart, Co-owner

Email: portsteilacoomdistillery@yahoo.com
Website: www.portsteilacoomdistillery.com
Facebook: Port Steilacoom Distillery

Type: Micro Distillery. Opened in 2012.

Hours of operation:
Wednesday through Sunday, 3:30 p.m. to 6:30 p.m.

Tours: Available

Types of spirits produced: Gin, vodka

Names of spirits:
- Homeport Craft Distilled Gin
- Chambers Bay Craft Distilled Vodka

Best known for / most popular: Not provided

Average bottle price: $22.55

Distribution: Not provided

Interesting facts:
- All products are made from local blackberry honey.
- Kevin learned to distill as a teenager spending summers with his moonshining grandfather who is now 100 years old.

Project V Distillery and Sausage Company

19495 144th Avenue NE
Woodinville, WA 98072
425-398-1738

Owners / Operators:
Mo Heck, President / Founder / Distiller

Email: projectvdistillery@gmail.com
Website: www.projectvdistillery.com
Facebook: Project V Distillery & Sausage Co.
Twitter: @ProjectVDistill
Yelp: Project V Distillery & Sausage Company
Flickr: ProjectVDistillery's protostream

Type: Micro Distillery. Opened in 2010.

Hours of operation: Not provided

Tours: Available Saturday and Sunday, noon to 5 p.m. or by appointment

Types of spirits produced: Vodka, gin, whiskey

Names of spirits:
- Single Silo Vodka
- Single Silo Distiller's Cut Vodka
- Single Silo Ultra Filtered Vodka
- Single Silo Chai Infused Vodka
- Double Silo (160 Proof)
- Douglas County Gin
- Mo's Wheat Whiskey

Best known for / most popular:
Chai Vodka Moscow Mule

Average bottle price: $30.00

Distribution: WA

Interesting facts: Not provided

Image by: Amy Louise Herndon

Rain City Spirits

4660 E. Marginal Way
South Seattle, WA 98134
206-464-7246

Owners / Operators:
Cory Duffy, Distiller / Managing Partner
Joe Matthys, VP Marketing / Sales / Partner

Email: cory@raincityvodka.com, joe@raincityvodka.com
Website: www.raincityvodka.com, www.raincitydistillery.com
Facebook: Rain City Spirits
Twitter: @RainCitySpirits

Type: Micro Distillery. Opened in 2011.

Hours of operation: Not open to the public

Tours: Available by appointment

Types of spirits produced: Vodka

Names of spirits:
- Rain Ciy Vodka
- Drip Coffee Liqueur

Best known for / most popular: Rain City Vodka

Average bottle price: $22.95

Distribution: WA

Interesting facts: Not provided

RiverSands Distillery

19 W. Canal Drive
Kennewick WA 99336
855-400-1974

Owners / Operators:
Paul Schiro, President
Russ Horn, GM / Distiller
Ida Horn, Finance Director

Email: support@riversandsdistillery.com
Website: www.riversandsdistillery.com
Facebook: Riversands Distillery

Type: Craft Distillery. Opened in November 2013.

Tasting room hours:
Tuesday through Friday, 11 a.m. to 6 p.m.
Saturday, 11 a.m. to 4 p.m.

Tours: Available

Types of spirits produced: Gin, vodka, whiskey, brandy

Names of spirits:
- Kennewick Fine Gin
- Kennewick Vodka

Best known for / most popular: Gin and vodka

Average bottle price: $32.00

Distribution:
On-site retail, Mid-Columbia Wine and Spirits

Interesting facts: Not provided

San Juan Island Distillery

12 Anderson Lane
Friday Harbor, WA 98250
360-378-2606

Owners / Operators:
Suzy Pingree, President
Hawk Pingree, Vice President
Rich Anderson, Treasurer

Email: suzy@sanjuanislanddistillery.com
Website: www.sanjuanislanddistillery.com
Facebook: San Juan Island Distillery
Twitter: @sjidistillery
Foursquare: San Juan Island Distillery

Type: Micro Distillery. Opened in 2011.

Hours of operation: Afternoons, Thursday through Sunday

Tours: Available

Types of spirits produced: Gin, brandy, liqueur

Names of spirits:
- Spy Hop Gin
- Apple Eau de vie
- Lavender and Wild Rose Liqueur
- Blackberry Brandy
- Thimbleberry Brandy
- Winterberry Brandy
- Madrone Brandy
- Red Sky at Night Cocktail
- Pommeau

Best known for / most popular: Spy Hop Gin

Average bottle price: $25.00 to $80.00

Distribution: WA

Interesting facts: Not provided

Sandstone Distillery LLC

840 Wright Road SE
Tenino, WA 98589
360-239-7272

Owners / Operators:
John Bourdon, Distiller / Sales
Jenni Bourdon, Office Manager
Justin Bourdon, Distiller

Email: john@spiritsofwashington.com
Website: TBA
Facebook: Sandstone Distillery

Type: Craft Distillery. Opening in Summer 2014.

Hours of operation: TBD

Tours: TBD

Types of spirits produced: Vodka, white whiskey, gin

Names of spirits:
- Sandstone Distillery Stone Carver Vodka
- Sandstone Distillery White Whiskey
- Sandstone Distillery Gin
- Sandstone Distillery Black Gin

Best known for / most popular: TBD

Average bottle price: $32.00

Distribution: WA

Interesting facts: Not provided

Seattle Distilling Company

19429 Vashon Highway SW
Vashon, WA 98070
206-463-0830

Owners / Operators:
Ishan D. Dillon, President
John P. (Paco) Joyce III, VP Head Distiller
David E. Waterworth, VP Marketing

Email: info@seattledistillingcompany.com
Website: www.seattledistillingcompany.com
Facebook: Seattle Distilling Company
Twitter: @SeattleDistills
Instagram: @seattledistillingcompany
Tumblr: seattledistillingcompany
Pinterest: seattledistills

Type: Micro Distillery. Opened in 2011.

Tasting room hours:
Thursday through Sunday, noon to 5 p.m. and by appointment
The tasting room is available for private events.

Tours: Available by appointment

Types of spirits produced:
Vodka, gin, whiskey, liqueur

Names of spirits:
- The Rocket Vodka
- The Alpinist Gin
- The Vashon Idle Hour Whiskey
- The Luana Beach Coffee Liqueur

Best known for / most popular: Rocket Vodka

Average bottle price: $25.00 to $30.00

Distribution: Vehr's, Marine View Beverage

Interesting facts:
- Custom built in-house still and columns
- Craft distilling workshop offered for those over 21
- 100% grain to bottle distillery, making all their spirits from scratch

Sidetrack Distillery

27010 78th Avenue S.
Kent, WA 98032
206-963-5079

Owners / Operators:
Larry Person, Partner
Linda Person, Partner
David O'Neal, Partner

Email: info@sidetrackdistillery.com
Website: www.sidetrackdistillery.com
Facebook: Sidetrack Distillery
Pinterest: Sidetrack Distillery

Type: Micro Distillery. Opened in 2011.

Hours of operation:
Saturdays, 11 a.m. to 5 p.m.
All other days by appointment

Tours: Available by appointment

Types of spirits produced:
Brandy, liqueurs, specialty spirits, eaux de vie

Names of spirits:
- Sidetrack Distillery Strawberry Liqueur
- Sidetrack Distillery Blueberry Liqueur
- Sidetrack Distillery Blackberry Liqueur
- Sidetrack Distillery Raspberry Liqueur
- Sidetrack Distillery Cassis
- Sidetrack Distillery Nocino
- Sidetrack Distillery BETE (a beet spirit)
- Sidetrack Distillery Strawberry Brandy
- Sidetrack Distillery Plum Brandy

Best known for / most popular: Raspberry Liqueur

Average bottle price: $24.95 to $49.95

Distribution: MA, WA

Awards and Recognitions:
Raspberry Liqueur
- Gold Medal, Best of Category
  2012 ADI Competition

Skip Rock Distillers

104 Avenue C
Snohomish, WA 98290
360-862-0272

Owners / Operators:
Ryan Hembree, Co-owner
Julie Hembree, Co-owner

Email: info@skiprockdistllers.com
Website: www.skiprockdistillers.com
Facebook: Skip Rock Distillers
Twitter: @SkipRockDistill

Type: Micro Distillery. Opened in 2009.

Hours of operation:
Monday through Friday, noon to 5 p.m.
Saturday, 11 a.m. to 5 p.m.

Tours: Available

Types of spirits produced:
Vodka, whiskey, liqueurs, gin

Names of spirits:
- Skip Rock Potato Vodka
- Headwaters White Whiskey
- Spiced Apple Liqueur
- Blackberry Liqueur
- Raspberry Liqueur
- Nocino, Walnut Liqueur
- Rye Whiskey
- Badger Pocket Black Peppercorn Vodka

Best known for / most popular:
Rye Whiskey, Skip Rock Potato Vodka, Spiced Apple Liqueur

Average bottle price: Vary

Distribution: CA, ID, LA, OR, WA

Interesting facts:
Ryan made beer, wine and cider at home before being interested in spirits. He has two year certificate in winemaking from Washington State University.

Sodo Spirits Distillery

2228 Occidental Ave. S.
Seattle, WA 98134
206-399-2645

Owners / Operators:
Not provided

Email: info@sodospirits.com
Website: www.sodospirits.com
Facebook: Sodo Spirits Distillery

Type: Micro Distillery. Opened in 2009.

Hours of operation: Not provided

Tours: Not provided

Types of spirits produced: Hankaku Shochu

Names of spirits:
- Evenstar
- Evenstar Mint
- Evenstar Ginger
- Evenstar Chiles

Best known for / most popular: Evenstar

Average bottle price: Not provided

Distribution: WA

Interesting facts: America's only craft shochu distillery.

Soft Tail Spirits

12280 NE Woodinville Drive, Ste. C
Woodinville, WA 98072

Second location:
14356 Woodinville Redmond Road
Redmond, WA 98052

425-770-1154, 425-770-1158

Owners / Operators:
Dennis Robertson, Owner
Tammy Robertson, Owner
Cameron Robertson, Distiller
Matthew Farmer, Distiller

Email: Dennis Robertson, dennis@softtailspirits.com
            Tammy Robertson, tammy@softtailspirits.com
            Matthew Farmer, matthew@softtailspirits.com
Website: www.softtailspirits.com
Facebook: Soft Tail Spirits
Twitter: @softtailspirits

Type: Micro Distillery.
Woodinville Distillery opened in 2008.
Redmond Distillery opened in 2011.

Hours of operation:
Woodinville, Monday through Saturday, noon to 5 p.m.
Redmond, Friday through Sunday, noon to 5 p.m.

Tours: Available

Types of spirits produced: Grappa, vodka

Names of spirits:
- Soft Tail Vodka
- Soft Tail Blanco Grappa
- Giallo Grappa
- Sangiovese Grappa
- Woodstock Reserve
  A 24- month aged Grappa blend of Merlot, Cab & Syrah

Best known for / most popular: Soft Tail Martini

Average bottle price: $32.00 to $38.00

Distribution: OR, WA

Interesting facts: Soft Tail Vodka is gluten free.

Sound Spirits

1630 15th Avenue West
Seattle, WA 98119
206-651-5166

Owners / Operators:
Steven Stone, Founder / Head Distiller

Email: info@drinksoundspirits.com
Website: www.drinksoundspirits.com
Facebook: Sound Spirits
Twitter: @Sound_Spirits

Type: Micro Distillery. Opened in 2010.

Hours of operation: Daily

Tours: Available

Types of spirits produced: Whiskey, vodka, gin, old tom gin, aquavit, liqueurs

Names of spirits:
- Ebb+Flow Gin
- Ebb+Flow Vodka
- Sound Spirits – Old Tom Gin
- Sound Spirits – Aquavit
- Depth Liqueurs - Cacao, Menthe, Herbal

Best known for / most popular: Ebb+Flow Gin

Average bottle price: $33.00

Distribution: ID, IL, MA, MN, OR, WA

Interesting facts:
Sound Spirits is Seattle's first craft distillery since Prohibition.

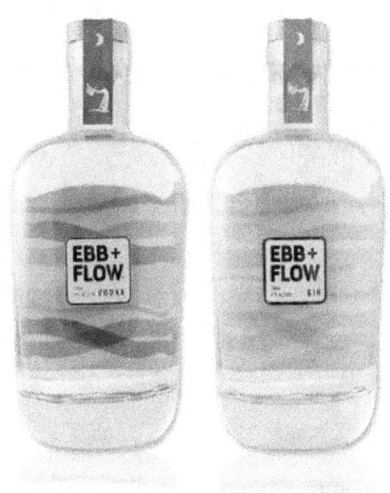

Sun Liquor Distillery

514 E. Pike Street
Seattle, WA 98122
206-720-1600

Owners / Operators:
Michael Klebeck, Founder / President
Erik Chapman, Manager / Head Distiller

Email: sunliquorseattle@gmail.com
  michael@sunliquor.com
Website: www.sunliquor.com
Facebook: Sun Liquor
Twitter: @SunLiquor
Tumblr: Sun Liquor

Type: Micro Distillery. Opened in 2011.

Hours of operation: Daily, 11 a.m. to 2 a.m.

Tours: Available by appointment

Types of spirits produced:
Gin, vodka, bitters, seasonal specialty products

Names of spirits:
- Gun Club Gin
- Hedge Trimmer Gin
- Sun Liquor Unxld Vodka
- Orange Bitters

Best known for / most popular: Gun Club 100 Proof Gin

Average bottle price: Not provided

Distribution: OR, WA

Interesting facts: The distillery is also a cocktail lounge.

Tatoosh Craft Distillery

Seattle, WA
206-412-1000

Owners / Operators:
Mark Simon, Co-founder / CEO
Troy Turner, Co-founder / COO
Michael Carrosino, Co-founder / CFO
Joe Eliasen, Co-founder / Head Distiller

Email: info@tatooshdistillery.com
Website: www.tatooshdistillery.com
Facebook: Tatoosh Distillery & Spirits
Twitter: @TatooshSpirits

Type: Micro Distillery. Opened in 2012.

Hours of operation: Not provided

Tours: Not provided

Types of spirits produced: Whiskey, bourbon

Names of spirits:
- Tatoosh Single Malt Whiskey
- Tatoosh Bourbon

Best known for / most popular: Tatoosh Bourbon

Average bottle price: Not provided

Distribution: Not provided

Interesting facts: Not provided

The Ellensburg Distillery

1000 N. Prospect Street
Ellensburg, WA 98926
509-925-1295

Owners / Operators:
Ralph Bullock, Owner

Email: info@WildcatWhite.com
Website: www.wildcatwhite.com
Facebook: The Ellensburg Distillery

Type: Micro Distillery. Opened in 2008.

Hours of operation: By appointment

Tours: Available by appointment

Types of spirits produced: Whisky, gin

Names of spirits:
- Wildcat White Whisky
- Amythyst Gin

Best known for / most popular: Gin and whisky

Average bottle price: $29.95

Distribution: WA

Interesting facts:
- The Ellensburg Distillery is Washington's second licensed distillery.
- It's known for making brandy and whisky.

The Hardware Distillery Co.

24210 N. Highway 101
Hoodsport, WA 98548
206-300-0877

Owners / Operators:
Chuck and Jan Morris, Owners

Email: jan@hardwaredistillery.com
chuck@hardwaredistillery.com
Website: www.thehardwaredistillery.com
Facebook: Hardware Distillery Co.
Twitter: @HDistillery

Hoodsport, Washington

Type: Craft Distillery. Opened in 2013.

Hours of operation:
Summer hours: Thursday through Sunday, 11 a.m. to 6 p.m.
Winter hours: Friday through Saturday, 11 a.m. to 6 p.m.

Tours: Available

Types of spirits produced: Gin, brandy, aquavit, specialty spirit

Names of spirits:
- Aquavit
- R Gin
- Crabby Ginny
- Bee's Knees Fig
- Bee's Knees Raspberry
- Bee's Knees Peachy Keen
- Bee's Knees Plumb
- Bee's Knees Merry Cherry

Best known for / most popular: Bee's Knees and Aquavit

Average bottle price: Not provided

Distribution: WA

Interesting facts:
The Hardware Distillery and tasting room are located in an old hardware store.

Valley Shine Distillery

22648 Chestnut Place
Mount Vernon, WA 98273
360-853-6702

Owners / Operators:
Benjamin Lazowski, Owner / Distiller / Manager
Stacey Lazowski, Owner

Email: info@valleyshinedistillery.com
Website: www.valleyshinedistillery.com
Facebook: Valley Shine Distillery LLC

Type: Craft Distillery. Opened in March 2013.

Hours of operation: Dictated by demand

Tours: Available by appointment

Types of spirits produced:
Vodka, bourbon, gin, limoncello, liqueur

Names of spirits:
- Glacier Vodka
- Benjamin's Bourbon
- Red X Gin
- Limoncello
- Spider Bite Black Licorice Liqueur

Best known for / most popular: Benjamin's Bourbon

Average bottle price: $37.00 to $45.00

Distribution: WA

Interesting facts: Not provided

Walla Walla Distilling Company
Walla Walla Wine & Spirits Inc.

1105 "C" Street (at the Regional Airport)
Walla Walla, WA 99362
509-301-8834

Owners / Operators:
Jeremy W. Barker, Co-founder
Katrina Roberts Barker, Co-founder

Email: info@wallawalladistillingcompany.com
Website: www.wallawalladistillingcompany.com
Facebook: Walla Walla Distilling Company

Type: Craft Distillery. Opened in 2008.

Hours of operation: Open only by appointment

Tours: Not available

Types of spirits produced:
Vodka, gin, whisky, grappa, eau de vie, brandy

Names of spirits:
- Walla Walla Gin
- Walla Walla Vodka
- Walla Walla Whisky
- Walla Walla Light Whisky
- Tytonidae Grappa
- Tytonidae Brandy
- Tytonidae Eau-de-Vie
- Tytonidae Gin

Best known for / most popular: Walla Walla Gin

Average bottle price: Not provided

Distribution: WA

Interesting facts:
Walla Walla Valley's first craft distillery.

Photos by Greg Lehman Photography

Westland Distillery

2931 First Avenue South, Ste. B
Seattle, WA 98134
206-767-7250

Owners / Operators:
Emerson Lamb, Co-founder / President
Matthew Hofmann, Co-founder / Master Distiller

Email: info@westlanddistillery.com
Website: www.westlanddistillery.com
Facebook: Westland Distillery
Twitter: @WestlandWhiskey
Yelp: Westland Distillery
Vimeo: Westland Distillery

Type: Craft Distillery. Opened in October 2013.

Hours of operation: Tuesday through Sunday, 11 a.m. to 6 p.m.

Tours: Wednesday through Saturday; 11 a.m., 2 p.m., 4 p.m., 6 p.m.

Types of spirits produced: American Single Malt Whiskey

Names of spirits:
- American Single Malt Whiskey
- Peated Malt Whiskey

Best known for / most popular:
American Single Malt Whiskey

Average bottle price: $55.00 to $65.00

Distribution: WA

Whidbey Island Distillery

3466 Craw Road
Langley, WA 98260
360-321-4715

Owners / Operators:
Steve Heising, Owner / Operator
Beverly Heising, Owner / Operator
James Heising, Owner / Operator
Kris Heising, Owner / Operator

Email: info@whidbeydistillery.com
Website: www.whidbeydistillery.com
Facebook: Whidbey Island Distillery
Twitter: @whidbeyspirits

Type: Micro Distillery. Opened in 2010.

Hours of operation: Saturday and Sunday, 11 a.m. to 5 p.m. or by appointment

Tours: Available

Types of spirits produced:
Neutral grapes spirits, whiskey, liqueur

Names of spirits:
- Whidbey Island Distillery Loganberry Liqueur
- Whidbey Island Distillery Raspberry Liqueur
- Whidbey Island Distillery Blackberry Liqueur
- Whidbey Island Distillery Whiskey

Best known for / most popular:
Whidbey Island Distillery Loganberry Liqueur

Average bottle price: $32.80

Distribution: WA

Awards and recognitions: Loganberry Liqueur has been rated a 94, exceptional rating, and Gold Medal with the Beverage Testing Institute.

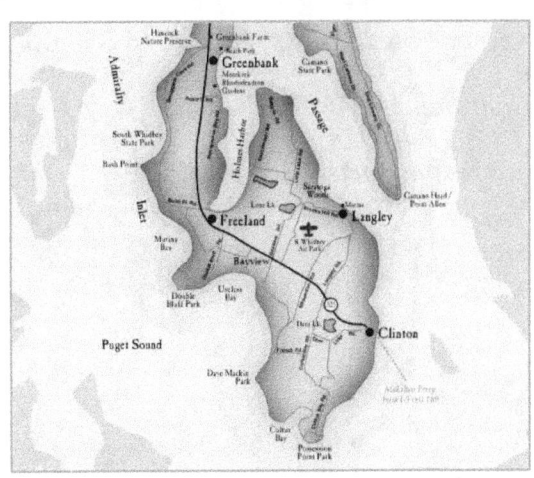

Wishkah River Distillery

2210 Port Industrial Road, Ste. A
Aberdeen, WA 98520
360-612-4756

Owners / Operators:
Josh Mayr, Co-owner / Lead Distiller
Patrick O'Donnell, Co-owner
Chris Olsen, Co-owner
Paul Stutzenburg, Co-owner

Email: josh@wishkahriver.com
tours@wishkahriver.com
Website: www.wishkahriver.com
Facebook: Wishkah River Distillery
Twitter: @WRDistillery

Type: Micro Distillery. Opened in 2011.

Hours of operation: Tuesday through Saturday, 12:30 p.m. to 5:30 p.m.

Tours: Available

Types of spirits produced:
Vodka, un-aged whiskey, aged whiskey, gin

Names of spirits:
- Wishkah River Distillery Vodka Distilled from Grains
- Wishkah River Distillery Vodka Distilled from Honey
- Thirteen Corners Virgin Cask American Malt Whiskey
- Bulfinch 83 Redistilled Gin

Best known for / most popular:
Wishkah River Distillery Vodka Distilled from Honey

Average bottle price: $20.00 to $50.00

Distribution: OR, WA

Interesting facts: Not provided

Woodinville Whiskey Co.

14508 Woodinville Redmond Road NE
Woodinville, WA 98052
425-486-1199

Owners / Operators:
Orlin Sorensen, Owner / Operator
Brett Carlile, Owner / Operator

Email: Orlin Sorensen, orlin@woodinvillewhiskeyco.com
Brett Carlile, brett@woodinvillewhiskeyco.com
Website: www.woodinvillewhiskeyco.com
Facebook: Woodinville Whiskey Co.

Type: Micro Distillery. Opened in 2010.

Hours of operation:
Monday through Sunday, 5 a.m. to 6 p.m.
Tasting room: Daily, noon to 5 p.m.

Tours: Daily

Types of spirits produced:
American whiskey , bourbon, rye whiskey

Names of spirits:
- The Microbarreled™ Collection - Bourbon and Rye Whiskey
- Age Your Own™ Whiskey Kit

Best known for / most popular:
The Microbarreled™ Collection

Average bottle price: $29.95 to $39.95

Distribution: WA

Interesting facts:
- Produced the first rye whiskey in WA State since Prohibition.
- Mentored by David Pickerell, former Master Distiller at Maker's Mark.

Bloomery Plantation Distillery

16357 Charles Town Road
Charles Town, WV 25414
304-725-3036

Owners / Operators:
Tom Kiefer, CEO / CFO / Owner
Linda Losey, COO / CCO / Owner
Rob Losey, Sales and Distribution

Email: LLosey@aol.com
Website: www.bloomerysweetshine.com
Facebook: Bloomery Plantation Distillery

Type: Micro Distillery. Opened in 2011.

Hours of operation:
Fridays and Saturday, 11 a.m. to 8 p.m.

Tours: Available Friday and Saturday

Types of spirits produced: Cordials

Names of spirits:
- Limoncello
- Raspberry Lemon
- Cremma Lemma
- Hard Lemonade
- Chocolate Raspberry
- Peach
- Ginger
- Pumpkin Spice
- Black Walnut

Best known for / most popular:
Raspberry Limoncello

Average bottle price: $20.00 to $30.00

Distribution: DC, TN, VA, WV

Interesting facts:
- The iron ore from the original Bloomery was used to make the ship carrying the Lewis and Clark Expedition in the early 1800s.
- The current distillery is housed in an original 1840s log cabin slave quarters that was on the plantation.
- In the mid-1800s, the historic site housed six stills.
- The tiny hamlet of Bloomery held the honor of being the largest bootlegging operation in WV. More illegal 'shine came through this area than in any other place in the state.

Forks of Cheat Distillery

2811 Stewartstown Road
Morgantown, WV 26508
304-598-2019

Owners / Operators:
Jerry Deal, Co-owner
Eric Deal, Co-owner / Distiller

Facebook: Forks of Cheat Distillery

Type: Micro Distillery. Opened in July 2006.

Hours of operation:
Monday through Saturday, 10 a.m. to 5 p.m.
Closed Sunday

Tours: Available daily.

Types of spirits produced:
Apple jack, rum, moonshine vodka, grappa, brandy

Names of spirits:
- Apple Jack
- Grappa
- Ridge Runner Rum (light and dark)
- Apple Pie Moonshine
- Seneca Brandy

Best known for / most popular: Apple Pie Moonshine

Average bottle price: $25.00

Distribution: On-site retail, WV

Interesting facts: Not provided

Pinchgut Hollow Distillery

1602 Tulip Lane
Fairmont, WV 26554
304-366-9463

Owners / Operators:
Mikey Heston, Owner

Email: info@hestonfarm.com
Website: www.hestonfarm.com
Facebook: Heston Farm
Twitter: @hestonfarm

Type: Craft Distillery. Opened in 2011.

Hours of operation:
Monday through Saturday, 9 a.m. to 9 p.m.
Sunday, 11 a.m. to 5 p.m.

Tours: Available

Types of spirits produced: Moonshine

Names of spirits:
- Pinchgut Hollow Distillery Buckwheat Moon
- Pinchgut Hollow Distillery Corn Shine
- Pinchgut Hollow Distillery Honey Peach Moon
- Pinchgut Hollow Distillery Apple Pie Shine

Best known for / most popular: Pinchgut Hollow Corn Shine

Average bottle price: Not provided

Distribution: Not provided

Interesting facts: Not provided

Smooth Ambler Spirits Company

745 Industrial Park Road
Maxwelton, WV 24957
304-497-3123

Owners / Operators:
John Little, Owner
TAG Galyean, Greg Parseghian, Owners
John Foster, Director of Sales & Marketing

Email: sales@smoothambler.com
Websites: www.smoothambler.com
Facebook: Smooth Ambler Spirits
Twitter: @SmoothAmbler

Type: Micro Distillery. Opened in 2010.

Hours of operation:
Monday through Friday, 10 a.m. to 6 p.m.;
Saturday, 11 a.m. to 3 p.m.

Tours: Friday, 2 p.m., 4 p.m.; Saturday, noon, 2 p.m.

Types of spirits produced: Vodka, gin, bourbon, rye

Names of spirits:
- Smooth Ambler Old Scout
- Smooth Ambler Greenbrier Gin
- Smooth Ambler Whitewater Vodka
- Smooth Ambler Yearling Bourbon
- Smooth Ambler Barrel Aged Gin
- Smooth Ambler Old Scout Straight Rye
- Smooth Ambler Old Scout Straight Bourbon Whiskey

Best known for / most popular: Smooth Ambler Old Scout

Average bottle price: $28.00 to $34.00

Distribution: AZ, CA, CO, CT, DC, DE, FL, IL, IN, KY, LA, MD, NC, NJ, NV, NY, OH, PA, RI, TN, VA, WA, WI, WV

WV Distilling Co. LLC

1380 Fenwick Avenue
Morgantown, WV 26505
304-599-0960

Owners / Operators:
Payton Fireman, Owner

Email: pfireman@frontier.com
Website: www.mountainmoonshine.com
Twitter: @wvdistilling

Type: Micro Distillery. Opened in 1999.

Hours of operation: Not provided

Tours: Not available

Types of spirits produced: Corn whiskey

Names of spirits:
- Mountain Moonshine Spirit Whiskey
- Mountain Moonshine Old Oak Recipe

Best known for / most popular: Mountain Moonshine Spirit Whiskey

Average bottle price: $15.00

Distribution: Not provided

Interesting facts: First legal distilled spirits company in WV since Prohibition.

45th Parallel Distillery

1570 Madison Avenue
New Richmond, WI 54017
715-246-0565

Owners / Operators:
Paul Werni Jr., Owner / Distiller
Scott Davis, Distiller
Tom Gunn, Distiller
Shafer Hartman, Sales Manager

Email: paul@45thparalleldistillery.com
   shafer@45thparalleldistillery.com
Website: www.45thparalleldistillery.com
Facebook: 45th Parallel Distillery
Twitter: @45th_Distillery

Type: Micro Distillery. Opened in 2007.

Hours of operation:
Tuesday through Friday, 9 a.m. to 7 p.m.
Saturday, noon to 6 p.m.

Tours:
Fridays and Saturdays by appointment
Exceptions are made by request

Types of spirits produced:
Grain based whiskies, vodka, gin, aquavit, cellos

Names of spirits:
- 45th Parallel Vodka
- Border Bourbon
- New Richmond Rye
- Midwest Vodka
- Midwest Gin
- Madison Avenue Limoncello
- Madison Avenue Orangecello

Contract Labels
- Referent Horseradish vodka
- Gamle Ode Dill Aquavit
- Gamle Ode Holiday Aquavit

Best known for / most popular:
45th Parallel Vodka, Border Bourbon,
New Richmond Rye

Average bottle price: $14.00 to $45.00

Distribution: GA, IL, MN, OR, WI

Interesting facts:
45th parallel is also the distillery's geographic location.

AEppelTreow Winery & Distillery

1072 288th Avenue
Burlington, WI 53105
262-878-5345

Owners / Operators:
Charles and Milissa McGonegal, Owners

Email: cider@appletrue.com
cpm@appletrue.com
Website: www.appletrue.com
Facebook: AEppelTreow Winery Artisan Ciders

Type: Winery / Micro Distillery. Opened in 2009.

Hours of operation:
Open seasonally, May through December. Visit website for details.

Tours: Available

Types of spirits produced: Apple brandy, hard cider

Names of spirits:
- AEppelTreow WI Apple Brandy
- Brown Dog Whiskey

Best known for / most popular:
Sparkling cider

Average bottle price: $20.00 to $30.00

Distribution: WI

Interesting facts:
AEppelTreow (pronounced Apple True) Winery & Distillery specializes in Wisconsin grown and produced artisan hard cider, brandy and specialty spirits to make craft beverages from heirloom apples.

Death's Door Spirits

2220 Eagle Drive
Middleton, WI 53562
608-831-1083

Owners / Operators:
Brian Ellison, President / Founder
John Jeffery, Distiller
John Kinder, National Brand Manager / Contract Sales

Email: Brian Ellison, brian@deathsdoorspirits.com
John Jeffery, johnny@deathsdoorspirits.com
John Kinder, john@deathsdoorspirits.com
Website: www.deathsdoorspirits.com
Facebook: Death's Door Spirits
Twitter: @deathsdoor

Type: Micro Distillery. Opened in 2007.

Hours of operation: Daily, 9 a.m. to 5 p.m.

Tours: Friday, 6 p.m.; Saturday, noon, 2 p.m.

Types of spirits produced: Gin, vodka, white whisky

Names of spirits:
- Death's Door Gin
- Death's Door Vodka
- Death's Door White Whisky

Best known for / most popular: Death's Door Gin

Average bottle price: $29.99 to $34.99

Distribution: 40 U.S. states; 9 countries

Interesting facts:
Death's Door takes its name from the body of water between Door County peninsula and Washington Island. Potowatami and Winnebego tribesmen originally named the waterway, while the French called it Port de Morts (Death's Door) when trading in the area to ward off other traders.

Door County Distillery

5806 Highway 42
Carlsville, WI 54235
920-746-8463

Owners / Operators:
Door County Distillery

Email: info@doorcountydistillery.com
Website: www.doorcountydistillery.com
Facebook: Door County Distillery
Twitter: @DoorDistillery

Type: Micro Distillery. Opened in 2011.

Hours of operation:
April to October, Daily 10 a.m. to 6 p.m.
Off-Season, Friday through Saturday vary

Tours: Not available

Types of spirits produced:
Brandy, bitters, gin, vodka, whiskey

Names of spirits:
- Door County Cherry Infused Vodka
- Door County Gin
- Door County Vodka
- Luminous Vodka
- Apple Brandy
- Cherry Brandy
- Cherry Infused Bitters
- Brandy – Aged in Oak Casks
- Whiskey

Best known for / most popular:
Luminous Vodka and Door County Gin

Average bottle price: $19.99 to $29.99

Distribution: IL, WI

Interesting facts: Not provided

Great Lakes Distillery LLC

616 W. Virginia Street
Milwaukee, WI 53204
414-431-8683

Owners / Operators:
Guy Rehorst, Owner

Email: info@greatlakesdistillery.com
Website: www.GreatLakesDistillery.com
Facebook: Great Lakes Distillery
Twitter: @GLDistillery
Foursquare: Great Lakes Distillery
Yelp: Great Lakes Distillery
Pinterest: Great Lakes Distillery
Google +: Great Lakes Distillery LLC
Instagram: #GLDistillery

Type: Micro Distillery. Opened in 2004.

Hours of operation: Sunday through Thursday, 11 a.m. to 8 p.m.
Friday and Saturday, 11 a.m. to 10 p.m.

Tours: Sunday through Thursday, 1 p.m., 3 p.m. and 5 p.m.
Friday, 1 p.m., 3 p.m., 5 p.m., 6 p.m.; Saturday, 1 p.m., 2 p.m., 3 p.m., 4 p.m.

Types of spirits produced:
Vodka, flavored vodka, gin, rum, brandy, absinthe, whiskey

Names of spirits:
- Rehorst Premium Milwaukee Vodka
- Rehorst Citrus Honey Flavored Vodka
- Rehorst Premium Milwaukee Gin
- Roaring Dan's Rum
- Kinnickinnic Whiskey
- Great Lakes Seasonal Pumpkin Spirit
- Amerique 1912 Absinthe Verte
- Amerique 1912 Absinthe Rouge
- Great Lakes Artisan Series Grappa
- Great Lakes Artisan Series Pear Eau-de-Vie
- Great Lakes Artisan Series Kirschwasser
- Various extremely small batch whiskeys

Best known for / most popular:
Rehorst Premium Milwaukee Vodka

Average bottle price: $33.00

Distribution: 23 states

Interesting facts:
Great Lakes Distillery was the first legal distillery in WI since Prohibition.

Hendricks Family Distillery LLC

3570 N. County Road K
Omro, WI 54963
920-685-6468

Owners / Operators:
James and Peggy Hendricks, Owners
Karl J. Hendricks, Distiller
Zachary Hendricks, Research and Development

Email: info@purclassvodka.com
Website: www.purclassvodka.com
Facebook: Pür Class Vodka
Twitter: @PurClassVodka

Type: Craft Distillery. Opened in April 2013.

Hours of operation: Not provided

Tours: Not available

Types of spirits produced: Vodka

Names of spirits:
- Pür Class Vodka

Best known for / most popular: Pür Class Vodka

Average bottle price: $25.00

Distribution:
Lee Beverage of Wisconsin, Johnson Brothers, and Phillips Distributing

Interesting facts: Family owned and operated.

Lo Artisan Distillery LLC

1607 South Stevenson Pier Road
Sturgeon Bay, WI 54235
337-660-1600

Owners / Operators:
Po Lo, Owner
Chong Va Lo, Operations Supervisor

Email: poclo@lo-artisandistillery.com
Website: www.lo-artisandistillery.com
Facebook: Yerlo Rice Spirits

Type: Micro Distillery. Opened in 2011.

Hours of operation: Not provided

Tours: Available by appointment

Types of spirits produced: Hmong Rice Spirits & Whiskey

Names of spirits:
- Yerlo (120 Proof)
- Yerlo Reserve (130 Proof)
- Yerlo X Rice Whiskey (90 Proof)
- Yerlo Silver (86 Proof)

Best known for / most popular: Hmong Rice Spirits

Average bottle price: $28.99 to $160.00

Distribution:
CA, CT, KS, LA, MA, MN, MO, MT, RI, SC, WI

Interesting facts:
- Lo Artisan Distillery uses all-natural rice grains; no additives or neutral spirits are added.
- Gluten free

Minhas Micro Distillery

1404 13th Street
Monroe, WI 53566
608-328-5550

Owners / Operators:
Gary Olson, Manager
Amos Gutknecht, MMD Coordinator
Michael Connolly, Head Distiller
Lance Ray, Tour / Tasting Room Manager

Email: tours@minhasdistillery.com
Website: www.minhasdistillery.com
Facebook: Minhas Micro Distillery
Twitter: @MinhasDistiller

Type: Micro Distillery. Opened in 2011.

Hours of operation:
Monday through Friday, 8 a.m. to 5 p.m.
Saturday and Sunday, 11 a.m. to 5 p.m.

Tours: Available. Check social media sites for times.

Types of spirits produced:
Vodka, whisky, rum, Irish Cream, Maya Horchata, tequila

Names of spirits:
Canada
Vodka (Aristo, Blackstone, Blackrock, Sailboat, Stars)
Rum (Aristo, Corsairs, Gold Coast, Golden Sands, Sailboat, Sam Lords, Stars)
Tequila (Alamo, Stars)
Whisky (Aristo, Chinook, Punjabi Club, Royal Crest, Sailboat, Stars, The Rockies)

U.S.
Chinook (Vodka, Whisky, Gold/Spiced/White Rum, Gold/Silver Tequila)
Wisconsin Club USA (Vodka, Whisky, Gold/Spiced/White Rum, Gold/Silver Tequila, (Country Cream)
Gold Coast XO Rum
Maya Horchata Cream Liqueur

Best known for / most popular: Maya Horchata

Average bottle price: $5.99 to $19.99

Distribution: IL, WI; Canada, AB, BC, ON, SK

Interesting facts:
Home to "GODSTILLA", a 1,000 gallon tank still located right in the tasting room.

Old Sugar Distillery

931 E. Main Street, Ste. 8
Madison, WI 53703
608-260-0812

Owners / Operators:
Nathan Greenawalt, Owner / Distiller

Email: madisondistillery@gmail.com
Website: www.madisondistillery.com
Facebook: Old Sugar Distillery

Type: Micro Distillery. Opened in 2010.

Hours of operation:
Thursday and Friday, 4 p.m. to 10 p.m.
Saturday, noon to 10 p.m.

Tours: Available

Types of spirits produced:
Sorghum whiskey, rum, honey liqueur, ouzo, and seasonal grappa and brandy

Names of spirits:
- Cane and Abe Small-Barrel Rum
- Old Sugar Factory Honey Liqueur
- Americanaki Ouzo
- Queen Jennie Sorghum Whiskey
- Brandy Station
  (brandy distilled from Wisconsin grapes)

Best known for / most popular: Rum

Average bottle price: $30.00 to $35.00

Distribution: DC, DE, FL, GA, IL, MD, MI, TN, WA, WI, WV

Interesting facts:
One of the only American ouzo producers.

The North Woods Distillery LLC

135 W. Main Street
Coleman, WI 54112
920-819-6083

Owners / Operators:
Curt A. Naegeli, Owner

Email: curt@northwoodsdistillery.com
Website: www.northwoodsdistillery.com
Facebook: The North Woods Distillery LLC

Type: Micro Distillery. Opened in 2011.

Hours of operation: Available by appointment

Tours: Available by appointment

Types of spirits produced: Rum

Names of spirits:
- Heath Rum
- Chocolat Mint Rum

Best known for / most popular: Heath Rum

Average bottle price: $21.00

Distribution: WI

Interesting facts:
"We operate under the assumption that today's consumer is health conscious and wants clean tasting spirits with little in the way of off flavors or burn.

Congeners in alcohol produce character and a sad feeling in the morning. Ethanol is what makes us happy, and by refining their rum through two careful distillations, little is left in the way of congeners. We take great strides to produce our rums' character through flavoring.

Heath Rum tastes like candy; it's sweet, smooth, and has a toffee flavor. It's good straight up or on the rocks, but also mixes well. The North Woods Distillery grows chocolat mint, a variety of peppermint, which is then distilled to make the flavoring. Mint is highlighted with a subtle chocolate flavor. Chocolat Mint Rum is great on the rocks and mixes well." - Curt Naegeli

Rum made by The North Woods Distillery is gluten free.

White Wolf Distillery

23396 Thompson Road
Shell Lake, WI 54871
715-468-4224

Owners / Operators:
Laura and Patrick Walters, Alexia and Jason Gannon, Owners
Ryan and Armani Walters and James Walters, Owners

Email: info@whitewolfdistillery.com
Website: www.whitewolfdistillery.com
Facebook: White Wolf Distillery

Type: Winery / Micro Distillery. Opened in 2011.

Hours of operation:
May 1 to October 31
Thursday through Saturday, noon to 9 p.m.; Sunday, noon to 6 p.m.

November 1 to April 30
Saturday and Sunday, noon to 4 p.m.

Tours: Not available

Types of spirits produced: Brandy, neutral spirit, whisky

Names of spirits:
- White Wolf Plum Brandy
- White Wolf Apple Brandy
- White Wolf Grape Brandy
- White Wolf Raspberry Brandy
- White Wolf Blackberry Brandy
- White Wolf Apple Neutral Spirit
- White Wolf Grape Neutral Spirit
- White Wolf Rye Whisky

Best known for / most popular: White Wolf Blackberry Brandy

Average bottle price: $35.00 to $70.00

Distribution: WI

Interesting facts:
- White Wolf Distillery is 100% certified organic and a travel green Wisconsin business.
- White Wolf Distillery generates 100% of their electricity needs using solar and wind energy.

Yahara Bay Distillers

3118 Kingsley Way
Madison, WI 53713
608-275-1050

Owners / Operators:
Nick Quint and Catherine Forde Quint, Owners
Lars Forde, Head Distiller
Jill Skowronski, VP of Sales and Marketing

Email: jill@yaharabay.com
Website: www.yaharabay.com
Facebook: Yahara Bay Distillery
Twitter: @SeraphineVodka
YouTube: Yahara Bay Distillery

Type: Micro Distillery. Opened in 2007.

Hours of operation:
Monday through Friday, 9 a.m. to 5 p.m.

Tours: Public house (tours/sampling) every Thursday, 5 p.m. to 10 p.m.. All others by appointment.

Types of spirits produced:
Gin, rum, vodka, whiskey, brandy, liqueur

Names of spirits:
- Yahara Bay Premium Rum
- Mad Bird Rum (aged)
- Yahara Bay Extra Dry Gin
- Yahara Bay Premium Vodka
- Seraphine Chai Tea Vodka
- Yahara Bay Whiskey
- V Bourbon Whiskey
- Lightning Whiskey
- Charred Oak Bourbon Whiskey
- Charred Oak Rye Whiskey
- Yahara Bay Apple Brandy
- Kirschwasser Cherry Brandy
- Yahara Bay Pear Brandy
- Cocoa Liqueur
- Coffee Liqueur
- Lemoncella

Average bottle price: $13.99 to $34.99

Distribution: CA, FL, GA, IA, IL, MD, MI, MN, OK, TX, WI, WY

Interesting facts: First legal distillery in Dane County WI.

Kolts Fine Spirits

Sheridan, WY 82801
307-673-5410

Owners / Operators:
Robert Koltiska, CEO
Jason Koltiska, Head of Distribution and Production
Justin Koltiska, Head of Marketing

Email: info@koltsfinespirits.com
Website: www.koltsfinespirits.com
Facebook: Koltiska Original & KO 90

Type: Micro Distillery. Opened in 2006.

Hours of operation: Not provided

Tours: Not provided

Types of spirits produced: Liqueur

Names of spirits:
- Koltiska 90 Proof Liqueur
- Koltiska Original Liqueur

Best known for / most popular: Not provided

Average bottle price: Not provided

Distribution: ID, MT, NE, WA, WY

Interesting facts: Not provided

Single Track Spirits

63 Sage Creek Road
Cody, WY 82414
307-761-1380

Owners / Operators:
Tom Pettinger, Owner

Email: Not provided
Website: www.singletrackspirits.com
Facebook: Not provided
Twitter: Not provided

Type: Micro Distillery. Opened in 2011.

Hours of operation: Not provided

Tours: Available by appointment

Types of spirits produced: Wheat whiskey

Names of spirits:
- TBA
- TBA

Best known for / most popular: TBA

Average bottle price: TBA

Distribution: Special order

Interesting facts:
The distillery is situated in a 75 year old log cattle barn on a small Wyoming ranch in a rural setting 3 miles east of Cody, WY.

Wyoming Whiskey Distillery

100 South Nelson
Kirby, WY 82430
307-864-2116

Owners / Operators:
Brad Mead, Owner
Kate Mead, Owner
David DeFazio, Owner / COO

Email: info@wyomingwhiskey.com
Website: www.wyomingwhiskey.com
Facebook: Wyoming Whiskey
Twitter: @WyoWhiskey

Type: Micro Distillery. Opened in 2009.

Hours of operation:
Monday, Tuesday, Thursday, Friday 10 a.m. to 4 p.m.

Tours: Available Monday through Saturday, 10 a.m. to 4 p.m.

Types of spirits produced: Bourbon

Names of spirits:
- Wyoming Whiskey

Best known for / most popular: Wyoming Whiskey

Average bottle price: $43.00

Distribution: Currently WY only. Additional select markets in 2014.

Interesting facts: The Meads are fourth generation Wyoming ranchers who run cattle in Kirby and in Jackson. Brad's grandfather, Cliff Hansen, was a US senator and governor. Brad's brother, Matt, is the current governor.

Central City Brewers and Distillers Ltd.

11411 Bridgeview Drive
Surrey, BC V3R 0C2
604-588-2337

Owners / Operators:
Darryll Frost, President
Gary Lohin, Brewmaster
Operations Manager, Tristan Warren
Tim Barnes, VP, Sales & Marketing
Head Distiller, Robert Barrett

Email: robert@centralcitybrewing.com
Website: www.centralcitybrewing.com
Facebook: Central City Brewing
Twitter: @CentralCityBrew
YouTube: CentralCityBrew

Type: Craft Distillery. Opened in August 2013.

Hours of operation: Daily until 9 p.m.

Tours: Saturday and Sunday, 1 p.m., 3 p.m., 5 p.m.

Types of spirits produced:
Gin, vodka, single malt, rye, whiskey

Names of spirits:
- Seraph Gin
- Seraph Vodka

Best known for / most popular: Not provided

Average bottle price: $35.00

Distribution: BC

Interesting facts: Not provided

Deep Cove Brewers and Distillers

170-2270 Dollarton Highway
North Vancouver, BC V7H 1A8
604-770-1136

Owners / Operators:
Shae DeJaray, Founder / Owner
Shawn Bethune, Founder / Owner
Kevin Emms, Brewmaster
Brett Jamieson, Head Distiller
Trish Garratt, Director of Sales and Marketing
Evan Cromshaw, Assistant Brewer and Distiller

Email: info@deepcovecraft.com
Website: www.deepcovecraft.com
Facebook: Deep Cove Brewers + Distillers
Twitter: @DeepcoveCraft
Instagram: DeepCoveCraft
Yelp: Deep Cove Brewers and Distillers
YouTube: Deepcove Brewers and Distillers

Type: Craft Distillery. Opened in August 2013.

Hours of operation:
Monday and Tuesday, 4 p.m. to 8 p.m.
Wednesday through Sunday, noon to 8 p.m.

Tours: Available

Types of spirits produced:
Vodka, gin, brandy, moonshine, eau de vie

Names of spirits:
- Deep Cove Brewers and Distillers Vodka
- Deep Cove Brewers and Distillers Gin

Best known for / most popular: Not provided

Average bottle price: $32.50 to $41.00

Distribution: Local

Interesting facts: Not provided

Island Spirits Distillery

4605 Roburn Road
Hornby Island, BC V0R 1Z0
250-335-0630

Owners / Operators:
Peter Kimmerly, Co-owner
Naz Abudurahman, Co-owner

Email: pckimmer@telus.net
Website: www.islandspirits.ca

Type: Micro Distillery. Opened in 2009.

Hours of operation: Not provided

Tours: Not provided

Types of spirits produced: Gin, vodka

Names of spirits:
- Phrog Premium Gin
- Phrog Premium Vodka

Best known for / most popular: Phrog Premium Gin

Average bottle price: Not provided

Distribution: Vancouver Island, Vancouver, Alberta

Interesting facts: Not provided

Long Table Distillery Ltd.

1451 Hornby Street
Vancouver, BC V6Z 1W8
604-266-0177

Owners / Operators:
Charles Tremewen, Founder / Distiller
Rita Tremewen, Distillery General Manager

Email: info@longtabledistillery.com
Website: www.longtabledistillery.com
Facebook: Long Table Distillery
Twitter: @LT_Distillery

Type: Craft Distillery. Opened in 2012.

Hours of operation:
Friday and Saturday, 11 a.m. to 6 p.m.
Sunday through Thursday by appointment only

Tours: Check distillery website for seasonally adjusted public tasting/sales room hours.

Types of spirits produced: Gin, vodka, whisky (2016)

Names of spirits:
- Long Table Distillery London Dry Gin
- Long Table Distillery Texada Vodka

Best known for / most popular: LTD Gin

Average bottle price: $45.00 to $50.00

Distribution: BC

Interesting facts:
- Vancouver's first micro distillery.
- Long Table Distillery focuses on handcrafted, small batch spirits incorporating locally produced and hand harvested botanicals and base ingredients.
- Spirits made on premises are available for purchase on site along with mixers, locally produced bitters and cocktail paraphernalia.
- Expect to release a wider range of spirits including a line of small batch apothecary spirits and liquors.

Maple Leaf Spirit Inc.

948 Naramata Road
Penticton, BC V2A 8V1
250-493-0180

Owners / Operators:
Jorg and Anette Engel, Owners

Email: info@engel.ca
          marketing@engel.ca
Website: www.mapleleafspirits.ca
Facebook: Maple Leaf Spirits Inc
Twitter: @mapleleafspirit

Type: Craft Distillery. Opened in 2006.

Hours of operation:
May to October: Wednesday through Sunday, 11 a.m. to 5 p.m.

Tours: Available by appointment. Call 250-493-0180.

Types of spirits produced: Eau de vie, liqueur

Names of spirits:
- Canadian Kirsch
- Pear Williams
- Apricot
- Italian Prune
- Aged Italian Prune
- Skinny Gewurztraminer
- Skinny Pinot Noir
- Skinny Syrah
- Quince Liqueur
- Pear Liqueur
- Cherry Liqueur
- Maple Liqueur

Best known for / most popular:
Canadian Kirsch, Skinny Pinot Noir, Cherry Liqueur, Maple Liqueur

Average bottle price: $30.00 to $50.00

Distribution: BC

Interesting facts:
- Pioneers in craft distilling in BC. First licensed distillery in the South Okanagan; second craft distillery in British Columbia; producing spirits since 2005 in Penticton in a European state of the art pot still.
- Skinny Pinot Noir won the Spirit of the Year in 2008 at the International Spirits and Liqueur Competition Destillata in Austria.

Merridale Ciderworks Corp.

1230 Merridale Road
P.O. Box 358
Cobble Hill, BC V0R 1L0
800-998-9908

Owners / Operators:
Janet Docherty and Rick Pipes, Owners
Laurent Lafuente and Rick Pipes, Distillers

Email: info@merridalecider.com
Website: www.merridalecider.com
Facebook: Merridale Ciderworks
Twitter: @merridalecider
Pinterest: Merridale Ciderworks

Type:
Micro Distillery and Cidery. Established 1991

Hours of operation:
Open 7 days a week. Visit website for hours.

Tours: Available by appointment

Types of spirits produced:
Fruit based brandies, eaux de vie, vodka

Names of spirits:
- Cowichan Cider Brandy
- Stairs Pear Brandy
- Frizz Vodka
- Apple Oh! De Vie
- Pomme Oh!
- Mure Oh!

Best known for / most popular:
Aged apple and pear brandies and fortified apple and blackberry wines

Average bottle price: $25.00 to $40.00

Distribution: BC

Interesting facts:
Largest Vancouver Island producer of exclusively field to table spirits.

apples expressed

Odd Society Spirits

1725 Powell Street
Vancouver, BC   V5L 1H6
604-559-6745

Owners / Operators:
Gordon Glanz, Founder / Distiller
Joshua Beach, Distiller

Email: info@oddsocietyspirits.com
Website: www.oddsocietyspirits.com
Facebook: Odd Society Spirits
Twitter: @oddspirits
Instagram: Odd Society Spirits

Type: Craft Distillery.
Opened in October 2013.

Hours of operation:
Thursday through Sunday, 1 p.m. to 9 p.m.

Tours: Weekends at 4 p.m.

Types of spirits produced:
Crème de Cassis, vodka, gin, whisky

Names of spirits:
- East Van Vodka
- Wallflower Gin
- Mongrel Whisky
- Crème de Cassis

Best known for / most popular:
Local spirits

Average bottle price:
$36.00 - $44.00

Distribution: BC

Okanagan Spirits

267 Bernard Avenue
Kelowna, BC   V1Y 6N2
250-549-3120

Owners / Operators:
Tyler Dyck, CEO
Tony Dyck, Owner
Peter von Hahn, Distiller
Rodney Goodchild, Sales & Marketing

Email: info@okanaganspirits.com
Website: www.okanaganspirits.com
Facebook: Okanagan Spirits
Twitter: @okspirits

Type: Craft Distillery. Opened in 2003.

Hours of operation: Daily

Tours: Available

Types of spirits produced:
Fruit spirits, fruit liqueurs, gin, rye whisky, vodka, absinthe, grappa, aquavit

Names of spirits:
- Okanagan Spirits Liqueur:
  Raspberry, Cherry, Blueberry, Black Currant, Cranberry, Blackberry, Sea Buckthorn

- Okanagan Spirits Eau de Vie:
  Poire Williams, Canados, Old Italian Prune, Italian Prune, Raspberry Framboise, Kirsch Danbue, Kirsch Virginiana, Apricot

- Okanagan Spirits Grappa:
  Gewurztraminer, Pinot Noir, Riesling

- Okanagan Spirits Gin
- Okanagan Spirits Whisky
- Okanagan Spirits Vodka
- Okanagan Spirits Single Malt Whisky
- Okanagan Spirits Aquavit – Aquavitus

- Absinthe:
  Okanagan Spirits Taboo Gold
  Okanagan Spirits Taboo Genuine

Average bottle price: $40.00

Distribution: Throughout Canada

Awards and Recognitions:
2013 World Spirits Awards, Distillery of the Year
2013 World Spirits Awards, Spirit of the Year 2013
2013 World Spirits Awards, "World Class Distillery"

Pemberton Distillery Inc.

1954 Venture Place
Pemberton, BC   V0N 2L0
604-894-0222

Owners / Operators:
Tyler Schramm, Owner / Master Distiller
Lorien Schramm, Owner

Email: info@pembertondistillery.ca
Website: www.pembertondistillery.ca
Facebook: Pemberton Distillery Inc.
Twitter: @pembydistillery
YouTube: Pemberton Distillery
Tripadvisor: Pemberton Distillery
Tumblr: Pemberton Distillery
Instagram: pembydistillery
Pinterest: Pemberton Distillery

Type:
Certified Organic Micro Distillery. Opened in 2009.

Hours of operation:
Winter (October 15 - May 15): Friday and Saturday
Summer (May 15 - October 15): Wed. through Sat.

Tours: Yes, tours run on Saturday at 4 p.m.

Types of spirits produced:
Vodka, gin, whisky, absinthe, brandy, liqueur

Names of spirits:
- Schramm Organic Gin
- Schramm Organic Potato Vodka
- Pemberton Distillery Organic Single Malt Whisky
- The Devil's Club Organic Absinthe

Best known for / most popular:
Schramm Organic Potato Vodka & Gin

Average bottle price: $40.00 to $50.00

Distribution: AB, BC

Interesting facts: The distillery uses a geothermal ground loop system to heat and cool water used in the distilling process reducing their energy usage by 35-70% depending on the function that it is providing.

Shelter Point Distillery

4650 Regent Road
Campbell River, BC V9H 1E3
778-420-2200

Owners / Operators:
Patrick Evans, Co-owner
James Marinus, Co-owner

Email: info@shelterpointdistillery.com
Website: www.shelterpointdistillery.com
Facebook: Shelter Point Distillery
Twitter: @ShelterPoint

Type: Micro Distillery. Opened in 2011.

Summer hours of operation:
Most days, 1 p.m. to 5 p.m.

Tours: Available

Types of spirits produced: Whisky, single malt whisky (release fall of 2014)

Names of spirits:
- Shelter Point Distillery Single Malt Whisky

Best known for / most popular: Shelter Point Distillery Single Malt Whisky

Average bottle price: $34.95

Distribution: U.S.; Japan

Interesting facts: Home of 42 resident deer, black bear, the odd cougar and thousands wintering migratory waterfowl including trumpeter swans. (Comox Valley has approximately 20% of the world population of swans in the winter).

Sons of Vancouver Distillery Ltd.

North Vancouver, BC V5N 3E2
778-773-4428

Owners / Operators:
James Lester, Director / Co-owner / Distiller
Richard Klaus, Director / Co-owner / Distiller

Email: james@sonsofvancouver.ca
Website: www.sonsofvancouver.ca
Twitter: @sovjames, @richardsov

Type: Craft Distillery. Opened in 2014.

Hours of operation: Not provided

Tours: Available evenings and weekends

Types of spirits produced:
Vodka, vodka infusions, white whiskey, amaretto

Names of spirits:
- 37 Black Vodka
- Before The Fire White Whiskey

Best known for / most popular: Not provided

Average bottle price: $40.00

Distribution: On-site retail, greater Vancouver area

Interesting facts: Not provided

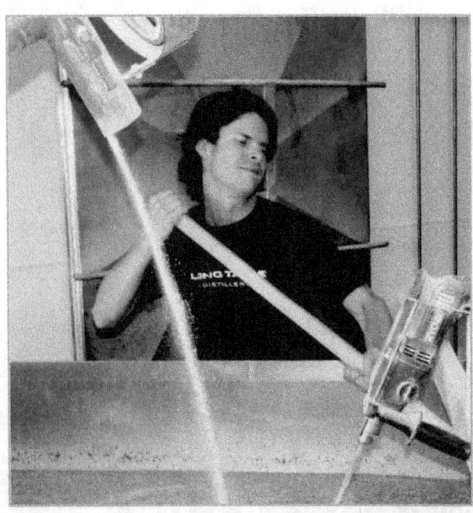

The Dubh Glas Distillery

8486 Gallagher Lake Frontage Road
Oliver, BC   V0H 1T2
250-486-7529

Owners / Operators:
Grant Stevely, Proprietor

Email: guestgervices@TheDubhGlasDistillery.com
Website: www.thedubhglasdistillery.com
Facebook: The Dubh Glas Distillery
Twitter: @TheDubhGlasD
Pinterest: TheDubhGlasD
Instagram: TheDubhGlasD
FourSquare: The Dubh Glas Distillery
Yelp: The Dubh Glas Distillery
YouTube: The Dubh Glas Distillery
Instagram: TheDubhGlasD
FourSquare: The Dubh Glas Distillery

Type: Craft Distillery. Opened in July 2014.

Hours of operation: Daily, 11 a.m. to 6 p.m.

Tours: Daily.   Appointment needed for groups of 10 or more.

Types of spirits produced: Whisky, gin and fruit liqueurs

Names of spirits:
- Noteworthy Gin
- Fruit Basket Liqueur
- Dubh Glas Whisky

Best known for / most popular: TBD

Average bottle price: $29.95 to $49.95

Distribution: On-site retail; AB, BC

Interesting facts: Not provided

The Liberty Distillery

Units 1 & 2 – 1494 Old Bridge Street
Granville Island
Vancouver, BC   V6H 3S6
604-558-1998

Owners / Operators:
Robert Simpson, Co-founder / Proprietor
Lisa Simpson-MBA, Co-founder, Director of Operations
Laurent Lafuente-Engineer HES, Master Distiller

Email: info@thelibertydistillery.com
Website: www.thelibertydistillery.com
Facebook: The Liberty Distillery
Twitter: @TLDistillery

Vimeo: The Liberty Distillery
Instagram: @thelibertydistillery
Linked In: The Liberty Distillery

Type: Craft Distillery. Established in May 2010.

Retail Hours:
Vary by season. Visit website for details.

Lounge Hours:
Vary by season. Visit website for details.

Tours: Available. Registration encouraged. Saturday and Sunday: 1 p.m. and 3 p.m. NOTE: Tours are also available at 1 p.m. and 3 p.m. on Mon. and Tue. (when not distilling).

Types of spirits produced: Vodka, whiskey, gin

Names of spirits:
- Truth Vodka 42% alc./vol.
- Railspur No 1 White 47% alc./vol. (ua whiskey)
- Endeavour Gin 45% alc./vol. (spring 2014)
- Trust Whiskey (spring 2016)

Best known for / most popular:
Liberty's spirits are known for being different and distinct.

Average bottle price: $6.99 to $49.99

Distribution: On-site retail, Lower Mainland

Interesting facts:
Uses 100% organic grown grains from BC to produce their handcrafted spirits.

Services offered other than production: Retail, tasting lounge, workshops

Urban Distilleries

6-325 Bay Avenue
Kelowna, BC   V1Y 7S3
778-478-0939

Owners / Operators:
Mike Urban, Owner / Master Distiller

Email: info@urbandistilleries.ca
Website: www.urbandistilleries.ca
Facebook: Urban Distilleries
Twitter: @SpiritBearVodka
YouTube: Urban Distilleries

Type: Micro Distillery. Opened in 2011.

Hours of operation:
May to October: Daily, 11 a.m. to 6 p.m.
November to April: Monday through Saturday, 11 a.m. to 5 p.m.

Tours: Available

Types of spirits produced: Gin, vodka, rum, whisky, brandy

Names of spirits:
- Spirit Bear Gin
- Spirit Bear Vodka
- Spirit Bear Espresso Vodka
- Urban White Rum
- Urban Amber Rum
- Urban Single Malt Whisky

Best known for / most popular: Spirit Bear Gin

Average bottle price: $48.00

Distribution: AB, BC

Interesting facts:
- Urban Distilleries is a hand craft micro producing top-shelf Okanagan gin, vodkas, rums and whisky including the signature "Spirit Bear" line in Kelowna, BC.
- Each batch is crafted in artesian copper stills from premium 100% British Columbia grains and agricultural inputs along with pure spring water from the Kootneys.
- All products are gluten free.

Victoria Spirits

6170 Old West Saanich Road
Victoria, BC V9E 2G8
250-544-8217

Owners / Operators:
Valerie and Bryan Murray, Owners
Peter Hunt, Distiller

Email: info@victoriaspirits.com
Website: www.victoriaspirits.com
Facebook: Victoria Spirits
Twitter: @victoriaspirits

Type: Micro Distillery. Opened in 2008.

Hours of operation:
Weekends and holidays, April through September, 10 a.m. to 5 p.m.

Tours: Available

Types of spirits produced:
Gin, vodka, oak barrel aged gin, whisky, bitters

Names of spirits:
- Victoria Gin
- Left Coast Hemp Vodka
- Oaken Gin
- Craigdarroch Whisky
- Twisted and Bitter Bitters

Best known for / most popular: Victoria Gin

Average bottle price: $50.00

Distribution: Provincial Government Liquor Stores; independent retail outlets in AB, BC, MB, ON, SK, QC.

Interesting facts:
First artisan producer of premium gin in Canada.

Yaletown Distilling Company

1132 Hamilton Street
Vancouver, BC V6B 2S2
604-669-2266

Owners / Operators:
Owned by Yaletown Brewing Company
Fraser Boyer, Director of Operations

Email: info@ytdistilling.com
Website: www.ytdistilling.com
Facebook: Yaletown Distilling Company
Twitter: @YTdistilling
YouTube: Yaletown Distilling Company
Instagram: @ytdistilling

Type: Craft Distillery. Opened in September 2013.

Hours of operation:
Sunday and Monday, Closed
Tuesday and Wednesday, noon to 5 p.m.
Thursday, noon to 7 p.m.
Friday, noon to 10 p.m.
Saturday, noon to 5 p.m.

Tours: Available. Call or email to book tour.

Types of spirits produced: Gin, vodka

Names of spirits:
- Yaletown Distilling Company Craft Vodka
- Yaletown Distilling Company BC Gin

Best known for / most popular: Gin, vodka

Average bottle price: $23.95 to $42.95

Distribution:
On-site retail, government and private liquor stores

Interesting facts:
After almost 20 years of making fresh beer at the Yaletown Brewing Company and pioneering the craft beer movement in Vancouver, it was an organic expansion for the Mark James Group to lead the way in artisian distilling. Launched on Repeal Day (December 5th) 2013, marking the anniversary for the end of Prohibition, the Yaletown Distilling Company is honouring the tradition of distilling by producing premium handcrafted spirits.

Winegarden Estate Ltd.

851 Route 970
Baie Verte, NB E4M 1Z7
506-538-7405

Owners / Operators:
The Rosswog Family, Owners / Operators
Steffen Rosswog, Distiller / Winemaker

Email: srosswog@nbnet.nb.ca
Website: www.winegardenestate.com

Type: Winery / Micro Distillery. Opened in 1991.

Hours of operation: Vary

Tours: Available

Types of spirits produced: Eau de vie, brandy, liqueur

Names of spirits:
- Johnny Ziegler Grappa
- Johnny Ziegler Sibowitz
- Johnny Ziegler Myrtille
- Johnny Ziegler Elderberry
- Johnny Ziegler Cassis
- Johnny Ziegler Kirsch
- Johnny Ziegler Obstler
- Johnny Ziegler Brandy
- Plaisir Apple Liqueur
- Blue Hill Blueberry Liqueur
- Wild Cherry Liqueur
- Maple Dream liqueur
- Elderberry Liqueur
- Pear Liqueur
- Cranberry Liqueur
- Cassis Liqueur
- Honey Liqueur
- Blackberry Liqueur
- Raspberry Liqueur
- Mocca Gino Coffee Liqueur

Best known for / most popular: Johnny Ziegler Apple Schnaps

Average bottle price: $16.00 to $45.00

Distribution: On-site, NB, co-op cottage wineries

Interesting facts:
First fruit wine distillery in Atlantic Canada, established in 1991
Pioneered New Brunswick's cottage distillery and winery industry

Glenora Distillery

13727 Route 19, Glenville
Cape Breton, NS B0E 1X0
902-258-2662, 1-800-839-0491

Owners / Operators:
Lauchie MacLean, President / CEO

Email: info@glenora1.ca
Website: www.glenoradistillery.com
Facebook: Glenora Inn & Distillery
Twitter: @GlenBreton

Type: Micro Distillery. Opened in 1990.

Hours of operation: Open May through October

Tours: Available on the hour, 9 a.m. to 5 p.m.

Types of spirits produced: Single malt whisky

Names of spirits:
- Glen Breton Canadian Single Malt Whisky
- Glen Breton Ice
- Battle of the Glen

Best known for / most popular: Glen Breton Rare Aged 10 years, 750 ml

Average bottle price: $50.00 to $300.00

Distribution: Canada, U.S., Europe

Interesting facts:
- In the early 1800s, Scottish immigrants chose Cape Breton Island for their new home as its beauty resembled the Highlands and Islands of Scotland. Many traditions and secrets came with these pioneers. The making of a spirited whisky was one of them. Scottish descendants passionately keep the dearest aspects of their colourful culture alive. This is especially evident in Inverness County, Nova Scotia, which is home to Glenora Distillery, the first single malt whisky distillery in North America.

Awards and Recognitions:
- Glen Breton Rare Aged 10 Years, Gold Medal, International Competition
- Glen Breton Ice, Silver Medal, 2008 International Competition.
- Battle of the Glen Aged 15 Years, 95 Points out of 100.

Ironworks Distillery

2 Kempt Street
Lunenburg, NS B0J 2C0
902-640-2424

Owners / Operators:
Lynne MacKay, Co-owner
Pierre Guevremont, Co-owner

Email: spirits@ironworksdistillery.com
Website: www.ironworksdistillery.com
Facebook: Ironworks Distillery
Twitter: @Ironworks_NS

Type: Micro Distillery. Opened in 2009.

Hours of operation: 2013 Schedule
January to May 18 – Thursday through Saturday, noon to 5 p.m.
May 19 to June 25 - Wednesday through Monday, noon to 5 p.m.
June 26 to September 2 – Daily, 11 a.m. to 7 p.m.
September 3 to December 31 – Daily, noon to 5 p.m.

Tours: Available

Types of spirits produced: Vodka, rum, eaux de vie, brandy, liqueur

Names of spirits:
- Amber Rum
- Bluenose Black Rum
- Ironworks Vodka
- Ironworks Eaux de Vie
- Ironworks Apple Brandy
- Ironworks Blueberry Liqueur
- Ironworks Cranberry Liqueur

Best known for / most popular:
Ironworks Vodka

Average bottle price: $25.00 to $38.00

Distribution: Lunenburg, Halifax NS

Interesting facts: Ironworks Distillery is housed in a heritage blacksmith shop built in the 1890s in the UNESCO - designated town of Lunenburg, NS.

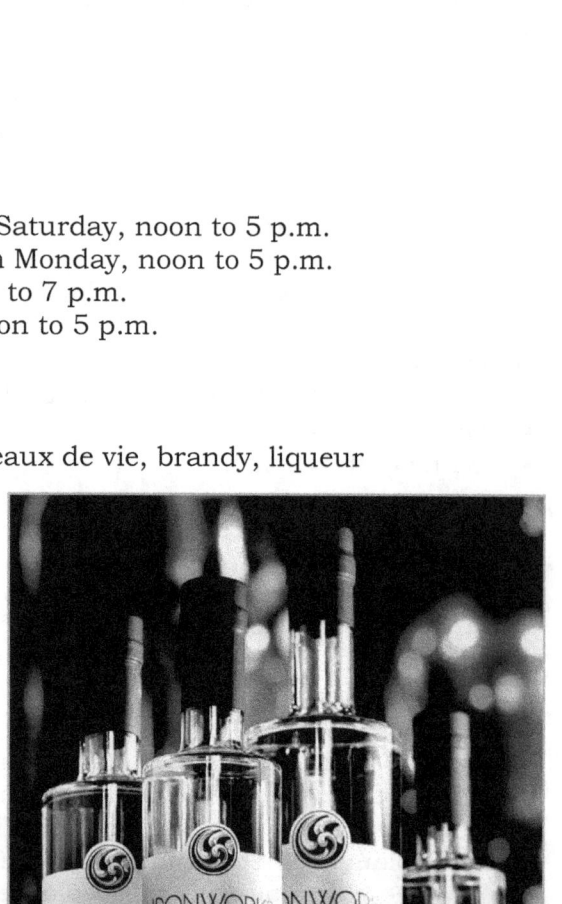

Jost Vineyards Ltd.

48 Vintage Lane
Malagash, NS   B0K 1E0
902-257-2636

Owners / Operators:
Hans Christian Jost, Owner
Carl Sparkes, CEO
Andrew Shelswell, Distiller

Email: info@jostwine.com
Website: www.jostwine.com
Facebook: Jost Vineyards Ltd.
Twitter: @JostVineyards

Type: Winery / Micro Distillery. Opened in 2008.

Hours of operation: Daily, 9 a.m. to 5 p.m.

Tours: Available from June 15 to September 15

Types of spirits produced: Eau de Vie

Names of spirits:
- Muscat Eau de Vie
- Red Plum Eau de Vie
- Maple Eau de Vie
- Yellow Plum Eau de Vie

Best known for / most popular:
Muscat Eau de Vie

Average bottle price: $17.99 to $24.99

Distribution: Malagash, NS

Interesting facts: Not provided

66 Gilead Distillery

66 Gilead Road
Bloomfield, ON K0K 1G0
613-393-1890

Owners / Operators:
Sophia Pantazi, Co-owner
Peter Stroz, Co-owner

Email: info@66gileaddistillery.com
Website: www.66gileaddistillery.com
Facebook: 66 Gilead Distillery
Twitter: @66Gilead

Type: Craft Distillery. Opened in 2011.

Hours of operation:
Daily from Victoria Day to Labour Day. Check website for exact hours.
Weekends year-round. Check website for exact hours.

Tours: Available on weekends from Victoria Day to Labour Day

Types of spirits produced:
Canadian rye whisky, vodka, gin, shochu, rum

Names of spirits:
- Loyalist Gin
- Duck Island Rum
- Whole Wheat Vodka
- Canadian Rye Vodka
- Canadian Pine Vodka
- White Dragon Shochu
- Black Dragon Shochu (barrel aged Shochu)

Best known for / most popular:
Canadian Pine Vodka

Average bottle price: $36.95 to $45.95

Distribution: AB, ON

Interesting facts:
- Ontario's first farm craft distillery.
- One of the only North American producers of shochu.

Forty Creek Distillery

297 South Service Road West
Grimsby, ON L3M 1Y6
905-945-9225

Owners / Operators:
John K. Hall, Owner

Email: Admin@FortyCreekDistillery.com
Website: www.fortycreekwhisky.com
            www.princeigorvodka.com, www.canadagoldwhisky.com
Facebook: Forty Creek Whisky
Twitter: @FortyCreek_John

Type: Micro Distillery. Opened in 1992.

Hours of operation:
Monday through Saturday, 10 a.m. to 6 p.m.
Sunday and Holidays, 11 a.m. to 5 p.m.

Tours: Available

Types of spirits produced:
Whisky, vodka, liqueur, brandy

Names of spirits:
- Forty Creek Barrel Select Whisky
- Forty Creek Copper Pot Whisky
- Forty Creek Port Wood Reserve
- Forty Creek Double Barrel Reserve
- Forty Creek Confederation Oak Reserve
- Canada Gold Premium Barrel Aged Canadian Whisky
- Forty Creek Whisky Cream Liquor
- Prince Igor Vodka

Best known for / most popular:
Not provided

Average bottle price: Not provided

Distribution: Throughout U.S. and Canada

Interesting facts: Not provided

Mary Jane's

Niagara Falls, ON L2H 2B5
289-257-0420

Owners / Operators:
Scott Collier, Owner

Email: drinkmaryjanes@live.com
Website: www.drinkmaryjanes.com
Facebook: Drink Mary Jane's

Type: Micro Distillery. Opened in 2012.

Hours of operation: Not provided

Tours: Not provided

Types of spirits produced: Vodka, gin

Names of spirits:
- Mary Jane's Primo Hemp Vodka
- Mary Jane's Premium Hemp Gin

Best known for / most popular: Mary Jane's Primo Hemp Vodka

Average bottle price: Not provided

Distribution: Not provided

Interesting facts: Handcrafted and multi-distilled in alembic copper using select grains and fastidiously filtered BC spring water.

Still Waters Distillery

150 Bradwick Drive, Unit # 26
Concord, ON L4K 4M7
905-482-2080

Owners / Operators:
Barry Bernstein and Barry Stein, Owners

Email: info@stillwatersdistillery.com
Website: www.stillwatersdistillery.com
Facebook: Still Waters Distillery
Twitter: @StillWatersD
Flickr: Still Water Distillery's photostream

Type: Micro Distillery. Opened in 2009

Hours of operation:
Monday through Friday, 10 a.m. to 5 p.m.
Weekends by appointment

Tours: Available by appointment

Types of spirits produced: Single malt whisky, rye whisky, Canadian whisky, vodka, brandy

Names of spirits:
- Stalk & Barrel Single Malt Whisky
- Special 1+11 Blend Canadian Whisky
- Still Waters Single Malt Vodka

Best known for / most popular:
Stalk & Barrel Single Malt Whisky

Average bottle price: $69.00

Distribution:
Liquor Control Board of Ontario and across Canada as well as through Purple Valley Imports for the U.S.

Interesting facts: The first micro distillery in Ontario.

The Ottawa Distillery Co.

356 Kirkwood
Ottawa, ON K1Z 8P1

Owners / Operators:
Jean Levac, Co-Founder

Email: Ottawadistillery@gmail.com
Website: TBA
Facebook: The Ottawa Distillery Co.
Twitter: @OttDistillery

Type: Craft Distillery. Opened in 2014.

Hours of operation: Not available

Tours: Not available

Types of spirits produced: Canadian whisky, rum, vodka

Names of spirits:
- TBA

Best known for / most popular: TBA

Average bottle price: TBA

Distribution: Not available

Interesting facts: Ottawa's first craft distillery in decades.

Waverley Spirits

34 Herriott Street
Perth, ON   K7H 1T2
613-601-8810

Owners / Operators:
James Snasdell-Taylor, Co-founder
Barbara Snasdell-Taylor, Co-founder

Email: info@waverleyspirits.com
Website: www.waverleyspirits.com
Facebook: Waverley Spirits Limited
Twitter: @waverleyspirits

Type: Micro Distillery under construction.

Hours of operation: TBA

Tours: TBA

Types of spirits produced: Vodka

Names of spirits:
- TBA

Best known for / most popular: TBA

Average bottle price: TBA

Distribution: TBA

Interesting facts: The first craft distillery in Perth, ON since 1916.

Myriad View Artisan Distillery Inc.

Prince Edward Island 2
Rollo Bay, PE C0A 2B0
902-687-1281

Owners / Operators:
Dr. Paul and Angie Berrow, Owners
Ken and Danielle Mill, Owners

Email: info@straitshine.com
Website: www.straitshine.com
Facebook: Strait Shine

Type: Micro Distillery. Opened in 2007.

Hours of operation: Vary

Tours: Available

Types of spirits produced: Moonshine, rum, gin, whisky, vodka

Names of spirits:
- Strait Shine
- Strait Lightning
- Strait Rum (historic 100 proof 57.1%)
- Strait Rum (40%)
- Strait Vodka
- Strait Gin
- Strait Pastis
- Strait Whisky

Best known for / most popular:
Strait Shine

Average bottle price: $26.00 to $42.00

Distribution: Calgary AB, PE

Interesting facts: Prince Edward Island's first distillery.

Prince Edward Distillery

9985 Route 16
Hermanville, PE C0A 2B0
902-687-2586

Owners / Operators:
Julie Shore, Co-owner
Arla Johnson, Co-owner

Email: info@princeedwarddistillery.com
Website: www.princeedwarddistillery.com
Facebook: Prince Edward Distillery

Type: Micro Distillery. Opened in 2008.

Hours of operation: Daily, 10 a.m. to 6 p.m.

Tours: Available

Types of spirits produced: Vodka, gin, rum, whiskey

Names of spirits:
- Prince Edward Potato Vodka
- Prince Edward Wild Blueberry Vodka
- Prince Edward Wild Blueberry Gin
- Prince Edward Merchantman Rum
- Prince Edward I.C. Shore Whiskey
- Prince Edward Canadian Rye

Best known for / most popular:
Prince Edward Potato Vodka

Average bottle price: Not provided

Distribution: NS, PE

Interesting facts: Not provided

Cidrerie Michel Jodoin

1130 Petite Caroline
Rougemont, QC J0L 1M0
450-469-2676

Owners / Operators:
Michel Jodoin, Owner

Email: info@micheljodoin.ca
Website: www.micheljodoin.ca
Facebook: Cidrerie Michel Jodoin
Twitter: @cidrerie

Type: Micro Distillery. Opened in 1999.

Hours of operation:
Monday through Friday, 9 a.m. to 5 p.m.
Saturday and Sunday, 10 a.m. to 4 p.m.

Tours: Available

Types of spirits produced:
Apple liquor, brandy, eau de vie, fortified cider

Names of spirits:
- Michel Jodoin Apple Brandy barrel-aged 3 years
- Michel Jodoin XO Apple Brandy barrel-aged 10 years
- Fine Caroline
- Pom de vie
- Ambre de pomme (fortified cider)

Best known for / most popular:
Michel Jodoin Apple Brandy barrel-aged 3 years

Average bottle price: $33.00

Distribution:
SAQ (Québec), Alberta, Germany

Interesting facts:
In 1999, the cidrerie became the first micro distillery of apples in Canada.

The Subersives Distillers

449 Gardenville
Longueuil, QC   J4H 2H5
514-316-6692

Owners / Operators:
Fernando Balthazard, Co-owner
Pascal Gervais, Co-owner
Stéphan Ruffo, Co-owner
Robert Paradis, Co-owner

Email: info@lat45.ca
Website: www.distillateurssubversifs.com, www.pigerhenricus.com
Facebook: Piger Henricus Gin
Twitter: @PigerHenricus

Type: Micro Distillery. Opened in 2012.

Hours of operation: Not provided

Tours: No provided

Types of spirits produced: Gin

Names of spirits:
- Piger Henricus Gin

Best known for / most popular: Piger Henricus Gin

Average bottle price: Not provided

Distribution: Not provided

Interesting facts: Not provided

Last Mountain Distillery Ltd.

70 Highway 20
Lumsden, SK S0G 3C0
306-731-3930

Owners / Operators:
Colin Schmidt, President / Distiller
Meredith Schmidt, Retail Manager / Secretary
Darryl Babey, Co-owner / Manager of Fixed Operations
Shannon Babey, Co-owner

Email: colin@lastmountaindistillery.com
Website: www.lastmountaindistillery.com
Facebook: Last Mountain Distillery
Twitter: @skdistillery

Type: Micro Distillery. Opened in 2011.

Hours of operation:
Tuesday through Saturday, noon to 6 p.m.

Tours: Available by appointment

Types of spirits produced: Vodka, whisky, liqueur

Names of spirits:
- Last Mountain Vodka
- Last Mountain Canadian Rye Whisky

Best known for / most popular: Last Mountain Vodka

Average bottle price: $35.00

Distribution: Saskatchewan

Interesting facts: Saskatchewan's first micro distillery.

LB Distillers

1925 Avenue B North
Saskatoon, SK   S7L 4K9
306-979-7280

Owners / Operators:
Cary Bowman, President of Good Times
Lacey Crocker, Chief Operating Officer Lady
Michael Goldney, President of Vice

Email: lucky@luckybastard.ca
Website: www.luckybastard.ca
Facebook: LB Distillers
Twitter: @luckybastardSK

Type: Micro Distillery. Opened in 2012.

Hours of operation:
Monday through Wednesday, 11 a.m. to 5 p.m.
Thursday through Saturday, 11 a.m. to 6 p.m.

Tours: Available

Types of spirits produced: Vodka, gin, whisky, rum

Names of spirits:
- Chai Vodka
- Lucky Bastard Vodka
- Gambit Gin
- Bettah Bitters
- Knock on Wood Rum
- Carmine Jewel Liqueur
- Saskatoon Liqueur
- Crème de Cassis Liqueur
- Seabuckthorn and Wildflower Honey Liqueur
- Blue Honeysuckle Liqueur

Best known for / most popular: Lucky Bastard Vodka

Average bottle price: $35.00 to $37.77

Distribution: AB, SK

Interesting facts: Not provided

Klondike River Distillery

Across the river from Dawson City, YT Y0B1G0
867-993-3487

Owners / Operators:
Dorian and Bridget Amos, Owners

Email: info@klondikeriverdistillery.com
Website: www.klondikeriverdistillery.com
Facebook: Klondike River Distillery

Type: Micro Distillery. Opened in 2007.

Hours of operation: Vary

Tours: Not available

Types of spirits produced: Vodka

Names of spirits:
- Klondike Vodka - The Spirit of the Yukon

Best known for / most popular: Klondike Vodka

Average bottle price: $39.99

Distribution: YT

Interesting facts:
Klondike Vodka is the first spirit to be legally produced in the Yukon Territory.

Yukon Spirits

102A Copper Road
Whitehorse, YT   Y1A 2Z6
867-668-4183

Owners / Operators:
Alan Hansen and Bob Baxter, Owners

Email: bob@yukonbeer.com
Website: www.yukonbeer.com, www.yukonspirits.ca
Facebook: Yukon Spirits
Twitter: @YukonSpirits

Type: Brewery / Micro Distillery. Opened in 2010.

Hours of operation: Monday through Sunday, 8 a.m. to 6 p.m.

Tours: Available

Types of spirits produced: Vodka, whisky (still aging)

Names of spirits:
- Solstice Infused Vodka

Best known for / most popular: Solstice Infused Vodka

Average bottle price: $44.95

Distribution: YT

Interesting facts: Not provided

Distilling Associations and Guilds

American Craft Distillers Association
Website: www.americancraftdistillers.org
Facebook: American Craft Distillers Accoc.
Twitter: @craftdistill

American Distilling Institute
Email: bill@distilling.com
Website: www.distilling.com
Facebook: American Distilling Institute
Twitter: @Distilling
Instagram: adiconf
YouTube: AmericanDistilling

Artisan Craft Distilling Institute
Email: info@artisancraftdistilling.com
Website: www.artisancraftdistilling.com
Facebook: Artisan Craft Distilling Institute
Pinterest: Artisan Craft Distilling Institute

California Artisanal Distillers Guild
Email: info@cadsp.org
Website: www.cadsp.org
Facebook: California Artisanal Distillers Guild

Colorado Distillers Guild
Email: coloradodistillers@gmail.com
Website: www.coloradodistillersguild.publishpath.com
Facebook: Colorado Distillers Guild

Craft Distillers Guild
LinkedIn: Craft Distillers Guild

Craft Distillers Guild of BC
Email: info@craftdistillersbc.ca
Website: www.craftdistillersbc.ca
Facebook: Craft Distillers Guild of British Columbia
Twitter: @CDG_BC
Google+: Craft Distillers Guild of BC

Distilled Spirits Council of Vermont
Website: www.distilledvermont.org
Facebook: Distilled Spirits Council of Vermont

Distillery Row Association – Portland, OR
Website: www.distilleryrowpdx.com
Facebook: Distillery Row
Twitter: @DistilleryRow

Distilled Spirits Council of the United States (DISCUS)
Website: www.discus.org
Facebook: Distilled Spirits Council of the United States
Twitter: @DistilledSpirit

Florida Craft Distillers Guild
Website: www.floridadistillers.org
Facebook: Florida Craft Distillers Guild

Illinois Craft Distillers Association
Email: info@illinoisdistillers.org
Website: www.illinoisdistillers.org
Facebook: Illinois Craft Distillers Association

Kentucky Distillers' Association (Kentucky Bourbon Trail)
Email: enjoy@kybourbon.com
Website: www.kybourbon.com, www.kybourbontrail.com
Facebook: Kentucky Bourbon Trail
Twitter: KentuckyBourbonTrail

Michigan Distillers Guild
Website: www.spiritsofmichigan.com
Facebook: Spirits of Michigan
Twitter: @MichiganSpirits

National Alcohol Beverage Control Association (NABCA)
Website: www.nabca.org
Facebook: National Alcohol Beverage Control Association (NABCA)
Twitter: @NABCA
YouTube: The NABCA

New York Distillers Guild
Website: www.nydistillers.org/wp
Facebook: New York State Distillers Guild

New York Craft Distillers Guild
Email: site_distiller@burningstill.com
Website: www.burningstill.com

Ohio Distillers Guild
Website: www.distillersguild.org

Oregon Distillers Guild
Email: director@oregondistillersguild.org
oregondistillerytrail@gmail.com
Website: www.oregondistillersguild.org
Facebook: Oregon Distillers Guild
Twitter: @OregonDistilled

Texas Distilled Spirits Association
Email: info@texasdistilledspirits.org
Website: www.texasdistilledspirits.org

United Craft Distillers Inc.
Email: info@unitedcraftdistillers.com
Website: www.unitedcraftdistillers.com
Facebook: United Craft Distillers, Inc.
LinkedIn: United Craft Distillers, Inc.

Washington Distilleries
Email: info@washingtondistilleries.com
Website: www.washingtondistilleries.com
Facebook: Washington Distilleries
Twitter: @WADistilleries

Washington Distillers Guild
Email: president@washingtondistillersguild.org
Website: www.washingtondistillersguild.org
Facebook: Washington Distillers Guild

Wine & Spirits Wholesalers of America
Email: info@wswa.org
Website: www.wswa.org

Wisconsin Distillers Association
Website: www.widistillers.org

Resources / Information / Publications

Alcohol and Tobacco Tax and Trade Bureau – Distilled Spirits
Website: www.ttb.gov/spirits

Alcoholmanac Magazine - Nightlife & Drink Culture Almanac
Website: www.alcoholmanac.com
Facebook: Alcoholmanac
Twitter: @alcoholmanac

American Craft Spirits – Reviews & Interviews
Email: info@americancraftspirits.com
Website: www.americancraftspirits.com
Facebook: American Craft Spirits

Artisan Spirit – The Magazine for Craft Distillers and Their Fans
Email: Rockwell@distilleryuniversity.com
Website: www.artisanspiritmag.com
Facebook: Artisan Spirit Magazine

Beverage Media Group
Email: info@bevmedia.com
Website: www.beveragemedia.com
Facebook: Beverage Media Group
Twitter: @BevMedia

Beverage World Magazine
Website: www.beverageworld.com
Facebook: Beverage World Magazine
Twitter: @Beverage_World

BevX – A Beverage & Lifestyle Magazine
Email: sean@bevx.com
Website: www.bevx.com
Facebook: BevX.com

Beverage Information Group – Info Source for the Beverage Alcohol Industry
Website: www.beveragenet.net

Burning Still
Website: www.burningstill.com

Canadian Whisky
Email: askhildamary@gmail.com
Website: www.canadianwhisky.org
Facebook: Davin de Kergommeaux
Twitter: @davindek

Cheers Magazine
Website: www.alturl.com/6v27z
Facebook: Cheers Magazine
Twitter: @cheersonline

Chilled Magazine
Website: www.chilledmagazine.com
Facebook: Chilled Magazine
Twitter: @chilledmagazine

Cigars & Spirits Magazine
Email: customerservice@cigarandspirits.com
Website: www.cigarandspirits.com
Facebook: Cigar & Spirits Magazine
Twitter: CigarSpiritsMag

Distillery News
Website: www.newsdistilleryonline.com
Twitter: @DistilleryNews

Drink Me – Lifestyle Beyond The Glass
Email: info@drinkmemag.com
Website: www.drinkmemag.com
Facebook: Drink Me Magazine
Twitter: Drink Me Magazine

Got Rum? Magazine
Website: www.gotrum.com
Facebook: Got Rum?
Twitter: @Got_Rum

Imbibe Magazine – Liquid Culture
Email: info@imbibemagazine.com
Website: www.imbibemagazine.com
Facebook: Imbibe Magazine
Twitter: Imbibe Magazine
Pinterest: Imbibe Magazine

Liquor.com
Email: info@liquor.com
Website: www.liquor.com
Facebook: Liquor.com
Twitter: @Liquor

Micro Liquor – Liquor Entrepreneurship + Innovation
Email: contact@MicroLiquor.com
Website: www.microliquor.com
Facebook: MicroLiquor
Twitter: MicroLiquor

MicroShiner Magazine
Email: microshiner@gmail.com
Website: www.microshiner.com
Facebook: MicroShiner
Twitter: @MicroShiner
Pinterest: MicroShiner

Modern Distillery Age – Spirits Business e-newsletter
Email: gregg@distilleryage.com
Website: www.distilleryage.com
Facebook: Modern Distillery Age

Mutineer Magazine
Email: info@mutineermagazine.com
Website: www.mutineermagazine.com
Facebook: Mutineer Magazine
Twitter: @mutineermag

F. Paul Pacult's Spirit Journal
Email: mail@spiritjournal.com
Website: www.spiritjournal.com

Sip Northwest Magazine
Website: www.sipnorthwest.com
Facebook: SIP Northwest Magazine
Twitter: @SIPnorthwest

The Distilled Life
Website: www.thedistilledlife.com
Facebook: The Distilled Life
Twitter: @TDistilledLife

The Hooch Life
Email: email@thehoochlife.com
Website: www.thehoochlife.com
Facebook: The Hooch Life
Twitter: @TheHoochLife

The Tasting Panel – Connection for Beverage Trends
Website: www.tastingpanelmag.com
Facebook: The Tasting Panel Magazine
Twitter: @TastingPanel

Washington Distilleries – Craft Distilleries of Seattle and the Pacific NW
Email: info@washingtondistilleries.com
Website: www.washingtondistilleries.com
Facebook: Washington Distilleries
Twitter: @WADistilleries

Whisky Advocate
Email: info@whiskyadvocate.com
Website: www.whiskyadvocate.com
Facebook: The Whisky Advocate Magazine
Twitter: @JohnHansell

Whisky Magazine
Website: www.whiskymag.com
Facebook: Whisky Magazine
Twitter: @Whisky_Magazine

Wine & Spirits Magazine
Email: info@wineandspiritsmagazine.com
Website: www.wineandspiritsmagazine.com
Facebook: Wine & Spirits Magazine
Twitter: Wine & Spirits Mag

Spirit Events and Festivals

American Craft Distillers Convention
Website: www.americancraftdistillers.org

Art of the Cocktail – Victoria BC, Canada
Email: sip@artofthecocktail.ca
Website: www.artofthecocktail.ca
Facebook: Art Of The Cocktail
Twitter: @ArtOfCocktail

Beverly Hills International Spirits Awards – Beverly Hills, CA
Email: info@beverlyhillsawards.com
Website: www.beverlyhillsawards.com
Facebook: Beverly Hills Awards
Twitter: @BeverlyHillsISA

Beverly Hills World Spirits Competition – Beverly Hills, CA
Email: info@bhspiritscomp.com
Website: www.bhspiritscomp.com
Facebook: Beverly Hills World Spirits Competition
Twitter: @BeverlyHillsISA

Breckenridge Craft Spirits Festival – Breckenridge, CO
Website: www.breckenridgecraftspiritsfestival.com
Facebook: Breckenridge Craft Spirits Festival

Chicago Craft Spirit Week – Chicago, IL
Email: chicagocraftspirits@gmail.com
Website: www.craftspiritweekchicago.com
Facebook: Chicago Craft Spirit Week

Chicago Independent Spirits Expo – Chicago, IL
Website: www.indiespiritsexpo.com
Facebook: The Chicago Independent Spirits Expo

Cocktail Camp – Portland, OR
Website: www.cocktailcamp.net
Twitter: @CocktailCamp

Colorado Distillers Festival – Denver, CO
Website: www.coloradodistillersfestival.com
Facebook: Colorado Distillers Festival
Twitter: CODistFest

Distill America – Madison, WI
Email: kevinguthrie80@gmail.com
Website: www.distillamerica.com
Facebook: Distill America
Twitter: @distill_america

Great American Distillers Festival – Portland, OR
Email: rogue@rogue.com
Website: www.distillersfestival.com
Facebook: Great American Distillers Festival
Twitter: @DistillersFest

Independent Spirits Expo – U.S. cities change
Email: indiespirits@gmail.com
Website: www.indiespiritsexpo.com
Twitter: @indyspirits

Kentucky Bourbon Festival – Bardstown, KY
Website: www.kybourbonfestival.com
Facebook: Kentucky Bourbon Festival
Twitter: @kybourbonfest

Los Angeles International Spirits Expo – Los Angeles, CA
Website: www.laspiritsexpo.com
Facebook: Los Angeles International Spirits Expo
Twitter: @LASPIRITSEXPO

Manhattan Cocktail Classic – New York, NY
Website: www.manhattancocktailclassic.com
Facebook: Manhattan Cocktail Classic
Twitter: @cocktailclassic

Midtown Cocktail Week – Sacramento, CA
Website: www.midtowncocktailweek.org
Facebook: Midtown Cocktail Week
Twitter: @SacMCW

Nashville Whiskey Festival – Nashville, TN
Website: www.nashvillewhiskeyfestival.com
Facebook: Nashville Whiskey Festival
Twitter: @NashWhiskeyFest

Northwest Food and Wine Festival – Portland, OR
Website: www.nwwinefestival.com
Facebook: Northwest Food & Wine Festival

Oregon Distillery Trail
Email: oregondistillerytrail@gmail.com
Website: www.oregondistillerytrail.com
Facebook: Oregon Distillery Trail
Twitter: @oregonspirits

Philadelphia Whiskey & Fine Spirits – Philadelphia, PA
Website: www.phillymag.com/whiskeyfest

Pittsburgh Whiskey & Fine Spirits Festival – Pittsburgh, PA
Email: dmarkham@pittsburghwinefestival.com
Website: www.pittsburghwhiskeyfestival.com

Portland Cocktail Week – Portland, OR
Email: questions@pdxcw.com
Website: www.portlandcocktailweek.com
Facebook: Portland Cocktail Week
Twitter: @PDXCocktailWeek

Proof - Washington Distillers Festival – Seattle, WA
Email: info@proofwashington.org
Website: www.proofwashington.org
Facebook: Proof Washington
Twitter: @ProofWashington

San Diego Spirits Festival – San Diego, CA
Email: info@sandiegospiritsfestival.com
Website: www.sandiegospiritsfestival.com
Facebook: San Diego Spirits Festival
Twitter: @spiritsfestival

San Francisco Cocktail Week – San Francisco Bay Area, CA
Website: www.sfcocktailweek.com
Facebook: SF Cocktail Week
Twitter: @CocktailWeek

Speakeasy Cocktail Festival – Atlanta, GA
Email: info@speakeasycocktailfestival.com
Website: www.speakeasycocktailfestival.com
Facebook: Speakeasy Cocktail Festival
Twitter: @speakeasyfest

St. Louis Classic Cocktail Party – St. Louis MO
Facebook: St. Louis Classic Cocktail Party

Tails of the Cocktail – New Orleans, LA
Email: info@talesofthecocktail.com
Website: www.talesofthecocktail.com
Facebook: Tales of the Cocktail
Twitter: @totc

Tennessee Whiskey Festival – Chattanooga, TN
Email: info@tnwhiskeyfestival.com
Website: www.tnwhiskeyfestival.com
Facebook: Tennessee Whiskey Festival
Twitter: @TNWhiskeyFest

The Great American Absinthe Festival
Email: info@absinthefestival.org
Website: www.absinthefestival.com
Facebook: The Great American Absinthe Festival
Twitter: @Absinthe_Fest

The Liquid Projects – Miami, FL
A Tasting Event, Craft Spirits & Beer
Email: info@theliquidprojects.com
Website: www.theliquidprojects.com
        www.craftspiritsandbeer.com
Facebook: Craft: Spirits & Beer, a Tasting Event
Twitter: @TLiquidProjects

Ultimate Beverage Challenge – New York, NY
Email: info@ultimate-beverage.com
Website: www.ultimate-beverage.com
Facebook: Ultimate Beverage Challenge

Whisky Live – U.S. / Canadian cities change
Email: info@whiskylive.com
Website: www.whiskylive.com
Facebook: Whisky Live
Twitter: @WhiskyLive

Miscellaneous

Museum of the American Cocktail – New Orleans, LA
Website: www.museumoftheamericancocktail.org
Facebook: Museum of the American Cocktail

National Absinthe Day – March 5
Facebook: National Absinthe Day

National Bourbon Day – June 14
Website: www.nationalbourbonday.com
Facebook: National Bourbon Day
Twitter: @BourbonDay

National Bourbon Heritage Month - September

National Daiquiri Day – July 19

National Margarita Day – February 22

National Piña Colada Day – July 10

National Repeal Day – December 5
Website: www.repealday.org

National Rum Punch Day – September 20

National Rum Day – August 16

National Vodka Day – October 4
Website: www.nationalvodkaday.com
Facebook: National Vodka Day
Twitter: @NtlVodkaDay

Small Business Saturday – November
Facebook: Small Business Saturday

Tequila Day – July 24

Whiskey Sour Day – August 25

World Gin Day – June 15
Website: www.worldginday.com
Facebook: World Gin Day
Twitter: @worldginday

World Whisky Day – May 18
Facebook: World Whisky Day
Twitter: @WorldWhiskyDay

Seminars and Certification for Craft Distilling

Artisan Craft Distilling Institute
Email: info@artisancraftdistilling.com
Website: www.artisancraftdistilling.com
Facebook: Artisan Craft Distilling Institute

Artisan Craft Distilling University
Email: info@distillinguniveristy.com
Website: www.distillinguniversity.com
Twitter: @distilleryU

Distilled Spirits Epicenter – Moonshine University
Website: www.ds-epicenter.com, www.moonshineuniversity.com
Facebook: Moonshine University
Twitter: @moonshine_U

Absinthe	Brimstone Absinthe	Rancho de Los Luceros Destilaría, NM
Absinthe	Delaware Phoenix Meadow of Love Absinthe	Delaware Phoenix Distillery, NY
Absinthe	Delaware Phoenix Walton Waters Absinthe	Delaware Phoenix Distillery, NY
Absinthe	Marteau Absinthe de la Belle Époque	Gnostalgic Spirits Distillery, WA
Absinthe	Okanagan Spirits Taboo Genuine Absinthe	Okanagan Spirits, BC
Absinthe	Redux Absinthe	Golden Moon Distillery, CO
Absinthe	Redux Absinthe No.2	Golden Moon Distillery, CO
Absinthe	Tree Spirits Absinthe	Tree Spirits, ME
Absinthe	Wild Card Absinthe	Oregon Spirit Distillers, OR
Absinthe, Barrel Aged	Absinthe Brun	Letherbee Distillers, IL
Absinthe, Blanche	Extrait d'Absinthe Blanche	Vilya Spirits LLC, MT
Absinthe, Bleue	La Sorciere Absinthe Bleue	Old World Spirits LLC, CA
Absinthe, Gold	Okanagan Spirits Taboo Gold Absinthe	Okanagan Spirits, BC
Absinthe, Organic	The Devil's Club Organic Absinthe	Pemberton Distillery Inc., BC
Absinthe, Red	Absinthia Rubra	Fish Hawk Spirits LLC, FL
Absinthe, Red	Amerique 1912 Absinthe Rouge	Great Lakes Distillery LLC, WI
Absinthe, Red	Corsair Red Absinthe	Corsair Artisan Distillery, TN
Absinthe, Red	Toulouse Red, Absinthe Rouge	Atelier Vie, LA
Absinthe, Superieure	Germain-Robin Absinthe Supérieure	Germain-Robin, CA
Absinthe, Superieure	Vieux Carré Absinthe Supérieure	Philadelphia Distilling, PA
Absinthe, Verte	Amerique 1912 Absinthe Verte	Great Lakes Distillery LLC, WI
Absinthe, Verte	Artemisia Superior Absinthe Verte	Fat Dog Spirits LLC, FL
Absinthe, Verte	Extrait d'Absinthe Verte	Vilya Spirits LLC, MT
Absinthe, Verte	Knarr Absinthe Verte	Immortal Spirits & Distilling Co., OR
Absinthe, Verte	La Sorciere Absinthe Verte	Old World Spirits LLC, CA
Absinthe, Verte	Leopold Bros. Absinthe Verte	Leopold Bros., CO
Absinthe, Verte	Pacifique Absinthe Verte	Pacific Distillery LLC, WA
Absinthe, Verte	Sirène Absinthe Verte	North Shore Distillery, IL
Absinthe, Verte	St. George Absinthe Verte	St. George Spirits, CA
Absinthe, Verte	Toulouse Green, Absinthe Verte	Atelier Vie, LA
Agave, see also Tequila		
Agave	D'agave Extra	Peach Street Distillers, CO

Agave	Tatanka Agave Spirit	Roundhouse Spirits, CO
Agave	Trail Town Still Colorado Agave Liquor Desert Water	Trail Town Still, CO
Agave	Colorado Gold's Own Agave Spirits	Colorado Gold Distillery, CO
Agave, Anejo	State 38 Agave Anejo	State 38 Distilling, CO
Agave, Blanco	State 38 Agave Blanco	State 38 Distilling, CO
Agave, Blue	Midnight Caye Rested 100% Blue Agave Spirit	Tailwinds Distilling Company, IL
Agave, Blue	Midnight Caye Silver 100% Blue Agave Spirit	Tailwinds Distilling Company, IL
Agave, Blue	Railean "El Perico" Blue Agave Reposado	Railean Distillers, TX
Agave, Blue	Railean "El Perico" 100% Blue Agave Spirit	Railean Distillers, TX
Agave, Blue	Spirits of St. Louis, Agave Blue	Square One Brewery and Distillery, MO
Agave, Gin	State 38 Agave Gin	State 38 Distilling, CO
Agave, Gold	California Gold Agave	Saint James Spirits, CA
Agave, Gold	D'agave Gold	Peach Street Distillers, CO
Agave, Liquor	State 38 Agave Liquor	State 38 Distilling, CO
Agave, Respsado	State 38 Agave Reposado	State 38 Distilling, CO
Agave, Silver	D'agave Silver	Peach Street Distillers, CO
Agave, Vodka	State 38 Agave Vodka	State 38 Distilling, CO
Akvavit, Organic	Ekström's Organic Akvavit	Bluewater Distilling, WA
Anise	Black Rope Anise	Dry County Distillery LLC, WA
Apple Jack	Apple Jack	Forks of Cheat Distillery, WV
Apple Jack	Coppercraft Applejack	Coppercraft Distillery LLC, MI
Apple Jack	Cornelius Applejack	Harvest Spirits LLC, NY
Apple Jack	Golden Moon Colorado Apple Jack	Golden Moon Distillery, CO
Apple Jack	Nickel Back Apple Jack	High Mark Distillery, AK
Apple Jack	Tom's Foolery Applejack	Tom's Foolery, OH
Apple Jack	Tree Spirits Applejack	Tree Spirits, ME
Aquavit	Älskar Aquavit	Old Ballard Liquor Co., WA
Aquavit	Aquavit	The Hardware Distillery Co., WA
Aquavit	Aquavit Private Reserve	North Shore Distillery, IL
Aquavit	Krogstad Festlig Aquavit	House Spirits Distillery, OR
Aquavit	Krogstad Gamel Aquavit	House Spirits Distillery, OR
Aquavit	Okanagan Spirits Aquavit	Okanagan Spirits, BC

Aquavit	Riktig Aquavit	Old Ballard Liquor Co., WA
Aquavit	Skadi Aquavit	Montgomery Distillery, MT
Aquavit	Sound Spirits Aquavit	Sound Spirits, WA
Beer Spirit	KOVAL Bierbrand	KOVAL Distillery, IL
Bierschnapps	Bierschnapps	Five & 20 Spirits, NY
Bitters	Basement Bitters	Tuthilltown Spirits Distillery, NY
Bitters	Bettah Bitters	LB Distillers, SK
Bitters	Bitter Face Bitters	Fremont Mischief, WA
Bitters	Breckenridge Bitters	Breckenridge Distillery, CO
Bitters	Cocktail Kingdom Bitters	Berkshire Mountain Distillers Inc., MA
Bitters	Turin-Style Bitters	Breckenridge Distillery, CO
Bitters	Twisted and Bitter Bitters	Victoria Spirits, BC
Bitters,	Cherry Cherry Infused Bitters	Door County Distillery, WI
Bitters,	Orange Orange Bitters	Sun Liquor Distillery, WA
Bourbon, see Whiskey, Bourbon		
Brandy	A & G Brandy	St. Julian Winery, MI
Brandy	Alambic 13 Brandy	McMenamins Edgefield Distillery, OR
Brandy	Autry Cellars American Oaked	Autry Cellars, CA
Brandy	Autry Cellars Hungarian Oaked	Autry Cellars, CA
Brandy	Baerenfang Fruit and Honey Blended Brandy	Nashoba Valley Spirits Ltd., MA
Brandy	Bickering Brothers Brandy	Dakota Spirits Distillery LLC, SD
Brandy	Black Heron Brandy	Black Heron Spirits Distillery, WA
Brandy	Blue Flame Brandy	Blue Flame Spirits, WA
Brandy	Brandy – Aged in Oak Casks	Door County Distillery, WI
Brandy	Brandy Station (brandy distilled from Wisconsin grapes)	Old Sugar Distillery, WI
Brandy	Buena Vista Brandy	Deerhammer Distilling Company, CO
Brandy	Catoctin Creek 1757 Virginia Brandy™	Catoctin Creek Distilling Co. LLC, VA
Brandy	Charbay Brandy No. 89	Charbay Distillers, CA
Brandy	Chateau Chantal Brandy – "Cinq à Sept"	Chateau Chantal, MI
Brandy	Chateau Chantal Cerise	Chateau Chantal, MI
Brandy	Chateau Chantal Cerise Noir	Chateau Chantal, MI
Brandy	Chateau Chantal Entice	Chateau Chantal, MI

Brandy	Chauvet Brandy	HelloCello, CA
Brandy	Colorado Gold Brandy	Colorado Gold Distillery, CO
Brandy	COMB Blossom Brandy	StilltheOne Distillery LLC, NY
Brandy	Cowichan Cider Brandy	Merridale Ciderworks Corp., BC
Brandy	Don Quixote Pisco	Don Quixote Distillery & Winery, NM
Brandy	Edgefield Potstill Brandy	McMenamins Edgefield Distillery, OR
Brandy	Foggy Bog Brandy	Nashoba Valley Spirits Ltd., MA
Brandy	Germain-Robin Brandy	Germain-Robin , CA
Brandy	Johnny Hop Appl and Hop flower-infused Brandy	Nashoba Valley Spirits Ltd., MA
Brandy	Johnny Ziegler Brandy	Winegarden Estate Ltd., NB
Brandy	Kuchan Alambic Brandy	Old World Spirits LLC, CA
Brandy	Longshot Brandy	McMenamins Edgefield Distillery, OR
Brandy	Madrone Brandy	San Juan Island Distillery, WA
Brandy	MiLi BiT Tuică	LiL'BiT Distillery Inc., OR
Brandy	Nevada Brandy	Churchill Vineyards and Distillery, NV
Brandy	Northern Comfort Brandy	Nashoba Valley Spirits Ltd., MA
Brandy	Oregon Pot Distilled Brandy	Clear Creek Distillery, OR
Brandy	Randy's Brandy	Mountain View Distillery, PA
Brandy	Seneca Brandy	Forks of Cheat Distillery, WV
Brandy	Spirit of Santa Fe Brandy	Don Quixote Distillery & Winery, NM
Brandy	St. George Brandy	St. George Spirits, CA
Brandy	Starlight Distillery Brandy	Huber's Starlight Distillery, IN
Brandy	Tytonidae Brandy	Walla Walla Distilling Company, WA
Brandy, Apple	AEppelTreow WI Apple Brandy	AEppelTreow Winery & Distillery, WI
Brandy, Apple	American Fruits™ Apple Brandy	Warwick Valley Distillery, NY
Brandy, Apple	Apple Brandy	Clear Creek Distillery, OR
Brandy, Apple	Apple Brandy	Door County Distillery, WI
Brandy, Apple	Apple Brandy	Fifth Element Spirits, OH
Brandy, Apple	Apple Brandy	Nashoba Valley Spirits Ltd., MA
Brandy, Apple	Apple in the Bottle	Of The Earth Farm Distillery LLC, MO
Brandy, Apple		Clear Creek Distillery, OR
Brandy, Apple	Autry Cellars Apple Brandy	Autry Cellars, CA

600

Brandy, Apple	BelleWood Aged Apple Brandy	BelleWood Distilling, WA
Brandy, Apple	Bitterroot Heritage Apple Brandy	Swanson's Mountain View Orchard, MT
Brandy, Apple	Cedar Ridge Apple Brandy	Cedar Ridge Distillery, IA
Brandy, Apple	Dead Bird Apple Brandy	Shelburne Orchards Distillery, VT
Brandy, Apple	Don Quixote Qalvados – Apple Brandy	Don Quixote Distillery & Winery, NM
Brandy, Apple	Fine Apple Brandy	Spirits of Maine Distillery, ME
Brandy, Apple	Germain-Robin Apple Brandy	Germain-Robin, CA
Brandy, Apple	Golden Apple Brandy	Golden Distillery, WA
Brandy, Apple	Hubbard's Apple Brandy	Corey Lake Orchards, MI
Brandy, Apple	Humboldt Distillery Apple Brandy	Humboldt Distillery, CA
Brandy, Apple	Ironworks Apple Brandy	Ironworks Distillery, NS
Brandy, Apple	Ivy Mountain Apple Brandy™	Ivy Mountain Distillery LLC, GA
Brandy, Apple	KOVAL Apple Brandy	KOVAL Distillery, IL
Brandy, Apple	Mad River Apple Brandy	Mad River Distillers, VT
Brandy, Apple	Maple River Distillery Brandy - Apple	Maple River Distillery, ND
Brandy, Apple	Moonrise Distillery Apple Brandy	Moonrise Distillery Inc., GA
Brandy, Apple	No. 14 Apple Brandy	Vermont Spirits Distilling Co., VT
Brandy, Apple	One Foot Cock Apple Brandy	Buffalo Distilling Co., NY
Brandy, Apple	Pomme de Vie - Vermont Apple Brandy	Flag Hill Farm, VT
Brandy, Apple	Rhine Hall Apple Brandy	Rhine Hall, IL
Brandy, Apple	Santa Fe Apple Brandy	Santa Fe Spirits, NM
Brandy, Apple	Starlight Distillery Apple Brandy	Huber's Starlight Distillery, IN
Brandy, Apple	White Wolf Apple Brandy	White Wolf Distillery, WI
Brandy, Apple	Woody Creek Colorado Apple Brandy	Woody Creek Distillers, CO
Brandy, Apple	Yahara Bay Apple Brandy	Yahara Bay Distillers, WI
Brandy, Apple	Harvest Apple Brandy	Woods Mill Distillery, VA
Brandy, Apple	Oregon Apple Brandy (oaked)	Stone Barn Brandyworks, OR
Brandy, Apple Jack	Starlight Distillery Applejack Brandy	Huber's Starlight Distillery, IN
Brandy, Apple, 10-Year Barrel Aged	Michel Jodoin XO Apple Brandy barrel-aged 10 years	Cidrerie Michel Jodoin, QC
Brandy, Apple, 3-Year Barrel Aged	Michel Jodoin Apple Brandy barrel-aged 3 years	Cidrerie Michel Jodoin, QC
Brandy, Apple, Aged	Aged Apple Brandy	Westford Hill Distillers, CT
Brandy, Apple, Barrel Aged	Josiah Bartlett Barrel Aged Apple Brandy	Flag Hill Winery & Distillery, NH

Brandy, Apple, Oaked	Rhine Hall Oaked Apple Brandy	Rhine Hall, IL
Brandy, Apricot	Apricot	Maple Leaf Spirit Inc., BC
Brandy, Apricot	Koenig Apricot Brandy	Koenig Distillery, ID
Brandy, Apricot	Maple River Distillery Brandy - Apricot	Maple River Distillery, ND
Brandy, Aronia	Maple River Distillery Brandy - Aronia	Maple River Distillery, ND
Brandy, Asian Pear	Stillwater Spirits Asian Pear Brandy	Stillwater Spirits, CA
Brandy, Blackberry	Blackberry Brandy	San Juan Island Distillery, WA
Brandy, Blackberry	Moonrise Distillery Blackberry Brandy	Moonrise Distillery Inc., GA
Brandy, Blackberry	White Wolf Blackberry Brandy	White Wolf Distillery, WI
Brandy, Blue Plum	Blue Plum Brandy (Slivovitz)	Clear Creek Distillery, OR
Brandy, Botanical	RE:FIND Botanical Brandy	RE:FIND Distillery, CA
Brandy, Cherry	Cherry Brandy	Door County Distillery, WI
Brandy, Cherry	Hubbard's Cherry Brandy	Corey Lake Orchards, MI
Brandy, Cherry	Kirschwasser (Cherry Brandy)	Clear Creek Distillery, OR
Brandy, Cherry	Kirschwasser Cherry Brandy	Glacier Basin Distillery, WA
Brandy, Cherry	Kirschwasser Cherry Brandy	Yahara Bay Distillers, WI
Brandy, Cherry	Koenig Cherry Brandy	Koenig Distillery, ID
Brandy, Cherry	Pacific Northwest Cherry Brandy	Stone Barn Brandyworks, OR
Brandy, Chokecherry	Maple River Distillery Brandy - Chokecherry	Maple River Distillery, ND
Brandy, Coffee, Dark Roast	Columbian Dark Roast Brandy	Artisan Distillery LLC, ME
Brandy, Coffee, Hazelnut	Hazelnut Coffee Brandy	Artisan Distillery LLC, ME
Brandy, Elderberry	Elderberry Brandy	Nashoba Valley Spirits Ltd., MA
Brandy, Elderberry	Elderberry Brandy	Fifth Element Spirits, OH
Brandy, French Vanilla Coffee	French Vanilla Coffee Brandy	Artisan Distillery LLC, ME
Brandy, Grape	Cedar Ridge Grape Brandy	Cedar Ridge Distillery, IA
Brandy, Grape	Grape Brandy	Finger Lakes Distilling, NY
Brandy, Grape	Hubbard's Grape Brandy	Corey Lake Orchards, MI
Brandy, Grape	Maple River Distillery Brandy - Grape	Maple River Distillery, ND
Brandy, Grape	White Wolf Grape Brandy	White Wolf Distillery, WI
Brandy, Grape, Aged	Brandy Peak Aged Grape Brandy	Brandy Peak Distillery, OR
Brandy, Muscat	Brandy Peak Spirit of Muscat Brandy	Brandy Peak Distillery, OR
Brandy, Muscat, Aged	Brandy Peak Aged Muscat Brandy	Brandy Peak Distillery, OR

Brandy, Neutral	RE:FIND Neutral Brandy	RE:FIND Distillery, CA
Brandy, Peach	Hubbard's Peach Brandy	Corey Lake Orchards, MI
Brandy, Peach	Jack & Jenny Peach Brandy	Peach Street Distillers, CO
Brandy, Peach	Moonrise Distillery Peach Brandy	Moonrise Distillery Inc., GA
Brandy, Peach	Silk Peach Brandy	Nashoba Valley Spirits Ltd., MA
Brandy, Peach, Aged	Aged Peach Brandy	Peach Street Distillers, CO
Brandy, Peach, Georgia	Ivy Mountain Georgia Peach Brandy™	Ivy Mountain Distillery LLC, GA
Brandy, Pear	American Fruits™ Pear Brandy	Warwick Valley Distillery, NY
Brandy, Pear	Bartlett Pear Brandy	Stone Barn Brandyworks, OR
Brandy, Pear	Brandy Peak Natural Pear Brandy	Brandy Peak Distillery, OR
Brandy, Pear	Catoctin Creek Pearousia®	Catoctin Creek Distilling Co. LLC, VA
Brandy, Pear	Comice Pear Brandy	Stone Barn Brandyworks, OR
Brandy, Pear	Hubbard's Pear Brandy	Corey Lake Orchards, MI
Brandy, Pear	Humboldt Distillery Pear Brandy	Humboldt Distillery, CA
Brandy, Pear	Jack & Jenny Pear Brandy	Peach Street Distillers, CO
Brandy, Pear	Koenig Pear Brandy	Koenig Distillery, ID
Brandy, Pear	KOVAL Pear Brandy (Williams)	KOVAL Distillery, IL
Brandy, Pear	Maple River Distillery Brandy - Pear	Maple River Distillery, ND
Brandy, Pear	Pear Brandy	Finger Lakes Distilling, NY
Brandy, Pear	Pear Brandy	McMenamins Edgefield Distillery, OR
Brandy, Pear	Poire Prisonniere	Westford Hill Distillers, CT
Brandy, Pear	Rare Pear Brandy	Harvest Spirits LLC, NY
Brandy, Pear	Stair's Pear - Vermont Pear Brandy	Flag Hill Farm, VT
Brandy, Pear	Stairs Pear Brandy	Merridale Ciderworks Corp., BC
Brandy, Pear	Tree Spirits Pear Brandy	Tree Spirits, ME
Brandy, Pear	Woody Creek Colorado Pear Brandy (Eau De Vie)	Woody Creek Distillers, CO
Brandy, Pear	Yahara Bay Pear Brandy	Yahara Bay Distillers, WI
Brandy, Pear, Aged	Aged Pear Brandy	Peach Street Distillers, CO
Brandy, Pear, Aged	Brandy Peak Aged Pear Brandy	Brandy Peak Distillery, OR
Brandy, Pear, Williams	Williams Pear Brandy	Clear Creek Distillery, OR
Brandy, Pineapple	Saint James Spirits Pineapple Brandy	Saint James Spirits, CA
Brandy, Pinot Noir, Aged	Brandy Peak Aged Pinot Noir Brandy	Brandy Peak Distillery, OR

Brandy, Plum	Elephant Heart Plum-infused Brandy	Nashoba Valley Spirits Ltd., MA
Brandy, Plum	Koenig Plum Brandy	Koenig Distillery, ID
Brandy, Plum	Pacific Northwest Plum Brandy	Stone Barn Brandyworks, OR
Brandy, Plum	Plum Brandy (Slivovitz)	Stringer's Orchard Winery and Dist., OR
Brandy, Plum	Sidetrack Distillery Plum Brandy	Sidetrack Distillery, WA
Brandy, Plum	White Wolf Plum Brandy	White Wolf Distillery, WI
Brandy, Plum, Wild	Maple River Distillery Brandy - Wild Plum	Maple River Distillery, ND
Brandy, Private Reserve	Starlight Distillery Private Reserve Brandy	Huber's Starlight Distillery, IN
Brandy, Raspberry	White Wolf Raspberry Brandy	White Wolf Distillery, WI
Brandy, Rhubarb	Maple River Distillery Brandy - Rhubarb	Maple River Distillery, ND
Brandy, Special Reserve	Demarest Hill Winery Special Reserve Brandy	Demarest Hill Winery, NY
Brandy, Strawberry	Sidetrack Distillery Strawberry Brandy	Sidetrack Distillery, WA
Brandy, Thimbleberry	Thimbleberry Brandy	San Juan Island Distillery, WA
Brandy, Winterberry	Winterberry Brandy	San Juan Island Distillery, WA
Cider	Harvest Legacy Dessert Cider	Swanson's Mountain View Orchard, MT
Cider, Apple, Sweet	1911 Hard Cider Sweet Apple	Beak & Skiff Distillery, NY
Cider, Blueberry	1911 Hard Cider Blueberry	Beak & Skiff Distillery, NY
Cider, Hard	1911 Hard Cider	Beak & Skiff Distillery, NY
Cider, Hard	Apple Knocker	Dark Moon Artisan Distillery, WA
Cider, Light	1911 Hard Cider Light	Beak & Skiff Distillery, NY
Cider, Raspberry	1911 Hard Cider Raspberry	Beak & Skiff Distillery, NY
Cocktail	Red Sky at Night Cocktail	San Juan Island Distillery, WA
Cocktail, Apple	Uncle Don's Country Cocktail Old Fashion Apple	Uncle Don's Apple Pie Craft Dist., MI
Cocktail, Barrel Aged	Barrel-Aged Cocktails (East India)	Napa Valley Distillery, CA
Cocktail, Barrel Aged	Barrel-Aged Cocktails (Manhattan)	Napa Valley Distillery, CA
Cocktail, Barrel Aged	Barrel-Aged Cocktails (Mint Julep)	Napa Valley Distillery, CA
Cocktail, Barrel Aged	Barrel-Aged Cocktails (Negroni)	Napa Valley Distillery, CA
Cocktail, Barrel Aged	Barrel-Aged Cocktails (Old Hollywood)	Napa Valley Distillery, CA
Cocktail, Black Cherry	Uncle Don's Country Cocktail Black Cherry	Uncle Don's Apple Pie Craft Dist., MI
Cocktail, Blueberry	Uncle Don's Country Cocktail Blueberry	Uncle Don's Apple Pie Craft Dist., MI
Cocktail, Boulevardier	The Barreled Boulevardier	High West Distillery, UT
Cocktail, Gingeroo	Gingeroo – an Old New Orleans Rum Bottled Cocktail	Celebration Distillation, LA

Cocktail, Mai Tai	Kōloa Rum Company, HI
Cocktail, Manhattan	High West Distillery, UT
Cocktail, Peach	Uncle Don's Apple Pie Craft Dist., MI
Cocktail, Raspberry	Uncle Don's Apple Pie Craft Dist., MI
Cocktail, Rum Punch	Kōloa Rum Company, HI
Cordials, see Liqueur, Cordials	
Eai de Vie	KyMar Farm Distillery, NY
Eau de Vie	Cidrerie Michel Jodoin, QC
Eau de Vie	Peak Spirits® Farm Distillery, CO
Eau de Vie	Ironworks Distillery, NS
Eau de Vie	Shinn Estate Vineyards, NY
Eau de Vie, Apple	Walla Walla Distilling Company, WA
Eau de Vie, Apple	San Juan Island Distillery, WA
Eau de Vie, Apple	Five & 20 Spirits, NY
Eau de Vie, Apple	Harvest Spirits LLC, NY
Eau de Vie, Apple	Of The Earth Farm Distillery LLC, MO
Eau de Vie, Apple	It's 5 Artisan Distillery, WA
Eau de Vie, Apple	Merridale Ciderworks Corp., BC
Eau de Vie, Apple	BelleWood Distilling, WA
Eau de Vie, Apple	Clear Creek Distillery, OR
Eau de Vie, Apple	Cidrerie Michel Jodoin, QC
Eau de Vie, Apple	San Juan Island Distillery, WA
Eau de Vie, Apple	Sea Hagg Distillery, NH
Eau de Vie, Apricot	It's 5 Artisan Distillery, WA
Eau de Vie, Apricot	Okanagan Spirits, BC
Eau de Vie, Canados	Okanagan Spirits, BC
Eau de Vie, Cherry	Chateau Chantal, MI
Eau de Vie, Cherry	Spirits Ltd., MA
Eau de Vie, Cherry	Five & 20 Spirits, NY
Eau de Vie, Cherry	It's 5 Artisan Distillery, WA
Eau de Vie, Cherry	Coppersea Distilling, NY
Eau de Vie, Cherry	Don Quixote Distillery & Winery, NM

Kōloa Mai Tai Cocktail	
The 36th Vote Barreled Manhattan	
Uncle Don's Country Cocktail Fuzzy Peach	
Uncle Don's Country Cocktail Raspberry	
Kōloa Rum Punch Cocktail	
Schoharie Eau de Vie de Pomme	
Ambre de pomme (fortified cider)	
CapRock® Organic Eaux de Vie	
Ironworks Eaux de Vie	
Shinn Estate Vineyards Eau de Vie	
Tytonidae Eau-de-Vie	
Apple Eau de vie	
Apple Eau de Vie	
Apple Eau de Vie	
Apple Eau de Vie	
Apple Eaux de Vie	
Apple Oh! De Vie	
BelleWood Apple Eau de Vie	
Eau de Vie de Pomme	
Pom de vie	
Pommeau	
Sea Hagg Eau de Vie Apple	
Apricot Eaux de Vie	
Okanagan Spirits Apricot Eau de Vie	
Okanagan Spirits Canados Eau de Vie	
Chateau Chantal Cherry Eau de Vie	
Cherry Eau de vie	
Cherry Eau de Vie	
Cherry Eaux de Vie	
Coppersea New York Cherry Eau de Vie	
Don Quixote Mon Cherie Cherry Eau de Vie	

605

Eau de Vie, Douglas Fir	Eau de Vie of Douglas Fir	Clear Creek Distillery, OR
Eau de Vie, Fraise	Fraise Eau de vie	Westford Hill Distillers, CT
Eau de Vie, Framboise	Framboise Eau de vie	Westford Hill Distillers, CT
Eau de Vie, Honey	Honey Eau de Vie	Spirits of Maine Distillery, ME
Eau de Vie, Kirsch	Kirsch Eau de vie	Westford Hill Distillers, CT
Eau de Vie, Kirsch	Saint James Spirits Kirsch (Eau de Vie)	Saint James Spirits, CA
Eau de Vie, Kirsch Dandue	Okanagan Spirits Kirsch Danbue Eau de Vie	Okanagan Spirits, BC
Eau de Vie, Kirsch Virginiana	Okanagan Spirits Kirsch Virginiana Eau de Vie	Okanagan Spirits, BC
Eau de Vie, Maple	Maple Eau de Vie	Jost Vineyards Ltd., NS
Eau de Vie, Muscat	Muscat Eau de Vie	Jost Vineyards Ltd., NS
Eau de Vie, Peach	Coppersea New York Peach Eau de Vie	Coppersea Distilling, NY
Eau de Vie, Peach	Peach Eau de Vie	Spirits of Maine Distillery, ME
Eau de Vie, Peach, Aged	Kuchan Eaux De Vie, O'Henry Oak Aged Peach	Old World Spirits LLC, CA
Eau de Vie, Peach, Indian Blood	Kuchan Eaux De Vie, Indian Blood Peach	Old World Spirits LLC, CA
Eau de Vie, Pear	Chateau Chantal Pear Eau de Vie	Chateau Chantal, MI
Eau de Vie, Pear	Classick Pure Pear Eau-de-Vie	Essential Spirits Alambic Distilleries, CA
Eau de Vie, Pear	Coppersea New York Pear Eau de Vie	Coppersea Distilling, NY
Eau de Vie, Pear	Great Lakes Artisan Series Pear Eau-de-Vie	Great Lakes Distillery LLC, WI
Eau de Vie, Pear	Pear Eau de Vie	Harvest Spirits LLC, NY
Eau de Vie, Pear	Pear Eau de Vie	Spirits of Maine Distillery, ME
Eau de Vie, Pear	Pear Eau de Vie	Five & 20 Spirits, NY
Eau de Vie, Pear	Pear Eaux de Vie	It's 5 Artisan Distillery, WA
Eau de Vie, Pear	Pear in the Bottle Pear Eau de Vie	Five & 20 Spirits, NY
Eau de Vie, Pear	Pear William Eau de vie	Westford Hill Distillers, CT
Eau de Vie, Pear	Pear Williams	Maple Leaf Spirit Inc., BC
Eau de Vie, Pear	Sea Hagg Eau de Vie Pear	Sea Hagg Distillery, NH
Eau de Vie, Pear	Pear in the Bottle	Clear Creek Distillery, OR
Eau de Vie, Plum	Chateau Chantal Plum Eau de Vie	Chateau Chantal, MI
Eau de Vie, Plum	Coppersea New York Plum Eau de Vie	Coppersea Distilling, NY
Eau de Vie, Plum	Plum Eau de Vie	Five & 20 Spirits, NY
Eau de Vie, Plum	Plum Eaux de Vie	It's 5 Artisan Distillery, WA
Eau de Vie, Plum, Red	Red Plum Eau de Vie	Jost Vineyards Ltd., NS

Eau de Vie, Plum, Yellow	Yellow Plum Eau de Vie	Jost Vineyards Ltd., NS
Eau de Vie, Poire	Eua de Vie Poire	Immortal Spirits & Distilling Co., OR
Eau de Vie, Poire Williams	Kuchan Eaux De Vie, Poire Williams	Old World Spirits LLC, CA
Eau de Vie, Poire Williams	Okanagan Spirits Poire Williams Eau de Vie	Okanagan Spirits, BC
Eau de Vie, Prune	Okanagan Spirits Italian Prune Eau de Vie	Okanagan Spirits, BC
Eau de Vie, Prune	Okanagan Spirits Old Italian Prune Eau de Vie	Okanagan Spirits, BC
Eau de Vie, Prune	Italian Prune	Maple Leaf Spirit Inc., BC
Eau de Vie, Prune, Aged	Aged Italian Prune	Maple Leaf Spirit Inc., BC
Eau de Vie, Raspberry	Okanagan Spirits Raspberry Framboise Eau de Vie	Okanagan Spirits, BC
Eau de Vie, Raspberry	Raspberry Eau de vie	Nashoba Valley Spirits Ltd., MA
Eau de Vie, Voignier	Voignier Eaux de Vie	It's 5 Artisan Distillery, WA
Fortified	Mure Oh!	Merridale Ciderworks Corp., BC
Fortified, Apple	Pomme Oh!	Merridale Ciderworks Corp., BC
Geist	Raspberry Geist	Spirits of Maine Distillery, ME
Gin	1542: California Native Botanical Gin	Old Harbor Distilling Company, CA
Gin	1911 Gin	Beak & Skiff Distillery, NY
Gin	3rd Ward Gin	Cajun Spirits Distillery, LA
Gin	50 Fathoms Gin Port	Chilkoot Distillery, AK
Gin	Abernathy Gin	Tenn South Distillery, TN
Gin	Adirondack ADK Gin	Adirondack Distilling Company, NY
Gin	Amador Distillery Gin	Amador Distillery, CA
Gin	Amythyst Gin	The Ellensburg Distillery, WA
Gin	Anselmo Gin	Headframe Spirits, MT
Gin	Autumnal Gin	Letherbee Distillers, IL
Gin	Back River Gin	Sweetgrass Farm Winery & Distillery, ME
Gin	BelleWood Gin	BelleWood Distilling, WA
Gin	Big Gin	Captive Spirits, WA
Gin	Bilberry Black Heart's Gin	Journeyman Distillery, MI
Gin	Black Button Citrus Forward Gin	Black Button Distilling, NY
Gin	Black Button Lilac Gin	Black Button Distilling, NY
Gin	Black Window Gin	Spirits of the USA LLC, FL
Gin	Blade California Small Batch Gin	Old World Spirits LLC, CA

Gin	Blaum Bros. Gin	Blaum Bros. Distilling Co., IL
Gin	Blue Flame Gin	Blue Flame Spirits, WA
Gin	Blue Flame Ultra Premium Gin	Blue Flame Spirits, WA
Gin	Blue Line Gin	Lake Placid Spirits LLC, NY
Gin	Blue Spirits Gin	Blue Spirits Distilling, WA
Gin	Bog Monster Gin	Dirty Water Distillery, MA
Gin	Botanica Spiritvs	Falcon Spirits LLC, CA
Gin	Brandon's Gin	Rock Town Distillery Inc., AR
Gin	Bristol Bay Glacier Gin	Alaska Distillery, AK
Gin	Bristow Gin	Cathead Distillery LLC, MS
Gin	Bulfinch 83 Redistilled Gin	Wishkah River Distillery, WA
Gin	Bull Run Gin	Bull Run Distilling Company, OR
Gin	Bullwheel Gin	Deerhammer Distilling Company, CO
Gin	Candy Manor Gin	Painted Stave Distilling, DE
Gin	Cardinal Gin	Southern Artisan Spirits, NC
Gin	CH Key Gin	CH Distillery, IL
Gin	Chief Gowanus – New-Netherland Gin	New York Distilling Company, NY
Gin	Chuckanut Bay Gin	Chuckanut Bay Distillery, WA
Gin	Civilized Gin	Northern United Brewing Co., MI
Gin	ClearHeart Gin	Cedar Ridge Distillery, IA
Gin	Cold River Gin	Maine Distilleries LLC, ME
Gin	Colorado Fog Gin	Mystic Mountain Distillery LLC, CO
Gin	Colorado Gold Premium Gin	Colorado Gold Distillery, CO
Gin	COMB 9 Gin	StilltheOne Distillery LLC, NY
Gin	Coopercraft Gin	Coppercraft Distillery LLC, MI
Gin	Coppers Gin	Vermont Spirits Distilling Co., VT
Gin	Copperworks Gin	Copperworks Distilling Company, WA
Gin	Corsair Gin	Corsair Artisan Distillery, TN
Gin	Counter Gin	Batch 206 Distillery, WA
Gin	Crabby Ginny	The Hardware Distillery Co., WA
Gin	Cranberry Gin	Sweetgrass Farm Winery & Distillery, ME
Gin	Crater Lake Gin	Bendistillery, OR

Gin	Cricket Club Gin	Indio Spirits, OR
Gin	Dancing Pines Gin	Dancing Pines Distillery, CO
Gin	Death's Door Gin	Death's Door Spirits, WI
Gin	Delaware Distilling Company Premium Gin	Delaware Distilling Company, DE
Gin	Dirty Gin	Two Guns Distillery, CO
Gin	Distiller's Gin No. 11	North Shore Distillery, IL
Gin	Distiller's Gin No. 6	North Shore Distillery, IL
Gin	Don Quixote Gin	Don Quixote Distillery & Winery, NM
Gin	Door County Gin	Door County Distillery, WI
Gin	Douglas County Gin	Project V Distillery and Sausage Co., WA
Gin	Down & Dirty	Black Sam Distillery Co., WA
Gin	Dry Fly Barrel Reserve Gin	Dry Fly Distilling, WA
Gin	Ebb+Flow Gin	Sound Spirits, WA
Gin	Elk Rider Crisp Gin	Heritage Distilling Company, WA
Gin	Endeavour Gin	The Liberty Distillery, BC
Gin	Ethereal Gin	Berkshire Mountain Distillers Inc., MA
Gin	Euphrosine Gin #9	Atelier Vie, LA
Gin	Fenimore Gin	Cooperstown Distillery, NY
Gin	Finn's Gin	Chicago Distilling Company, IL
Gin	Fitzgerald Gin	Du Nord Craft Spirits, MN
Gin	Fremont Mischief Gin	Fremont Mischief, WA
Gin	Gables Gin	McMenamins Cornelius Pass, OR
Gin	Gale Force Gin	Triple Eight Distillery, MA
Gin	Gambit Gin	LB Distillers, SK
Gin	Gin No. 1	New Deal Distillery, OR
Gin	Glorious Gin	Breuckelen Distilling Company Inc., NY
Gin	Golden Moon Gin	Golden Moon Distillery, CO
Gin	Good Old Fashioned Gin	3 Howls Distillery, WA
Gin	Green Hat Gin	New Columbia Distillers, DC
Gin	Green Hat Seasonal Gin	New Columbia Distillers, DC
Gin	Greylock Gin	Berkshire Mountain Distillers Inc., MA
Gin	Griffon	Double V Distillery, WA

Gin	Gun Club Gin	Sun Liquor Distillery, WA
Gin	Half Moon Orchard Gin	Tuthilltown Spirits Distillery, NY
Gin	Hat Trick Botanical Gin	High Wire Distilling, SC
Gin	Healy's Gin	Trailhead Spirits, MT
Gin	Hedge Trimmer Gin	Sun Liquor Distillery, WA
Gin	Heirloom Gin	Norseman Distillery, MN
Gin	Homeport Craft Distilled Gin	Port Steilacoom Distillery, WA
Gin	Ingenium Gin	New England Distilling, ME
Gin	Isis Premium Gin	Mac Donald Distillery, WA
Gin	Jack Pine Gin	Northern Latitudes Distillery, MI
Gin	Jackelope and Jenny Gin	Peach Street Distillers, CO
Gin	Jackelope Gin	Peach Street Distillers, CO
Gin	Jagged Peaks Gin	Tahoe Moonshine Distillery Inc., CA
Gin	Jinn Gin	K J Wood Distillers LLC, CO
Gin	Karner Blue Gin	Flag Hill Winery & Distillery, NH
Gin	Kennewick Fine Gin	RiverSands Distillery, WA
Gin	Knickerbocker Gin	New Holland Artisan Spirits, MI
Gin	Knockabout Gin	Ryan & Wood Inc., MA
Gin	Leopold Bros. American Small Batch Gin	Leopold Bros., CO
Gin	Letherbee Gin	Letherbee Distillers, IL
Gin	Los Luceros Hacienda Gin	Rancho de Los Luceros Destilaria, NM
Gin	Loyalist Gin	66 Gilead Distillery, ON
Gin	McKenzie Distiller's Reserve Gin	Finger Lakes Distilling, NY
Gin	MetropoliGin	Loon Liquors, MN
Gin	Midwest Gin	45th Parallel Distillery, WI
Gin	Missouri Spirits Gin	Missouri Spirits, MO
Gin	Myer Farm Gin	Myer Farm Distillers, NY
Gin	Navy Strength Gin	3 Howls Distillery, WA
Gin	Nicholas Gin	Fat Dog Spirits LLC, FL
Gin	No. 209 Gin	Distillery No. 209, CA
Gin	Noteworthy Gin	The Dubh Glas Distillery, BC
Gin	Oaken Gin	Victoria Spirits, BC

Gin	Okanagan Spirits Gin	Okanagan Spirits, BC
Gin	Old Grove Gin	Ballast Point Spirits, CA
Gin	Old Hollywood Gin	Napa Valley Distillery, CA
Gin	Old No. 176™ Railroad Gin	Quincy Street Distillery, IL
Gin	Old Point Comfort Gin	Three Brothers' Whiskey Distillery, VA
Gin	OOLA Gin	OOLA Distillery, WA
Gin	Oryza Gin	Donner-Peltier Distillers, LA
Gin	Peninsula Gin	Grand Traverse Distillery, MI
Gin	Penny's Gin	McMenamins Edgefield Distillery, OR
Gin	Perry's Tot - Navy Strength Gin	New York Distilling Company, NY
Gin	Phrog Premium Gin	Island Spirits Distillery, BC
Gin	Piger Henricus Gin	The Subersives Distillers, QC
Gin	Professors Gin	McMenamins Edgefield Distillery, OR
Gin	Prohibition Gin	Heartland Distillers, IN
Gin	R Gin	The Hardware Distillery Co., WA
Gin	RE:FIND Gin	RE:FIND Distillery, CA
Gin	Red X Gin	Valley Shine Distillery, WA
Gin	Rehorst Premium Milwaukee Gin	Great Lakes Distillery LLC, WI
Gin	River Rose Gin	Mississippi River Distilling Company, IA
Gin	RMD Gin	Artesian Distillers, MI
Gin	Rob's Mountain Gin	Spring44 Distilling, CO
Gin	Rogue Pink Gin	Rogue Spirits, OR
Gin	Rogue Spruce Gin	Rogue Spirits, OR
Gin	Rolling River Spirits Gin	Rolling River Spirits, OR
Gin	Roundhouse Gin	Roundhouse Spirits, CO
Gin	San Miguel: Southwestern Gin	Old Harbor Distilling Company, CA
Gin	Sandstone Distillery Black Gin	Sandstone Distillery LLC, WA
Gin	Sandstone Distillery Gin	Sandstone Distillery LLC, WA
Gin	Seneca Drums Gin	Finger Lakes Distilling, NY
Gin	Seraph Gin	Central City Brewers and Distillers, BC
Gin	Shoal Finder Gin	Clayton Distillery, NY
Gin	Show Pony Gin	Steel Toe Distillery, MT

Gin	Six Mile Creek Gin	Six Mile Creek Winery & Distillery, NY
Gin	Small's Gin	Ransom Spirits, OR
Gin	Smooth Ambler Greenbrier Gin	Smooth Ambler Spirits Company, WV
Gin	Smugglers' Notch Gin	Smugglers' Notch Distillery, VT
Gin	Solveig	Far North Spirits, MN
Gin	Southern Gin	Thirteenth Colony Distilleries, GA
Gin	Spirit Bear Gin	Urban Distilleries, BC
Gin	Spirit Hound Gin	Spirit Hound Distillers, CO
Gin	Spirit of Santa Fe Gin	Don Quixote Distillery & Winery, NM
Gin	Spirit Works Gin	Spirit Works Distillery, CA
Gin	Spirits of St. Louis, Regatta Bay Gin	Square One Brewery and Distillery, MO
Gin	Spring44 Gin	Spring44 Distilling, CO
Gin	Spy Hop Gin	San Juan Island Distillery, WA
Gin	Starling Gin	25th Street Spirits, OH
Gin	Stay Tuned Distillery PathoGin	Stay Tuned Distillery LLC, PA
Gin	Stillwater Spirits Gin	Stillwater Spirits, CA
Gin	Stoutridge Gin	Stoutridge Distillery, NY
Gin	Strait Gin	Myriad View Artisan Distillery Inc., PE
Gin	Summer Harvest Gin	Ursa Major Distilling, AK
Gin	Sunset Hills Virginia Gin	A. Smith Bowman Distillery, VA
Gin	The Alpinist Gin	Seattle Distilling Company, WA
Gin	TOPO Piedmont Gin	Top of the Hill Distillery, NC
Gin	Trail Town Still Colorado Gin	Trail Town Still, CO
Gin	Treeline Gin	Wood's High Mountain Distillery, CO
Gin	TRU Gin	GreenBar Collective, CA
Gin	Two James Gin	Two James Spirits, MI
Gin	Tytonidae Gin	Walla Walla Distilling Company, WA
Gin	Ugly Dog Gin	Ugly Dog Distillery LLC, MI
Gin	Union Gin	Dogwood Distilling, OR
Gin	Valentine Liberator Gin	Valentine Distilling Company, MI
Gin	Vernal Gin	Letherbee Distillers, IL
Gin	Victoria Gin	Victoria Spirits, BC

Gin	Vivacity Bankers' Gin	Vivacity Spirits, OR
Gin	Vivacity Native Gin	Vivacity Spirits, OR
Gin	Voyager Single Batch Distilled Gin	Pacific Distillery LLC, WA
Gin	Walla Walla Gin	Walla Walla Distilling Company, WA
Gin	Wallflower Gin	Odd Society Spirits, BC
Gin	Waterloo Gin	Treaty Oak Distilling Co., TX
Gin	Wheat State Distilling Gin	Wheat State Distilling, KS
Gin	Wheelers Gin	Santa Fe Spirits, NM
Gin	Whistling Andy Gin	Whistling Andy Distillery, MT
Gin	Whyte Laydie Gin	Montgomery Distillery, MT
Gin	Wildflower Gin	Honey House Distillery, CO
Gin	Yaletown Distilling Company BC Gin	Yaletown Distilling Company, BC
Gin, Aged	Corsair Barrel Aged Gin	Corsair Artisan Distillery, TN
Gin, Aged	Rusty Blade Barrel Aged Gin	Old World Spirits LLC, CA
Gin, Aged	Waterloo Antique Aged Gin	Treaty Oak Distilling Co., TX
Gin, American	Aviation American Gin	House Spirits Distillery, OR
Gin, American	Dorothy Parker - American Gin	New York Distilling Company, NY
Gin, American	Few American Gin	Few Spirits LLC, IL
Gin, American	Pinckney Bend American Gin	Pinckney Bend Distillery, MO
Gin, American	Warwick Rustic American Gin	Warwick Valley Distillery, NY
Gin, American	Wire Works American Gin	GrandTen Distilling, MA
Gin, Barrel Aged	Barrel Aged Ethereal Gin	Berkshire Mountain Distillers Inc., MA
Gin, Barrel Aged	Bilberry Black Heart's Gin Barrel Aged	Journeyman Distillery, MI
Gin, Barrel Aged	Bourbon Barrel Aged Big Gin	Captive Spirits, WA
Gin, Barrel Aged	Coppercraft Barrel Aged Gin	Coppercraft Distillery LLC, MI
Gin, Barrel Aged	Imperial Barrel Aged Gin	Roundhouse Spirits, CO
Gin, Barrel Aged	Smooth Ambler Barrel Aged Gin	Smooth Ambler Spirits Company, WV
Gin, Barrel Finished	OOLA Waitsburg Barrel-Finished Gin	OOLA Distillery, WA
Gin, Barrel Reserve	Brandon's Gin Barrel Reserve	Rock Town Distillery Inc. , AR
Gin, Barrel Reserve	No. 209 Cabernet Sauvignon Barrel Reserve Gin	Distillery No. 209, CA
Gin, Barrel Reserve	Old No. 176™ Barrel Reserve Gin	Quincy Street Distillery, IL
Gin, Barrel Reserve, Blanc	No. 209 Sauvignon Blanc Barrel Reserve Gin	Distillery No. 209, CA

613

Gin, Barrel Rested	Wheat State Distilling Barrel Rested Gin	Wheat State Distilling, KS
Gin, Blueberry, Wild	Prince Edward Wild Blueberry Gin	Prince Edward Distillery, PE
Gin, Botanivore	St. George Botanivore Gin	St. George Spirits, CA
Gin, Bourbon Barrel	Watershed Distillery Bourbon Barrel Gin	Watershed Distillery, OH
Gin, Cask Rested	Healy's Reserve - Cask Rested Gin	Trailhead Spirits, MT
Gin, Dry	Corbin Western Dry Gin	Sweet Potato Spirits, CA
Gin, Dry	Desert Dry Gin	Arizona High Spirits Distillery, AZ
Gin, Dry	Dry County Gin	Dry County Distillery LLC, WA
Gin, Dry	Northwest Dry Gin	It's 5 Artisan Distillery, WA
Gin, Dry	Portland Dry Gin 33	New Deal Distillery, OR
Gin, Dry	Quimby and Jack's Distilled Dry Gin	Carbon Glacier Distillery, WA
Gin, Dry	Denver Dry Gin	Mile High Spirits LLC, CO
Gin, Dry, American	Bluecoat American Dry Gin	Philadelphia Distilling, PA
Gin, Dry, American	Greenhook Ginsmiths American Dry Gin	Greenhook Ginsmiths, NY
Gin, Dry, American	Moody June American Dry Gin	Bone Spirits, TX
Gin, Dry, American	Silvertip American Dry Gin	Vilya Spirits LLC, MT
Gin, Dry, London	Bardenay London Dry Gin	Bardenay Inc., ID
Gin, Dry, London	CH London Dry Gin	CH Distillery, IL
Gin, Dry, London	Long Table Distillery London Dry Gin	Long Table Distillery Ltd., BC
Gin, Dry, Rye	St. George Dry Rye Gin	St. George Spirits, CA
Gin, Extra Dry	Yahara Bay Extra Dry Gin	Yahara Bay Distillers, WI
Gin, Four Peel	Watershed Distillery Four Peel Gin	Watershed Distillery, OH
Gin, Genever	Corsair Genever	Corsair Artisan Distillery, TN
Gin, Genever	Merrylegs Genever	Oregon Spirit Distillers, OR
Gin, Hemp	Mary Jane's Premium Hemp Gin	Mary Jane's, ON
Gin, Hopped	Smugglers' Notch Hopped Gin	Smugglers' Notch Distillery, VT
Gin, Kosher	No. 209 Kosher-for-Passover Gin	Distillery No. 209, CA
Gin, Old Tom	Old Tom Gin	Ransom Spirits, OR
Gin, Old Tom	Sound Spirits – Old Tom Gin	Sound Spirits, WA
Gin, Old Tom	Spring44 Old Tom Gin	Spring44 Distilling, CO
Gin, Old Tom	Valentine Liberator Old Tom Gin	Valentine Distilling Company, MI
Gin, Organic	Bainbridge Heritage Organic Gin	Bainbridge Organic Distillers, WA

Gin, Organic	CapRock® Organic Gin	Peak Spirits® Farm Distillery, CO
Gin, Organic	Catoctin Creek Organic Watershed Gin®	Catoctin Creek Distilling Co. LLC, VA
Gin, Organic	Green Mountain Organic Gin	Green Mountain Distillers, VT
Gin, Organic	Halcyon Organic Distilled Gin	Bluewater Distilling, WA
Gin, Organic	Organic Nation Gin	Cascade Peak Spirits Distillery, OR
Gin, Organic	Schramm Organic Gin	Pemberton Distillery Inc., BC
Gin, Organic	Wigle Organic Ginever	Pittsburgh Distilling Co., PA
Gin, Plum	Pacific Plum Gin	Stringer's Orchard Winery, OR
Gin, Sloe	Spirit Works Sloe Gin	Spirit Works Distillery, CA
Gin, Soft	HDC Soft Gin	Heritage Distilling Company, WA
Gin, Special Reserve	Wire Works Special Reserve Gin	GrandTen Distilling, MA
Gin, Spicebush	Fifth Element Spirits Spicebush Gin	Fifth Element Spirits, OH
Gin, Terroir	St. George Terroir Gin	St. George Spirits, CA
Gin, Wheat	Dry Fly Washington Wheat Gin	Dry Fly Distilling, WA
Grappa	1512 Spirits Grappa	1512 Spirits, CA
Grappa	A 24- month aged Grappa blend of Merlot, Cab & Syrah	Soft Tail Spirits, wa
Grappa	Autry Cellars Grappa	Autry Cellars, CA
Grappa	Blue Flame Grappa	Blue Flame Spirits, WA
Grappa	Brandy Peak Grappa	Brandy Peak Distillery, OR
Grappa	CapRock® Biodynamic® Estate Grappa	Peak Spirits® Farm Distillery, CO
Grappa	Cavatappi Nebbiolo Grappa	Clear Creek Distillery, OR
Grappa	Cavatappi Sangiovese Grappa	Clear Creek Distillery, OR
Grappa	Cedar Ridge Grappa	Cedar Ridge Distillery, IA
Grappa	Classick Grappa di Cabernet - Stags Leap	Essential Spirits Alambic Distilleries, CA
Grappa	Demarest Hill Winery Grappa	Demarest Hill Winery, NY
Grappa	Don Quixote Grappa	Don Quixote Distillery & Winery, NM
Grappa	Don Quixote Malvasia Bianca Grappa	Don Quixote Distillery & Winery, NM
Grappa	Fiore Grappa	Fiore Winery & Distillery, MD
Grappa	Germain-Robin Grappa	Germain-Robin , CA
Grappa	Gewurztraminer Grappa	Finger Lakes Distilling, NY
Grappa	Gewürztraminer Grappa	Ransom Spirits, OR
Grappa	Giallo Grappa	Soft Tail Spirits, wa

Grappa	Golden Moon Colorado Grappa	Golden Moon Distillery, CO
Grappa	Graham's Grappa	Flag Hill Winery & Distillery, NH
Grappa	Grappa	Broadbent Distillery, IA
Grappa	Grappa	Harvest Spirits LLC, NY
Grappa	Grappa	It's 5 Artisan Distillery, WA
Grappa	Grappa	Of The Earth Farm Distillery LLC, MO
Grappa	Grappa	Forks of Cheat Distillery, WV
Grappa	Grappa	Glacier Basin Distillery, WA
Grappa	Grappa & Limone	Magnanini Farm Winery Inc., NY
Grappa	Grappa & Miele	Magnanini Farm Winery Inc., NY
Grappa	Grappa & Walnut	Magnanini Farm Winery Inc., NY
Grappa	Grappa Del Nonno	Magnanini Farm Winery Inc., NY
Grappa	Grappa Moscato	Clear Creek Distillery, OR
Grappa	Grappa Muscat	Peach Street Distillers, CO
Grappa	Grappa of Gewurztraminer	Peach Street Distillers, CO
Grappa	Grappa of Steuben	Five & 20 Spirits, NY
Grappa	Grappa of Viognier	Peach Street Distillers, CO
Grappa	Great Lakes Artisan Series Grappa	Great Lakes Distillery LLC, WI
Grappa	Johnny Ziegler Grappa	Winegarden Estate Ltd., NB
Grappa	Koenig Grappa	Koenig Distillery, ID
Grappa	Marc de Gewürztraminer	Clear Creek Distillery, OR
Grappa	Mill St. Grappa	Mill St. Distillery LLC, OH
Grappa	Red Hook Grappa	Van Brunt Stillhouse, NY
Grappa	Rhine Hall Grappa	Rhine Hall, IL
Grappa	Saint James Spirits Grappa	Saint James Spirits, CA
Grappa	Sangiovese Grappa	Soft Tail Spirits, wa
Grappa	Six Mile Creek Grappa	Six Mile Creek Winery & Distillery, NY
Grappa	Skinny Gewurztraminer	Maple Leaf Spirit Inc., BC
Grappa	Skinny Syrah	Maple Leaf Spirit Inc., BC
Grappa	Starlight Distillery Grappa	Huber's Starlight Distillery, IN
Grappa	Stillwater Spirits Cabernet Sauvignon Grappa	Stillwater Spirits, CA
Grappa	T & W Grappa Di Muscatto	Empire Winery & Distillery, FL

Grappa	Tytonidae Grappa	Walla Walla Distilling Company, WA
Grappa	Vidal Grappa	Nashoba Valley Spirits Ltd., MA
Grappa	Woodstock Reserve	Soft Tail Spirits, WA
Grappa, Blanco	Soft Tail Blanco Grappa	Soft Tail Spirits, wa
Grappa, Chardonnay	Chardonnay Grappa	Fifth Element Spirits, OH
Grappa, Gewurztraminer	Okanagan Spirits Gewurztraminer Grappa	Okanagan Spirits, BC
Grappa, Oaked	Rhine Hall Oaked Grappa	Rhine Hall, IL
Grappa, Pinot Grigio	Grappa of Pinot Grigio	Clear Creek Distillery, OR
Grappa, Pinot Noir	Grappa of Oregon Pinot Noir	Clear Creek Distillery, OR
Grappa, Pinot Noir	Okanagan Spirits Pinot Noir Grappa	Okanagan Spirits, BC
Grappa, Pinot Noir	Pinot Noir Grappa	Stone Barn Brandyworks, OR
Grappa, Pinot Noir	Skinny Pinot Noir	Maple Leaf Spirit Inc., BC
Grappa, Riesling	Okanagan Spirits Riesling Grappa	Okanagan Spirits, BC
Grappa, Riesling	Riesling Grappa	Finger Lakes Distilling, NY
Kirsch	Canadian Kirsch	Maple Leaf Spirit Inc., BC
Kirschwasser	Great Lakes Artisan Series Kirschwasser	Great Lakes Distillery LLC, WI
Liqueur	broVo Amaro No 1	broVo Spirits, WA
Liqueur	broVo Amaro No 2	broVo Spirits, WA
Liqueur	broVo Amaro No 3	broVo Spirits, WA
Liqueur	broVo Amaro No 4	broVo Spirits, WA
Liqueur	broVo Amaro No 5	broVo Spirits, WA
Liqueur	broVo Amaro No 6	broVo Spirits, WA
Liqueur	Calisaya®	Elixir Inc., OR
Liqueur	Carmine Jewel Liqueur	LB Distillers, SK
Liqueur	Cassis Liqueur	Clear Creek Distillery, OR
Liqueur	Cassis Liqueur	Winegarden Estate Ltd., NB
Liqueur	Crème de Cassis Liqueur	LB Distillers, SK
Liqueur	Demarest Hill Winery Amarena Aperitivo	Demarest Hill Winery, NY
Liqueur	Demarest Hill Winery Tropical Liqueur	Demarest Hill Winery, NY
Liqueur	Deputy Dave's Contraband Liquor	Three Brothers' Whiskey Distillery, VA
Liqueur	Distroya Liqueur	Mile High Spirits LLC, CO
Liqueur	Fine Caroline	Cidrerie Michel Jodoin, QC

617

Liqueur	Fruit Basket Liqueur	The Dubh Glas Distillery, BC
Liqueur	FRUITLAB Liqueur	GreenBar Collective, CA
Liqueur	Golden Moon Amer dit Picon	Golden Moon Distillery, CO
Liqueur	Golden Moon Dry Curacao	Golden Moon Distillery, CO
Liqueur	GRAND POPPY Bitter Liqueur	GreenBar Collective, CA
Liqueur	Hideous Liqueur	Hideous LC, TX
Liqueur	Holiday Spiced Liqueur	Eastside Distilling, OR
Liqueur	Hoodoo Chicory Liqueur	Cathead Distillery LLC, MS
Liqueur	Iris™	Elixir Inc., OR
Liqueur	Koltiska 90 Proof Liqueur	Kolts Fine Spirits, WY
Liqueur	Koltiska Original Liqueur	Kolts Fine Spirits, WY
Liqueur	Lavender and Wild Rose Liqueur	San Juan Island Distillery, WA
Liqueur	Love Potion	Old Republic Distillery, PA
Liqueur	Malört Liqueur	Letherbee Distillers, IL
Liqueur	Maple Dream liqueur	Winegarden Estate Ltd., NB
Liqueur	Maui Okolehao ® (made from Ti root)	Haleakala Distillers, HI
Liqueur	Nocino	HelloCello, CA
Liqueur	Plum Jam and Syrup	Stringer's Orchard Winery, OR
Liqueur	Pumpkin King Cordial	Roundhouse Spirits, CO
Liqueur	Saskatoon Liqueur	LB Distillers, SK
Liqueur	Seabuckthorn and Wildflower Honey Liqueur	LB Distillers, SK
Liqueur	Sorel	Jack From Brooklyn Inc., NY
Liqueur	Southern Accents Liqueur	Firefly Distillery, SC
Liqueur	Spiritopia	Oregon Ryegrass Spirits, OR
Liqueur	St. George Liqueur	St. George Spirits, CA
Liqueur	Strait Pastis	Myriad View Artisan Distillery Inc., PE
Liqueur	Whisper Creek Tennessee Sipping Cream	SPEAKeasy Spirits, TN
Liqueur	Wisconsin Club USA Country Cream	Minhas Micro Distillery, WI
Liqueur	Wisconsin Club USA Maya Horchata Cream Liqueur	Minhas Micro Distillery, WI
Liqueur	Germain-Robin Créme de Poète Liqueur	Germain-Robin , CA
Liqueur	Sidetrack Distillery Nocino	Sidetrack Distillery, WA
Liqueur, Almond, Barrel Aged	mandine - Barrel Aged Almond Liqueur	GrandTen Distilling, MA

618

Liqueur, Alpine Herbal	Leopold Bros. Three Pins Alpine Herbal Liqueur	Leopold Bros., CO
Liqueur, Apple	Plaisir Apple Liqueur	Winegarden Estate Ltd., NB
Liqueur, Apple	Spiced Apple Liqueur	Skip Rock Distillers, WA
Liqueur, Apple Crème	Vermont Ice Apple Crème	Boyden Valley Winery & Spirits, VT
Liqueur, Apple, Barrel Aged	American Fruits™ Burbon Barrel Aged Apple Liqueur	Warwick Valley Distillery, NY
Liqueur, Apricot	Apricot Liqueur	It's 5 Artisan Distillery, WA
Liqueur, Apricot	Biggs Junction Apricot Liqueur	Stone Barn Brandyworks, OR
Liqueur, Banana	Pollyodd Bananacreamcello	Naoj and Mot Inc., PA
Liqueur, Black Cherry	Love Potion Black Cherry	Old Republic Distillery, PA
Liqueur, Black Currant	Okanagan Spirits Black Currant Liqueur	Okanagan Spirits, BC
Liqueur, Black Currant	Sidetrack Distillery Cassis	Sidetrack Distillery, WA
Liqueur, Black Licorice	Spider Bite Black Licorice Liqueur	Valley Shine Distillery, WA
Liqueur, Black Walnut	Charbay Black Walnut Liqueur	Charbay Distillers, CA
Liqueur, Black Walnut	Kuchan Nocino Black Walnut Liqueur	Old World Spirits LLC, CA
Liqueur, Blackberry	Blackberry Liqueur	Skip Rock Distillers, WA
Liqueur, Blackberry	Blackberry Liqueur	It's 5 Artisan Distillery, WA
Liqueur, Blackberry	Blackberry Liqueur	Winegarden Estate Ltd., NB
Liqueur, Blackberry	Brandy Peak Blackberry Liqueur	Brandy Peak Distillery, OR
Liqueur, Blackberry	Buckeye Distillery Blackberry Liqueur	Buckeye Distillery Inc., OH
Liqueur, Blackberry	Leopold Bros. Rocky Mountain Blackberry Liqueur	Leopold Bros., CO
Liqueur, Blackberry	Marion Blackberry Liqueur	Clear Creek Distillery, OR
Liqueur, Blackberry	Okanagan Spirits Blackberry Liqueur	Okanagan Spirits, BC
Liqueur, Blackberry	Sidetrack Distillery Blackberry Liqueur	Sidetrack Distillery, WA
Liqueur, Blackberry	Whidbey Island Distillery Blackberry Liqueur	Whidbey Island Distillery, WA
Liqueur, Blueberry	Blue Hill Blueberry Liqueur	Winegarden Estate Ltd., NB
Liqueur, Blueberry	Blueberry Liqueur	Flag Hill Winery & Distillery, NH
Liqueur, Blueberry	Blueberry Liqueur	It's 5 Artisan Distillery, WA
Liqueur, Blueberry	Ironworks Blueberry Liqueur	Ironworks Distillery, NS
Liqueur, Blueberry	Johnny Ziegler Myrtille	Winegarden Estate Ltd., NB
Liqueur, Blueberry	Okanagan Spirits Blueberry Liqueur	Okanagan Spirits, BC
Liqueur, Blueberry	Sidetrack Distillery Blueberry Liqueur	Sidetrack Distillery, WA
Liqueur, Botanical	Angelica - Botanical Liqueur	GrandTen Distilling, MA

Liqueur, Bourbon	Benjamin Prichard's Sweet Lucy Bourbon Liqueur	Prichard's Distillery Inc., TN
Liqueur, Bourbon Cream	Benjamin Prichard's Sweet Lucy Bourbon Cream Liqueur	Prichard's Distillery Inc., TN
Liqueur, Bourbon Cream	Orphan Girl Bourbon Cream Liqueur	Headframe Spirits, MT
Liqueur, Brulee	Dancing Pines Brulee Liqueur	Dancing Pines Distillery, CO
Liqueur, Cacao Rum	Cacao Prieto Don Daniel Cacao Rum Liqueur	Cacao Prieto LLC, NY
Liqueur, Cacao Rum	Cacao Prieto Don Esteban Cacao Rum Liqueur	Cacao Prieto LLC, NY
Liqueur, Caraway	KOVAL Caraway Liqueur	KOVAL Distillery, IL
Liqueur, Chai	Dancing Pines Chai Liqueur	Dancing Pines Distillery, CO
Liqueur, Cherry	Buckeye Distillery Cherry Liqueur	Buckeye Distillery Inc., OH
Liqueur, Cherry	Cherry Bounce	Old Ballard Liquor Co., WA
Liqueur, Cherry	Cherry Liqueur	Clear Creek Distillery, OR
Liqueur, Cherry	Cherry Liqueur	Finger Lakes Distilling, NY
Liqueur, Cherry	Cherry Liqueur	It's 5 Artisan Distillery, WA
Liqueur, Cherry	Cherry Liqueur	Maple Leaf Spirit Inc., BC
Liqueur, Cherry	Johnny Ziegler Kirsch	Winegarden Estate Ltd., NB
Liqueur, Cherry	Okanagan Spirits Cherry Liqueur	Okanagan Spirits, BC
Liqueur, Cherry Tart	Dancing Pines Cherry Tart Liqueur	Dancing Pines Distillery, CO
Liqueur, Cherry, Tart	Leopold Bros. Michigan Tart Cherry Liqueur	Leopold Bros., CO
Liqueur, Cherry, Wild	Wild Cherry Liqueur	Winegarden Estate Ltd., NB
Liqueur, Chocolate	Pollyodd Chocolatecello	Naoj and Mot Inc., PA
Liqueur, Chocolate	Pollyodd Chocolatecreamcello	Naoj and Mot Inc., PA
Liqueur, Chokecherry, Wild	Montana Wild Chokecherry Liqueur	Willie's Distillery, MT
Liqueur, Chrysanthemum	KOVAL Chrysanthemum & Honey Liqueur	KOVAL Distillery, IL
Liqueur, Cocoa	Cocoa Liqueur	Yahara Bay Distillers, WI
Liqueur, Cocoa	Depth Liqueur - Cacao	Sound Spirits, WA
Liqueur, Coffee	Ampersand: Cold Brew Coffee Liqueur	Old Harbor Distilling Company, CA
Liqueur, Coffee	Black Cat Coffee Liquor	Mt. Index Brewery & Distillery, WA
Liqueur, Coffee	Brooklyn Roasting Company Coffee Liqueur	Cacao Prieto LLC, NY
Liqueur, Coffee	Coffee Liqueur	New Deal Distillery, OR
Liqueur, Coffee	Coffee Liqueur	Yahara Bay Distillers, WI
Liqueur, Coffee	Coffee Liqueur	McMenamins Edgefield Distillery, OR
Liqueur, Coffee	Colorado Coffee Liqueur	Mancos Valley Distillery, CO

Liqueur, Coffee	Corretto Coffee Liqueur	Roundhouse Spirits, CO
Liqueur, Coffee	DARK (Coffee Liqueur)	Prairie Wolf Spirits, OK
Liqueur, Coffee	Drip Coffee Liqueur	Rain City Spirits, WA
Liqueur, Coffee	Fifth Element Spirits Coffee Liqueur	Fifth Element Spirits, OH
Liqueur, Coffee	House Spirits Coffee Liqueur	House Spirits Distillery, OR
Liqueur, Coffee	KOVAL Coffee Liqueur	KOVAL Distillery, IL
Liqueur, Coffee	Leopold Bros. Frenchpress Style American Coffee Liqueur	Leopold Bros., CO
Liqueur, Coffee	Mocca Gino Coffee Liqueur	Winegarden Estate Ltd., NB
Liqueur, Coffee	Perc Coffee Liqueur	Saxtons River Distillery LLC, VT
Liqueur, Coffee	Red Wing Roast Coffee Liqueur	Stone Barn Brandyworks, OR
Liqueur, Coffee	Richardo's Coffee Liqueur	Spirit Hound Distillers, CO
Liqueur, Coffee	Snaggle Tooth Coffee Liqueur	Journeyman Distillery, MI
Liqueur, Coffee	The Luana Beach Coffee Liqueur	Seattle Distilling Company, WA
Liqueur, Coffee	Turkish Coffee Liqueur	Vivacity Spirits, OR
Liqueur, Cordial, Apple	Maple River Distillery Cordial - Apple	Maple River Distillery, ND
Liqueur, Cordial, Berry	Berry Berry Cordial	Wood Hat Spirits LLC, MO
Liqueur, Cordial, Cherry, Sour	American Fruits™ Sour Cherry Cordial	Warwick Valley Distillery, NY
Liqueur, Cordial, Chocolate Raspberry	Chocolate Raspberry	Bloomery Plantation Distillery, WV
Liqueur, Cordial, Chokecherry	Maple River Distillery Cordial - Chokecherry	Maple River Distillery, ND
Liqueur, Cordial, Currant, Black	American Fruits™ Black Currant Cordial	Warwick Valley Distillery, NY
Liqueur, Cordial, Currant, Black	Maple River Distillery Cordial - Aronia Black Currant	Maple River Distillery, ND
Liqueur, Cordial, Currant, Red	Maple River Distillery Cordial - Red Currant	Maple River Distillery, ND
Liqueur, Cordial, Elderberry	Caledonia Spirits Elderberry Cordial	Caledonia Spirits Inc., VT
Liqueur, Cordial, Ginger	Ginger	Bloomery Plantation Distillery, WV
Liqueur, Cordial, Huckleberry	Huckleberry Cordial	Black Heron Spirits Distillery, WA
Liqueur, Cordial, Lemon	Cremma Lemma	Bloomery Plantation Distillery, WV
Liqueur, Cordial, Lemonade	Hard Lemonade	Bloomery Plantation Distillery, WV
Liqueur, Cordial, Lime	Limoncello	Bloomery Plantation Distillery, WV
Liqueur, Cordial, Marionberry	Black Mariah	Oregon Spirit Distillers, OR
Liqueur, Cordial, Peach	Peach	Bloomery Plantation Distillery, WV
Liqueur, Cordial, Pear	Maple River Distillery Cordial - Pear	Maple River Distillery, ND
Liqueur, Cordial, Plum, Wild	Maple River Distillery Cordial - Wild Plum	Maple River Distillery, ND

Liqueur, Cordial, Pumpkin Spice	Pumpkin Spice	Bloomery Plantation Distillery, WV
Liqueur, Cordial, Raspberry Lemon	Raspberry Lemon	Bloomery Plantation Distillery, WV
Liqueur, Cordial, Walnut, Black	Black Walnut	Bloomery Plantation Distillery, WV
Liqueur, Cranberry	Benjamin Prichard's Cranberry Liqueur	Prichard's Distillery Inc., TN
Liqueur, Cranberry	Cranberry Liqueur	Clear Creek Distillery, OR
Liqueur, Cranberry	Cranberry Liqueur	Stone Barn Brandyworks, OR
Liqueur, Cranberry	Cranberry Liqueur	Flag Hill Winery & Distillery, NH
Liqueur, Cranberry	Cranberry Liqueur	Winegarden Estate Ltd., NB
Liqueur, Cranberry	Craneberry - Massachusetts Cranberry Liqueur	GrandTen Distilling, MA
Liqueur, Cranberry	Ironworks Cranberry Liqueur	Ironworks Distillery, NS
Liqueur, Cranberry	Leopold Bros. New England Cranberry Liqueur	Leopold Bros., CO
Liqueur, Cranberry	Okanagan Spirits Cranberry Liqueur	Okanagan Spirits, BC
Liqueur, Cream	Forty Creek Whisky Cream Liquor	Forty Creek Distillery, ON
Liqueur, Currant	Johnny Ziegler Cassis	Winegarden Estate Ltd., NB
Liqueur, Douglas Fire	broVo+DF Douglas Fir Liqueur	broVo Spirits, WA
Liqueur, Egg Nog	Egg Nog Advocaat Liqueur	Eastside Distilling, OR
Liqueur, Elderberry	Elderberry Liqueur	Hidden Marsh Distillery, NY
Liqueur, Elderberry	Elderberry Liqueur	It's 5 Artisan Distillery, WA
Liqueur, Elderberry	Elderberry Liqueur	Winegarden Estate Ltd., NB
Liqueur, Elderberry	Johnny Ziegler Elderberry	Winegarden Estate Ltd., NB
Liqueur, Espresso	Dancing Pines Espresso Liqueur	Dancing Pines Distillery, CO
Liqueur, Figcello	FigCello di Sonoma	HelloCello, CA
Liqueur, Fudge Chocolate	Mackinac Island Fudge Chocolate Liqueur	Northern Latitudes Distillery, MI
Liqueur, Geranium	broVo+RG Rose Geranium Liqueur	broVo Spirits, WA
Liqueur, Ginger	300 Joules Ginger Infusion	Big Still Liquors LLC, NJ
Liqueur, Ginger	Barrow's Intense Ginger Liqueur	Proof of Concept LLC, NY
Liqueur, Ginger	broVo+G Ginger Liqueur	broVo Spirits, WA
Liqueur, Ginger	Ginger Liqueur	New Deal Distillery, OR
Liqueur, Ginger	KOVAL Ginger Liqueur	KOVAL Distillery, IL
Liqueur, Ginger	Northern Roots Ginger Liqueur	Northern Latitudes Distillery, MI
Liqueur, Hazelnut	Hazelnut Liqueur (Nov. 2014)	McMenamins Cornelius Pass, OR
Liqueur, Herbal	Depth Liqueur - Herbal	Sound Spirits, WA

Liqueur, Herbal	Herbal Liqueur	McMenamins Edgefield Distillery, OR
Liqueur, Honey	Honey Liqueur	Winegarden Estate Ltd., NB
Liqueur, Honey	Old Sugar Factory Honey Liqueur	Old Sugar Distillery, WI
Liqueur, Honey, Spiced	Krupnikas	The Brothers Vilgalys Spirits Co., NC
Liqueur, Honey, Spiced	Velnias Spiced Honey Liqueur	Dirty Water Distillery, MA
Liqueur, Honeysuckle, Blue	Blue Honeysuckle Liqueur	LB Distillers, SK
Liqueur, Jasmine	KOVAL Jasmine Liqueur	KOVAL Distillery, IL
Liqueur, Lavender	broVo+L Lavender Liqueur	broVo Spirits, WA
Liqueur, Lemon	300 Joules Lemon Infusion	Big Still Liquors LLC, NJ
Liqueur, Lemon	Cedar Ridge Lemoncella	Cedar Ridge Distillery, IA
Liqueur, Lemon	Lemoncella	Yahara Bay Distillers, WI
Liqueur, Lemon	Lemoncello	Black Heron Spirits Distillery, WA
Liqueur, Lemon	T & W Lemonela Liqueur	Empire Winery & Distillery, FL
Liqueur, Lemon	broVo+LB Lemon Balm Liqueur	broVo Spirits, WA
Liqueur, Lemon	Limoncello di Leelanau Lemon Liqueur	Northern Latitudes Distillery, MI
Liqueur, Lemon	Paula's Texas Lemon	Texacello LLC, TX
Liqueur, Lemon	Pollyodd Lemoncello	Naoj and Mot Inc., PA
Liqueur, Lemon	Pollyodd Lemoncreamcello	Naoj and Mot Inc., PA
Liqueur, Lemon	Sorbetta Liqueurs - Lemon	Long Island Spirits, NY
Liqueur, Lemon, Meyer	Napa Valley Meyer Lemon Liqueur	Napa Valley Distillery, CA
Liqueur, Lime	Ciriaco's Limoncello	Vermont Distillers, VT
Liqueur, Lime	Demarest Hill Winery Limoncella	Demarest Hill Winery, NY
Liqueur, Lime	Fiore Limoncello	Fiore Winery & Distillery, MD
Liqueur, Lime	Giuliana's Crema di Limoncello	CH Distillery, IL
Liqueur, Lime	Letterpress Limoncello	Letterpress Distilling, WA
Liqueur, Lime	Limoncello	Valley Shine Distillery, WA
Liqueur, Lime	Limoncello	Five & 20 Spirits, NY
Liqueur, Lime	Limoncello di Sonoma	HelloCello, CA
Liqueur, Lime	Limoncello Lemon Liqueur	Clayton Distillery, NY
Liqueur, Lime	Madison Avenue Limoncello	45th Parallel Distillery, WI
Liqueur, Lime	Pollyodd Limecello	Naoj and Mot Inc, PA
Liqueur, Lime	RE:FIND Limoncello	RE:FIND Distillery, CA

Liqueur, Lime	Six Mile Creek Limoncella	Six Mile Creek Winery & Distillery, NY
Liqueur, Lime	Sorbetta Liqueurs - Lime	Long Island Spirits, NY
Liqueur, Lime	T &W Limonela Liqueur	Empire Winery & Distillery, FL
Liqueur, Lime	Ventura Limoncello Crema	Ventura Limoncello Company, CA
Liqueur, Lime	Ventura Limoncello Originale	Ventura Limoncello Company, CA
Liqueur, Lime	Yvelise Limoncello	Lifted Spirits LLC, LA
Liqueur, Loganberry	Loganberry Liqueur	Clear Creek Distillery, OR
Liqueur, Loganberry	Whidbey Island Distillery Loganberry Liqueur	Whidbey Island Distillery, WA
Liqueur, Mango	Pollyodd Mangocello	Naoj and Mot Inc., PA
Liqueur, Maple	Green Mountain Organic Maple Liqueur	Green Mountain Distillers, VT
Liqueur, Maple	Maple Liqueur	Maple Leaf Spirit Inc., BC
Liqueur, Maple	Maple Smash Liqueur	Sweetgrass Farm Winery & Distillery, ME
Liqueur, Maple	Sapling Vermont Maple Liqueur	Saxtons River Distillery LLC, VT
Liqueur, Maple Cream	Metcalfe's Vermont Maple Cream Liqueur	Vermont Distillers, VT
Liqueur, Maple Crème	Vermont Ice Maple Crème	Caledonia Spirits Inc., VT
Liqueur, Maple Strawberry	Maple Strawberry Liqueur	Clayton Distillery, NY
Liqueur, Maplejack	Maplejack Liqueur	Finger Lakes Distilling, NY
Liqueur, Menthe	Depth Liqueur - Menthe	Sound Spirits, WA
Liqueur, Mixed Fruit	Johnny Ziegler Obstler	Winegarden Estate Ltd., NB
Liqueur, Orange	Demarest Hill Winery Orancella	Demarest Hill Winery, NY
Liqueur, Orange	Leopold Bros. American Orange Liqueur	Leopold Bros., CO
Liqueur, Orange	Madison Avenue Orangecello	45th Parallel Distillery, WI
Liqueur, Orange	Naranjo Orange Liqueur	Rancho de Los Luceros Destilaría, NM
Liqueur, Orange	OrangeCello di Sonoma	HelloCello, CA
Liqueur, Orange	Paula's Texas Orange	Texacello LLC, TX
Liqueur, Orange	Pollyodd Orangecello	Naoj and Mot Inc., PA
Liqueur, Orange	Pollyodd Orangecreamcello	Naoj and Mot Inc, PA
Liqueur, Orange	Sorbetta Liqueurs - Orange	Long Island Spirits, NY
Liqueur, Orange	T & W Orangela Liqueur	Empire Winery & Distillery, FL
Liqueur, Orange Blossom	KOVAL Orange Blossom Liqueur	KOVAL Distillery, IL
Liqueur, Orange, Blood	Ventura Orangecello Blood Orange	Ventura Limoncello Company, CA
Liqueur, Pear	American Fruits™ Bartlett Pear Liqueur	Warwick Valley Distillery, NY

Liqueur, Pear	Pear Liqueur	Clear Creek Distillery, OR
Liqueur, Pear	Pear Liqueur	It's 5 Artisan Distillery, WA
Liqueur, Pear	Pear Liqueur	Magnanini Farm Winery Inc., NY
Liqueur, Pear	Pear Liqueur	Maple Leaf Spirit Inc., BC
Liqueur, Pear	Pear Liqueur	Winegarden Estate Ltd., NB
Liqueur, Pear, Prickly	Prickly Pear Liqueur	Arizona High Spirits Distillery, AZ
Liqueur, Peppermint Bark	Peppermint Bark Liqueur	Eastside Distilling, OR
Liqueur, Plum	Johnny Ziegler Sibowitz	Winegarden Estate Ltd., NB
Liqueur, Plum	Pacific Plum Liqueur	Stringer's Orchard Winery, OR
Liqueur, Plum Gin	Greenhook Ginsmiths Beach Plum Gin Liqueur	Greenhook Ginsmiths, NY
Liqueur, Pumpkin Spice	BelleWood Pumpkin Spice Liqueur	BelleWood Distilling, WA
Liqueur, Quince	Golden Quince Liqueur	Stone Barn Brandyworks, OR
Liqueur, Quince	Quince Liqueur	Maple Leaf Spirit Inc., BC
Liqueur, Raspberry	Buckeye Distillery Raspberry Liqueur	Buckeye Distillery Inc., OH
Liqueur, Raspberry	Cedar Ridge Lamponcella	Cedar Ridge Distillery, IA
Liqueur, Raspberry	Metcalfe's Raspberry Liqueur	Vermont Distillers, VT
Liqueur, Raspberry	Okanagan Spirits Raspberry Liqueur	Okanagan Spirits, BC
Liqueur, Raspberry	Raspberry Liqueur	Clayton Distillery, NY
Liqueur, Raspberry	Raspberry Liqueur	Clear Creek Distillery, OR
Liqueur, Raspberry	Raspberry Liqueur	Finger Lakes Distilling, NY
Liqueur, Raspberry	Raspberry Liqueur	Flag Hill Winery & Distillery, NH
Liqueur, Raspberry	Raspberry Liqueur	It's 5 Artisan Distillery, WA
Liqueur, Raspberry	Raspberry Liqueur	Skip Rock Distillers, WA
Liqueur, Raspberry	Raspberry Liqueur	Winegarden Estate Ltd., NB
Liqueur, Raspberry	Sidetrack Distillery Raspberry Liqueur	Sidetrack Distillery, WA
Liqueur, Raspberry	Sorbetta Liqueurs - Raspberry	Long Island Spirits, NY
Liqueur, Raspberry	Whidbey Island Distillery Raspberry Liqueur	Whidbey Island Distillery, WA
Liqueur, Rhubarb	Oregon Blush Rhubarb Liqueur	Stone Barn Brandyworks, OR
Liqueur, Rose Hip	KOVAL Rose Hip Liqueur	KOVAL Distillery, IL
Liqueur, Sea Buckthorn	Okanagan Spirits Sea Buckthorn	Okanagan Spirits, BC
Liqueur, Strawberry	Pollyodd Strawberrycreamcello	Naoj and Mot Inc., PA
Liqueur, Strawberry	Sidetrack Distillery Strawberry Liqueur	Sidetrack Distillery, WA

Liqueur, Strawberry	Strawberry Liqueur	Stone Barn Brandyworks, OR
Liqueur, Strawberry	Sorbetta Liqueurs - Strawberry	Long Island Spirits, NY
Liqueur, Strawberry, Rhubarb	Rhubarbe Fraise, Strawberry rhubarb liqueur	Clayton Distillery, NY
Liqueur, Sugar Maple	Sugar Maple Liqueur	Flag Hill Winery & Distillery, NH
Liqueur, Violette	Golden Moon Crème de Violette	Golden Moon Distillery, CO
Liqueur, Walnut	KOVAL Walnut Liqueur	KOVAL Distillery, IL
Liqueur, Walnut Nocino,	Walnut Liqueur	Skip Rock Distillers, WA
Liqueur, Walnut, Green	Nocino Green Walnut Liqueur	Stone Barn Brandyworks, OR
Liqueur, Whiskey	Spirits of St. Louis, Vermont Night Whiskey Liqueur	Square One Brewery and Distillery, MO
Maple Jack	Schoharie Mapple Jack	KyMar Farm Distillery, NY
Mead	T & W Royal Mead Honey Wine	Empire Winery & Distillery, FL
Misc., Energy Drink	Runner Energy Drink	Spirits of the USA LLC, FL
Moonshine, see Whiskey, White		
Neutral Spirit	Technical Reserve Neutral Spirit	Industry City Distillery Inc., NY
Ouzo	Americanaki Ouzo	Old Sugar Distillery, WI
Ouzo	Eastside Ouzo	Stone Barn Brandyworks, OR
Poitin	1512 Spirits Signature Poitin	1512 Spirits, CA
Potcheen	Sturgis Shine	Black Hills Dakota Distillery, SD
Rhum	Shipwreck Spiced Pirate Rhum	Artesian Distillers, MI
Rum	1492 Cristobal Rum	Artesian Distillers, MI
Rum	Älander (Rum)	Far North Spirits, MN
Rum	Alchemist Distillery Rum	Alchemist Distilleries Inc., FL
Rum	Amador Distillery Rum	Amador Distillery, CA
Rum	Aristo Rum	Minhas Micro Distillery, WI
Rum	Bardenay Small Batch Rum	Bardenay Inc., ID
Rum	Barrelman: Navy Strength Rum	Old Harbor Distilling Company, CA
Rum	Belle 1775 Colonial Reserve Rum	Belle of Dayton, OH
Rum	Bluenose Black Rum	Ironworks Distillery, NS
Rum	Braddah Kimo's Extreme 155 Proof Rum ®	Haleakala Distillers, HI
Rum	Bull Run Pacific Rum	Bull Run Distilling Company, OR
Rum	Bully Boy Boston Rum	Bully Boy Distillers, MA
Rum	California Dreamin' Rum	Tahoe Moonshine Distillery Inc., CA

626

Rum	Cane and Abe Small-Barrel Rum	Old Sugar Distillery, WI
Rum	Carolina Coast Rum	Broadslab Distillery LLC, NC
Rum	Carolina Rum	Muddy River Distillery, NC
Rum	CH Rum (cocktail bar only)	CH Distillery, IL
Rum	Chamomile Rum	Cacao Prieto LLC, NY
Rum	Chick's Beach Rum	Chesapeake Bay Distillery LLC, VA
Rum	Chinook White Rum	Minhas Micro Distillery, WI
Rum	Civilized Rum	Northern United Brewing Company, MI
Rum	Coppercraft Rum	Coppercraft Distillery LLC, MI
Rum	Corsairs Rum	Minhas Micro Distillery, WI
Rum	CRUSOE Rum	GreenBar Collective, CA
Rum	Cypress Creek Reserve Crystal Rum	D.E.W. Distillation LLC, TX
Rum	Dancing Pines Rum	Dancing Pines Distillery, CO
Rum	Desert Diamond Distillery Gold Miner Rum	Desert Diamond Distillery, AZ
Rum	Devil's Own Wicked Rum	Stillwagon Distillery, OR
Rum	Distiller's Workshop Rum	New Deal Distillery, OR
Rum	DiVine Rum	Entente Spirits LLC, MI
Rum	Dry County Rum	Dry County Distillery LLC, WA
Rum	Dry Dock Rum	Big Thicket Distilling Company, TX
Rum	Duck Island Rum	66 Gilead Distillery, ON
Rum	Due North Rum	Van Brunt Stillhouse, NY
Rum	Edgefield Rum	McMenamins Edgefield Distillery, OR
Rum	Eight Bells Rum	New England Distilling, ME
Rum	Esprit de Krewe™ Crystal Rum	Rollins Distillery, FL
Rum	Expedition Rum	StiL 630, MO
Rum	Folly Cove Rum	Ryan & Wood Inc., MA
Rum	Gold Coast Rum	Minhas Micro Distillery, WI
Rum	Gold Label Rum	3 Howls Distillery, WA
Rum	Golden Sands Rum	Minhas Micro Distillery, WI
Rum	Heath Rum	The North Woods Distillery LLC, WI
Rum	High Wire Distilling Co. Belonger's Rum	High Wire Distilling, SC
Rum	Holstein Rum	Werner Distilling LLC, IA

Rum	House Spirits Rum	House Spirits Distillery, OR
Rum	Hurricane Rum	Triple Eight Distillery, MA
Rum	Ian's Alley Rum	Mancos Valley Distillery, CO
Rum	Jug Dealer Rum	Tahoe Moonshine Distillery Inc., CA
Rum	Knock on Wood Rum	LB Distillers, SK
Rum	Lyon Distilling Company Rum	Lyon Distilling Company, MD
Rum	Mad River Rum	Mad River Distillers, VT
Rum	Maggie's Farm Rum	Allegheny Distilling LLC, PA
Rum	Malahat Spirits Rum	Malahat Spirits, CA
Rum	Mischief Mariner Rum	Fremont Mischief, WA
Rum	Missouri Spirits Rum	Missouri Spirits, MO
Rum	Mountain Bum Rum	Spirit Hound Distillers, CO
Rum	Old Ipswich "Tavern Style" Rum	Turkey Shore Distilleries, MA
Rum	Old Ipswich "White Cap" Rum	Turkey Shore Distilleries, MA
Rum	Owney's NYC Rum	The Noble Experiment NYC, NY
Rum	Pecan Street Rum	Spirit of Texas LLC, TX
Rum	Peg Leg Rum	Mile High Spirits LLC, CO
Rum	Petty's Island Rum	Cooper River Distillers, NJ
Rum	Pitorro Añejo	Port Morris Distillery, NY
Rum	Pitorro Shine	Port Morris Distillery, NY
Rum	Prichard's Fine Rum	Prichard's Distillery Inc., TN
Rum	Prichard's Sweet Georgia Bell	Prichard's Distillery Inc., TN
Rum	Prince Edward Merchantman Rum	Prince Edward Distillery, PE
Rum	Privateer True American Rum	Privateer Rum, MA
Rum	Quackenbush Still House Rum	Albany Distilling Company, NY
Rum	Queen's Share Overproof	Allegheny Distilling LLC, PA
Rum	Ragged Mountain Rum	Berkshire Mountain Distillers Inc., MA
Rum	Red Island Rum	Indio Spirits, OR
Rum	Richland Rum	Richland Distilling Company, GA
Rum	RMD Rum	Artesian Distillers, MI
Rum	Road's End Rum	Journeyman Distillery, MI
Rum	Roaring Dan's Rum	Great Lakes Distillery LLC, WI

Rum	Roggen's Rum	Tuthilltown Spirits Distillery, NY
Rum	Rougaroux 13 Pennies Praline Rum	Donner-Peltier Distillers, LA
Rum	Rougaroux Sugarshine Rum	Donner-Peltier Distillers, LA
Rum	Sailboat Rum	Minhas Micro Distillery, WI
Rum	Sam Lords Rum	Minhas Micro Distillery, WI
Rum	Shipmate Rum	Hewn Spirits LLC, PA
Rum	Smugglers' Notch Rum	Smugglers' Notch Distillery, VT
Rum	Spirit of Texas Rum	Spirit of Texas LLC, TX
Rum	Stars Rum	Minhas Micro Distillery, WI
Rum	State of Jefferson Rum	Immortal Spirits & Distilling Co., OR
Rum	Steel Drum Rum	Iowa Distilling Company, IA
Rum	Strait Rum (40%)	Myriad View Artisan Distillery Inc., PE
Rum	Strait Rum (historic 100 proof 57.1%)	Myriad View Artisan Distillery Inc., PE
Rum	Striped Rum	Striped Pig Distillery, SC
Rum	Tesouro Rum	Tesouro Distillery, CO
Rum	Three Crow Rum	Sweetgrass Farm Winery & Distillery, ME
Rum	Tirado El Pitito Rum	Tirado Distillery, NY
Rum	Tresillo Rum	Cajun Spirits Distillery, LA
Rum	Ugly Dog Rum	Ugly Dog Distillery LLC, MI
Rum	Whaleback Spiced Rum	Northern Latitudes Distillery, MI
Rum	Wheat State Distilling Rum	Wheat State Distilling, KS
Rum	White Hat Rum	South Congress Distillery, TX
Rum	White Label Rum	3 Howls Distillery, WA
Rum	Wicked Dolphin Rum	Cape Spirits Inc., FL
Rum	Wiggly Bridge Rum	Wiggly Bridge Distillery, ME
Rum	Wigle Landlocked	Pittsburgh Distilling Co., PA
Rum	Yahara Bay Premium Rum	Yahara Bay Distillers, WI
Rum, 10-Year Aged	Old New Orleans 10 Year Rum	Celebration Distillation, LA
Rum, 4-Year Aged	Calhoun Bros. Aged Rum 4 Years	Big Bottom Distilling, OR
Rum, Agave	Desert Diamond Distillery Gold Miner Agave Rum	Desert Diamond Distillery, AZ
Rum, Aged	Mad Bird Rum (aged)	Yahara Bay Distillers, WI
Rum, Aged	Rock Town Barrel Aged Rum	Rock Town Distillery Inc., AR

Rum, Aged	Treaty Oak Aged Rum	Treaty Oak Distilling Co., TX
Rum, Agricole	St. George California Agricole Rum	St. George Spirits, CA
Rum, Amber	Amber Rum	Ironworks Distillery, NS
Rum, Amber	Freshwater Michigan Amber Rum	New Holland Artisan Spirits, MI
Rum, Amber	Old New Orleans Amber Rum	Celebration Distillation, LA
Rum, Amber	Sea Hagg Rum (Amber)	Sea Hagg Distillery, NH
Rum, Amber	Spirits of St. Louis, Island Time Amber Rum	Square One Brewery and Distillery, MO
Rum, Amber	Sugar Daddy Amber Rum	HelloCello, CA
Rum, Amber	Taildragger Amber Rum	Tailwinds Distilling Company, IL
Rum, Amber	Urban Amber Rum	Urban Distilleries, BC
Rum, Barrel Aged	Cut Spike Barrel-Aged Rum	Cut Spike Distillery, NE
Rum, Barrel Aged	Queen Charlotte's Reserve (barrel aged rum)	Muddy River Distillery, NC
Rum, Barrel Aged	Road's End Rum Barrel Aged (Navy Strength)	Journeyman Distillery, MI
Rum, Barrel Aged	Three Sheets Barrel Aged Rum	Ballast Point Spirits, CA
Rum, Barrel Reserve	Desert Diamond Distillery Gold Miner Barrel Reserve Rum	Desert Diamond Distillery, AZ
Rum, Blueberry	Sea Hagg Blueberry Rum	Sea Hagg Distillery, NH
Rum, Bourbon Barrel	Belle Bourbon Barrel Rum	Belle of Dayton, OH
Rum, Brown Honey	Brown Honey Rum	Dogfish Head Craft Brewery, DE
Rum, Cacao	Cacao Prieto Don Rafael Cacao Rum	Cacao Prieto LLC, NY
Rum, Cask	Dancing Pines Cask Rum	Dancing Pines Distillery, CO
Rum, Chocolat Mint	Chocolat Mint Rum	The North Woods Distillery LLC, WI
Rum, Coconut	Holstein Coconut Flavored Rum	Werner Distilling LLC, IA
Rum, Coconut	Kaua`i Coconut Rum	Kōloa Rum Company, HI
Rum, Coffee	Below Deck Coffee Rum	Eastside Distilling, OR
Rum, Cranberry	Prichard's Cranberry Rum	Prichard's Distillery Inc., TN
Rum, Dark	Busted Barrel Dark Rum	Jersey Artisan Distilling, NJ
Rum, Dark	Cedar Ridge Dark Rum	Cedar Ridge Distillery, IA
Rum, Dark	Dark Rum	Spirits of Maine Distillery, ME
Rum, Dark	Deadman's Dark Rum	Spirits of the USA LLC, FL
Rum, Dark	Desert Diamond Distillery Gold Miner Dark Rum	Desert Diamond Distillery, AZ
Rum, Dark	George Bowman Colonial Era Dark Caribbean Rum	A. Smith Bowman Distillery, VA
Rum, Dark	Kaua`i Dark Rum	Kōloa Rum Company, HI

Category	Product	Distillery
Rum, Dark	Maui Dark Rum ®	Haleakala Distillers, HI
Rum, Dark	Railean Reserve XO Dark Rum	Railean Distillers, TX
Rum, Dark	Ridge Runner Dark Rum	Forks of Cheat Distillery, WV
Rum, Dark	Rogue Dark Rum	Rogue Spirits, OR
Rum, Dark	Rougaroux Full Moon Dark Rum	Donner-Peltier Distillers, LA
Rum, Dark	Sugar Daddy Dark Rum	HelloCello, CA
Rum, Dark, Aged	Manatawny Hearts of Darkness Rum - Dark/Aged Rum	Manatawny Still Works, PA
Rum, Dark, Single Barrel	Railean Small Cask Single Barrel Dark Rum	Railean Distillers, TX
Rum, Elderflower	Dunc's Mill Elderflower Flavored Rum	Dunc's Mill, VT
Rum, Ginger	Below Deck Ginger Rum	Eastside Distilling, OR
Rum, Gold	California Gold Rum	Stark Spirits, CA
Rum, Gold	Chinook Gold Rum	Minhas Micro Distillery, WI
Rum, Gold	Devil's Own Gold Rum	Stillwagon Distillery, OR
Rum, Gold	Downslope Gold Rum	Downslope Distilling, CO
Rum, Gold	Island Gold Rum	Copper Run Distillery, MO
Rum, Gold	Kaua'i Gold	Kōloa Rum Company, HI
Rum, Gold	Maui Gold Rum ®	Haleakala Distillers, HI
Rum, Gold	Maui Reserve Gold Rum ®	Haleakala Distillers, HI
Rum, Gold	Sea Island Gold Rum	Firefly Distillery, SC
Rum, Gold	Sergeant Classick Hawaiian Rum (Gold)	Essential Spirits Alambic Distilleries, CA
Rum, Gold	Siesta Key Gold Rum	Drum Circle Distilling, FL
Rum, Gold	Wisconsin Club USA Gold Coast XO Rum	Minhas Micro Distillery, WI
Rum, Gold	Wisconsin Club USA Gold Rum	Minhas Micro Distillery, WI
Rum, Heavy Oaked	White Sand Rum - a 80 Proof Heavy Oaked rum	Paradise Distilling Company LLC, IA
Rum, Hibiscus, Coconut	Whistling Andy Hibiscus-Coconut Rum	Whistling Andy Distillery, MT
Rum, Honey	Kentucky Honey (rum)	Barrel House Distilling Co., KY
Rum, Java	Sea Island Java Rum	Firefly Distillery, SC
Rum, Key Lime	Prichard's Key Lime Rum	Prichard's Distillery Inc., TN
Rum, Light	ClearHeart Light Rum	Cedar Ridge Distillery, IA
Rum, Light	Light Rum	Spirits of Maine Distillery, ME
Rum, Light	Ridge Runner Light Rum	Forks of Cheat Distillery, WV
Rum, Light	Rutter Rum - Light Rum	Manatawny Still Works, PA

Product	Brand	Distillery
Rum, Light	Sugar Daddy Light Rum	HelloCello, CA
Rum, Light	White Light Rum	Dogfish Head Craft Brewery, DE
Rum, Mango	Deadman's Mango Flavored Rum	Spirits of the USA LLC, FL
Rum, Maple	Dunc's Mill Maple Flavored Rum	Dunc's Mill, VT
Rum, Organic, Spiced	Humboldt Distillery Organic Spiced Rum	Humboldt Distillery, CA
Rum, Oro	Montanya Oro Rum	Montanya Distillers LLC, CO
Rum, Peach	Sea Hagg Peach Rum	Sea Hagg Distillery, NH
Rum, Pineapple	Maui Pineapple Flavored Rum ®	Haleakala Distillers, HI
Rum, Pineapple, Hawaiian	Royale Hawaiian Pineapple Rum	Saint James Spirits, CA
Rum, Platino	Montanya Platino Rum	Montanya Distillers LLC, CO
Rum, Platinum	Maui Platinum Rum ®	Haleakala Distillers, HI
Rum, Platinum	Treaty Oak Platinum Rum	Treaty Oak Distilling Co., TX
Rum, Private Stock	Prichard's Private Stock Rum	Prichard's Distillery Inc., TN
Rum, Rye Oak Reserve	Petty's Island Rum Rye Oak Reserve (aged rum)	Cooper River Distillers, NJ
Rum, Silver	Below Deck Silver Rum	Eastside Distilling, OR
Rum, Silver	Busted Barrel Silver Rum	Jersey Artisan Distilling, NJ
Rum, Silver	California Silver Rum	Stark Spirits, CA
Rum, Silver	Portside Distillery Silver Rum	Portside Distillery, OH
Rum, Silver	Privateer Silver Reserve Rum	Privateer Rum, MA
Rum, Silver	Sea Hagg Silver Rum	Sea Hagg Distillery, NH
Rum, Silver	Sergeant Classick Hawaiian Rum (Silver)	Essential Spirits Alambic Distilleries, CA
Rum, Silver	Seven Brothers Silver Rum	Seven Brothers Distilling Company, OH
Rum, Silver	Siesta Key Silver Rum	Drum Circle Distilling, FL
Rum, Silver	Silver Bayou Rum	Louisiana Spirits LLC, LA
Rum, Silver	Whistling Andy Silver Rum	Whistling Andy Distillery, MT
Rum, Silver	Witherspoon's River Rum	Quentin D. Witherspoon Distillery, TX
Rum, Single Barrel	Freshwater Superior Single Barrel Rum	New Holland Artisan Spirits, MI
Rum, Single Barrel	Holstein Single Barrel Sippin' Rum	Werner Distilling LLC, IA
Rum, Single Barrel	Thomas Tew Single Barrel Rum	Newport Distilling Company, RI
Rum, Sorghum	Sorghum Rum	Fifth Element Spirits, OH
Rum, Spiced	Breckenridge Spiced Rum	Breckenridge Distillery, CO
Rum, Spiced	Caribbean Mist Rum - a 80 Proof Spiced Rum	Paradise Distilling Company LLC, IA

Rum, Spiced	Chinook Spiced Rum	Minhas Micro Distillery, WI
Rum, Spiced	Corsair Spiced Rum	Corsair Artisan Distillery, TN
Rum, Spiced	Dancing Pines Spice Rum	Dancing Pines Distillery, CO
Rum, Spiced	Deadman's Spice Rum	Spirits of the USA LLC, FL
Rum, Spiced	Delaware Distilling Company Spiced Rum	Delaware Distilling Company, DE
Rum, Spiced	Downslope Spiced Rum	Downslope Distilling, CO
Rum, Spiced	Esprit de Krewe™ Spiced Rum	Rollins Distillery, FL
Rum, Spiced	Ginger Spiced Rum	Bardenay Inc., ID
Rum, Spiced	Ian's Alley Spiced Rum	Mancos Valley Distillery, CO
Rum, Spiced	Kaua'i Spice Rum	Kōloa Rum Company, HI
Rum, Spiced	Malahat Spirits Spiced Rum	Malahat Spirits, CA
Rum, Spiced	Old Ipswich "Golden Marsh" Spiced Rum	Turkey Shore Distilleries, MA
Rum, Spiced	Old Ipswich "Greenhead" Spiced Rum	Turkey Shore Distilleries, MA
Rum, Spiced	One-Eyed Jon Spiced Rum	Oregon Spirit Distillers, OR
Rum, Spiced	Pieces of Eight Spiced Rum	Arizona High Spirits Distillery, AZ
Rum, Spiced	Railean Spiced Rum	Railean Distillers, TX
Rum, Spiced	Rogue Hazelnut Spice Rum	Rogue Spirits, OR
Rum, Spiced	Sea Island Spiced Rum	Firefly Distillery, SC
Rum, Spiced	Seven Brothers 100-Proof Spiced Rum	Seven Brothers Distilling Company, OH
Rum, Spiced	Siesta Key Spiced Rum	Drum Circle Distilling, FL
Rum, Spiced	Spiced Bayou Rum	Louisiana Spirits LLC, LA
Rum, Spiced	Stingray Spiced Rum	JEM Beverage Company, TX
Rum, Spiced	Wheat State Distilling Spiced Rum	Wheat State Distilling, KS
Rum, Spiced	Wicked Dolphin Spiced Rum	Cape Spirits Inc., FL
Rum, Spiced	Wisconsin Club USA Spiced Rum	Minhas Micro Distillery, WI
Rum, Spiced	Wit Spiced Rhum	Dogfish Head Craft Brewery, DE
Rum, Spiced, Cajun	Old New Orleans Cajun Spice Rum	Celebration Distillation, LA
Rum, Straight, Reserve	Backwoods Reserve Straight Rum	Dunc's Mill, VT
Rum, Sweet	Sweet Crude Rum	Rank Wildcat Spirits LLC, LA
Rum, Vanilla	Cypress Creek Reserve Vanilla Flavored Rum	D.E.W. Distillation LLC, TX
Rum, Vanilla	Downslope Vanilla Rum	Downslope Distilling, CO
Rum, Vanilla Bean	Charbay Tahitian Vanilla Bean Rum	Charbay Distillers, CA

633

Rum, White	Bully Boy Bully Boy White Rum	Bully Boy Distillers, MA
Rum, White	Cacao Prieto White Rum	Cacao Prieto LLC, NY
Rum, White	Delaware Distilling Company White Rum	Delaware Distilling Company, DE
Rum, White	Downslope White Rum	Downslope Distilling, CO
Rum, White	Flag Hill White Rum	Flag Hill Winery & Distillery, NH
Rum, White	Freshwater Huron White Rum	New Holland Artisan Spirits, MI
Rum, White	Island Bay Rum - a 90 Proof Clear Rum	Paradise Distilling Company LLC, IA
Rum, White	Kaua`i White	Kōloa Rum Company, HI
Rum, White	Manitou Passage Rum - White Rum	Northern Latitudes Distillery, MI
Rum, White	Old New Orleans Crystal Rum	Celebration Distillation, LA
Rum, White	Powder™ White Rum	Syntax Spirits LLC, CO
Rum, White	Prichard's Crystal Rum	Prichard's Distillery Inc., TN
Rum, White	Railean Texas White Rum	Railean Distillers, TX
Rum, White	Taildragger White Rum	Tailwinds Distilling Company, IL
Rum, White	Three Sheets White Rum	Ballast Point Spirits, CA
Rum, White	Urban White Rum	Urban Distilleries, BC
Rum, White	What Knot White Rum	Dirty Water Distillery, MA
Rum, White	Wisconsin Club USA White Rum	Minhas Micro Distillery, WI
Rum, Wine Barrel Aged	Downslope Wine Barrel Aged Rum	Downslope Distilling, CO
Rumskey	White Rumskey	Las Vegas Distillery, NV
Schnapps, Beer	Moylan's Distilling Beer Schnapps	Stillwater Spirits, CA
Shochu	White Dragon Shochu	66 Gilead Distillery, ON
Shochu, Barrel Aged	Black Dragon Shochu (barrel aged Shochu)	66 Gilead Distillery, ON
Shochu, Hankaku	Evenstar	Sodo Spirits Distillery, WA
Shochu, Hankaku	Evenstar Chiles	Sodo Spirits Distillery, WA
Shochu, Hankaku	Evenstar Ginger	Sodo Spirits Distillery, WA
Shochu, Hankaku	Evenstar Mint	Sodo Spirits Distillery, WA
Shochu, Hankaku	Sodo Spirits Distillery	Sodo Spirits Distillery, WA
Sorgrhum	Sorgrhum White – America's First Sweet Sorghum Spirit	Heartland Distillers, IN
Sorgrhum, Barrel Aged	Sorgrhum Barrel Aged	Heartland Distillers, IN
Spirit	8	Rumshine Distilling LLC, IL
Spirit	A Buck and a Quarter	Rumshine Distilling LLC, IL

Spirit	Brass	Rumshine Distilling LLC, IL
Spirit	Don Quixote Angelica	Don Quixote Distillery & Winery, NM
Spirit	Mamajuana	Cacao Prieto LLC, NY
Spirit	Rex Velvet Sinister Spirit	Fremont Mischief, WA
Spirit	River Baron Artisan Spirit	Mississippi River Distilling Company, IA
Spirit	Rumble	Balcones Distillery, TX
Spirit	Rumble Cask Reserve	Balcones Distillery, TX
Spirit	Temperance Small Batch	Bull Run Distilling Company, OR
Spirit	That Purple Stuff	Rumshine Distilling LLC, IL
Spirit	Whistling Andy Harvest Select	Whistling Andy Distillery, MT
Spirit	Whistling Andy Hopshnop	Whistling Andy Distillery, MT
Spirit	Uncle Don's Shining Spirit	Uncle Don's Apple Pie Craft Dist., MI
Spirit	Apple Strudel	Rumshine Distilling LLC, IL
Spirit, Apple	Still Cellars Apple Straightup	Still Cellars, CO
Spirit, Apple	White Wolf Apple Neutral Spirit	White Wolf Distillery, WI
Spirit, Apple	Still Cellars Apple Cinnamon	Still Cellars, CO
Spirit, Apple Cinnamon	Still Cellars Apple Ginger	Still Cellars, CO
Spirit, Apple Ginger	Vinn Baiju (pronounced "By-Je-oh")	Vinn Distillery, OR
Spirit, Baijiu	Sidetrack Distillery BETE	Sidetrack Distillery, WA
Spirit, Beet	Hum Botanical Spirit	Hum Spirits Company, IL
Spirit, Botanical	Bee's Knees Merry Cherry	The Hardware Distillery Co., WA
Spirit, Cherry	MBR St. Elmo's Fire	MB Roland Distillery, KY
Spirit, Cinnamon, Cayenne	Prairie Moonshine™ Corn & Honey Spirit	Quincy Street Distillery, IL
Spirit, Corn, Honey	Bee's Knees Fig	The Hardware Distillery Co., WA
Spirit, Fig	Mahia	Nahmias et Fils, NY
Spirit, Fig	White Wolf Grape Neutral Spirit	White Wolf Distillery, WI
Spirit, Grape	Dutch Harbor Breeze Grog	Ye Ol' Grog Distillery, OR
Spirit, Grog	Underground Herbal Spirit	Ogden's Own Distillery, UT
Spirit, Herbal	Yerlo (120 Proof)	Lo Artisan Distillery LLC, WI
Spirit, Hmong Rice	Yerlo Reserve (130 Proof)	Lo Artisan Distillery LLC, WI
Spirit, Hmong Rice	Yerlo Silver (86 Proof)	Lo Artisan Distillery LLC, WI
Spirit, Hmong Rice	Legendary Gold Honey Spirit	Swanson's Mountain View Orchard, MT
Spirit, Honey		

635

Spirit, Honey	Prairie Sunshine™ Wildflower Honey Spirit	Quincy Street Distillery, IL
Spirit, Jalapeno	Humdinger Jalapeno Spirit	Journeyman Distillery, MI
Spirit, Malt	Wasmund's Single Malt Spirit	Copper Fox Distillery, VA
Spirit, Maple	Rail Dog Barrel Aged Maple Spirit	Elm Brook Farm, VT
Spirit, Maple	Tree Spirits Knotted Maple	Tree Spirits, ME
Spirit, Mijiu	Vinn Mijiu (pronounced "Mee-Je-oh") Fire	Vinn Distillery, OR
Spirit, Mijiu	Vinn Mijiu (pronounced "Mee-Je-oh") Ice	Vinn Distillery, OR
Spirit, Mint	MBR Kentucky Mint Julep	MB Roland Distillery, KY
Spirit, Peach	Bee's Knees Peachy Keen	The Hardware Distillery Co., WA
Spirit, Plum	Bee's Knees Plumb	The Hardware Distillery Co., WA
Spirit, Plum	Mirabelle Plum	Clear Creek Distillery, OR
Spirit, Pumpkin	Great Lakes Seasonal Pumpkin Spirit	Great Lakes Distillery LLC, WI
Spirit, Raspberry	Bee's Knees Raspberry	The Hardware Distillery Co., WA
Spirit, Raspberry	Framboise (Raspberry)	Clear Creek Distillery, OR
Spirit, Rum	Turtle Island Rum-style Spirit	Dark Moon Artisan Distillery, WA
Spirit, Rye	Wasmund's Rye Spirit	Copper Fox Distillery, VA
Spirit, Tangerine, American White Oak	Marion Black 106	Fish Hawk Spirits LLC, FL
Sprit, Grog	Good Morning Glory Grog	Ye Ol' Grog Distillery, OR
Straight Bourbon	Spring44 Straight Bourbon	Spring44 Distilling, CO
Tequila, see also Agave		
Tequila	Alamo Tequila	Minhas Micro Distillery, WI
Tequila	IXÁ Tequila	GreenBar Collective, CA
Tequila	Rattlesnake Tequila	Spirits of the USA LLC, FL
Tequila	Stars Tequila	Minhas Micro Distillery, WI
Tequila, Blanco	Charbay Tequila Blanco	Charbay Distillers, CA
Tequila, Gold	Chinook Gold Tequila	Minhas Micro Distillery, WI
Tequila, Gold	Wisconsin Club USA Gold Tequila	Minhas Micro Distillery, WI
Tequila, Jalapeño	Rattlesnake Jalapeño Tequila	Spirits of the USA LLC, FL
Tequila, Silver	Chinook Silver Tequila	Minhas Micro Distillery, WI
Tequila, Silver	Wisconsin Club USA Silver Tequila	Minhas Micro Distillery, WI
Vermouth	Vermouth	Sweetgrass Farm Winery & Distillery, ME
Vodka	18 Vodka	Virtuoso Distillers LLC, IN

Vodka	1911 Vodka	Beak & Skiff Distillery, NY
Vodka	2bar Vodka	2bar® Spirits, WA
Vodka	37 Black Vodka	Sons of Vancouver Distillery Ltd., BC
Vodka	3BEES Vodka	Sherwoods Winery & Distillery LLC, MN
Vodka	4 Spirits Vodka	4 Spirits Distillery, OR
Vodka	44° North Magic Valley Vodka	44° North Vodka, ID
Vodka	45th Parallel Vodka	45th Parallel Distillery, WI
Vodka	46 Peaks Potato Vodka	Lake Placid Spirits LLC, NY
Vodka	9 Rocks Vodka	Black Rock Distillery LLC, OR
Vodka	Abner Doubleday Double-play Vodka	Cooperstown Distillery, NY
Vodka	Adirondack ADK Vodka	Adirondack Distilling Company, NY
Vodka	Aeroplano Vodka	Good Spirits Distilling, KS
Vodka	Alchemist Distillery Vodka	Alchemist Distilleries Inc., FL
Vodka	Amador Distillery Vodka	Amador Distillery, CA
Vodka	American Star Vodka	Ascendant Spirits, CA
Vodka	American Vodka Arizona	High Spirits Distillery, AZ
Vodka	Aristo Vodka	Minhas Micro Distillery, WI
Vodka	B4 Premium Handcrafted Vodka	Carbon Glacier Distillery, WA
Vodka	Baker Beach San Francisco Vodka	Treasure Island Distillery, CA
Vodka	Bakon Vodka	Black Rock Spirits LLC, WA
Vodka	Banner Natural Vodka	Banner Distilling Co., TX
Vodka	Bardenay Vodka	Bardenay Inc., ID
Vodka	Barr Hill Vodka	Caledonia Spirits Inc., VT
Vodka	Batch 206 Mad Mint Vodka	Batch 206 Distillery, WA
Vodka	Batch 206 Vodka	Batch 206 Distillery, WA
Vodka	Battlefield Vodka	Old Republic Distillery, PA
Vodka	Beauport Vodka	Ryan & Wood Inc, MA
Vodka	Belle Vodka	Belle of Dayton, OH
Vodka	BelleWood Vodka, (distilled from apples)	BelleWood Distilling, WA
Vodka	Big Gun Vodka	Uncle Don's Apple Pie Craft Dist., MI
Vodka	Birch Syrup Vodka	Alaska Distillery, AK
Vodka	Black Button Professional Proof Vodka	Black Button Distilling, NY

Vodka	Black Heron Vodka	Black Heron Spirits Distillery, WA
Vodka	Black Mule Vodka	Tenn South Distillery, TN
Vodka	Blackrock Vodka	Minhas Micro Distillery, WI
Vodka	Blackstone Vodka	Minhas Micro Distillery, WI
Vodka	Blaum Bros. Vodka	Blaum Bros. Distilling Co., IL
Vodka	Blue Flame Ultra Premium Vodka	Blue Flame Spirits, WA
Vodka	Blue Flame Vodka	Blue Flame Spirits, WA
Vodka	Blue Hen Vodka	Dogfish Head Craft Brewery, DE
Vodka	Blüe Heron Premium Vodka	Wilderness Trace Distillery, KY
Vodka	Blue Spirits Vodka	Blue Spirits Distilling, WA
Vodka	BOHICA Vodka	Mystic Mountain Distillery LLC, CO
Vodka	Bootlegger 21 Vodka	Prohibition Distillery LLC, NY
Vodka	Brandon's Vodka	Rock Town Distillery Inc., AR
Vodka	Breckenridge Vodka	Breckenridge Distillery, CO
Vodka	Buck 25 Vodka	Atelier Vie, LA
Vodka	Buckeye Vodka	Crystal Spirits LLC, OH
Vodka	Bully Boy Vodka	Bully Boy Distillers, MA
Vodka	Cane Vodka	The Florida Distillery, FL
Vodka	Cardinal Sin Vodka	St. Louis Distillery, MO
Vodka	Cathead Vodka	Cathead Distillery LLC, MS
Vodka	CD Vodka	Mid-Oak Distillery, IL
Vodka	Ceres Vodka	Chicago Distilling Company, IL
Vodka	CH Vodka	CH Distillery, IL
Vodka	Chai Vodka	LB Distillers, SK
Vodka	Chambers Bay Craft Distilled Vodka	Port Steilacoom Distillery, WA
Vodka	Charbay Vodka	Charbay Distillers, CA
Vodka	Chase Nebraska Vodka	Cooper's Chase Distillery LLC, NE
Vodka	China Beach San Francisco Vodka	Treasure Island Distillery, CA
Vodka	Chinook Vodka	Minhas Micro Distillery, WI
Vodka	Chuckanut Bay Vodka	Chuckanut Bay Distillery, WA
Vodka	Cinco ~ The Five Star Vodka	Azar Distillery, TX
Vodka	Cirrus Vodka	Parched Group LLC, VA

Vodka	Civilized Vodka	Northern United Brewing Company, MI
Vodka	Class V™ Vodka	Syntax Spirits LLC, CO
Vodka	CLEAR10 Vodka	Good Spirits Distilling, KS
Vodka	ClearHeart Vodka	Cedar Ridge Distillery, IA
Vodka	Cold House Vodka	Valley Spirits LLC, CA
Vodka	Cold River Classic Vodka	Maine Distilleries LLC, ME
Vodka	Colorado Blue Vodka	Mystic Mountain Distillery LLC, CO
Vodka	Colorado Crystal Vodka	Mystic Mountain Distillery LLC, CO
Vodka	Colorado Gold Premium Vodka	Colorado Gold Distillery, CO
Vodka	COMB Vodka	StilltheOne Distillery LLC, NY
Vodka	Coopercraft Vodka	Coppercraft Distillery LLC, MI
Vodka	Copperworks Vodka	Copperworks Distilling Company, WA
Vodka	Core Vodka	Harvest Spirits LLC, NY
Vodka	Covington Gourmet Vodka	Covington Spirits LLC, NC
Vodka	Coyote Vodka	Spirits of the USA LLC, FL
Vodka	Crater Lake Reserve Vodka	Bendistillery, OR
Vodka	Crater Lake Vodka	Bendistillery, OR
Vodka	Crescent Vodka	Cajun Spirits Distillery, LA
Vodka	Cut Spike Premium Vodka	Cut Spike Distillery, NE
Vodka	Czar	Good Spirits Distilling, KS
Vodka	Death's Door Vodka	Death's Door Spirits, WI
Vodka	Deception Vodka	Deception Distilling LLC, WA
Vodka	Deep Run Virginia Vodka	A. Smith Bowman Distillery, VA
Vodka	Deer Camp Vodka	Northern Latitudes Distillery, MI
Vodka	Delaware Distilling Company Potato Vodka	Delaware Distilling Company, DE
Vodka	Delaware Distilling Company Premium Vodka	Delaware Distilling Company, DE
Vodka	Desert Diamond Distillery Gold Miner Vodka	Desert Diamond Distillery, AZ
Vodka	DiVine Vodka	Entente Spirits LLC, MI
Vodka	Dizzythree Expresso Vodka	Good Spirits Distilling, KS
Vodka	DL Franklin Vodka	Dogwood Distilling, OR
Vodka	Dog Trot Vodka	Big Thicket Distilling Company, TX
Vodka	Dog Watch Vodka	Ye Ol' Grog Distillery, OR

Vodka	Door County Vodka	Door County Distillery, WI
Vodka	Double Silo (160 Proof)	Project V Distillery and Sausage Co., WA
Vodka	Dripping Springs Vodka	San Luis Spirits, TX
Vodka	Dry County Copper Still Vodka	Dry County Distillery LLC, WA
Vodka	Dutchess Vodka	New Holland Artisan Spirits, MI
Vodka	E Vodka	Evanson Handcrafted Distilling LLC, WA
Vodka	East Van Vodka	Odd Society Spirits, BC
Vodka	Ebb+Flow Vodka	Sound Spirits, WA
Vodka	Elevate Vodka	Mile High Spirits LLC, CO
Vodka	Elk Rider Vodka	Heritage Distilling Company, WA
Vodka	Enchanted Rock Vodka	Rebecca Creek Distillery LLC, TX
Vodka	Esprit de Krewe™ Vodka	Rollins Distillery, FL
Vodka	E-VO-DKA Vodka	Evanson Handcrafted Distilling LLC, WA
Vodka	Expedition Vodka	Santa Fe Spirits, NM
Vodka	Fifth Element Spirits Vodka from grains	Fifth Element Spirits, OH
Vodka	Fifth Element Spirits Vodka from grapes	Fifth Element Spirits, OH
Vodka	Fire Puncher Vodka	GrandTen Distilling, MA
Vodka	Firefly Handcrafted Vodka	Firefly Distillery, SC
Vodka	Firefly Skinny Tea	Firefly Distillery, SC
Vodka	Fireweed Vodka	Alaska Distillery, AK
Vodka	Five Wives Vodka	Ogden's Own Distillery, UT
Vodka	Flagship Vodka	Clayton Distillery, NY
Vodka	Flathead Vodka	The Montana Distillery-1889, MT
Vodka	Fremont Mischief Vodka	Fremont Mischief, WA
Vodka	Frizz Vodka	Merridale Ciderworks Corp., BC
Vodka	FrostBite Alaska Vodka	Alaska Distillery, AK
Vodka	Fugu Vodka	Ballast Point Spirits, CA
Vodka	General John Stark Vodka	Flag Hill Winery & Distillery, NH
Vodka	Georgia Vodka	Georgia Distilling Company, GA
Vodka	Glacier Vodka	Valley Shine Distillery, WA
Vodka	Glass Vodka	Glass Distillery, WA
Vodka	Glimmerglass Vodka	Cooperstown Distillery, NY

Vodka	Goat Artisan Vodka	Peach Street Distillers, CO
Vodka	Grand Teton Vodka	Grand Teton Distillery, ID
Vodka	Great North Vodka	Trailhead Spirits, MT
Vodka	Green Geisha	Hard Times Distillery LLC, OR
Vodka	Grey Heron Vodka	St. Julian Winery, MI
Vodka	Gridiron Vodka	Glass Distillery, WA
Vodka	Hard Times Blue Collar Vodka	Hard Times Distillery LLC, OR
Vodka	Hawaiian Vodka	Island Distillers Inc., HI
Vodka	HDC Vodka	Heritage Distilling Company, WA
Vodka	Heartland Distiller's Reserve Vodka	Heartland Distillers, IN
Vodka	High Mark Vodka	High Mark Distillery, AK
Vodka	High Ore Vodka	Headframe Spirits, MT
Vodka	High Roller Premium Vodka	High Roller Spirits, CA
Vodka	High West Vodka 7000' ®	High West Distillery, UT
Vodka	High Wire Distilling Co. Home Team Vodka	High Wire Distilling, SC
Vodka	Honor Vodka	D and J Distilling
Vodka	Ice Dunes Vodka	Northern Latitudes Distillery, MI
Vodka	Ice Glen Vodka	Berkshire Mountain Distillers Inc., MA
Vodka	Icy Strait Vodka	Port Chilkoot Distillery, AK
Vodka	Incentive Vodka	Big Cedar Distilling Inc., MI
Vodka	Indiana Vodka	Heartland Distillers, IN
Vodka	Indigenous Vodka: Empire State Wheat and Fresh Pressed Apple	Tuthilltown Spirits Distillery, NY
Vodka	Indio Vodka	Indio Spirits, OR
Vodka	Industry Standard Vodka	Industry City Distillery Inc., NY
Vodka	Ironworks Vodka	Ironworks Distillery, NS
Vodka	Isis Vodka	Mac Donald Distillery, WA
Vodka	Kennewick Vodka	RiverSands Distillery, WA
Vodka	Klondike Vodka - The Spirit of the Yukon	Klondike River Distillery, YT
Vodka	L'etoile Vodka	Du Nord Craft Spirits, MN
Vodka	Last Mountain Vodka	Last Mountain Distillery Ltd., SK
Vodka	Lavender Vodka	Alaska Distillery, AK
Vodka	Letterpress Vodka	Letterpress Distilling, WA

Vodka	Literary Dog Premium Sipping Vodka	Elm Brook Farm, VT
Vodka	Lockhouse Vodka	Lockhouse Distillery, NY
Vodka	Long Table Distillery Texada Vodka	Long Table Distillery Ltd., BC
Vodka	Long Winter Vodka	Ursa Major Distilling, AK
Vodka	Loyal 9 Vodka	Sons of Liberty Spirits Co., RI
Vodka	Lucky Bastard Vodka	LB Distillers, SK
Vodka	Luminous Vodka	Door County Distillery, WI
Vodka	Mastermind Vodka	Mastermind Vodka, IL
Vodka	Medoyeff Vodka	Bull Run Distilling Company, OR
Vodka	Michigan Dew Vodka	St. Julian Winery, MI
Vodka	Midwest Vodka	45th Parallel Distillery, WI
Vodka	Miss Kitty's Velvet Vodka	Good Spirits Distilling, KS
Vodka	Miss Kitty's Velvet Vodka	Dodge City Distillery, KS
Vodka	Missouri Spirits Vodka	Missouri Spirits, MO
Vodka	Mojo Vodka	Saint James Spirits, CA
Vodka	Mount Baker Vodka	Mount Baker Distillery, WA
Vodka	Mount Snow Vodka	Vermont Distillers, VT
Vodka	Mt. Index Vodka	Mt. Index Brewery & Distillery, WA
Vodka	Myer Farm Vodka	Myer Farm Distillers, NY
Vodka	Napa Vodka Vintage Reserve	Napa Valley Distillery, CA
Vodka	Nashoba Vodka	Nashoba Valley Spirits Ltd., MA
Vodka	Nevada Vodka	Churchill Vineyards and Distillery, NV
Vodka	Nevada Vodka	Las Vegas Distillery, NV
Vodka	New Deal Vodka	New Deal Distillery, OR
Vodka	Nick the Sipper, (a gently filtered vodka)	Damnation Alley Distillery, MA
Vodka	No. 209 Kosher-for-Passover Vodka	Distillery No. 209, CA
Vodka	Norseman Vodka	Norseman Distillery, MN
Vodka	North Shore Vodka	North Shore Distillery, IL
Vodka	Ocean Beach San Francisco Vodka	Treasure Island Distillery, CA
Vodka	Ocean Vodka	Hawaii Sea Spirits LLC, HI
Vodka	Okanagan Spirits Vodka	Okanagan Spirits, BC
Vodka	OOLA Rosemary Vodka	OOLA Distillery, WA

Vodka	OOLA Vodka	OOLA Distillery, WA
Vodka	Orchard Vodka (distilled from apples)	Hidden Marsh Distillery, NY
Vodka	Oregon Spirit Vodka	Oregon Spirit Distillers, OR
Vodka	Oryza Vodka	Donner-Peltier Distillers, LA
Vodka	OYO Stone Fruit Vodka	Middle West Spirits LLC, OH
Vodka	OYO Vodka	Middle West Spirits LLC, OH
Vodka	Ozark Premium Vodka	Ozark Distillery LLC, MO
Vodka	P3 Placid Vodka	Lake Placid Spirits LLC, NY
Vodka	Peace Vodka	Catskill Distilling Company Ltd., NY
Vodka	Permafrost Alaska Vodka	Alaska Distillery, AK
Vodka	Phrog Premium Vodka	Island Spirits Distillery, BC
Vodka	Plantation Vodka	Thirteenth Colony Distilleries, GA
Vodka	Portland 88 Vodka	New Deal Distillery, OR
Vodka	Prairie Wolf Vodka	Prairie Wolf Spirits, OK
Vodka	Prince Igor Vodka	Forty Creek Distillery, ON
Vodka	Pür Class Vodka	Hendricks Family Distillery LLC, WI
Vodka	Pure Blue Vodka	Barrel House Distilling Co., KY
Vodka	Quicksilver Vodka	Montgomery Distillery, MT
Vodka	Railean Vodka	Railean Distillers, TX
Vodka	Rain Ciy Vodka	Rain City Spirits, WA
Vodka	RE:FIND Vodka	RE:FIND Distillery, CA
Vodka	Real Russian Vodka	Premiere Distillery LLC, IL
Vodka	Red Arrow Vodka	Journeyman Distillery, MI
Vodka	Rehorst Premium Milwaukee Vodka	Great Lakes Distillery LLC, WI
Vodka	Rider Vodka	Dark Horse Distillery, KS
Vodka	Ringneck Vodka	Dakota Spirits Distillery LLC, SD
Vodka	River Pilot Vodka	Mississippi River Distilling Company, IA
Vodka	RMD Vodka	Artesian Distillers, MI
Vodka	Rock Town Vodka	Rock Town Distillery Inc., AR
Vodka	Rogue Vintage Vodka	Rogue Spirits, OR
Vodka	Rolling River Spirits Vodka	Rolling River Spirits, OR
Vodka	Rosemary Vodka	3 Howls Distillery, WA

Vodka	Rx Vodka	Kill Devil Spirit Company, CA
Vodka	S.D. Strong Vodka	S. D. Strong Distilling, MO
Vodka	Sailboat Vodka	Minhas Micro Distillery, WI
Vodka	Sandstone Distillery Stone Carver Vodka	Sandstone Distillery LLC, WA
Vodka	SAVVY Vodka	SAVVY Distillers LP, TX
Vodka	Seersucker Vodka	VooDoo Distillery, LA
Vodka	Seraph Vodka	Central City Brewers and Dist. Ltd, BC
Vodka	Seven Brothers Vodka	Seven Brothers Distilling Company, OH
Vodka	Seven Grain Vodka	Las Vegas Distillery, NV
Vodka	Sherlock's "Mischief Well" Vodka	Fremont Mischief, WA
Vodka	Silver Screen Vodka	Painted Stave Distilling, DE
Vodka	Silver Tree American Small Batch Vodka	Leopold Bros., CO
Vodka	Singing Whale Vodka	Dark Moon Artisan Distillery, WA
Vodka	Single Silo Distiller's Cut Vodka	Project V Distillery and Sausage Co., WA
Vodka	Single Silo Ultra Filtered Vodka	Project V Distillery and Sausage Co., WA
Vodka	Single Silo Vodka	Project V Distillery and Sausage Co., WA
Vodka	Sintillation Low Calorie Vodka	Fremont Mischief, WA
Vodka	Six Mile Creek Vodka	Six Mile Creek Winery & Distillery, NY
Vodka	SlapTail Vodka	4 Spirits Distillery, OR
Vodka	Sloop Betty	Blackwater Distilling Inc., MD
Vodka	Smiths Premium Vodka	Bone Spirits, TX
Vodka	Smooth Ambler Whitewater Vodka	Smooth Ambler Spirits Company, WV
Vodka	Smugglers' Notch Vodka	Smugglers' Notch Distillery, VT
Vodka	Snow Creek Vodka	Collier and McKeel, TN
Vodka	Snowcrest Vodka	Willie's Distillery, MT
Vodka	Snowflake Vodka	Tahoe Moonshine Distillery Inc., CA
Vodka	Soft Tail Vodka	Soft Tail Spirits, WA
Vodka	Solano Vodka	HelloCello, CA
Vodka	Solstice Infused Vodka	Yukon Spirits, YT
Vodka	Southern Son Vodka	JEM Beverage Company, TX
Vodka	Southern Vodka	Thirteenth Colony Distilleries, GA
Vodka	Space City Vodka	Whitmeyer's Distilling Co. LLC, TX

Vodka	Speakeasy Vodka	Meriwether Distilling Co., WA
Vodka	Spike Vodka	Spink Distillery, TX
Vodka	Spirit Bear Vodka	Urban Distilleries, BC
Vodka	Spirit of Santa Fe Vodka	Don Quixote Distillery & Winery, NM
Vodka	Spirit Works Vodka	Spirit Works Distillery, CA
Vodka	Spirits of the Blue Ridge Vodka	Chesapeake Bay Distillery LLC, VA
Vodka	Spring44 Vodka	Spring44 Distilling, CO
Vodka	St Helens Vodka	Ye Ol' Grog Distillery, OR
Vodka	Starlite Vodka	Treaty Oak Distilling Co., TX
Vodka	Stars Vodka	Minhas Micro Distillery, WI
Vodka	Still Cellars Vodka	Still Cellars, CO
Vodka	Stillwater Spirits Vodka 100°	Stillwater Spirits, CA
Vodka	Stillwater Spirits Vodka 80°	Stillwater Spirits, CA
Vodka	Stoutridge Vodka	Stoutridge Distillery, NY
Vodka	Strait Vodka	Myriad View Artisan Distillery Inc., PE
Vodka	Striped Vodka	Striped Pig Distillery, SC
Vodka	Sub Rosa Saffron Vodka	Sub Rosa Spirits, OR
Vodka	Sub Rosa Tarragon Vodka	Sub Rosa Spirits, OR
Vodka	Sun Liquor Unxld Vodka	Sun Liquor Distillery, WA
Vodka	Superfly Vodka	Superfly Distilling Company, OR
Vodka	Tailgater's Vodka	Good Spirits Distilling, KS
Vodka	The Re-Mixer (Vodka)	Damnation Alley Distillery, MA
Vodka	The Rocket Vodka	Seattle Distilling Company, WA
Vodka	The Vodka	Ransom Spirits, OR
Vodka	Thunderbeast Stampede Vodka	Mad Buffalo Distillery, MO
Vodka	Tito's Handmade Vodka	Tito's Handmade Vodka, TX
Vodka	TOPO Vodka	Top of the Hill Distillery, NC
Vodka	Touch Vodka-Original	Fat Dog Spirits LLC, FL
Vodka	Trail Town Still Colorado Vodka	Trail Town Still, CO
Vodka	Tree Vodka	Celk Distilling, NY
Vodka	Triple Divide Spirits Vodka	Triple Divide Spirits, MT
Vodka	Triple Eight Vodka	Triple Eight Distillery, MA

Vodka	Troubadour Vodka	The Original Texas Legend Distillery, TX
Vodka	TRU Vodka	GreenBar Collective, CA
Vodka	True North Vodka	Grand Traverse Distillery, MI
Vodka	Truth Vodka	The Liberty Distillery, BC
Vodka	Truuli Peak Vodka	Bare Distillery, AK
Vodka	Twenty 2 Create	Northern Maine Distilling Company, ME
Vodka	Twenty 2 Vodka	Northern Maine Distilling Company, ME
Vodka	Twister Vodka	Good Spirits Distilling, KS
Vodka	Two James Vodka	Two James Spirits, MI
Vodka	Ugly Dog Vodka	Ugly Dog Distillery LLC, MI
Vodka	Valentine Vodka	Valentine Distilling Company, MI
Vodka	Velocipede Vodka	Elm City Distillery LLC, CT
Vodka	Vermont Crimson Vodka	Vermont Spirits Distilling Co., VT
Vodka	Vermont Gold Vodka	Vermont Spirits Distilling Co., VT
Vodka	Vermont White Vodka	Vermont Spirits Distilling Co., VT
Vodka	Viezbicke 303 Vodka	Boulder Distillery, CO
Vodka	Vinn Vodka	Vinn Distillery, OR
Vodka	Vintner's Vodka	Finger Lakes Distilling, NY
Vodka	Viscova	Double V Distillery, WA
Vodka	Vivacity Fine Vodka	Vivacity Spirits, OR
Vodka	Vodka	It's 5 Artisan Distillery, WA
Vodka	Vodka 14	Altitude Spirits, CO
Vodka	Vodka Morava	Cal-Czech Distillery, CA
Vodka	Vodka Viracocha	Rancho de Los Luceros Destilaría, NM
Vodka	Volstead Vodka	House Spirits Distillery, OR
Vodka	VR Vodka	Rocky Mountain Distilling Co., CO
Vodka	VS Limited Release Vodka	Vermont Spirits Distilling Co., VT
Vodka	Walla Walla Vodka	Walla Walla Distilling Company, WA
Vodka	Watershed Distillery Vodka	Watershed Distillery, OH
Vodka	WebFoot Vodka	4 Spirits Distillery, OR
Vodka	Well No 1876	San Luis Spirits, TX
Vodka	Well Vodka	Old Ballard Liquor Co., WA

Vodka	Western Son Texas Vodka	JEM Beverage Company, TX
Vodka	Whistling Andy Vodka	Whistling Andy Distillery, MT
Vodka	Wiggly Bridge Vodka	Wiggly Bridge Distillery, ME
Vodka	Wisconsin Club USA Vodka	Minhas Micro Distillery, WI
Vodka	Wishkah River Distillery Vodka Distilled from Grains	Wishkah River Distillery, WA
Vodka	Wishkah River Distillery Vodka Distilled from Honey	Wishkah River Distillery, WA
Vodka	Woodstone Creek Vodka	Woodstone Creek, OH
Vodka	Woody Creek Colorado 100% Potato Vodka	Woody Creek Distillers, CO
Vodka	Woody Creek Colorado Reserve Vodka	Woody Creek Distillers, CO
Vodka	Worker's No 9 Vodka	Fremont Mischief, WA
Vodka	Yahara Bay Premium Vodka	Yahara Bay Distillers, WI
Vodka	Yaletown Distilling Company Craft Vodka	Yaletown Distilling Company, BC
Vodka	Five Wives Sinful Vodka	Ogden's Own Distillery, UT
Vodka, Apple	Maple River Distillery Flavored Vodka - Apple	Maple River Distillery, ND
Vodka, Apricot	Maple River Distillery Flavored Vodka - Apricot	Maple River Distillery, ND
Vodka, Bacon	Ugly Dog Bacon Vodka	Ugly Dog Distillery LLC, MI
Vodka, Banana	Bananas Foster Vodka	3 Howls Distillery, WA
Vodka, Black Peppercorn	Badger Pocket Black Peppercorn Vodka	Skip Rock Distillers, WA
Vodka, Blackberry	Blackberry Vodka	Old Republic Distillery, PA
Vodka, Blackberry	Mountain Blackberry Vodka	Alaska Distillery, AK
Vodka, Blood Orange	Charbay Fresh Fruit Vodka (Blood Orange)	Charbay Distillers, CA
Vodka, Blue Corn	Don Quixote Blue Corn Vodka	Don Quixote Distillery & Winery, NM
Vodka, Blueberry	Blueberry Vodka	Alaska Distillery, AK
Vodka, Blueberry	Cane Vodka Buccaneer Blueberry	The Florida Distillery, FL
Vodka, Blueberry	Cold River Blueberry Vodka	Maine Distilleries LLC, ME
Vodka, Blueberry	Blueberry Vodka – Coming soon	Mountain View Distillery, PA
Vodka, Blueberry Orange	Myer Farm Blueberry Orange Vodka	Myer Farm Distillers, NY
Vodka, Blueberry, Wild	Prince Edward Wild Blueberry Vodka	Prince Edward Distillery, PE
Vodka, Boysenberry	Hanson of Sonoma Organic Vodka - Boysenberry	Hanson Spirits LLC, CA
Vodka, Cane	Downslope Cane Vodka	Downslope Distilling, CO
Vodka, Chai	Single Silo Chai Infused Vodka	Project V Distillery and Sausage Co., WA
Vodka, Chai Tea	Seraphine Chai Tea Vodka	Yahara Bay Distillers, WI

Vodka, Charr Barrel Finished	HDC Charr Barrel Finished Vodka	Heritage Distilling Company, WA
Vodka, Cherry	44° North Rainier Cherry Vodka	44° North Vodka, ID
Vodka, Cherry	Civilized Sakura	Northern United Brewing Company, MI
Vodka, Cherry	Door County Cherry Infused Vodka	Door County Distillery, WI
Vodka, Cherry	Flathead Cherry Vodka	The Montana Distillery-1889, MT
Vodka, Cherry	True North Cherry Flavored Vodka	Grand Traverse Distillery, MI
Vodka, Cherry	Ugly Dog Black Cherry Vodka	Ugly Dog Distillery LLC, MI
Vodka, Cherry	Vishnovka, Russian style cherry vodka	Grand Teton Distillery, ID
Vodka, Chili	Chili Vodka	Arizona High Spirits Distillery, AZ
Vodka, Chocolate	Chocolate Vodka	Dogfish Head Craft Brewery, DE
Vodka, Chocolate	True North Chocolate Flavored Vodka	Grand Traverse Distillery, MI
Vodka, Chocolate Moouse	Chocolate Moouse Vodka	Alaska Distillery, AK
Vodka, Chocolate Vanilla Bean	Loyal 9 Dark Chocolate Vanilla Bean Flavored Vodka	Sons of Liberty Spirits Co., RI
Vodka, Chocolate, Bitter	Mud Puddle Bitter Chocolate Vodka	New Deal Distillery, OR
Vodka, Chokecherry	Maple River Distillery Flavored Vodka - Chokecherry	Maple River Distillery, ND
Vodka, Citrus	Coopercraft Citrus Vodka	Coppercraft Distillery LLC, MI
Vodka, Citrus	Dutchess Citrus Vodka	New Holland Artisan Spirits, MI
Vodka, Citrus	OOLA Citrus Vodka	OOLA Distillery, WA
Vodka, Citrus	Sol Chamomile Citrus Vodka	North Shore Distillery, IL
Vodka, Citrus Honey	Rehorst Citrus Honey Flavored Vodka	Great Lakes Distillery LLC, WI
Vodka, Clementine	Dirty Water Clementine Vodka	Dirty Water Distillery, MA
Vodka, Coconut	Hawaiian Coconut Vodka	Island Distillers Inc., HI
Vodka, Coffee	Flathead Coffee Vodka	The Montana Distillery-1889, MT
Vodka, Coffee	Glass Kona Coffee Vodka	Glass Distillery, WA
Vodka, Coriander	Mt. Index Coriander Flavored Vodka	Mt. Index Brewery & Distillery, WA
Vodka, Corn	TLD Vodka, Neutral Spirit Corn Vodka, 80 proof	The Original Texas Legend Distillery, TX
Vodka, Cranberry	Dirty Water Cranberry Vodka	Dirty Water Distillery, MA
Vodka, Cranberry	High Bush Cranberry Vodka	Alaska Distillery, AK
Vodka, Cranberry, Maple	Alpenglow Cranberry Maple Vodka	Lake Placid Spirits LLC, NY
Vodka, Cucumber	Hanson of Sonoma Organic Vodka - Cucumber	Hanson Spirits LLC, CA
Vodka, Cucumber	Loyal 9 Mint Cucumber Flavored Vodka (Spring/Summer)	Sons of Liberty Spirits Co., RI
Vodka, Cucumber	RE:FIND Cucumber Vodka	RE:FIND Distillery, CA

Vodka, Elderflower	Valentine White Blossom Elderflower Flavored Vodka	Valentine Distilling Company, MI
Vodka, Espresso	Hanson of Sonoma Organic Vodka - Espresso	Hanson Spirits LLC, CA
Vodka, Espresso	LiV Vodka - Original LiV, Ristretto Espresso Flavored Vodka	Long Island Spirits, NY
Vodka, Espresso	Spirit Bear Espresso Vodka	Urban Distilleries, BC
Vodka, Garlic	Hot Stinkin' Garlic Vodka	Tahoe Moonshine Distillery Inc., CA
Vodka, Ginger	Hanson of Sonoma Organic Vodka - Ginger	Hanson Spirits LLC, CA
Vodka, Ginger	Myer Farm Ginger Vodka	Myer Farm Distillers, NY
Vodka, Grain	Downslope Grain Vodka	Downslope Distilling, CO
Vodka, Grape	Maple River Distillery Flavored Vodka - Grape	Maple River Distillery, ND
Vodka, Grapefruit	Cane Vodka Gator Grape	The Florida Distillery, FL
Vodka, Grapefruit	Touch Red Grapefruit Flavored Vodka	Fat Dog Spirits LLC, FL
Vodka, Grapefruit, Ruby Red	Charbay Fresh Fruit Vodka	Charbay Distillers, CA
Vodka, Green Tea	Charbay Fresh Fruit Vodka (Green Tea)	Charbay Distillers, CA
Vodka, Hazelnut Espresso	Crater Lake Hazelnut Espresso Vodka	Bendistillery, OR
Vodka, Hemp	Left Coast Hemp Vodka	Victoria Spirits, BC
Vodka, Hemp	Mary Jane's Primo Hemp Vodka	Mary Jane's, ON
Vodka, Hemp Seed	Purgatory Hemp Seed Vodka	Alaska Distillery, AK
Vodka, Honey	Barr Hill Honey Vodka	Caledonia Spirits Inc., VT
Vodka, Honey	Glass Honey Vodka	Glass Distillery, WA
Vodka, Honey	Honey Vodka	Alaska Distillery, AK
Vodka, Honey	Spring44 Honey Vodka	Spring44 Distilling, CO
Vodka, Honeysuckle	Cathead Honeysuckle Vodka	Cathead Distillery LLC, MS
Vodka, Horseradish	Apollo Horseradish Vodka	Northern Latitudes Distillery, MI
Vodka, Huckleberry	44° North Mountain Huckleberry Vodka	44° North Vodka, ID
Vodka, Huckleberry	Finn Huckleberry Vodka	Black Heron Spirits Distillery, WA
Vodka, Huckleberry	Koenig Huckleberry Flavored Vodka	Koenig Distillery, ID
Vodka, Ice Peppermint	Coyote Ice Peppermint Flavored Vodka	Spirits of the USA LLC, FL
Vodka, Infusions	Indiana Infusions	Heartland Distillers, IN
Vodka, Jalapeño	Coyote Jalapeño Flavored Vodka	Spirits of the USA LLC, FL
Vodka, Lemon	Green Mountain Organic Lemon Vodka	Green Mountain Distillers, VT
Vodka, Lemon	Lemon Vodka	Bardenay Inc., ID
Vodka, Lime	American Star Caviar Lime Vodka	Ascendant Spirits, CA

Vodka, Lime	Touch Key Lime Flavored Vodka	Fat Dog Spirits LLC, FL
Vodka, Mandarin	Hanson of Sonoma Organic Vodka - Mandarin	Hanson Spirits LLC, CA
Vodka, Mango	Coyote Mango Flavored Vodka	Spirits of the USA LLC, FL
Vodka, Meyer Lemon	Charbay Fresh Fruit Vodka (Meyer Lemon)	Charbay Distillers, CA
Vodka, Orange	Blood Orange Vodka	3 Howls Distillery, WA
Vodka, Orange	Cane Vodka Orlando Orange	The Florida Distillery, FL
Vodka, Orange	Dripping Springs Orange	San Luis Spirits, TX
Vodka, Orange	Green Mountain Organic Orange Vodka	Green Mountain Distillers, VT
Vodka, Orange	Orange Vodka	Manzanita Distilling Company, CA
Vodka, Orange	Touch Valencia Orange Flavored Vodka	Fat Dog Spirits LLC, FL
Vodka, Organic	Bainbridge Legacy Organic Vodka	Bainbridge Organic Distillers, WA
Vodka, Organic	Bluewater Organic Vodka	Bluewater Distilling, WA
Vodka, Organic	CapRock® Organic Vodka	Peak Spirits® Farm Distillery, CO
Vodka, Organic	Green Mountain Organic Sunshine Vodka	Green Mountain Distillers, VT
Vodka, Organic	Hanson of Sonoma Organic Vodka - Original	Hanson Spirits LLC, CA
Vodka, Organic	Humboldt Distillery Organic Vodka	Humboldt Distillery, CA
Vodka, Organic	Organic Nation Vodka	Cascade Peak Spirits Distillery, OR
Vodka, Organic	Rime Organic Vodka	Westford Hill Distillers, CT
Vodka, Organic, Potato	Schramm Organic Potato Vodka	Pemberton Distillery Inc., BC
Vodka, Peach	High West Vodka 7000' ® Peach	High West Distillery, UT
Vodka, Peach	Peach Vodka	Mountain View Distillery, PA
Vodka, Peach Tea	Firefly Peach Flavored Tea Vodka	Firefly Distillery, SC
Vodka, Peanut Butter	Peanut Butter Vodka	Dogfish Head Craft Brewery, DE
Vodka, Peanut Butter	Peanut Butter Vodka	Tahoe Moonshine Distillery Inc., CA
Vodka, Pear	Maple River Distillery Flavored Vodka	Maple River Distillery, ND
Vodka, Pear	Pear Vodka	Mountain View Distillery, PA
Vodka, Pear, Prickly	Prickly Pear Vodka	Arizona High Spirits Distillery, AZ
Vodka, Pepper	BEE Hot Vodka	Hidden Marsh Distillery, NY
Vodka, Pepper	Blue Flame Peppered Vodka	Blue Flame Spirits, WA
Vodka, Pepper	Crater Lake Pepper Vodka	Bendistillery, OR
Vodka, Pepper	Downslope Pepper Vodka	Downslope Distilling, CO
Vodka, Pepper	Hot Monkey Pepper-Flavored Vodka	New Deal Distillery, OR

Vodka, Pepper	One Night in Bangkok Flavored Vodka	Damnation Alley Distillery, MA
Vodka, Pepper	OOLA Chili Pepper Vodka	OOLA Distillery, WA
Vodka, Pepper	Perky Pepper™ Pepper Flavored Vodka	Syntax Spirits LLC, CO
Vodka, Pepper, Barrel Aged	Fire Puncher Black Vodka	GrandTen Distilling, MA
Vodka, Pine, Canadian	Canadian Pine Vodka	66 Gilead Distillery, ON
Vodka, Pomegranate	Charbay Fresh Fruit Vodka	Charbay Distillers, CA
Vodka, Potato	Boyd & Blair Potato Vodka (80 proof)	Pennsylvania Pure Distilleries LLC, PA
Vodka, Potato	Boyd & Blair Professional Proof 151 Potato Vodka	Pennsylvania Pure Distilleries LLC, PA
Vodka, Potato	Koenig Potato Vodka	Koenig Distillery, ID
Vodka, Potato	Portland Potato Vodka	Eastside Distilling, OR
Vodka, Potato	Prince Edward Potato Vodka	Prince Edward Distillery, PE
Vodka, Potato	Skip Rock Potato Vodka	Skip Rock Distillers, WA
Vodka, Potato	BelleWood Vodka	BelleWood Distilling, WA
Vodka, Raspberry	Raspberry Vodka	Alaska Distillery, AK
Vodka, Raspberry	Red Raspberry Vodka	Mountain View Distillery, PA
Vodka, Raspberry	Ugly Dog Raspberry Vodka	Ugly Dog Distillery LLC, MI
Vodka, Raspberry Tea	Firefly Raspberry Flavored Tea Vodka	Firefly Distillery, SC
Vodka, Rhubarb	Maple River Distillery Flavored Vodka	Maple River Distillery, ND
Vodka, Rhubarb	Rhubarb Vodka	Alaska Distillery, AK
Vodka, Rye	Canadian Rye Vodka	66 Gilead Distillery, ON
Vodka, Rye	Penn 1681 Rye Vodka	Philadelphia Distilling, PA
Vodka, Rye	T & W V6 Rye Vodka	Empire Winery & Distillery, FL
Vodka, Seasoned	The Bay Seasoned Vodka	Philadelphia Distilling, PA
Vodka, Single Malt	Ezra Cox Single Malt Vodka	Ezra Cox Distillery, WA
Vodka, Single Malt	Rogue Oregon Single Malt Vodka	Rogue Spirits, OR
Vodka, Single Malt	Still Waters Single Malt Vodka	Still Waters Distillery, ON
Vodka, Smoked Salmon	Smoked Salmon Vodka	Alaska Distillery, AK
Vodka, Strawberry	American Star Strawberry Vodka	Ascendant Spirits, CA
Vodka, Strawberry	Cane Vodka Plant City Strawberry	The Florida Distillery, FL
Vodka, Sweet Ginger	Crater Lake Sweet Ginger Vodka	Bendistillery, OR
Vodka, Sweet Potato	Corbin California Estate Grown Sweet Potato Vodka	Sweet Potato Spirits, CA
Vodka, Sweet Tea	Firefly Sweet Tea Flavored Vodka	Firefly Distillery, SC

Vodka, Sweet Tea	Graham's Texas Tea	Treaty Oak Distilling Co., TX
Vodka, Three Grain	Pinckney Bend Three-Grain Vodka	Pinckney Bend Distillery, MO
Vodka, Vanilla Bean	Corsair Vanilla Vodka	Corsair Artisan Distillery, TN
Vodka, Vanilla Bean	OYO Honey Vanilla Bean Vodka	Middle West Spirits LLC, OH
Vodka, Wheat	Black Button Wheat Vodka	Black Button Distilling, NY
Vodka, Wheat	Dry Fly Washington Wheat Vodka	Dry Fly Distilling, WA
Vodka, Wheat	Spirits of St. Louis, Midwest Spring Wheat Vodka	Square One Brewery and Distillery, MO
Vodka, Wheat	True North Wheat Vodka	Grand Traverse Distillery, MI
Vodka, Wheat	Wheat State Distilling Wheat Vodka	Wheat State Distilling, KS
Vodka, Wheat, Whole	Whole Wheat Vodka	66 Gilead Distillery, ON
Vodka, Whipped Cream	Ugly Dog Whipped Cream Vodka	Ugly Dog Distillery LLC, MI
Vodka, Wild Berry	Maple River Distillery Flavored Vodka	Maple River Distillery, ND
Vodka, Wild Berry	Vintner's Wild Berry Vodka	Finger Lakes Distilling, NY
Whiskey, see also Whisky		
Whiskey	1816 Cask	Chattanooga Whiskey Company, TN
Whiskey	1816 Reserve	Chattanooga Whiskey Company, TN
Whiskey	4 Spirits Whiskey	4 Spirits Distillery, OR
Whiskey	77 Whiskey	Breuckelen Distilling Company Inc., NY
Whiskey	Abraham Bowman Limited Edition Whiskey	A. Smith Bowman Distillery, VA
Whiskey	Alaska Outlaw Whiskey	Alaska Distillery, AK
Whiskey	Alchemist Distillery Whiskey	Alchemist Distilleries Inc., FL
Whiskey	Amador Distillery Whiskey	Amador Distillery, CA
Whiskey	Barrel Master	StiLL 630, MO
Whiskey	Bighorn Whiskey	Willie's Distillery, MT
Whiskey	Black Canyon Rita	Black Canyon Distillery, CO
Whiskey	Black Sam	Black Sam Distillery Co., WA
Whiskey	Black Snake Whiskey	Vermont Spirits Distilling Co., VT
Whiskey	Blackjack Aces High Whiskey	Mystic Mountain Distillery LLC, CO
Whiskey	Blonde Whiskey	Asheville Distilling Company, NC
Whiskey	Blue Spirits Whiskey	Blue Spirits Distilling, WA
Whiskey	Bowen's Whiskey	Bowen's Spirits Inc., CA
Whiskey	CH Whiskey	CH Distillery, IL

Type	Product	Distillery
Whiskey	Charbay R5 Whiskey	Charbay Distillers, CA
Whiskey	Charbay 'S' Whiskey	Charbay Distillers, CA
Whiskey	Charbay Whiskey, Release III	Charbay Distillers, CA
Whiskey	Civilized Whiskey	Northern United Brewing Company, MI
Whiskey	Coal Yard New Make Whiskey	Albany Distilling Company, NY
Whiskey	Colorado's Own Corn Whiskey	Colorado Gold Distillery, CO
Whiskey	Coppercraft Whiskey	Coppercraft Distillery LLC, MI
Whiskey	Corsair Quinoa Whiskey	Corsair Artisan Distillery, TN
Whiskey	Corsair Rasputin Hopped Whiskey	Corsair Artisan Distillery, TN
Whiskey	Dead Drift Whiskey	K J Wood Distillers LLC, CO
Whiskey	Destroying Angel Whiskey	Headframe Spirits, MT
Whiskey	Devil's Share Whiskey	Ballast Point Spirits, CA
Whiskey	Devils Bit Whiskey	McMenamins Edgefield Distillery, OR
Whiskey	Distiller's Workshop Whiskey	New Deal Distillery, OR
Whiskey	Downslope Double-Diamond Whiskey	Downslope Distilling, CO
Whiskey	Elk Rider Whiskey	Heritage Distilling Company, WA
Whiskey	Feisty Spirits Elementals	Feisty Spirits, CO
Whiskey	Ghost Owl Whisky	Parliament Distillery, WA
Whiskey	Grandaddy Mimm's Whiskey	Georgia Distilling Company, GA
Whiskey	High West Silver Whiskey OMG Pure Rye®	High West Distillery, UT
Whiskey	High West Silver Whiskey® Western Oat	High West Distillery, UT
Whiskey	High West Whiskey American Prairie Reserve	High West Distillery, UT
Whiskey	High West Whiskey Campfire®	High West Distillery, UT
Whiskey	High West Whiskey Son of Bourye®	High West Distillery, UT
Whiskey	Hogshead Whiskey	McMenamins Edgefield Distillery, OR
Whiskey	Hop Flavored Whiskey (Spring/Summer)	Sons of Liberty Spirits Co., RI
Whiskey	Hoppin' Eights Whiskey	Stone Barn Brandyworks, OR
Whiskey	Ironweed Whiskey	Albany Distilling Company, NY
Whiskey	JP Trodden Small Batch Bourbon	J.P. Trodden Small Batch Bourbon, WA
Whiskey	Kinnickinnic Whiskey	Great Lakes Distillery LLC, WI
Whiskey	Kopper Kettle Virginian Whiskey	Appalachian Mountain Spirits LLC, VA
Whiskey	LA 1 Whiskey	Donner-Peltier Distillers, LA

Whiskey	Legs Diamond Whiskey	Nahmias et Fils, NY
Whiskey	Leopold Bros. American Small Batch Whiskey	Leopold Bros., CO
Whiskey	Malthouse Whiskey	New Holland Artisan Spirits, MI
Whiskey	MBR Kentucky Black Patch Whiskey	MB Roland Distillery, KY
Whiskey	McKenzie Pure Potstill Whiskey	Finger Lakes Distilling, NY
Whiskey	McNulty Whiskey	25th Street Spirits, OH
Whiskey	Monkey Puzzle Whiskey	McMenamins Edgefield Distillery, OR
Whiskey	Moonshine	Flag Hill Winery & Distillery, NH
Whiskey	Morning Dew	McMenamins Cornelius Pass, OR
Whiskey	New Age Spirit Whiskey	Tiger Juice Distillery, SC
Whiskey	North Fork Whiskey	Glacier Distilling Company, MT
Whiskey	Old Homicide	Ernest Scarano Distillery, OH
Whiskey	One Foot Cock Whiskey	Buffalo Distilling Co., NY
Whiskey	Palm Ridge Reserve	Florida Farm Distillers, FL
Whiskey	Primo Aqua Ardiente	Fog's End Distillery, CA
Whiskey	Prince Edward I.C. Shore Whiskey	Prince Edward Distillery, PE
Whiskey	Prohibition Spirits	Valley Spirits LLC, CA
Whiskey	Pump Trolley Whiskey	Carbon Glacier Distillery, WA
Whiskey	Rebecca Creek Fine Texas Whiskey	Rebecca Creek Distillery LLC, TX
Whiskey	Rogue Dead Guy Whiskey	Rogue Spirits, OR
Whiskey	Rolling River Spirits Whiskey	Rolling River Spirits, OR
Whiskey	S.S. Sorghum Whiskey	StiL 630, MO
Whiskey	Silver Cross Whiskey	Journeyman Distillery, MI
Whiskey	Sinner	Sinister Distilling Company, OR
Whiskey	Sir Whisquila	StiL 630, MO
Whiskey	Small Batch Spirit Whiskey	Copper Run Distillery, MO
Whiskey	Snowflake	Stranahan's Colorado Whiskey, CO
Whiskey	Stocking Stuffer Whiskey	Carbon Glacier Distillery, WA
Whiskey	Stormin' Whiskey	Tahoe Moonshine Distillery Inc., CA
Whiskey	Stranahan's Colorado Whiskey	Stranahan's Colorado Whiskey, CO
Whiskey	Stumphouse Whiskey	Dark Corner Distillery, SC
Whiskey	Tenderfoot Whiskey	Wood's High Mountain Distillery, CO

Whiskey	The Indiana Straight Leg Infantry Whiskey	The Indiana Whiskey Company, IN
Whiskey	The Microbarreled™ Collection - Bourbon and Rye Whiskey	Woodinville Whiskey Co., WA
Whiskey	The Vashon Idle Hour Whiskey	Seattle Distilling Company, WA
Whiskey	Tirado El Caribe Whiskey	Tirado Distillery, NY
Whiskey	Tirado Gold	Tirado Distillery, NY
Whiskey	Tirado Maple Delight	Tirado Distillery, NY
Whiskey	TOPO Carolina Whiskey	Top of the Hill Distillery, NC
Whiskey	Two Guns Wild West Whiskey	Two Guns Distillery, CO
Whiskey	Ty Wolfe Whiskey	Mac Donald Distillery, WA
Whiskey	Uncle Carls Prohibition Style Whiskey	Steel Toe Distillery, MT
Whiskey	Van Brunt Stillhouse Whiskey	Van Brunt Stillhouse, NY
Whiskey	Viezbicke 303 Whiskey	Boulder Distillery, CO
Whiskey	Virginia Gentleman	A. Smith Bowman Distillery, VA
Whiskey	War Horn Whiskey	Appalachian Mountain Spirits LLC, VA
Whiskey	Westchester Whiskey	StilltheOne Distillery LLC, NY
Whiskey	Wheatfish Whiskey	Glacier Distilling Company, MT
Whiskey	Whidbey Island Distillery Whiskey	Whidbey Island Distillery, WA
Whiskey	WhipperSnapper Oregon Spirit Whiskey	Ransom Spirits, OR
Whiskey	Whiskey	Great Lakes Distillery LLC, WI
Whiskey	Whiskey Dick	Ernest Scarano Distillery, OH
Whiskey	Whiskey Is In The Wood	Fifth Element Spirits, OH
Whiskey	White Cat™ Whiskey	Syntax Spirits LLC, CO
Whiskey	White Owl Whiskey	McMenamins Cornelius Pass, OR
Whiskey	White Pike Whiskey	Finger Lakes Distilling, NY
Whiskey	White Water Whiskey	Panther Distilling, MN
Whiskey	Whitewater Whiskey	Deerhammer Distilling Company, CO
Whiskey	Wiggly Bridge Whiskey	Wiggly Bridge Distillery, ME
Whiskey	Wild Buck Whiskey	NJoy Spirits LLC, FL
Whiskey	Yahara Bay Whiskey	Yahara Bay Distillers, WI
Whiskey	Vinn Whiskey	Vinn Distillery, OR
Whiskey, 1-Year Aged	Manatawny Batch Whiskey - One-Year Old Aged	Manatawny Still Works, PA
Whiskey, 2-Year Aged	Manatawny Pennsylvania Whiskey - Two-Year Old Aged	Manatawny Still Works, PA

Whiskey, 3-Year	3 Year Old Whiskey (Sept. 2014)	McMenamins Cornelius Pass, OR
Whiskey, 4-Grain	Woody Creek Colorado 4 Grain Whiskey	Woody Creek Distillers, CO
Whiskey, 8-Year Aged	Fremont Mischief Whiskey, aged 8 years	Fremont Mischief, WA
Whiskey, Age Your Own Kit	Age Your Own™ Whiskey Kit	Woodinville Whiskey Co., WA
Whiskey, Age Your Own Kit	TOPO Age Your Own Whiskey Kits	Top of the Hill Distillery, NC
Whiskey, Aged	Massachusetts Whiskey	Damnation Alley Distillery, MA
Whiskey, Aged, Blue Corn	Aged Blue Corn Whiskey	Wood Hat Spirits LLC, MO
Whiskey, American	291 American Whiskey	Distillery 291, CO
Whiskey, American	American Whiskey	StilL 630, MO
Whiskey, American Malt	Spirits of St. Louis JJ Neukomm American Malt Whiskey	Square One Brewery and Distillery, MO
Whiskey, American Malt	Thirteen Corners Virgin Cask American Malt Whiskey	Wishkah River Distillery, WA
Whiskey, American Straight	Bully Boy American Straight Whiskey	Bully Boy Distillers, MA
Whiskey, American Straight Bourbon	Big Bottom Whiskey American Straight Bourbon Whiskey	Big Bottom Distilling, OR
Whiskey, Apple	Leopold Bros. New York Apple Whiskey	Leopold Bros., CO
Whiskey, Apple Cider	HDC Fall Classic – Apple Cider Flavored Whiskey	Heritage Distilling Company, WA
Whiskey, Apple Pie	MBR Kentucky Apple Pie	MB Roland Distillery, KY
Whiskey, Apple Pie	Smitty's Apple Pie Whiskey	J.K. Williams Distilling LLC, IL
Whiskey, Apple Pie	Tootsie's Apple Pie Whiskey	Georgia Distilling Company, GA
Whiskey, Apple, Cinnamon	Spiked Apple Spirits	Panther Distillery, MN
Whiskey, Aspen Stave Finished	291 Colorado Whiskey Aspen Stave Finished (aged)	Distillery 291, CO
Whiskey, Barley	Double Down Barley Whiskey	New Holland Artisan Spirits, MI
Whiskey, Barley	Still Cellars Whiskey Barley	Still Cellars, CO
Whiskey, Barrel Aged	James Henry Barrel Aged Whiskey	Moonrise Distillery Inc., GA
Whiskey, Barrel Aged	Tuthilltown Barrel Aged Cassis	Tuthilltown Spirits Distillery, NY
Whiskey, Beer Barrel Bourbon	Beer Barrel Bourbon	New Holland Artisan Spirits, MI
Whiskey, Black Label	RoughStock Montana Black Label Whiskey	RoughStock Distillery, MT
Whiskey, Blackberry	Leopold Bros. Rocky Mountain Blackberry Whiskey	Leopold Bros., CO
Whiskey, Blended	Blended Whiskey	Dakota Spirits Distillery LLC, SD
Whiskey, Blended	Blended Whiskey	Yellow Rose Distilling LLC, TX
Whiskey, Blended	Troubadour Blended Whiskey	The Original Texas Legend Distillery, TX
Whiskey, Blended	TX Blended Whiskey	Firestone & Robertson Distilling Co., TX
Whiskey, Blue	Six & Twenty Whiskey "Blue"	Six & Twenty Distillery, SC

656

1512 Spirits Bourbon #1	1512 Spirits, CA	Whiskey, Bourbon
2bar Bourbon	2bar® Spirits, WA	Whiskey, Bourbon
601 Bourbon	Adirondack Distilling Company, NY	Whiskey, Bourbon
Amador Distillery Bourbon	Amador Distillery, CA	Whiskey, Bourbon
Baby Bourbon	Tuthilltown Spirits Distillery, NY	Whiskey, Bourbon
Beanball Bourbon	Cooperstown Distillery, NY	Whiskey, Bourbon
Bell Bourbon	StiLL 630, MO	Whiskey, Bourbon
Belle Bourbon	Belle of Dayton, OH	Whiskey, Bourbon
Belle Meade™ Bourbon	Nelson's Green Brier Distillery, TN	Whiskey, Bourbon
Benjamin Prichard's Double Barreled Bourbon	Prichard's Distillery Inc., TN	Whiskey, Bourbon
Benjamin's Bourbon	Valley Shine Distillery, WA	Whiskey, Bourbon
Berkshire Bourbon	Berkshire Mountain Distillers Inc., MA	Whiskey, Bourbon
Black Dirt Bourbon	Black Dirt Distillery, NY	Whiskey, Bourbon
Black Heron Bourbon	Black Heron Spirits Distillery, WA	Whiskey, Bourbon
Black Reserve Bourbon Whiskey	Cleveland Whiskey LLC, OH	Whiskey, Bourbon
Border Bourbon	45th Parallel Distillery, WI	Whiskey, Bourbon
Bourbon	Clayton Distillery, NY	Whiskey, Bourbon
Bourbon (coming soon)	Five & 20 Spirits, NY	Whiskey, Bourbon
Bourbon Rubenesque	Wood Hat Spirits LLC, MO	Whiskey, Bourbon
Bourbon Spring™ Young Rested Illinois Bourbon Whiskey	Quincy Street Distillery, IL	Whiskey, Bourbon
Breaker Bourbon	Ascendant Spirits, CA	Whiskey, Bourbon
Breaking & Entering Bourbon	St. George Spirits, CA	Whiskey, Bourbon
Breckenridge Bourbon	Breckenridge Distillery, CO	Whiskey, Bourbon
Bullhead Bourbon	Lake George Distilling Company, NY	Whiskey, Bourbon
Burnside Bourbon	Eastside Distilling, OR	Whiskey, Bourbon
Cask Strength Straight Bourbon Whiskey	Whitmeyer's Distilling Co. LLC, TX	Whiskey, Bourbon
Cedar Ridge Iowa Bourbon Whiskey	Cedar Ridge Distillery, IA	Whiskey, Bourbon
CH Bourbon	CH Distillery, IL	Whiskey, Bourbon
Charred Oak Bourbon Whiskey	Yahara Bay Distillers, WI	Whiskey, Bourbon
Cody Road Bourbon Whiskey	Mississippi River Distilling Company, IA	Whiskey, Bourbon
Colorado Bourbon	Boathouse Distillery, CO	Whiskey, Bourbon
Colorado Gold Straight Bourbon Whiskey	Colorado Gold Distillery, CO	Whiskey, Bourbon

Whiskey, Bourbon	Coopercraft Bourbon	Coppercraft Distillery LLC, MI
Whiskey, Bourbon	Dancing Pines Bourbon	Dancing Pines Distillery, CO
Whiskey, Bourbon	Dark Horse Distillery Reserve Bourbon Whiskey	Dark Horse Distillery, KS
Whiskey, Bourbon	Delaware Distilling Company Bourbon	Delaware Distilling Company, DE
Whiskey, Bourbon	Devils' Share Bourbon	Ballast Point Spirits, CA
Whiskey, Bourbon	DiVine Bourbon	Entente Spirits LLC, MI
Whiskey, Bourbon	Dodge City Distillery Bourbon Whiskey	Good Spirits Distilling, KS
Whiskey, Bourbon	Double Barrel Bourbon Whiskey	Yellow Rose Distilling LLC, TX
Whiskey, Bourbon	Featherbone Bourbon	Journeyman Distillery, MI
Whiskey, Bourbon	Few Bourbon	Few Spirits LLC, IL
Whiskey, Bourbon	Fireside Bourbon	Mile High Spirits LLC, CO
Whiskey, Bourbon	Galena Bourbon Whiskey	Blaum Bros. Distilling Co., IL
Whiskey, Bourbon	Gold Coast Bourbon	Cathead Distillery LLC, MS
Whiskey, Bourbon	Heartland Distiller's Reserve Bourbon	Heartland Distillers, IN
Whiskey, Bourbon	Hooker's House Bourbon	HelloCello, CA
Whiskey, Bourbon	John Myer Bourbon Whiskey	Myer Farm Distillers, NY
Whiskey, Bourbon	Kings County Bourbon	Kings County Distillery, NY
Whiskey, Bourbon	Lewis Redmond Carolina Bourbon Whiskey	Dark Corner Distillery, SC
Whiskey, Bourbon	Lone Loggers Bourbon Whiskey	Hidden Marsh Distillery, NY
Whiskey, Bourbon	Mad River Bourbon	Mad River Distillers, VT
Whiskey, Bourbon	McKenzie Bourbon Whiskey	Finger Lakes Distilling, NY
Whiskey, Bourbon	Mill Street Bourbon / Aged Whiskey	Mill St. Distillery LLC, OH
Whiskey, Bourbon	Missouri Spirits Bourbon	Missouri Spirits, MO
Whiskey, Bourbon	Montgomery County Bourbon	Wood Hat Spirits LLC, MO
Whiskey, Bourbon	Mosswood American Whiskey Apple Brandy Barreled Bourbon	Mosswood Distillers Inc, CA
Whiskey, Bourbon	Mosswood American Whiskey California Ale Barreled Bourbon	Mosswood Distillers Inc, CA
Whiskey, Bourbon	Mosswood American Whiskey Espresso Barreled Bourbon	Mosswood Distillers Inc, CA
Whiskey, Bourbon	Neversweat Bourbon Whiskey	Headframe Spirits, MT
Whiskey, Bourbon	No. 14 Bourbon	Vermont Spirits Distilling Co., VT
Whiskey, Bourbon	Noah's Mill	Willett Distillery, KY
Whiskey, Bourbon	Northern Threat Yankee Bourbon	Stoutridge Distillery, NY
Whiskey, Bourbon	One Foot Cock Bourbon	Buffalo Distilling Co., NY

Whiskey, Bourbon	OOLA Waitsburg Bourbon Whiskey	OOLA Distillery, WA
Whiskey, Bourbon	Outlaw Bourbon Whiskey	Yellow Rose Distilling LLC, TX
Whiskey, Bourbon	Ozark Bourbon Whiskey	Ozark Distillery LLC, MO
Whiskey, Bourbon	Prohibition Edition Bourbon	Artesian Distillers, MI
Whiskey, Bourbon	Ranger Creek .36 Texas Bourbon Whiskey	Ranger Creek Brewing & Distilling, TX
Whiskey, Bourbon	Red Handed Bourbon	Treaty Oak Distilling Co, TX
Whiskey, Bourbon	Red River Texas Bourbon Whiskey	JEM Beverage Company, TX
Whiskey, Bourbon	Reserve Bourbon (aged 4 years)	It's 5 Artisan Distillery, WA
Whiskey, Bourbon	Rock Town Arkansas Bourbon Whiskey	Rock Town Distillery Inc., AR
Whiskey, Bourbon	Seven Devils Straight Bourbon Whiskey	Koenig Distillery, ID
Whiskey, Bourbon	Smooth Ambler Yearling Bourbon	Smooth Ambler Spirits Company, WV
Whiskey, Bourbon	Spring Mill Straight Bourbon Whiskey	Heartland Distillers, IN
Whiskey, Bourbon	Stillwrights Bourbon	Flat Rock Spirits, OH
Whiskey, Bourbon	Tatoosh Bourbon	Tatoosh Craft Distillery, WA
Whiskey, Bourbon	Thunderbeast Baby Buffalo Bourbon	Mad Buffalo Distillery, MO
Whiskey, Bourbon	Troubadour Barrel Strength Bourbon, 116 proof	The Original Texas Legend Distillery, TX
Whiskey, Bourbon	Troubadour Texas Bourbon	The Original Texas Legend Distillery, TX
Whiskey, Bourbon	Two James Bourbon	Two James Spirits, MI
Whiskey, Bourbon	V Bourbon Whiskey	Yahara Bay Distillers, WI
Whiskey, Bourbon	Watershed Distillery Bourbon	Watershed Distillery, OH
Whiskey, Bourbon	Wheat State Distilling Bella Bahre's Bourbon	Wheat State Distilling, KS
Whiskey, Bourbon	Widow Jane Bourbon Whiskey	Cacao Prieto LLC, NY
Whiskey, Bourbon	Widow Jane Wapsie Valley Bourbon Whiskey	Cacao Prieto LLC, NY
Whiskey, Bourbon	Wiggly Bridge Bourbon	Wiggly Bridge Distillery, ME
Whiskey, Bourbon	Willett Family Estate Bottled Bourbon	Willett Distillery, KY
Whiskey, Bourbon	Willett Pot Still Reserve Bourbon	Willett Distillery, KY
Whiskey, Bourbon	Wyoming Whiskey	Wyoming Whiskey Distillery, WY
Whiskey, Bourbon	Young Buck Bourbon	J.K. Williams Distilling LLC, IL
Whiskey, Bourbon	Bloody Butcher Bourbon Whiskey	Cacao Prieto LLC, NY
Whiskey, Bourbon	MBR Kentucky Bourbon Whiskey	MB Roland Distillery, KY
Whiskey, Bourbon, Aged	Hillrock Soera Aged Bourbon Whiskey	Hillrock Estate Distillery, NY
Whiskey, Bourbon, Aged	KOVAL Bourbon Aged Whiskey	KOVAL Distillery, IL

Whiskey, Bourbon, Barrel Aged	Harvest Rum Bourbon Barrel Aged	Wilderness Trace Distillery, KY
Whiskey, Bourbon, Barrel Strength	Temperance Trader Barrel Strength Bourbon	Bull Run Distilling Company, OR
Whiskey, Bourbon, Black Walnut	Dancing Pines Black Walnut Bourbon	Dancing Pines Distillery, CO
Whiskey, Bourbon, Blue Corn	Don Quixote Blue Corn Bourbon	Don Quixote Distillery & Winery, NM
Whiskey, Bourbon, Blue Corn	Feisty Spirits Blue Corn Bourbon	Feisty Spirits, CO
Whiskey, Bourbon, Cask Strength	Moylan's Distilling Bourbon Cask Strength	Stillwater Spirits, CA
Whiskey, Bourbon, Double Barrel	Double Barrel Bourbon	Dodge City Distillery, KS
Whiskey, Bourbon, Double Barrel	Double Barrel Burnside Bourbon	Eastside Distilling, OR
Whiskey, Bourbon, Double Chocolate	Benjamin Prichard's Double Chocolate Bourbon Whiskey	Prichard's Distillery Inc., TN
Whiskey, Bourbon, Four Grain	Black Button Four Grain Bourbon	Black Button Distilling, NY
Whiskey, Bourbon, Four Grain	Four Grain Bourbon	Tuthilltown Spirits Distillery, NY
Whiskey, Bourbon, Four Grain	OYO Bourbon, Michelone Reserve (4-Grain)	Middle West Spirits LLC, OH
Whiskey, Bourbon, Honey	Colorado Honey	Honey House Distillery, CO
Whiskey, Bourbon, Maple	Sapling Maple Bourbon	Saxtons River Distillery LLC, VT
Whiskey, Bourbon, Rye	Bloody Butcher High Rye Bourbon Whiskey	Cacao Prieto LLC, NY
Whiskey, Bourbon, Single Barrel	Saratoga Single Barrel Bourbon	Saratoga Distilleries Inc., NY
Whiskey, Bourbon, Single Barrel	Thomas Tate Tobin's Taos Lightning	Rancho de Los Luceros Destilaría, NM
Whiskey, Bourbon, Single Barrel	Thunderbeast Baby Buffalo Bourbon Single Barrel	Mad Buffalo Distillery, MO
Whiskey, Bourbon, Single Barrel, 6 Year	Simeon Turley's Taos Lightning	Rancho de Los Luceros Destilaría, NM
Whiskey, Bourbon, Straight	Bowman Brothers Small Batch Virginia Straight Bourbon Whiskey	A. Smith Bowman Distillery, VA
Whiskey, Bourbon, Straight	Colorado Straight Bourbon	Peach Street Distillers, CO
Whiskey, Bourbon, Straight	Dry Fly Washington Straight Bourbon Whiskey	Dry Fly Distilling, WA
Whiskey, Bourbon, Straight	Garrison Brothers Texas Straight Bourbon Whiskey	Garrison Brothers Distillery, TX
Whiskey, Bourbon, Straight	J.K.'s Straight Bourbon	J.K. Williams Distilling LLC, IL
Whiskey, Bourbon, Straight	Straight Bourbon	Firestone & Robertson Distilling Co., TX
Whiskey, Bourbon, Straight, SB	John J. Bowman Single Barrel Virginia Straight Bourbon Whiskey	A. Smith Bowman Distillery, VA
Whiskey, Bourdon, Single Barrel	Spring44 Single Barrel Bourbon	Spring44 Distilling, CO
Whiskey, Charred Oak	American Shine - Charred Oak	Blackbird Distillery, PA
Whiskey, Cherry	Cherry Bomb Whiskey	Eastside Distilling, OR
Whiskey, Cherry	Cherry Whiskey	Grand Traverse Distillery, MI
Whiskey, Chipotle	Rogue Chipotle Whiskey	Rogue Spirits, OR
Whiskey, Chocolate	Kings County Chocolate Whiskey	Kings County Distillery, NY

Whiskey, Cinnamon	Collier and McKeel Fiery Gizzard Cinnamon Whiskey	Collier and McKeel, TN
Whiskey, Cinnamon	Prairie Fire Cinnamon Whiskey	Iowa Distilling Company, IA
Whiskey, Coffee Infused	Cowboy Coffee	Two Guns Distillery, CO
Whiskey, Corn	Corn Whiskey	Five & 20 Spirits, NY
Whiskey, Corn	Dawsonville Moonshine Georgia Corn Whiskey	Dawsonville Moonshine Distillery, GA
Whiskey, Corn	Fitch's Goat 100% Corn Whiskey	Bone Spirits, TX
Whiskey, Corn	Glen Thunder Corn Whiskey	Finger Lakes Distilling, NY
Whiskey, Corn	Iowa Shine Corn Whiskey	Iowa Distilling Company, IA
Whiskey, Corn	J.K.'s Original Corn Whiskey	J.K. Williams Distilling LLC, IL
Whiskey, Corn	Judd's Wreckin' Ball Corn Whiskey	Hidden Marsh Distillery, NY
Whiskey, Corn	Mad River Corn Whiskey	Mad River Distillers, VT
Whiskey, Corn	New England Corn Whiskey	Berkshire Mountain Distillers Inc., MA
Whiskey, Corn	New York Corn Whiskey	Tuthilltown Spirits Distillery, NY
Whiskey, Corn	Old Cooch's Corn Whiskey	Painted Stave Distilling, DE
Whiskey, Corn	Pinckney Bend Corn Whiskey	Pinckney Bend Distillery, MO
Whiskey, Corn	Southern Corn Whiskey	Thirteenth Colony Distilleries, GA
Whiskey, Corn	Tangle Foot Corn Whiskey	Hidden Marsh Distillery, NY
Whiskey, Corn	The Silver Sweet Corn Whiskey	The Indiana Whiskey Company, IN
Whiskey, Corn	Tirado NY Corn Whiskey	Tirado Distillery, NY
Whiskey, Corn	Two Jays Corn Whiskey	Broadbent Distillery, IA
Whiskey, Corn	Two Jays Corn Whiskey Country Style	Broadbent Distillery, IA
Whiskey, Corn, Blue	Blue Corn Whiskey	Wood Hat Spirits LLC, MO
Whiskey, Four Grain	John Myer Four Grain Whiskey	Myer Farm Distillers, NY
Whiskey, Four Grain, Aged	KOVAL Four Grain Aged Whiskey	KOVAL Distillery, IL
Whiskey, Gold	Golden White Gold Whiskey	Golden Distillery, WA
Whiskey, Hopped	Hatter Royale Hopquila	New Holland Artisan Spirits, MI
Whiskey, Hopped	Hopped Whiskey	3 Howls Distillery, WA
Whiskey, Irish	South Boston Irish Whiskey	GrandTen Distilling, MA
Whiskey, Kentucky	TJ Pottinger Kentucky Whiskey	Limestone Branch Distillery, KY
Whiskey, Kentucky Bourbon	Rowan's Creek	Willett Distillery, KY
Whiskey, Lemon	J.K.'s Lemon Whiskey	J.K. Williams Distilling LLC, IL
Whiskey, Light	Coyote 100 Light Whiskey	Dakota Spirits Distillery LLC, SD

Whiskey, Light	Trail Town Still Coyote Light Whiskey	Trail Town Still, CO
Whiskey, Limited	Valentine Woodward Limited Whiskey	Valentine Distilling Company, MI
Whiskey, Malt	Blaum Bros. Malt Whiskey	Blaum Bros. Distilling Co., IL
Whiskey, Malt	Cross Timbers Texas Malt Whiskey	Quentin D. Witherspoon Distillery, TX
Whiskey, Malt	Downslope Malt Whiskey	Downslope Distilling, CO
Whiskey, Malt	Virginia Highland Malt Whisky	Virginia Distillery Company, VA
Whiskey, Millet, Aged	KOVAL Limited Edition Toasted Barrel Millet Aged Whiskey	KOVAL Distillery, IL
Whiskey, Millet, Aged	KOVAL Millet Aged Whiskey	KOVAL Distillery, IL
Whiskey, Millet, White	KOVAL Limited Edition White Millet	KOVAL Distillery, IL
Whiskey, Oak Reserve	Troy & Sons Oak Reserve Whiskey	Asheville Distilling Company, NC
Whiskey, Oak, White	KOVAL Limited Edition White Oat	KOVAL Distillery, IL
Whiskey, Oat, Aged	KOVAL Limited Edition Toasted Barrel Oat Aged Whiskey	KOVAL Distillery, IL
Whiskey, Oat, Aged	KOVAL Oat Aged Whiskey	KOVAL Distillery, IL
Whiskey, Organic	Bainbridge Battle Point Organic Whiskey	Bainbridge Organic Distillers, WA
Whiskey, Organic	Bainbridge 'The Whiskey Forty Saloon' Organic Whiskey	Bainbridge Organic Distillers, WA
Whiskey, Peach	J.K.'s Peach Whiskey	J.K. Williams Distilling LLC, IL
Whiskey, Peach	Leopold Bros. Georgia Peach Whiskey	Leopold Bros., CO
Whiskey, Peach	Leopold Bros. Rocky Mountain Peach Whiskey	Leopold Bros., CO
Whiskey, Peated Malt	Peated Malt Whiskey	Westland Distillery, WA
Whiskey, Peated Single Malt	Leviathan American Peated Single Malt Whiskey	Lost Spirits Distillery, CA
Whiskey, Peated Single Malt	Paradiso Peated American Single Malt Whiskey	Lost Spirits Distillery, CA
Whiskey, Peated Single Malt, SB	Woodstone Creek Single Barrel Peated Single Malt Whisky	Woodstone Creek, OH
Whiskey, Pumpkin Spice	Pumpkin Spice Flavored Whiskey (Fall/Winter)	Sons of Liberty Spirits Co., RI
Whiskey, Pure Malt	Peregrine Rock – California Pure Malt Whisky	Saint James Spirits, CA
Whiskey, Pure Malt	RoughStock Montana Pure Malt Whiskey	RoughStock Distillery, MT
Whiskey, Reserve	Broadslab Legacy Reserve	Broadslab Distillery LLC, NC
Whiskey, Reserve	Golden Samish Bay Whiskey Reserve	Golden Distillery, WA
Whiskey, Reserve	Hooker's House General's Reserve	HelloCello, CA
Whiskey, Rested American	Pinckney Bend Rested American Whiskey	Pinckney Bend Distillery, MO
Whiskey, Rice	Riz, Louisiana Rice Whiskey	Atelier Vie, LA
Whiskey, Rice	Yerlo X Rice Whiskey (90 Proof)	Lo Artisan Distillery LLC, WI
Whiskey, Rye	1512 Barbershop Rye Whiskey	1512 Spirits, CA

Whiskey, Rye	Bad Rock Rye	Glacier Distilling Company, MT
Whiskey, Rye	Benjamin Prichard's Rye Whiskey	Prichard's Distillery Inc., TN
Whiskey, Rye	Blue Flame Rye	Blue Flame Spirits, WA
Whiskey, Rye	Catoctin Creek Organic Roundstone Rye™	Catoctin Creek Distilling Co. LLC, VA
Whiskey, Rye	Charred Oak Rye Whiskey	Yahara Bay Distillers, WI
Whiskey, Rye	Cody Road Rye Whiskey	Mississippi River Distilling Company, IA
Whiskey, Rye	Commander's Rye Whiskey	Heritage Distilling Company, WA
Whiskey, Rye	Coppersea New York Raw Rye	Coppersea Distilling, NY
Whiskey, Rye	Corbin Cash Merced Rye Whiskey	Sweet Potato Spirits, CA
Whiskey, Rye	Corsair Ryemageddon Whiskey	Corsair Artisan Distillery, TN
Whiskey, Rye	Corsair Wry Moon Un-aged Rye Whiskey	Corsair Artisan Distillery, TN
Whiskey, Rye	Crater Lake Rye Whiskey	Bendistillery, OR
Whiskey, Rye	Dad's Hat™ Pennsylvania Rye Whiskey	Mountain Laurel Spirits LLC, PA
Whiskey, Rye	Dark Horse Distillery Reunion Rye Whiskey	Dark Horse Distillery, KS
Whiskey, Rye	Delaware Phoenix Rye Dog	Delaware Phoenix Distillery, NY
Whiskey, Rye	Delaware Phoenix Rye Whiskey	Delaware Phoenix Distillery, NY
Whiskey, Rye	Doc Holliday Rye Whiskey	Georgia Distilling Company, GA
Whiskey, Rye	Estate Rye	Hillrock Estate Distillery, NY
Whiskey, Rye	Feisty Spirits Rye	Feisty Spirits, CO
Whiskey, Rye	Fever River Rye Whiskey	Blaum Bros. Distilling Co., IL
Whiskey, Rye	Few Rye	Few Spirits LLC, IL
Whiskey, Rye	George (Rye Whiskey)	Three Brothers' Whiskey Distillery, VA
Whiskey, Rye	Goldrun Rye Whiskey	Old World Spirits LLC, CA
Whiskey, Rye	Gunpowder Rye Whiskey	New England Distilling, ME
Whiskey, Rye	Hard Eight Rye Whiskey	Stone Barn Brandyworks, OR
Whiskey, Rye	High West Double Rye! ®	High West Distillery, UT
Whiskey, Rye	High West Whiskey Rendezvous® Rye	High West Distillery, UT
Whiskey, Rye	Hooker's House Rye	HelloCello, CA
Whiskey, Rye	James Oliver Rye	Indio Spirits, OR
Whiskey, Rye	John Jacob Rye Whiskey	Fremont Mischief, WA
Whiskey, Rye	John Myer Rye Whiskey	Myer Farm Distillers, NY
Whiskey, Rye	KOVAL Aged Rye Whiskey	KOVAL Distillery, IL

Whiskey, Rye	Mad River Rye	Mad River Distillers, VT
Whiskey, Rye	Manhattan Rye	Tuthilltown Spirits Distillery, NY
Whiskey, Rye	McKenzie Rye Whiskey	Finger Lakes Distilling, NY
Whiskey, Rye	Monterey Rye	Fog's End Distillery, CA
Whiskey, Rye	New Richmond Rye	45th Parallel Distillery, WI
Whiskey, Rye	Nine Square Rye	Elm City Distillery LLC, CT
Whiskey, Rye	Old Maysville Club Rye Whiskey Old	Pogue Distillery, KY
Whiskey, Rye	Oldfield Rye Whiskey	Cascade Peak Spirits Distillery, OR
Whiskey, Rye	Organic Aged Rye Whiskey-Small Cask Series	Pittsburgh Distilling Co., PA
Whiskey, Rye	OYO Rye Whiskey (100% Dark Pumpernickel)	Middle West Spirits LLC, OH
Whiskey, Rye	Prince Edward Canadian Rye	Prince Edward Distillery, PE
Whiskey, Rye	Railroad Rye Whiskey	Hidden Marsh Distillery, NY
Whiskey, Rye	Rally Point Rye Whiskey	StilL 630, MO
Whiskey, Rye	Ranger Creek. 44 Texas Rye Whiskey	Ranger Creek Brewing & Distilling, TX
Whiskey, Rye	Ravenswood Rye (Rye Whiskey)	Journeyman Distillery, MI
Whiskey, Rye	Ray County Rye	Of The Earth Farm Distillery LLC, MO
Whiskey, Rye	RE:FIND Rye Whiskey	RE:FIND Distillery, CA
Whiskey, Rye	Red Barn Rye	Hewn Spirits LLC, PA
Whiskey, Rye	Red Rock Rye	Lake George Distilling Company, NY
Whiskey, Rye	Reservoir Rye Whiskey	Reservoir Distillery, VA
Whiskey, Rye	Rock Town Arkansas Rye Whiskey	Rock Town Distillery Inc., AR
Whiskey, Rye	Rogue Oregon Rye Whiskey	Rogue Spirits, OR
Whiskey, Rye	Roknar (Rye Whiskey)	Far North Spirits, MN
Whiskey, Rye	Rough Rider Rye	Long Island Spirits, NY
Whiskey, Rye	Rye Whiskey	3 Howls Distillery, WA
Whiskey, Rye	Rye Whiskey	Five & 20 Spirits, NY
Whiskey, Rye	Rye Whiskey	Skip Rock Distillers, WA
Whiskey, Rye	Rye Whiskey	Stark Spirits, CA
Whiskey, Rye	Settlers Select Rye Whiskey	Wilderness Trace Distillery, KY
Whiskey, Rye	Silver Fox Rye (unaged rye spirits)	Cooper River Distillers, NJ
Whiskey, Rye	Smugglers' Notch Rye	Smugglers' Notch Distillery, VT
Whiskey, Rye	Spirit Works Rye Whiskey	Spirit Works Distillery, CA

Whiskey, Rye	Staley Rye Whiskey	Indian Creek Distillery, OH
Whiskey, Rye	Templeton Rye Whiskey	Templeton Rye Distillery, IA
Whiskey, Rye	The Judge: Rye Whiskey	Old Harbor Distilling Company, CA
Whiskey, Rye	Two James Rye Whiskey	Two James Spirits, MI
Whiskey, Rye	Walleye Rye Whiskey	New Holland Artisan Spirits, MI
Whiskey, Rye	Widmer Winter Rye	Ernest Scarano Distillery, OH
Whiskey, Rye	Widow Jane Rye	Cacao Prieto LLC, NY
Whiskey, Rye	Willett Family Estate Bottled Rye	Willett Distillery, KY
Whiskey, Rye	Woody Creek Colorado Rye Whiskey	Woody Creek Distillers, CO
Whiskey, Rye, Aged	1512 Spirits Aged 100% Rye Whiskey	1512 Spirits, CA
Whiskey, Rye, Aged	KOVAL Limited Edition Toasted Barrel Rye Aged Whiskey	KOVAL Distillery, IL
Whiskey, Rye, Citrus	Mister Katz's Rock & Rye	New York Distilling Company, NY
Whiskey, Rye, Maple	Sapling Maple Rye	Saxtons River Distillery LLC, VT
Whiskey, Rye, Organic	Bainbridge Rolling Bay Organic Rye	Bainbridge Organic Distillers, WA
Whiskey, Rye, Single Barrel, 15 Year	Ceran St. Vrain's Taos Lightning	Rancho de Los Luceros Destilaría, NM
Whiskey, Rye, Single Barrel, 5 Year	John David Albert's Taos Lightning	Rancho de Los Luceros Destilaría, NM
Whiskey, Rye, Straight	Straight Rye Whiskey	Yellow Rose Distilling LLC, TX
Whiskey, Rye, Straight	WhistlePig Straight Rye Whiskey	WhistlePig Farm, VT
Whiskey, Rye, Straight, Double Barreled	Double Barreled Ole George 100% Straight Rye Whiskey	Grand Traverse Distillery, MI
Whiskey, Rye, Strawberry	Pennington's Strawberry Rye Whiskey	SPEAKeasy Spirits, TN
Whiskey, Rye, Sweet Wine Barrel Aged	Dad's Hat™ Pennsylvania Rye Whiskey	Mountain Laurel Spirits LLC, PA
Whiskey, Rye, Vermouth Barrel Aged	Dad's Hat™ Pennsylvania Rye Whiskey	Mountain Laurel Spirits LLC, PA
Whiskey, Rye, White	KOVAL White Rye	KOVAL Distillery, IL
Whiskey, Rye, Young	Red River Texas Young Rye Whiskey	JEM Beverage Company, TX
Whiskey, Single Barrel	Whitmeyer's Texas Single Barrel American Single Malt Whiskey	Whitmeyer's Distilling Co. LLC, TX
Whiskey, Single Malt	BATTLE CRY American Single Malt Whiskey	Westland Distillery, WA
Whiskey, Single Malt	Belle Single Malt	Sons of Liberty Spirits Co., RI
Whiskey, Single Malt	Benjamin Prichard's Single Malt Whiskey	Belle of Dayton, OH
Whiskey, Single Malt	Cedar Ridge Single Malt Whiskey	Prichard's Distillery Inc., TN
Whiskey, Single Malt	Civilized Single Malt Whiskey	Cedar Ridge Distillery, IA
Whiskey, Single Malt	Colkegan Single Malt	Northern United Brewing Co., MI
		Santa Fe Spirits, NM

665

Whiskey, Single Malt	Corsair Triple Smoke Single Malt Whiskey	Corsair Artisan Distillery, TN
Whiskey, Single Malt	Cut Spike Single Malt Whiskey	Cut Spike Distillery, NE
Whiskey, Single Malt	Down Time Single Malt Whiskey	Deerhammer Distilling Company, CO
Whiskey, Single Malt	Estate Single Malt	Hillrock Estate Distillery, NY
Whiskey, Single Malt	Ezra Cox Single Malt Whiskey	Ezra Cox Distillery, WA
Whiskey, Single Malt	Golden Samish Bay Single Malt Whiskey	Golden Distillery, WA
Whiskey, Single Malt	McCarthy's Oregon Single Malt Whiskey	Clear Creek Distillery, OR
Whiskey, Single Malt	Missouri Spirits Single Malt Whiskey	Missouri Spirits, MO
Whiskey, Single Malt	Nashoba Single Malt Whiskey	Nashoba Valley Spirits Ltd., MA
Whiskey, Single Malt	Nevada Single Malt Whiskey	Churchill Vineyards and Distillery, NV
Whiskey, Single Malt	New Zealand Single Malt (Around the World Series)	Journeyman Distillery, MI
Whiskey, Single Malt	North American Steamship Rye™ Single Malt Rye Whiskey	Quincy Street Distillery, IL
Whiskey, Single Malt	Oregon Single Malt Whiskey	Immortal Spirits & Distilling Co., OR
Whiskey, Single Malt	Oregon Single Malt Whiskey	Bull Run Distilling Company, OR
Whiskey, Single Malt	Ranger Creek Rimfire Mesquite Smoked Texas Single Malt Whiskey	Ranger Creek Brewing, TX
Whiskey, Single Malt	Rogue Oregon Single Malt Whiskey	Rogue Spirits, OR
Whiskey, Single Malt	Single Malt	Tuthilltown Spirits Distillery, NY
Whiskey, Single Malt	Single Malt Whiskey	3 Howls Distillery, WA
Whiskey, Single Malt	Single Malt Whiskey	Stark Spirits, CA
Whiskey, Single Malt	St. George Single Malt Whiskey	St. George Spirits, CA
Whiskey, Single Malt	Tatoosh Single Malt Whiskey	Tatoosh Craft Distillery, WA
Whiskey, Single Malt	Three Oaks Single Malt	Journeyman Distillery, MI
Whiskey, Single Malt	Two James "Reserve" Single Malt Whiskey	Two James Spirits, MI
Whiskey, Single Malt	UPRISING American Single Malt Whiskey	Sons of Liberty Spirits Co., RI
Whiskey, Smoked	Rock Town Hickory Smoked Whiskey	Rock Town Distillery Inc., AR
Whiskey, Smoked Corn	Indian Kettles Smoke	Lake George Distilling Company, NY
Whiskey, Sorghum	High Wire Distilling Co. Quarter Acre Sorghum Whiskey	High Wire Distilling, SC
Whiskey, Sorghum	Queen Jennie Sorghum Whiskey	Old Sugar Distillery, WI
Whiskey, Sour Mash	Collier and McKeel Sour Mash Whiskey	Collier and McKeel, TN
Whiskey, Sour Mash	Ivy Mountain Georgia Sour Mash Spirits™	Ivy Mountain Distillery LLC, GA
Whiskey, Sour Mash	Ivy Mountain Georgia Sour Mash Whiskey™	Ivy Mountain Distillery LLC, GA
Whiskey, Sour Mash	Copperhead Georgia Sour Mash	Georgia Distilling Company, GA

Whiskey, Sour Mash, Corn	Black Canyon Sour Mash Corn Whiskey	Black Canyon Distillery, CO
Whiskey, Spelt, Aged	KOVAL Limited Edition Charred Barrel Spelt Aged Whiskey	KOVAL Distillery, IL
Whiskey, Spelt, Aged	KOVAL Limited Edition Toasted Barrel Spelt Aged Whiskey	KOVAL Distillery, IL
Whiskey, Straight	Zeppelin Bend Straight Whiskey	New Holland Artisan Spirits, MI
Whiskey, Straight Bourbon	Smooth Ambler Old Scout Straight Bourbon Whiskey	Smooth Ambler Spirits Company, WV
Whiskey, Straight Bourbon	Big Bottom Whiskey Straight Bourbon Whiskey (Port casks)	Big Bottom Distilling, OR
Whiskey, Straight Bourbon	Big Bottom Whiskey Straight Bourbon Whiskey (Zinfandel casks)	Big Bottom Distilling, OR
Whiskey, Straight Bourbon	Big Bottom Whiskey, Straight Bourbon Whiskey (Cabernet Sauvignon casks)	Big Bottom Dist., OR
Whiskey, Straight Bourbon	Big Bottom Whiskey, Straight Bourbon Whiskey 111 Proof	Big Bottom Distilling, OR
Whiskey, Straight Bourbon	C.W. Irwin Straight Bourbon	Oregon Spirit Distillers, OR
Whiskey, Straight Bourbon	Calhoun Bros. Straight Bourbon Whiskey	Big Bottom Distilling, OR
Whiskey, Straight Bourbon	Smooth Ambler Old Scout Straight Bourbon Whiskey	Smooth Ambler Spirits Company, WV
Whiskey, Straight Bourbon	Straight Bourbon Whiskey	Grand Traverse Distillery, MI
Whiskey, Straight Bourbon	Temperance Trader Straight Bourbon Whiskey	Bull Run Distilling Company, OR
Whiskey, Straight Bourbon, 5-Grain	Woodstone Creek 5 Grain Straight Bourbon Whisky	Woodstone Creek, OH
Whiskey, Straight KY Bourbon	E.H. Taylor, Jr. Straight Kentucky Bourbon Whiskey	E.H. Taylor, Jr. Old Fashioned, KY
Whiskey, Straight KY Bourbon	Johnny Drum Private Stock	Willett Distillery, KY
Whiskey, Straight KY Bourbon	Kentucky Straight Bourbon	Wilderness Trace Distillery, KY
Whiskey, Straight KY Bourbon	Old Pogue "Master's Select" Kentucky Straight Bourbon	Old Pogue Distillery, KY
Whiskey, Straight Malt	Westward Oregon Straight Malt Whiskey	House Spirits Distillery, OR
Whiskey, Straight Rye	Ole George 100% Straight Rye Whiskey	Grand Traverse Distillery, MI
Whiskey, Straight Rye	RoughStock Montana Straight Rye Whiskey	RoughStock Distillery, MT
Whiskey, Straight Rye	Ryan & Wood Straight Rye Whiskey	Ryan & Wood Inc., MA
Whiskey, Straight Rye	Smooth Ambler Old Scout Straight Rye	Smooth Ambler Spirits Company, WV
Whiskey, Straight Wheat	Ryan & Wood Straight Wheat Whiskey	Ryan & Wood Inc, MA
Whiskey, Sugar, Double Barrel	Revenge	Limestone Branch Distillery, KY
Whiskey, Sweet Corn	RoughStock Montana Sweet Corn Whiskey	RoughStock Distillery, MT
Whiskey, Tennessee	Benjamin Prichard's Tennessee Whiskey	Prichard's Distillery Inc., TN
Whiskey, Tennessee	Clayton James Tennessee Whiskey	Tenn South Distillery, TN
Whiskey, Tennessee	Collier and McKeel Tennessee Whiskey	Collier and McKeel, TN
Whiskey, Triticale	Dry Fly Washington Straight Triticale Whiskey	Dry Fly Distilling, WA
Whiskey, Wheat	1512 Spirits 2nd Chance Wheat Whiskey	1512 Spirits, CA

Whiskey, Wheat	Banner Texas Wheat Whiskey	Banner Distilling Co., TX
Whiskey, Wheat	Bill's Michigan Wheat Whiskey	New Holland Artisan Spirits, MI
Whiskey, Wheat	Blue Flame Wheat Whiskey	Blue Flame Spirits, WA
Whiskey, Wheat	Buggy Whip Wheat (Wheat Whiskey)	Journeyman Distillery, MI
Whiskey, Wheat	Carolina Virgin Wheat Whiskey	Six & Twenty Distillery, SC
Whiskey, Wheat	Dry Fly Cask Straight Wheat Whiskey	Dry Fly Distilling, WA
Whiskey, Wheat	Dry Fly Port Barrel Finish Wheat Whiskey	Dry Fly Distilling, WA
Whiskey, Wheat	Dry Fly Washington Straight Wheat Whiskey	Dry Fly Distilling, WA
Whiskey, Wheat	Duck Blind Shine Wheat Whiskey	Hidden Marsh Distillery, NY
Whiskey, Wheat	John Myer Wheat Whiskey	Myer Farm Distillers, NY
Whiskey, Wheat	Mo's Wheat Whiskey	Project V Distillery and Sausage Co., WA
Whiskey, Wheat	Organic Aged Wheat Whiskey – Small Cask Series	Pittsburgh Distilling Co., PA
Whiskey, Wheat	OYO Whiskey (100% Wheat)	Middle West Spirits LLC, OH
Whiskey, Wheat	Reservoir Wheat Whiskey	Reservoir Distillery, VA
Whiskey, Wheat	RoughStock Montana Spring Wheat Whiskey	RoughStock Distillery, MT
Whiskey, Wheat	Spirit Works Wheat Whiskey	Spirit Works Distillery, CA
Whiskey, Wheat	Wheat State Distilling Wheat Whiskey	Wheat State Distilling, KS
Whiskey, Wheat Spelt, White	KOVAL Limited Edition White Spelt	KOVAL Distillery, IL
Whiskey, Wheat, Aged	KOVAL Limited Edition Charred Barrel Wheat Aged Whiskey	KOVAL Distillery, IL
Whiskey, Wheat, Aged	KOVAL Limited Edition Toasted Barrel Wheat Aged Whiskey	KOVAL Distillery, IL
Whiskey, Wheat, White	KOVAL Limited Edition White Wheat	KOVAL Distillery, IL
Whiskey, White	1,000 Stills White Whiskey	Adirondack Distilling Company, NY
Whiskey, White	100% Corn Whiskey (un-aged)	Grand Traverse Distillery, MI
Whiskey, White	12 Volts Moonshine	Port Chilkoot Distillery, AK
Whiskey, White	291 Colorado Rye Whiskey White Dog	Distillery 291, CO
Whiskey, White	2bar Moonshine	2bar® Spirits, WA
Whiskey, White	32 Mile Moonshine	Lake George Distilling Company, NY
Whiskey, White	All Purpose Shine	Tenn South Distillery, TN
Whiskey, White	Apple-achian Shine	Dark Corner Distillery, SC
Whiskey, White	Arkansas Lightning	Rock Town Distillery Inc., AR
Whiskey, White	Bear Creek Sippin' Shine	Georgia Distilling Company, GA
Whiskey, White	Benjamin Prichard's Lincoln County Lightning	Prichard's Distillery Inc., TN

668

Whiskey, White	Big Jake White Dog Whiskey	StilL 630, MO
Whiskey, White	Black Heron Moonshine	Black Heron Spirits Distillery, WA
Whiskey, White	Blackbird's - Straight Shine	Blackbird Distillery, PA
Whiskey, White	Blind Cat Moonshine	High Mark Distillery, AK
Whiskey, White	Blue Flame Moonshine	Arkansas Moonshine Inc., AR
Whiskey, White	Broadslab Legacy Shine	Broadslab Distillery LLC, NC
Whiskey, White	Brown Dog Whiskey	Death's Door Spirits, WI
Whiskey, White	Bully Boy White Whiskey	Bully Boy Distillers, MA
Whiskey, White	California Moonshine	Fog's End Distillery, CA
Whiskey, White	Catoctin Creek Organic Mosby's Spirit™	Catoctin Creek Distilling Co. LLC, VA
Whiskey, White	Civilized White Dog	Northern United Brewing Co., MI
Whiskey, White	Collier and McKeel White Dog	Collier and McKeel, TN
Whiskey, White	Colorado Moonshine	Boathouse Distillery, CO
Whiskey, White	Corn Squeezins (Moonshine)	Moonrise Distillery Inc., GA
Whiskey, White	Delaware Distilling Company White Whiskey	Delaware Distilling Company, DE
Whiskey, White	Desert Lightning Corn Whisky	Black Heron Spirits Distillery, WA
Whiskey, White	Devil John Moonshine	Barrel House Distilling Co., KY
Whiskey, White	Devil's Share Moonshine	Ballast Point Spirits, CA
Whiskey, White	Downhome Sweetwater	Crown Valley Distilling Company, MO
Whiskey, White	Ezra Cox Moonshine	Ezra Cox Distillery, WA
Whiskey, White	Few White Whiskey	Few Spirits LLC, IL
Whiskey, White	Firefly Moonshine - White Lightning	Firefly Distillery, SC
Whiskey, White	Fitch's Goat Moonshine	Bone Spirits, TX
Whiskey, White	Fletcher's Finest	Lucky Duck Distillery, SC
Whiskey, White	Foggy Dog Whiskey	Whiskey Thief Distilling Company, KY
Whiskey, White	Gold Coast White Whiskey	Cathead Distillery LLC, MS
Whiskey, White	Hawaiian Moonshine	Island Distillers Inc., HI
Whiskey, White	Headwaters White Whiskey	Skip Rock Distillers, WA
Whiskey, White	Hooker's House Corn Whiskey	HelloCello, CA
Whiskey, White	House Spirits White Dog	House Spirits Distillery, OR
Whiskey, White	J. Potts Whiskey - White Whiskey	Manatawny Still Works, PA
Whiskey, White	Junior Johnson's Midnight Moon	Piedmont Distillers, NC

Whiskey, White	Kings County Moonshine	Kings County Distillery, NY
Whiskey, White	LBL Most Wanted Moonshine	Silver Trail Distillery, KY
Whiskey, White	Lead Mine Moonshine	Blaum Bros. Distilling Co., IL
Whiskey, White	Lightning Whiskey	Yahara Bay Distillers, WI
Whiskey, White	Long Shot White Whiskey	Dark Horse Distillery, KS
Whiskey, White	Loonshine	Loon Liquors, MN
Whiskey, White	LPR Moonshine	Mastermind Vodka, IL
Whiskey, White	Manzanita Moonshine	Manzanita Distilling Company, CA
Whiskey, White	Massachusetts Moonshine	Cape Cod Distilling Company LLC, MA
Whiskey, White	Massachusetts Whiskey	Damnation Alley Distillery, MA
Whiskey, White	MBR Kentucky White Dog	MB Roland Distillery, KY
Whiskey, White	MBR True Kentucky Shine	MB Roland Distillery, KY
Whiskey, White	Mill St. Moonshine	Mill St. Distillery LLC, OH
Whiskey, White	Missouri Moonshine	Crown Valley Distilling Company, MO
Whiskey, White	Moonshine	Dark Corner Distillery, SC
Whiskey, White	Moonshine Bandits Outlaw Moonshine	Valley Spirits LLC, CA
Whiskey, White	Moose Shine Pacific Northwest Un-aged Whiskey	Carbon Glacier Distillery, WA
Whiskey, White	Mount Baker Moonshine	Mount Baker Distillery, WA
Whiskey, White	Mountain Moonshine	Howling Moon Distillery, NC
Whiskey, White	Mountain Moonshine Old Oak Recipe	WV Distilling Co. LLC, WV
Whiskey, White	Mountain Moonshine Spirit Whiskey	WV Distilling Co. LLC, WV
Whiskey, White	Ole Smoky® Hunch Punch Moonshine™ (seasonal)	Ole Smoky Distillery LLC, TN
Whiskey, White	Ole Smoky® White Lightnin'™ (Neutral Spirits)	Ole Smoky Distillery LLC, TN
Whiskey, White	Onyx Moonshine	Onyx Spirits Company LLC, CT
Whiskey, White	Original Shine	Mountain View Distillery, PA
Whiskey, White	Overproof Ozark Mountain Moonshine	Copper Run Distillery, MO
Whiskey, White	Ozark Apple Pie Moonshine	Ozark Distillery LLC, MO
Whiskey, White	Ozark Moonshine	Ozark Distillery LLC, MO
Whiskey, White	Ozark Mountain Moonshine	Copper Run Distillery, MO
Whiskey, White	Pink Lightning Moonshine	Ascendant Spirits, CA
Whiskey, White	Ranger Creek La Bestia Defavorable Belgian White Whiskey	Ranger Creek Brewing & Distilling, TX
Whiskey, White	Really Fine Drink – Heritage Appalachian Moonshine	Mayberry Spirits, NC

Whiskey, White	Reservoir Bourbon	Reservoir Distillery, VA
Whiskey, White	Roberson's Tennessee Mellomoon	East Tennessee Distillery, TN
Whiskey, White	Roberson's Tennessee Mellomoon 100 Proof Straight	East Tennessee Distillery, TN
Whiskey, White	Roberson's Tennessee Mellomoon 150 Proof	East Tennessee Distillery, TN
Whiskey, White	Roberson's Tennessee Mellomoon 70 proof Caramel	East Tennessee Distillery, TN
Whiskey, White	Rocky Mountain Moonshine	Mystic Mountain Distillery LLC, CO
Whiskey, White	Sandstone Distillery White Whiskey	Sandstone Distillery LLC, WA
Whiskey, White	Schoharie Shine	KyMar Farm Distillery, NY
Whiskey, White	See 7 Stars Moonshine	Batch 206 Distillery, WA
Whiskey, White	Sempre Fi Moonshine	Ascendant Spirits, CA
Whiskey, White	Shinn Estate Vineyards Shine	Shinn Estate Vineyards, NY
Whiskey, White	Short Mountain Shine	Short Mountain Distillery, TN
Whiskey, White	Shorty's White Whiskey	Chicago Distilling Company, IL
Whiskey, White	Silver Coyote Un-aged Whiskey	Santa Fe Spirits, NM
Whiskey, White	Silver Lightning Moonshine	Ascendant Spirits, CA
Whiskey, White	Single Six Rocky Mountain Moonshine	Two Guns Distillery, CO
Whiskey, White	Skagit Moon Moonshine	Deception Distilling LLC, WA
Whiskey, White	South House Southern Moonshine	JEM Beverage Company, TX
Whiskey, White	Stills Crossroads Shine	High Ridge Spirits
Whiskey, White	Striped 'Shine	Striped Pig Distillery, SC
Whiskey, White	Teton Moonshine	Grand Teton Distillery, ID
Whiskey, White	Thunderbeast Storm Moonshine Corn Whiskey	Mad Buffalo Distillery, MO
Whiskey, White	TJ Pottinger Sugar Shine	Limestone Branch Distillery, KY
Whiskey, White	Troy & Sons Platinum Heirloom Moonshine Whiskey	Asheville Distilling Company, NC
Whiskey, White	Ugly California Moonshine	Kill Devil Spirit Company, CA
Whiskey, White	Virginia Lightning Whiskey	Appalachian Mountain Spirits LLC, VA
Whiskey, White	Virginia Sweetwater Moonshine	Appalachian Mountain Spirits LLC, VA
Whiskey, White	W.R. Whiskey (White Whiskey)	Journeyman Distillery, MI
Whiskey, White	Water Tower White Lightning™ Un-aged Illinois Corn Whiskey	Quincy Street Distillery, IL
Whiskey, White	Whistling Andy Moonshine	Whistling Andy Distillery, MT
Whiskey, White	White Dog	Fog's End Distillery, CA
Whiskey, White	White Dog Moonshine	Spirit Hound Distillers, CO

Whiskey, White	White Dog Whiskey	Whiskey Thief Distilling Company, KY
Whiskey, White	White Dog Whiskey	McMenamins Edgefield Distillery, OR
Whiskey, White	White Lightning, 105 proof	Palmetto Moonshine, SC
Whiskey, White	White Widow	Adam Dalton Distillery, NC
Whiskey, White	Woody Creek Colorado White Whiskey (100% Olathe Sweet Corn)	Woody Creek Distillers, CO
Whiskey, White	XXX Shine Whiskey (range)	Philadelphia Distilling, PA
Whiskey, White	Apple Pie Shine (40 & 80 Proof)	Mountain View Distillery, PA
Whiskey, White	Montana Moonshine	Willie's Distillery, MT
Whiskey, White	New Moon White Whiskey	Hewn Spirits LLC, PA
Whiskey, White	Sweet Baby Moonshine	Hard Times Distillery LLC, OR
Whiskey, White	Wagner's White Lightning	Stoutridge Distillery, NY
Whiskey, White	Whitmeyer's Texas Moonshine Whiskey	Whitmeyer's Distilling Co. LLC, TX
Whiskey, White, Apple	Apple Betty	Black Swamp Distillery, OH
Whiskey, White, Apple	Apple Shine	Hard Times Distillery LLC, OR
Whiskey, White, Apple Pie	Alaska Apple Pie Moonshine	Alaska Distillery, AK
Whiskey, White, Apple Pie	Apple Pie Arkansas Lightning	Rock Town Distillery Inc., AR
Whiskey, White, Apple Pie	Apple Pie Moonshine	Clayton Distillery, NY
Whiskey, White, Apple Pie	Apple Pie Moonshine	Old Republic Distillery, PA
Whiskey, White, Apple Pie	Apple Pie Moonshine	Forks of Cheat Distillery, WV
Whiskey, White, Apple Pie	Apple Pie Moonshine	Howling Moon Distillery, NC
Whiskey, White, Apple Pie	Apple Pie Shine	Lake George Distilling Company, NY
Whiskey, White, Apple Pie	Blueberry Apple Pie Moonshine	Tenn South Distillery, TN
Whiskey, White, Apple Pie	Colonel Cobb Apple Pie	Old Republic Distillery, PA
Whiskey, White, Apple Pie	Dry County Apple Pie	Double V Distillery, WA
Whiskey, White, Apple Pie	Dutch Apple Pie	Dry County Distillery LLC, WA
Whiskey, White, Apple Pie	Firefly Moonshine - Apple Pie	Mayberry Spirits, NC
Whiskey, White, Apple Pie	Homemade ApplePie - Corn Shine	Firefly Distillery, SC
Whiskey, White, Apple Pie	Ole Smoky® Apple Pie Moonshine™	Blackbird Distillery, PA
Whiskey, White, Apple Pie	Palmetto Apple Pie Moonshine, 45 proof	Ole Smoky Distillery LLC, TN
Whiskey, White, Apple Pie	Pinchgut Hollow Distillery Apple Pie Shine	Palmetto Moonshine, SC
Whiskey, White, Apple Pie	Rack House Apple Pie w/ Graham Cracker Crust	Pinchgut Hollow Distillery, WV
		Parliament Distillery, WA

Whiskey, White, Apple Pie	Roberson's Tennessee Mellomoon Apple Pie	East Tennessee Distillery, TN
Whiskey, White, Apple Pie	Short Mountain Apple Pie Shine	Short Mountain Distillery, TN
Whiskey, White, Apple Pie	South House Southern Moonshine Apple Pie	JEM Beverage Company, TX
Whiskey, White, Apple Pie	Spiced Apple Pie Moonshine	Grand Teton Distillery, ID
Whiskey, White, Apple Pie	The Spirits of Yellow Springs® Apple Pie Moonshine	S and G Artisan Distillery LLC, OH
Whiskey, White, Apple Pie	Virginia Lightning Apple Pie	Appalachian Mountain Spirits LLC, VA
Whiskey, White, Apple, Caramel	Rack House Caramel Apple	Parliament Distillery, WA
Whiskey, White, Banana	Banana - Corn Shine	Blackbird Distillery, PA
Whiskey, White, Banana	Roberson's Tennessee Mellomoon Banana	East Tennessee Distillery, TN
Whiskey, White, Blackberry	Blackberry Bev	Black Swamp Distillery, OH
Whiskey, White, Blackberry	Blackberry Cobbler Arkansas Lightning	Rock Town Distillery Inc., AR
Whiskey, White, Blackberry	Blackberry Moonshine	Ozark Distillery LLC, MO
Whiskey, White, Blackberry	Blackberry Shine	Tenn South Distillery, TN
Whiskey, White, Blackberry	Firefly Moonshine - Blackberry	Firefly Distillery, SC
Whiskey, White, Blackberry	Ole Smoky® Blackberry Moonshine™	Ole Smoky Distillery LLC, TN
Whiskey, White, Blackberry	Palmetto Blackberry Moonshine, 45 proof	Palmetto Moonshine, SC
Whiskey, White, Blackcherry	Blackcherry - Corn Shine	Blackbird Distillery, PA
Whiskey, White, Blueberry	MBR Kentucky Blackberry Shine	MB Roland Distillery, KY
Whiskey, White, Blueberry	MBR Kentucky Blueberry Shine	MB Roland Distillery, KY
Whiskey, White, Buckwheat	Pinchgut Hollow Distillery Buckwheat Moon	Pinchgut Hollow Distillery, WV
Whiskey, White, Butterscotch	Butterscotch Moonshine	Ozark Distillery LLC, MO
Whiskey, White, Butterscotch	Butterscotch Shine	Dark Corner Distillery, SC
Whiskey, White, Caramel	Firefly Moonshine - Caramel	Firefly Distillery, SC
Whiskey, White, Cherries	Ole Smoky® Moonshine Cherries™	Ole Smoky Distillery LLC, TN
Whiskey, White, Cherry	Cherry Moonshine	Clayton Distillery, NY
Whiskey, White, Cherry	Firefly Moonshine - Cherry	Firefly Distillery, SC
Whiskey, White, Cherry	Virginia Lightning Cherry	Appalachian Mountain Spirits LLC, VA
Whiskey, White, Cherry Lemonade	South House Southern Moonshine Cherry Lemonade	JEM Beverage Company, TX
Whiskey, White, Cherry, Dark	MBR Kentucky Dark Cherry Shine	MB Roland Distillery, KY
Whiskey, White, Cinnamon Roll	Roberson's Tennessee Mellomoon Cinnamon Roll	East Tennessee Distillery, TN
Whiskey, White, Coconut	Roberson's Tennessee Mellomoon Coconut	East Tennessee Distillery, TN
Whiskey, White, Corn	291 Fresh Colorado Whiskey	Distillery 291, CO

Whiskey, White, Corn	Block and Tackle Moonshine 100% Corn Whiskey Un-aged	It's 5 Artisan Distillery, WA
Whiskey, White, Corn	Colonel Cobb Corn Whiskey	Double V Distillery, WA
Whiskey, White, Corn	Corn Whiskey Moonshine 100% Corn Whiskey Aged	It's 5 Artisan Distillery, WA
Whiskey, White, Corn	Delaware Phoenix Corn Whiskey	Delaware Phoenix Distillery, NY
Whiskey, White, Corn	Myer Farm White Dog Corn Whiskey	Myer Farm Distillers, NY
Whiskey, White, Corn	Ole Smoky® Original Moonshine (Corn Whiskey)	Ole Smoky Distillery LLC, TN
Whiskey, White, Corn	Pinchgut Hollow Distillery Corn Shine	Pinchgut Hollow Distillery, WV
Whiskey, White, Corn	Two Dog Moonshine, Un-aged corn whisky	Clayton Distillery, NY
Whiskey, White, Corn, Apple	AppleBlack - Corn Shine	Blackbird Distillery, PA
Whiskey, White, Grape	Grape Arkansas Lightning	Rock Town Distillery Inc., AR
Whiskey, White, Grape	Ole Smoky® Grape Moonshine™ (seasonal)	Ole Smoky Distillery LLC, TN
Whiskey, White, Grape	Roberson's Tennessee Mellomoon Grape	East Tennessee Distillery, TN
Whiskey, White, Honey	Montana Honey Moonshine	Willie's Distillery, MT
Whiskey, White, Honey Ginseng	Roberson's Tennessee Mellomoon Honey Ginseng	East Tennessee Distillery, TN
Whiskey, White, Honey Peach	Pinchgut Hollow Distillery Honey Peach Moon	Pinchgut Hollow Distillery, WV
Whiskey, White, Hot Cinnamon	Lightning Hot Cinnamon Arkansas Lightning	Rock Town Distillery Inc., AR
Whiskey, White, Lemon	LemonDrop - Corn Shine	Blackbird Distillery, PA
Whiskey, White, Lemon	Old Smoky® Lemon Drop Moonshine™	Ole Smoky Distillery LLC, TN
Whiskey, White, Lemonade	Lake George Lemonade	Lake George Distilling Company, NY
Whiskey, White, Lemonade	Lemonade Moonshine	Clayton Distillery, NY
Whiskey, White, Lemonade	Rack House Yucca	Parliament Distillery, WA
Whiskey, White, Mango	Mango Marge	Black Swamp Distillery, OH
Whiskey, White, Oaked	Manzanita Oaked Moonshine	Manzanita Distilling Company, CA
Whiskey, White, Oat	Easy Eight Unoaked Oat Whiskey	Stone Barn Brandyworks, OR
Whiskey, White, Peach	Carolina Peach Shine	Dark Corner Distillery, SC
Whiskey, White, Peach	Firefly Moonshine - Peach	Firefly Distillery, SC
Whiskey, White, Peach	Ole Smoky® Peach Moonshine™ (seasonal)	Ole Smoky Distillery LLC, TN
Whiskey, White, Peach	Palmetto Peach Moonshine, 45 proof	Palmetto Moonshine, SC
Whiskey, White, Peach	Peach - Corn Shine	Blackbird Distillery, PA
Whiskey, White, Peach	Peach Arkansas Lightning	Rock Town Distillery Inc., AR
Whiskey, White, Peach	Roberson's Tennessee Mellomoon Peach	East Tennessee Distillery, TN
Whiskey, White, Peach	South House Southern Moonshine Peach	JEM Beverage Company, TX

Index Entry	Product	Distillery
Whiskey, White, Peach	Whitmeyer's Texas Peach Whiskey	Whitmeyer's Distilling Co. LLC, TX
Whiskey, White, Peach	Pattys Peach	Black Swamp Distillery, OH
Whiskey, White, Peach Pie	Peach Pie Shine	Tenn South Distillery, TN
Whiskey, White, Pineapple	Pineapple – Corn Shine	Blackbird Distillery, PA
Whiskey, White, Pink Lemonade	MBR Kentucky Pink Lemonade	MB Roland Distillery, KY
Whiskey, White, Pink Lemonade	Pink Lemonade Moonshine	Ozark Distillery LLC, MO
Whiskey, White, Pumpkin Spice	Corsair Pumpkin Spice Moonshine	Corsair Artisan Distillery, TN
Whiskey, White, Rye	Black Button Unaged Rye	Black Button Distilling, NY
Whiskey, White, Rye	Dad's Hat™ Pennsylvania White Rye	Mountain Laurel Spirits LLC, PA
Whiskey, White, Rye	Elias Staley Un aged Rye Whiskey	Indian Creek Distillery, OH
Whiskey, White, Rye	Glacier Dew Rye Spirit	Glacier Distilling Company, MT
Whiskey, White, Rye	Small Batch White Rye Whiskey	Thistle Finch Distilling, PA
Whiskey, White, Rye	White Rye Whiskey (coming soon)	Five & 20 Spirits, NY
Whiskey, White, Rye	Wigle Organic White Rye Whiskey	Pittsburgh Distilling Co., PA
Whiskey, White, Single Malt	Limestone Landing Single Malt Rye Un-aged Whiskey	Old Pogue Distillery, KY
Whiskey, White, Single Malt	SPOKANE FALLS-Single Malt-White Dog Whiskey	Evanson Handcrafted Distilling LLC, WA
Whiskey, White, Smoked White Corn	MBR Kentucky Black Dog	MB Roland Distillery, KY
Whiskey, White, Spiced	Catdaddy Spiced Moonshine	Piedmont Distillers, NC
Whiskey, White, Strawberry	Firefly Moonshine - Strawberry	Firefly Distillery, SC
Whiskey, White, Strawberry	MBR Kentucky Strawberry Shine	MB Roland Distillery, KY
Whiskey, White, Strawberry	Ole Smoky® Strawberry Moonshine™	Ole Smoky Distillery LLC, TN
Whiskey, White, Strawberry	Roberson's Tennessee Mellomoon Strawberry	East Tennessee Distillery, TN
Whiskey, White, Strawberry	Shellys Strawberry	Black Swamp Distillery, OH
Whiskey, White, Strawberry	Strawberry Moonshine	Howling Moon Distillery, NC
Whiskey, White, Tennessee	Popcorn Sutton's Tennessee White Whiskey	Popcorn Sutton's Distillery, TN
Whiskey, White, Vanilla Bean	Vanilla Bean Moonshine	Ozark Distillery LLC, MO
Whiskey, White, Wheat	Myer Farm White Dog Wheat Spirit	Myer Farm Distillers, NY
Whiskey, White, Wheat	Wigle Organic White Wheat Whiskey	Pittsburgh Distilling Co., PA
Whisky, see also Whiskey		
Whisky	Aristo Whisky	Minhas Micro Distillery, WI
Whisky	Baby Blue Whisky	Balcones Distillery, TX
Whisky	Battle of the Glen	Glenora Distillery, NS

Whisky	Big Cat™ Whisky	Syntax Spirits LLC, CO
Whisky	Brimstone Whisky	Balcones Distillery, TX
Whisky	Chinook Whisky	Minhas Micro Distillery, WI
Whisky	Chinook Whisky	Minhas Micro Distillery, WI
Whisky	Coyote Howl Whisky	Black Heron Spirits Distillery, WA
Whisky	Craigdarroch Whisky	Victoria Spirits, BC
Whisky	Dubh Glas Whisky	The Dubh Glas Distillery, BC
Whisky	Forty Creek Barrel Select Whisky	Forty Creek Distillery, ON
Whisky	Forty Creek Copper Pot Whisky	Forty Creek Distillery, ON
Whisky	Glen Breton Ice	Glenora Distillery, NS
Whisky	Mongrel Whisky	Odd Society Spirits, BC
Whisky	Okanagan Spirits Whisky	Okanagan Spirits, BC
Whisky	Punjabi Club Whisky	Minhas Micro Distillery, WI
Whisky	Royal Crest Whisky	Minhas Micro Distillery, WI
Whisky	Sailboat Whisky	Minhas Micro Distillery, WI
Whisky	Snake River Stampede	Indio Spirits, OR
Whisky	Special 1+11 Blend Canadian Whisky	Still Waters Distillery, ON
Whisky	Stars Whisky	Minhas Micro Distillery, WI
Whisky	Strait Whisky	Myriad View Artisan Distillery Inc., PE
Whisky	The Rockies Whisky	Minhas Micro Distillery, WI
Whisky	True Blue Whisky	Balcones Distillery, TX
Whisky	Walla Walla Whisky	Walla Walla Distilling Company, WA
Whisky	Wisconsin Club USA Whisky	Minhas Micro Distillery, WI
Whisky, American Single Malt	Defiant Whisky, An American Single Malt	Blue Ridge Distilling Company, NC
Whisky, American Single Malt	Old Barnstable American Single Malt Whisky	Cape Cod Distilling Company LLC, MA
Whisky, Barrel Aged	Canada Gold Premium Barrel Aged Canadian Whisky	Forty Creek Distillery, ON
Whisky, Bourbon	Rough Rider Straight Bourbon Whisky	Long Island Spirits, NY
Whisky, Light	Walla Walla Light Whisky	Walla Walla Distilling Company, WA
Whisky, Mesquite Smoked	Single Malt Mesquite Smoked Whisky	Arizona High Spirits Distillery, AZ
Whisky, Organic, Single Malt	Pemberton Distillery Organic Single Malt Whisky	Pemberton Distillery Inc., BC
Whisky, Reserve	Forty Creek Confederation Oak Reserve	Forty Creek Distillery, ON
Whisky, Reserve	Forty Creek Double Barrel Reserve	Forty Creek Distillery, ON

Whisky, Reserve	Forty Creek Port Wood Reserve	Forty Creek Distillery, ON
Whisky, Rye	Copper Fox Rye Whisky	Copper Fox Distillery, VA
Whisky, Rye	Five Fathers Pure Rye Whisky	Old Pogue Distillery, KY
Whisky, Rye	Last Mountain Canadian Rye Whisky	Last Mountain Distillery Ltd., SK
Whisky, Rye	Moylan's Distilling Rye Whisky	Stillwater Spirits, CA
Whisky, Rye	White Wolf Rye Whisky	White Wolf Distillery, WI
Whisky, Scotch	Glen Scotch Whisky	Artesian Distillers, MI
Whisky, Single Malt	'1' Texas Single Malt Whisky	Balcones Distillery, TX
Whisky, Single Malt	Notch Single Malt Whisky	Triple Eight Distillery, MA
Whisky, Single Malt	Okanagan Spirits Single Malt Whisky	Okanagan Spirits, BC
Whisky, Single Malt	Pine Barrens Single Malt Whisky	Long Island Spirits, NY
Whisky, Single Malt	Shelter Point Distillery Single Malt Whisky	Shelter Point Distillery, BC
Whisky, Single Malt	Stalk & Barrel Single Malt Whisky	Still Waters Distillery, ON
Whisky, Single Malt	The Kid: Single Malt Whisky	Old Harbor Distilling Company, CA
Whisky, Single Malt	Urban Single Malt Whisky	Urban Distilleries, BC
Whisky, Single Malt	Wasmund's Single Malt Whisky	Copper Fox Distillery, VA
Whisky, Single Malt	Glen Breton Canadian Single Malt Whisky	Glenora Distillery, NS
Whisky, Single Malt	Moylan's Distilling American Single Malt Whisky	Stillwater Spirits, CA
Whisky, Single Malt, Cask Strength	Moylan's Distilling American Single Malt Cask Strength	Stillwater Spirits, CA
Whisky, Single Malt, Cask Strength	Moylan's Distilling Cherry Wood Malt Cask Strength	Stillwater Spirits, CA
Whisky, White	Before The Fire White Whiskey	Sons of Vancouver Distillery Ltd., BC
Whisky, White	Black Button Moonshine	Black Button Distilling, NY
Whisky, White	Death's Door White Whisky	Death's Door Spirits, WI
Whisky, White	Railspur No 1 White	The Liberty Distillery, BC
Whisky, White	Strait Lightning	Myriad View Artisan Distillery Inc., PE
Whisky, White	Strait Shine	Myriad View Artisan Distillery Inc., PE
Whisky, White	Wildcat White Whisky	The Ellensburg Distillery, WA
Wine, Plum	Wild Plum Wine	Stringer's Orchard Winery and Dist., OR

www.ingramcontent.com/pod-product-compliance
Lightning Source LLC
Chambersburg PA
CBHW080918180426
43192CB00040B/2442